PSYCHOLOGY

AN INTRODUCTION

Second Edition

PSYCHOLOGY

AN INTRODUCTION

Benjamin B. Lahey
University of Georgia

Wm. C. Brown Publishers
Dubuque, Iowa

Book Team

James M. McNeil Editor
Sandra E. Schmidt Associate Editor
Michael E. Warrell Designer
Gloria G. Schiesl Senior Production Editor
Michelle Oberhoffer Photo Editor
Mavis M. Oeth Permissions Editor

Wm. C. Brown Chairman of the Board
Mark C. Falb President and Chief Executive Officer

wcb
Wm. C. Brown Publishers, College Division

Lawrence E. Cremer President
James L. Romig Vice-President, Product Development
David A. Corona Vice-President, Production and Design
E. F. Jogerst Vice-President, Cost Analyst
Bob McLaughlin National Sales Manager
Catherine M. Faduska Director of Marketing Services
Craig S. Marty Director of Marketing Research
Marilyn A. Phelps Manager of Design
Eugenia M. Collins Production Editorial Manager
Mary M. Heller Photo Research Manager

Cover photograph © Patricia Fisher/Folio, Inc.

Library of Congress Catalog Card Number: 85–71374

ISBN 0-697-00844-4 (Cloth)
ISBN 0-697-00617-1 (Paper)

Printed in the United States of America
10 9 8 7 6 5 4 3 2 1

To my children

Megan, Ted, and Erin Lahey

B R I E F C O N T E N T S

C O N T E N T S

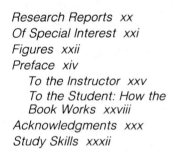
PART ONE

Introduction

C O N T E N T S

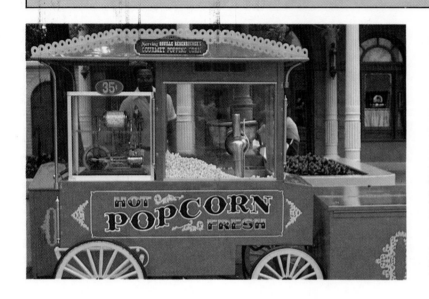

PART THREE

Learning and Cognition

Chapter 5

Basic Principles of Learning 170

RESEARCH REPORT

OF SPECIAL INTEREST

F I G U R E S

FIGURES

*These figures are included in the transparency sets that are available free to instructors adopting *Psychology: An Introduction*, Second Edition.

P R E F A C E

Reactions to the first edition of *Psychology: An Introduction* have been among the most gratifying of my career. Many students and instructors told us that we had achieved our goal—that we had provided them with a textbook from which learning about psychology was both enjoyable and effective. But from the moment that the first edition appeared, I was anxious to write the second one. New research suggested important ways to improve further the book's pedagogy and provided many important and fascinating additions to the knowledge-base of psychology itself. These changes in what is known begged for a second edition. For me personally, the most enjoyable aspect of revising the text was the opportunity to polish what had already been written and to repeatedly pore over the text with a passion for accuracy and detail. The revision process was helped enormously by the input of numerous superb reviewers with a knowledge both of psychology and of the art and science of teaching. The results of that combined effort are before you, and I hope that it will serve the needs of students and instructors even better than did the first edition.

From the conception of the first edition seven years ago and through every stage of its development, *Psychology: An Introduction* has been built with a single purpose in mind: to create a teaching tool from which students will learn a great deal of basic information about psychology. The accent is on meaningful and efficient learning by students.

Although psychologists devote a great deal of time to studying human learning, we have rarely put the information we have acquired to use in writing textbooks. Because I enjoy teaching psychology and have an interest in human learning, I decided to organize a textbook based on what current research tells us about how people learn. I began by talking with psychologists Bruce Britton and Ellen Gagné, who are experts on the psychology of learning from written text. We discussed the idea at length, and they directed me to additional research. To help me synthesize the available information, Professor Britton was kind enough to write a highly useful summary of the research on this topic.

From that beginning, I developed a tentative plan for the first edition of this textbook. I then contacted James L. Romig at Wm. C. Brown Publishers. Dr. Romig's first step was to obtain the advice of additional experts on the psychology of learning from textbooks. He assembled a meeting of researchers at the 1981 meeting of the American Psychological Association. During that meeting and in follow-up contacts, several people provided us with the benefit of their expert knowledge: Thomas André (Iowa State University); Bruce K. Britton, Ellen D. Gagné, and Shawn M. Glynn (University of Georgia); Lawrence T. Frase and Ernst Z. Rothkopf (Bell Telephone Laboratories); Arthur C. Graesser (California State University, Fullerton); James Hartley (University of Keele); Richard E. Mayer (University of California, Santa Barbara); Gary M. Schumacher (Ohio University); Robert H. W. Waller and Peter Whalley (The Open University); and G. Michael Pressley (University of Western Ontario). These experts were asked the question, "What does research tell us about the way a textbook should be written to make learning most efficient?" Based on their answers and my own research, we settled on a final plan for the first edition of the book and I began writing in earnest.

In the two sections that follow, the mechanics of *Psychology: An Introduction* are explained in detail. "To the Instructor" describes the pedagogical strategy used in the text and my reasons for selecting the elements that are included. The next section, entitled "To the Student: How the Book Works," explains in a step-by-step manner each teaching device I have used. It's essential that the student understand the purpose of each teaching device to derive maximum benefit from this text.

To the Instructor

Psychology: An Introduction offers thorough topic coverage and standard organization designed to fit courses as they are most commonly taught. But, it differs significantly from other texts in two main ways.

First, every effort has been made to create a writing style that is—as one former student kindly described it—"friendly." This book is not a pompous attempt to impress students with the complexities of the science of psychology. It was written to provide a clear, informative, challenging, exciting, and personal introduction to psychology.

Second, *Psychology: An Introduction* differs from other texts in its emphasis on meaningful learning. This text contains many elements that are designed to enhance learning and remembering. The book is based on an *organizational model of semantic memory*. The content of the first course in psychology can be thought of as a hierarchical organization of concepts and facts. To improve learning and memory, it is as important for students to understand the overall organization of new information as it is for them to understand the individual concepts and facts.

Based on what is now known about learning from written text, the student is given an understanding of organizational structure in four primary ways:

1. *Advance organizers.* Considerable research now indicates that students learn and retain information better when they have an advance understanding of the hierarchical organization of the information being learned. To accomplish this, the student is given two kinds of advance organizers before reading the main body of the text. The student is presented first with an **outline** of the major topics covered within the chapter, a device common to many textbooks. But to add to the effectiveness of this bare-bones overview, a prose advance organizer, called the **preview,** highlights the major concepts and shows how they are *related* to one another before the chapter opens. Thus, the student is provided with two forward looks at the chapter to create a cognitive organization upon which to "hang" new facts and concepts.

2. *Nested hierarchical reviews.* The interrelationship of the new information is further strengthened in the **review** and **summary** sections. Following each major section within each chapter, the content of that section is briefly reviewed in prose. At the end of each chapter, the main content of the chapter is again summarized, but this time in a hierarchical outline that visually highlights the organization of the material.

3. *Visual organizational cues.* Using hierarchical outlines in the end-of-chapter summaries is only one way in which the student is actually *shown* the organization of the new material. Close attention has been paid to the use of visual cues—such as typeface, type size, color of type, and indentations—to indicate the organization of the text. The difference between this text and others is intentionally subtle in this respect, but students should have little trouble distinguishing the superordinate-subordinate structure of *A, B,* and *C* sections in the text. In diagrams and figures, colors were chosen not to be decorative, but to show students which elements are related and which are different. In addition, lists—like the one you are reading now—have been frequently (but not excessively) used to show that each element in the list is at the same level of organization and subordinate to the title of the list ("four ways to help students understand organizational structure" in the case of the list you are reading now).

4. *Verbal cues to organization.* Another important way to help readers see how concepts and facts are related is to simply *tell* them in words. Many references are made in the text, therefore, to the organization of the new information. This is done in two main ways. First, when a newly introduced concept is related to another concept that was discussed in an earlier section, this fact is specifically pointed out. Second, information that is subordinate to a concept is frequently introduced in a way that makes that relationship very clear (i.e., "The two factors that cause forgetting in short-term memory are . . ."). Although these cues are subtle so as not to interrupt the flow of the text, they have been added to help improve the student's comprehension and memory.

The use of these pedagogical devices in the text was chosen over two other pedagogical approaches after much consideration. I chose not to use the SQ3R (survey, question, read, recite, review) method of organizing the text because the author, not the student, must ask the questions, which reduces student involvement and is distracting to many students. However, the SQ3R approach is useful as a general study method and can be used with any text, including this one. Therefore, I have included its application in the study skills section that begins on preliminary page xxxii.

I also chose not to use specific instructional objectives and review questions on empirical grounds. Research suggests that while these devices do improve learning for the specific information targeted in the objectives and questions, they *reduce* learning for all other material in the chapter. In other words, they focus learning, but they do not increase the overall amount of material learned by the student. So as not to exclude the use of instructional objectives altogether, however, a list of **key terms** with page references has been provided at the start of each chapter and can be used to focus learning to some extent. For those instructors who wish to use instructional objectives, we have included them in the study guide and the instructor's manual that accompany this text.

An appendix on measurement, research design, and statistics appears at the end of the book for those professors who wish to teach a more research-oriented course.

Learning and Instructional Aids

Instructor's Manual by Steven A. Schneider (Pima Community College, Tucson, Arizona) contains, for each chapter in the text, an overview, page-referenced learning objectives, a page-referenced list of key terms, essay questions, discussion questions, student projects, and film suggestions.

Lecture Enrichment Kit by Steven A. Schneider includes the following elements for each chapter: an extended outline, instructional strategies for teaching the chapter and using the transparencies; classroom activities; and a section entitled "Issues, Implications, and Applications: Going beyond the Chapter." A supplement on using **wcb** PSYCOM, Psychology on Computer: Simulations, Experiments, and Projects will be added.

Test Item File by William O. Dwyer (Memphis State University) includes 3,000 multiple-choice test questions that are page-referenced to the text, identified by topic, and designated as *factual, conceptual,* or *applied.*

Student Study Guide by Steven A. Schneider includes, for each chapter in the text, page-referenced learning objectives, an overview, a key terms matching exercise, "Who Am I?" (an exercise matching famous psychologists to their scientific contributions), a page-referenced guided review, special interest questions, discussion questions, "For Further Thought" questions and exercises, and multiple-choice questions with answers.

Transparency Set of 160 acetate transparencies, many in full-color, includes graphics from the text and outside sources. These transparencies have been expressly designed to help you teach your classes and organize lectures.

wcb TestPak is the free, computerized testing service available to adopters of *Psychology: An Introduction.* All questions in the Test Item File are available on TestPak. Two options are available. The call-in/mail-in TestPak service guarantees that we will put in the mail to you a test master, a student answer sheet, and an answer key within two working days of receiving your request. Call-in hours are 8:30–1:30, Central time, Monday through Thursday. **wcb** TestPak is also available for instructors who want to use their Apple ®*IIe* or *IIc,* or IBM®PC to create their own tests. Upon request, adopters of *Psychology: An Introduction* will receive the Test Item File, program diskettes, and user's guide. With these, the instructor will be able to create tests, answer sheets, and answer keys. The program allows for adding, deleting, or modifying test questions. No programming experience is necessary.

wcb QuizPak, the interactive self-testing, self-scoring quiz program, will help your students review text material from any chapter by testing themselves on an Apple® *IIe* or *IIc,* or an IBM®PC. Adopters will receive the QuizPak program, question disks, and an easy-to-follow user's guide. QuizPak may be used at a number of work stations simultaneously and requires only one disk drive.

wcb StudyPak is a computerized study guide that will help your students master the material in *Psychology: An Introduction.* StudyPak includes guided reviews with fill-in-the-blank, short-answer, multiple-choice, and matching items; quizzes; and games. The easy-to-use program includes a built-in diagnostic scoring system that identifies the learning objectives the student has not mastered. StudyPak is available on the Apple® *IIe* and *IIc,* and the IBM®PC.

PSYCOM, Psychology on Computer: Simulations, Experiments, and Projects, is an interactive software package for introductory psychology, which is available for the Apple® *IIe* and *IIc,* and the IBM®PC. The various activities teach students to collect data, analyze it, and discuss the results within the context of scientific study. Results of the experiments can be tabulated for individual students or the entire class. A brief student workbook accompanies the software, providing background reading, instructions, worksheets, and other material necessary to complete the projects.

To the Student: How the Book Works

This book contains several learning devices, each of which is included for a reason. In general, the learning devices are designed to accomplish three things:

1. To focus your attention on the subject of the chapter.

2. To give you an advance overall view of what you are about to learn.

3. To show you how each fact and concept is related to the overall subject matter of the chapter.

These three goals must be accomplished if you are going to learn about psychology in a meaningful way, rather than just blindly memorizing facts and definitions. Let me show you how each feature of the book contributes to these three goals.

Chapter Outline

Each chapter begins with an outline that organizes the key ideas of the chapter. Examine the outline carefully to see what topics will be studied, but notice also how the topics are arranged. The major topics are called *A* heads; they define the breadth of coverage in each chapter. Subsumed under each *A* head are *B* heads and *C* heads; these heads (indented and in smaller type) reveal the depth and detail of coverage. Studying the outline for a few minutes will give you an advance look at the content of the chapter and show you how topics are related to one another. When you read a chapter, you may wish to refer to the outline from time to time. It will reinforce the relationship among topics and help you understand the structure of the chapter.

Key Terms

A list of the most important terms you will encounter in the chapter are presented on the same page as the chapter outline. You can use these key terms to focus and check your learning. Because learning new vocabulary is half the battle in psychology, be sure you understand the meaning of each of these terms by the time you have finished studying a chapter. They will help you make sure you have learned the most important terms when you are reviewing for a test. Page references have been added to the key terms in this second edition to help you locate definitions while studying.

Prologue

Following the chapter outline and key terms is a short section designed to focus your attention on the theme of the chapter. It is a high-interest essay that introduces a bit of research or history to prepare you for the content of the chapter. No specialized knowledge is needed to understand the prologue, but if you reread it after you have studied the chapter, you will see it in a different light.

Chapter Preview

The chapter preview is perhaps the single most useful learning aid in the book. It highlights the most important concepts and facts that will be covered in the chapter. Along with the chapter outline, it allows you to see what the chapter is going to be about before you attempt to read and understand details. A great deal of research suggests that having a general understanding of what is going to be learned will improve learning and memory of the new material. The preview will help you *understand* what you are learning, which is better than rote memorization of details.

Section Reviews

Within each chapter, there are from three to seven major sections. These are self-contained in the sense that they can be understood without an extensive understanding of the sections that precede or follow them. This will allow your instructor to assign sections to be read instead of an entire chapter when the need arises. This helps promote easy mastery.

Following each major section is a brief review that summarizes the main ideas introduced in that section. Again, this will help you keep the *overall* organization of the new material in mind as you study the details.

Chapter Summaries

At the end of each chapter, the content of the entire chapter is summarized in sentence outline form. This outline format is designed to give you one last look at the content of the chapter to see how all the pieces of new information fit together.

Other Features of the Text

In addition to the main learning aids just described, the book contains many other features. Two kinds of inserts are provided: "Of Special Interest" entries introduce highly interesting materials that illustrate the meaning and importance of the topics at hand; "Research Reports" help show the experimental foundations of the science of psychology by describing interesting experiments or clinical case studies that relate to the chapters.

A running glossary with pronunciation guide defines new terms and shows you how to pronounce those that may be difficult. You will find these definitions and pronunciations along the outside margin of the text near the new terms that appear in boldface type within the text. They provide a convenient way of learning definitions without disrupting your reading. At the end of the text, a full alphabetical glossary with page references is provided so that you can easily find the definition of any major term. A list of suggested readings is presented at the end of each chapter if you want to learn more about a specific topic covered in the chapter, and charts, drawings, and photographs are used throughout to clarify and illustrate the information presented in the text.

Special Section on Study Skills

To help you improve your study skills in this or any other college course, a special section follows on page xxxii to provide you with a set of useful hints. These are based on the latest that the psychology of human learning has to offer.

A C K N O W L E D G M E N T S

The editorial contributions of Jim Romig, Richard Owen, Susan Soley, and Gloria Schiesl to the first edition were enormous and sincerely appreciated. And, perhaps knowing what a tough act they were following, the editorial team for the second edition was no less excellent. Jim McNeil, the genius behind the visual design of the first edition, proved to be an equally valuable acquisitions editor. Gloria Schiesl's excellent production editing of the first edition could only be duplicated by having Gloria as the production editor for the second edition. Finally, the success or failure of any writing project hinges directly on the pivotal role played by the developmental editor. No one makes more decisions, keeps track of more deadlines, and spends more time taking care of authors during our frequent neurotic and slothful episodes. My sincere thanks go to Sandy Schmidt for her genuinely excellent work and frequently needed support.

I was also very fortunate to have the assistance of Steven A. Schneider, Pima Community College (Arizona), who wrote the *Instructor's Manual, Lecture Enrichment Kit,* and *Student Study Guide* that accompany this text; and William O. Dwyer, Memphis State University, who wrote the Test Item File.

Many other persons helped very significantly in the development of the text. Thanks go to Linda Iverson; Michael E. Warrell, designer; Mary Heller, photo research manager; and Mavis Oeth, permissions editor. Thanks also to the many unnamed persons at Wm. C. Brown Publishers who did their jobs so well but without coming as directly to my attention.

Special thanks go to William B. Pavlik and Roger Thomas of the University of Georgia for their generous support.

Many of my fellow psychology instructors provided assistance in the development and writing of this book. I'd like to thank the following professors for reviewing parts or all of the manuscript for the first and/or second edition:

Henry E. Adams *University of Georgia*
Vincent J. Adesso *University of Wisconsin, Milwaukee*
John B. Benson *Texarkana Community College*
Tom Bourbon *Stephen F. Austin State University*
Thomas Brothen *University of Minnesota*
Hazel J. Brown *Harrisburg Area Community College*
Francis B. Colavita *University of Pittsburgh*
Ed Donnerstein *University of Wisconsin, Madison*
George J. Downing *Gloucester Community College*
William O. Dwyer *Memphis State University*
David C. Edwards *Iowa State University*
Henry C. Ellis *University of New Mexico*
Joseph D. Eubanks *San Antonio College*
Laura Freberg *Cuesta College*
Ajaipal S. Gill *Anne Arundel Community College*
Megan R. Gunnar *University of Minnesota*

John Hensley *Midwestern State University*
A. Herschberger *Greater Hartford Community College*
Lyllian B. Hix *Houston Community College*
Robert H. Hodgens *Florence-Darlington Technical College*
Neil B. Holliman *Midwestern State University*
R. Reed Hunt *University of North Carolina*
Chester Karwoski *University of Georgia*
Daniel S. Kirschenbaum *University of Wisconsin, Madison*
Kathryn Ann Lambers *Beal College*
James T. Lamiell *Georgetown University*
Joseph T. Lawton *University of Wisconsin, Madison*
Donald H. McBurney *University of Pittsburgh*
Caven S. Mcloughlin *Kent State University*
Lynn E. McCutcheon *Northern Virginia Community College*
Richard E. Mayer *University of California, Santa Barbara*
Daniel D. Moriarty *University of San Diego*
Paul Muhs *University of Wisconsin, Green Bay*
Thomas P. Petzel *Loyola University of Chicago*
William Pfohl *Western Kentucky University*
Daniel W. Richards *Houston Community College*
Deborah Richardson *University of Georgia*
Ronald W. Rogers *University of Alabama*
Gary Schaumberg *Cerritos College*
Steven A. Schneider *Pima Community College*
Pamela E. Stewart *Northern Virginia Community College*
Lawrence L. Stofan *University of Maine*
Roger K. Thomas *University of Georgia*
Edward A. Thompson *Southern Connecticut State University*
M. E. Thrasher *San Bernardino Valley College*
William H. Van Hoose *University of Virginia*
Maureen Rousset Worth *Southern Seminary Junior College*

STUDY SKILLS

Before You Begin:
The Psychology of Study Skills

A glance at the table of contents for this book reveals the complexity and diversity of the field of psychology. It's a science that includes a great many topics, most of which have some direct relevance to our lives. One topic that has long been of interest to psychologists is human learning—the ways in which we learn and remember new information, such as the new information that you will soon learn about the field of psychology. Much has been discovered about learning and memory that can be translated into suggestions for more efficient learning. We do not absorb information like a sponge absorbs water; we are highly effective learners, but we learn better in some ways than we do in others. If we understand the characteristics and quirks of the human learner, we can make better use of our study time. These characteristics will be discussed in some detail in chapters 5 and 6, but before you begin to study the science of psychology, it may be useful to summarize some of the more helpful hints provided by psychologists for more effective learning and recall.

I have kept this section brief because I know how busy the beginning of the term can be. But I believe the information contained in this section is worth your attention. From my own personal experience as a student and from working with many students since that time, I know that learning better ways to study can make the learning process more enjoyable, can increase the amount of information that you learn and retain, and can improve your grades. I hope that the following suggestions will help you.

The SQ3R Method

Many years ago, the late Francis Robinson of Ohio State University suggested a method for studying textbooks known as the *SQ3R* method. These initials stand for the five steps in effective textbook study outlined by Robinson.

S: *Survey.* Look ahead at the content of the text before you begin to read.

Q: *Question.* Ask yourself questions about the material you are reading before and as you read.

R: *Read.* Read through the material in the normal way.

R: *Recite.* Recite the new information that you are learning, out loud or silently to yourself.

R: *Review.* Go over the material that you have learned several times before you are tested on it.

Let's go through these steps in more detail to get a better feel for them.

Survey

Most of us think there is just one way to read—you start at the beginning and read to the end. That is the best way to read a novel because you do not want to know about the next twist of the plot or the surprise ending until you get there. But a very different strategy is needed when reading a textbook. It's important to *survey,* or *look ahead,* at what you are going to read. In fact, you should try to find out as much as possible about the text material you are going to read *before* you read it.

The reason behind this strategy of surveying before reading is based on the way humans learn and store new information in memory. Speaking loosely, we "hang" new information on what we already know. If we learn a new fact about marijuana, we hang that information on what we already know about mind-altering drugs; and the more organized knowledge we have of a topic, the better we are able to learn and remember new information about it. In particular, the more *general* information we possess about a topic, the easier it is to learn and remember new *specific* information about the topic (Ausubel, 1960; Deese & Deese, 1979).

There are several effective ways to survey this textbook. As in studying any text, you should look at the general content of each chapter by reading the headings within it. For your convenience, the headings within each chapter of this text are placed in an outline on the chapter opening page. Novels do not have headings because there is no reason to survey their content in advance; textbooks have them because they greatly aid surveying and reviewing. For example, did you look ahead at the headings in this section before beginning to read it? If you did, you developed an overall view of its content.

Next look at the preview section at the beginning of each chapter. It is there to give you an advance look at the highpoints of the content you will be reading. Study this preview section carefully before going on and it will increase the amount of information you learn as you read. When surveying some textbooks, you may need to add to what you learn from the headings by briefly skimming sections and looking at illustrations, but in this text, the chapter outlines and previews provide the best sources of advance information.

Question

After you have surveyed the material you will be reading, Robinson suggests that you ask questions. Do this before and as you are reading. These questions should be those raised during your survey and first reading. They should reflect your own personal struggle to understand and digest the contents of this book. For example, included here are sample questions that you might ask while studying the thyroid gland in chapter 2, page 73. Asking such questions will help you become actively involved in the learning process and will focus your attention on relevant information. As you locate the information that answers your questions, you may find it helpful to underline or highlight such information with a felt-tip pen.

The **thyroid gland,** located just below the larynx, or voice box, plays an important role in the regulation of **metabolism.** It does so by secreting a hormone called **thyroxin.** The level of thyroxin in a person's bloodstream, and the resulting metabolic rate, are important in many ways. In children, proper functioning of the thyroid is necessary for proper mental development. A serious thyroid deficiency in childhood will produce sluggishness, poor muscle tone, and a type of mental retardation called **cretinism.**

Where is the thyroid gland located?

What role does the thyroid gland play in metabolism?

What are the effects of thyroxin?

Read

After the S and Q steps, you are ready to begin reading in the usual way. Although you have put in a lot of time preparing for this step, your reading probably will be so much more efficient that it's worth the extra time. In fact, if you have the time to invest, you could improve the efficiency of your reading even more by *skimming* the material quickly before reading it more closely.

Recite

When studying, is it more beneficial to spend your time reading the material over and over again, or to read it and then practice reciting it (repeating it to yourself)? Reciting is definitely the most useful part of the study process. If nothing else, it alerts you to those things you do not really know yet (the things you cannot recite), and it may actually make learning more efficient. Regardless of how recitation works, it works. A. I. Gates (1917) found that subjects who spent 80 percent of their time reciting lists and only 20 percent reading them recalled *twice* as much as subjects who spent all of their time reading. This seems to be especially true of students who take the time to understand the meaning of what they are learning rather than memorizing it in rote fashion (Honeck, 1973). The list of key terms found at the beginning of each chapter and the marginal glossary should help you with this recitation step. If you can recite the basic definitions of these terms, you will have learned critical material.

Review

After you have learned the new information in the text by reading and reciting, you will need to add one final step that most students neglect: *Review* what you have learned several times before you are tested on it. The goal of the review process is to *overlearn* the material, which means to continue studying material *after* you have first mastered it. The learning process is not over when you can first recite the new information to yourself without error. Your ability to recall this information can be significantly strengthened later by reciting it several more times before you are tested (Krueger, 1929). To aid you with the review step, this text provides you with a review section following each major heading within the chapter and a sentence outline summary at the end of each chapter.

Other Strategies for Studying

The SQ3R method can improve your ability to learn information from textbooks. Several other strategies may help you make even more efficient use of your study time.

Be Sure That You Are Actually Learning

The most common reason why students "forget" information when taking tests is that they did not actually learn it in the first place. Since studying is not much fun, even when you are efficient at it, it's far too easy to *act* as if you are studying when in fact you are really listening to the radio, thinking about your sweetheart, or clipping your nails. If you are good at *acting* as if you are studying—I was a master of it during my first two years of college—you can easily fool your roommate, your best friend, or even *yourself*. Fooling yourself is the most dangerous possibility; do not fool yourself into thinking that you are studying when you are not really exerting the effort to become absorbed in the material. When you study, really study.

Study in One Place, and Only Study There

One way to help you really study during your study periods is to study only in *one place*. The goal is to associate that place *only* with effective studying. Begin by choosing a spot that is *free* from distractions. Some places in libraries are ideal for studying, but other places in libraries are great for talking and making new friends. Avoid the latter when you are studying, but feel free to visit these places when you are taking breaks. After you find a good place to study, never do anything there except study. If a friend comes over for conversation, get up and move to another area to talk. Return only when you are ready to study. Similarly, if you are in your study place and find that your mind is wandering, *leave* it until you are ready to study again. If you do this consistently—if you *only study* in your study place—this spot will soon "feel" like a place to study, and you will be more apt to study efficiently while you are there.

Space Out Your Study Time

As long ago as 1885, Hermann Ebbinghaus found that studying a list of new information once a day for several days resulted in better recall of that information than studying the list several times in one day. Since his time, a great deal of research has shown that *spaced practice* often results in better learning and memory than *massed practice*. This is especially true in learning motor skills (such as learning to play a musical instrument) or in learning large amounts of unfamiliar verbal material (such as studying for a psychology test). This is why cramming (massing all your study time into one long session) is terribly inefficient. You can get better grades by spacing the same amount of study time over a longer period.

Use Mnemonic Devices

The suggestions given thus far concern how to study. The following suggestions are about *how to memorize. Mnemonic devices* are methods for storing memories so that they will be easier to recall. In each mnemonic device, an additional indexing cue is memorized along with the material to be learned. *More is less* with mnemonics; memorizing something more will improve retrieval and result in less forgetting.

Method of Loci
Loci is the Latin word for "places." In this method, the items in a list are mentally placed in a series of logically connected places. For example, if you are trying to remember a grocery list, you might think of a bag of sugar hanging on your garage door, a gallon of milk sitting in the front seat of your car, a carton of eggs perched on your steering wheel, and a box of donuts sitting in front of the grocery store door. Stanford University psychologist Gordon Bower (1973) found that subjects who used the method of loci were able to recall almost three times as many words from lists as subjects who did not.

Acronyms

My favorite mnemonic device is the method of *acronyms*. Nearly every list I know in psychology was memorized in terms of acronyms. In this simple method, the first letters of each word in a list are combined to form an acronym. For example, the four stages of alcoholism, which are *P*realcoholic, *P*rodromal, *C*rucial, and *C*hronic, can be memorized using the acronym PPCC. Acronyms are even more useful if they form a real word. For most people, the word *ape* means an animal in a zoo, but the acronym APE helps me remember the names of the three subscales of the psychological test called the Semantic Differential: *A*ctivity, *P*otency, *E*valuation.

A system closely related to acronyms takes the first letter of each word in an ordered series but uses them in a new sentence. My high school biology teacher taught me to remember the hierarchy of biological classification using the sentence "*K*athy *P*ulls *C*andy *O*n *F*riday, *G*ood *S*tuff." Notice that the first letter in each word of this sentence is the same as in *K*ingdom, *P*hylum, *C*lass, *O*rder, *F*amily, *G*enus, *S*pecies. As with acronyms, memory of a phrase or sentence is likely to spark recall of an entire list.

Another useful mnemonic device called the *keyword method* is discussed in *Research Report:* "Memory of Rote vs. Meaningful Learning" in chapter 6, page 235.

Try some of these prescriptions for better learning and memory; they could make a big difference. If you are interested in learning more about study skills, you might want to consult three books that deal with the topic in more depth.

Annis, L. F. (1983). *Study techniques.* Dubuque, Ia.: Wm. C. Brown Publishers.

Deese, J., & Deese, E. K. (1979). *How to study.* 3d ed. New York: McGraw-Hill.

Langan, J. (1978). *Reading and study skills.* New York: McGraw-Hill.

PSYCHOLOGY
AN INTRODUCTION

P A R T

Introduction

What Is Psychology?

OUTLINE

KEY TERMS

Aristotle was born in 384 B.C. in an area of northern Greece. His father was a royal physician who trained his son to follow in his footsteps, but Aristotle was a less practical man than his father. Aristotle pursued knowledge for the sake of knowledge—a pursuit that led him to become one of Ancient Greece's most famous and influential philosophers.

In Aristotle's day, philosophy was much broader than it is now and also encompassed the modern fields of science and mathematics. The topics of his writings were wide-ranging, but most of them had a common theme—*life.* Aristotle was interested in learning everything he could about living things. He and his students collected and dissected plants and animals in an attempt to see how their organs sustained life. They studied the process of reproduction to see how life was recreated in each generation. And they studied the everyday actions of living people as they reasoned, remembered, learned, and attempted to persuade one another.

It was Aristotle's habit in his later years to discuss philosophy with his students as they strolled the covered walks of his school, the Lyceum. Imagine that they were talking about his favorite subject—the nature of life itself. Listen to what he might have said to them:

> You'll understand what life is if you think about the act of dying. You know I'm getting up in years: I might pass from life to death soon. When I do, how will I be different from the way I am right now? When I breathe my last dying breath, what changes will take place?

> In the first moment after death, my body will be scarcely different than it was in the last seconds of life, yet I will be vastly different. I will no longer move, no longer sense, nor speak, nor feel, nor care. It's precisely these characteristics of life, and many more like them, that pass out of a living thing with the last breath. At that moment the psyche takes flight.

Aristotle used the term *psyche* to refer to the essence of life. This term is translated to mean soul or mind, but it is closely linked in meaning to the word *breath.* To Aristotle, psyche escaped as the last dying breath was exhaled. Modern psychologists no longer speak of Aristotle's "breath of life," but they are interested in the same actions, thoughts, and feelings of human beings. Indeed, the term *psychology* comes from Aristotle's word *psyche* plus the Greek word *logos* signifying "the study of." Although we use a more restricted definition in this text, it would not be inaccurate to define psychology as the study of life.

Aristotle not only first defined the subject matter for the science that would later be called psychology, but also laid the basic foundation for the *methods* that psychologists and other scientists use in carrying out their studies. Aristotle received much of his own training in philosophical methods from the famous philosopher Plato, but he disagreed with Plato's belief that one could achieve a full understanding of anything simply by thinking about it. Instead, Aristotle felt that one must also *observe* the thing being studied—look at it, listen to it, touch it. Aristotle studied life by observing it. Although he was not a scientist in the modern sense of the word, Aristotle's emphasis on the importance of observation is the basis for the methods of contemporary science. Progress in scientific methods from Aristotle to the present has involved no basic changes in this idea; scientists have only developed more precise and careful ways of observing. Thus, Aristotle launched the study of life that evolved, some 2,200 years later, into the modern science of psychology.

P R E V I E W

Psychologists are interested in the actions, thoughts, motives, and feelings that make up our lives. They seek to describe them, predict them, understand them, and influence them in helpful ways. In contrast to philosophers who seek to understand human nature only by thinking about it, psychologists are scientists who also gather new information about behavior by systematically observing it. Observation is the heart of the scientific method. Psychologists use a variety of scientific methods ranging from surveys to formal experiments; each has special advantages in helping us fit new pieces into the puzzle of human behavior and mental processes.

The first systematic writings about human behavior date back over 2,000 years to the time of Aristotle, but psychology did not become an independent science until 1879 when Wilhelm Wundt founded the first laboratory of psychology in Germany. Psychology had other "beginnings" in the late 1800s by a number of scientists who were interested in different aspects of human behavior and mental processes. Even today there are many different theories and specialties in psychology focusing on different facets of the human condition.

Psyche and Science=Psychology

Welcome to psychology! You are invited to learn about one of life's interesting subjects—yourself. You enrolled in this psychology course knowing that it had something to do with people. Botany is about plants; history is about the past; psychology is about people. You may even know someone who is a psychologist, or you may have some knowledge about how psychology is put to use in society. But, what exactly is psychology? What will you learn about people and of what use is it?

Definition of Psychology

In the Prologue to this chapter, we stated that it would not be incorrect to define psychology as the "study of life"—psychologists want to understand the nature of people's lives. The only thing that is incorrect about this definition is that it's not specific enough to characterize the modern discipline of psychology and to distinguish it from other sciences, such as biology, that also study the processes of life. Today, **psychology** *is defined as the science of behavior and mental processes.* Notice that this definition contains three key terms—science, behavior, and mental processes. Let's look at each of these terms separately. Psychology is considered a **science** because psychologists attempt to understand people not only by thinking about them, but by learning about them through careful, controlled observation. It is this reliance on rigorous scientific methods of observation that is the basis of all sciences, including psychology. The term **behavior** refers to all of a person's overt actions that others can directly observe. When you walk, speak, throw a Frisbee, or show a facial expression, you are behaving in this sense. The term **mental processes** refers to the thoughts, feelings, and motives that each of us experiences privately, which others cannot directly observe. Your thoughts and feelings about the Frisbee that your dog just caught in mid-air are mental processes.

psychology
The science of behavior and mental processes.

science
Approach to knowledge based on systematic observation.

behavior
Directly observable and measurable human actions.

mental processes
Private psychological activities that include thinking, perceiving, and feeling.

CATHY   **by Cathy Guisewite**

Some psychologists prefer to limit the science of psychology to the study of behavior. They believe that a science can only study directly observable phenomena. For example, a psychologist could see what I did and said if I lost my wallet, but could not observe what I was thinking or feeling about losing it. Most psychologists, however, believe that although mental processes cannot be directly observed, they are so important that they must be included in the field of psychology for us to have a complete understanding of human lives. Some argue that this can be done by making careful **inferences** about mental processes. This text takes the latter position; while recognizing the difficulties involved in making inferences, a science of psychology that does not deal with both behavioral and mental processes seems incomplete.

inference
Logical conclusion based on available evidence.

Goals of Psychology

What are the goals of the science of psychology? What are psychologists trying to accomplish?

Psychologists study people by using scientific methods. The goals of this scientific enterprise are to be able to describe, predict, understand, and influence behavior and mental processes. More on these four goals:

1. *Describe.* The information gathered through scientific research helps us describe psychological phenomena more accurately. Information gathered in a survey on sexual behavior, for example, would enable psychologists to describe this aspect of human life more knowledgeably.

2. *Predict.* In some cases, psychologists are able to predict behavior, such as predicting how much anxiety a group of employees will experience from knowledge of how much stress they are under on the job.

3. *Understanding behavior.* The third goal of psychology—requires us to add an *explanation* to our descriptive and predictive knowledge of facts and relationships. We understand behavior and mental processes when we can explain them. That is not to say, however, that we understand psychological phenomena when we know the *truth* about them. Science is not a set of finished truths; it's a method of gaining information that may never be finished. At the very least, it's safe to say that psychology is not a finished science because there is still much more to know. And if there is more to

The goals of psychology are to describe, predict, understand, and influence human behavior.

know, that means our current explanations *must be tentative;* in other words, our explanations are **theories,** not truths. Theories are tentative explanations of facts and relationships in sciences. It's essential for you to understand this basic fact about science as you read this or any other textbook. The knowledge that we can offer you is always tentative. As the science of psychology progresses through research, our theories are always subject to revision.

The business of science, in fact, can be thought of as the revision of theories using the scientific methods. Scientists make predictions, or **hypotheses,** based on a theory, then they test them in experiments. If the predictions are borne out, the theory is supported; if not, the theory is disconfirmed. Eventually, a theory that is often disconfirmed and rarely supported will be discarded and a new theory offered in its place. If a theory is consistently supported, on the other hand, it may acquire the status of a **law,** a strongly supported and widely accepted theory. However, a law is still not the equivalent of the truth; it's just a well-supported, tentative theory. There are few laws in psychology. Those that could be reasonably labeled as laws deal with relatively simple phenomena. As we said earlier, psychology is hardly a finished science; yet, as you will see, much is already known.

4. *Influence.* Finally, we hope to go beyond description, understanding, and prediction to influence behavior in desirable ways: What can we do to help a teenage boy climb out of a period of severe depression? How can we help parents raise their rambunctious children better? What is the best way to help a 38-year-old woman decide on a career when she returns to the work force? It's not until we can intentionally influence behavior that psychology completely fulfills its promise.

theory
Tentative explanation of facts and relationships in sciences.

hypothesis (hi-poth′ĕ-sis)
A proposed explanation for a phenomenon that can be tested.

law
A strongly supported and widely accepted theory.

R E V I E W

We have defined psychology as the science of behavior and mental processes. Many psychologists believe that sciences can only deal with directly observable phenomena—in this case, overt behavior. Other psychologists believe that we can do justice to the human condition only by making careful inferences about private mental processes. The goals of psychology are to describe, predict, understand, and influence behavior and mental processes. Using the methods of science, we gather information through systematic observation that enables us to accurately describe psychological facts and relationships. When adequate descriptive information has been acquired, reasonably accurate predictions can be made and explanations proposed to help us understand these facts and relationships. Finally, when enough understanding and ability to predict has been acquired, we can sometimes intentionally influence people in ways that improve and enrich their lives. Psychology is an ongoing process of gathering new information, but a great deal is already known. That is, the goals of psychology have been partially met in some cases.

OF SPECIAL INTEREST

What Will This Course Be About?

You may have already glanced through the book and noticed illustrations of nerve cells, discussions of binocular cues in the perception of distance, and photos of dogs being taught to salivate to the sound of a bell. *This is psychology?* If you are like me when I opened my first introductory psychology book, you were surprised to see such topics in a book about psychology. I had expected tales of madness, love, and social ills, but instead I got brain structures, salivating dogs, and odor receptors. Had I not had an instructor who explained how these topics were related to my interests in people, I would have surely changed majors. I hope this book will help your instructor do the same for you.

This text surveys the *basics* of psychological principles and shows you how these principles can be *applied* to solve significant human problems. Because the solution of problems requires an understanding of basic concepts and facts, we begin with the basics and move toward the applications as the course unfolds. And, because this is a first course in psychology, we cover far more basics than applications. But to help you make better sense of the fundamental concepts, this book describes many applications throughout the course to illustrate the concrete importance of the data and abstract principles upon which psychology is built.

Will This Course Help Me with My Personal Adjustment?

All of the material in this book, even the most basic material, is relevant to human lives in some way. In discussing the basic topics, I point out some of these implications. More importantly, contemporary psychology textbooks contain many topics that relate directly to everyone's personal efforts to make sense out of life. In this text we discuss emotions, love, sex, ways of improving memory, and other important personal topics. Helping you to better understand yourself is a primary goal of this book, but be careful! It has been wisely said that a little knowledge is a dangerous thing. So do not be overconfident that you'll learn enough in this course to solve all of the problems that life can toss at you. If you find yourself playing amateur psychologist with a serious personal issue, you might want to consult a professional psychologist just to make sure you are on the right track.

OF SPECIAL INTEREST

Will This Course Help Me with My Career?

Two chapters in the book are directly concerned with career topics. Chapter 13 on therapies for psychological problems is relevant to the careers of clinical and counseling psychology, and chapter 15 discusses applications of psychology to business, medicine, law, and education. In addition, all of the chapters on basic psychology are relevant to careers. All careers involve people in some way—even if it's only the employees themselves. For this reason, any understanding of a profession that does not include a psychological understanding of the people involved will be inadequate.

Will This Course Cover Some Topics That are Just Interesting?

Many facets of psychology are inherently interesting. Topics such as the meaning of dreams, compulsive gambling, out-of-body experiences, hypnosis, and the like are covered in this book. In part, we discuss such topics just because they are fun to learn about—fun is a legitimate goal for education if kept in proper perspective. But we also study such topics because they can teach us about more basic psychological principles. Ultimately, a firm understanding of the basic concepts will be most useful to you in later life because they can be applied to any issue or situation you might encounter.

Will This Course Shed Some Light on the "Big" Issues in Life?

You cannot open a newspaper or turn on the television without being confronted with one of the major issues facing human beings today. Crime, war, job pressures, divorce, prejudice, and unemployment affect us all either directly or indirectly. Can a knowledge of psychology help you understand and deal more effectively with these issues? Let's compare the approach that psychology takes in dealing with an issue like crime to the approach that would be taken by other disciplines that are interested in human welfare.

A philosopher might approach this issue by asking about the ethics of crime. When is it moral or immoral to commit a crime? Is it moral to obey a law that you consider unjust? Would it be immoral to steal to feed a child if you had no other alternative? A lawyer might take a different approach. He or she would be interested in

[Continued on page 12]

OF SPECIAL INTEREST

[*Continued from page 11*]

the laws designed to prevent crime. Do existing laws adequately protect citizens? Are they so extensive that they unnecessarily limit our freedoms? Are laws designed to protect our freedom during arrest, allowing criminals too much of an edge over the police?

A psychologist would take yet another approach. The psychologist would use methods of science to understand criminal behavior itself. One question might concern the conditions under which a specific type of crime occurs most frequently. Psychologists are also interested in whether habitual criminals are psychologically different from noncriminals. Other experiments have explored the effectiveness of different methods of rehabilitating criminals.

The information covered in this text will sometimes seem far removed from important issues such as crime. It will often seem to focus so closely on details that the application of psychology to everyday life is obscured. This is because a huge amount of basic information must be surveyed in a brief span of time in an introductory psychology course. This book will try not to let you miss the forest for the trees, however. As we study the way nerve cells influence one another, for instance, you will be reminded that knowledge of this mechanism led to the development of modern tranquilizing drugs. When we study the way the eyes sense color, it will be pointed out that such knowledge led to an understanding of color blindness and the invention of color television. In psychology you are never far from an application to a human problem, no matter how technical the subject matter.

The Many Faces of Psychology and Their Origins

Behavior is superbly complex and varied. A scientist could spend an entire career studying any part of it: the causes of abnormal behavior, the way we recall facts, the ways to improve job satisfaction among factory workers, the role of the brain in emotions, the nature of racial prejudice, and so on. When we consider the range of possibilities, it's not surprising that there are many fields within the science of psychology, each focusing on a different facet of human behavior. To better understand this diversity, we need to look back briefly in history.

The Early Psychologists

There was no formal discipline of psychology during the time of Aristotle or for 2,200 years after he lived. Like the other sciences, psychology was simply part of "philosophy." It wasn't until modern times that the sciences emerged from the general field of philosophy. In the seventeenth and eighteenth centuries physics, biology, medicine, and other disciplines began to accumulate knowledge that set each somewhat apart from the others. Each developed distinct ways of viewing phenomena and solving problems, which taken as a whole represented a scientific way of thinking that spawned psychology.

The formal launching of the separate field of psychology is usually credited to Wilhelm Wundt for establishing the first Laboratory of Psychology in Leipzig, Germany, in 1879. However, some psychologists and historians feel that William James deserves the honor for a less publicized laboratory at Harvard University, which opened in 1875. Actually, many people "founded" psychology. Their varied interests and talents laid the foundations for the diverse field surveyed in this text. As you read about some of the most influential early psychologists, imagine how different their answers would be if you asked each of them, "What is the most important question in psychology?"

Wundt and Titchener: The Structure of the Mind

Wilhelm Wundt was a professor of biology who was fascinated by human consciousness and culture. He was familiar with the scientific methods used by other scientists and applied them to the phenomena of human consciousness. This part of Wundt's work was taken over and expanded by his student, Edward Titchener. Just as physicists sought to discover the basic particles that make up physical matter, Titchener wanted to identify the basic elements of conscious experience. He and Wundt studied consciousness using a method of looking inward at one's own experiences called **introspection.** They rigorously trained themselves to observe the contents of their own minds as accurately and unemotionally as possible in an attempt to isolate the basic elements of the mind. What does that mean exactly?

Wilhelm Wundt (1832–1920)

introspection
(in″tro-spek′shun)
The process of looking inward at one's own consciousness.

Well, suppose that I visit your city some day and your instructor prevails upon me to give a guest lecture on the history of psychology. Suppose further that I am in a particularly dramatic mood and decide to give the lecture playing the role of Edward Titchener. I arrive wearing a fake beard and the flowing black academic robes that he always wore, and without any explanation at all, I choose you to be the subject of a demonstration of introspection. I ask you to close your eyes and I place a bit of apple in your mouth. Then I ask you to describe to me the *sensations* that this physical stimulus creates in your mind.

You hesitate for a moment, then announce with a smile, "It's an apple!"

"Nein! Nein! Nein!" I shout, using the only word I can remember from German 101. "I asked you to tell me what you *sense,* not what the stimulus is. Don't tell me what the thing is on your tongue—describe the sensations in your mind."

You hesitate for yet another moment, regain your composure, and hesitatingly say, "Sweet?"

"Yes! Yes!" I cry. "What else do you sense?"

"A little bit of sourness, and a grainy texture, and a wetness."

"Wonderful!" I shout, leading you to break into a grin. "Now, you're introspecting. Now, you're describing the elemental contents of your mind. Sweet, sour, grainy . . . those are a few of the building blocks that the mind is structured from."

Because they were interested in the elements of the mind and how they are organized, Wundt and Titchener are known as **structuralists;** that is, they sought to determine the structure of the mind through controlled introspection. Structuralists are important to the history of psychology not so much for what they learned about human experience as for their emphasis on careful and precise methods of observation. That emphasis made a true science of psychology possible.

structuralism
(struk′tūr-al-izm)
The nineteenth-century school of psychology that sought to determine the structure of the mind through controlled introspection.

William James (1842–1910)

functionalism
(funk′shun-al-izm)
The nineteenth-century
school of psychology that
emphasized the useful
functions of consciousness.

William James: The Functions of Consciousness

In 1875 a young professor of biology and philosophy at Harvard University named William James taught the first course on "psychology." In 1890 he published an influential early textbook of psychology. Like Wundt, James borrowed concepts and scientific methods from biology to use in his study of consciousness, but James took a very different view of psychology from Wundt and Titchener's.

James was impressed with the work of biologist Charles Darwin, who suggested in his theory of evolution that every physical characteristic evolved in a species because it serves some *purpose*. James suspected that the same thing could be said about the human mind. He speculated that thinking, feeling, learning, remembering, and other processes of human consciousness exist *only because they help us survive as a species*. Because we can think, for example, we are better able to find food, avoid danger, and care for our children—all of which help the human species survive. Because of its emphasis on the *functions* of consciousness, a school of thought known as **functionalism** emerged based on the work of William James.

James was particularly interested in topics he considered to be evolutionarily important: the emotions of fear and rage, the learning of unconscious habits, volition (the exercise of "free will"), and the flow of conscious thought. Because he was concerned with what the mind could do rather than what it was made of, James criticized the structuralists for creating a barren, meaningless approach to psychology. He likened human consciousness to a flowing stream: We could study that stream by isolating single molecules of water, but by doing so we would miss the nature and beauty of the whole stream. Moreover, studying the water molecules in a stream would tell us nothing about what the stream *does*—that it erodes riverbanks, provides a home for fish, carries barges, and so on. Similarly, studying the elements of the mind tells us nothing about how it *functions* to help us adapt to the demands of life. The functions of the mind, not its raw elements, were the subject matter of psychology to the functionalists.

Functionalism continues to have a strong influence on contemporary psychology, even though it's no longer viewed as a separate school of thought. The way American psychologists view thinking, learning, self-control, and the biological basis of behavior still bears the mark of William James. In particular, the contemporary emphasis in American psychology on the active role played by thinking and perception in human behavior can be thought of as a return to the basic tenets of functionalism.

Pavlov and Watson: Behaviorism

In the 1890s Russian **physiologist** Ivan Pavlov was conducting research on digestion in dogs when he noticed a curious thing. He had surgically implanted tubes in the cheeks of the dogs to gather saliva during eating. He noticed that after several feedings the dogs started salivating when they heard the food being brought to them rather than when it was placed in their mouths. Pavlov recognized that the dogs had learned to associate the sound with the food. Because the sound had immediately preceded the food on many occasions, the dogs came to respond to the sound as if it were food. He demonstrated that this interpretation was correct by conducting careful experiments using a clicking metronome—instead of the sound of food's being brought—and small quantities of powdered meat. When the metronome and the meat powder were presented together, the dogs quickly learned to salivate to the metronome alone.

Ivan Pavlov (1849–1936)

physiologist
(fiz′′e-ol′o-jist)
A scientist who studies the functions of living organs.

Although teaching dogs to salivate to the sound of a metronome is not important in its own right, Pavlov's accidental discovery was of tremendous importance to the new field of psychology. He had identified a simple form of learning—or **conditioning** to use his term—and a precise scientific way to study it. By measuring the number of drops of saliva produced by a dog who heard the metronome, Pavlov was able to study many aspects of the learning process, such as the time interval between the sound and the food that produced the most rapid conditioning (one-half second). Pavlov felt that the study of conditioning was such an important breakthrough that he completed his research on digestion, for which he had already won the Nobel Prize, and he spent the rest of his career studying his new discovery. Pavlov eventually came to believe that all human thought, emotion, and language derived largely from this simple form of learning that we now call *classical* or *Pavlovian conditioning*.

Pavlov's research and theories were slow to be recognized in the United States, but by the 1920s the concepts were taken up in the writings of John B. Watson. Watson was trained in functionalism, but he rejected the ideas of the functionalists and structuralists and founded his own approach to psychology. He felt that it was impossible to study consciousness because only outward behavior could be scientifically understood. He was deeply impressed by the first reports of Pavlov's work on conditioning because of its scientific precision and the absence of introspection. Watson also agreed with Pavlov that the importance of conditioning went far beyond salivating dogs, and that most human behavior is learned through classical conditioning.

Because of the emphasis on the precise measurement of overt behavior, Watson called the new school of thought, founded on his principles and those of Pavlov, **behaviorism.** Behaviorism continues to be an important force in psychology today in its emphasis on overt behavior and learning, but many contemporary behaviorists now believe that it's also important to study human consciousness.

Max Wertheimer: Gestalt Psychology

A relative "latecomer" to the early schools of thought in psychology was **Gestalt psychology.** Max Wertheimer, a professor of psychology at the University of Frankfurt, and his associates in Germany began developing their own ideas on perception about 25 years after the pioneering work of Wundt.

The key concept in their school of thought was the concept of the **gestalt** or *whole.* Like William James, the Gestalt psychologists felt that human consciousness could not be meaningfully broken down into raw elements as the structuralists proposed to do. Instead, the mind must be studied in terms of large, meaningful units. This is necessary, as they were fond of saying, because "the whole is different from the sum of its parts." To illustrate, the two examples in figure 1.1 are drawn from exactly the same angled lines, but their organization greatly changes your perception of them. While the parts are the same in each example, the *whole* shows a triangle in one example and arrows in the other. Similarly the second element in the two rows in figure 1.1 is exactly the same each time, but it's perceived as a "13" in the first row and as a "B" in the second. A perception only has meaning when it's seen as a whole, rather than as a collection of parts.

conditioning
(kon-dish'-un-ing)
A simple form of learning.

John B. Watson
(1878–1958)

behaviorism
(be-hāv'yor-izm)
The school of psychology that emphasizes the process of learning and the measurement of overt behavior.

Max Wertheimer
(1880–1943)

gestalt (ges-tawlt')
An organized or unified whole.

Figure 1.1 The organization of the lines in these two illustrations shows that only "whole" perceptions have meaning. The lines do not change but their meaning does.

phi phenomenon
(fī fĕ-nom′ĕ-non)
The perception of apparent movement between two stationary stimuli.

Figure 1.2 If two lights are briefly presented in rapid sequence to a person, a single moving light will be seen instead of two stationary lights. This apparent movement, or *phi phenomenon*, is an important demonstration that the whole of a perception is different from the sum of its parts.

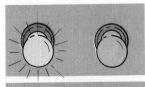

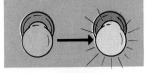

Alfred Binet (1857–1911)

Gestalt psychologists also used the so-called **phi phenomenon** to demonstrate that the whole is different from the sum of its parts (see fig. 1.2). When two lights are presented in rapid sequence, the viewer sees an apparent movement in the stimuli. That is, rather than perceiving two separate stationary lights, the viewer sees one light moving from one position to another. This is a highly important perception to Gestalt psychologists, since what is seen—a moving light—is not present in the two parts of the stimulus at all. Movement is a property of the whole perception—the Gestalt—but not of the individual parts of that perception. Motion picture projectors rely on a similar principle of perception to present a series of motionless images that appear to be moving. Perception was not the only topic that interested Gestaltists; in chapter 5 you will learn that they contributed important insights on learning and problem solving as well.

The Gestalt psychologists were historically important for their criticisms, not only of the structuralists but of the behaviorists as well. They felt that the behaviorists reduced behavior to meaningless elements when they studied simple conditioned responses. Similarly, they believed that behaviorists left the very essence of human existence out of psychology when they rejected the study of consciousness and private mental processes.

Alfred Binet: Measuring Intelligence

In the 1890s the Paris Ministry of Education was faced with a difficult problem. They wanted to provide extensive education for all "intelligent" children and more practical, less academic kinds of schooling for less intelligent children. They wanted to be fair about choosing the children who would be given advanced academic training, but they also wanted to make the decision when the children were fairly young. How could they "measure" something so intangible as a child's intelligence?

The Ministry of Education turned for advice to a professor at the University of the Sorbonne who had just founded France's first psychology laboratory. Alfred Binet's interests were quite different from other early psychologists. Rather than analyzing the mind's structure or functions, Binet sought to *measure* its intellectual capacities. By experimenting with a large number of test items, Binet and his collaborators were able to find a set of questions (e.g., arithmetic problems, word definitions, memory tasks) that could be answered by most children of a given age, but not by younger children or by children with subnormal intelligence. These questions were used to create an intelligence test that was later revised and translated in America to become the current, widely used Stanford–Binet Intelligence Scale. To Alfred Binet, this test was the heart of his definition of psychology as the science that measured the mind for practical purposes. As such, he gave impetus to the branch of psychology that specializes in the measurement of intelligence, personality, job aptitude, and so on.

Sigmund Freud: Psychoanalysis

As is obvious from our discussion so far, psychology developed into a separate science during the late nineteenth century in a number of different places in Europe and the United States, and in a number of different ways through the independent work of people with very strong views. One more "founder" of psychology must be added to our list. In many ways, his view of psychology was the most distinctly different and, until recently, the most influential one in applied psychology.

Sigmund Freud (1856–1939)

Sigmund Freud was an Austrian physician who practiced neurology, the treatment of diseases of the nervous system. Unlike other early psychologists, he was not trained as a philosopher and did not hold a professorship that allowed him to conduct research. Instead, he was responsible for the day-to-day care of a large number of patients, many of whom had psychological problems. This fact, perhaps more than anything else, explains the enormous differences between his view of psychology and those of the other founders. To Freud, the most important topic in psychology was abnormal motivation because he saw it as the cause of psychological problems. Learning, memory, thinking, and other processes so important to the other founding psychologists were of little interest to Freud.

Moreover, Freud believed that conscious experience was of trivial importance when compared to the workings of the **unconscious mind.** Freud felt that the roots of psychological problems were **motives,** particularly sexual and aggressive ones, that reside in a part of the mind of which we are not consciously aware. He believed that these unconscious motives, and the conflicts that surround them, influence our behavior even though we are not aware of their existence. They are manifested in disguised, symbolic ways in dreams, slips of the tongue ("Freudian slips"), and sometimes psychological problems.

unconscious mind
All mental activity of which we are unaware.

motives
Internal states or conditions that activate behavior and give it direction.

Freud attempted to help people with psychological problems through the process of **psychoanalysis.** He believed that the conscious mind actively kept itself from becoming aware of troubles in the unconscious mind. Somehow, this conscious "censor" had to be bypassed to learn about unconscious motives and conflicts. By encouraging the person to speak in a loose, uncontrolled way about whatever came to mind, Freud hoped that enough information about the unconscious would slip into consciousness for the therapist to interpret the problem to the person. Through this method (the so-called "talking cure") and other ways of bringing the unconscious out in the open, Freud hoped that the person would be able to use his or her powers of reason to deal with strong motives and resolve conflicts.

psychoanalysis
(si″ko-ah-nal′ĭ-sis)
The technique of helping persons with emotional problems based on Sigmund Freud's theory of the unconscious mind.

Contemporary Theories of Psychology

We have just looked at the early days of psychology by seeing how a number of turn-of-the-century scientists launched six different versions of psychology. Each had different interests and assumptions about human nature, so each defined the methods and subject matter of psychology in distinctly different ways. It's important for us to have an understanding of these points of view, because the way we view human beings determines how we study them. For example, Wundt and Titchener thought that personal conscious experiences were highly interesting and important, so to them the method of introspection was the cornerstone of psychology. Watson, on the other hand, felt that consciousness was of so little importance—and could not be studied scientifically anyway—that he never demanded introspection from the subjects in his experiments. Indeed, the subjects would not have told Watson much, since they were usually animals or infants!

OF SPECIAL INTEREST

What's the Difference between a Psychologist and a Psychiatrist?

Perhaps the question most often asked of a psychologist is what is the difference between a psychologist and a psychiatrist. While these two professionals do roughly the same thing—help people with psychological problems—their training is quite different.

A *psychiatrist* has completed medical school and has obtained the M.D. (doctor of medicine) or D.O. (doctor of osteopathy) degree, usually has done an internship in general medicine, and has completed residency training in psychiatry. Because of their medical training, psychiatrists are licensed to prescribe drugs and use other medical treatments such as electroconvulsive shock therapy.

A *psychologist* has been trained strictly in psychology. The closest specialty within psychology to psychiatry is clinical psychology. Clinical psychologists have attended graduate school in psychology and have obtained the degree of Ph.D. (doctor of philosophy) or Psy.D. (doctor of psychology) and have completed an internship in clinical psychology. Because of their lack of medical training, they do not prescribe drugs or other medical treatments.

In addition to these professions, people with psychological problems often also seek help from social workers, counselors, and other individuals. It's worth noting, however, that while nearly every state regulates the practice of psychology and psychiatry, most states do not regulate other helping professions. It's good advice, then, to ask about the training and professional background of anyone who is not licensed in his or her profession by the state.

Where are we today in psychology? Do these six theoretical views still divide psychology? Two of the theories from the turn of the century still exist as important perspectives in contemporary psychology—*psychoanalysis* and *behaviorism*—but Wundt's structuralism and James's functionalism no longer play a role in modern psychology as separate schools of thought. Binet's applied approach has had quite a different fate. Although he never developed an influential theoretical position, Binet's approach to the measurement of intelligence is still very much alive in applied psychology today. In more recent times, a third major theoretical viewpoint, *humanism,* has emerged, and in the last decade a fourth position, *cognitive psychology,* appears to have become a major force. All in all, however, there are fewer staunch adherents to a particular point of view than in the past. Many contemporary psychologists are *eclectic;* that is, they blend the insights of several approaches in their work.

Contemporary Psychoanalysis

Psychoanalysis remains a significant point of view in modern psychology even though the theory has been subjected to a number of revisions since Freud's death. Modern psychoanalysts still adhere to Freud's view that conflicts in the unconscious mind are the chief source of psychological problems. However, there are few "orthodox" psychoanalysts today. Most disagree with Freud's emphasis on sexual and aggressive motives and feel that other motives, such as the need to feel adequate in social relationships, are of greater importance. In addition, contemporary psychoanalysts believe that the cognitive processes of the conscious mind are more significant than did Freud. Even with these changes, Sigmund Freud's view of the human condition continues to exert influence in the modern field of psychology.

B. F. Skinner (1904–   )

Humanistic Psychology

During the 1950s and 1960s, a third important theoretical movement emerged in psychology often known as the "third force" in psychology. Led by the late Carl Rogers, Abraham Maslow, and Viktor Frankl, **humanistic psychology** paints a very different picture of human beings than either psychoanalysis or behaviorism. Rather than being creatures who are pushed by their unconscious motives (as Freud would have it) or passively shaped by their learning experiences (as Watson says), human beings determine their own fates through the decisions they make. In this view, people have a powerful inborn tendency to grow, improve, and to take control of their own lives. While humans can be influenced by outside forces, nothing *determines* their behavior but their own free will.

    Humanistic psychologists are the least scientific of all psychologists. This is not to say that humanistic psychologists never use scientific methods. It's just that many of the issues with which they are concerned would be difficult to investigate in a scientific manner. Topics such as free will, values, the essential goodness of people, the motives that stimulate the creation of art and philosophy, and the uniqueness of each human personality are of prime importance to humanistic psychologists, but these issues are more philosophical than scientific in nature. On the other hand, leading humanistic psychologist Carl Rogers has been particularly interested in methods of psychotherapy and has conducted a great deal of research evaluating his approach.

Abraham Maslow
(1908–1970)

Cognitive Psychology

Recently, there has been an impressive increase of interest among both experimental and applied psychologists in the intellectual processes of **cognition**—perceiving, believing, thinking, remembering, knowing, deciding, and so on. The human mind is thought to resemble a computer as it receives, codes, changes, stores, and uses information. But, unlike mechanical computers, the mind is an information-processing system that actively seeks out information and transforms it to create a view of reality. As you read the word *cognitive,* for example, you may try to make sense out of it in several ways: by reading ahead to see how it's discussed in this section; by looking at the definition in the running glossary; or, if you took Latin in high school, by recalling that *cogito* means "I think." From all of these sources of information, you will construct a perception of what cognitive psychology is all about.

Carl Rogers (1902–   )

humanistic psychology
The psychological view that human beings possess an innate tendency to improve and determine their lives by the decisions they make.

cognition (kog-nish′un)
Mental processes of perceiving, believing, thinking, remembering, knowing, deciding, and so on.

The focus of cognitive psychology reflects a belief that our behavior and emotions are caused in large part by our cognitions. I might stop to offer assistance to a motorist on a highway if I *perceive* him to be in need of help, *believe* that his car is broken, and *remember* that someone once helped me in a similar situation. On the other hand, if I perceive him as not being in need of help, believe that he is planning to rob me at gunpoint, or remember a bad incident with a similar situation, I would not offer him assistance.

Contemporary Behaviorism

Behaviorism has also survived as an independent school of thought in contemporary psychology, but there are a number of different versions of the behavioral perspective today. One version is a "pure" descendant of Watson's behaviorism that rules out the study of mental processes and emphasizes the importance of learning in shaping our behavior. B. F. Skinner of Harvard University is the leading exponent of this brand of behaviorism. The other, more widely accepted version of contemporary behaviorism is quite different. While it continues to emphasize the process of learning, this version departs dramatically from the position of Watson and Skinner by stating that mental processes—particularly cognition—can be scientifically studied. Indeed, these cognitive behaviorists, as they are called, believe that any conception of human behavior that ignores mental processes is incomplete. Stanford University's Albert Bandura is perhaps the leading spokesperson for this viewpoint. Thus, modern behaviorism comes in at least two types: a pure Harvard version and a broadened Stanford version.

Specialty Fields of Modern Psychology

Psychology is, as we have seen, an unusually broad and diverse field. From the very beginnings of psychology, different founders studied different aspects of human behavior and declared their own theories and methods to be the correct way to look at psychology. Today, theoretical divisions still exist, but the greatest diversity in modern psychology is in terms of subject-matter specialties. Even though a basic core of knowledge is shared by all psychologists, the interests and expertise of a psychologist who studies the sense of taste, for example, are quite distinct from one who evaluates employees in a large company for possible promotion to management positions, or one who works in a mental institution.

For starters, contemporary psychology can be roughly divided into *experimental* fields and *applied* fields (see fig. 1.3). Experimental psychologists conduct research on basic psychological processes such as emotion, thinking, and learning by using the scientific methods described in the next section of this chapter. Applied psychologists use knowledge acquired by experimental psychologists—and by their own applied research studies—to solve and prevent significant human problems such as emotional instability, marital difficulties, underachievement in school, and job dissatisfaction.

Experimental Fields of Modern Psychology

experimental psychologist
A psychologist who conducts basic research.

About a third of all psychologists are **experimental psychologists** (Boneau & Cuca, 1974; Gottfredson & Dyer, 1978). They are generally broadly trained but they tend to specialize in the study of a single psychological process. Nearly all experimental psychologists work in colleges and universities where they teach and

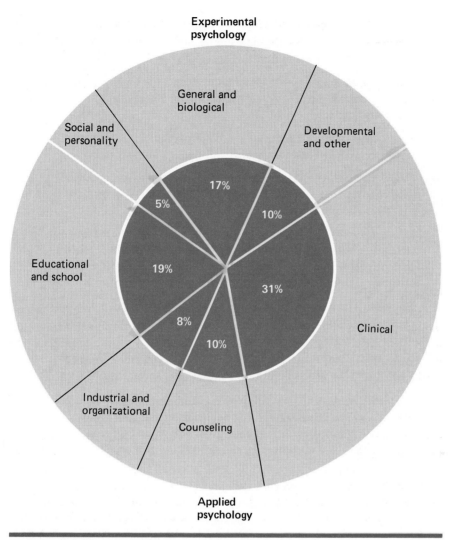

Figure 1.3 The percentage of psychologists engaged in each of the major experimental and applied fields within psychology (Based on Cates, 1970; Boneau & Cuca, 1974; and Gottfredson & Dyer, 1978).

do research, but a few work in research institutions, government agencies, or other settings. Their domain is the basic knowledge of psychology upon which all applications are built. The largest specialties within experimental psychology are as follows:

1. *Biological psychology.* Psychologists in this specialty field study the ways in which the nervous system and other organs provide the basis for behavior. For example, they examine the ways in which inheritance influences our behavior. Biological psychologists also study animal behavior both to compare it to human behavior and to better understand other species of animals.

2. *Sensation and perception.* This specialty is concerned with the way sense organs operate and the way we interpret incoming sensory information in the process of perception.

3. *Learning and memory*. The ways in which we learn and remember new information, new skills, new habits, and new ways of relating to other people are studied in this specialty.

4. *Cognition*. Psychologists in this area are concerned with intelligent action: thinking, perceiving, planning, imagining, creating, dreaming, and solving problems.

5. *Psycholinguistics*. This specialty area of psychology is concerned with how we learn and use spoken and written language.

6. *Developmental psychology*. This field of psychology is concerned with changes that take place in people during their life span, as they grow from birth to old age.

7. *Motivation*. In this specialty, psychologists study the needs and states that activate and guide behavior, such as hunger, thirst, sex, the need for achievement, and the need to have relationships with others.

8. *Emotion*. The nature of the feelings and moods that color human experience, in addition to factors such as stress and learning that are related to them, are the topics for this specialty.

9. *Personality*. The field of personality focuses on the more-or-less consistent ways of behaving that characterize our personalities.

10. *Social psychology*. This specialty area studies the influence of other people on our behavior: the behavior of people in groups, mobs, or organizations; interpersonal attraction and intimate relationships; and attitudes and prejudice toward others.

Applied Fields of Modern Psychology

applied psychologist
A psychologist who uses knowledge of psychology to solve and prevent human problems.

The other two-thirds of psychologists use basic psychological knowledge to solve human problems. Some **applied psychologists** teach and do research, but most work in mental health centers, industries, school systems, medical centers, and other applied settings. The following are the major specialties within applied psychology.

1. *Clinical psychology*. Clinical psychologists are concerned with understanding and treating personal problems and abnormal behavior.

2. *Counseling psychology*. Specialists in this field help people with personal or school problems and with career choices.

3. *Industrial-organizational psychology*. This field focuses on ways to match employees to jobs, to train and motivate workers, and to promote job satisfaction and good relationships among workers.

4. *Educational and school psychology.* Educational psychology is concerned with the ways children learn in the classroom and with the construction of psychological and educational tests. School psychologists consult with teachers about children who have learning or behavior problems as well as test children to see if they could benefit from special educational programs.

5. *Behavioral medicine.* Specialists in this field are concerned with the ways in which pressures, conflicts, hardships, and other factors can contribute to poor health. They seek to prevent health problems such as heart disease by teaching people to relax, exercise, control their diets, and stop smoking, for example.

There is something in psychology to interest or help just about everyone. And if you glance ahead, you will see that the chapters of this book are organized to cover these basic and applied facets of psychology.

R E V I E W

There was no formal science of psychology for 2,200 years after the time of Aristotle. Then, a number of events occurred in the late nineteenth century that led to the emergence of an independent discipline. Wilhelm Wundt founded his psychology laboratory in 1879 and, with his student Edward Titchener, began a controlled introspective study of the structure of human consciousness. William James offered the first psychology course at Harvard and published an influential textbook stressing the evolutionary significance of consciousness. Max Wertheimer and his associates in Germany developed Gestalt psychology, which emphasized the need to study consciousness in whole, meaningful units rather than the artificial elements studied by Wundt and Titchener. Alfred Binet developed a useful intelligence test for use in selecting children for advanced education in Paris. John B. Watson introduced to the United States the research on classical conditioning conducted by Russian biologist Ivan Pavlov. Watson advocated a science of psychology that included only overt behavior and made no attempt to study mental processes. Physician Sigmund Freud began publishing his observations on psychoanalysis and the origins of abnormal behavior.

It's clear that there were many origins of psychology rather than a single one. Given this diversity of origins, it's easy to understand why psychology is still a diverse discipline today. Psychoanalysis and behaviorism still exist as independent schools of thought, although in both cases, there are "pure" and more popular "modified" versions of these points of view. Humanistic psychology has emerged as a rather philosophical new perspective in recent years that emphasizes people's inherent tendency to grow and ability to control their own lives. A fourth major viewpoint that has emerged in contemporary times is cognitive psychology. This approach places its emphasis on the importance of cognition in the control of behavior. In general, however, psychologists tend to be more eclectic in recent years and are less likely to align themselves with a single theoretical position.

While studying the diversity that exists within psychology in terms of theoretical perspectives is useful, studying the diversity in subject matter that exists is more important. Psychology can be divided into experimental fields, which use a variety of scientific methods to study psychological processes, and applied fields, which apply psychological knowledge to the solution of human problems. This distinction is only a rough one, however, since psychological research often leads directly to applications and since many applied psychologists conduct research. Each of these two major divisions of psychology can be further subdivided in terms of the specific subject matter studied or the kind of human problems to which the application is addressed.

Scientific Methods: How We Learn about Behavior

As we discussed above, psychologists use scientific methods to describe, predict, understand, and influence behavior. But while it's easy to see how we might use the methods of science to study chemicals in a test tube, it's sometimes difficult to see how something as varied, complex, and apparently capricious as human behavior can be the subject matter of science. How can this be?

scientific methods
Methods of gathering information based on systematic observation.

The answer to this question requires our returning to a discussion of the fundamental nature of **scientific methods**—*systematic observation*. It's not necessary for a science to possess what most of us identify as the hallmarks of the scientific method: white lab coats, test tubes, and electron microscopes. Science has to do with *the way information is gathered and hypotheses are tested*. In contrast to philosophy in which one tries to understand human nature only by thinking about it, scientific psychologists follow Aristotle's advice both to reason and gather new information through observation. This is the essence of the scientific method. While we cannot profitably learn about human behavior by putting people into test tubes or under microscopes, we can scientifically study them using our intelligence and our senses.

Before we discuss several of the specific methods of science, one additional prerequisite to understanding how it's possible to have a science of human behavior is worth mentioning: All scientists must believe that their subject matter is *orderly and lawful* before they begin their research. For example, if astronomers felt that the planets wandered aimlessly and randomly through space, there would be little reason to study their paths. If, on the other hand, it appeared that the planets moved in predictable orbits, it would be very useful to study their movements.

The same thing is true of people. To have a science of psychology, we must believe that human behavior is at least somewhat predictable. Often, though, we see ourselves as being able to do whatever we choose and not subject to the laws of nature. While there may be some truth to that, psychologists believe that our behavior is much more orderly and predictable than most of us think. (See *Of Special Interest:* "Is Human Behavior Predictable Enough to Study Scientifically?")

OF SPECIAL INTEREST

Is Human Behavior Predictable Enough to Study Scientifically?

I regularly begin teaching my courses in psychology with a disguised demonstration that human behavior is actually fairly predictable under some circumstances. It's a little corny, but it makes the point. After telling the students that I'm a democratic fellow, I ask the class to decide how they want to be evaluated in the course. I tell them that I have to require a cumulative final examination, but that everything else is open to a vote. I give them the option of doing a term paper (to give themselves a way of being evaluated that is free from the pressure of classroom testing), and I also give them the options of having one, two, or three tests plus the final, or no tests plus the final. Then a vote is taken.

In every class, a couple of students vote for the term paper (one student who writes well and one who thinks I'm too lazy to read the papers), but that option is always soundly defeated. There are also a few students who vote for no test or one test, and about 20 percent who vote for two tests, but about three-quarters always choose three tests plus the final.

When the voting is over, I thank the students for their judicious decision and hand out the course syllabus. Only then do I point out that 250 copies of the syllabus have already been printed including no requirement of a term paper and giving the dates of three tests plus the final examination. After the laughing, booing, and hissing have subsided, I generally say something like, "The science of psychology rests on the assumption that your behavior is a good deal more predictable than you might think. That's not to take anything away from the mysteries and complexities of human existence; it's just to say that we aren't immune to the laws of nature. We're predictable enough to study scientifically."

Let's look for a moment at the kinds of methods that psychologists use to study human behavior and mental processes. In the sections that follow, we will briefly examine three general types of scientific methods used by psychologists—descriptive methods, correlational methods, and formal experiments—and also examine some of the more specific strategies that psychologists employ in attempting to reach the goals of the science of psychology.

Descriptive Methods

As mentioned earlier, there are actually a number of different scientific methods used in psychology, each with its own advantages and disadvantages. The different methods are best suited for answering different kinds of questions, so they tend to be relied upon to varying extents by individual specialties within psychology. The simplest methods of scientific inquiry involve *description*. Three descriptive methods are used in psychology: surveys, naturalistic observation, and the clinical method.

Surveys

survey method
A research method that utilizes interviews and questionnaires with individuals in the community.

The most direct way to answer a question about people is to *ask* the question of several people, hence the **survey method.** Surveys are perhaps most widely used today by psychologists interested in consumer opinions about television programs, soft drinks, political candidates, and similar subjects. Surveys are frequently used for other purposes as well, however. For example, the myth-shattering surveys of sex researcher Alfred Kinsey (Kinsey, Pomeroy, & Martin, 1948) revealed that the number of people who engage in masturbation and extramarital intercourse was much higher in completely normal individuals than expected. Similarly, surveys have shown us that relatively brief periods of mild depression are quite common in normal college students (Bosse, Croghan, Greenstein, Katz, Oliver, Powell, & Smith, 1975). The primary advantage of this method is that you can gather a great deal of information in a relatively short period of time. The main disadvantage is that there are often questions about the accuracy of information obtained in surveys. We cannot always be sure that the answers are honest, especially to controversial questions about such topics as sex and drug use.

Naturalistic Observation

naturalistic observation
A research method based on recording behavior as it occurs in natural life settings.

Another straightforward way to learn about behavior is simply to watch and describe it as it naturally occurs. The careful observation and recording of behavior in real-life settings is called **naturalistic observation.** When internationally known scientist Jane Goodall goes to Africa and sits down in the jungle and watches a troop of apes, she is using the method of naturalistic observation. She watches the apes over long periods of time, taking careful notes of the things she sees until specific patterns of behavior become evident. Using this method, she and her coworkers have learned that the social behavior and use of tools by apes is often strikingly similar to that of humans. Sadly, she has recently discovered that apes are also capable of "murder"—ambushing and killing other apes over relatively minor incidents in a way that looks "intentional."

The method of naturalistic observation is not restricted to the study of animal behavior. It's a method also used to study such topics as the play and friendship patterns of young children, the leadership tactics of effective business managers, and the ways that juvenile delinquents encourage antisocial behavior in one another.

Clinical Method

clinical method
The method of observing people while they are receiving psychological help from a psychologist.

An important variation on naturalistic observation is the **clinical method.** This involves simply observing people while they receive help for their psychological problems from a psychologist. Although not as useful as observing them in the natural situations where they have problems—at home, school, or work—clinical observation does provide useful information. Sigmund Freud, for example, developed his theories of abnormal behavior from years of intensive work with patients in his "consulting room." He was able to observe their behavior in this one

situation over long periods of time until he felt he saw consistent patterns in what they did, thought, and felt. The clinical method is also often used today for the evaluation of clinical treatment methods. For example, daily measures of anxiety might be taken on an individual before, during, and after treatment to evaluate a new method of treating excessive anxiety. When information is gathered in this way, the term *single-subject research* is often used.

Naturalistic observation is the careful recording of behavior as it occurs in real-life settings.

Correlational Methods

Being able to *predict* behavior and mental processes requires a knowledge of the *relationship* between two or more psychological **variables.** A variable is a factor whose numerical value can *vary*. The **correlational method** examines the relationship between variables. The first step in such studies is to measure each variable in a **quantitative** fashion, that is, to measure each variable in numerical units. For example, an industrial psychologist might want to know about the relationship between intelligence and the job performance of medical laboratory technicians. First, intelligence and job performance would need to be quantitatively measured in a group of technicians. Intelligence could be measured using a standard intelligence test, but a special measure of job performance might need to be devised. If, for example, accuracy in performing medical tests were singled out as an aspect of job performance, the test results of the group of technicians could be double-checked for a period of time by a team of experts to provide a measure of accuracy.

If a relationship existed between intelligence and job performance of laboratory technicians, then we would expect those with higher intelligence scores to make fewer mistakes in performing medical tests. Because many other factors probably also influence job performance (e.g., laboratory conditions and emotional stability), the relationship with intelligence would not be a perfect one, but it still should be noticeable. Mathematicians have developed a quantified way of expressing the strength of the relationship, called the **coefficient of correlation** (see the appendix).

variable
A factor whose numerical value can change.

correlational method
(kor″ĕ-la′shun-al)
A research method that measures the strength of the relation between variables.

quantitative
(kwon′ti-ta-tiv)
Capable of being measured in numerical terms.

coefficient of correlation
The numerical expression of the strength of a relationship between two variables.

Correlation methods have also been used to show, for example, that college students who have experienced considerable stress in their lives during the past year are somewhat more likely to feel depressed and anxious (Sarason, Johnson, & Siegel, 1978), and parents who frequently use legal drugs (alcohol, cigarettes, and tranquilizers) are more likely to have teenagers who frequently use illegal drugs (Smart & Fejer, 1972).

When interpreting correlational data, we must remember that a relationship between two variables does not mean that one *causes* the other. Let's look at the relationship between the use of drugs by teenagers and their parents. This correlation *might* mean that seeing one's parents use drugs causes teenagers to use more drugs. It *might* be, however, that worrying about their teenagers taking drugs causes parents to use alcohol or tranquilizers to reduce their worries. Correlations tell us little about which variable is the cause in cause-and-effect relationships. In fact, correlations often exist between two variables that are not causally related at all, but are related through some other factor. For example, it might be that some parents and their teenagers use drugs frequently to calm the emotions they feel because of the unpleasant and unrewarding circumstances in which their families live. That is, the drug uses of some parents and teenagers might be caused by the same factor, but are not causally related to one another. We must be very careful not to misinterpret correlational findings.

Formal Experiments

formal experiments
Research methods that allow the researcher to manipulate the independent variable in order to study the effect on the dependent variable.

The most sophisticated and rigorous scientific method of observation is the **formal experiment.** Experiments are particularly helpful in reaching the goals of understanding and influencing behavior. Like the correlational method, experiments are designed to tell us about the relationship between two or more variables. Unlike other methods, however, the experiment involves deliberate arrangement of the variables involved. And unlike correlational methods, a carefully conducted experiment allows the researcher to draw conclusions about cause-and-effect relationships.

The heart of an experiment is the *comparison* of quantitative measures of behavior *under different conditions*. For example, we have all heard about the supposedly damaging effects of "noise pollution." Do high levels of noise have a negative effect on our behavior and mental processes? Two psychologists (Mathews & Canon, 1975) conducted a simple, but very informative, study to shed experimental light on this question. They examined the effects of high levels of noise on one of the more admirable aspects of human behavior—our tendency to help others when they are in need. In this experiment, a person wearing a cast on his arm emerged from a car and dropped a large pile of books in front of a pedestrian. If you were the pedestrian, would you have stopped to help him pick up his books? You might not have if there had been a lot of noise in the background. Remember, the purpose of an experiment is to compare measures of behavior under different conditions. In this case, the number of people who stopped

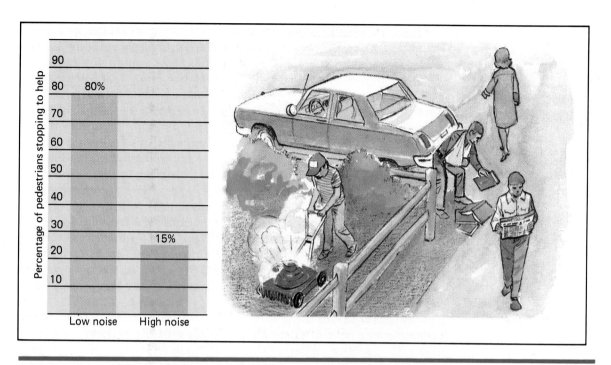

Figure 1.4 The percentage of pedestrians who stop to help a man with an arm cast who had dropped his books under conditions of low and high noise (Mathews & Canon, 1975).

to help was compared under conditions of low noise or high noise (when a loud lawn mower without a muffler was running). Figure 1.4 shows the results of this study in graphic form. When there was little noise in the background, over five times as many pedestrians stopped to help the fellow with the broken arm than when there was a high noise level.

An important advantage of formal experiments is that they allow us to *control,* or eliminate, the influence of variables other than the ones on which the experiment focuses. The goal is to eliminate all explanations for differences between the groups except the relevant one. This was accomplished in the study of noise levels by not changing anything in the two conditions except the amount of noise.

The number of people who stopped to help in this experiment is termed the **dependent variable** because its value *depends* on the effects of the noise. The amount of noise is the **independent variable,** because the experimenter can *independently* control it. In a study of the effects of different-sized doses of alcohol on memory, the independent variable would be the amount of alcohol given to each group and the dependent variable would be the number of words recalled from a list. All formal experiments have at least one independent and one dependent variable.

dependent variable
The variable whose quantitative value depends on the effects of the independent variable.

independent variable
The variable whose quantitative value can be independently controlled by the researcher.

control group
The group in simple experiments that receives none of the independent variable and is used for comparisons with the treatment group.

experimental group
The group in an experiment that receives some value of the independent variable.

In the simplest experiments, one group receives *none* of the independent variable and is called the **control group.** The group that receives the independent variable is called the **experimental group.** Often there is more than one experimental group (such as giving three experimental groups 2, 4, or 6 ounces of alcohol in the hypothetical study of memory), and sometimes there is more than one control group designed to rule out different alternative explanations for the results of the study.

Through the logic and control of experiments, it's possible to test hypotheses about causal relationships. That is the primary advantage of formal experiments over other scientific methods. For all their utility, however, experiments also have their drawbacks. First and foremost, all experiments require some degree of *artificiality.* Experimenters do not study naturally-occurring phenomena but create and control conditions. In doing so, scientists risk creating experiments that are so artificial that the findings are difficult to apply to the real world, or they may even be entirely inapplicable. For example, the results of studies in which college students are crowded into small rooms for an hour may not have much relevance to the long-term effects of crowded urban living conditions on behavior.

Second, experiments can also lead us to believe that because a scientist conducted them, the conclusions are necessarily valid. Experiments are complicated affairs and even the best experimenters make errors. We should be careful when evaluating experimental conclusions to question the logic, control, and relevance of the experiment. Finally, the power of formal experiments often leads us to reject the other scientific methods. Each method is valid within its restrictions and weaknesses. Psychology, like all sciences, depends on a blend of scientific methods and a healthy skepticism about results drawn from them.

Ethical Principles of Research with Human Subjects

Psychology depends heavily on research conducted with human subjects for its data base. But while researchers have an obligation to collect meaningful information through research, they also have an ethical responsibility to protect the welfare of their subjects. Often the ethics of research with human subjects pose complicated issues for the researcher—issues that do not have simple solutions. As a human being, and especially as one who may be asked to serve as a subject in psychological research, you may find it of interest to review some of the key ethical issues involved in psychological research with human subjects. A more complete discussion of these issues can be found in the American Psychological Association's *Ethical Principles in the Conduct of Research with Human Participants* (1973).

1. *Freedom from coercion.* It's not ethical to coerce or pressure a subject into participating in an experiment. Students in college courses, for example, cannot be required to participate. They must be given an alternative way to meet any course requirement. Similarly, it would be considered unethical to offer special consideration in parole hearings to prisoners who volunteer to participate in psychological studies, since the promise of special considerations might constitute undue coercion.

2. *Informed consent*. The experimenter must, under most circumstances, give potential subjects a full description of the experiment, in language they can understand, before they are asked to participate. It's not ethical to allow subjects to participate in an experiment without knowing what they are getting into. Furthermore, once the experiment has begun, it must be made clear to participants that they are fully free to change their minds and withdraw from the experiment without penalty, such as embarrassment, loss of course credit, and so on.

3. *Deception*. Sometimes it's necessary to conduct experiments without the subject's knowing the true purpose of the study. For example, chapter 14 discusses a study in which subjects were asked to make judgments about the relative lengths of three lines after other subjects (actually the experimenter's confederates who were acting out parts in the experiment) had given the wrong answer. The question was, would the real subjects give the wrong answer, too, under these conditions? Obviously, it was necessary to deceive the subjects into thinking that the other subjects really believed their erroneous judgments about the lines. Is it ethical to deceive subjects in this manner? The current guidelines suggest that deceptions can be used only if two conditions are met. First, the potential subjects must be told everything they could reasonably be expected to need to know to make an informed decision about participation. That is, the deception can only involve aspects of the study that do not influence the decision to participate. Second, the nature of the deception must be fully revealed to the subjects immediately after their participation in the experiment. Under these conditions, it's considered ethical to deceive subjects in research.

4. *Debriefing*. Research participants have a right to know the results of the study. Current practice dictates that all subjects be provided with a summary of the study in language that they can understand. If the results are not immediately available, the subjects have a right to receive it when it's available.

These are not all of the ethical issues raised by psychological research with humans by any means, but they are some of the major ones. Most institutions where research is conducted now require that all proposals for human experimentation be approved by a board of other scientists so as to protect subjects from the full range of potential abuses. Separate ethical standards and review boards ensure ethical research using animal subjects. (See *Of Special Interest:* "Animal Psychologists" for another perspective on the ethics of psychological research.)

OF SPECIAL INTEREST

Phrenology and Sarcognomy: Psychological Pseudosciences

In our efforts through the years to understand a complex topic like ourselves, we have inevitably made some mistakes. As complicated as human beings are, it would be surprising if we did not bark up the wrong tree occasionally. The advantage of taking a scientific approach to the understanding of human beings, however, is that science is *self-correcting*. If we are careful to test all of our hypotheses in experiments, we should find out which hypotheses work and which do not.

Unfortunately, not everyone who talks like a scientist *is* a scientist. The fields of medicine and psychology have long been plagued by individuals who dress up their ideas in scientific-sounding language but who have not scientifically validated their hypotheses at all. Such individuals are known as pseudoscientists, or quacks in the vernacular. Medicine-show vendors who sell cure-all potions are classic examples of pseudoscientists in medicine, while *phrenologists* are classic examples in psychology.

Phrenology was founded by Viennese physician Franz Gall. He believed that the bumps on the skull reflect the structure of the brain underneath. When these bumps are read by an expert—similar to reading tea leaves—they supposedly reveal much about the personality of the individual. The bumps were even used to predict the future. Phrenology was widely practiced in the United States during the eighteenth and nineteenth centuries, and was briefly an accepted part of psychiatry from about 1820 to 1850. Benjamin Rush, the founder of the American Psychiatric Association, used phrenology in his practice for a while.

An imaginative phrenologist by the name of J. R. Buchanan apparently became bored feeling bumps on his clients' heads and enlarged the practice of phrenology. In his method, called *sarcognomy*, it was necessary to feel "bumps" all over the body to fully understand an individual's personality. Buchanan was successful in attracting clients, but he eventually got into trouble over his method of "diagnosing" the bodies of female clients.

OF SPECIAL INTEREST

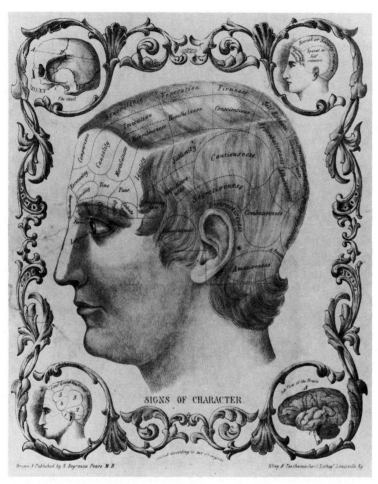

The locations of bumps that phrenologists claimed reveal our personality and predict our future.

OF SPECIAL INTEREST

Animal Psychologists

A sizable minority of psychologists can be described as *animal psychologists*. No, I'm not talking about a pipe-smoking psychoanalyst who helps Bowser the family pet solve his deep-seated psychological problems. Rather, the term *animal psychologist* refers to the fact that some psychologists conduct research using animals as subjects.

Why would anyone want to do that? Why would some psychologists study animals when they could be studying people? There are a number of important reasons why psychologists study animal behavior:

1. Some kinds of studies are conducted using animals because it would not be ethical to do the research with humans. Studies of the brain, for example, often require surgically destroying a part of the brain to discover its precise role in behavior. All psychologists feel that it would be unethical to conduct such research with human subjects. For similar reasons, studies in which infants are isolated from all social contact to study the absence of parental and peer relationships on development must be conducted with animals rather than humans. While we must be very careful not to assume automatically that what is learned about animal behavior will apply to human behavior, much useful information has been learned from animal research.

R E V I E W

Psychology is a science, which means that it uses scientific methods to gather information and test ideas. In addition to thinking about behavior, psychologists acquire new information about it through carefully controlled methods of observation. Although they are many and varied, scientific methods are all based on the assumption that behavior is lawful and orderly, and capable of being understood in scientific terms. Each scientific method has different advantages and disadvantages and is best suited to answering different types of questions. The simplest scientific methods are descriptive methods. Information that allows us to describe knowledgeably a psychological phenomenon is gathered by asking questions about it in surveys, by observing it in natural settings, or through extensive experience with it in clinical cases.

When the scientific question concerns the relationship between two variables, correlational methods are often used. Both variables are measured quantitatively and the relationship between the two is noted; however, it's not possible to determine from such information whether one variable causes the other to change. To determine whether cause-and-effect relationships exist, formal experiments must be conducted.

OF SPECIAL INTEREST

2. It's possible to conduct experiments using animals that are far more precisely controlled than human experiments. It's possible for a researcher to know and control almost every detail of a laboratory animal's life from birth: its environment, diet, and social experiences. This makes it possible to control a multiplicity of factors that must be left uncontrolled when using human subjects.

3. A great deal can be learned by comparing the behavior of animals of different species. For example, a number of insights about human aggression have come from studies of aggression in other animal species. Similarly, much has been learned about the brain structures involved in sleep by identifying animals who have differing sleep patterns and comparing the evolutionary development of the sleep centers in these different species.

4. Many psychologists study animal behavior not to learn anything at all about humans, however, but to learn more about another animal species. If we are going to protect endangered species, we must understand their patterns of behavior. We must know, for example, how a species hunts, mates, and raises its young before we can protect its ability to survive.

In formal experiments, scientists rigorously control the conditions of the experiment so that only one explanation for the results is most plausible. In the simplest experiments, one factor—the independent variable—is artificially manipulated by the experimenter to see what effect it has on another variable—the dependent variable. Often one group of subjects—the control group—receives none of the independent variable, while the independent variable is present in another group—the experimental group. In a study of the effects of alcohol on memory of a list of words, for example, the alcohol is the independent variable. Alcohol is given to subjects in the experimental group and not given to the subjects in the control group, so its effects on the dependent variable, memory of the list, can be compared.

While it's important to conduct psychological research using human subjects, it's essential that we protect the rights of subjects. Subjects must not be coerced in any way into participating and must be informed about the nature of the study before they participate. Subjects can only be deceived about a study if (1) the information withheld is not relevant to their decision to participate, and (2) they are informed about the true nature of the study immediately after it's over.

What We Know about Human Behavior: Some Starting Places

Now that we have looked at psychology's origins, discussed the different beginnings of modern psychology around the turn of the century, gone over psychology's basic assumptions and scientific methods, and surveyed its different theories and areas of specialization, we are ready to begin talking about the substance of psychology. The diversity in this large field is striking. Nevertheless, psychology is a *unified* science with many shared assumptions and beliefs. Lest we overemphasize the diversity within the field, let's identify some ideas that all psychologists *have in common* besides their history and scientific methods.

I have prepared a list of the most important things that contemporary psychologists "know" about human lives. This is not a list of universally accepted "truths." Since psychologists are known for their tendency to disagree with one another, there are sure to be differences of opinion about this or any similar list. My intent, though, is to come as close as possible to a summary of the most important concepts that *all* psychologists share. These are educated guesses as to the "true nature" of human beings as seen from the perspective of the science of psychology.

1. *Human beings are biological creatures.* We take our biological nature so much for granted that we often do not realize how much it influences our behavior. We experience emotional highs and lows because of the way part of our nervous system is constructed. We spend much of our time preparing and eating food to satisfy the needs of our cells for energy.

   But even though our biology determines our behavior to a great extent, the limits it places on us are *elastic,* that is, we can easily stretch them. The muscles given to us by heredity can be strengthened through exercise. Our native intelligence can be stretched to the limit by a stimulating home environment. We can build airplanes to fly, and aqualungs for breathing underwater to overcome physical limitations. At times, biological processes that are normally part of involuntary emotional reactions can even be brought under voluntary control through special types of practice. Although creatures of our biological nature, we are not rigidly programmed by it.

2. *Every person is different, yet the same.* Every human being is truly unique. With the exception of identical twins, each person's heredity is unique, even compared to one's own family members. And each person's experiences are different from anyone else's. It's inevitable that we should differ from one another in significant ways, and perhaps almost as inevitable that psychologists would devote much of their time to studying the ways in which our personalities, intellects, and interests differ. Differences are a normal part of life that greatly interest psychologists.

   Yet as members of the human race, we are similar in our capacities to think, feel, remember, and so on. Thus it's possible to have a single science of human psychology. If we were not alike in

Each human is unique, and yet we all share certain characteristics of the species.

human qualities, we would have to develop a different psychology for each person. Fortunately, we are enough alike to be understood using one science of psychology and different enough to be interesting.

3. *Human lives are a continuous process of change.* From birth to death, humans are changing, developing organisms. We grow from helpless infancy through the time of playing with toys, through the time of adult work and rearing children, to the age of retirement. Change is almost continual; standing still is rare in human lives. Much of this developmental change is inevitably the result of our biological nature: Unless the process is disturbed, all creatures must grow from infancy to old age. Other aspects of change come from our experiences in life. Every time we learn a new concept from a college course, memorize a friend's telephone number, or adjust to a tragedy in our life, we change in some way.

    These changes are usually so gradual that they slip by unnoticed. But the next time you ask yourself the question "Who am I?" remember that the answer you give today will be different from the answer you will give tomorrow. This is not to say that nothing stays constant in our personalities over time—I feel as strongly about prejudice as an adult as I did as a teenager—but change is an enormously important aspect of human life.

4. *Behavior is motivated.* Human behavior is not aimless. Rather, most of our actions can be viewed as attempts to meet our needs. We work to earn money that buys food, shelter, and clothing. We go on dates for companionship and perhaps to meet sexual needs. We tell a joke at a party because of the sweet feeling of approval

that laughter brings. However, all of our motives are not simple and selfish. Some of us are also willing to put in long hours tutoring handicapped children just to see the joy of accomplishment in these children's faces. Others are internally motivated to express themselves in a painting or poem.

Most basic motives (i.e., for food, warmth, companionship, sex) are shared by all people and seem to be part of our biological makeup. Other motives differ among different cultures and seem to be learned from others. For example, in some cultures most people want to be rich, famous, and important, while in other cultures most people try to avoid anything that will make them stand out from others in the community. Regardless of their origins, motives are important forces in guiding our lives.

5. *Humans are social animals.* Like hives of bees or flocks of geese, people gather in social groups. The progress of modern civilization, and indeed the very survival of the human species, has only been possible because people are able to work together in groups for the mutual benefit of all. From hunting large animals in the jungle to operating an assembly line, social groups are able to accomplish things that single individuals cannot.

The social nature of human lives extends beyond mutual benefit, however. People *need* to have contact and relationships with one another. Imprisonment in solitary confinement is a harsh punishment because it deprives a person of human interactions. People seek out social support, friendships, and romantic relationships. When deprived of these social relationships for even short periods of time—a condition relatively common among university students, incidentally—we know the pain that loneliness brings. Social relationships are a significant part of our lives.

6. *People play an active part in creating their experiences.* Aristotle compared the mind of an infant to a blank clay tablet on which experiences leave their mark. In his view, we passively let experiences teach us about the world and become the person that they lead us to become. This is one of the few ideas of Aristotle that most contemporary psychologists have rejected. It seems to us today that people play a more active role in creating their experiences. The phi phenomenon discussed earlier was used by Gestalt psychologists to make this point: Often what we see— motion in this case—is not in the outside world at all; we create it.

At a different level, it's clear that people even play an active role in determining what kinds of experiences they will have by seeking out particular kinds of situations. Some people regularly choose to be in relaxed, low-pressure situations, while others get themselves into frenetic, exciting circumstances. We are shaped by these experiences, to be sure, but we play a role in choosing the experiences to which we will be exposed. We are active participants in the flow of life, not passive, blank tablets.

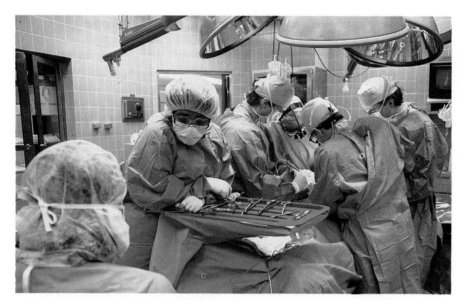

Survival of the human species has been possible because people are able to work together in groups for the benefit of all.

7. *Behavior has multiple causes.* The answer to the question "Why did I do that?" is rarely a single reason. Behavior can be influenced by many factors, and it is usually influenced by many of them at once. Think about the factors that went into the decision to go to the restaurant up the street to have a hamburger at 10:30 last night. You went because your body needed food; you had finished studying; you wanted to have some companionship; you had just heard the place advertised on the radio; you had been there last week and had a good time; and so on. Behavior is influenced simultaneously by many "causes."

8. *Behavior can be adaptive or maladaptive.* Humans have an amazing ability to adapt to the demands of life. We are flexible, capable creatures who generally use our wits to successfully adjust to whatever life dishes out in the way of challenges or pressures. Sometimes, however, we deal with life in ways that are harmful to us or to others. For example, some of us are excessively aggressive, some are much too timid, while some of us use a clinging dependency to get our way. These maladaptive ways of living can result from a combination of biological influences, excessive stress, or improper learning experiences. They are correctable, however, under the right conditions—such as advice from friends, a change in life circumstances that encourages us to behave in more adaptive ways, or professional help.

These ideas will serve as starting places for our study of psychology. They provide an overview of the science we are about to explore, and as unifying concepts that link together its many diverse specialties. It might be useful as you read the following chapters to glance back from time to time to these ideas to see how what you are studying relates to them.

S U M M A R Y

Chapter 1 defines psychology, introduces scientific methods that psychologists use, discusses the history of psychology, and reviews what psychologists have learned about human behavior.

I. Psychology is defined as "the science of behavior and mental processes."
   A. Psychology is considered to be a science because—like all sciences—knowledge is acquired through systematic observation.
   B. The goals of psychology are to
      1. Describe,
      2. Predict,
      3. Understand, and
      4. Influence behavior and mental processes.

II. The general scientific method involves careful observation, forming hypotheses, and testing hypotheses against empirical facts.
   A. Psychologists use three major scientific methods: descriptive methods, correlational methods, and formal experiments.
      1. Descriptive methods include the use of surveys, naturalistic observation, and clinical methods to describe behavior and mental processes; these help reach the goal of description.
      2. Correlational methods are used to study the relationships between variables; these help us reach the goal of prediction.
      3. Formal experiments can be used to reach conclusions about cause-and-effect relationships between variables; these help us reach the goals of understanding and influencing behavior.
   B. Experiments usually involve an *experimental group,* which receives the independent variable, and a *control group.* Differences between the groups in the *dependent variable* are thought to be caused by the *independent variable.*
   C. Ethical research carefully protects the rights of human subjects by avoiding coercion, uninformed participation, and unnecessary deception.

III. Modern psychology developed from beginnings in the late nineteenth century.
   A. Important early psychologists and their schools of thought were
      1. Wilhelm Wundt and Edward Titchener (Structuralism)
      2. William James (Functionalism)
      3. Ivan Pavlov and John B. Watson (Behaviorism)
      4. Max Wertheimer (Gestalt psychology)
      5. Alfred Binet (Psychological measurement)
      6. Sigmund Freud (Psychoanalysis)
   B. The four major contemporary theories of psychology are
      1. Psychoanalysis, emphasizing unconscious motives
      2. Humanistic psychology, emphasizing the inherent human tendency to grow and personal freedom
      3. Cognitive psychology, emphasizing conscious intellectual processes
      4. Behaviorism, emphasizing learning and overt behavior

C. Modern psychology can be divided into experimental and applied fields.
   1. Experimental psychologists conduct basic research on the biological basis of behavior, the processes of sensation and perception, learning and memory, cognition, psycholinguistics, human development, emotion, personality, and social behavior.
   2. Applied psychologists put the knowledge of psychology to work helping people. Then they specialize in applied fields such as clinical treatment, personal or marital counseling, industrial or educational applications, or behavioral medicine.
IV. Most psychologists would agree that the following statements accurately describe human behavior and mental processes.
   A. Human beings are biological creatures whose structure and physiology influence and limit behavior.
   B. Each person is unique, yet enough similarities exist between individuals to allow a true science of behavior.
   C. Human lives are a continuous process of change, evolving from birth to death.
   D. Behavior is motivated, not random or aimless.
   E. Humans are social animals working together in groups.
   F. People play an active part in choosing their experiences and constructing perceptions.
   G. Behavior has multiple causes.
   H. Behavior can be either adaptive or maladaptive.

Suggested Readings

1. For a closer look at the early days of the history of psychology:
   Watson, R. I. (1971). *The great psychologists* (3rd ed.). Philadelphia: J. B. Lippincott.

2. For a firsthand look at the writings of some of the most important psychologists through the history of science:
   Marks, R. W. (Ed.). (1966). *Great ideas in psychology.* New York: Bantam.

3. For information on career opportunities in psychology:
   American Psychological Association. *A career in psychology.* Can be obtained free from the American Psychological Association, 1200 17th Street, N.W., Washington, DC 20036.

4. You might also be interested in another view of the value of the science of psychology:
   Lunneborg, P. (1978). *Why study psychology?* Monterey, CA: Brooks/Cole.

5. A concise introduction to the history of psychology:
   Wertheimer, M. (1979). *A brief history of psychology.* New York: Holt, Rinehart & Winston.

6. An extremely readable introduction to scientific methods for the life sciences (although it was written over 20 years ago, it's entirely up-to-date):
   Dethier, V. G. (1962). *To know a fly.* San Francisco: Holden–Day.

7. For a sophisticated recent history of psychology:
   Gilgen, A. R. (1982). *American psychology since World War II.* Westport, CT: Greenwood Press.

Biological Foundations
of Behavior

OUTLINE

KEY TERMS

Where do you live? We don't think about it much, but the thinking, feeling, acting part of you cannot live apart from your *body.* Psychological life depends on biological life for its existence. The ways we behave are even determined in part by the nature of the body. If humans did not have hands that grasp, we would never have learned to write, paint, or play racquetball. If we did not have eyes that could see color, we would think the world existed only in shades of black and white.

Some parts of the body are more intimately linked to psychological life than others. An experience of Canadian brain surgeon Wilder Penfield in the late 1930s dramatically revealed the essential role played by the brain. Dr. Penfield was conducting surgery on the surface layer of the brain known as the cerebral cortex. The patient, who was awake under local anesthesia, had consented to be part of a brief experiment that was conducted during surgery. When Penfield placed a small rod that carried a mild electric current against the brain, there were astonishing results. The patient felt no pain, but instead she began to recall in vivid detail an incident from years before. She was in her kitchen, listening to the voice of her little boy playing out in the yard. In the background, she could hear the noises of the neighborhood, the cars passing in the street. Penfield was amazed to discover that stimulation of particular spots on the brain could produce flashbacks recalled by the patient in cinematic detail. One young man recalled a small-town baseball game that included a boy trying to crawl under a fence. Another woman recalled a melody each time a certain point on the cortex was stimulated. Penfield tried to fool her by stimulating other points in alternation with the one that produced the melody, claiming he was stimulating one point when in fact he was stimulating another. Still, each time the rod touched the same point on the cortex, the woman heard the melody.

The importance of the brain in behavior has also been dramatized in another way by the recent legal controversies surrounding the issue of "brain death." When is a person considered legally dead? There is no doubt that a person is dead when the heart stops beating, breathing stops, and all behavior ceases. But many states now allow a physician to declare a patient dead even though the heart and lungs are still working if those parts of the brain involved in thinking, feeling, and acting are no longer alive. When these parts of the brain are dead, psychological life is gone and the person is considered dead. To understand behavior, we must understand the workings of the brain and other biological organs.

P R E V I E W

We are psychological beings who live in biological machines. Our psychological existence is dependent upon the healthy functioning of the body, and our behavior is limited and influenced by the nature of that body. All parts of our biological selves are involved in one way or another with behavior, but the nervous system, endocrine glands, and genetic mechanisms are the bodily structures that are most intimately related to what we experience and do.

Just as electronic machines are built out of wires, transistors, and other components, the nervous system is built out of specialized cells called neurons. Billions of neurons in your nervous system transmit messages to one another in complex ways that make the nervous system both the computer and communication system of the body. The biological control center of the nervous system is the brain. The brain has many parts that carry out different functions but operate together in an integrated way. It communicates to the body through an intricate network of neurons that fan out to every part of the body.

In terms of functions, the nervous system can be thought of as two largely separate systems. The somatic nervous system is involved in conscious actions and awareness. The autonomic nervous system regulates the internal body organs and activates motivation and emotion more or less automatically. The fact that the autonomic nervous system performs three functions helps explain why our emotions, motives, and internal organs so often get churned up at the same time. And the fact that thought and emotion operate in separate nervous systems partially explains why we often have difficulty logically controlling our feelings.

The communication function of the nervous system is implemented in part by the endocrine glands. Under the control of the brain, these glands secrete chemical messengers called hormones into the bloodstream. These hormones regulate the functions of the body and also indirectly influence our behavior and experience.

Heredity exerts its influence on behavior through genes in the nucleus of the body's cells. These genes contain the codes that allow heredity to influence the development of our bodies and behavior. We do not inherit behavior directly like we do eye color, but inheritance is one of the factors that controls the development of the brain, endocrine glands, and other body structures that, in turn, influence broad dimensions of our behavior.

This chapter was written to help you understand *psychology* better. We'll discuss only those aspects of human biology that are directly relevant to understanding behavior: the brain and nervous system, endocrine glands, and genetic mechanisms. Without these biological systems, human life could not exist. They provide the basis for and place limits on our behavior and mental processes.

Nervous System: The Biological Control Center

The nervous system is both a powerful computer and a complex communication system. The complex mass of nerve cells called the **brain** is a computer that not only thinks and calculates, but also feels and controls actions. The brain is connected to a thick bundle of long nerves running through the spine, called the **spinal cord.** Individual nerves exit or enter the spinal cord and brain, linking every part of the body to the brain. Some of these nerves carry messages from the body to the brain to keep the brain informed about what is going on in the body. Other nerves carry messages from the brain to the body to regulate the body's functions and the person's behavior. Without the nervous system, the body would be no more than a mass of uncoordinated parts that could not act, reason, or experience emotions. In other words, without a nervous system, there would be no psychological life.

brain
The complex mass of neural cells and related cells encased in the skull.

spinal cord
The nerve fibers in the spinal column.

Neurons: The Units of the Nervous System

The basic units of which computers, telephone systems, and other electronic systems are made consist of individual wires, transistors, and other components that transmit and regulate electricity. These components are put together in complex patterns to create functioning systems. The nervous system is similarly made up of components. The most important unit of the nervous system is the individual nerve cell, or **neuron.** We begin our discussion of the nervous system with the neuron, then progress to a discussion of the larger parts of the nervous system.

neuron (nu'ron)
An individual nerve cell.

Parts of Neurons

Neurons range in length from less than a millimeter to more than a meter in length. Yet all neurons are made up of essentially the same parts (see fig. 2.1). The **cell body** is the central part of the nerve cell. It contains the cell's control center, or *nucleus,* and other components of the cell necessary for the cell's preservation and nourishment. **Dendrites** are small branches that extend out from the cell body and receive messages from other neurons.

The **axons** are small branches at the other end of the neuron that perform a function opposite that of the dendrites. They carry messages away from the axon and transmit these messages to the next neuron. (It's easy to remember the difference between the functions of the dendrites and axons by remembering that the axon "acts on" the next cell.) The message transmitted along the axon may be picked up by the dendrites of one or more other neurons. Neurons, then, have a cell body, dendrites, and an axon. But the shape and size of these parts can vary greatly, depending on what function the neuron serves.

Neurons are grouped together in complex networks that make the largest computer seem like a child's toy. The nervous system is composed of something on the order of 100 billion neurons (Hubel, 1979; Stevens, 1979), about as many as the number of stars in our galaxy. Each neuron can receive from or transmit messages to a total of 1,000 to 10,000 other neural cells. All told, your body

cell body
The central part of the neuron that includes the nucleus.

dendrites (den'drīts)
Small extensions on the cell body that receive messages from other neurons.

axons (ak'sonz)
Neuron endings that transmit messages to other neurons.

Figure 2.1 Two common shapes of neurons. Neurons are typically composed of a cell body, dendrites that receive neural messages, and an axon that passes the neural message on to the next neuron.

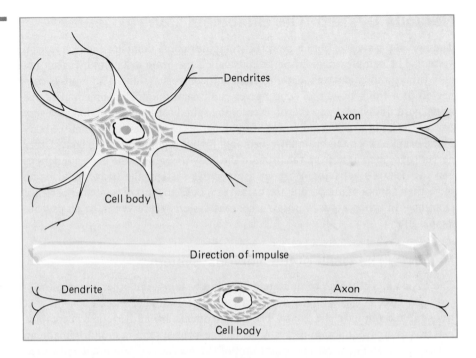

Dendrites

Axon

Cell body

Direction of impulse

Dendrite

Axon

Cell body

A neuron in the human brain showing the cell body and dendrites.

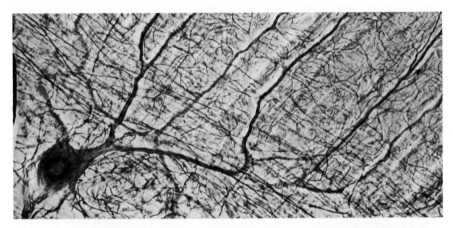

Knoblike tips of the axons; the small branches of the neuron that transmit messages to the next nerve cell.

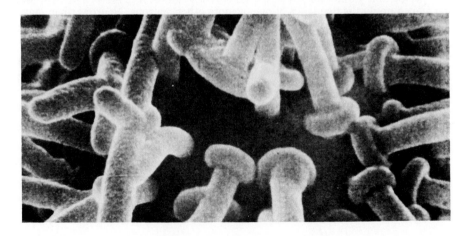

contains trillions of neural connections, most of them in the brain. These numbers are not important in their own right, but they may help us understand the incredibly rich network of neural interconnections that makes us humans (Iverson, 1979). Incidentally, be careful not to confuse the term neuron with the term **nerve;** they are not synonyms. A nerve is a bundle of many long neurons—sometimes thousands of them—outside the brain and the spinal cord.

Neural Transmission

In a sense, each neuron is able to conduct an electrical impulse from the tip of its dendrite to the end of its axon because of two special characteristics of neural cells. First, electrically charged molecules fill the neuron and the fluid that surrounds it. Second, neurons have a "skin," or a **cell membrane,** that allows some molecules to pass through it while blocking others out. During a neural impulse, electrically charged particles move in and out of the membrane in a way that creates a flowing electrical current.

Many of the chemical particles that make up the inside of the neuron are called **ions** because they possess an electrical charge. The charge of most ions within the neuron are negative, thus giving the inside of the cell a negative charge. This negative charge attracts positively charged particles like the negative pole of a magnet attracts the positive pole of another magnet. One positively charged particle that is attracted in significant quantities by the negative particles inside the neuron is sodium (Na^+). However, the membrane of the neuron keeps the sodium ions outside of the neuron. The neural membrane is **semipermeable.** In essence, this means that it has "holes" in it that allow some particles to pass through it, but keep other particles out. Not only does the membrane of the neuron keep sodium ions out, but when they do get inside, it actively "pumps" them out.

Thus, in its normal resting state, the neuron has mostly negative ions on the inside and mostly positive ions on the outside. In this condition, the neuron is said to be electrically **polarized** (see fig. 2.2). When the membrane is stimulated by an adjacent neuron, however, the semipermeability of the membrane is changed. Generally, positively charged sodium ions are allowed to enter the neuron making the inside less negative. This process is termed **depolarization.** If sufficient depolarization occurs, a dramatic change takes place in the neural membrane near the spot where the axon emerges from the cell body. This change results in a rapid and massive influx of positive sodium ions that strongly depolarizes that part of the axon. Very quickly, however, the membrane regains its semipermeability and "pumps" the positive sodium ions back out, reestablishing its polarization. This tiny storm of sodium ions flowing in and out of the membrane does not stop there, however. It disturbs the adjacent section of membrane of the axon so that it depolarizes, which in turn disturbs the next section of membrane, and so on. Thus, the neural impulse—a flowing storm of depolarization—travels the length of the axon.

Local anesthetics, such as the Novocain that your dentist injects, stop pain by chemically interrupting this flowing process of depolarization in the axons of nerves that carry pain messages to the brain.

nerve
A bundle of long neurons outside the brain and spinal cord.

cell membrane
The covering of a neuron or other cell.

ions (ī′ons)
Electrically charged particles.

semipermeable
(sem″e-per′me-ah-b′l)
A surface that allows some, but not all, particles to pass through.

polarized state
(po′lar iz′d)
The resting state of a neuron when mostly negative ions are inside and mostly positive ions are outside the cell membrane.

depolarization
The process during which positively charged ions flow into the axon making it less negatively charged inside.

Figure 2.2 Short sections of a neuron are shown to illustrate neural transmission. (a) When an axon is in its resting state, there is a balance between the number of positively and negatively charged ions along the membrane. (b) When the axon is sufficiently stimulated, the membrane allows positively charged sodium ions to pass into the cell, depolarizing that spot on the membrane. (c) This depolarization disturbs the adjacent section of membrane, allowing sodium ions to flow in again, while sodium ions are being pumped back out of the first section. (d) This process continues as the swirling storm of depolarization continues to the end of the axon.

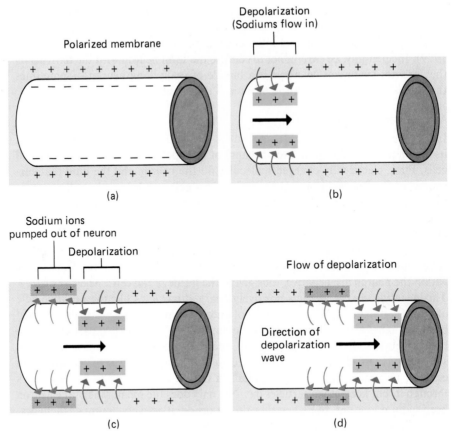

myelin sheath (mi′e-lin)
The protective fatty covering wrapped around part of the neuron.

nodes of Ranvier
(rahn′-vē-ā)
Gaps in the myelin sheath covering the nerves.

synapse (sin aps′)
The space between the axon of one neuron and the dendrite of another.

neurotransmitters
(nu″ro-tranz′-mit-erz)
Chemical substances produced by axons that transmit messages across the synapse.

　　Many axons are encased in a white fatty coating known as the **myelin sheath.** This sheath, which is wrapped around the axon like the layers of a jelly roll, provides insulation to the axon and greatly improves its capacity to conduct neural impulses. In simplified terms, it speeds neural conduction by allowing the electrical disturbance to skip between widely spaced gaps in the myelin sheath—known as the **nodes of Ranvier**—rather than flow the entire length of the neuron (see fig. 2.3). Sadly, the importance of the myelin sheath in neural transmission can be seen in victims of *multiple sclerosis.* This disease destroys the myelin sheaths of many neurons and leaves them unable to operate at normal efficiency. The result is that the individuals with multiple sclerosis have severe difficulties controlling their muscles and suffer serious vision problems (Morell & Norton, 1980).

Synaptic Transmission

Neurons are linked together in complex chains, but they are not directly connected to each other. Between the axon of one neuron and the dendrite of another, there is a small gap called the **synapse.** The ability of a neural message to cross this gap depends on chemical substances called **neurotransmitters.** They are released from the knoblike tips of the axons across the gap, exciting the adjacent dendrite, causing the neural message to continue along the next neuron (see fig. 2.4).

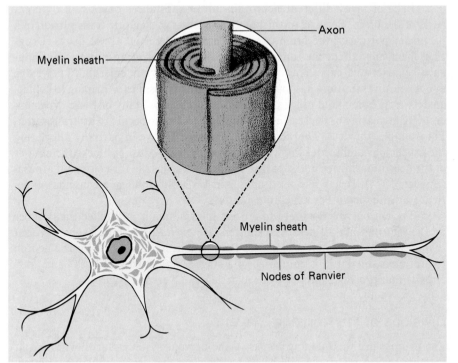

Figure 2.3 Many neurons are wrapped like a jelly roll in a white fatty substance called myelin. The myelin sheath speeds neural transmission by allowing the electrical disturbance to jump between widely spaced gaps in the myelin sheath called the nodes of Ranvier.

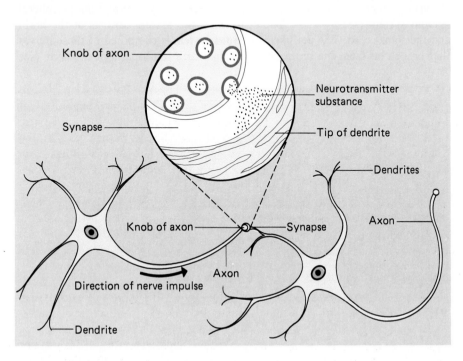

Figure 2.4 Neural messages are transmitted across synaptic gaps when neurotransmitters are secreted that stimulate the next dendrite (Hole, 1984).

Each of many different neurotransmitter substances operate in different parts of the brain. Because of this fact, the process of synaptic transmission in a particular portion of the brain can be altered through the use of drugs. Drugs that chemically affect the function of one of these neurotransmitters can influence behavior and experience in specific ways. Thus, our emerging knowledge about neurotransmitters has made the use of drugs possible for helping to control anxiety, depression, and other psychological problems. Many of these drugs operate by increasing or decreasing the effectiveness of a specific neurotransmitter. For example, the drug *Thorazine* is apparently effective in partially alleviating the psychological disorder known as schizophrenia because it blocks the actions of the neurotransmitter in the part of the brain responsible for emotional arousal (Snyder, 1974). Drugs like marijuana and LSD also influence conscious experience by affecting other neurotransmitters.

The capacity of the brain to process information is multiplied many times by the fact that not all neurotransmitters are *excitatory*. Some axons transmit *inhibitory* substances across synapses that make it more difficult for the neuron to fire. Thus, the brain is composed of a staggering network of "yes" and "no" circuits that process and create our experiences (Iverson, 1979).

Divisions of the Nervous System

The neurons are the building blocks of the nervous system. But they do not fit together to create a single, simple nervous system that serves only one function. Ours is a nervous system with many different parts or divisions. The major divisions of the nervous system are the central nervous system and the peripheral nervous system (see fig. 2.5). The **central nervous system** consists of the brain and the spinal cord. The **peripheral nervous system** is composed of those nerves that branch off from the brain and the spinal cord to all parts of the body (see

central nervous system
The brain and the nerve fibers that make up the spinal cord.

peripheral nervous system
(pĕ-rif'er-al)
The network of nerves that branch off the brain and spinal cord to all parts of the body.

Figure 2.5 The relationships of the divisions of the nervous system to one another.

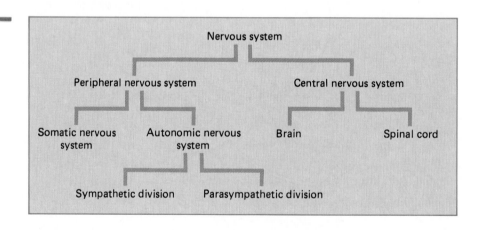

fig. 2.6). Nerves of the peripheral nervous system transmit messages from the body to the central nervous system. They also transmit messages from the central nervous system to the muscles, glands, and organs that put the messages into action.

Messages can only travel across the synapse in one direction. So messages coming from the body *into* the central nervous system are carried by one set of neurons, the **afferent neurons.** Messages going *out from* the central nervous system to the organs and muscles are carried by another set, the **efferent neurons.**

The spinal cord's primary function is to relay messages between the brain and the body, but it also does some rudimentary processing of information on its own. A simple reflex, such as the reflexive withdrawal from a hot object, is a good example. The impulse caused by the hot object travels up an afferent nerve

afferent neurons
(af'er-ent)
Neurons that transmit messages from sense organs to the central nervous system.

efferent neurons
(ef'er-ent)
Neurons that transmit messages from the central nervous system to organs and muscles.

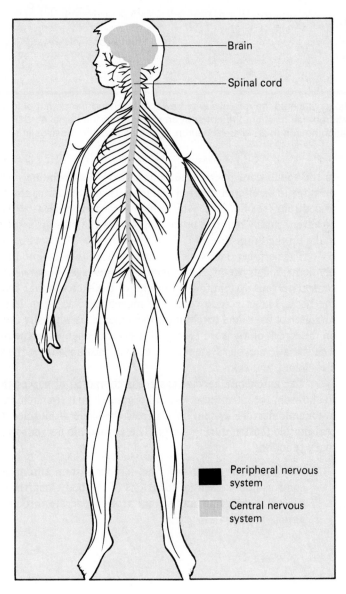

Brain

Spinal cord

Peripheral nervous system

Central nervous system

Figure 2.6 The nervous system can be divided into the central nervous system (brain and spinal cord) and the peripheral nervous system (the nerves that branch out to all parts of the body from the central nervous system).

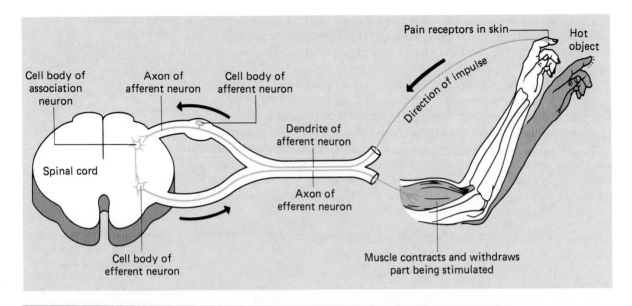

Figure 2.7 Some simple reflexes, such as the reflexive withdrawal of the hand from a hot object, involve a message traveling along an afferent neuron from the hot spot on the hand to the spinal cord. In the spinal cord, it travels across a short association neuron to an efferent neuron, which causes the muscles in the limb to contract.

association neurons
Neurons in the brain and spinal cord that process neural messages.

somatic nervous system
(so-mat′ik)
Division of the nervous system that carries messages from the sense organs, muscles, joints, and skin to the central nervous system, and from the central nervous system to the skeletal muscles.

autonomic nervous system
(aw″to-nom′ik)
The division of the nervous system that controls the involuntary actions of internal body organs, such as heartbeat and breathing, and is important in motivation and the experience of emotion.

to the spinal cord. Here a neuron, called an **association neuron,** transmits the message to an efferent neuron which, in turn, stimulates the muscles of the limb to contract (see fig. 2.7). Any behavior more complicated than a simple reflex, however, usually requires processing within the mass of association neurons that make up the brain.

The peripheral nervous system is further divided into the somatic and autonomic nervous systems. The **somatic nervous system** carries messages from the central nervous system to the muscles of the skeleton that control movements of the body. These include voluntary movements, as when I type the words on a manuscript page, and involuntary movements, as when my eyes maintain fixation on the screen of my word processor in spite of changes in the position of my head. The somatic nervous system also receives messages from the sense organs, muscles, joints, and skin.

The **autonomic nervous system** is composed of nerves that carry messages to and from the glands and visceral organs (heart, stomach, intestines, etc.). The autonomic nervous system only affects the skeletal muscles by influencing general muscle tension during stress. The autonomic nervous system has three primary functions:

1. *Essential body functions.* The nervous system automatically controls many essential functions of the body: heartbeat, breathing, digestion, sweating, and sexual arousal operate through the autonomic nervous system.

2. *Emotion.* The autonomic nervous system also regulates emotion. Have you ever wondered why you sometimes get a stomachache, diarrhea, a pounding heart, or a headache when you feel anxious? It's because the autonomic nervous system serves the function of regulating both the internal organs and the emotions. When a person gets very emotional, the autonomic system often overdoes its job and throws our internal organs out of balance in minor, but uncomfortable, ways.

3. *Motivation.* Finally, the autonomic nervous system also plays an important role in the control of our motivations. That is why we tend to overeat or experience other changes in our motives when anxious or depressed.

The autonomic nervous system can itself be divided into two separate parts. In general, the **sympathetic division** of the autonomic nervous system tends to activate the visceral organs during emotional arousal or when there are physical demands on the body. The **parasympathetic division** tends to "calm" the visceral organs after arousal (see fig. 2.8). For example, the sympathetic division increases the rate of heartbeat while the parasympathetic division decreases heartbeat. In tandem, therefore, these two divisions of the autonomic nervous system operate to control and balance the functioning of the visceral organs. Not all of the functions of the two autonomic divisions are in opposition to one another, however. For example, the parasympathetic division is responsible for vaginal lubrication and erection of the penis during sexual arousal, while the sympathetic division controls sexual orgasm.

The structure and the functions of these two divisions of the autonomic nervous system can be seen more clearly by referring to figure 2.8. Essentially all organs that are served by the sympathetic division are also served by the parasympathetic division. Note also that the clusters of cell bodies of neurons—called **ganglia**—are organized in different ways in the two divisions. The ganglia of the sympathetic division are linked together in a chain that is near the spinal column. This arrangement results in the sympathetic division's operating in a diffuse manner. That is, when the sympathetic division is aroused, it tends to stimulate all of the organs served by it to some extent—because all of its parts are chained together. The ganglia of the parasympathetic division, in contrast, are separate and located near the individual organs. This allows the parasympathetic division to operate more selectively which is particularly fortunate—otherwise we would wet our pants every time we salivated!

sympathetic division (sim″pah-thet′ik) The division of the autonomic nervous system that generally activates internal organs during emotional arousal or when physical demands are placed on the body.

parasympathetic division (par″ah-sim″pah-thet′ik) The division of the autonomic nervous system that generally "calms" internal organs.

ganglia (gang′gle-ah) Clusters of cell bodies of neurons outside of the central nervous system.

Figure 2.8 The sympathetic and parasympathetic divisions of the autonomic nervous system regulate many of the body's organs and play key roles in emotions and motivations (Hole, 1984).

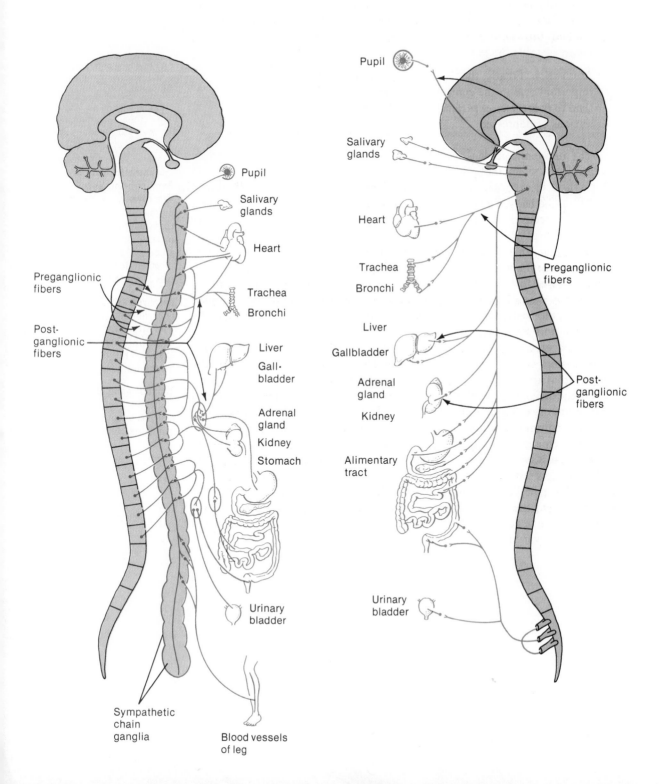

SYMPATHETIC DIVISION   PARASYMPATHETIC DIVISION

We generally are not conscious of the actions of the autonomic nervous system. It carries out its regulation of the heart, lungs, intestines, sweat glands, and so on in an automatic way that does not require our awareness or intentional control. It plays its role in motivation and emotion in an equally automatic way. It is possible, however, to learn to exert more conscious control over the actions of the autonomic nervous system. Through practice—and perhaps with the help of a psychologist—we can learn to think in ways that reduce emotional arousal or learn to relax the body in ways that accomplish the same thing. Sometimes, people need to develop voluntary control over a particular function of the autonomic nervous system. Individuals with high blood pressure, for example, can often learn to control their blood pressure if they are given precise information (feedback from a special recording instrument) on how well that biological function is being controlled. The term **biofeedback** is now commonly used to describe this technique. (See *Research Report:* "Biofeedback.") Biofeedback has been successfully used in the treatment of migraine and tension headaches, some cases of high blood pressure, and other problems related to sympathetic arousal (Blanchard & Epstein, 1978).

biofeedback
(bi''o-fēd'bak)
A technique for providing an individual with precise information about the functioning of an internal organ to help him or her learn to control it voluntarily.

R E V I E W

The nervous system is a highly efficient living computer and communication system built of neurons. These specialized cells transmit neural messages from their dendrites to their axons in a flowing swirl of electrically charged molecules produced by the changing semipermeability of their membranes. When the neural message reaches the tip of the axon, it is transmitted across the synaptic gap to the next neuron by a neurotransmitter substance.

The nervous system can be divided into a central nervous system composed of the brain and spinal cord, and a peripheral nervous system composed of nerves that carry messages to and from the body. The peripheral nervous system is further divided into the somatic and autonomic nervous systems. The somatic nervous system carries messages from the sense organs, muscles, and joints to the central nervous system, and from the central nervous system to the skeletal muscles. The autonomic nervous system is responsible for the regulation of the internal organs, emotion, and motivation. Even the autonomic nervous system can be divided into two working parts: the sympathetic division that primarily activates visceral organs and the parasympathetic division that primarily calms these organs.

R E S E A R C H   R E P O R T

Biofeedback: Learning to Control Voluntarily the Autonomic Nervous System

A lot of our aches, pains, and ailments involve organs served by the autonomic nervous system. For example, tension headaches, migraine headaches, stomachaches, nocturnal bruxism ("tooth grinding" during sleep), and some forms of joint pain are believed to be caused by excessive and prolonged arousal of the sympathetic division of the autonomic nervous system. Ordinarily we are not aware of the "automatic" operations of the autonomic nervous system, but if people who have such problems could voluntarily "turn down" their sympathetic arousal, they could save themselves a great deal of discomfort.

Is it possible to learn voluntary control of the autonomic nervous system, or is it biologically impossible to control such an independent, automatic system? Fortunately, an effective method for teaching people to control autonomic arousal called *biofeedback* has been developed. According to this method, the autonomic nervous system is not constructed in such a way that makes voluntary control totally impossible. Rather, we usually cannot control its functions because we do not get enough *feedback* from the organs themselves to know what is going on. What is your blood pressure right now? If you tried to make it go down, would you know if it had changed? Ordinarily, we have very little information about what the organs are doing. In contrast, if you raised your left hand, you would have no trouble sensing that it was up in the air.

As the name implies, *biofeedback* teaches people to control voluntarily their autonomic nervous systems by giving them additional *feedback* on the biological organs that the autonomic nervous system controls. Recently, biofeedback has been used successfully in the treatment of a number of problems associated with abnormal autonomic arousal. Migraine headaches, for example, are believed to be caused by excessive blood flow to the brain. When the sympathetic division of the autonomic nervous system is aroused, as during stress, the blood vessels near the skin constrict, while the blood vessels serving the brain dilate (open wider). If this increased blood flow to the brain persists due to unresolved stress, migraine headaches can result (Kallman & Gilmore, 1981).

RESEARCH REPORT

Ellie Sturgis, David Tollison, and Henry Adams (1978) conducted a clinical study of the use of biofeedback in the treatment of migraine headaches. They taught patients how to regulate the amount of blood flowing through the temporal artery by using a special instrument to measure blood flow and give feedback about it to the patient. The amount of blood flowing through the temporal artery—the one you can sometimes feel pulsing in your temples—is closely related to the amount of blood flowing to the brain. Patients were asked to try to reduce the amount of blood flow by relaxing. When the amount of blood flowing through the temporal artery fell below a preset level, the patient heard a tone from the instrument, indicating that the blood flow had decreased to a normal rate. By using this tone as feedback, the patients learned to consistently reduce temporal artery blood flow. The effects of biofeedback training on the migraine headaches of one of the patients—a 54-year-old woman with a 40-year history of migraines—are shown in figure 2.9. Before treatment, the patient averaged 6.2 hours of migraine headaches every two weeks. During biofeedback treatment, however, she stopped having migraines altogether and continued to have virtually no migraines during a one-year follow-up period.

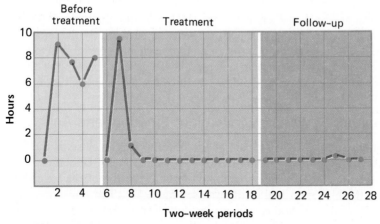

Figure 2.9 The average number of hours of migraine headaches experienced during two-week periods before, during, and after biofeedback treatment in which the individual was taught to voluntarily reduce the amount of blood flowing through the temporal artery (Sturgis, Tollison & Adams, 1978).

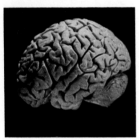

The human brain.

Structures and Functions of the Brain: The Living Computer

All mental functions require the integrated functioning of many parts of the brain; no single function of the brain is carried out solely in one part. Still, the brain does have a number of specialized parts, each bearing primary responsibility for certain activities. The brain's many and complex structures can be classified in various ways. The most convenient classification divides the brain into three major parts. These are the hindbrain, the midbrain, and the forebrain. The major structures and functions of each part are described below. As we look at the brain, we start at the bottom and work our way up.

Hindbrain and Midbrain: Housekeeping Chores and Reflexes

hindbrain
The lowest part of the brain, located at the base of the skull.

medulla (mĕ-dul'ah)
The swelling at the top of the spinal cord responsible for controlling breathing and a variety of reflexes.

pons (ponz)
Part of the hindbrain that is involved in balance, hearing, and some parasympathetic functions.

cerebellum (ser''e-bel'um)
Two rounded lumps behind the medulla responsible for maintaining muscle tone and muscular coordination.

midbrain
The small area at the top of the hindbrain that primarily serves as a reflex center for orienting the eyes and ears.

forebrain
The parts of the brain, including the thalamus, hypothalamus, and cerebral cortex, that cover the hindbrain and midbrain and fill much of the skull.

thalamus (thal'-ah-mus)
That part of the forebrain that primarily routes messages to appropriate parts of the brain.

The **hindbrain** is the lowest part of the brain, located at the rear base of the skull. It primarily carries out routine "housekeeping" functions that keep the body working properly. The hindbrain has three principal parts, the medulla, the pons, and the cerebellum (see fig. 2.10). The **medulla** is a swelling at the top of the spinal cord, where the cord enters the brain. The medulla is responsible for controlling breathing and a variety of reflexes, including those that enable you to maintain an upright posture. The **pons** is concerned with balance, hearing, and some parasympathetic functions. It is located just above the medulla. The **cerebellum** consists of two rounded structures located to the rear of the pons. It is chiefly responsible for maintaining muscle tone and coordination of muscular movements.

The **midbrain** is a small area at the top of the hindbrain that serves primarily as a center for several postural reflexes, particularly the ones associated with the senses. For example, the automatic movement of the eyes to keep them fixed on an object as the head moves, and the reflexive moving of the head to better orient the ears to a sound, are both controlled in the midbrain.

Forebrain: Cognition, Motivation, Emotion, and Action

By far the most interesting part of the brain to psychologists is the forebrain. Structurally, the **forebrain** consists of two distinct areas. One area, which contains the thalamus and hypothalamus, rests at the top of the long stalk comprising the hindbrain and midbrain (see fig. 2.11). The other area, made up primarily of the cerebral cortex, covers the lower part of the brain like a fat cap of an acorn covering its kernel. Not only are these two areas distinctly different in terms of structure, but they control very different functions as well.

Thalamus and Hypothalamus

The **thalamus** is primarily a switching station for messages going to and from the brain. It routes incoming stimuli from the sense organs to the appropriate parts of the brain and links the upper and lower centers of the brain.

The **hypothalamus** is a small, but vitally important, part of the brain. It lies underneath the thalamus, just forward of the midbrain. The hypothalamus is intimately involved in our *motives* and *emotions:* eating, drinking, sexual motivation, pleasure, anger, and fear. It also plays a key role in regulating body temperature, sleep, endocrine gland activity; controlling glandular secretions of the

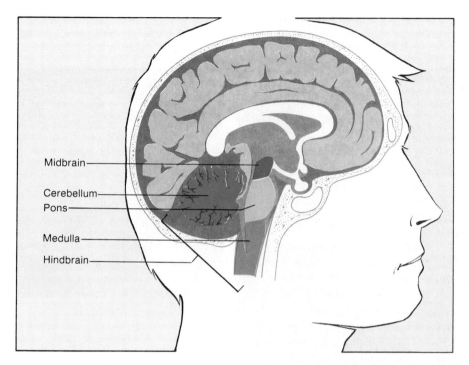

Figure 2.10 Important structures of the hindbrain and midbrain.

Midbrain

Cerebellum

Pons

Medulla

Hindbrain

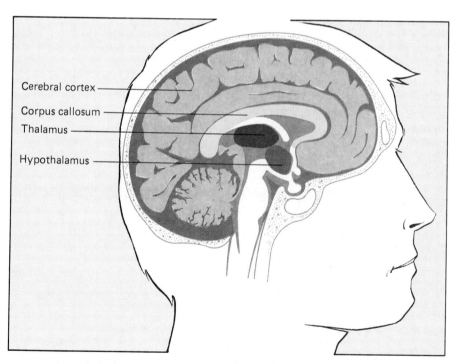

Figure 2.11 Key structures of the forebrain.

Cerebral cortex

Corpus callosum

Thalamus

Hypothalamus

Figure 2.12 (a) A coronal cross section through the human brain corresponding to the diagrams in figures 2.10 and 2.11. (b) A posterior view of the human brain showing both hemispheres. Most of what is visible is cerebral cortex.

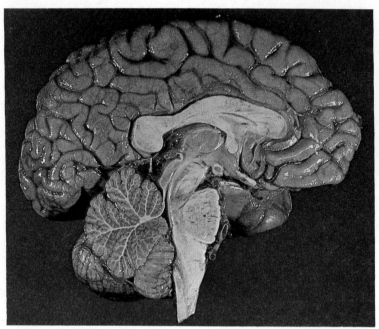

(a)

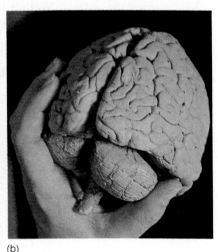

(b)

hypothalamus
(hi″po-thal′ah-mus)
The small part of the forebrain involved with motives, emotions, and the functions of the autonomic nervous system.

stomach and intestines; and maintaining the normal pace and rhythm of such body functions as blood pressure and heartbeat. Thus, the hypothalamus is the brain center most directly linked to the functions of the autonomic nervous system.

The **hypothalamus** is also involved in *aggression*. Laboratory studies have found that the degree of aggression in rats can be altered by chemically controlling the hypothalamus. Rats that normally kill mice on sight will stop this behavior when a drug that inhibits the actions of the hypothalamus is injected directly into it. In contrast, rats that normally do not attack mice will kill them when a stimulating drug is injected into the hypothalamus (Smith, King, & Hoebel, 1970).

The hypothalamus also appears to contain specific *pleasure centers*. Rats will repeatedly press a lever for hours in order to receive electrical stimulation in certain parts of the hypothalamus (Olds & Milner, 1954). Jose Delgado (1969), working with human subjects, appears to have identified particular parts of the hypothalamus where electrical stimulation produces intense generalized sensations of pleasure, and other parts where electrical stimulation produces strong specific sensations of sexual pleasure. Apparently, these parts of the hypothalamus are active when we experience pleasure in our daily lives.

Cerebral Cortex

cerebral cortex
(ser′ĕ-bral)
The largest structure in the forebrain, controlling conscious experience and intelligence, and involved with the somatic nervous system.

The largest structure in the forebrain is the **cerebral cortex,** which controls the conscious experience and intelligence that make us uniquely human (see fig. 2.12). As such, it is the primary brain structure related to the somatic nervous system.

Drawing by Lorenz; © 1980
The New Yorker Magazine, Inc.

"It's finally happening, Helen. The hemispheres of my brain are drifting apart."

The cerebral cortex is made up of two nearly separate halves called the **cerebral hemispheres.** These two hemispheres are joined by the **corpus callosum,** a collection of axons that provides a communication link between them. Some of the brain's functions, such as vision and touch, are shared by both cerebral hemispheres. Interestingly, this sensory input is processed differently than one might think. Information from receptors on the left side of the body (the left hand and the left visual field of each eye, for example) is processed in the right hemisphere. Input from the right side of the body is processed by the left hemisphere. To accomplish this, the major nerves entering the brain from the spinal cord twist and cross-over each other.

Many of the other functions of the forebrain are carried out by only one of the hemispheres. In other words, the two sides of the brain are not symmetrical mirror images of one another in terms of their functions. As a rough generalization, the right side of the brain is chiefly involved in music, fantasy, intuition, art, visualizing spatial relationships, and the understanding of unhappy events. The left side is less cultured, but more pragmatic. It is involved in logic, mathematics, language, writing, and the understanding of happy situations (Kinsbourne, 1981; Levy, 1985). (See *Research Report:* "Split Brains.")

Although the right and left cerebral hemispheres ordinarily work together in an integrated fashion, there is reason to believe that different individuals show different amounts of activity in the two hemispheres (Levy, 1985). In a sense, then, different people may tend to rely more on either their left or right hemisphere in dealing with life. How can you tell whether you are right- or left-hemisphere dominant? The answer comes from a very unlikely source—the way you hold a pencil to write. The first clue comes from the hand in which you hold the pencil; 97 percent of right-handed people are left-hemisphere dominant, whereas only about 60 percent of left-handed people are left-hemisphere dominant. The

cerebral hemispheres
The two main parts of the cerebral cortex.

corpus callosum
(kor′pus kah-lo′-sum)
The link between the cerebral hemispheres.

RESEARCH REPORT

Split Brains: The Left Brain Doesn't Know What the Right Brain Is Doing

It's sometimes necessary to control the neurological disease of epilepsy by surgically cutting the corpus callosum to keep seizures from spreading from one cerebral hemisphere to the other. When this is done, the right and left hemispheres have no way of exchanging information; the left brain literally does not know what the right brain is doing and vice versa. A number of experiments have been performed on these patients (referred to as *split-brain* patients) that are a major source of our knowledge about the different functions of the two cerebral hemispheres.

The general procedure for these experiments is to send information to one hemisphere at a time to see how it's processed. Information from the left side of the visual field of each eye is sent to the right hemisphere, while information received from the right side of the visual field of each eye is sent to the left hemisphere (see fig. 2.13). To present information to only one side of the visual field, a special apparatus is used. As illustrated in figure 2.14, the split-brain patient is asked to fix his vision on a spot in the center of a screen directly in front of him. This keeps his eyes in a fixed position while a word is presented on one side of the screen for such a brief interval that eye movements are impossible (less than .2 of a second). If the word is presented to the left visual field on the left side of the screen, then the image of the word is transmitted only to the right cerebral hemisphere. Images presented to the right side of the screen travel the opposite path to the left hemisphere (more on this when we discuss vision in the next chapter).

If the word *pencil* is presented in the right visual field, the information travels to the language control areas in the left hemisphere. In this situation, the subject has no difficulty reading aloud the word *pencil*. But if the same word is presented to the left visual field, the split-brain patient would typically not be able to respond when asked what word had been presented. This does not mean that the right side of the brain did not receive or understand the word *pencil*, however. It means that the patient cannot verbalize what he saw. Using the sense of touch, the split-brain patient can easily pick out a pencil as the object that matched the word from among a number of unseen objects—but only if he uses his left hand, which has received the message from the right cerebral cortex.

[*Continued on page 64*]

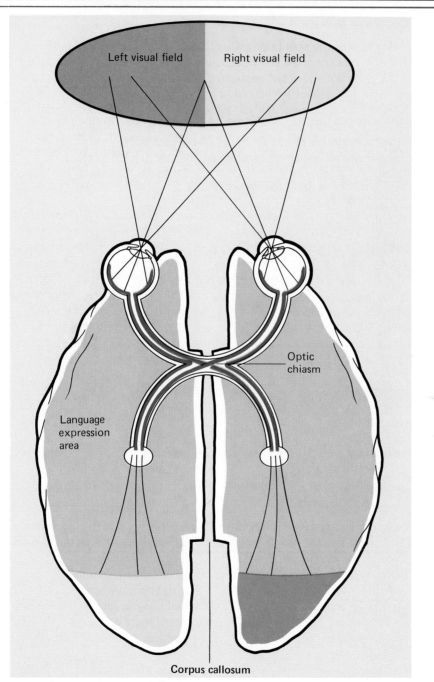

Figure 2.13 Diagram of a "split-brain" patient showing the pathways traveled by information from the left and right visual fields of the eyes to the left and right cerebral hemispheres.
From The split brain in man, *by M. S. Gazzaniga. Copyright © 1967 by Scientific American, Inc. All rights reserved.*

RESEARCH REPORT

[*Continued from page 62*]

However, if the split-brain patient holds an unseen pencil in his left hand, he cannot tell you what he is holding. It's not that the right cortex does not know, but because it has no area controlling verbal expression, it cannot *tell* you what it knows. The left cortex that is "talking" to you cannot tell you either, because information in the right cortex cannot reach it in the split-brain patient. Such studies with split-brain patients clearly reveal the localization of language expression abilities in the left cerebral hemisphere (Gazzaniga, 1967; 1983).

Figure 2.14 Apparatus used to study split-brain patients.
From The split brain in man, *by M. S. Gazzaniga. Copyright © 1967 by Scientific American, Inc. All rights reserved.*

second clue comes from *how* you hold your pencil when you write. As shown in figure 2.15, right-handed people who write with their hand below the line and left-handed people who invert their hand are left-hemisphere dominant (Levy & Reid, 1976). Which is better, to be left- or right-hemisphere dominant? Nobody knows for sure, but there is some evidence that right-hemisphere dominant individuals may be better at tasks that involve visual images, such as drawing and painting. Picasso and Michelangelo were right-hemisphere dominant artists, but there are many examples of successful left-hemisphere dominant artists as well (Pines, 1980).

The location of some specific kinds of functions within each of the cerebral hemispheres has been known for some time (see fig. 2.16). The fact that language abilities are located primarily in an area of the left hemisphere was discovered in the mid-nineteenth century by the French neurologist Paul Broca. Broca performed autopsies on a number of people who had suffered from the serious speech disorder termed **aphasia.** He discovered that these individuals had sustained damage to the left cerebral hemisphere. Today we know that two primary areas

aphasia (ah-fa′ze-ah)
An impairment of the ability to understand or use language.

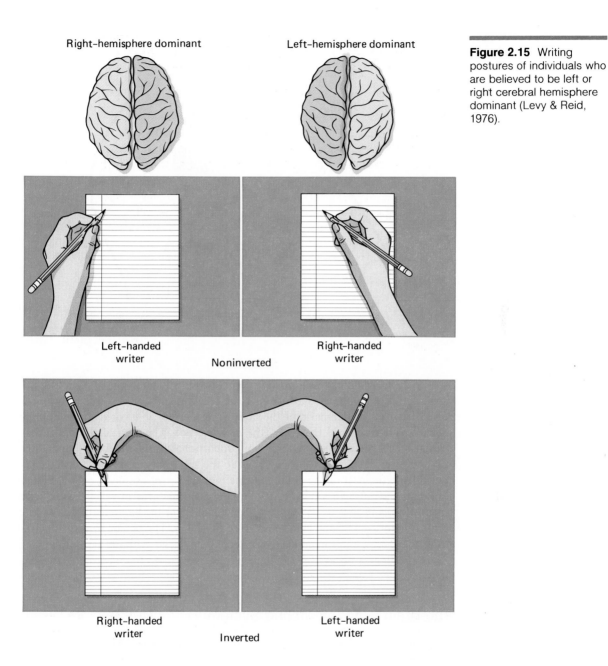

Right-hemisphere dominant   Left-hemisphere dominant

Left-handed
writer   Noninverted   Right-handed
writer

Right-handed
writer   Inverted   Left-handed
writer

Figure 2.15 Writing postures of individuals who are believed to be left or right cerebral hemisphere dominant (Levy & Reid, 1976).

in the left hemisphere are important in language (see fig. 2.16). *Broca's area* controls our use of language to communicate with others, whereas *Wernicke's area* is involved in our understanding of language. Damage to either of these areas, as from a stroke that ruptures or blocks a blood vessel in the brain, will produce aphasia.

The location of many other functions of the cerebral cortex is also known. For example, figure 2.16 shows the location of structures of the left cerebral cortex involved in thinking, vision, hearing, the skin senses, motor control, and language. Similar areas for all of these functions except language are found in the right hemisphere.

Figure 2.16 Location of several major functions in the left cerebral hemisphere.

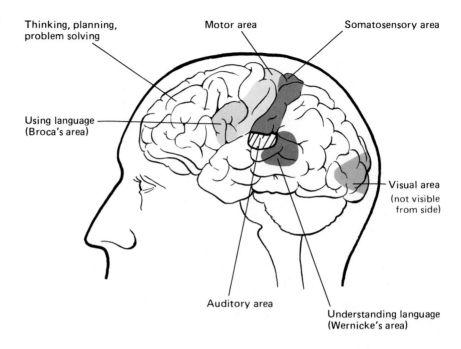

Thinking, planning, problem solving

Motor area

Somatosensory area

Using language (Broca's area)

Visual area (not visible from side)

Auditory area

Understanding language (Wernicke's area)

Within each area of the cortex, there is often a further localization of functions. For example, particular areas of the cerebral cortex control sensations received from particular parts of the body (the *sensory area*) or neural impulses sent to various parts of the body (the *motor area*). The area of the brain that regulates a particular body part is not proportional to the physical size of that part, however. Rather, it is proportional to the sensitivity of neural messages received from the part or the degree of fine motor control exercised over the part. Biologists have drawn amusing, yet informative, pictures of people with body features proportional to the space allocated to them in the areas of the cortex serving motor control and skin senses (see fig. 2.17). The person that results has small arms, legs, and torso but a very large face, large genitals, as well as huge hands and fingers because many neural messages travel to and from these sensitive areas.

The Brain Is an Interacting System

Even though we find it convenient to think of the brain as being divided into many separate parts, you should know that the parts commonly *work together* in intellectual and emotional functioning. Consider, for example, your reaction in the following situation. You are waiting at a bus stop late at night. A poorly dressed man approaches, smelling of alcohol. He asks you if you can spare five dollars. In his pocket, you see the outline of what might be a gun. Your reaction to this scene would involve many parts of your brain working together. Your cerebral hemispheres are evaluating the possible threat to you and the alternative courses of action open to you. Your hypothalamus is involved in a process of emotional arousal. If you fight, run, or even reach in your pocket to hand over the money, your hindbrain and midbrain will coordinate the muscular movements involved. Many parts of the brain must work together in this situation.

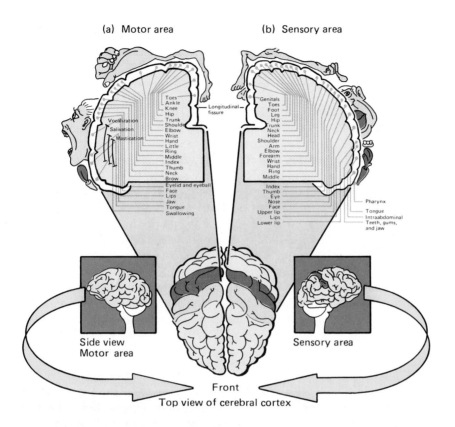

(a) Motor area   (b) Sensory area

Top view of cerebral cortex

Figure 2.17 A cross section of the cerebral cortex in the (a) motor control area and (b) the skin sense area showing the areas in the cortex serving each part of the body. The size of the body feature in the drawing is proportional to the size of the related brain area (Peele, 1961).

There are even some structures that can be said to cross the lines between the hindbrain, midbrain, and forebrain. One such system is the network of neural structures called the **reticular formation.** This neural system plays an important role in arousing the cerebral cortex. When sensory impulses reach the reticular formation, it activates the cerebral cortex. Without this activation, the cortex would not be able to process sensory information, carry out thought processes, and the like. The reticular formation also plays a role in the process of attention. All of the sense organs have nerve fibers that go to the reticular formation. It "screens" sensory input, letting "important" sensory messages—such as those having to do with pain—pass through to the cerebral cortex, while not allowing less important sensory messages to pass on—such as information about the location of your left foot as you sit reading. This frees the cortex from processing the seemingly unmanageable number of sensory inputs that constantly reach the brain.

The reticular formation also plays an important role in the regulation of sleep and wakefulness through its activating function. Input to the cortex from the reticular formation is one of the factors that results in wakefulness. Indeed, when the reticular formation is severely damaged, the result is a state of coma.

One more fact about the reticular formation for you to think about: The nerves between the reticular formation and the cerebral cortex run in both directions. This means that not only can the reticular formation affect the cortex, but also the cortex can affect the reticular formation. Cortical activity—such as

reticular formation (re-tik′u-lar) The system of neural structures spanning parts of the hindbrain, midbrain, and forebrain that plays a role in cortical arousal and attention.

RESEARCH REPORT

Exciting New Images of the Brain at Work

Exciting new tools have recently been developed for the study of brain functions. These techniques create images of the activities of the living brain by using computers to compile and interpret large amounts of information. One of these new brain-imaging techniques uses recordings of the brain's electrical activity, termed electroencephalograph or EEG recordings. The head is covered with electrodes placed 1 centimeter apart to record brain activity. The computer converts these recordings into color images of the brain. The images in figure 2.18 show the pattern of activity in the brain of psychiatric researcher Monte Buchsbaum during the moments following the administration of a mild electrical shock to his arm. Predictably, the area of greatest activity (red and orange) is at the top of the sensory and motor strips of the cerebral cortex—the area that receives skin sensations and controls movements of the arm (Buchsbaum, 1983).

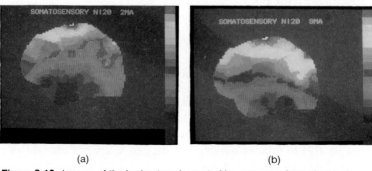

(a)   (b)

Figure 2.18 Images of the brain at work created by computer from electrical recordings of the activity of the brain. Here, the images show the activation of areas of the cerebral cortex of Dr. Monte Buchsbaum immediately after the administration of a mild electric shock to his arm (Buchsbaum, 1983).

lying in bed thinking about the new object of your love and passion—tends to activate the reticular formation. This, in turn, leads the reticular formation to further activate the cerebral cortex and keep you awake. This is part of the reason that it is often difficult to fall asleep when you "can't turn your thoughts off."

Thus, the brain does not function like many separate computers that each handle different jobs. Rather, it's a single complex system composed of many specialized parts that operate together as the basis for human experience and behavior. (See *Of Special Interest:* "Living with a Hole in the Head.")

RESEARCH REPORT

A different kind of image is shown in figure 2.19. These images were created by computer interpretation of multiple X rays (emission-computed tomography). The subject is shown at left resting with his eyes closed. The image at the right shows the same subject when naming visually presented objects. Note the increased activity in several regions: the frontal and visual areas of the cerebral cortex, the two language areas of the left hemisphere of the cerebral cortex, and two areas of the right hemisphere. Several different areas of the brain are activated during this task because naming objects involves vision, spatial interpretation, and language processes (Lou, Henriksen, & Bruhn, 1984). These powerful new brain-imaging techniques promise new breakthroughs in our understanding of brain functions in the near future.

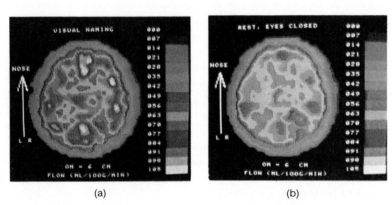

(a)   (b)

Figure 2.19 Images of the activity of the living brain created by computer interpretation of multiple X rays. The image on the left is of an individual who is resting with eyes closed. The image on the right shows increased activity in the language areas of the left cerebral hemisphere and two areas of the right hemisphere when looking at objects and naming them (Lou, Henriksen, & Bruhn, 1984).

REVIEW

While they work together in an integrated fashion, the many different parts of the brain carry out different functions. The hindbrain and midbrain handle housekeeping responsibilities of the body such as breathing, posture, reflexes, and other basic processes. The more "psychological" functions of the brain are carried out in the larger forebrain area. The thalamus—which integrates sensory input—and the hypothalamus—which controls motivation, emotion, sleep, and other basic bodily processes—lie beneath

OF SPECIAL INTEREST

Living with a Hole in the Head: The Case of Phineas Gage

In 1848 Phineas Gage was excavating rock to make way for a new section of track for the Rutland and Burlington Railroad in Vermont. Gage was known as a reasonable, polite, and hardworking man and had been made a foreman by the railroad. On one particular afternoon in the fall, he was hard at work preparing to blast a section of rock when an accident happened. Gage was tamping blasting powder into a hole with a long tamping rod when a spark ignited the powder. The explosion shot the rod up through his upper left jaw and completely through his head (see fig. 2.20).

When Gage's coworkers reached him, he was conscious and able to tell them what had happened. He was rushed to a physician who was able to stop the bleeding and save his life, but the destruction of such a large amount of brain tissue took a terrible toll on his emotions and intelligence. Gage became irritable, publicly profane, and impossible to reason with. He also seemed to lose much of his ability to think rationally and plan. As a result, he had trouble holding a job and was regarded as a "totally changed" man by his former friends (Bigelow, 1850).

The case of Phineas Gage is surprising in part because he lived through his accident. It's highly unlikely that injuries to the brain as extensive as his could occur without destroying areas that are vital to survival. But the dramatic alteration in Gage's personality is also impressive in what it reveals about behavior. Even though his wounds healed, Gage's brain never functioned in the same way again. Because brain and behavior are inseparably linked, destruction of important parts of the brain leads to destruction of important parts of personality as well.

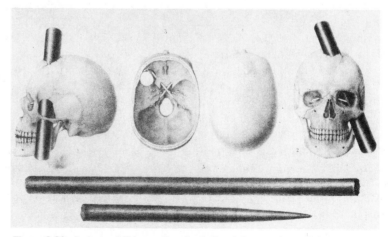

Figure 2.20 A photo of Phineas Gage's skull and the tamping rod that passed through his brain.

the cap of the cerebral cortex. The cerebral cortex provides the neurological basis for thinking, language, control of motor movements, perception, and other cognitive processes. The cortex is composed of two halves, the cerebral hemispheres, that are connected to each other by the corpus callosum. Except for areas of the cortex that serve language, those that provide the basis for the other cognitive processes are found in both hemispheres. The two cerebral hemispheres are involved in different aspects of these cognitive processes, however. The right hemisphere serves intuitive, spatial, and artistic cognitive processes, while the left hemisphere is involved in logical, mathematical, and language-based processes.

Endocrine System: Chemical Messengers of the Body

The nervous system, as we have just seen, is the vital computer and communication system that forms the biological basis for behavior and conscious experience. Another biological system also plays an important role in communication and the regulation of bodily processes—the **endocrine system.** This system consists of a number of **glands** that secrete chemical messengers called **hormones** into the bloodstream. The action of hormones is closely related to that of the nervous system in three ways. First, the hormones are directly regulated by the brain, particularly the hypothalamus. Second, some of the hormones are chemically identical to some of the neurotransmitters. Third, the hormones aid the nervous system in a number of ways. Principally, they activate the visceral organs during physical stress or emotional arousal, influencing such things as metabolism, the level of blood sugar, and sexual functioning. Let's look briefly at the six endocrine glands that are most important psychologically (see fig. 2.21).

Adrenal Glands

The **adrenal glands** are a pair of glands that sit atop the two kidneys like stocking caps. They play an important role in emotional arousal and secrete a variety of hormones important to metabolism and sexual arousal. When stimulated by the sympathetic division of the autonomic nervous system, the adrenal glands secrete two hormones, among others, that are particularly important in reactions to stress. **Epinephrine** and **norepinephrine** (which are also neurotransmitters) stimulate changes to prepare the body to deal with physical demands that require intense bodily activity, including psychological threats or danger (even when the danger cannot be dealt with physically). The effects of these two adrenal hormones are quite similar, but they can be distinguished in terms of their most potent effects. Epinephrine increases blood pressure by increasing heart rate and blood flow; causes the liver to convert and release some of its supply of stored sugar into the bloodstream; and increases the rate with which the body uses energy (i.e., metabolism), sometimes by as much as 100 percent over normal. Norepinephrine also increases blood pressure by constricting the diameter of blood vessels in the body's muscles and reducing the activity of the digestive system (Groves & Schlesinger, 1979).

endocrine system (en′do-krin)
The system of glands that secretes hormones.

glands
Structures in the body that secrete substances.

hormones (hor′mōnz)
Chemical substances, produced by endocrine glands, that influence internal organs.

adrenal glands (ah-dre′nal)
Two glands near the kidneys that secrete epinephrine and norepinephrine and that are involved in emotional arousal.

epinephrine (ep″i-nef′rin)
A hormone produced by the adrenal glands.

norepinephrine (nor″ep-i-nef′rin)
A hormone produced by the adrenal glands.

Figure 2.21 Locations of major endocrine glands.

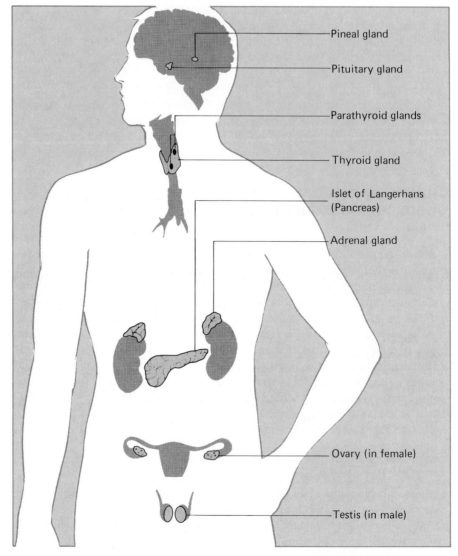

Pineal gland

Pituitary gland

Parathyroid glands

Thyroid gland

Islet of Langerhans (Pancreas)

Adrenal gland

Ovary (in female)

Testis (in male)

islets of Langerhans
(i'lets *of* lahng'er-hanz)
Endocrine cells in the pancreas that regulate the level of sugar in the blood.

pancreas (pan'kre-as)
The organ near the stomach that contains the islets of Langerhans.

glucagon (gloo'kah-gon)
A hormone produced by the islets of Langerhans that causes the liver to release sugar into the bloodstream.

insulin (in'su-lin)
A hormone produced by the islets of Langerhans that reduces the amount of sugar in the bloodstream.

ovaries (o'vah-rez)
Female endocrine glands that secrete sex-related hormones and produce ova, or eggs.

testes (tes'tēz)
Male endocrine glands that secrete sex-related hormones and produce sperm cells.

Note that these effects are very similar to the ones that sympathetic arousal produces on its own. Thus, the autonomic nervous system has two ways to activate the internal bodily organs: through direct action and by stimulating the adrenals and other endocrine glands. Incidentally, one reason that it takes so long to feel calm after a stressful event has passed is because of this second route to activating the body. It takes quite a while for the hormones to leave the bloodstream, so their effects are rather long lasting.

Islets of Langerhans

The **islets of Langerhans,** which are embedded in the **pancreas,** regulate the level of sugar in the blood by secreting two hormones that have opposing actions. **Glucagon** causes the liver to convert its stored sugar into blood sugar and dump it into the bloodstream. **Insulin,** in contrast, reduces the amount of blood sugar by helping the body's cells absorb it more easily from the bloodstream. Blood sugar level is important psychologically because it's one of the factors that determines how energetic a person feels.

Gonads

There are two sex glands—the **ovaries** in females, the **testes** in males. The **gonads** produce the sex cells—ova or eggs in females, sperm in males. They also secrete hormones that are important in sexual arousal and contribute to the development of so-called secondary sex characteristics, e.g., breast development in women, growth of chest hair in men, deepening of the voice in males at adolescence, and growth of pubic hair in both sexes. The most important sex hormones are **estrogen** in females and **testosterone** in males.

Thyroid Gland

The **thyroid gland,** located just below the larynx, or voice box, plays an important role in the regulation of **metabolism.** It does so by secreting a hormone called **thyroxin.** The level of thyroxin in a person's bloodstream, and the resulting metabolic rate, are important in many ways. In children, proper functioning of the thyroid is necessary for proper mental development. A serious thyroid deficiency in childhood will produce sluggishness, poor muscle tone, and a type of mental retardation called **cretinism.**

In adults, the thyroxin level helps determine one's weight and level of activity. People whose thyroid glands secrete unusually large amounts of thyroxin are typically very active. They may eat large amounts of food but still not gain weight because their rapid metabolic rate burns off calories so quickly. Conversely, people with low thyroxin levels will tend to be inactive and overweight. A "thyroid problem" is rarely the main cause of a weight problem, however. In still other cases, thyroid disturbances can lead to depression in adults. But, as with weight problems, most depression is not caused by a malfunctioning thyroid.

Parathyroid Glands

The four small glands imbedded in the thyroid gland are the **parathyroid glands.** They secrete **parathormone,** which is important in the functioning of the nervous system. Parathormone controls the excitability of the nervous system by regulating ion levels in the neurons. Too much parathormone inhibits nervous activity and leads to lethargy; too little of it may lead to excessive nervous activity and tension.

Pituitary Gland

The **pituitary gland** is located near the bottom of the brain, connected to and largely controlled by the hypothalamus. It's the body's *master gland* because its hormones help to regulate the activity of the other glands in the endocrine system. The pituitary gland secretes hormones that have other important effects on the body, notably in controlling blood pressure, thirst, and body growth. Too little or too much of the pituitary's growth hormone will make a person develop into a dwarf or giant. One special function of the pituitary gland is of particular importance to newborn infants. When the infant sucks the mother's nipples, a neural message is sent to the mother's hypothalamus, which sends a message to the pituitary gland. This causes the pituitary to secrete a hormone that releases breast milk for the baby.

gonads (gō′nadz)
The glands that produce sex cells and hormones important in sexual arousal and that contribute to the development of secondary sex characteristics.

estrogen (es′tro-jen)
A female sex hormone.

testosterone
(tes-tos′ter-ōn)
A male sex hormone.

thyroid (thi′roid)
The gland below the voice box that regulates metabolism.

metabolism
(mĕ-tab′o-lizm)
The process through which the body burns energy.

thyroxin (thi-rok′sin)
A hormone produced by the thyroid that is necessary for proper mental development in children and helps determine weight and level of activity in adults.

cretinism (kre′tin-izm)
A type of mental retardation in children caused by a deficiency of thyroxin.

parathyroid
(par″ah-thi′roid)
Four glands embedded in the thyroid that produce parathormone.

parathormone
(par″ah-thor′mōn)
A hormone that regulates ion levels in neurons and controls excitability of the nervous system.

pituitary (pi-tu′i-tār″e)
The body's master gland, located near the bottom of the brain, whose hormones help regulate the activity of the other glands in the endocrine system.

R E V I E W

The hormones of the endocrine glands supplement the brain's ability to coordinate the body's activities. These chemical messengers are involved in the regulation of metabolism, blood sugar level, sexual functioning, and other body functions. Most important from the viewpoint of psychology is the role of epinephrine and norepinephrine secreted by the adrenal glands in emotional arousal. These hormones activate the bodily organs in a diffuse and long-lasting way that is partially responsible for the length of time necessary for us to feel calm following a stressful event.

Genetic Influences on Behavior: Biological Blueprints?

If you speak loudly like your father, is it because you inherited a loud voice from him or because you learned to talk that way by living with him? If you are good in math like your mother, was that inherited or learned? In general, what is the role of heredity in human behavior?

What Is Inherited?

It's obvious that children inherit many of their physical characteristics from their parents. Light or dark skin, blue or brown eyes, tall or short stature—these are all traits we routinely expect to be passed from parents to children. Many aspects of behavior are also influenced by inheritance, but at this point it becomes difficult to separate the influence of heredity from that of the environment—to separate "*nature* from *nurture*," as the saying goes.

Research on animals can provide some valuable insights. For example, considerable research has been done on the nest-building behavior of a seabird called the tern. The question is: How does every female tern know how to build a nest? Is it a learned skill, or are the instructions for this behavior biologically programmed into the bird from birth? Experiments have made it clear that the latter is the case. If you raise a female tern in a laboratory, depriving it of the opportunity to see any tern nests from the time it hatches, it will still proceed to build precisely the same kind of nest its mother built. Obviously, "knowledge" of nest building is part of the tern's genetic inheritance.

Inheritance does not play so direct and complete a role in governing the behavior of humans. Humans do not inherit specific patterns of behavior like nest building in terns; rather, inheritance seems to *influence* broad dimensions of our behavior such as sociability, anxiousness, and intelligence (Lahey & Ciminero, 1980). Psychologists are not yet sure *how much* heredity influences these dimensions of behavior. It's probably never the sole cause but operates in conjunction with the effects of the environment.

Research on nest building has shown that all terns are biologically programmed to build the same type of nest.

Biological Mechanisms of Inheritance: Genetic Codes

People have long wondered how inherited characteristics are passed on. For many years it was thought that they were transmitted through the blood—hence, old sayings like, "He has his father's bad blood." We now know that inheritance operates through genetic material called **genes** found in the nuclei of all human cells. The existence of genes was guessed more than a century ago by Gregor Mendel, the Austrian monk who helped found the science of genetics. It has been only in the last half of this century, however, that genes have actually been seen with the aid of electron microscopes.

Mendel's theory that there are genes for a wide variety of traits, or characteristics, was based on a study of pea plants. If a pea was wrinkled, it was because it had a gene for wrinkled skin. If a pea plant (or by extension a person) was tall, it was because it (or he or she) had a gene for tallness. The genes, Mendel reasoned, were passed on from parents to children. If both parents passed on a gene for a particular trait, clearly that trait would be perpetuated. If the parents passed on conflicting genes, however, only one of the genes would dominate, and the child would show the trait reflecting the dominant gene. Although Mendel's theory attracted little notice in the nineteenth century, it gained a widespread following in the twentieth century and research has largely borne it out.

Individual genes for the hormone insulin.

Genes and Chromosomes

Genes provide their instructions to the organism through a complex substance called **DNA,** short for *deoxyribonucleic acid.* Not until the early 1950s did scientists begin to unravel the structure of DNA and begin to understand the way in which strands of DNA form a code that, in effect, instructs an organism how to develop and function. Research on DNA and its role in the genetic process is still continuing at an intense pace today.

gene (jēn)
The hereditary unit made up of deoxyribonucleic acid.

deoxyribonucleic acid (DNA)
(de-ok″se-ri″bo-nu-kla′ik)
The complex molecule that contains the genetic code.

Figure 2.22 A typical human cell contains 46 chromosomes.

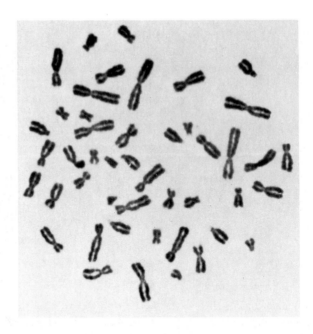

chromosome
(kro′mo-sōm)
The strip in the cell nucleus that contains genes.

gamete (gam′ēt)
A sex cell that contains 23 chromosomes instead of the normal 46.

fertilization
(fer′tĭ-lĭ-za′shun)
The uniting of sperm and ovum that produces a zygote.

zygote (zi′gōt)
The stable cell resulting from fertilization; it has 46 chromosomes—23 from the sperm and 23 from the ovum.

How many genes do you have? We don't know exactly, but a conservative guess is that you have something like 46,000 genes in each cell of your body. They are arrayed on strips called **chromosomes,** which are found within the nucleus of each body cell (see fig. 2.22). All human cells, except the sex cells, have 46 chromosomes, each carrying approximately 1,000 genes.

The 46 chromosomes of a normal cell are arranged in 23 pairs. When cells divide in the normal process of tissue growth and repair, they create exact copies of themselves. However, when sex cells (sperm or ova) are formed, the chromosome pairs split so that the resulting sex cell has only 23 unpaired chromosomes. These sex cells, or **gametes,** are short-lived, but when a sperm unites successfully with an ovum in the act of **fertilization,** a stable cell, capable of life, is formed. The new cell, called a **zygote,** has a full complement of 23 *pairs* of chromosomes, 23 from the father (sperm) and 23 from the mother (ovum). If conditions are right, the zygote will become implanted in the lining of the mother's uterus, and the embryo will develop.

Which chromosomes you receive from a particular parent is a matter of chance. That is why brothers and sisters can have substantially different genes and substantially different inherited traits. Think of each of your parents' 23 pairs of chromosomes for a moment as if they were labeled A and B. Let's say, for the sake of speculation, that the gene for blue eyes is found on chromosome pair 18. You might inherit chromosome 18A from your father, and 18B from your mother. Your sister might inherit 18B from your father and 18A from your mother. In regard to this trait, you and your sister would have no genetic inheritance in common. On the average, brothers and sisters will have about 50 percent of their genes in common. The exception is identical (monozygotic) twins. Since they are formed from a single zygote, they share all their genes.

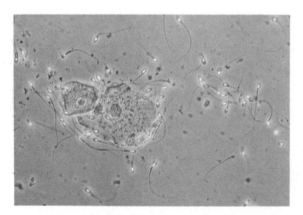

Human sperm, the tiny
cells with the long tails.

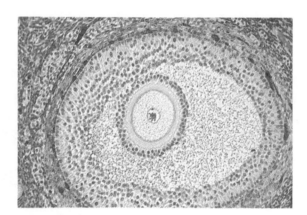

A human egg cell.

Dominant and Recessive Traits

As we have just seen, the 23 chromosomes you get from your father are matched to the 23 you get from your mother. Each pair of chromosomes carries a gene from each of the two parents for the same characteristic. But what if they conflict? What if the gene from father says "blue eyes" and the gene from mother says "brown eyes?" The answer depends on which is the **dominant gene.** In the case of eye color, a gene for brown eyes is typically dominant over one for blue eyes. The gene for blue eyes is said to be recessive. A dominant gene will normally reveal its trait whenever the gene is present. A **recessive gene** will reveal a trait only when the same recessive gene has been inherited from *both* parents and there is no dominant gene giving instructions to the contrary. Brown eyes, dark hair, curly hair, farsightedness, and dimples are common examples of dominant traits; while blue eyes, light hair, normal vision, and freckles are recessive traits.

The description given here of genetic inheritance is a simplified one. You should understand that many physical and behavioral traits appear to be controlled, not simply by one gene, but by the interaction of several genes. A person's height is controlled by four genes, for example. Still, the basic principles described here are the same in all aspects of genetic inheritance.

Sex-linked Traits

The 23rd pair of chromosomes determines what sex a person will have. The other 22 pairs of chromosomes are uniform in appearance. In this pair, however, the two chromosomes may or may not look alike. The so-called **sex chromosomes** are called X or Y chromosomes, after their distinctive appearance (see fig. 2.23). All females have two X chromosomes. All males have one X and one Y. Since females have two Xs, they always pass on an X to the zygote. Therefore, it's the male whose chromosome determines the sex of the child. If he passes on an X, the child will be a girl. If he passes on a Y, the child will be a boy.

Some genetic traits are said to be *sex linked,* because the relevant genes are carried on the 23rd chromosome pair. A good example is color blindness. The gene for color blindness is an uncommon recessive gene, carried only on the X

dominant gene
The gene that produces a trait in the individual when paired with a recessive gene.

recessive gene
The gene that produces a trait in the individual only when the same recessive gene has been inherited from both parents.

sex chromosomes
Chromosome pair number 23, which determines the sex of the individual.

Figure 2.23 Photo of X and Y chromosomes.

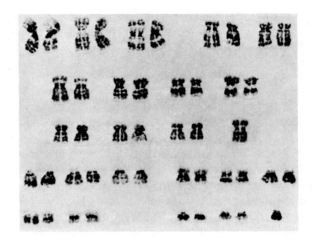

chromosome. Since most females who carry this recessive gene also have a dominant gene for normal color vision on the other X chromosome, females are not likely to be color blind. Since the trait is recessive, they would need to have a gene for color blindness on *both* of their X chromosomes for the trait to show up.

Males, however, only have one X chromosome. If it contains a gene for color blindness, they cannot have a gene on their Y chromosome to cancel it out (since the gene for color blindness can be carried only by X chromosomes). If males inherit the gene, the trait will appear. However, a mother who is not color blind may still pass the trait to her son. The son cannot pass the trait to his own son, because he can only pass on his Y chromosome to a son (if the child is to have a Y chromosome and be a male), but he may pass it on to a daughter, who will probably be a symptomless carrier of the trait.

Chromosome Abnormalities

Unfortunately, the genetic mechanism does not always work properly. When chromosomes are damaged or malformed, abnormalities of body and behavior often result. A common example is **Down's syndrome,** formerly called mongolism, which stems from a malformation in the 21st chromosome pair. Children with Down's syndrome have obvious physical irregularities, including a thickened tongue and a skinfold at the corner of the eye. The most serious aspect of Down's syndrome, as with many chromosomal abnormalities, is mental retardation. (See *Of Special Interest*: "Amniocentesis.")

Down's syndrome
A human abnormality resulting from a chromosomal malformation of chromosome pair number 21.

Research on Inheritance in Humans

When Mendel wanted to study genetic influences on the physical characteristics of pea plants, he was able to breed selectively those plants with a particular characteristic, such as smooth skins, to see what that characteristic would be like in the next generation. That research strategy has been successfully used with animals, showing, for example, that aggressiveness and learning ability in rats is partially determined by heredity (Cooper & Zubek, 1958; Ebert & Hyde, 1976). Selective breeding experiments cannot be carried out with humans for ethical reasons, however, so it's much harder to untangle the strands of nature and nurture in human behavior.

OF SPECIAL INTEREST

Amniocentesis:
Diagnosing Birth Defects during Early Pregnancy

Sharon is pregnant for the second time and worried that there will be something wrong with her baby. Most expectant parents have some moments of worry over the same thing, but Sharon has considerable reason to be concerned: She is 40 years old and knows that the risk of having a mentally retarded child is higher for her than for younger women. Her first child was born with a deformity of the spine that will leave this child at least partially crippled for life. Very shortly, however, Sharon's doctor will tell her that the test results show that the child she is carrying probably does not have the same spinal problem and probably doesn't have any of the forms of deformity or mental retardation caused by chromosome abnormalities that are more common in infants of older mothers.

The test Sharon's physician performed when she was only 14 weeks pregnant is called *amniocentesis* (see fig. 2.24), a process by which a needle is used to extract an ounce of amniotic fluid (the fluid that fills the sac holding the fetus). The amniotic fluid contains some cells from the fetus that are isolated and examined for chromosomal and other abnormalities. The test is not foolproof, but it does provide important information. If serious defects had been detected using this test, Sharon would have had time to consider having an abortion.

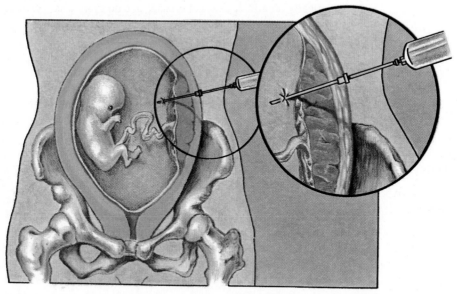

Figure 2.24 The procedure of amniocentesis involves extracting fetal cells contained by the fluid surrounding the fetus. These cells are studied to determine whether the fetus will have certain forms of mental retardation or other birth defects (Batshaw & Perret, 1981).

Instead, researchers interested in hereditary influences have had to use two descriptive methods of research. These are based on unusual situations that are not contrived by the experimenter, but nevertheless allow some conclusions to be reached about the role of the variable being studied. Because these studies do not allow for the same degree of experimental control as do formal experiments, conclusions drawn from them must be viewed cautiously. Still, they are of great importance in research on heredity. The two most common types of naturally occurring experiments in this area involve the study of twins and the study of adopted children.

Studies of Twins

monozygotic twins
(mon"o-zi-got'ik)
Twins formed from a single ovum; they are identical in appearance because they have the same genetic structure.

There are two kinds of twins formed in two very different ways. In the case of *identical,* or **monozygotic twins,** a single fertilized egg begins to grow in the normal way through cell division in the mother's womb. Ordinarily, this cluster of cells will grow over the course of about nine months until it emerges as a baby. Monozygotic twins are formed, however, when that cluster of cells breaks apart into two clusters early in the growth process. If conditions are right, each of these clusters will grow into a baby. These infants will be "identical" not only in appearance but also in genetic structure, since they came from the same fertilized egg.

dizygotic twins
(di"zi-got'ik)
Twins formed from the fertilization of two ova by two sperm.

Dizygotic twins, in contrast, are formed when the female produces two separate eggs that are fertilized by two different sperm cells. These two fertilized eggs each grow into babies that are born at about the same time, but they are not genetically identical. Dizygotic twins are no more alike genetically than siblings who are born at different times. Like other siblings, dizygotic twins share only about 50 percent of their genes.

The natural experiment comes from the fact that both types of twins provide us with pairs of children that grow up in essentially the same home environments. They have the same parents; they are reared during the same time period; and they have the same brothers and sisters. On the other hand, the two kinds of twins differ genetically. If a characteristic of behavior is influenced by heredity, therefore, monozygotic twin pairs would be considerably more similar to one another than would dizygotic twin pairs.

Many experiments have been conducted using twins that reveal the influence of heredity on behavior. For example, studies of twins have suggested that intelligence or IQ is partly determined by heredity. Table 2.1 summarizes the findings of a number of studies indicating the degree of similarity in the intelligence test scores of various types of twins and siblings. Monozygotic twin pairs who share both identical genetic structure and common environments have almost identical IQ scores. Dizygotic twins, on the other hand, are no more similar in their IQ scores than are other pairs of siblings who are not twins.

Adoption Studies

Studies of adopted children have also shown that inheritance plays a role in influencing behavior. Take the case of IQ again. It's well known that the IQs of children are pretty similar to those of their parents. But why is this so? Is it because bright parents provide a stimulating intellectual environment that makes

Identical, or monozygotic, twins have the same genetic structure because they come from the same fertilized egg.

Fraternal, or dizygotic, twins share an average of 50 percent of their genes.

Table 2.1 The degree of similarity between monozygotic and dizygotic twins on measures of intelligence

Monozygotic twins	.85
Dizygotic twins (same sex pairs only)	.54
Siblings	.47
Unrelated children	.00

Note: The numbers cited here are coefficients of correlation (see the appendix). They are a measure of the degree of similarity between pairs of measures. A correlation coefficient of .00 indicates no similarity in scores, while coefficients nearer 1.00 (perfect similarity) indicate greater similarity.

their children bright like they are, while unintelligent parents do just the opposite? Or is it because the children inherit their intellectual potential from their parents? As it turns out, both heredity and environment influence IQ, but studies of adopted children have helped show us that the role played by heredity is a fairly strong one. These studies have shown that the IQs of adopted children are more similar to those of their biological parents than the adoptive parents by whom they were raised since infancy. Since they spent no time living with their biological parents, the only explanation for the similarity in IQs is the link of inheritance. (See *Research Report:* "Is Alcoholism Inherited?" for a closer look at adoption studies.)

R E S E A R C H   R E P O R T

Is Alcoholism Inherited?

As a serious social problem affecting roughly 10 million Americans, alcoholism obviously cries out for study. One issue to which researchers have devoted attention is the question of whether alcoholism is in any sense inherited. If it is, then the problem might have solutions that are different, at least in part, from the solutions we would seek if it were known that alcoholism is caused solely by one's personal experiences.

Recent data suggest that some degree of predisposition to alcoholism may be inherited by some individuals. Two key studies in this area were done in Denmark because of the availability of extensive records on citizens there. Psychologist Donald Goodwin and his colleagues (Goodwin, Schulsinger, Hermansen, Guze, & Winokur, 1973) compared a group of 55 males who were adopted from alcoholic biological parents to a matched group of 78 individuals who were also adopted, but whose biological parents were not alcoholics. All of the subjects were evaluated by psychiatrists who had no information about their biological parents. Result: 18 percent of those with alcoholic parents were alcoholic themselves, in contrast to only 5 percent of the control group. In addition to being almost four times as likely to become alcoholics, the individuals adopted from alcoholic parents were also more likely to have experienced divorce or psychiatric hospitalization.

A second study by Goodwin's research team (Goodwin, Schulsinger, Moller, Hermansen, Winokur, & Guze, 1974) added additional information. This time, the research team compared the rate of alcoholism in individuals who were adopted from alcoholic biological parents to their own siblings who had not been adopted but had been reared by the alcoholic parents. Result: The rate of alcoholism did not differ significantly between the two groups. This finding strongly supports the idea of a biological predisposition toward alcoholism. But to put these data into proper perspective, we must remember that more than 80 percent of the offspring of alcoholic parents did not exhibit alcoholism, even if they had been reared by the alcoholic parents themselves. It should also be noted that the data on a possible genetic predisposition to alcoholism in women are much less convincing.

Alcoholism, like most other behavior disorders and social problems, is a highly complex phenomenon. Clearly, learning and experience play a role in its origins, but the results of these studies suggest that heredity also plays at least some role.

The Implications of Inheritance

Many among both the public and scientific sectors are skeptical about the notion that human behavior is even partially influenced by heredity. Such a belief seems to run counter to our philosophical belief that any person can be what he or she wants to be. If you are *born* more or less intelligent, more or less aggressive, more or less prone to be depressed than your neighbor, then in some sense you are not "created equal." This offends our sense of fairness and makes us question any claim that genetic factors are significant influences on behavior.

We have a perfect right to be skeptical. Until recently, evidence for genetic influences on behavior was not strong enough to be convincing. And we as a society have not had much time to think through the implications of the more convincing new findings. (See *Of Special Interest*: "Superkids.")

Let's take the example of schizophrenia. Schizophrenia is a psychological disorder that appears to be partially genetic in origin. Does it mean that the child of a schizophrenic parent will necessarily be schizophrenic, too? No, it definitely does not. Only 10 percent of children of schizophrenic parents become schizophrenic at any time during their lives. Fully 90 percent of children with schizophrenic parents do not develop the disorder. The role of inheritance in schizophrenia is real, but limited.

Research on schizophrenia among twins leads to similar conclusions. If your fraternal (dizygotic) twin is schizophrenic, there is a 6 percent chance of your also being or becoming schizophrenic. If your identical (monozygotic) twin is schizophrenic, the chance rises to 24 percent (Lahey & Ciminero, 1980). Note, however, that 76 percent of identical twins who have a schizophrenic twin never develop the disorder, even though both have precisely the same genetic inheritance. Clearly, experience is very potent. Heredity, while significant, is certainly not the sole cause of schizophrenia.

Schizophrenia, in the example used here, is considered a negative trait. In general, there is probably a wider and deeper body of research on negative traits than on positive ones, perhaps because social scientists react to problems by studying them. In any case, if your chances of inheriting a negative behavioral trait are relatively small, what about your chances of inheriting a positive trait? Unfortunately, they are no better. If your mother is a brilliant physicist or concert pianist, your chances of being the same are only slightly better than anyone else in the population. The workings of genetics tend to bring about a *regression to the mean*. In other words, the offspring of exceptional parents are usually a little closer to average than their parents. This notion is consistent with commonsense observation. If your father is Kareem Abdul-Jabbar, you are likely to be taller than average, but the odds do not favor your being over 7'. If your father is Albert Einstein, it's likely you will be more intelligent than average, but the odds are you would not discover a new theory of relativity. Heredity doesn't work strongly against you, but it doesn't work strongly for you either. A lot is left up to you.

OF SPECIAL INTEREST

Superkids:
A Sperm Bank for Nobel Prize Winners?

If you were married to a man who was sterile—that is, he could not produce sperm cells—would you want to become pregnant through artificial insemination (medically placing sperm cells from another man in the uterus of the woman so that conception can take place)? If so, who would you want to be the father? "Sperm banks" that store sperm from anonymous donors have long been available for use in artificial insemination, but a wealthy California businessman has supported the development of an unusual type of sperm bank, one that only stores the sperm of Nobel Prize winners. Since research from twin and adoption studies suggest that inheritance plays a significant role in determining intelligence, you might want the donor of the sperm to be intelligent. So why not a highly intelligent and creative scholar? In fact, a California woman gave birth to the sperm bank's first Nobel baby in April 1982.

The donor of the sperm was identified only as a Nobel Prize-winning mathematics professor in his 30s. Most of the potential prize-winning sperm donors—several have publicly said that they are opposed to the idea—are in their 60s and 70s, however. Since the chances of having a mentally retarded child due to chromosome abnormalities increase when the father is older than age 55, however, it's possible that use of the Nobel sperm bank would produce a child of very low, rather than very high, intelligence.

REVIEW

Specific patterns of behavior are not inherited by humans, but heredity does influence broad dimensions of behavior. The hereditary blueprints that exert this influence are coded in thousands of genes arranged on pairs of chromosome strips in the nuclei of cells. One member of each chromosome pair comes from each parent, giving each individual two sets of genes. Sometimes these genes are in conflict, as when a person inherits a gene for blue eyes from her mother and brown eyes from her father. When this happens, some genes are dominant because they suppress the influence of the other conflicting gene for the same trait; other genes are recessive and will only have an effect when the same recessive gene is inherited from both parents.

The effects of heredity on human behavior have been studied in experiments using twins and adopted children. For example, the fact that monozygotic (identical) twins have exactly the same genes, while dizygotic twins share only about 50 percent of their genes can be used to study the role of heredity. Even though both kinds of twins grow up in comparably similar environments, monozygotic twins are more similar to each other on several dimensions of behavior, suggesting that genetics plays some role in behavior. In addition, the role of inheritance can also be seen in the fact that adopted children resemble their biological parents in some ways more than they resemble adoptive parents who reared them. While the influence of heredity on behavior is a significant one, many other factors influence behavior as well. We are far from being as rigidly programmed by our inheritance as some species of animals are.

S U M M A R Y

Chapter 2 describes people as psychological beings who live in biological machines; it looks at the role played by the *nervous system* and the human *brain*, the *endocrine system,* and *genetic mechanisms* in our behavior and mental processes.

  I. The human nervous system is a complex network of neural cells that carry messages and regulate bodily functions and personal behavior.

    A. The individual cells of the nervous system *(neurons)* transmit electrical signals along the length of the neuron.

    B. Chemical substances transmit neural messages across the gap (*synapse*) between the axon of one neuron and the dendrite of the next.

    C. The *central nervous system* is composed of the brain and spinal cord. The *peripheral nervous system* carries messages to and from the rest of the body. It is composed of the *somatic* and *autonomic* nervous systems:

        1. The somatic nervous system carries messages from the sense organs, skeletal muscles, and joints to the central nervous system; and carries messages from the central nervous system to the skeletal muscles.

        2. The autonomic nervous system regulates the visceral organs and other body functions, motivation, and emotional activity.

  II. The *brain* has three basic parts: the hindbrain, the midbrain, and the forebrain.

    A. The *hindbrain* consists of the *medulla,* the *pons,* and the *cerebellum.*

        1. The medulla controls breathing and a variety of reflexes.

        2. The pons is concerned with balance, hearing, and several parasympathetic functions.

        3. The cerebellum is chiefly responsible for maintaining muscle tone and coordination of muscular movements.

    B. The *midbrain* is a center for reflexes related to vision and hearing.

    C. Most cognitive, motivational, and emotional activity is controlled by the *forebrain,* which includes the thalamus, hypothalamus, and cerebral cortex.

        1. The *thalamus* is a switching station for routing sensory information to appropriate areas of the brain.

        2. The *hypothalamus* is involved with our motives and emotions.

        3. The largest part of the brain is the *cerebral cortex,* made up of two *cerebral hemispheres* connected by the *corpus callosum.* The cortex controls conscious experience, intellectual activities, the senses, and voluntary actions.

    D. Each part of the brain interacts with the entire nervous system, and the parts work together in intellectual, physical, and emotional functions.

III. While the nervous system forms the primary biological basis for behavior and mental processes, the *endocrine system* of *hormone-secreting glands* influences emotional arousal, metabolism, sexual functioning, and other bodily processes.

    A. *Adrenal glands* secrete *epinephrine* and *norepinephrine*, which are involved in emotional arousal, increase heart rate and metabolism, and stimulate sexual arousal.

    B. *Islets of Langerhans* secrete *glucagon* and *insulin,* which control blood sugar and energy levels.

    C. *Gonads* produce sex cells (*ova* and *sperm*) for human reproduction, and *estrogen* and *testosterone* hormones important to sexual functioning and the development of secondary sex characteristics.

    D. The *thyroid gland* secretes *thyroxin,* which controls the rate of metabolism.

    E. *Parathyroid glands* secrete *parathormone,* which controls the level of nervous activity.

    F. The *pituitary gland* secretes various hormones that control the activities of other endocrine glands and have important effects on general body processes.

IV. Human characteristics and behaviors are influenced by genetic inheritance.

    A. Inherited characteristics are passed on through *genes* (containing *DNA* found in chromosome strips).

    B. Most normal human cells contain 46 chromosomes (23 pairs).

    C. The sex cells contain only 23 chromosomes each and are capable of combining into a new *zygote* with a unique set of chromosomes.

    D. Research has shown that inheritance plays a significant role in influencing behavior, but environmental and other personal factors leave much to the individual.

Suggested Readings

1. For more information on the brain written for educated nonexperts:
   Scientific American. (1979), *241.* [Special issue on the brain].

2. Biofeedback is described further in:
   Blanchard, E. B., & Epstein, L. H. (1978). *A biofeedback primer.* Reading, MA.: Addison-Wesley.

3. Research on patients with "split brains" is described in readable detail in:
   Gazzaniga, M. S. (1970). *The bisected brain.* New York: Appleton-Century-Crofts.

4. A fascinating look at the possible role played by neural factors in mental disorders is provided by:

   Andreasen, N. C. (1983). *The broken brain: The biological revolution in psychiatry.* New York: Harper & Row.

5. For more on the genetic basis of behavior:

   Dixon, L. K., & Johnson, R. C. (1980). *The roots of individuality: A survey of human behavior genetics.* Monterey, CA: Brooks/Cole.

6. For a more in-depth look at the biological foundations of behavior:

   Groves, P. & Schlesinger, K. (1982). *Biological psychology* (2nd ed.). Dubuque, IA: Wm. C. Brown Publishers.

Awareness

THREE

Sensation and Perception

OUTLINE

KEY TERMS

Last night I "saw" the University of North Carolina play Notre Dame in basketball by listening to the radio: The play-by-play announcer sat in Chapel Hill watching the action of the game; he translated what he saw into a kind of information (words) that could be transmitted over the radio; and I used the information to form a mental picture of the game. I did not see with my eyes, yet I was able to watch the game in my head. I realized this morning that my way of seeing the game was not really that different from when I see games in person. We never really "see" with our eyes alone; we use our eyes to gather information and translate it into a form that can be transmitted to the brain. It's in the brain that visual perception is created out of the incoming sensory information, and influenced according to our moods and memories.

This point can be made more vividly by considering the pictorial images of people who have been totally blind since birth. Psychologist John Kennedy of the University of Toronto asked blind individuals to draw pictures to learn if they had formed an accurate perception of the shapes of things from their sense of touch. He found that they drew surprisingly good pictures of people, cups, tables, and other common objects. Perhaps most strikingly, Kennedy found that when his blind subjects drew a hand with crossed fingers, their drawings indicated they knew that the closest finger would partially block the other finger from view.

The blind subjects created these visual perceptions *in much the same way that sighted people do,* only they created them from information transmitted from their fingertips rather than their eyes. Interestingly, when adults who have been blind since birth obtain eyesight through surgery, they often cannot make sense out of what their eyes are picking up at first. They have to learn how to use the new confusing blur of information from their eyes to create visual images the way sighted persons do. Often the formerly blind do this by touching the objects they are looking at to help themselves "see" the objects. It's only after practice that they can recognize objects solely on the basis of what their eyes tell them. Some are never able to learn to "see" in spite of having normally functioning eyes.

It's easy for us to naively assume that we simply "see" what is "there." The processes of seeing or smelling or touching seem so simple and straightforward. Yet, perception is based on a complex chain of receiving, transmitting, and interpreting. Each step actively *changes* the information in significant ways. Since we know "reality" only through perception, we must understand the biological machinery of our senses and the psychological uses to which sensory information is put.

Human life would be very different without our ability to sense and perceive. Take friendships, for example. How could we have friends if we could not distinguish one person from another by being sensitive to their differences? How could we communicate with our friends if we could not hear their words properly or read their notes accurately or notice the expressions on their faces? How could we let them know that we cared if they could not feel the difference between a pat on the back and a push? And that is only one example of the importance of sensation and perception to our lives. Without these processes, life would be so different that we might not call it life at all. Without the ability to sense and perceive, we could not move (we would have no sense of balance or ability to avoid dangerous objects) or even safely eat (edible and spoiled food would smell and taste the same). No friends, no racquetball, and no food. Would that be living?

A cold glass of water depicted by a thirteen-year-old blind girl, including an ice cube at the bottom and "mist" on the sides of the glass.

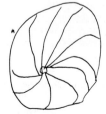

A wheel drawn by a totally blind woman. The curved spokes suggest movement, but she said the spokes are not really curved in a moving wheel.

P R E V I E W

We can see, hear, feel, and in other ways *sense* the outside world because our bodies possess sense organs and nervous systems. When a piano is played, specialized sensory receptor cells in your ears translate the sound waves from the piano into neural messages; neurons transmit the messages to your brain where the information is interpreted, and you hear a Beethoven melody.

We have four basic kinds of senses: Body senses, chemical senses, vision, and hearing. Body senses provide information from the skin about temperature, touch, and pain; information from the inner ear, muscles, and joints tells us about the position and movement of our bodies. Chemical senses use receptor cells in the tongue and nose to provide smell and taste information about chemicals in the air and in what we eat and drink. The eye collects and transmits light energy to the brain for the sense of vision. And the sense of hearing translates vibrations into sound through the sense organ of the ear.

Individual sensations have little meaning until they are organized and interpreted in the process of *perception*. Perception is an active process that often goes beyond the immediate sensory information available, as when we perceive a series of rapidly changing still photographs to be moving in a motion picture. Many perceptual patterns appear to be inborn and are common to all individuals, but our perceptions of reality are sometimes colored by individual expectations, cultural learning experiences, or needs. All people experience the world with the same sensory machinery, but individual differences in perception sometimes mean that we have different views of the world.

sense organs
Organs that receive stimuli.

sensory receptor cells
Cells in sense organs that translate messages into neural impulses that are sent to the brain.

sensation (sen-sa´-shun)
The process of receiving, translating, and transmitting messages from the outside world to the brain.

perception
(per-sep´-shun)
The process of organizing and interpreting information received from the outside world.

stimulus (stim´u-lus)
Any aspect of the outside world that directly influences our behavior or conscious experience.

Sensation: Receiving Messages about the World

We take no aspect of human existence more for granted than our ability to "experience" life. We savor the sights, sounds, smells, and other sensations provided by the world around us, but rarely do we stop to think about sensory processes. We are aware of an outside world, and the internal world of our own bodies, only because we have a number of **sense organs** able to receive messages. These organs enable us to see, hear, taste, smell, touch, balance, and experience such feelings as body stiffness, soreness, fullness, warmth, pleasure, pain, and movement. Sense organs operate through **sensory receptor cells** that *receive* outside forms of energy (light, vibrations, heat) and *translate* them into *neural impulses* that can be *transmitted* to the brain for interpretation. Sense organs do the job of the basketball announcer who translates what he sees into words that can be transmitted on the radio. The process of receiving information from the outside world, translating it, and transmitting it to the brain is called **sensation.** The process of interpreting that information and forming ideas about the world is called **perception.**

Stimuli: What Messages Can Be Received?

A key concept that you will run into frequently throughout this text is **stimulus,** which refers to any aspect of the outside world that directly influences our behavior or conscious experience. The name *stimulus* comes from the action of *stimulating* sensory receptor cells.

Sensory receptor cells translate stimuli, including blows to the skin, into neural impulses that are sent to the brain.

Eating too much food produces an uncomfortable sensation from the stomach.

Virtually anything that can excite receptor cells can be a stimulus. When you take a seat at a dinner party, the chair is a stimulus through your senses of sight and touch. When you begin to eat, the food becomes a stimulus through your sense of taste, smell, and sight. If the room is too hot, the temperature acts as a stimulus through the sensory receptors in your skin. The compliments you lavish on your host and hostess are also stimuli that increase your chances of being asked over for dinner again. Whenever a person is aware of, or in some other way responds to, a part of the outside world, he or she receives a stimulus.

Selective attention helps us to screen out interfering stimuli.

When I say that any part of the outside world can be a stimulus, I am using the term *outside* broadly. Even parts of the internal world of the body can be stimuli. If you eat too much at the dinner party, the bloated stretching of your stomach is a very noticeable stimulus.

Selective Attention: The First Step

The first step in receiving and interpreting a sensory message is to pay attention to it. We are being bombarded constantly with far more potential stimuli from the external and internal world than we can possibly respond to at one time. To deal with this overload of information, we must process only a small portion of it and filter out the rest. The process of allowing only certain potential stimuli to be responded to is called **selective attention.** This is the process that makes it possible for you to pay attention to what that gorgeous person who sits next to you in class is saying in spite of the fact that the professor up front is lecturing loudly. It's also the reason you are able to hear your favorite song on the radio while your eyes stare blindly at the textbook sitting in your lap.

What makes us pay attention to one stimulus and not another? The list of reasons is long, but some key factors that influence our attention are presented here.

1. *Meaning.* Things that have meaning for us—such as your own name mentioned on the radio, restaurant signs when you are hungry, a song that reminds you of a lost love, attractive people of the preferred sex, noises made by your approaching supervisor when you are goofing off—will usually be attended to.

2. *Intensity.* The most intense of the incoming sensory messages will usually grab our attention. A tiny splinter in the bottom of your foot might go unnoticed while you are jogging, but a large dog biting your ankle definitely would be noticed.

selective attention
The mental process of selecting only certain stimuli to be responded to.

3. *Novelty and change.* When spring first comes, the sight of shorts is novel because you have not seen people wearing them in a while. When people wearing shorts go walking by, they will attract your attention. Also, changes in familiar things attract your attention. A friend's new haircut or a new sign in the student parking lot is likely to be noticed.

4. *Others.* Many other factors such as color, complexity, and repetition also influence selective attention.

Transduction: Translating Messages for the Brain

Energy from stimuli cannot go directly to the brain. Light, sound, and other kinds of energy from the outside world are not able to travel through the nerves, and the brain cannot "understand" what they mean. To be useful to the brain, sensory messages must be translated into neural impulses that the neurons carry and the brain understands. The translation of one form of energy into another is called **transduction.** Sense organs transduce sensory energy into neural energy. This is accomplished in the sense organ by the sensory receptor cells, which are specialized neurons that are excited by specific kinds of sensory energy and give off neural impulses from their axons. Some sensory receptor cells are sensitive to sound, some to light, some to chemicals, and so on. But in every case, the receptor cells give off coded neural impulses that carry the transduced sensory message to one of the sensory areas of the brain. The sense organs themselves (such as the ear, eye, and nose) are constructed in special ways that expose the receptor cells to sensory energy and help them translate it into coded neural impulses. At the center of every sense organ are the receptor cells that do the transducing.

transduction
(trans-duk'shun)
The translation of energy from one form to another.

Note that we can only be aware of a stimulus if the receptor cells can transduce it. We cannot see radio waves or hear some high-frequency tones, for example. And we find some chemicals to be "tasteless" and "odorless" because we do not have receptors that can transduce these kinds of stimuli. But a radio wave is just as real as the light reflected to our eyes from an apple, even though we cannot transduce the radio wave. We know of the existence of radio waves only because radios mechanically transduce them into sound waves that are in turn transduced by our ears into neural messages to the brain. Probably there are forms of energy in the world that we are not aware of at all because we do not have receptor cells that can transduce them. There may not even be mechanical devices that can transduce them into a form of energy that we can sense. If our planet were visited by aliens who had sensory receptors that were sensitive *only* to different forms of energy from our own, they would experience an entirely different world from what we do.

Sensory Limits: How Strong Must Messages Be?

Even when we have receptor cells that can transduce a kind of sensory message, not every message will be strong enough to be detected. The term *threshold* refers to the lower limits of sensory experience. There are two primary kinds of thresholds: (1) the smallest *magnitude* of a stimulus that can be detected and (2) the smallest *difference* between two stimuli that can be detected.

The **absolute threshold** is the smallest magnitude of a stimulus that can be detected. Look at the absolute thresholds for a number of common stimuli shown in table 3.1 to gain a fuller appreciation of your remarkably sensitive receptor

absolute threshold
The smallest magnitude of a stimulus that can be detected half the time.

Table 3.1 The sensitivity of our senses

The human senses are remarkably sensitive systems. Psychologist Eugene Galanter (1962) has offered these illustrative estimates of the weakest stimuli that we are capable of sensing.

Sense	Weakest Detectable Stimulus
Light	A candle flame seen at 30 miles on a clear dark night
Sound	The tick of a watch under quiet conditions at 20 feet
Taste	One teaspoon of sugar in 2 gallons of water
Smell	One drop of perfume diffused into the entire volume of a 3-room apartment
Touch	The wing of a bee falling on your cheek from a height of 1 centimeter

From Brown, R., E. Galanter, E. H. Hess, and Mandler (eds.), New Directions in Psychology. © *1962 Holt, Rinehart and Winston, Inc., New York. Reprinted by permission of the author.*

difference threshold
The smallest difference between two stimuli that can be detected half the time.

cells. Measuring such thresholds is no simple matter. People differ considerably in their sensitivity to weak stimuli, and the sensitivity of each of us differs from time to time. For this reason, absolute thresholds are defined as the magnitude of a stimulus that subjects can detect half the time. The smallest difference between two stimuli that can be detected *half the time* is called the **difference threshold.** For example, the smallest change in intensity of your stereo that you can distinguish as "louder" 50 percent of the time would be your difference threshold for that stimulus. Detailed knowledge of absolute and difference thresholds has, in fact, been used by the electronics industry to design better stereo systems.

Sensory Adaptation

sensory adaptation
Weakened magnitude of a sensation resulting from prolonged presentation of the stimulus.

I just mentioned that an individual's sensitivity to a given stimulus differs from time to time. There are many reasons why this happens, such as fatigue or inattention, but **sensory adaptation** is one of the major causes. When a stimulus is continuously present, or repeated at short intervals, the sensation that the same amount of sensory energy causes becomes gradually weaker, probably because the receptor cells become fatigued. When I was a teenager, I frequently went skin diving in an extremely cold spring in central Florida. At first the water was almost unbearably cold; when I jumped in from the dock, the intensity of the cold grabbed my attention so totally that for a moment I felt like only a cold skin of a person rather than a whole person. But after a few minutes the water felt comfortably cool. The water did not change in temperature, of course, but the sensation changed considerably because the temperature receptors in the skin adapted to the temperature of the water. This is sensory adaptation. It happens to some extent in all the senses; loud sounds and offensive odors, fortunately, also seem less intense as time goes by.

Psychophysics

psychophysics
(si″ko-fiz′iks)
A specialty area of psychology that studies sensory limits, sensory adaptation, and related topics.

The specialty area within the field of psychology that studies sensory limits, sensory adaptation, and related topics is called **psychophysics.** The subject matter of this field is the relationship between the *physical* properties of stimuli and the *psychological* sensations they produce. The name *psychophysics* derives from the terms *psychology* and *physics.*

Psychophysics is an important field because frequently there is *not* a direct or simple relationship between stimuli and sensations. Since our knowledge of

Receptors in the skin adapt to changes in temperature and lessen the sensation of coldness, but most of us would never claim to enjoy a cup of hot tea while sitting in ice water.

the outside world is limited to what our sensations tell us, we need to understand under what conditions our sensations do not directly reflect the physical nature of the stimulus. Sensory adaptation is a process that alters the relationship between stimuli and sensations, but there are numerous other circumstances that provide examples of this lack of a one-to-one relationship. The concept of the difference threshold provides another good example.

A fact about difference thresholds that has captured the attention of psychophysicists since the nineteenth century is that the size of the difference threshold increases as the strength of the stimulus increases. When a stimulus is strong, change in it must be bigger to be noticed than when the stimulus is weak. You can demonstrate this phenomenon for yourself by conducting a simple experiment using two small flashlights. Go into a small room at night that has light-colored walls, close the door, and turn off the lights. Wait about 10 minutes for your eyes to adjust and then direct the beam of a small flashlight on the rear wall behind you. You can easily see the change in brightness in the room because the difference threshold for changes in brightness is very slight when there is almost no light prior to the change.

Now turn on a second flashlight behind you, pointing it to the same rear wall. With most flashlights in most rooms, you can just barely notice a change in brightness, even though the second flashlight added the same amount of light as the first flashlight did. This is because the difference threshold is greater now that the brightness in the room is greater. You could see this further by turning off both flashlights and turning on the overhead lights in the room. If you wait a little while for your eyes to adjust to the light and then turn on a flashlight, you probably will not see any change at all because at that level of intensity the difference threshold is so much greater than the amount of light the flashlight adds to the room.

The fact that we are able to detect small changes in the intensity of weak stimuli, and only large changes in the intensity of strong stimuli, was first formally noted by German psychophysicist Ernst Weber. Today this phenomenon

Weber's law
A law stating that the amount of change in a stimulus needed to detect a difference is always in direct proportion to the intensity of the original stimulus.

is known as **Weber's law.** Interestingly, the amount of the change needed to be detected half the time (the difference threshold) is almost always in direct proportion to the intensity of the original stimulus. Thus, if a waiter holding a tray on which four glasses had been placed is just able to detect the added weight of one glass, he would only feel the added weight from *two* more glasses if the tray were already holding eight glasses. The amount of detectable added weight would always be in the same proportion: In this case ¼.

The relevance of this bit of information? Weber's law tells us that what we see is not always the same thing that enters the eye. The same magnitude of physical change in intensity can be obvious one time, yet go unseen under different circumstances. This fact has important practical implications. Suppose, for example, that you are chosen to help design the instruments for the next space shuttle built by NASA. The pilot wants an easier way to monitor the altitude of the shuttle, so you put in a light that increases in intensity as the shuttle nears the earth—the lower the altitude the more intense the light. That way, you assume, the pilot can easily monitor changes in altitude by seeing changes in brightness. Right?

According to Weber's Law, this would be a dangerous way to monitor altitude. At high altitudes, the intensity of the light would be low, so small changes could be easily detected; but at low altitudes, the intensity would be so great that large changes in altitude—even fatal ones—might not be noticed. That is why the people who design instruments for airplanes, cars, and the like need to know about psychophysics.

R E V I E W

The world is known to us only indirectly because our brains are not in direct contact with the outside world. But sensory receptor cells have the ability to transduce physical energy into coded neural messages that are sent to the brain (sensation) where they are interpreted (perception). Not all forms of physical energy can become part of our perception of the world: We must have sensory receptor cells that can transduce that form of energy; the stimulation must be strong enough to exceed the sensory threshold; and the stimulus must be attended to because of its importance, intensity, or for some other reason. Our perception of external reality is complicated by the fact that there is not a simple and direct relationship between the properties of physical stimuli and our conscious sensations. For example, a small change in the intensity of a stereo is noticeable when the stereo is being played softly, but the same size change would go unnoticed if the stereo were at high volume. The complicated relationship between physical stimuli and conscious sensations is the subject matter of psychophysics.

Body Senses: Messages from Myself

The body senses tell us how the body is oriented, where it moves, the things it touches, and so on. Information about orientation and movement comes from a sense organ located in the inner ear and from individual receptors spread throughout the body. Information about touch and temperature is provided by a variety of receptors located below the surface of the skin. Information about pain comes from receptors in the skin and inside the body. Although we usually are not aware that we are using this information, the body senses play an important role in keeping us upright, moving straight ahead, and out of hot water.

The vestibular organ and kinesthetic receptors help orient us even in unusual situations.

Orientation and Movement

Messages about the orientation, balance, and movement of the body come to us from two kinds of sense organs. A complicated set of sensory structures called the **vestibular organ** is located in the inner section of the ear where it provides the somatic sensory area of the cerebral cortex with information about movement. Individual sensory receptors called **kinesthetic receptors** located in the muscles, joints, and skin provide additional messages about movement, posture, and orientation.

Vestibular Organ

The vestibular organ is composed of two smaller sensory structures: the *semicircular canals* and the linked *saccule* and *utricle* structure (see fig. 3.1). The **saccule** and **utricle** are fluid-filled sacs in the inner ear that contain sensory receptors that keep the brain informed about the body's orientation. The part of the vestibular organ that provides the most sensitive messages to the brain about orientation is the **semicircular canals.** This organ constitutes a marvelous bit of natural engineering perfectly suited to its purpose. The semicircular canals are composed of three nearly circular tubes (canals) that lie at right angles to one another, providing information on orientation of the body in three planes—left and right, up and down, and front to back. Think of the semicircular canals as the corner of a room, with one in the plane of the floor and the other two in the planes of the two walls. At the base of each canal is an enlargement that holds the sensory receptors. A tuft of these hairlike cells are formed together in a gelatinlike structure called the **cupula** that sticks out into the enlargement of the canal (see fig. 3.2). As the head is tilted, the fluid flows through the canal in the opposite direction. This bends the cupula and causes its receptors to fire, sending a message of "tilt" to the brain. While the vestibular organ provides the brain with vital information about orientation and movement, it can turn from a friend to an enemy at times. When overloaded and confused by rocking boats, bumping airplanes, or twisting circus rides, it can produce dizziness and nausea.

vestibular organ
(ves-tib′u-lar)
The sensory structures in the inner ear that provide the brain with information about movement.

kinesthetic receptors
(kin″es-thet′ik)
Receptors in the muscles, joints, and skin that provide information about movement, posture, and orientation.

saccule and utricle
(sak′ul *and* u′tre-k′l)
Fluid-filled sacs of the vestibular organ that inform the brain about the body's orientation.

semicircular canals
(sem″e-ser′ku-lar)
Three nearly circular tubes in the vestibular organ that inform the brain about tilts of the head and body.

cupula (ku′-pu-lah)
A gelatinlike structure containing a tuft of hairlike sensory receptor cells in the semicircular canals.

Figure 3.1 Illustration of the major structures of the vestibular organ.

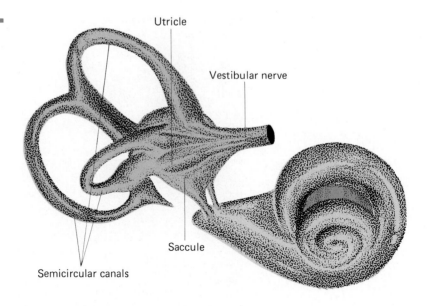

Utricle

Vestibular nerve

Saccule

Semicircular canals

Figure 3.2 Diagram of the internal structure of the semicircular canals.

Semicircular canal

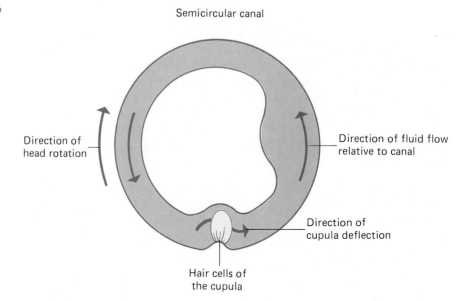

Direction of head rotation

Direction of fluid flow relative to canal

Direction of cupula deflection

Hair cells of the cupula

Kinesthetic Sense

Throughout the skin, muscles, joints, and tendons are kinesthetic receptors that signal when they are moved. As the body walks, bends, writes, and so on, these receptors provide information about the location and movement of each part. Close your eyes, take off your shoes, and wiggle your toes. You can tell they are wiggling because of your kinesthetic sense. Unlike the vestibular organ, the kinesthetic receptors are individual receptors that are not clumped together into sense organs. But as reflected in the skilled movements of a musician, painter, or discus thrower, they are remarkably sensitive to fine and complicated patterns of movement.

Basket cell around hair   Hair   Specialized end bulbs   Tactile discs   Free nerve endings

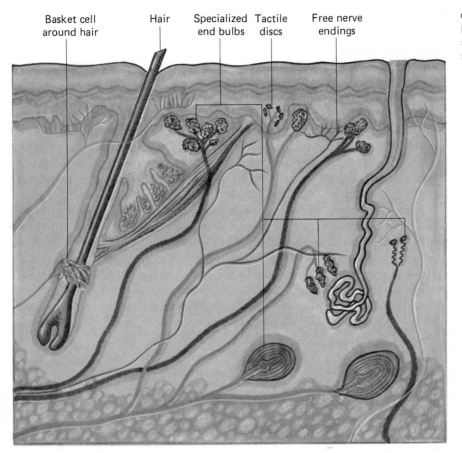

Figure 3.3 Diagram of the skin showing the major skin receptor cells.

Skin Senses

We usually do not think of the skin as a sense organ, yet it's capable of picking up a number of different kinds of sensory information. The skin can detect *pressure, temperature,* and *pain.* Feeling a kiss on the cheek, cold in the winter, hurt by a rock, and all other sensations involving the skin are made up of combinations of these three skin sensations.

Although the skin can detect only three kinds of sensory information, there are at least four different general types of receptors in the skin: the **free nerve endings,** the **basket cells** wound around the base of hairs, the **tactile discs,** and the **specialized end bulbs.** These are shown in figure 3.3. In spite of much research, it's not yet completely clear which receptors operate in which of the skin senses.

Pressure

The skin is amazingly sensitive to pressure, but sensitivity differs considerably from one region of the skin to another depending on how many skin receptors are present. In the most sensitive regions—the fingertips, the lips, and the genitals—a pressure that pushes the skin in less than 0.001 mm can be felt, but sensitivity in other areas is considerably less (Schiffman, 1976). Perhaps the most striking example of the sensitivity of the skin is its ability to "read." Many blind

free nerve endings
Sensory receptor cells in the skin that apparently detect pressure, temperature, and pain.

basket cells
Sensory receptor cells at the bases of hairs that apparently detect pressure, temperature, and pain.

tactile discs (tak'til)
Sensory receptor cells in the skin whose function is not clearly established.

specialized end bulbs
Sensory receptor cells in the skin whose function is not clearly established.

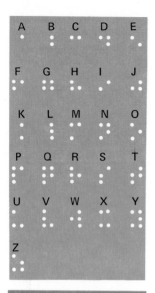

Figure 3.4 Raised dots are used in the Braille alphabet and are "read" with the fingertips.

people can read books using the Braille alphabet, patterns of small raised dots that stand for the letters of the alphabet. An experienced Braille user can read up to fifty words per minute using the sensitive skin on the tips of the fingers (see fig. 3.4).

Temperature

When the air outside is hot or cold, how do you sense this fact? It seems to most of us that the entire surface of the skin is able to detect temperature, but we actually sense skin temperature only through sensory receptors that are located in rather widely spaced "spots" on the skin. One set of spots detects warmth and one detects coldness. The information sent to the brain by these spots creates the feeling of temperature across the entire skin surface.

When the skin is warmed (for example, by air, sunlight, or water), the receptors in the warm spots send messages about warmness to the brain; when the skin is cooled, the cold spots send messages about coldness. The sensation of intense heat, however, is created by *both* the warm and cold spots. High temperatures stimulate the receptors in both sets of spots to send messages simultaneously to the brain that are interpreted as hotness. At dangerously high or low temperatures, pain receptors also send messages that lead to a sense of burning or freezing. Thus, the sensing of skin temperatures is far more complicated than it first appears.

The fact that the sensation of hotness involves both the cold and warmth receptors can be easily demonstrated in a simple experiment. If you warm a number of BBs under a light bulb and cool another set in a refrigerator and then quickly mix them together and pick them up in your hand, they would feel HOT! Both the warmth and cold receptors would be fired by the warm and cold BBs and the brain would interpret the temperature as being very hot.

Pain

How do you know you have been hurt? Psychologists have only recently learned enough to begin answering this question. We know that free nerve endings in the skin and body are involved, but whether other kinds of skin receptors can also detect pain or how they operate is not known. A little more is known about the neural pathways that pain messages travel on their way to the brain. For instance, we know that the sensation of pain is transmitted along two different nerve pathways in the spinal cord—*rapid* and *slow* neural pathways. This is why we often experience "first and second pain" (Sternbach, 1978).

The difference in speed of transmission in these pathways is based in part on the facts that the rapid pathway neurons tend to be thicker and sheathed in myelin. The slow pathway neurons, in contrast, are smaller unmyelinated neurons. The first pain sensation is a clear, localized feeling that does not "hurt" much. The second pain is a more diffuse, long-lasting pain that hurts much more. When you cut your finger with a knife, an initial pain tells you where you are hurt, followed quickly by a second, more diffuse painful sensation. The first sensation makes you drop the knife and grab your finger, the second makes you jump up and down and scream.

Pain involves more than the simple direct transmission of a pain message to the brain, however. There is not a direct relationship between the pain stimulus and the amount of pain experienced. Under certain circumstances, pain messages can even be blocked out of the brain. A football player whose attention is on a

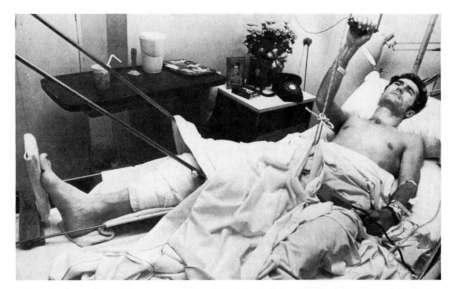

Guy Gertsch, who finished the 1982 Boston Marathon in a respectable two hours and forty-seven minutes, discovered at the finish line that he had run the last nineteen miles with a broken thigh bone.

big game may not notice a painful cut until after the game is over. The pain receptors transmit the pain message during the game, but the message is not fully processed by the brain until the player is no longer concentrating on the game. Similarly, hypnosis has been used to block pain messages during surgery and childbirth (Hilgard, 1978).

In the opposite way, circumstances can sometimes make pain more intense or longer lasting. If a person is injured in an accident and the resulting pain means that he will be pampered by his wife, and be able to quit his boring job and receive insurance benefits, his pain may last longer than if he received no benefits from it. In such a case, he is not faking his pain; the pain is very real. But it can be prolonged by the emotional benefits that it produces for the victim. The most effective treatment for such cases is to provide the person with rewards for *not* feeling the pain (a more enjoyable job, social activities, sports, etc.) that outweigh the gains produced by the pain (Fordyce, 1978).

Canadian psychologist Ronald Melzack of McGill University has proposed the *gate control theory of pain* to explain such phenomena (Melzack & Dennis, 1978). Melzack believes that pain signals are allowed in or blocked from the brain by neural "gates" in the spinal cord and brain stem. For example, placing a sore foot in a tub of warm water helps to close the gate on pain from the toe. The warm sensations block some of the pain sensations by closing the neural gates. Melzack believes that emotion, mental attitudes, distracting stimuli, hypnosis, and sometimes even acupuncture can close the pain gates. (See *Research Report:* "Acupuncture.") There is intriguing evidence that the pain gates are operated by substances that chemically resemble the pain-killing drug morphine, called *endorphins* made by the body in the nervous system.

Perhaps the strongest demonstration that pain involves more than the simple transmission of pain messages to the brain is the phenomenon of *phantom limb pain.* People who have had arms or legs amputated sometimes "feel" pain *in the* limb that is no longer there. The sensation of pain is located in the missing limb just as it would be if an injured limb were present. The pain does not arise from a pain receptor in the missing limb, of course. It probably originates with irritation of the severed afferent nerves that served the limb. But, the "pain" in the

acupuncture
(ak''u-pungk'chūr)
The ancient Chinese
practice of inserting needles
into specific parts of the
body to control pain or cure
illness.

RESEARCH REPORT

Acupuncture: How Does It Work?

Acupuncture is the ancient Chinese practice of inserting thin needles into specific parts of the body to cure illnesses. Chinese physicians also use this practice to produce anesthesia (lack of feeling) during surgical operations. During the 1970s, a group of American physicians visiting China watched in amazement while a man's stomach was removed using no anesthesia other than acupuncture.

Although the original Chinese theory was that acupuncture works by restoring the balance between yin and yang (the spirit and the blood), many in both the East and West now believe that acupuncture works by stimulating nerves that close *pain gates* on other nerves (Melzack & Dennis, 1978). It is believed that the needles, which are inserted, twirled, and sometimes warmed, stimulate the large *rapid* pain fibers. As mentioned in the text, these fibers quickly transmit a sharp, but not particularly uncomfortable pain message to the brain. Ironically, activation of the rapid fibers is also believed to close the pain gate to the slow fibers, and perhaps even to impulses of the rapid fibers. In this way, the dull uncomfortable type of pain is kept from reaching the brain. This process may be based on the release of endorphins and related substances in the pain-gate regions of the spinal cord and brain stem (Melzack & Dennis, 1978).

missing limb is "in the head." It's as if the somatic sensory area of the cerebral cortex, which has been receiving information from the limb since infancy, interprets the lack of other information from the limb as a mistake and constructs a perception of the missing limb anyway—including pain in that limb.

REVIEW

The body contains a number of sense organs that provide vital information about the body's movement and orientation in space and about the world as it contacts our skin. Information about posture, movement, and orientation is coded and sent to the somatic sensory area of the cortex by the vestibular organ in the inner ear and by kinesthetic receptors spread throughout the body. Skin receptors feed information about temperature, pressure, and pain to the same area of the brain. The phenomenon of pain provides a good example of the lack of direct relationship between physical stimuli and conscious sensations in that a number of psychological factors serve to increase or decrease the experience of pain. Phantom limb pain particularly illustrates the complex relationship between stimulus and sensation.

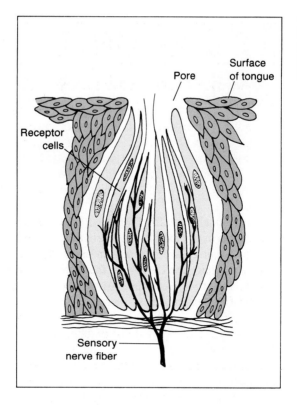

Figure 3.5 Taste buds contain clusters of taste (gustatory) receptor cells (Hole, 1984).

Chemical Senses: The Flavors and Aromas of Life

The senses of **gustation** (taste) or **olfaction** (smell) differ from the other senses in that they respond to chemicals rather than to energy in the environment. The chemical senses tell us about the things we eat, drink, and breathe.

Taste

We are able to taste food because of the 10,000 *taste buds* on the tongue. Each taste bud contains approximately a dozen sensory receptors called **taste cells,** which are sensitive to chemicals in our food and drink (Brown & Deffenbacher, 1979) (see fig. 3.5). Taste buds are clustered together in bumps called **papillae** that can be easily seen on the tongue. The taste buds are responsive to only four different primary qualities: *sweet, sour, bitter,* and *salty.* Every flavor that we experience from veal cacciatore to peanut butter is made up of combinations of these four basic qualities. However, our perception of food also includes the sensations from the skin surfaces of the tongue and mouth: touch (food texture), temperature (cold coffee tastes very different from hot coffee), and pain (as in Jalapeño peppers!). The sight and aroma of food also greatly affect our perception of food.

Although each taste bud seems to be primarily responsive to one of the four primary qualities, each responds to some extent to some or all of the other qualities as well (Arvidson & Friberg, 1980). Interestingly, the taste buds that are most sensitive to the four primary tastes are not evenly distributed over the tongue.

gustation (gus-ta′-shun) The sense of taste.

olfaction (ol-fak′-shun) The sense of smell.

taste cells The sensory receptor cells for gustation located in the taste buds.

papillae (pah-pil′e) Clusters of taste buds on the tongue.

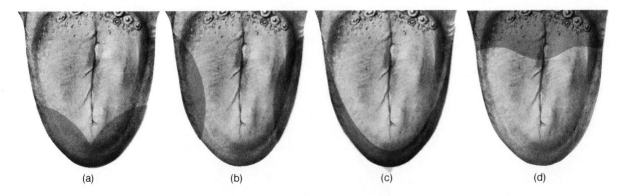

(a)   (b)   (c)   (d)

Figure 3.6 Areas of the tongue that are most sensitive to the four primary qualities of taste: (a) sweet, (b) sour, (c) salty, and (d) bitter (Hole, 1984).

They are bunched in different areas as shown in figure 3.6. This means that different parts of the tongue are sensitive to different tastes. We do not usually notice this because the differences in sensitivity are not great and because our food usually reaches all parts of the tongue during the tasting and chewing process anyway. But if you ever have to swallow a bitter pill, try placing it in the exact middle of the tongue where there are no bitter receptors.

Smell

olfactory epithelium
(ol-fak′to-re ep″i-the′le-um)
The sheet of receptor cells at the top of the nasal cavity.

Chemicals in the air we breathe pass by the olfactory receptors on their way to the lungs. These receptor cells are located in a dime-sized mucous-coated sheet at the top of the nasal cavity called the **olfactory epithelium** (see fig. 3.7). As with taste, we seem to be able to smell only a limited number of primary odors. There is much less agreement among psychologists about primary odors than primary tastes. But, some psychologists have suggested that all of the complex aromas and odors of life are made up of combinations of seven primary qualities: *camphoraceous* (camphor), *floral, pepperminty, ethereal* (dry-cleaning fluid), *musky* (musk oil), *pungent* (spices), and *putrid* (rotten eggs) (Amoore, Johnston, & Rubin, 1964).

stereochemical theory
The theory that different odor receptors can only be stimulated by molecules of a specific size and shape that fit them like a "key" in a lock.

According to the **stereochemical theory,** the complex molecules that are responsible for each of these primary odors are different shapes and will "fit" into only one type of receptor cell each, like a key into a lock. Only when molecules of a particular shape are present will the corresponding olfactory receptor send its distinctive message to the brain.

R E V I E W

Chemicals in the air we breathe and the things we eat and drink are sensed by the gustatory receptors (taste buds) on the tongue and the olfactory receptors in the nose. For both chemical senses, combinations of a small number of primary sensations apparently make up the entire variety of our experiences of taste and smell.

You probably never thought to credit your olfactory epithelium for your ability to detect the aroma of hot buttered popcorn.

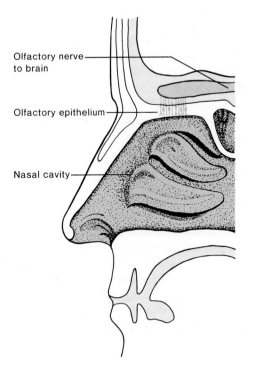

Olfactory nerve to brain

Olfactory epithelium

Nasal cavity

Figure 3.7 Olfactory receptor cells are located in the olfactory epithelium at the top of the nasal cavity (Hole, 1984).

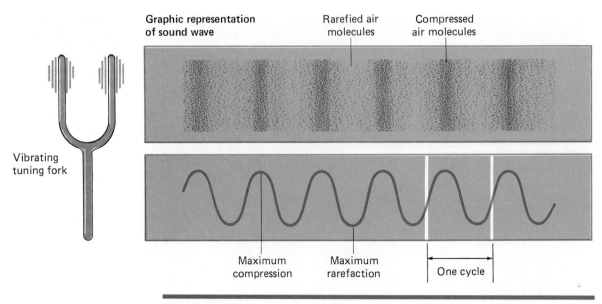

Graphic representation
of sound wave

Rarefied air
molecules

Compressed
air molecules

Vibrating
tuning fork

Maximum
compression

Maximum
rarefaction

One cycle

Figure 3.8 Vibrating objects such as a tuning fork create a sound wave of successive compression and rarefaction (expansion) in the air, which can be represented graphically as shown.

Hearing: Sensing Sound Waves

While all of the senses are important to a full appreciation of life, the last two senses that we will discuss are of particular importance. Without hearing and vision, there probably would be no spoken or written languages, and without language most of the cultural and scientific accomplishments of human beings probably would have been impossible. The sense of hearing depends on the ear, a complex sensory instrument that transduces the physical properties of sound waves into neural messages that can be sent to the brain.

Sound: What Is It?

audition (aw-dish'un)
The sense of hearing.

sound waves
Vibratory changes in the air that carry sound.

frequency of cycles
Rate of vibration of sound waves; determines pitch.

hertz (Hz)
Measurement of the frequency of sound waves in cycles per second.

intensity
Density of vibrating air molecules; determines the loudness of sound.

Hearing, or **audition,** is the sense that detects the vibratory changes in the air known as **sound waves.** When an object such as a tuning fork vibrates back and forth it sets in motion successive waves of *compression* and *rarefaction* (expansion) of the molecules of the air (see fig. 3.8). When the waves reach the ear, the reception of sound begins. As we shall see in a moment, the sound waves in the air cause a chain of parts in the ear to vibrate in a way that is eventually translated into a neural message to the brain.

Not all sound waves are alike, however, and the nature of a sound wave determines to a great extent how we will sense it. For one thing, sound waves differ in the **frequency of cycles** of compression and rarefaction of the air (see fig. 3.8). Objects that vibrate slowly create low-frequency sound waves, while rapidly vibrating objects produce high-frequency sound waves. The frequency of sound waves is measured in **hertz (Hz)** units, the number of cycles per second. The human ear is sensitive to sound waves in the range of 20 to 20,000 Hz. Sound waves also differ in terms of **intensity,** or how densely compacted the air molecules are in the sound wave.

Table 3.2 The loudness of common sounds as measured in decibel units

Decibels	Sounds
120	Loud thunder and painful sound
110	
100	Subway
90	City bus
85	Maximum level of industrial noise considered safe
80	Noisy automobile
70	
60	Normal conversation
50	
40	Quiet office
30	Whisper
20	
10	
0	Absolute threshold of human hearing

Source: Modified from Schiffman, 1976; Brown & Deffenbacher, 1979.

Note: Prolonged exposure to sounds over 85 decibels can lead to permanent hearing loss. Even brief exposure to loudness of 150 decibels (being close to an explosion or the speakers at some rock concerts) can permanently damage hearing.

The frequency of the sound wave largely determines its **pitch,** or how high or low it sounds to us. For example, striking a glass with a spoon causes a higher frequency sound wave—which we hear as a higher pitch—than striking a bass drum. The loudness of a sound is largely determined by its intensity. Gently tapping a bass drum produces less dense compression and rarefaction, and a quieter sound, than striking it hard. Intensity is measured in **decibel (db)** units. This scale begins at zero at the absolute threshold for detecting a 1,000-Hz tone (and increases by 20 db as the intensity of the stimulus is multiplied by 10). Normal conversation averages about 60 db, while sounds of 120 db or more are quite painful (see table 3.2). The **timbre** of a sound (its characteristic quality) is determined by the complexity of the sound wave—that is, the extent to which it is composed of many waves of different frequency and intensity. Different human voices sound different to us largely because of their different timbres.

The relationship between the physical properties of sound waves and the sensation of sound is not as simple as I have just made it seem, however. Take loudness, for example. Two tones of equal intensity may not be heard as equally loud if they are not equal in frequency. Loudness seems greatest for tones of about 3,000 to 4,000 Hz; higher- or lower-frequency sounds seem less loud to us.

The Ear: How Does It Work?

The ear is a sensitive sensory instrument that transduces sound waves into neural impulses to the brain. It is composed of three major sections: the outer, middle, and inner ear (see fig. 3.9).

Outer Ear

The external part of the ear, or **pinna,** that we think of as the "ear," does serve some function as a sound collector, but we could hear quite well without it. Connecting the outer and middle ear is the hollow **external auditory canal.** It's the part that gets waxy and the part through which sound waves reach the *eardrum,* the first structure of the middle ear.

pitch
The experience of sound vibrations sensed as high or low.

decibel (db) (des'i-bel)
Measurement of the intensity of perceived sound.

timbre (tim'ber, tam'br)
The characteristic quality of a sound as determined by the complexity of the sound wave.

pinna (pin'nah)
The external part of the ear.

external auditory canal
The tube that connects the pinna to the middle ear.

Figure 3.9 Diagram of the major structures of the ear (Hole, 1984).

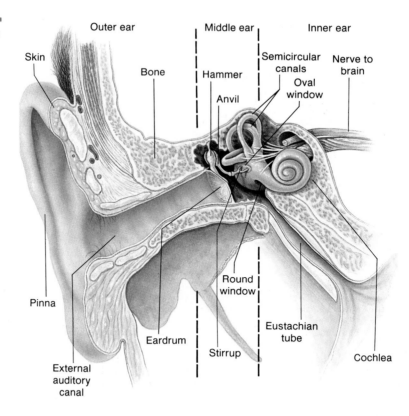

Middle Ear

The sound wave is transduced into mechanical energy in the middle ear. Sound waves set the thin **eardrum,** which resembles the skin on a drum, into vibratory movement. The eardrum is connected to a series of three movable, interconnected bones: the **hammer,** the **anvil,** and the **stirrup,** so named because of their shapes. The vibrating eardrum sets these bones into mechanical movement, passing the energy on to the inner ear.

Inner ear

The vibrating stirrup shakes another eardrumlike structure called the **oval window** into motion. This membrane is at the end of a long, curled structure called the **cochlea** that is filled with fluid. The vibrating oval window creates waves in the fluid of the cochlea (see fig. 3.10). The cochlea contains two long tubes that double back on themselves and are connected only at the tip end of the spiral. The pressure of the vibrating waves is relieved by a third eardrumlike membrane at the other end of the cochlea called the **round window.** Running almost the entire length of the cochlea are several layers of membranes that separate the two tubes. The lower membrane, called the **basilar membrane,** forms a floor upon which the ear's sensory receptors sit. These hairlike cells are contained in the **organ of Corti.** Vibrations in the cochlear fluid set the basilar membrane in motion. This movement, in turn, moves the organ of Corti and stimulates the receptor cells that it contains. These receptors transduce the sound waves in the cochlear fluid into coded neural impulses.

eardrum
Thin membrane that sound waves cause to vibrate; the first structure of the middle ear.

hammer
A hammer-shaped bone of the middle ear that helps pass sound waves to the inner ear.

anvil
An anvil-shaped bone of the middle ear that helps pass sound waves to the inner ear.

stirrup
A stirrup-shaped bone of the middle ear that helps pass sound waves to the inner ear.

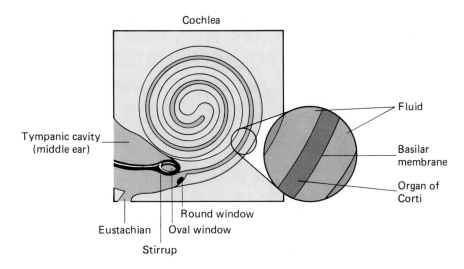

Cochlea

Tympanic cavity
(middle ear)

Eustachian   Oval window

Round window

Stirrup

Fluid

Basilar
membrane

Organ of
Corti

Figure 3.10 Vibrations from sound waves enter the cochlea through the oval window, travel the length of the cochlea where they are transduced into neural messages by receptors in the organ of Corti.

How does the organ of Corti code neural messages to the brain? The *intensity* of a sound wave is coded by the number of receptors in the organ of Corti that fire. Low-intensity sounds stimulate only a few receptors; high-intensity sounds stimulate many receptors.

The *frequency* of the sound wave is apparently coded in at least two ways. First, sound waves of different frequencies will stimulate firings of receptor cells at different *places* along the organ of Corti. Higher-frequency waves stimulate the organ of Corti close to the oval window; lower-frequency waves stimulate it farther along the cochlea (except for very low frequencies). Second, to some extent the frequency of the sound waves is duplicated in the *frequency* of the firings of the auditory receptors. But only at lower frequencies is each individual neuron able to fire at the same frequency as the sound wave. At higher frequencies, the coding of frequency is achieved by the firing of *volleys* of neural impulses by different groups of neurons that fire in turns at the same frequency as the sound wave.

Not all sounds go through this full process from outer ear to cochlea. Some sounds are transmitted through the bones of the head directly to the cochlear fluid. We hear ourselves speak (and eat) largely through **bone conduction hearing.** This fact is important in the diagnosis of hearing problems. People who have suffered damage to the hearing apparatus of the middle ear can hear bone conducted sounds fairly well, but not airborne sounds. People with damage to the auditory nerve—nerve deafness—cannot hear either type of sound.

One more thing about ears deserves mentioning. Ever wonder why most of us have two of them? For one thing, a pair of ears gives us a spare in case something goes wrong with one, but the fact that we have two ears also serves an important function in *locating* the origin of sounds. The ears locate sounds in two ways—one for high-frequency sounds and another for low-frequency sounds.

When a sound wave is coming from straight ahead or from straight behind us, the sound reaches both ears simultaneously. But when a sound is coming from the sides or from an angle, it arrives at slightly different times to the two ears. The ears are sensitive enough to this difference that they allow us to locate the direction of low-frequency sounds. The reason you know that the person to the left of you is blowing her nose again is because your left ear heard it before your right ear did. With high-frequency sounds, the difference in the intensity of the sound waves reaching the two ears provides the cue for the location of the sound.

oval window
The membrane of the inner ear that vibrates, creating sound waves in the fluid of the cochlea.

cochlea (cok′le-ah)
A curved structure of the inner ear that is filled with fluid.

round window
The membrane that relieves pressure from the vibrating waves in the cochlear fluid.

basilar membrane (bas′i-lar)
One of the membranes that separates the two tubes of the cochlea and upon which the organ of Corti rests.

organ of Corti (kor′te)
Sensory receptor in the cochlea that transduces sound waves into coded neural impulses.

bone conduction hearing
Sounds transmitted through the bones of the head directly to the cochlear fluid.

R E V I E W

Sound is a physical stimulus made up of successive waves of densely and sparsely compressed air. The ear is composed of a series of structures that transmit the sound wave from the outer ear to the inner ear where it produces vibrations in the fluid of the cochlea. The vibrations of the cochlear fluid are transduced by the ear's receptor cells that are located in the organ of Corti. Coded neural messages are sent to the auditory sensory areas of the brain where frequency, intensity, and complexity are interpreted as pitch, loudness, and timbre.

Table 3.3 Physical properties of light and sound waves and corresponding psychological dimensions in vision and hearing

Property of Physical Stimulus	Corresponding Dimension	
	In Color Vision	**In Hearing**
Wavelength/Frequency	Hue	Pitch
Intensity	Brightness	Loudness
Complexity	Saturation	Timbre

Vision: Your Human Camera

In 1950 psychologist George Wald wrote an important paper comparing the eye to a camera. This is still a good analogy today. Both are instruments that use a lens to focus light onto a light-sensitive surface on which the visual image is registered. The gross anatomy of the human eye shown in figure 3.11 makes the resemblance to a camera very apparent. This intricate and efficient instrument transduces the physical properties of light into elaborately coded neural messages.

Light: What Is It?

electromagnetic radiation (e-lek″tro-mag-net′ik) A form of energy including electricity, radio waves, and X rays, of which visible light is a part.

We need to have some knowledge of the nature of light to understand vision. Light is one small part of the form of energy known as **electromagnetic radiation** that also includes radio waves and X rays. Only a small portion of this radiation is visible—that is, our senses can transduce only a small part of it. Like sound, we can best think of light as being composed of *waves* that have *frequency* and *intensity*. These two properties of light waves provide us with most of our information in vision.

The *intensity* of the light largely determines the *brightness* of the visual sensation. The light reflected by an apple that is lighted by a single candle would be low in intensity, so we would see the red of the apple as a dim rather than a bright sensation. The frequency of the light wave (the term **wavelength** is generally used instead of frequency when referring to light waves) largely determines the *color*, or *hue*, that we see—that is, light waves of different wavelengths are seen as different colors. But most light waves are not made up of a single

wavelength Frequency of light waves; determines the color we see.

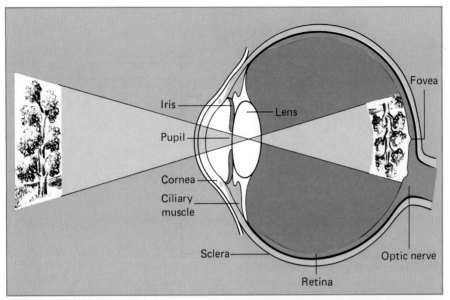

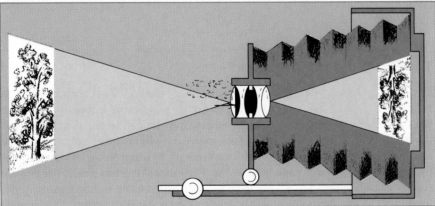

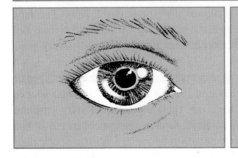

Figure 3.11 Optical similarities of eye and camera are apparent in their cross sections. Both utilize a lens to focus an inverted image on a light-sensitive surface. Both possess an iris to adjust to various intensities of light. The single lens of the eye, however, cannot bring light of all colors to a focus at the same point. The compound lens of the camera is better corrected for color because it is composed of two kinds of glass.
From Eye and camera, *by George Wald. Copyright ©* 1950 by Scientific American, Inc. All rights reserved.

wavelength and so are not seen as a pure color. Rather, they are made up of light waves of more than one wavelength. The more a color is composed of multiple wavelengths, the less *saturated* (or pure) the color is said to be. Like sound, however, the relationship between the physical properties of light and what is seen is not always simple and direct.

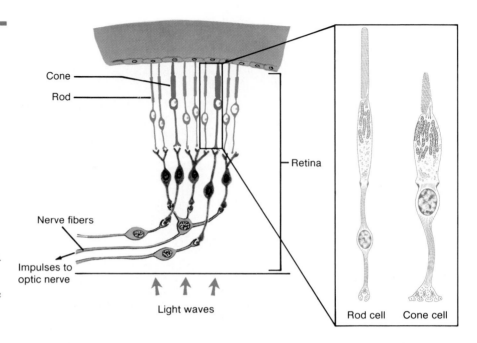

cornea (kor′ne-ah)
The protective coating on the surface of the eye through which light passes.

iris (i′ris)
The colored part of the eye behind the cornea that regulates the amount of light that enters.

pupil (pu′pil)
The opening of the iris.

lens
Transparent portion of the eye that focuses light on the retina.

ciliary muscle (sil′e-er″e)
The muscle in the eye that controls the shape of the lens.

retina (ret′i-nah)
The area at the back of the eye on which images are formed and that contains the rods and cones.

rods
The 120 million cells located outside the center of the retina that transduce light waves into neural impulses, thereby coding information about light and dark.

cones
The 6 million receptor cells located mostly in the center of the retina that transduce light waves into neural impulses, thereby coding information about light, dark, and color.

The Eye: How Does It Work?

The eye is an almost perfect sphere composed of two fluid-filled chambers. Light passes through the clear **cornea** into the first chamber. At the back of this chamber, the colored **iris** opens and closes to regulate how much light will pass through the **pupil** into the **lens.** The lens is held in place by ligaments that are attached to the **ciliary muscle.** This muscle focuses images by controlling the thickness of the lens so that a clear image falls on the light-sensitive **retina** at the back of the second chamber (see fig. 3.11). When the ciliary muscle is uncontracted, the tension of the ligaments stretches the lens relatively flat. When the ciliary muscle contracts, it lessens the tension of the ligaments and the lens thickens. The lens must be thickened to focus on close objects; that is why reading for long periods—which involves prolonged contraction of the ciliary muscle—makes your eyes feel tired.

The real business of transducing light waves is carried out by two types of receptor cells in the retina named the **rods** and the **cones** because of their shapes (see fig. 3.12). The cones are far less numerous than the rods—about 6 million cones compared to 120 million rods in each eye. Cones are concentrated in the center of the retina, with the greatest concentration being at a central spot called the **fovea.** In good light, **visual acuity** (the clearness and sharpness of vision) is best for images that are focused directly on the fovea, largely because of the high concentration of cones.

The rods are located throughout the retina except in the center (the fovea). They play a role in vision that differs from that of the cones in four main ways. First, because of their location, they are largely responsible for peripheral vision—vision at the top, bottom, and sides of the visual field—while the cones play little role in this aspect of seeing. Second, the rods are hundreds of times more sensitive to light than the cones. This means that they play a far more important

The color of this red apple hasn't changed, but in a dim light its brilliance appears to fade. Cones in the eye pick up color but they work well only in bright light.

Figure 3.13 Demonstration of the blind spot. You can demonstrate to yourself the existence of the ''blind spot'' in the following way. Hold your book at about arm's length with the word *spot* in front of your eyes. Close your right eye and stare at the word *spot*. Move the book in slowly until the word *blind* disappears. At this point, its image is falling on the spot in the retina where the optic nerve is attached and there are no receptors. We are not normally aware of the existence of this blind spot because we ''fill in'' a perception to compensate for the missing information. In this case, we see the dotted line as continuous after the word *blind* disappears.

□ □ □ Blind □ □ □ □ □ □ □ □ □ □ □ □ Spot □ □

role in vision in dim light than the cones. Third, the rods produce images that are perceived with less visual acuity than cones. This is largely due to the fact that neurons leading from several rods often converge so that their impulses are sent to the brain on a single nerve fiber (shown in fig. 3.12). In contrast, cones more commonly send their messages to the brain along separate nerve fibers, giving the brain more precise information about the location of the stimulation on the retina.

The fourth difference between the rods and cones concerns color vision. Both types of receptors respond to variations in light and dark (in terms of the number of receptors that fire and the frequency with which they fire), but only the cones can code information about color. Because the rods do not detect color, and because the cones can respond only in bright light, we can see only indistinct forms of black and gray in an almost totally dark room. Light of different wavelengths is still present in the room during near darkness, but the rods have no way of sending messages about them to the brain, so colors "disappear" from view.

Would you be surprised to learn that you are partially blind in each eye? The spot near the center of the retina where the **optic nerve** is attached contains no rods or cones. Because there is no visual reception at this point, it is known as the **blind spot.** We are not normally aware of the existence of this blind spot because we "fill in" the missing information during the process of seeing by using information coming in from the other parts of the retina. However, look at figure 3.13 for a demonstration of its existence.

fovea (fo′ve-ah)
The central spot of the retina containing the greatest concentration of cones.

visual acuity
(vizh′-u-al ah-ku′ĭ-te)
Clearness and sharpness of vision.

optic nerve
The nerve that carries neural messages about vision to the brain.

blind spot
The spot where the optic nerve is attached to the retina, containing no rods or cones.

Dark and Light Adaptation

When you walk into a dark movie theater from the daylight, you are "blind" at first; your eyes can pick up very little visual information. Within about 5 minutes, however, your vision in the darkened room has improved considerably, and very slowly it improves over the next 25 minutes until you can see fairly well. When you step out of the theater from the matinee performance, you have the opposite experience. At first the intense light "blinds" you. You squint and block out the painful light, but in a little while you can see normally again. What is going on? How can you be sighted one moment and blind the next just because the intensity of light has suddenly changed?

The phenomena are called *dark adaptation* and *light adaptation.* Here is what happens in the retina during **dark adaptation.** During vision in high intensity light, the rods and cones are being used frequently, so they are tired and not very sensitive. When we enter darkness, the rods and cones are not sensitive enough to be stimulated by the low-intensity light and they stop firing almost completely. This gives the receptors a "rest" before they begin to regain their sensitivity by making a fresh supply of the chemicals used in light reception that have been literally "bleached out" by the intense light.

dark adaptation
Increased sensitivity of the eye in semidarkness following an abrupt reduction in overall illumination.

At first, both the rods and the cones are recovering their sensitivity, so there is fairly rapid improvement. But the cones become as sensitive as they can (remember they are not very sensitive in weak light) within about five minutes, so the rate of improvement slows after that. The rods continue to improve in sensitivity slowly, reaching a level of sensitivity to light that is 100,000 times greater than in bright illumination after about 30 minutes in the dark.

In **light adaptation,** eyes that have been in the dark for a while have built up a full supply of the chemicals used in light reception and are very responsive to light. When we are suddenly exposed to intense light, a barrage of rods and cones fires almost at once and, in essence, "overloads" the visual circuits. It's not until the intense light has had a chance to bleach out some of the receptor chemicals and reduce the sensitivity of the receptors to a normal level that we can see comfortably again. Fortunately, this process takes place in about a minute.

light adaptation
Regaining sensitivity of the eye to bright light following an abrupt increase in overall illumination.

By the way, your mother was right about carrots and good vision. The chemical involved in light reception in the rods is largely made up of vitamin A. This is why a deficiency of vitamin A can lead to "night blindness." And yes, there is a lot of vitamin A in carrots.

Color Vision

Energy of any wavelength within the spectrum of visible light will evoke a sensation of a specific color when it stimulates the human visual system. But note that light energy is just that—energy; it has no color inherent in it. Color, like all sensations, has no existence outside the human observer. Rather, color is the conscious experience that results from the processing of light energy by the eye and brain.

It's obviously advantageous from an evolutionary perspective to be able to discriminate among lights of different wavelengths: "blue" berries are ready to be eaten; "green" berries are not. But, how does the human visual system produce the sensation of color? Two theories of color vision have received considerable attention from psychologists over the last century: trichromatic theory and opponent-process theory.

Trichromatic Theory

Trichromatic theory states that there are three kinds of cones in the retina—those that respond primarily to light in either the red, green, or blue range of wavelengths. We see myriad colors, not just three, because all visual stimuli activate more than one of these three cones to different degrees. Suggested in the early 1800s by Thomas Young and Hermann von Helmholz, trichromatic theory is based primarily on the observation that any color can be made by mixing a certain combination of the wavelengths for red, blue, and green.

Today, we know that the trichromatic theory of color vision accurately describes the properties of the receptors that transduce wavelength into color—the cones. There are, in fact, three types of cones in the human retina that respond to different, but overlapping, ranges of wavelengths. However, to understand color processing in the rest of the visual system, concepts from the opponent-process theory first stated by Ewald Hering in the 1870s must also be considered.

trichromatic theory
(tri″kro-mat′ik)
The theory of color vision that contends that the eye has three different kinds of cones, each of which responds to light of one range of wavelength.

Opponent-Process Theory

Opponent-process theory suggests that there are two different kinds of color-processing mechanisms in the visual system that respond in opposite ways to light of specific wavelengths: the red-green (R-G) and yellow-blue (Y-B) processing mechanisms. These are systems of neurons in the retina that are stimulated by the cones. If the R-G mechanism is "activated" by light in the red range of wavelengths, it will be "shut down" by light in the green range, thus sending opposite signals along the visual system of neurons to the brain. Similarly, the Y-B mechanism sends opposite signals in response to light in the yellow and blue ranges. The combinations of signals from the opponent-processing mechanisms provides the brain with the information necessary for color sensations.

Support for the opponent-process theory of color vision is provided by the fact that it successfully explains several phenomena:

opponent-process theory
The theory of color vision that contends that the eye has two kinds of cones that respond to light in either the red-green or yellow-blue ranges of wavelength.

1. *Complementary colors.* Artists know that yellow and blue as well as red and green are complementary colors—that is, you cannot mix lights of these colors to produce a yellowish-blue or a reddish-green. Opponent-process theory accounts for this fact because an opponent system cannot signal both of its opponent colors at the same time. It signals either red or green and either yellow or blue. In fact, simultaneous presentations of both colors of a single opponent process usually result in the perception of white. In contrast, "orange" light apparently excites the R of the R-G mechanism and the Y of the Y-B mechanism, resulting in the sensation of orange.

2. *Color afterimages.* If a patch of color is viewed for a period of time, and then the eyes are shifted to a neutral (white or gray) surface, the image of the patch then appears to have the complementary color to that originally viewed. For example, stare intensely for about thirty seconds at the white dot in the center of the word *red* that is printed in the color of red in figure 3.14. Then stare at the blank white space next to it. You will still be able to see an image of the word *red,* but it will be colored green. Opponent-process theory suggests that staring at the red stimulus

Figure 3.14 Stimulus used in the demonstration of afterimages.

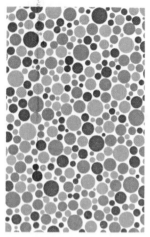

Normal individuals read this as 8. Red/green color-blind individuals see a 3 here.

reduces the ability of the R-G opponent system to respond to red so much that the white light (containing all of the wavelengths of the spectrum) from the paper is now only able to stimulate "green" signals from the R-G system. Comparable phenomena can be demonstrated using any of the four opponent colors.

3. *Neuron responses.* Perhaps the strongest evidence for the opponent-process theory is that neurons throughout the visual system respond to light in an opponent-process fashion. For example, if a specific neuron is excited by green light, then it is inhibited from firing by red light. This is true of most neurons in the visual parts of the brain, and even for neurons in the retina that receive synaptic information from the cone receptors.

Thus, trichromatic theory accurately describes events at the first level of neurons in the visual system—the cones within the retina. However, the opponent-process theory best describes the activities of neurons in the rest of the visual system, and better explains a large number of perceptual phenomena. Does this mean the trichromatic theory is wrong? No—it's exactly right at the level of the cones. However, the three cone signals apparently are immediately combined in a two-way opponent fashion, and these resulting opponent-process mechanisms then appear to be the dominant color processors in the rest of the visual system and in the determination of color perception.

Color Blindness

monochromacy
(mon″o-kro′mah-se)
Color blindness in which the individual sees no color at all.

dichromacy
(di-kro′mah-se)
Color blindness in which the individual is unable to distinguish either red and green or yellow and blue.

Some people cannot see in color at all; such total color blindness (**monochromacy**) is rare, however. Partial color blindness is more common, affecting about 8 percent of males, but only 0.7 percent of females. Most people with partial color blindness seem to see the world almost normally. However, in extreme cases (called **dichromacy**), the afflicted individual is unable to distinguish red from green or, much less commonly, yellow from blue. Both major theories of color vision have been used to explain dichromatic color blindness. Note that the colors that cannot be distinguished are the colors of only one of the opponent processes. It's as if something is wrong with one of the opponent-process mechanisms. Although the explanation is more technical, the trichromatic theory explains dichromatic color blindness in terms of a dysfunction of one of the three kinds of cones. For example, a person whose blue-sensitive cones did not function properly would still be able to discriminate between red and green.

R E V I E W

The eye operates much like a human camera. The lens focuses a visual image on the retina of the eye, which contains two kinds of sensory receptor cells, the rods and cones. These transduce the wavelength, amplitude, and complexity of the light waves into neural messages. The two kinds of receptor cells perform their jobs somewhat differently: Cones work best in intense light, provide good visual acuity, and transduce information about color; rods work well in weak light, do not provide good acuity, and do not transduce color. The eye does not function well when the intensity of light suddenly changes, but quickly regains its sensitivity through the processes of light and dark adaptation. There are two major theoretical explanations of how the visual system transduces color. One states that three different kinds of cones are most sensitive to light of different wavelengths. The other suggests that there are two kinds of color-processing mechanisms in the visual system that process complementary colors. Each theory seems to be better able to describe different aspects of color vision.

Perception: Interpreting Sensory Messages

Sensations that are transmitted to the brain have little "meaning" of their own. They are in the form of raw neural energy that must be organized and interpreted in the process we call *perception*. The process is pretty much the same in all of us. If this were not the case—if we each interpreted sensory input in different ways—there would be no common "reality" in the sense of a perceived world that we all share. But there are some aspects of perception that are unique to a particular individual or members of a particular culture. The specific learning experiences, memories, motives, and emotions of the individual can influence perception. For example, we all perceive the visual stimuli of a knife in pretty much the same way because of the inborn ways we organize visual information. But a knife also has unique perceptual meaning to each individual depending on whether the person has been cut by a similar knife, has a similar favorite hunting knife, or has just been asked to carve a turkey for dinner.

In this section, we will describe the inborn organizational properties that all humans share and briefly discuss some of the ways in which each individual's perceptions are unique. For another view of perceptual abilities claimed by some, see *Research Report:* "Experimental Studies of Extrasensory Perception."

Keep in mind as we discuss perception that while it's easy to distinguish between sensation and perception in theory, it's very difficult to do so in practice. Visual perception, for example, begins in the complex neural structures of the eye before sensory messages are transmitted to the brain (Brown & Deffenbacher, 1979). The distinction between sensation and perception, then, is largely an arbitrary one to make our discussion of information processing by the sense organs and brain easier to understand.

Visual Perception

In the discussion that follows, we will describe the major ways in which sensory information is interpreted in meaningful perceptions, including both those ways that are common to us all and those that are unique to each individual. This discussion will focus on visual perception rather than on all the perceptual systems for several reasons: Visual perception is a highly important sensing system; scientists understand how it works better than other systems; and it is representative enough of other systems to tell us something about the process of perception in general.

RESEARCH REPORT

Experimental Studies of Extrasensory Perception (ESP)

parapsychology
(par″ah-si-kol′o-je)
The study of psychic
phenomena such as ESP.

extrasensory perception
(ESP)
Perception not accounted
for by the five senses.

When I was a freshman in college, I took an unusual psychology course in **parapsychology,** the study of psychic phenomena such as **extrasensory perception (ESP).** As I look back on the course, my professor was less interested in teaching us about ESP than in teaching us how to study scientifically any phenomenon using the fascinating question of ESP as an example. His point was this: If you are skeptical about ESP, you will thoroughly examine experiments that seem to prove the existence of ESP to find flaws in the logic or procedure of the experiments. That is good, because you should be careful in your evaluation of experiments. But you should be equally careful about all experiments whether you are skeptical about the phenomenon studied or not.

A special guest professor was brought in to lecture and lead discussions for a week. He was the late J. B. Rhine, the psychologist who pioneered serious, controlled research on ESP in the United States. I still remember my surprise upon meeting Dr. Rhine. A serious, quiet man with close-cropped white hair who was invariably dressed in a suit and tie, he fit my image of a retired banker far more than my image of a true believer in psychic powers.

While visiting our campus, he showed us his favorite and best-known method for experimentally studying ESP. ESP means being able to perceive something without using any of the usual senses (vision, hearing, touch, etc.); rather the individual is thought to use a *psychic sense.* Rhine frequently studied ESP using a deck of twenty-five cards called Zener cards that resemble ordinary playing cards. One side of the cards is blank while the other side has a figure printed on it (see fig. 3.15). There are five of each figure in the deck.

To see if an individual "has ESP," the experimenter shuffles the deck in a way to insure that they are in random order. Then the experimenter looks at the cards one at a time and concentrates on the figure. The subject whose ESP is being tested does not look at the cards but tries to read the experimenter's mind and write down the figures in the same order that the experimenter is seeing them.

RESEARCH REPORT

Figure 3.15 Zener cards like the ones used by J. B. Rhine and other researchers in the study of extrasensory perception.

The original studies conducted by Rhine and his colleagues were justifiably criticized for their lack of control. For example, the subjects could see the experimenter's face during the tests and might have been detecting subtle reactions in the experimenter (such as eye movements and facial expressions) rather than reading his or her mind. Later studies controlled for such alternative explanations much better through such measures as having the experimenter look at the cards in a different building so that there could be no unintentional transmission of clues through the regular sensory channels.

When tested in this way, no one—not even subjects who believe they have sensitive powers of ESP—is able to get all, or even most of the cards right. However, when the performance of some subjects is compared to what would be expected on the basis of chance alone (if you randomly guessed an equal number of each figure, you would expect to get five out of twenty-five right through chance), *some* of the subjects can hit more than a chance number (such as 9 or 10 correct in each deck of twenty-five) *some of the time.*

Critics of recent ESP research point to the fact that only some of the subjects can perform at better than a chance level, and that even they can do so only some of the time. This could mean that the data reported in journals reflects only "streaks of luck." Believers in ESP, on the other hand, believe that these facts only mean that ESP is a delicate, sensitive ability that can easily be disturbed by the experimental situation (Wolman, 1977). Which explanation is correct? Until we have more evidence, your guess is as good as mine.

a

b

c

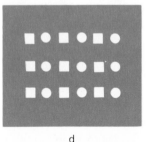

d

e

Figure 3.16 Illustrations of principles of perceptual organization.

Perceptual Organization

Raw visual sensations are like the unassembled parts of a washing machine: they must be put together in an organized way before they are useful to us. Some of the fundamental ways in which the eye and brain organize visual sensations were described about 75 years ago by Gestalt psychologists in their pioneering writings on perception (see chapter 1). These principles of perceptual organization are still worth studying today (see fig. 3.16 for examples of each).

a. *Figure-ground.* When we perceive a visual stimulus, part of what we see is the center of our attention, the *figure,* and the rest is indistinct background, the *ground.* All perceptions have this quality, but the reversible drawing in figure 3.16a shows that this way of seeing does not simply reflect the nature of reality. The fact that figure and ground of this drawing can be reversed to perceive either a goblet or two opposing faces shows that sensations can be organized by the brain in different ways.

b. *Proximity.* Things that are proximal (close together) are usually seen as belonging together. In figure 3.16b, we see three sets of three circles, not one set of nine.

c. *Continuity.* A baby seen behind a set of bars on a crib is seen as a complete baby, even though only "stripes" of the baby can be seen in figure 3.16c. We "fill in" the missing information to complete our perception.

d. *Similarity.* Figure 3.16d is seen as three vertical rows of circles and three rows of squares, rather than three horizontal rows of alternating circles and squares, because similar things tend to be perceived together.

e. *Closure.* Incomplete figures, such as in figure 3.16e tend to be perceived as complete wholes. Again, we fill in missing sensory information to create complete and whole perceptions.

Our perceptions are actively organized according to these and other similar inborn principles.

Perceptual Constancy

We perceive the world as being a fairly constant and unchanging place: tables, lamps, and people do not change in size, shape, or color from moment to moment, but stay the same. Yet, the sensations that tell us about these things do change considerably from moment to moment. The size of the image that falls on the retina changes as a person walks away, but we do not perceive the person as shrinking in size. The shape of a pot seen from different angles is different on the retina, but we do not believe that the pot is changing shape. This characteristic of perception is called **perceptual constancy.**

1. *Brightness constancy.* A piece of white paper does not change in perceived brightness when it moves from a weakly lit room to an intensely lit room even though the intensity of the light reaching the eye does change considerably. Fortunately for our ability to cope with the world, our perception corresponds to the unchanging

Perceptual constancy
helps us to recognize this
vase as unchanging, even
though we are viewing it
from different angles and
from different distances.

"Excuse me for shouting—I thought you were further away."

physical properties of the paper rather than to the changing sensory
information about its brightness. When you stop to think about it,
this is a remarkable accomplishment, but one that we take so much
for granted that you may not have been aware that it was
happening until you read this paragraph.

2. *Color constancy.* Colors do not appear to change much in spite of
    different conditions of light and surroundings that change incoming
    visual information.

perceptual constancy
The tendency for
perceptions of objects to
remain relatively
unchanged in spite of
changes in raw sensations.

OF SPECIAL INTEREST

The Moon Illusion

There are few things more beautiful than a huge full moon on the horizon. But have you ever stopped to wonder why it always looks *bigger* on the horizon than overhead? It does not really grow, you know; it's an *illusion*. In fact, it's an illusion that has puzzled scientists for a long time. Many explanations have been offered, such as the dense air close to the horizon magnifies the moon's image—which it does not. But it has been only recently that a fully acceptable explanation has been offered by psychologist Irvin Rock (Rock & Kaufman, 1972).

The explanation involves an understanding of the role of depth cues in the perception of the size of objects. As shown in figure 3.17 an object that our senses tells us is *farther away* is perceived as being *larger* than an object that casts the same size image on the retina but appears to be closer. The two triangles in this figure are the same size, but the one at the top is perceived as larger because it appears to be farther away. Ordinarily the top triangle *would* be larger if it were farther away, but could still cast as large a retinal image as a closer object.

The moon illusion is based on the same principle. When the moon is overhead we have no cues of distance at all, so depth cues do not influence our perception of the moon's size. When it's near the horizon, however, we can see the moon is farther away than objects such as distant trees and buildings, which we know to be large but which cast a small image on the retina. When the size of the moon

3. *Size constancy.* A dollar bill seen from one foot and from ten feet casts different-sized images on the retina, but we do not perceive it as changing in size. Familiar objects do not change in perceived size at different distances.

4. *Shape constancy.* A penny seen from straight ahead casts a circular image on the retina. When seen at a slight angle, however, the image it casts is in the shape of an oval, yet we continue to perceive it as circular.

Through the process of perceptual constancy we automatically adjust our interpretations to correspond with what we have learned the physical world to be like rather than placing sole reliance on changing stimulus input.

Depth Perception

The retina is a two-dimensional surface. It has an up and down, and a left and right, but no depth. How is it then that we are able to *perceive* a three-dimensional world using a two-dimensional retina? The eye and brain accomplish this by using a number of two-dimensional cues to create a perceptual distance. The

OF SPECIAL INTEREST

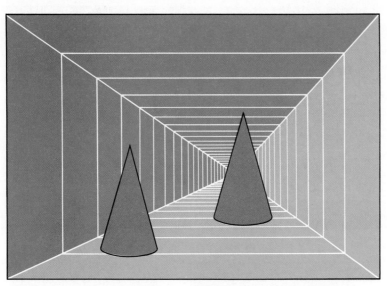

Figure 3.17 When two objects of the same size are perceived as being at different distances, the one farthest away is perceived as being larger.
From The moon illusion, *by Lloyd Kaufman & Irvin Rock. Copyright © 1962 by Scientific American, Inc. All rights reserved.*

is perceived in comparison to these objects, it looks much bigger. You can test this explanation by blocking out the horizon with your hand placed horizontally close to your eye the next time you look at a rising moon; you will see that it looks smaller.

nine major cues used in depth perception are listed below. The first seven are known as **monocular cues** because they can be seen by one eye; the last two factors are known as **binocular cues** because they can only be perceived using both eyes. The monocular cues are as follows.

1. *Texture gradient.* The texture of objects is more distinctive and visible up close (such as the bricks on the side of a building), and less distinct than far away (see fig. 3.18).

2. *Linear perspective.* Parallel lines appear to grow closer together the farther away they are, such as railroad tracks. Similarly, objects farther away cast a smaller image on the retina.

3. *Superposition.* Closer objects tend to be partially in front of or partially cover up more distant objects.

4. *Shadowing.* The shadows cast by objects suggest their depth.

5. *Speed of movement.* Objects far away appear to be moving across the field of vision more slowly than closer objects.

monocular cues
(mon-ok′u-lar)
Seven visual cues that can be seen with one eye that allow us to perceive distance.

binocular cues
(bin-ok′u-lar)
Visual cues that require both eyes to allow us to perceive distance.

Artists, including those whose works appear on the walls of buildings, have long understood monocular cues of depth perception.

Figure 3.18 Monocular cues create a perception of depth in these flat photographs.

6. *Aerial perspective.* Water vapor and pollution in the air scatter light waves and give distant objects a bluish and hazy appearance compared to nearby objects.

7. *Accommodation.* As discussed earlier in the chapter, the shape of the lens of the eye must change to focus the visual image on the retina from stimuli that are different distances from the eye. This process is called *accommodation.* Kinesthetic receptors in the ciliary muscle, therefore, provide a source of information about the distance of different objects. This information is only useful, however, for short distances up to about 4 feet.

 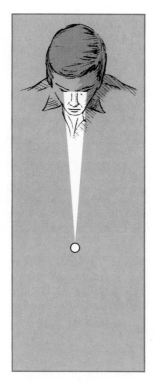 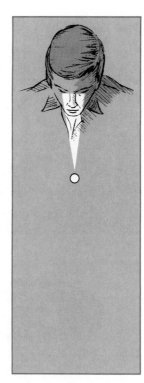

Figure 3.19 The degree to which the eyes must look inward (convergence) to focus on objects at different distances provides information on the distance of that object. It's a binocular cue in depth perception because it requires the use of both eyes.

The binocular cues are as follows:

8. *Convergence.* When both eyes are looking at an object in the center of the visual field, they must angle inward more sharply for a near object than for a distant object (see fig. 3.19). Information from the muscles that move the eyes thus provide a clue as to the distance an object is from the viewer.

9. *Retinal disparity.* Because the two eyes are a couple of inches apart, they do not see the same view of three-dimensional objects, especially when the object is close to the eyes. This disparity, or difference, between the images on the two retinas is a key factor in depth perception. Retinal disparity is the principle behind the old-fashioned *stereopticon.* As shown in figure 3.20, the individual looks at two pictures of the same scene in a special viewer that lets each eye see only one of the two images. The images were photographed from two slightly different spots to duplicate the disparity between two retinal images. When seen in the stereopticon, the two images fuse into a single scene perceived in startlingly good three-dimension. Try placing a sheet of white paper edgewise between the two pictures and the bridge of your nose to allow each eye to see only one of the pictures. Look at them for a while to see if they fuse into a single three-dimensional scene.

Through a combination of these monocular and binocular cues we are able to perceive our three-dimensional world using only two-dimensional information.

Figure 3.20 Two photos taken from slightly different angles are used in a stereopticon to create an illusion of depth through retinal disparity.

Figure 3.21 An illustration of the Müller-Lyer illusion.

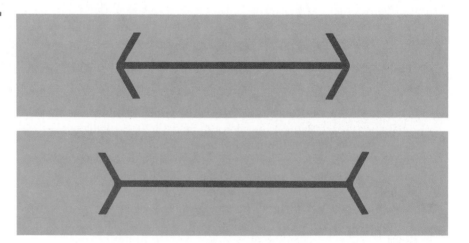

Visual Illusions

Instructors of introductory psychology have long enjoyed amusing their classes with visual illusions. These illusions intentionally manipulate the cues that we use in perception to create a perception of something that is not real. They are instructive, therefore, in showing us more about the process of perception, and for showing us in yet *another* way that what we see is not always the same as the visual information that enters the eyes. For example, the two horizontal lines in figure 3.21 are of different lengths—or are they? Actually they just look different because of the context they are in. Similarly, the two central circles in figure 3.22 are the same size, but they do not look it because of their contexts.

Perhaps the most impressive visual illusion of all is the *Ames room*. This is an entire room constructed to create a powerful illusion. When viewed through a peephole at one end (used to restrict the availability of binocular cues) the room appears to be a normal square. Actually, however, the room is much deeper on one side than the other, but many cues of depth perception have been altered to give the illusion of equal depth for all sides of the back wall. The effect this room has on perception is startling when people are in the room (see fig. 3.23).

Individual and Cultural Influences on Perception

Up to this point, we have been discussing factors in perception that are common to all individuals. As mentioned earlier, however, there are a number of factors that are unique to specific individuals or groups and thus give an individualized flavor to the process of perception.

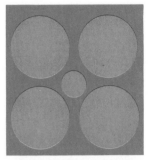

Figure 3.22 Context influences our perception of the size of the middle circle.

Figure 3.23 The Ames Room, which was constructed to illustrate how the monocular cues used in depth perception can be used to create illusions.

OF SPECIAL INTEREST

Perceiving Depth: The Case of Xavier X

In 1978 Xavier X. was just starting a tour of duty with the U.S. Navy in Antarctica. Now a professor of psychology, Xavier recalls an incident that tells us something about the way our sense of vision provides information about distance.

One summer day when it was about 25 degrees below zero, a group of Navy buddies decided to hike to the foot of a nearby mountain that looked to them to be about a mile away. Setting out in warm clothing, but without food or survival gear, they expected to return to the base in about an hour. But after walking for at least 2 miles, the mountain still seemed about a mile away! When one member of the party looked at a map, he discovered to everyone's surprise that the mountain was over 10 miles distant. Fortunately, the group discovered that they could no longer "believe their own eyes" before it was too late to return safely to camp.

What is it about Antarctic landscape that so dramatically fooled eight trained men? What cues misled their eyes and brains? As you have just read in the text, the eye and brain construct three-dimensional perceptions of depth out of two-dimensional cues. Many of the normal depth cues were not present for Xavier and his friends in this circumstance, so they were unable to judge accurately the distance to the mountain. The dry, clear air of the Antarctic does not give distant objects a hazy appearance, so there was little aerial perspective. The uniform whiteness of the snow that covered everything also reduced cues available from texture gradients. Because the landscape did not include any parallel straight lines, and because the sailors did not know how big the mountain was, there was no linear perspective. And finally, there were no moving objects available to provide cues from speed of movement. The lack of all these cues led to a nearly fatal misperception of distances.

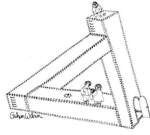

"Let's have another look at the blueprint."

Reproduced by special permission of Playboy *Magazine. Copyright © 1974 by* Playboy.

A number of characteristics of the person doing the perceiving can influence the process of perception. Psychologist Jerome Bruner (Bruner & Goodman, 1947), for example, has demonstrated that poor children estimate the size of coins to be larger than do children from higher-income families. Similarly, hungry people, as opposed to people who have just eaten, are more likely to perceive ambiguous pictures as being food (McClelland & Atkinson, 1948). Similarly, women are perceived as more attractive by sexually aroused men than unaroused men (Stephan, Berscheid, & Walster, 1971). And new Cadillacs look bigger than 1968 Chevrolets even though they are the same size.

Cultural factors may even influence more basic aspects of the perceptual process. A major study conducted by a group of Northwestern University psychologists directly addresses this issue (Segall, Campbell, & Herskovits, 1963). Some 1,800 people from numerous industrialized and nonindustrialized cultures were asked to make perceptual judgments about difficult stimuli such as the "Müller–Lyer" lines in figure 3.21 and the "horizontal-vertical" drawing shown in figure 3.24. If inborn organization factors were the only determinants of visual perception, we would expect no difference among the cultures in the frequency of inaccurate judgments. If, on the other hand, the different learning experiences of people growing up in these very different cultures can influence perception, differences could be expected to show up in these judgments.

The results did reveal some differences between cultures, suggesting that learning does play some role in the development of perceptual abilities. For example, the Zulu people of southern Africa were tested in this study. In their native environment, Zulus see few angles and corners like the ones we see on rectangular buildings. Perhaps as a result, the Zulus were less susceptible to the Müller–Lyer and the horizontal-vertical illusions. That is, they were less likely to see lines such as those in figures 3.21 and 3.24 as being of different lengths. Impressively, however, Zulus who were living in a large African city with rectangular buildings were susceptible to these illusions. This suggests that the difference in perception was not inborn, but depended upon differences in experience.

Similarly, pygmies who live in the dense rain forests of the African Congo rarely see objects at long distances. In their world thick vegetation blocks the sight of distant objects. It is interesting, then, that if they travel to the African plains, distant buffalo are at first seen as tiny "insects" (Turnbull, 1962). Their lack of perceptual constancy for the size of objects appears to be based on their lack of experience with distant objects.

Such evidence certainly suggests that individual and cultural factors are important in perception. Not all of the evidence is consistent with this conclusion, however. We will have to wait for future research to resolve fully this issue.

Figure 3.24 The horizontal figure often produces an illusory judgment of length. Which line is longer, the horizontal or the vertical line? Actually, they are both the same length.

R E V I E W

Perception is the interpretation of meaningless sensations. It's an active process in which impressions are created that often go beyond the minimal information provided by the senses. Many of the ways in which we organize and interpret sensations are inborn and common to all humans. The Gestalt principles of perceptual organization, perceptual constancies, depth perception, and visual illusions provide examples of the active, creative nature of perception. Other factors that enter into the process of perception are more unique to the individual, such as motivational states and cultural learning experiences. These factors ensure that we will perceive the world in a way that is largely universal and common to all humans, but with some individuality.

S U M M A R Y

Chapter 3 recognizes that we live in a physical world that is sensed through our *sense organs* and processed (*perceived*) by our nervous systems.

I. External *stimuli* are received through specialized *sensory receptor cells.*
   A. *Selective attention* is the process of selecting the stimuli to which we will attend.
   B. Sense organs receive stimuli, *transduce* sensory energy into *neural impulses,* and send neural messages to the brain for interpretation.
   C. Psychophysics is the field of psychology that studies the relationships between physical stimuli and psychological sensations and perceptions.

II. Internal stimuli are also received by the sensory system.
   A. The *vestibular organ* provides information about body orientation, while the *kinesthetic sense* reports bodily position and movement.
   B. The various *skin senses* can detect pressure, temperature, and pain.

III. *Chemical senses* respond to chemicals rather than to energy in the environment.
   A. In the sense of *taste,* chemicals produce the qualities of sweet, sour, bitter, and salty.
   B. In the sense of *smell,* chemicals produce odors.

IV. The sense of *hearing* detects sound waves.
   A. The *frequency* of sound waves determines pitch, while the *intensity* determines loudness.
   B. The ear is the primary sense organ for hearing.
      1. The *outer ear* functions as a sound wave collector.
      2. Sound waves vibrate the eardrum, which is connected to a series of three movable bones (*hammer, anvil, stirrup*) in the *middle ear.*
      3. The *inner ear,* containing the *cochlea* and the *organ of Corti,* transduces the sound wave energy into neural impulses for transportation to the brain.

V. The sense of *sight* detects light energy.
   A. The intensity of light waves largely determines brightness, while the wavelength (frequency) largely determines color.
   B. The eye, working much like a camera, is the primary sense organ for seeing.
      1. Light enters the eye through the *cornea* (with the *iris* regulating the size of the *pupil*) and the *lens* into the *retina.*
      2. *Rods* and *cones* then transduce light waves into neural impulses for transportation to the brain.
      3. The 100 million rods are located throughout the retina except for the fovea and are active in peripheral vision and vision in dim light, but do not play a role in color vision.
      4. The 6 million cones clustered mostly near the fovea code information for color.
      5. Both *trichromatic theory* and *opponent-process theory* can be helpful in understanding color vision.

VI. Sensory neural impulses, when transmitted to the brain, are interpreted in a process called perception; examining visual perception demonstrates the general nature of the process.
   A. Perception is an active mental process. Gestalt principles explain many of the ways in which humans tend to organize sensory information.
   B. Individual factors, such as motivation and previous learning, also affect our perceptions.

Suggested Readings

1. For an in-depth look at sensation and perception:
   McBurney, D. H., & Collings, V. B. (1984). *Introduction to Sensation-Perception,* Second Edition. New York: Prentice-Hall.

2. A closer examination of the sensation of pain and its psychological control is provided in:
   Sternbach, R. A. (Ed.). (1978). *The psychology of pain.* New York: Raven Press.

3. A readable but sophisticated examination of perception and illusions is supplied by:
   Held, R., & Richards, W. (Eds.). (1972). *Perception: Mechanisms and models.* San Francisco: W. H. Freeman.

4. For a scientific view of extrasensory perception (ESP):
   Hansel, C. E. M. (1966). *ESP: A scientific evaluation.* New York: Charles Scribner.

FOUR

States of Consciousness

O U T L I N E

K E Y   T E R M S

How often do you dream? A couple of times per month? Several times per week? Every night? Even if you said every night, you are probably greatly underestimating the frequency of your dreams. We spend a great deal more time in the strange world of dreams than most of us realize. I dream about five times per night. Does that seem like an unusually high frequency? It's not at all. The average person dreams four to six times each night but rarely remembers more than a fraction of those dreams. If we only remember a few of our dreams, how do psychologists know that the frequency of dreams is so high? Let's go back to the early days of sleep research and witness the accidental discovery that led to our modern understanding of dreams.

The year was 1952. Dr. Nathaniel Kleitman of the University of Chicago had given his graduate student Eugene Aserinsky instructions to spend another sleepless night watching a subject sleep in his laboratory. Kleitman was interested in the slow, rolling eye movements that occur during the first moments of sleep and was curious to see if they occurred during later sleep. His subject was connected to a complicated network of wires that led from instruments monitoring many aspects of the body's functioning (such as brain waves, heartbeat, breathing) and a special instrument to measure eye movements.

As Aserinsky dutifully watched the instruments, he was startled to see an unexpected pattern of eye movements. Half a dozen times during the night, the subject's eyes darted back and forth rapidly and irregularly. At first Aserinsky thought his instruments were not working properly, but he could easily see the eye movements beneath the closed eyelids of the subject. When Aserinsky looked again at his instruments, he saw an even more startling fact: The brain waves of the subject looked more like he was awake than asleep. Each time the rapid eye movements returned, the same brain pattern resembling wakefulness returned.

When Aserinsky showed Kleitman the unexpected findings, the conclusion was almost inescapable—the subject must be dreaming. During the next several years, a number of studies were carried out in which the sleeping subjects were awakened whenever they entered this peculiar stage of sleep characterized by rapid eye movements. By 1957, they had awakened subjects 191 times during this stage, and 80 percent had said that they were dreaming at the time. In contrast, sleeping subjects had been awakened 160 times during other stages of sleep and had recalled dreams only 7 percent of the time. Aserinsky and Kleitman had discovered a simple and objective way to determine when a subject was dreaming. Through their efforts, a scientific door had been opened on the partially hidden world of consciousness that we call dreams.

P R E V I E W

Consciousness is a state of awareness—awareness of the outside world, of our own thoughts and feelings, and sometimes even of our own consciousness. But consciousness is not a single state; rather, there are many different states of conscious awareness. Even being awake during the course of a typical day is composed of a variety of states of consciousness: focused consciousness, loosely drifting consciousness, and daydreams.

When the waking day ends, moreover, we do not cease to be aware, rather we experience other kinds of consciousness. As we drift off to sleep, we pass through a dreamlike "twilight" phase, and even amidst the shifting stages of sleep itself, we experience the strange reality of dreams. Although we are able to recall only a small proportion of our dreams, we dream a surprising four to six times per night on the average. Apparently, these dreams are important to our well-being; it's known that sleep does not rest and restore us for the next day if we do not dream sufficiently. But we still have not developed a widely accepted method of interpreting the meaning of dreams.

Other states of consciousness are experienced much less often. Some altered conscious awareness occurs spontaneously, such as hallucinations and other distorted perceptual experiences. Other altered states of consciousness are achieved in part through deep concentration and relaxation, such as during meditation and hypnosis. Still other altered states are induced by taking certain kinds of drugs.

Wide Awake: Normal Waking Consciousness

What does it mean to be conscious? Clearly, it has something to do with awareness. When conscious, we are aware of the sights and sounds of the outside world, of our feelings, our thoughts, and sometimes even of our own consciousness. When unconscious, we are not aware of any of these things. **Consciousness,** simply defined, is *a state of awareness.*

consciousness
(kon'shus-nes)
A state of awareness.

Yet, there is more than one kind of conscious state; it comes in more than the wide-awake-and-thinking variety. The qualities of conscious awareness that we experience when daydreaming, when hypnotized, when high on drugs, or when dreaming are so different from one another that we clearly need to think of consciousness as being many different states of awareness. To understand consciousness fully, we need to explore its many varieties and the conditions under which they occur. In this chapter we speak of dreams, trances, highs, and the like, both to understand the nature of these states and to help us better understand being awake.

We spend our lives passing from one state of consciousness to another. We read a book, we daydream, we drift off to sleep, we dream, and so on. Each of these states of conscious awareness is so different from the next that the very sense of reality they impart differs. What is logical and possible in a dream may seem absurd when considered the next day. We seldom wonder which state contains the ultimate reality, however. We assume without questioning that the waking state in which we spend most of our lives is the "real" consciousness. It's the standard by which we judge other states and find them to be "distorted" or "unreal."

Waking consciousness is so much a part of us, in fact, that it's difficult to step back and look at it objectively. When we do, we see that it is not a single state of consciousness; instead it includes at least three varieties: directed consciousness, flowing consciousness, and daydreaming.

Directed Consciousness

Sometimes our conscious awareness is directed toward a single focus. When we are reading a book, our awareness is mostly absorbed by the words and phrases on the page. During such an experience, our conscious awareness is focused, ordered, and one-tracked. The same is true during any intellectual activity that absorbs awareness, such as during intense emotions or intense sensations. This state is known as **directed consciousness.**

directed consciousness
Focused and orderly awareness.

The next time you drink a cola, notice how easy it is to focus directed awareness to intensify the experience. Pay close attention to how wet the cola feels, how cold it is in your mouth. Feel the tingle of the bubbles, and the cold pieces of ice against your lips. Taste the sweet flavor and try to imagine which taste receptors the flavor is stimulating. You will taste that cola like you never tasted one before—you will be aware of it in an intense, absorbing way. Try to focus your consciousness in the same way the next time you stop to look at a flower, kiss someone you care about, or shake your father's hand. You may even find that you can direct your awareness in the same intense way the next time you study for a test!

Flowing Consciousness

Most of our waking days are spent in a kind of consciousness that is less directed and single-purposed. In **flowing consciousness,** our awareness drifts from one thought to another, from an emotion to an irritating itch, and back to a reminiscence. The changing pattern of this kind of consciousness was compared to the flow of water in a stream by founding American psychologist William James (1890). He used this analogy to convey to students of psychology the idea that conscious experience is a process of changes following changes that flow so smoothly from one to another that there is never a gap in between. Stop yourself sometime in the midst of your flowing consciousness, and try to remember what you were aware of during the previous two minutes. You may be surprised by the flowing, swirling mixture of consciousness that you experienced. In one experiment, university students were asked to "think aloud"—describe the contents of their conscious awareness—when they were not performing any other task. Note the "flowing" nature of awareness in the following excerpt:

flowing consciousness
Drifting, unfocused awareness.

> The thud in my head matches people walking, the sound of people walking across the floor. There's a piece of floor that looks like a fish. Paula has some fish. No, I wonder if she's going to take them home. My mother seems to get lonely. The tape doesn't stick too

"I'm sorry, dear, I must have lost consciousness.
What were you saying?"

well. I hate looking at people. I keep listening to the sound upstairs. Somebody said "hail!" She ought to go to a class this morning. (Name)'s probably given me her cough. She should have gone to the doctor. I had a dream that I had a two-room double. I might have swore that I have one now. I'll probably have a good time next year. (Name) and I get along very well. The room feels like it's shaking. People don't seem to give this girl a rest. It sorta kind of sounds like someone's swinging on a swing. Jungle Jim. I remember the time I fell off the swing at home. It was the time I broke my ankle. I had a pain behind my left eye. It feels like I have something in it. (Pope & Singer, 1980, p. 173)

Daydreams

Many of the features of directed consciousness and dreams are combined in the state of waking consciousness called **daydreams.** They are a period of focused, directed thinking and feeling, yet they are fantasies that are not bound by what is logical or likely to happen. Daydreams are not a sometime thing; most of us daydream many times each day. Why do we spend time in these dreamlike reveries instead of focusing all of our awareness productively on the concerns of the day?

Sigmund Freud, the Austrian founder of psychoanalysis, believed that daydreams reduce the tension left by our unfulfilled needs and wishes. What we cannot do in reality, we accomplish in the fantasy world of daydreams. While daydreaming, we win the race, see our lost love return, and build a rustic home in the country with our own hands.

Was Freud right? Are daydreams a way of reducing the tension of unmet needs and unfulfilled wishes? To answer this question, researchers have asked college students to jot down a summary of each of their daydreams for several days (Pope & Singer, 1978). As predicted by Freud, many daydreams involve the fulfilling of a wish. Also consistent with Freud's theory is the fact that most people feel quite relaxed during this type of daydreaming. Contrary to Freud's predictions, however, many daydreams are filled with regret, sorrow, and guilt. Other daydreams are highly sexual, such as those focusing on that gorgeous person you would love to know better. These daydreams *create* rather than release tension, casting doubt on Freud's theory of daydreaming. Instead of reducing tension, daydreams may be merely a slightly distorted reflection of our current concerns and emotions (Pope & Singer, 1978). (See *Of Special Interest:* "The Concept of the Unconscious Mind.")

When do we do all of this daydreaming? You will not be surprised to learn that a series of studies has shown that we are most likely to daydream when we are in boring or routine situations and when we are sitting or lying down instead of moving about (Pope & Singer, 1980). Daydreams are turned on when our active behavior and directed awareness are turned off. To repeat yet another observation made by William James (1890), when we are awake, something is always going on in consciousness—there are no gaps. If it's not productive behavior or thinking, it's flowing awareness or daydreaming.

daydreams
Relatively focused thinking about fantasies.

R E V I E W

Consciousness is composed of many different states of awareness. Even normal waking consciousness can be divided into three different states. During each day, we shift many times among focused consciousness, directed consciousness, a less organized flowing consciousness, and daydreaming. Each is real, but each carries with it a somewhat different sense of conscious reality.

OF SPECIAL INTEREST

The Concept of the Unconscious Mind

In discussing conscious experience, it's important to compare the term *conscious* with the term *unconscious.* Most people beginning to study psychology expect that they will be studying about the "unconscious mind." It may surprise you to know, then, that until recently the term was not even mentioned in most modern introductory psychology textbooks. Psychology is taught in most American colleges and universities from a scientific viewpoint. The term *unconscious,* in contrast, is used primarily by psychologists who take a more philosophical approach to the understanding of people and their problems. But it's wrong to dismiss the unconscious simply as "unscientific" and not discuss it at all. Today, most scientists agree that it's time to apply scientific thinking to the study of the unconscious (e.g., Hilgard, 1980).

Freud and others used the concept of the unconscious mind to explain things about human behavior for which they had no other satisfactory explanation. Why, for example, would a man compulsively touch his hand to his genitals several times each minute? (Such problems are uncommon, but they do exist.) If you were to ask this man why he did it, he would tell you that he not only did not know why, but that he would very much like to stop doing it. That is to say, the man would tell you that he had *no* conscious reason for the behavior. Freud believed that the mind had a reason for everything that it did, so that if the man had no conscious reason for touching his genitals, then he must have an *un*conscious reason. Freud might have suggested that the man had an unconscious fear of being castrated by his father (because of the man's lustful thoughts, also unconscious, for his mother), so he was checking his genitals periodically just to be sure they were still there.

Although this may seem like a silly explanation to you, the inference is not completely illogical. The real problem with explanations that refer to the unconscious mind is that they are hard to prove or disprove. Recently, however, a number of psychologists have begun trying to study unconscious mental processes (if indeed it is meaningful to talk of such things) in very rigorous ways. Although their steps are quite small and may even seem dull compared to the way Freud talked of the unconscious, they seem to be steps in the right direction. For example, researchers are now studying the role of unconscious processes in selective attention. When a person is listening to two voices at the same time (such as at a party), but is paying attention to one only, what happens to the other voice? There is evidence that it reaches the brain, but the person is never consciously aware of it. In that sense, the voice is processed unconsciously by the brain. If that is true, it may be that other important unconscious processes exist and in time can be scientifically demonstrated.

Sleep is not a single, continuous state. Most researchers distinguish between several levels of sleep that we all experience.

Sleeping and Dreaming: Conscious While Asleep

Most nights, we slip gently from wakefulness into sleep, only to return from our mental vacation the next morning. Is this all there is to sleeping? Is it a mere gap in awareness that consumes one-third of our lives? Sleep is not a single state; instead, it's a complex combination of states, some of which involve conscious awareness. We do not leave consciousness for the entire night when we sleep; rather we enter worlds of awareness with very different properties from the wide-awake world's.

Stages of Sleep

Actually, several states of conscious awareness are a part of the sleep process. As we fall asleep, we pass from waking consciousness into a semiwakeful state, into four stages of progressively deeper sleep (all of which contain little or no conscious awareness), then into dream sleep, which brings a kind of conscious awareness with a reality all its own. We need to look carefully at each of these steps in the sleep cycle.

Hypnogogic State

We do not go from wakefulness to sleep in one step. Generally, we daydream for a while, then gradually pass into a "twilight" state that is neither daydreaming nor dreaming. This is the **hypnogogic state.** We begin to lose voluntary control over our body movements; our sensitivity to outside stimuli diminishes; and our thoughts become more fanciful, less bound by reality. For most people, it's a highly relaxed, enjoyable state. On some occasions, however, we are rudely snapped out of the peaceful hypnogogic state; we suddenly feel like we are falling and our body experiences a sudden jerk called a **myoclonia.**

hypnogogic state
(hip″nah-goj′ik)
A relaxed state of dreamlike awareness between wakefulness and sleep.

myoclonia
(mi″o-klo′ne-ah)
An abrupt movement that sometimes occurs during the hypnogogic state in which the sleeper often experiences a sense of falling.

electroencephalogram (EEG)
(e-lek"tro-en-sef'ah-lo-
gram)
Measures of electrical brain
activity recorded on an
electroencephalograph.

Stages of Light and Deep Sleep

After making the transition from the hypnogogic state to sleep, we pass through four stages of progressively deeper sleep. Most sleep researchers distinguish between four different levels of sleep defined on the basis of **electroencephalogram (EEG)** measures of electrical brain activity (Webb, 1968). There is clearly a range of light to deep sleep that we pass through, but the depth of sleep alternates upward and downward many times during the night. Indeed, young adults show an average of 34 shifts in the depth of sleep during the first six hours (Webb, 1968). Sleep, then, is not a single, continuous state; it is an almost constantly changing one (see fig. 4.1).

Dream Sleep

dream sleep
A stage of sleep that
typically occurs four to six
times each night during
which the individual
experiences dreams.

Many times per night, however, the sleeper passes into an even more interesting stage of sleep called **dream sleep.** As previously mentioned, not only do most of us dream nearly every night, but we generally dream more than once each night. This may not fit with the way you see your pattern of dreaming; you may feel that you dream far less often than that. This is because unless we awaken for some reason during or shortly after a dream, we are usually unable to remember that we were dreaming at all. Dreams are very quickly forgotten if we pass back to a period of nondream sleep. Studies of dreaming conducted during the past 20 years show that the average college student spends about two hours per night dreaming, divided into about four to six dreams per night. The length of these dreams varies, but the longest dream—generally about an hour in duration—usually occurs during the last part of the sleep cycle (Webb, 1982).

The fact that dreams are quickly forgotten unless the dreamer awakens soon after the dream has long made the scientific study of dreams unfeasible; we cannot wake up sleeping subjects every five minutes to see if they are dreaming. The era of the scientific study of this elusive state of consciousness was ushered in, however, by Aserinsky and Kleitman's surprising discovery of the relationship between dreaming and movements of the eyeball (see *Prologue*). Their discovery that dreams were accompanied by eye movements and brain-wave activity suggesting the presence of conscious awareness provided a convenient way for scientists to know when dreams were occurring and study them. Because of the characteristic eye movement during dreaming, dream sleep is often referred to as *rapid eye movement sleep* or **REM sleep.**

REM sleep
Rapid-eye-movement sleep,
characterized by movement
of the eyes under the lids;
often accompanies dreams.

After three decades of study, it's now known that the eyeballs are not the only parts of the body that are busy during dreams. Sleep researcher Wilse Webb (1968) has likened dream sleep to an *"autonomic storm."* The autonomic nervous system (see chapter 2) is very active during dreams, causing noticeable changes in many parts of the body: Blood flow to the brain increases; heartbeat becomes irregular; the muscles of the face and fingers twitch involuntarily; breathing becomes irregular; and there is erection of the male penis and the female clitoris. Anyone who has watched a sleeping beagle begin to twitch in the face, make miniature running movements, and rasp muffled barks at dream rabbits knows about these autonomic storms and knows that REM sleep is not limited to humans. Interestingly, voluntary control of the large body muscles is lost during REM sleep, serving perhaps to keep us from acting out our dreams.

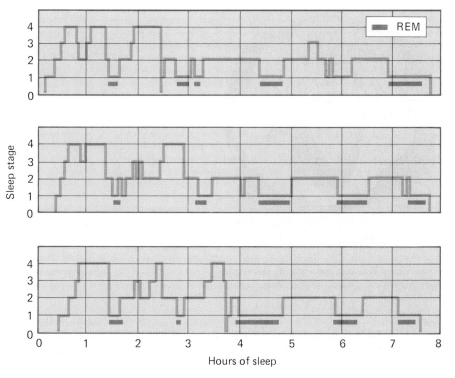

Figure 4.1 Each night we pass through a complicated and irregular pattern of shifts from one stage of sleep to another. The three patterns exhibited by one subject during three nights of sleep are shown here (Meyer, 1979).

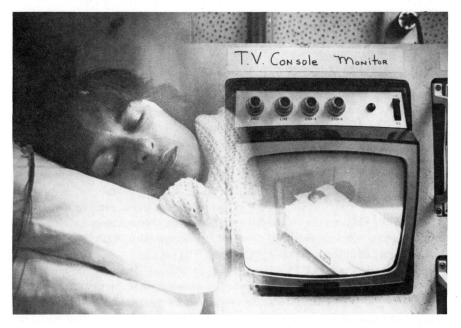

Studies show that the average college student has four to six dreams per night that last a total of two hours.

"Greetings. You are now entering the Rapid
Eye Movement phase of your sleep cycle."

Dreams may also occur during other parts of the sleep cycle. Although it's uncommon, dreams are sometimes recalled when people are awakened during non-REM sleep. It's not clear, however, whether the people are reporting dreams that actually occurred during the non-REM period, or whether they are just occasionally remembering a dream from the last period of REM sleep. It's interesting, however, that dreams recalled when awakened during non-REM sleep are briefer, less fragmented, less vivid, and less emotional than REM sleep dreams (Foulkes & Schmidt, 1983; Monroe, Rechtschaffen, Foulkes, & Jensen, 1965).

The Content and Meaning of Dreams

Dreams are one of the most fascinating aspects of human consciousness. Since at least the time of the Egyptian pharaohs, people have attempted to decipher their meaning. What do dreams tell us about ourselves? The answer to that question depends greatly on who you listen to. Different psychologists take very different views of dreams, ranging from the opinion that they tell us virtually nothing, to the belief that they provide a rich source of information about hidden aspects of our personalities that cannot be gotten easily in other ways.

To followers of Sigmund Freud, dreams are the *"royal road to the unconscious."* They allow us to travel deep into the unconscious mind and view hidden conflicts and motives cloaked only by the symbols of dreams. There are two levels of the content of dreams, according to Freud. The events that happen in a dream are their **manifest content.** This level held little interest for Freud; he felt that it was necessary to get beyond the surface and find out what the manifest content of the dream *symbolized* to discover its true meaning, or **latent content.** For example, the manifest content of a young woman's dream might involve riding on a train and becoming frightened as it enters a tunnel. On the surface the dream was about trains and tunnels. But what does the manifest content of the dream symbolize? Freud might see the train as symbolizing a penis (a *phallic symbol* in Freud's terms) and the tunnel as symbolizing a vagina. Hence, the hidden or latent content of the dream might concern the young woman's conflicts about having sex with a male friend.

manifest content
According to Freud, the obvious, but superficial, meaning of dreams.

latent content
According to Freud, the true meaning of dreams that is found in the symbols of their manifest content.

Such interpretations are provocative and fascinating. But can we be sure they are accurate? After years of trying, psychologists have found no way to determine if such symbolic interpretations are right or wrong. Since symbols can be interpreted in an infinite number of ways, we can never be sure we are correct. Perhaps as a result, most Freudian psychologists have placed less emphasis on dream interpretation in recent years.

If clinical experience with the interpretation of dreams does not give us any sure answers about their meaning, what does research tell us? The most extensive study of dreams was conducted by Calvin Hall (1951). He analyzed the content of thousands of dreams to give us a composite picture of their content. As it turns out, most dreams are rather commonplace; they take place in familiar surroundings and involve ordinary rather than strange activities, such as walking, talking, and thinking. Most dreams do not involve familiar people, however. The dreamer appears in only about 15 percent of his or her own dreams, while strangers— entirely imaginary people—make up 55 percent of the characters. The rest are friends, family members, and acquaintances.

The emotional content of dreams is mostly negative, but only a small proportion of dreams are negative enough to be considered "nightmares." About 70 percent of dreams concern worries and hostility. The content of recurrent dreams, paticularly, seems to be negative. In a survey of over a thousand readers of *Psychology Today,* the most frequently reported recurrent dreams were of being chased or falling. Flying, appearing naked or scantily clothed in public, and taking exams when unprepared were also common themes (Stark, 1984). The particular content of dreams usually cannot be traced to any obvious cause, but it often reflects ongoing concerns of the dreamer. For example, a person who has gone a long period of time without sexual activity might dream of sex. Such dreams, some of which lead to orgasm ("wet dreams"), are quite common among adolescents and young adults who do not have a steady sexual partner. Or a dream may simply reflect unimportant events of the day (seeing a new kind of tennis racket), or may incorporate events that are currently happening (such as your telephone ringing during the night).

This research does suggest that dreams may tell us something about what is going on in a person's life, but they may or may not reflect important issues. If a woman dreams about the same man three nights in a row, it *may* mean that she has strong feelings for him, or it may simply reflect that she has seen him three days in a row. The three dreams may mean nothing at all about her feelings toward the man, and if they do, they may reveal any of a number of very different feelings about him (affection, amusement, disgust). Interpreting dreams, in other words, may mislead us more often than they aid us.

Going without Sleep

Obviously, people need to sleep, but what happens when we do not sleep? What effects does lack of sleep have on us? First of all, if we miss sleep we apparently create a "sleep debt" that needs to be made up. College students at the University of Florida who participated in a sleep experiment were limited to two hours sleep for one night. They suffered no ill effects the next day, but the next night they fell asleep more quickly and slept longer than usual (Webb & Bonnet, 1979).

Longer periods of sleep deprivation have some unpleasant psychological effects, but people are remarkably able to do without a lot of sleep. When the length of sleep was *gradually* reduced in a group of volunteers from eight to four

RESEARCH REPORT

Insomnia: A Simple Solution

Sleep is essential in maintaining health and the quality of normal waking consciousness. Disorders of the sleep process are quite common, however. These can turn the gentle healer of sleep into something of an opponent.

The most common sleep disorder is **insomnia,** or the inability to sleep a normal length of time. There are actually two types of insomnia: *sleep-onset insomnia* in which a person has difficulty falling asleep and *early-waking insomnia* in which a person cannot stay asleep for a normal sleep period. Both types of insomnia are experienced by nearly everyone at one time or another and are, in that sense, quite normal. These brief episodes of insomnia are most common during periods of high stress. Some individuals experience long periods of nearly chronic insomnia, however.

A simple, effective method of treating sleep-onset insomnia has been developed and tested by Richard Bootzin of Northwestern University (1973). The idea is to make being in bed at night a stimulus for only one thing, falling asleep. The person, who must give up daytime naps to ensure sleepiness at night, follows a five-step procedure:

1. You go to bed only when sleepy.

2. You must *not* eat, study, watch television, or read in bed. Until the insomnia is solved, the bed is to be used only for sleeping.

3. If you do not fall asleep in 10 minutes, get out of bed and leave the bedroom. Do other things until you feel sleepy, then go back to bed.

4. Repeat step 3 until you fall asleep rapidly.

5. Get up everyday at the same time regardless of how much sleep you got the night before to establish a regular sleep-wake cycle.

Over 60 percent of the people who followed Bootzin's plan for four weeks were able to get their sleep onset time down below 20 minutes, which is within the normal range.

---

insomnia (in-som'ne-ah) Chronic inability to fall asleep in a reasonable amount of time or to stay asleep.

---

hours per night for a period of two months, there were no detectable effects in one experiment (Webb & Bonnet, 1979). When we *abruptly* reduce the amount of nightly sleep, or reduce it to less than four hours, however, we become irritable, fatigued, intellectually inefficient, and feel an intense need for sleep. (See *Research Report:* "Insomnia" for a look at losing sleep because we cannot fall asleep, and a simple psychological solution for this problem.)

The most dramatic experiments in sleep deprivation are ones in which volunteers are continuously deprived of sleep for long periods of time. People have gone without sleep for as long as 265 hours without lasting psychological damage. In a few widely publicized cases, long-term sleep deprivation has led to temporary disorientation and hallucinations. This is quite rare, however. In most cases, prolonged sleep deprivation simply produces the same effects as shorter deprivation—fatigue, intellectual inefficiency, irritability, and the need for sleep.

Why do we need to sleep? When we do not get enough, what did we miss? From a psychological viewpoint, it's interesting that dreams may be the key element. In a number of experiments, sleeping subjects were awakened whenever they entered REM sleep. They were otherwise allowed to get a normal amount of sleep each night. Depriving subjects of approximately two hours of dream sleep per night had the same effects as much longer deprivations of sleep in general. The subjects were irritable, inefficient, and fatigued. On subsequent nights, they showed an increase in the amount of REM sleep, suggesting that they had a need to catch up on their dreaming. Other studies have also shown that deprivation of the deepest part of nondream sleep has much the same effects (Webb & Bonnet, 1979).

The importance of dreaming has been shown in another way in sleep research. When volunteers are able to get by on greatly reduced amounts of sleep, it's apparently because they pack their two hours of dream sleep tightly into their shortened sleeping time. The amount of nondream sleep that occurs between dreams is greatly reduced when total sleep time is cut, but the amount of dream sleep stays fairly constant. Only when the total amount of sleep time is reduced abruptly do we feel the effects of lack of sleep. The sleeper in this case does not have time to adopt a more packed dream schedule or the sleep time is reduced so much that there is not time for adequate dreaming.

As of yet, we have no solid explanation of why dreams are so important, but they appear to be essential in restoring us for the next day. Clearly, dreams are a larger and more important part of our conscious lives than most of us realized prior to Eugene Aserinsky's fortunate discovery.

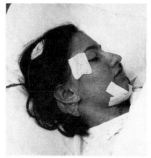

Apparently we need to dream. Individuals deprived of REM sleep become irritable, inefficient, and fatigued; and when given the chance to sleep, they increase their amount of REM sleep in order to catch up on their dreaming.

Nightmares and Other Sleep Phenomena

We have all had the terrifying kind of dreams known as **nightmares.** These are dreams that occur during REM sleep whose content is exceptionally frightening, saddening, provoking, or in some other way uncomfortable. They are upsetting enough to wake us up during the dream, so we can vividly remember our nightmares, even though they account for only a small proportion of the dreams that we have.

Night terrors are a less common, but perhaps even more upsetting nocturnal experience. The individual awakens suddenly in a state of panic, sometimes screaming, usually with no clear recollection of an accompanying dream. A sense of calm usually returns within a few minutes, but these are terrifying experiences. Unlike nightmares, they do not occur during REM sleep, but occur during the deepest phases of non-REM sleep. Night terrors are most common in preschool-age children, but sometimes occur in adults.

Sleepwalking is another interesting phenomenon that occurs primarily during the deepest parts of non-REM sleep. Sleepwalkers rise from the bed and carry on complicated activities, such as walking from one room to another, even

nightmare
A dream that occurs during REM sleep whose content is exceptionally frightening, sad, angry, or in some other way uncomfortable.

night terror
An upsetting nocturnal experience that occurs most often in preschool-age children during deep non-REM sleep.

sleepwalking
Walking and carrying on complicated activities during the deepest part of non-REM sleep.

though they are sound asleep. Sleepwalking is most common in children before the age of puberty, but is not particularly unusual in adults. Sleepwalking usually reappears in adults only during periods of stress, but except for the danger of accidents while wandering around in the dark, it's not an abnormal behavior.

sleeptalking
Talking during any phase of the sleep cycle.

Sleeptalking is a fairly common phenomenon that can occur during any phase of the sleep cycle. In this, the soundly sleeping person says words, sometimes making fairly coherent statements for a brief period of time. It's most common in young adults, but occurs at all ages.

R E V I E W

Each night, we depart the world of waking consciousness and enter another world that we will scarcely remember the next morning. Alternating among stages of sleep that contain little or no conscious experience, we live a distorted life of dreams. These dreams consist of a flurry of activity in the body, but when studied systematically, they are found to be less bizarre in content than we would expect. Still, the meaning of dreams has long fascinated us and played a major role in Freud's attempts to understand the hidden workings of the mind. A reliable way to interpret dreams still eludes us, however.

Altered States of Consciousness

We have talked about states of consciousness that we are all familiar with to this point. We all know what it feels like to think about a problem, to dream, to let our minds wander. Next we turn to more unusual and less familiar realms of conscious experience, the so-called altered states of consciousness. We begin by looking at some general characteristics of altered states of consciousness.

There are many kinds of altered states of consciousness that differ from one another in important ways. Yet, these states—whether they occur during meditation, when taking drugs, during an unusually intense sexual orgasm, or during a moment of religious conversion—have been described as having a number of important characteristics in common (Deikman, 1980; Pahnke, 1980; Tart, 1975):

1. *Distortions of perception.* In altered states of consciousness, distortions often occur in what is seen, heard, and felt. Time passes differently, and the body may seem to be distorted—indeed, the body may even seem to have been left behind and observed from the outside.

2. *Intense positive emotions.* People who have experienced altered states of consciousness frequently describe them as being joyful, ecstatic, loving, and tranquil.

3. *Sense of unity.* Individuals often experience a sense of being unified with nature, blended with the universe, or "one" with a spiritual force.

4. *Illogical.* Many of the experiences and "revelations" of the altered states of consciousness do not make sense by the standards of everyday logic. For example, the experience that "I exist as a separate person, yet I am one with the universe" is typical of altered states.

5. *Indescribable.* Individuals who have experienced altered states of consciousness usually feel that words cannot adequately express the nature of their experience. Our languages may not have words for many of the qualities of the experience, but the difficulty may come from trying to describe illogical experiences in language.

6. *Transcendent.* The altered states are experienced as transcending—going beyond—what is normally experienced. In particular, the individual may experience a new perspective that goes beyond ordinary conceptions of space and time limitations.

7. *Self-evident reality.* New revelations and insights are experienced that concern "ultimate reality" and are felt to be "real" in a way that requires no proof. The insight is intuitively and immediately understood as the truth; it requires no explanation or justification.

Given these qualities—particularly the euphoric emotionality of experiencing self-evident revelations—it may be wise to state the obvious here. Our evaluation of the insights obtained through altered states of consciousness clearly depends on the perspective that we take. From the standpoint of a logical science, it can only be stated that altered states of consciousness are *different* from everyday waking consciousness—no claims can be made that one "reality" is more "real" than another. From the perspective of those who have experienced the "self-evident reality" of altered states, however, our everyday reality is often seen as false. Who is right? It depends on which perspective you believe is correct (which is a question for philosophy, not science).

Meditation

While most of us think of waking consciousness as the normal state, others seek a different, more "perfect" state. One method of searching for an alternative to waking consciousness is **meditation.** This was a popular exercise in the United States in the 1960s and 1970s and continues to be rather popular today. Its popularity in the Western world is dwarfed, however, by the fact that meditation is an important part of yoga, Zen Buddhism, and other religions for many tens of millions of Asians.

There are many varieties of meditation, some very difficult to master and others much simpler. In its simplest form, meditation involves assuming a relaxed sitting or lying position and breathing deeply, slowly, and rhythmically. Attention is directed only at the breathing movements of the diaphragm and all other thoughts and feelings are gently blocked from consciousness. While this feat is very difficult to accomplish at first, if you do not pressure yourself, it becomes easier with practice. In some forms of meditation, the individual also repeats a word or sound silently to himself or herself. Often these words have special religious meaning (**mantras**), but researchers have found that any pleasant word (such as *calm* or *one*) or sound has the same effect of further focusing attention away from thoughts and feelings (Benson, 1975).

Meditation, which has been practiced by Buddhists for many centuries, became popular in the United States during the 1970s.

meditation
(med″i-ta′shun)
Several methods of focusing concentration away from thoughts and feelings and generating a sense of relaxation.

mantra (man′trah)
A word or sound containing religious meaning used during meditation.

RESEARCH REPORT

Are There Unique Physiological Benefits of Meditation?

Meditation is a practice through which some individuals achieve distinct altered states of consciousness and many others simply obtain a sense of relaxation. Because of its ability to induce relaxation, a number of psychologists and physicians have suggested that the meditative state involves a reduction in sympathetic autonomic arousal (e.g., Wallace & Benson, 1972). Based on this theory, meditation has been prescribed for over a decade as a "natural remedy" for stress-related medical problems ranging from high blood pressure to insomnia. As a result, many thousands of individuals practice meditation in the belief that it counteracts the physiological effects of stress. Is this assumption correct? Does meditation beneficially dampen sympathetic autonomic arousal?

Although a few early studies appeared to support the assumption of reduced sympathetic arousal, more recent and better-controlled research does not. In a cogent review of research on this topic, psychologist David Holmes (1984) convincingly argues that teaching individuals to meditate does not lead to greater reductions in blood pressure, heart rate, oxygen consumption, general muscle tension, skin sweat, or any other measure of sympathetic arousal than produced by simple relaxation. Meditation does not appear to be a more effective treatment for stress-related problems than other forms of relaxation. The possibility remains that some very experienced meditators experience greater physiological benefits, but this possibility has not been unequivocally documented (Wallace & Benson, 1972). That is not to say that meditation is not beneficial, however. Any form of relaxation, including meditation, is a good antidote to stress.

Once mastered, the practice of meditation can produce what many describe as a desirable altered state of consciousness. If nothing else, meditation generally produces a relaxed state (Beiman, Majestic, Johnson, Puente, & Graham, 1976). Some experienced meditators also report achieving an altered state of consciousness—the so-called **transcendental state**—that is very different from normal consciousness.

Mesmerism: The Hypnotic Trance

Did you ever watch a stage hypnotist convince a subject that she is standing in a snowstorm without a coat and then see her shiver? Or have you seen a hypnotist tell a subject he is going back to his fourth birthday party and watched him act like he is playing with other four-year-olds instead of standing on a stage? People who have been hypnotized like this often tell us that they actually felt the cold wind and experienced the birthday party. What is it about this state of **hypnosis** that makes it so fascinatingly different from waking consciousness?

transcendental state
An altered state of consciousness, sometimes achieved during meditation, that transcends normal human experience.

hypnotism (hip'no-tizm)
An altered state of consciousness in which the individual is highly relaxed and susceptible to suggestions.

The Hypnotic Experience

The person becoming hypnotized focuses his or her attention firmly on the hypnotist's voice and then is talked and lulled into an altered state of consciousness. This stage differs from individual to individual, but typically has the following characteristics:

1. *Relaxation.* A sense of deep relaxation and peacefulness exists, often accompanied by changes in the way the body feels, such as floating, sinking, and shrinking.

2. *Hypnotic hallucinations.* When told to do so, the subject may see, feel, or hear things in distorted ways, or may even experience things that are not there, such as smelling a flower that does not exist.

3. *Hypnotic analgesia.* When told to do so, the subject may lose the sense of touch or pain in some region of the body.

4. *Hypnotic age regression.* The subject can sometimes be made to feel that he or she is passing back in time to an earlier stage of life, such as childhood. It's not known whether individuals undergoing age regression actually remember forgotten events, but the process often seems convincing to the subject.

5. *Hypnotic control.* The actions of the hypnotized individual sometimes seem as if they are out of the individual's control. When told that her arm can float, a hypnotized person's arm may seem to float up as if it were lifted by invisible balloons rather than her own muscles (Bowers, 1976).

What is the nature of this altered state of consciousness? To understand it best, we should look back briefly at the fascinating history of hypnosis. (See also *Of Special Interest:* "Stage Hypnotism.")

Mesmer and Mesmerism

Franz Anton Mesmer was a practicing physician in Paris in the late 1700s. Although he was trained in classical medicine, his medical practice was decidedly unusual—so unusual that he earlier had been driven from his native Austria by the medical establishment for alleged "quackery." He treated patients with medical or psychological problems in what he called *"magnetic seances."* Mesmer believed that all living bodies were filled with magnetic energy and that diseases were the result of the magnetic forces being out of balance. His treatment, therefore, consisted of passing his hands, which he believed had become magnetized, over the afflicted part of the patient's body and having them touch metal rods that protruded from a large tub called a *baquet.* The baquet was filled with water, chemicals, ground glass, and iron filings—a mixture that Mesmer thought created magnetism.

The magnetic seances were not merely mechanical procedures involving the laying on of hands and metal instruments, however. Mesmer created an atmosphere that induced a mysterious and powerful hypnotic trance. He entered the darkened and silent room wearing flowing lilac-colored robes. He lulled his patients into a deep state of relaxation and made them believe deeply in his healing powers; that is, he hypnotized them. He told them that their problems would go away, and some of them did.

OF SPECIAL INTEREST

Stage Hypnotism: Real or Fake?

I opened the section on hypnotism with the words: "Have you ever watched a stage hypnotist . . . ?" The closest most of us have come to hypnotism has been in a nightclub watching a stage hypnotist, but have you ever wondered whether it's really on the up and up? Or does stage hypnotism have more in common with the "magic" performed by stage magicians—is it all just an illusion?

Although it would be unfair for me to pass judgment on all stage hypnotists, it would be reasonable to say that most of them perform entertaining acts that do not involve real hypnosis at all. If that is so, how do they get people to cluck like chickens, cry like babies, and drop their pants on stage? The answer is twofold: an exaggeration of normal suggestibility and tricks (Bowers, 1976).

Stage hypnotists rely on the use of highly suggestible and cooperative subjects. They only use volunteers from the audience, never hecklers, and often "hypnotize" a number of volunteers and choose only the ones that appear most cooperative. In other words, hypnotists choose people who are so willing to go along with what others want, that if they do not fall into a trance, they will fake it. The suggestibility of these individuals is no doubt heightened by the fact that they are on stage and would embarrass the hypnotist if they admitted that they had not been hypnotized.

In addition to capitalizing on the suggestibility and cooperation of their volunteers, stage hypnotists use outright trickery; after all, they are entertainers! For example, stage hypnotists often convince their audiences of the power of hypnotism by having a subject perform an "astounding" physical feat that almost anyone can do without being hypnotized. The "hypnotized" subject is told to lie on three chairs and is told to stiffen like a board. Then the middle chair is pulled out and the person stays suspended between the two remaining chairs. It looks like something a person could do only when hypnotically turned into a living board, but it's really not difficult (Bowers, 1976).

Novelist Mark Twain recounted in his autobiography the story of his own "hypnosis" by a stage hypnotist as a boy. He did not fall into a deep trance but still was too embarrassed to admit it to the audience. So intense was his desire to play along that he allowed needles to be stuck in his flesh and endured extreme pain. When he later told his mother of his faking, she had been so convinced by his "painless" performance that she did not believe him (Bowers, 1976; Clemens, 1959).

Because of the controversy surrounding Mesmer, the king of France appointed a blue-ribbon commission in 1784 led by Benjamin Franklin, who was then serving as ambassador to France, to investigate Mesmer. The commission concluded that while Mesmer was sometimes able to help his patients, there was no validity to his theories. When Mesmer was able to reduce pain temporarily or help in some other way, it was due to the patient's belief rather than the power of magnetism (Bowers, 1976).

Benjamin Franklin's evaluation was not flattering to Mesmer. It focused correctly on the fact that his "cures" were only temporary and often kept his patients from seeking more effective forms of treatment. What Franklin did not see, however, was that Mesmer was inadvertently teaching us something about altered states of human consciousness. The process of putting people into hypnotic trances came to be known for many years as *mesmerism.* Only much later was it referred to as *hypnosis.*

In more recent years, hypnotism has been intensively studied, and understood to some extent. It took psychologists a long time to decide that it was respectable to study a phenomenon with such a shady and controversial past, but in the past 20 years, hypnosis has finally seen the hard light of scientific inquiry (Barber, 1969; Bowers, 1976; Hilgard, 1975). It now appears that the hypnotic trance is best thought of as a highly relaxed state in which the person's conscious awareness is highly focused, imagination is intensified, and the person is highly susceptible to the instructions of the hypnotist.

In recent years hypnosis has gained some limited acceptance by the medical and dental professions for the relief of pain through *hypnotic analgesia.* Patients who could not use analgesic medications for a variety of reasons have been able to have extensive operations under hypnosis with little or no pain. Hypnosis has also been found to be particularly successful in the relief of phantom limb pain, discussed in chapter 3 (Hilgard & Hilgard, 1975).

Depersonalization

Not all altered states of consciousness occur when we are striving to attain them; some occur quite spontaneously. This section describes one of the more common of these experiences. The term **depersonalization** refers to the perceptual experience of one's body becoming "distorted" or "unreal" in some way or the sense of strange distortions in one's surroundings. While very bizarre, such experiences are not necessarily abnormal or even uncommon among young adults. British researchers interviewed 891 university students and found 76 who had experienced depersonalization. Excerpts from the accounts of a number of different students help to portray these experiences (Myers & Grant, 1972):

> I felt slightly unreal and as though I wasn't part of my surroundings, but watching from a distance; my voice sounded strange to me and did not seem to be part of me.

> The feeling of not belonging to my body but being outside it.

> I do not feel the sensation of it being my hand; it is something else which is there but nothing to do with me.

depersonalization
(de-per″sun-al-i-za′shun)
The perceptual experience of one's body or surroundings becoming distorted or unreal in some way.

OF SPECIAL INTEREST

Hallucinations in Normal Individuals: Monotony's Mirages

Recall from the opening of chapter 2 the revealing studies of neurosurgeon Wilder Penfield. When he touched an electrically charged rod to the brain of surgery patients, they experienced vivid visual or auditory perceptions. Because the brain has so much stored information, it's perfectly capable of producing complete perceptions in the absence of any incoming sensory stimulation. And that is what an hallucination is: a perceptual experience in the absence of normal sensation. Hallucinations are not something that can occur only in a disturbed mind. It seems that all human brains have the capacity to create hallucinations.

If all of us are capable of having hallucinations, why is it that normal people generally do not experience them? Psychologist Daniel Goleman (1976) thinks he knows what keeps hallucinations from popping into our consciousness during most of our waking lives. Goleman and others have suggested that the brain's ability to create false perceptual experiences is suppressed during the hours that we are awake, probably to keep us from confusing reality with fantasy in our daily lives. The stimulation of day-to-day activities seems to activate a chemical mechanism in the brain stem that blocks out hallucinations (Jacobs, 1976). At night, however, when the lack of stimulation leads the blockade to be dropped, hallucinations do occur but we call them dreams.

This line of reasoning is pretty speculative, but there is enough evidence to make the idea at least seem credible. For example, when cats are injected with a drug that diminishes the supply of the chemical that supposedly blocks hallucinations, they stay awake, but their brain waves show the pattern characteristic of dream sleep (Jacobs, 1976). Are they dreaming while awake (hallucinating)? Additional evidence comes from the experiences of individuals who must endure long periods of minimal stimulation in their work (such as airline pilots, radar operators, truck drivers). If Goleman is correct, the prolonged lack of stimulation should sometimes fool the brain into thinking it's asleep and unlock the blockade on hallucinations. In fact, one survey of long-distance truck drivers who endure long hours of monotonous driving found that 3 percent of them had experienced at least one full-fledged hallucination.

I suddenly felt that I was really behind myself, not watching myself but detached from everything including my body to some extent.

My mother and I were walking towards each other from opposite ends of a street, and I suddenly felt an odd sense of estrangement, as if I had never seen her face in my life before.

I felt disembodied . . . only my mind seemed to exist . . . I would have to pinch myself to reassure myself that I did exist. (p. 60)

Suppose that this afternoon your mind leaves your body and floats up to the ceiling where it watches you. Does this mean you have gone crazy? Have you had a psychic or religious experience? Depersonalization experiences sometimes include the illusion that the mind has left the body and traveled about in a so-called *out-of-body experience* or **astral projection.** When such experiences are recurrent, they *may* be an indication of psychological problems, but isolated experiences seem to be quite normal, even if somewhat unnerving.

astral projection
(as'tral)
Depersonalization that includes the illusion that the mind has left the body.

R E V I E W

Sometimes a kind of consciousness is experienced that is greatly different from normal waking consciousness. These altered states of consciousness may be unwelcome and upsetting occurrences (as with depersonalization), but others are intentionally induced through meditation and hypnosis. Meditation produces a transcendent sense of relaxation that is helpful in combating stress; and hypnosis has been found to be useful in relieving pain under some circumstances. (See *Research Report:* "Altering Consciousness through Sensory Deprivation.")

Altering Consciousness with Drugs

Up to this point we have been discussing altered states of consciousness that are "natural" in the sense that they can be experienced by anyone without artificial inducements. Perhaps the most distinctly different types of altered consciousness, however, involve taking chemicals into the body or using drugs. Specifically, we are talking about **psychotropic drugs,** that class of drugs that alters conscious experience. These drugs exert their effects by influencing specific neurotransmitters in the brain or by chemically altering the action of neurons in other ways. The range of effects of psychotropic drugs is enormous, from mild relaxation to vivid hallucinations. But perhaps more enormous than the range of their effects is the frequency and casualness of their use in contemporary society.

Psychotropic drugs can be divided into four major categories. **Stimulants** are drugs that increase the activity of the central nervous system, providing a sense of energy and well-being. **Depressants** reduce the activity of the central nervous system, leading to a sense of relaxation, drowsiness, and lowered inhibitions. **Hallucinogens** produce dreamlike alterations in perceptual experience.

psychotropic drugs
(si"ko-trop'pik)
The class of drugs that alters conscious experience.

stimulants
Drugs that increase the activity of the central nervous system, providing a sense of energy and well-being.

depressants
Drugs that reduce the activity of the central nervous system, leading to a sense of relaxation, drowsiness, and lowered inhibitions.

hallucinogens
(hah-lu'si"no-jenz)
Drugs that alter perceptual experiences.

RESEARCH REPORT

Altering Consciousness through Sensory Deprivation

An interesting series of studies conducted at Montreal's McGill University in the 1950s looked at the psychological effects of extreme restrictions in sensory input (Heron, 1957). The results of these and subsequent studies (Zubek, 1973) suggest that prolonged sensory deprivation can lead to altered states of consciousness. The subjects in these studies were placed in a special sound-deadened chamber and were padded, masked, and bandaged to reduce stimulus input to a minimum. Except for brief breaks for meals and other necessities of life, the subjects were kept in isolation for several days (see fig. 4.2). In time the subjects began to see minor visual hallucinations; they also became irritable and could not concentrate. In short, they found it a strange and unpleasant experience.

Ironically, sensory deprivation has more recently become a fad in some parts of the country, the goal being the attainment of a particularly *enjoyable* state of consciousness. Sensory deprivation chambers have been designed that are sound deadened and filled with salty water just deep enough to float gently in. This chamber minimizes sensations, even the sensation of gravity. Proponents of these chambers claim that they produce a blissfully relaxed state and vivid, enjoyable hallucinations.

Why is it that Heron's experiments led to an uncomfortable state and users of the sensory deprivation tank find it so enjoyable? It may be because the tank is used for much shorter periods of time and involves much less deprivation of sensory input. But, the power of suggestion may also be operating: if told you are going to love floating in the salt water, that expectation just might lead you to like it. Heron's subjects, on the other hand, were probably led to expect something unpleasant.

---

inhalants (in-ha′lants)
Toxic substances that
produce a sense of
intoxication when inhaled.

Inhalants are common household chemicals that are put to dangerous use by being inhaled, producing feelings of intoxication. Not fitting easily into this classification is the drug *marijuana,* which induces a relaxed sense of well-being. Common members of these classes of drugs are summarized in table 4.1. They will be discussed in the section that follows in terms of their patterns of usage.

Drug Use: Some Basic Considerations

While the effects of psychotropic drugs are quite varied, we need to consider a number of issues that are relevant to all of them. These issues include the wide variation in responses to drugs and the problems that are associated with their use.

RESEARCH REPORT

Figure 4.2 The apparatus used by Heron to study the effects on consciousness of extreme deprivation of sensory input.
From Pathology of boredom, *by Woodburn Heron. Copyright © 1957 by Scientific American, Inc. All rights reserved.*

Variable Response to Drugs

In the sections that follow, we look at the psychological effects of a number of widely used drugs. In discussing these effects, we must keep in mind the fact that the effects that drugs have on us are far from perfectly reliable and predictable. Many factors influence the individual's response to a drug; most important among them are:

1. *Dose and purity.* Obviously the amount of the drug taken will influence its effect. Less obvious is the fact that drugs purchased on the street are often cut—mixed—with other substances that can alter the effects of the drug.

Table 4.1 Major psychotropic drugs

Stimulants

Amphetamines
    Benzedrine (amphetamine)
    Dexedrine (dextroamphetamine)
    Methedrine (methamphetamine)
Cocaine
Caffeine (in coffee, tea, and colas)
Nicotine (in tobacco)

Depressants

Tranquilizers
    Equanil (meprobamate)
    Librium (chlordiazepoxide)
    Miltown (meprobamate)
    Valium (diazepam)
Narcotics
    Opiates (opium and its derivatives)
        Codeine
        Heroin
        Morphine
        Opium
    Synthetic narcotics
        Demerol
        Methadone
        Percodan
Sedatives
    Alcohol (ethanol)
    Barbiturates
        Nembutal (pentobarbital)
        Quaalude (methaqualone)
        Seconal (secobarbital)
        Tuinal (secobarbital and amobarbital)
        Veronal (barbital)

Hallucinogens

LSD (lysergic acid diethylamide-25)
Mescaline (peyote)
PCP (phencyclidine hydrochloride)
Psilocybin (psychotogenic mushrooms)

Inhalants (volatile hydrocarbons)

Cleaning fluids
Gasoline
Glue
Nail-polish remover (acetone)
Paint thinner

Marijuana Family

Marijuana
Hashish

2. *Personal characteristics.* The weight, health, age, and even the personality of the person taking a drug can influence the drug's effect.

3. *Expectations.* The effect that we expect a drug to have, based on our own past experiences and what we have heard from others, will partly determine the effect of the drug.

4. *Social situation.* Other people influence our response to the drug; we may respond differently if the drug is taken alone versus in the midst of an upbeat party.

5. *Moods.* The mood that we are in at the time of taking the drug can dramatically alter its effects. Alcohol, for example, can make a happy person happier, a sad person more depressed, and can unleash violence in an angry individual.

When you consider the interplay of the list of factors that influence our response to drugs, it's easy to see how their effects are at least partly unpredictable.

Problems Associated with Drug Use

The use of drugs to alter conscious experience carries with it certain risks. These risks differ considerably from drug to drug, but the risks associated with all drugs involve the same basic issues.

1. *Drug abuse.* A drug is being abused if taking it causes some kind of biological damage (as in liver damage caused by alcohol) or impairment of psychological functioning (as in heroin addiction leading to crime or loss of employment).

2. *Psychological dependence.* A psychological dependence has been developed when the individual needs to use the drug regularly to maintain a comfortable psychological state, as when a person gets edgy if he or she does not smoke marijuana daily.

3. *Physiological addiction.* Many drugs quickly become involved in the chemical functioning of the individual's body. The body chemistry adjusts to accept the drug into it to such a degree that when the drug is not present, the body cannot function properly and the person experiences painful *withdrawal* symptoms. Addictive drugs produce progressively stronger addiction, because over time the body learns to adapt more easily to the drug in its system. As this *tolerance* for the drug increases, larger doses are needed to produce the same effect on consciousness. Therefore, the addicted person's body chemistry becomes progressively more tied to the drug.

The Everyday Drugs

We consume enormous quantities of psychotropic drugs on an almost daily basis, often without being aware that we are taking "drugs."

(left)
The average American drinks 36 gallons of coffee each year that contain 125 mg of the stimulant caffeine per cup.

(right)
A 25-year-old who never smokes has a life expectancy of 8 years longer than a person who smokes two packs of cigarettes a day.

Caffeine

Each year the average person in the United States drinks 36 gallons of coffee, 7 gallons of tea, and 30 gallons of cola, and uses untold amounts of over-the-counter drugs containing caffeine (Ray, 1974). At approximately 125 milligrams (mg) per cup of coffee, that is an enormous consumption of a psychotropic stimulant. For most people, consumption of eight or more cups of caffeinated coffee per day (1,000 mg) constitutes a dangerously high level of intake (Greden, 1974). Common effects of such consumption for a prolonged period of time include excessive stomach acid and ulcers, abnormal heart rhythms and accelerated heart rate, increased kidney activity, anxiety, irritability, insomnia, and sensory disturbances (Greden, 1974). Prolonged use of caffeine at even moderate levels can also result in a physiological addiction to the substance.

Nicotine

The drug nicotine found in tobacco is another drug widely used to alter consciousness. Although it's technically a stimulant like caffeine, it can also have relaxing effects under some circumstances. Its effects on consciousness are so mild, however, that they are often not noticed by experienced smokers.

The wonder, in fact, is that so many people (about 40 percent of all adults) use this relatively ineffective psychotropic drug. Not only are its pleasant effects minimal, but nicotine is a highly dangerous drug. The life expectancy of regular smokers is reduced because smoking greatly increases the chances of lung and mouth cancer, heart attacks, pneumonia, emphysema, and other life-threatening diseases. A person aged 25 who never smokes has a life expectancy that is over eight years longer than a person who smokes two packs a day. Why do people smoke then?

The answer to that question seems to have two parts. First, it appears that most people *start* smoking because they see others do it. Adolescents see adults smoking and perhaps imitate it because of its association with adult status. They also see their friends smoking and are thus subjected to peer pressure to smoke. But whatever the reason they begin smoking, other factors soon begin to take over. Smokers are quick to develop a psychological dependence on cigarettes and soon become physically addicted to the nicotine. At this point, smokers smoke

*Drawing by Saxon; © 1962
The New Yorker Magazine, Inc.*

"Oh, for goodness' sake! Smoke!"

primarily to avoid the discomfort of not smoking rather than for any positive effects the drug might have. As a result of this two-stage process, 95 percent or more of smokers become addicted smokers in a relatively short time (Russell, 1971). As their tolerance for nicotine increases, their need for higher daily doses increases. As a result, it's very difficult to stop smoking cigarettes once the habit becomes regular. Only about 20 percent of all smokers are able to stop completely without help (Russell, 1971). But see chapter 15, page 623, for a suggestion on how to make quitting a little easier.

Alcohol

Although we generally do not think of alcohol as a "drug," it's a very powerful and widely abused drug. Alcohol works principally as a depressant, but it's an enjoyable drug because it reduces inhibitions, facilitates social interaction, and may augment a good mood (it can also worsen a bad mood).

Alcohol is the most widely abused drug in the United States and is probably the drug to which the most individuals are physiologically addicted. Assessing the exact extent of alcohol abuse is difficult for two main reasons. First, the amount of alcohol consumption that can lead to harmful effects varies markedly from person to person and situation to situation. An individual who only drinks four drinks every New Year's Eve is an alcohol abuser if he drives himself home when intoxicated; a surgeon who has two drinks a day may be an alcohol abuser if she drinks them right before performing surgery. Second, the potential harmful effects of alcohol abuse are so varied. Heavy drinking can affect job performance, disrupt marriages, and harm one's health. It is involved in about half of all fatal fire and automobile accidents, one-third of all suicides, and two-thirds of all murders (Marlatt & Rose, 1980).

In spite of the difficulties involved in defining alcohol abuse, surveys have been taken with eye-opening results. Using a broad definition of alcohol abuse, it has been found that while about two-thirds of all adults drink at least occasionally, nearly one-third of the individuals surveyed reported at least one serious alcohol-related problem (for 41 percent of males and 21 percent of females) (Cahalan, 1970; Cahalan & Room, 1974). This is not to say that alcohol is always a harmful drug that leads to problems; in the survey cited above, half of all drinkers report no harmful side effects. Indeed, used in some ways, alcohol may be beneficial for some individuals. It has now been rather well-established that individuals who drink an average of one drink (a glass of wine, beer, or a mixed drink) per day are less likely to die of heart attacks than individuals who drink either more or less alcohol (Hennekens, Rosner, & Cole, 1978).

alcoholism
Addiction to alcohol.

Because of its powerful mood-altering qualities, alcohol can rapidly result in psychological dependence and physiological addiction (**alcoholism**). In about one-third of all addicted individuals, this addiction results in a progressively deteriorating series of changes known as *classic alcoholism*. The four stages of classic alcoholism are well-known:

1. *Prealcoholic stage.* During this stage drinking begins to serve the important function of releasing tension. As drinking continues, the tolerance for alcohol increases, so the amount that must be consumed to provide the same release of tension increases.

2. *Prodromal stage.* The drinking level is excessive in this stage. Blackouts or memory losses begin to occur, and drinking behavior shifts from sipping to gulping. Guilt, anxiety, and promises to stop drinking are also common during this period.

3. *Crucial stage.* During the crucial stage, deterioration occurs in self-esteem and in general social functioning, including loss of friends. Once the individual begins to drink, the drinking is uncontrollable ("binges"), but the individual can still avoid taking the first drink for relatively long periods of time. He or she begins to rationalize drinking as acceptable. Excessive drinking generally leads to neglect of nutrition.

4. *Chronic stage.* The alcoholic has reached a stage of almost constant drinking, with little or no control over either starting or continuing to drink. Impairment of thinking and loss of social standards are very common. Fears, hallucinations, and tremors often develop along with serious medical complications.

Other Psychotropic Drugs

Many other drugs are used and abused in the United States today. The drugs described below are powerful in their effects on conscious experience, are powerfully addictive, and are used illegally in most circumstances.

Stimulants

A number of stimulants (*uppers*) more powerful than caffeine and nicotine are widely abused in the United States. **Amphetamines** (trade names *Dexedrine, Benzedrine,* and *Methedrine*) are stimulant drugs that generally produce a conscious sense of increased energy, alertness, enthusiasm, and a euphoric high. They are not physically addictive but produce rapid and intense psychological dependence. Hence, the possibility for abuse is very high. The amphetamines are dangerous physically, particularly in their effects on the heart. Psychologically, the greatest risk is known as **amphetamine psychosis**—a prolonged reaction to excessive use of stimulants that is characterized by distorted thinking, confused and rapidly changing emotions, and intense suspiciousness.

Cocaine is quickly becoming one of the more widely abused drugs in the United States. It is estimated that 4–5 million Americans use this drug at least once a month (Andersen, 1983). Cocaine is a stimulant much like amphetamine that is made from the leaves of the coca plant. It is taken in many forms, but is most commonly inhaled as a powder. It produces alertness, high energy, optimism, self-confidence, happiness, exhilaration, and talkativeness. It raises body temperature, breathing rate, and heart rate, and reduces the desire for food and sleep. This pleasant effect generally lasts no longer that 30 minutes. At times, particularly after repeated or prolonged use, the high is followed by anxiety, irritability, and depression. Repeated use also often causes a paranoid suspiciousness that resembles amphetamine psychosis.

Most users of cocaine consider it to be a harmless, occasional recreation. But, the uncomfortable aftereffects that sometimes follow the cocaine high are definitely not the only dangers of this drug. The high is so pleasurable that users often repeat its use for many hours. Eventually, they come down with a painful, exhausted crash. And, although cocaine is not a physiologically addictive drug, it's so effective at wiping out the pains of daily life that some individuals soon become powerfully dependent on the drug—and can no more resist its lure than an addicted heroin junkie can resist heroin.

Interestingly, cocaine was once a legal drug in the United States. Coca-Cola, which was originally marketed as a "nerve tonic," at first contained cocaine as part of its "secret formula." In 1906 the cocaine was replaced by the milder stimulant caffeine.

Sedatives and Tranquilizers

Sedatives, often called *downers,* are depressants that in mild doses generally produce a state of calm relaxation. They are commonly prescribed in the United States as drugs to aid sleep and sometimes to combat anxiety. Common trade names for these drugs are *Seconal, Tuinal, Nembutal,* and *Quaaludes* (which are no longer sold in the United States, but are still abused). Because they are highly addictive and dangerous to withdraw from without medical supervision and because overdoses are highly dangerous (and even small doses are dangerous when taken with alcohol), they are prescribed by physicians less frequently now than in the past. They are still widely abused through illegal drug markets.

amphetamines
(am-fet′ah-minz)
Powerful stimulants that produce a conscious sense of increased energy and a euphoric high.

amphetamine psychosis
(si-ko′sis)
A prolonged reaction to the excessive use of stimulants, characterized by disordered thinking, confused and rapidly changing emotions, and intense suspiciousness.

Cocaine originally appeared in Coca-Cola at a time when use of the drug was legal. It is now an expensive and illicit stimulant, which can lead to psychological dependence.

Tranquilizers are milder drugs that are similar to sedatives in that they typically produce a sense of calm relaxation for a brief period of time. As such, they are often prescribed to reduce anxiety. Common trade names are *Valium, Librium, Miltown,* and *Equanil.* Like sedatives, they are dangerously addictive, often difficult to withdraw from, and are very dangerous when mixed with alcohol; they must be taken with great care. Also like sedatives, these types of downers are widely sold illegally.

Narcotics

Narcotics are powerful and highly addictive depressants. The use of the narcotic drug opium derived from the opium poppy dates back at least 7,000 years in the Middle East. Derivatives of opium, including *morphine, heroin,* and *codeine,* are powerful narcotic drugs that dramatically alter consciousness. They generally relieve pain and induce a sudden, rushing high, followed by a relaxed, lethargic drowsiness. Narcotics create a powerful physiological addiction very rapidly. With prolonged addiction, the physical effects on the body are profoundly damaging. Compared with other drugs, narcotic use in the United States is not high, but the drastic effects of opiates, including the crimes that many addicts commit to maintain their increasingly expensive habits, make it an extremely significant drug abuse problem. It became an especially difficult problem during the Vietnam War. Perhaps due to a combination of its availability and the stresses of war, it was estimated that 20 percent of all Vietnam veterans tried heroin at least once (Harris, 1973).

opiates (o'pe-ats)
Narcotic drugs derived
from the opium poppy.

Opium and its derivatives (the **opiates**) are not the only kinds of narcotic drugs. In recent years, synthetic narcotics have been artificially produced in drug laboratories. These synthetic narcotics include widely used painkilling drugs with trade names such as *Demerol, Percodan,* and *Methadone.*

Inhalants

Substances that when inhaled produce a sense of intoxication are called *inhalants.* Toxic (poisonous) substances such as glue, cleaning fluid, paint, and so on are typically placed in paper bags and inhaled ("sniffed"). This type of intoxication is common among children because the materials are relatively easy to obtain. This is particularly sad, because inhalants are highly addictive and extremely dangerous. These toxic fumes often cause permanent brain damage and other serious complications.

Hallucinogens

The drugs that most powerfully alter consciousness are hallucinogens such as *d-lysergic acid* (*LSD*), *mescaline* (derived from the peyote cactus), and *psilocybin* (derived from a kind of mushroom). These drugs typically alter perceptual experiences, but only large doses cause vivid hallucinations. In these unusual states, the drugged individual experiences imaginary visions and realities that, ironically, sometimes seem more "real" to the drug user than waking consciousness. This latter fact, however, may be more attributable to the drug-taker's dissatisfaction with everyday life than to the powers of the drug itself.

The hallucinogens are generally not physiologically addictive, but individuals can quickly become psychologically dependent on them. In addition, while many of the drug-induced states (*trips*) produced by hallucinogens are experienced as pleasant, frightening, and dangerous, "bad trips" are not uncommon

(McWilliams & Tuttle, 1973). Individuals who are frightened about taking the drug but do so because of peer pressure are more likely to experience bad trips. These trips, both good and bad, can sometimes recur in *flashbacks* without the individual taking the drug again. About 65 percent of flashbacks are bad trips, apparently being triggered by stress or anxiety. About 25 percent of all regular LSD users experience flashbacks, sometimes several months after the original trip (Matefy & Kroll, 1974).

Considerable research has looked into the possibility that LSD causes damage to the chromosomes of reproductive cells and may lead to birth defects. At this point in the research effort, it appears that LSD is capable of doing this only in rare instances, if at all. In this respect, it should be pointed out that even widely used drugs such as aspirin are suspected of having the same potential to create very rare birth defects in the offspring of its users (Maugh, 1973).

One other hallucinogenic drug needs to be discussed because of its dangers. The drug *phencyclidine* or *PCP* (angel dust), which was originally developed as an animal tranquilizer, has come into common use in recent years, especially among adolescents. The effects of PCP typically last from four to six hours. In some cases, the individual experiences auditory or visual hallucinations, but more likely the experience includes feelings of numbness, lack of muscular coordination, anxiety, and a sense of detachment from the environment. Euphoria, a sense of strength, and "dreaminess" may also be present. The individual on PCP may also engage in unconventional behavior such as going into public places nude. Violent behavior toward others, suicide, and psychotic episodes are other possible reactions to this drug. It's generally considered one of the most dangerous drugs now on the street (Petersen & Stillman, 1978).

Marijuana

Marijuana is a popular consciousness-altering drug that generally produces a sense of relaxation and well-being. In some cases, the drug alters sensory experiences and the perception of time. Not since the time of Prohibition has any drug been so hotly debated or so widely used in spite of being illegal. It's not physically addictive, and in fact many users experience a *reverse tolerance,* in which smaller amounts of the drug eventually come to produce the same high. However, some psychological dependence is possible. Although the evidence as to possible physical or psychological harm is not conclusive, there is some evidence that prolonged marijuana use decreases the efficiency of cognitive processing, weakens the body's immune response, and decreases the action of male sex hormones (Wallace & Fisher, 1983). Moreover, like smoking any type of cigarette, marijuana increases the risk of lung cancer over time. Driving an automobile or using any other form of machinery when intoxicated by marijuana (or any other substance) is also obviously dangerous.

Polydrug Abuse

In many ways, the most difficult problem that consciousness-altering drugs present is that there are so many of them. Unfortunately, it's not uncommon for the same individual to abuse many of these drugs at the same time—so-called *polydrug abuse.* This greatly increases the possibilities of addiction and dependence; the chances that the use of drugs will interfere with an individual's adjustment to school, work, or family; and the chances that the drugs will interact chemically to produce toxic effects. The use of any drug carries dangers with it, but polydrug abuse is especially dangerous. Perhaps it is not surprising, therefore, that polydrug abusers have a particularly high rate of previous emotional problems (Halikas & Rimmer, 1974). Polydrug abuse is not a very "sane" thing to do.

R E V I E W

Altered states can be induced by taking psychotropic drugs that alter conscious experience by influencing the action of neurons in the brain. These drugs produce varying changes in consciousness ranging from mild alterations of mood to vivid hallucinations, but they also carry with them the danger of abuse, dependence, addiction, and direct physical damage in some cases. The use of many drugs (caffeine, nicotine, and alcohol) is legal and routine in the United States, while the use of illegal drugs varies greatly in frequency.

S U M M A R Y

Chapter 4 explores human awareness, normal waking consciousness, sleeping and dreaming, and altered states of consciousness.

   I. *Consciousness* is defined as "a state of awareness" and is experienced in a variety of states.
     A. *Directed consciousness* occurs when our awareness is directed toward a single focus.
     B. In the state of *flowing consciousness,* awareness drifts from one thought to another.
     C. *Daydreams* combine the features of directed consciousness and dreamlike fantasies.
   II. Approximately one-third of our lives is spent in sleep.
     A. Sleep begins with a semiwakeful *hypnogogic state* and moves through stages of progressively deeper sleep to *dreaming* or *REM sleep.*
     B. Dreams include alterations of reality, which Freudian psychologists believe offer clues to the unconscious mind.
     C. Sleeping and dreaming seem essential to physical and psychological health; sleep deprivation brings on fatigue, inefficiency, and irritability.
     D. Nightmares, night terrors, sleepwalking, and sleeptalking are fairly common sleep phenomena.
   III. We sometimes experience more unusual *altered states of consciousness.*
     A. Many individuals practice *meditation* to achieve a highly relaxed state.
     B. *Hypnosis* is sometimes used to alter consciousness and to relieve pain.
     C. Disturbed consciousness is sometimes experienced in the form of *depersonalization.*

IV. Consciousness can also be altered through the use of various *psycho-tropic drugs.*
    A. Psychotropic drugs may be classified as *stimulants, depressants, hallucinogens,* and *inhalants;* the drug *marijuana* does not fit easily into the classification.
    B. Though risks differ from drug to drug, all drug use runs the risk of *abuse, dependence,* or *addiction.*
    C. Even the more common drugs (caffeine, nicotine, alcohol) produce definite physical and psychological effects and can be quite harmful if used in excess.
    D. The more powerful drugs cause radical changes in consciousness, can lead to serious physical and psychological problems, and are often illegal.
        1. *Stimulants* are not physically addictive but produce psychological dependence; they can be dangerous, particularly in their effects on the heart.
        2. *Sedatives* and *tranquilizers* are highly addictive and can be highly dangerous, particularly when taken in large doses or with alcohol.
        3. *Narcotics* are powerful and dangerous depressants; physiological addiction occurs rapidly, and prolonged use has profoundly damaging effects on the body.
        4. *Inhalants* are usually toxic and often cause permanent brain damage.
        5. *Hallucinogens* radically alter perception, cause hallucinations, and are often associated with bizarre or even violent behavior; though not physiologically addictive, psychological dependence is common.
        6. *Marijuana* is a popular, though illegal, drug that produces a sense of well-being and sometimes alters perception.

Suggested Readings

1. For a readable discussion of meditation without its metaphysical or religious trimmings, read:
    Benson, H. (1975). *The relaxation response.* New York: Morrow.

2. For a fascinating and sensible look at hypnosis:
    Bowers, K. S. (1976). *Hypnosis for the seriously curious.* Monterey, CA: Brooks/Cole.

3. For more on the contents of dreams, written by a Freudian psychologist:
    Hall, C. S. (1951). What people dream about. *Scientific American, 84,* 60–63.

4. For additional information on the study of sleeping and dreaming:
    Webb, W. B., & Agnew, H. W. (1973). *Sleep and dreams.* Dubuque, IA: Wm. C. Brown Publishers.

5. A thoroughly scientific statement on mind-altering drugs:
    Leavitt, F. (1974). *Drugs and behavior.* Philadelphia: W. B. Saunders.

6. An interesting view of human consciousness is given by:
    Ornstein, R. (1977). *The psychology of consciousness.* New York: Harcourt Brace Jovanovich.

7. An excellent broad overview of the topic of consciousness is provided by:
    Wallace, B., & Fisher, L. E. (1983). *Consciousness and behavior.* Boston: Allyn & Bacon.

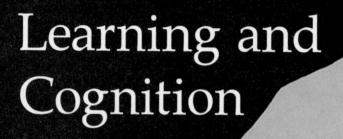

Learning and Cognition

Basic Principles of Learning

OUTLINE

KEY TERMS

P R O L O G U E

In 1938 a young scientist named Ruth Benedict published a book summarizing what had been learned from expeditions studying three remote cultures. At that time, these cultures did not have extensive contact with industrialized societies and still existed as they had for centuries before. Benedict used the three cultures as examples to argue against the concept of a fixed "human nature." Then, as now, it was common to explain such traits as greed, drive, and ambition as unchangeable, inborn aspects of the nature of all humans. Using the three tribes, Benedict showed that any trait that was typical of one culture could be found in the *opposite* form in one of the other two cultures. For example, the Dobu Indians of New Guinea were a people who generally did everything they could to acquire more wealth and fame than anyone else. The Zuñi Indians of the American Southwest, on the other hand, shared all wealth equally with other members of the tribe and actively avoided doing anything that would bring them individual fame.

Courtship and marriage provided another example of the differences between these two cultures. In Zuñi society, male and female children were strictly separated until adolescence, allowing almost no contact with their opposite-sex peers before marriage. Courtship consisted of no more than the male's asking a young woman, whom he had probably seen only at a distance until that moment, for a drink of water as she returned from her daily trip to the stream with a filled water jug. If she gave him a drink, they were soon married.

In Dobu society, male and female children were not only allowed to play with each other, but sex play among children was approved by adults. When children reached puberty, frequent sexual relationships were common among the unmarried males and females, with the lovemaking generally occurring openly in the one-room home of the girl's parents. The only restriction was that the male had to leave before sunrise. If he failed to leave, the young Dobu man had to serve a harsh year as the family's servant, after which his father bought him out of servitude and the young man was allowed to marry his sweetheart.

Benedict's point was this: If patterns of behavior exist in opposite forms in different cultures, then they cannot be an inborn characteristic of all humans. In other words, there cannot be an inevitable or fixed aspect of human nature. Rather, the patterns of behavior seem to be *learned* from other members of each society. Consider this: What if a Dobu infant were adopted by a Zuñi family? The child would grow up speaking the language of the Zuñi and would behave like a Zuñi rather than a Dobu. If you had been adopted as an infant by a family in China, France, or Saudi Arabia, you would have learned a different language and acquired the ways of behaving that characterize that different culture. In short, if your learning experiences had been different, you would have been a different person. Learning is a powerful force in our lives and, hence, an important topic in psychology.

P R E V I E W

You behave the way you do largely because you *learned* to act that way; learning is a major factor in the origin of your personality. If you had been adopted as an infant by a family in another part of the world, you would speak a different language, prefer different kinds of food and clothes, and act in ways that are characteristic of that culture, all because your learning experiences would have been different.

As an infant, you responded to very few of the stimuli in your environment and had a limited repertoire of behavior. In time, though, a great many stimuli acquired the ability to influence you and your range of behavior greatly expanded. In this way, a helpless infant became a competent adult. How did this happen? Much of the change took place because of biological growth, but a great deal of it occurred through the several processes of learning.

Through learning, parts of the environment that you hardly noticed before can become stimuli that strongly influence your behavior through simple association with already effective stimuli. If your water pipes began to groan one night, you probably would not pay much attention to the sound. But if the groaning always immediately preceded a sudden change in the temperature of your shower—from warm to icy cold—you would soon learn to jump at the first groan. Association of the water pipe's groan with the icy water would turn the groan into an effective stimulus.

Learning also results from the consequences of your behavior. Was the consequence of your action positive or negative? Positive consequences will lead you to repeat the same behavior again; negative consequences will make you less likely to engage in the behavior. If studying all night for a test brings you only bloodshot eyes and a poor grade, you will probably not study that way again. But if spacing out your study time over three days results in your first score of 100, you will be more likely to use that strategy again. Consequences change the probability of the behavior that produces them.

There are many kinds of phenomena of learning, most of which are variations on these two themes of association between stimuli and the consequences of behavior. Through learning, our experiences powerfully shape our behavior. Indeed, the ability to learn is one of humanity's most adaptive tools in coping with the demands of a changing world.

Definition of Learning

time between childhood and adulthood.

learning
Any relatively permanent change in behavior brought about through experience.

Life is a process of continual change. From infancy to adolescence to adulthood to death, we are changing. Many factors work together to produce those changes, but one of the most important is the process of **learning.** Through our experiences, we learn new information, new attitudes, new fears, and new skills; we also learn to understand new concepts, to solve problems in new ways, and even to develop a personality over a lifetime. And in the course of reading textbooks, we learn new definitions for words like learning: In psychology the term *learning* refers to any relatively permanent change in behavior brought about through experience.

Learning is any relatively permanent change in behavior brought about through experience.

As the definition states, not *all* changes in behavior are considered the result of learning. The term is restricted to relatively permanent, as opposed to temporary, changes that are the result of experience, rather than changes due to biological causes such as drugs, fatigue, maturation, injury, or the like. If a baseball pitcher throws the ball differently this season because his pitching coach demonstrated a new way to pitch, we would say that learning has occurred—a relatively permanent change in pitching due to the experience of the coach's demonstration. But if the pitcher's changed style was due to recovery from an injury, fatigue from throwing too much before each game, an arm strengthened by weight lifting, or biological maturation (if he was a seven-year-old little league pitcher), we would not refer to the change in pitching behavior as learning (Tarpy & Mayer, 1978).

Keep in mind when you interpret the phrase *change in behavior* that the change is not always immediately obvious. If you watch a film on the proper way to hit backhands in tennis this winter, the change in your behavior will not be evident until you are on the tennis court again next spring. Notice also that the definition of learning does not restrict its usage to intentionally produced changes in behavior or even to desirable changes in behavior. For instance, if you begin to loathe barbecue sandwiches because you get sick after eating one, learning has occurred. The new disgust for barbecue sandwiches is undesirable and certainly unintentional, but it's still the result of learning.

Over the years, psychologists have isolated and studied a number of ways that learning takes place. As a result, we now understand a number of different principles of learning. In the following sections we describe those principles of learning and indicate some of the ways that they can influence us in our daily lives.

Ivan Pavlov accidentally discovered that dogs learn to associate the sounds of food being prepared with the food itself.

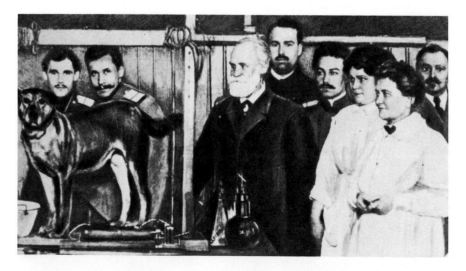

Classical Conditioning: Learning by Association

We begin our study of specific types of learning with a simple form called *classical conditioning*. The scientific study of classical conditioning began around the turn of the century with an accidental discovery made in the Leningrad laboratory of Ivan Pavlov. Pavlov was a Russian physiologist who was studying the role of saliva in digestion at the time of the discovery. In order to study the reflexive response of the salivary glands to the presence of food in the mouth, he had surgically implanted tubes in the cheeks of dogs so that saliva could be drained and precisely measured when small amounts of food were placed in the dogs' mouths (see fig. 5.1). Pavlov noticed, however, that dogs that had been in the experiment a few days started salivating when the attendant entered the room with the food dish *before* food was placed in their mouths. The sights (and probably sounds) of the attendant had come to *elicit* (evoke or produce) a reflexive response that only the food had originally elicited. This fact would have gone quite unnoticed had the tubes not been placed in the dogs' cheeks—that is the accidental part of the discovery. A dog that salivates whenever he or she sees a laboratory attendant may not seem like a great step forward for science at first glance. But from the experiment Pavlov recognized that a reflexive response to food, which was biologically "wired into" the nervous system, had come under the control of an *arbitrary* stimulus—the sight of the attendant.

Stated in a different way, Pavlov knew he had witnessed a form of learning that was based on nothing more than the repeated association of two stimuli. Remember from chapter 3 that a *stimulus* is anything that can directly influence behavior or conscious experience. Because the dog's experience of food was linked to the sight of the attendant, the behavior of the dog was changed—the dog now salivated to the stimuli of the approaching attendant. That is, the stimuli elicited a *response*. When you were born, you could only respond to the outside world with a limited repertoire of inborn reflexes, but now you are a marvelously complex product of your learning experiences. Pavlov wanted to understand this process of learning, so over his colleagues' objections, he hastily completed his studies of digestion and devoted the rest of his career to the study of learning (Watson, 1971).

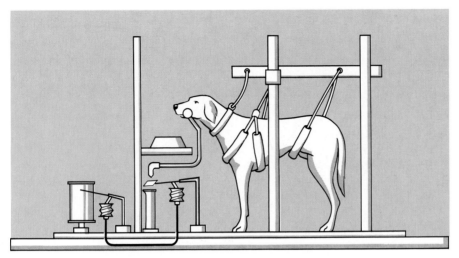

Figure 5.1 Apparatus originally used by Pavlov to study the role of salivation in digestion, and later in his studies of classical conditioning.

Dennis the Menace® Used by permission of Hank Ketcham and © by Field Enterprises, Inc.

Association: The Key Element in Classical Conditioning

It had been noted by Aristotle more than 2,000 years before Pavlov that two sensations repeatedly experienced together will become *associated*. If you have frequently visited the seashore with a friend, visiting the seashore alone will probably trigger memories of that friend. If you got sick the last time you ate a hot dog, you will likely feel nauseous the next time you see one. Learning through association is a common part of our lives.

Pavlov considered classical conditioning to be a form of learning through association—the association in time of a neutral stimulus (one that originally does not elicit the response) and a stimulus that does elicit the response. Pavlov used the apparatus that was already constructed in his laboratory to measure the progress of learning, and he used food as the stimulus to elicit the response (of salivation).

Specifically, Pavlov presented (as the neutral stimulus) a clicking metronome that the dog could easily hear. After a precisely measured interval of time, he would blow a small quantity of meat powder into the dog's mouth to elicit salivation. Every 15 minutes the same procedure was repeated, and soon the dog began salivating to the metronome when it was presented alone. By continuously measuring the amount of saliva drained through the tube in the dog's cheek, the strength of the new learning was accurately monitored throughout the process of classical conditioning.

Figure 5.2 In Pavlov's studies, the more often the metronome was associated in time with meat powder, the more effective it was in eliciting salivation.

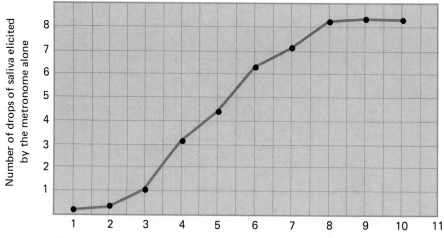

Number of times metronome and meat powder have been presented together

Keep in mind that the key phrase in classical conditioning is the "association in time" of the two stimuli. The more *frequently* the metronome and the food are associated, the more often the metronome will come to elicit salivation (see fig. 5.2). The *timing* of the association of the two stimuli is also highly important. Pavlov found, for example, that he obtained the best results when the metronome preceded the food powder by about a half a second. Longer time intervals were less effective, and almost no learning occurred when the metronome was presented at the same time as the food or when the food was presented slightly before the metronome.

Thus, Pavlov took advantage of a chance observation and began a systematic study of one aspect of the learning process. Although learning had been studied before Pavlov, his experiments were highly influential because of their extensiveness and precision. But, perhaps his true genius lay in seeing that this simple form of learning had important implications far beyond clicking metronomes and salivating dogs. Pavlov's writings became an important part of American psychology when they came to the attention of John B. Watson who expanded upon and popularized Pavlov's views in English.

Terminology of Classical Conditioning

Before we can proceed much further in our understanding of classical conditioning, we need to learn some new terminology. Although a bit awkward and confusing at first, these new terms will allow us to expand our discussion of classical conditioning to topics more relevant to your own experiences than salivating dogs without losing sight of the basic concept. First, we use each of these four new terms to refer to the specific stimuli and responses in Pavlov's experiments, then we use them with new examples. The new terms are as follows.

unconditioned stimulus (UCS)
A stimulus that can elicit a response without any learning.

1. *Unconditioned stimulus.* The meat powder was the **unconditioned stimulus (UCS)** in Pavlov's experiment. This is a stimulus that can elicit the response without any learning. In other words, the response to an unconditioned stimulus is essentially inborn.

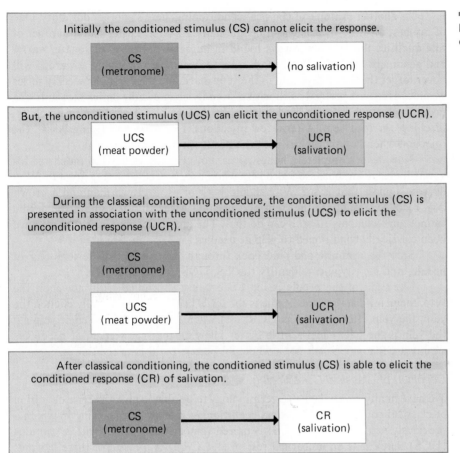

Figure 5.3 Diagram of classical conditioning.

2. *Conditioned stimulus*. The metronome was originally unable to elicit the response of salivation, but it acquired the ability to elicit the response through the process of classical conditioning. It was the **conditioned stimulus (CS)** in Pavlov's studies.

3. *Unconditioned response*. Salivation was the **unconditioned response (UCR)**. It's an unlearned, inborn reaction to the unconditioned stimulus.

4. *Conditioned response*. When the dog began salivating to the conditioned stimulus, salivation became the **conditioned response (CR)**. When the previously unconditioned response is elicited by the conditioned stimulus, it's referred to as the conditioned response.

To summarize: The meat powder was the unconditioned stimulus (UCS); the metronome was the conditioned stimulus (CS); salivation was the unconditioned response (UCR); and when the salivation was elicited by the conditioned stimulus, it became the conditioned response (CR). These are difficult terms to keep straight at first; it may help to read through the diagram in figure 5.3 to review the meaning of these terms.

conditioned stimulus (CS)
A stimulus that comes to elicit responses as a result of being paired with an unconditioned stimulus.

unconditioned response (UCR)
An unlearned, inborn reaction to an unconditioned stimulus.

conditioned response (CR)
A response that is similar or identical to the unconditioned response that comes to be elicited by a conditioned stimulus.

As another example of classical conditioning, here's another dog story. One of my best all-time friends was a beagle named Lester. Lester had a number of fine qualities that are not always found in humans; he was affectionate, warm, and genuinely loyal. But in all candor, Lester was also a profound coward. I will never forget the time I took him to the veterinarian for the first of a weekly series of shots: He stood perfectly still with a friendly beagle smile on his face until the needle was stuck into his hindquarter. At that point, he produced a flinching, lurching, terrified yelp. After a few injections, Lester began yelping before the injection when he saw the vet with the needle in her hand.

Now, to be completely honest, I cannot criticize Lester too much for his cowardly behavior, because I also yelp when I see a needle coming my way. Why do you suppose that is so? Why should both of us, a grown man and a grown dog, react so strongly to the sight of a needle? After all, the sight of the needle cannot hurt you; only its stab can do that. The answer, of course, is that we have been classically conditioned to yelp at needles.

Stop for a minute and read back through the example of Lester's fear of needles and see if you can identify the CS, UCS, UCR, and CR.

The sight of the needle is the CS because it originally did not elicit the yelp; the painful stab of the needle is the UCS because it biologically elicited the yelp; the yelp after the stab is UCR; and when the CS comes to elicit yelping, the yelp is the CR. I feel a little better knowing that my yelping at needles is simply a CR to a CS, but not a whole lot better; I still hate the things.

Definition of Classical Conditioning

We have finally covered enough terminology to be able to give a precise definition of classical conditioning. **Classical conditioning** is a form of learning in which a previously neutral stimulus (CS) is paired (associated in time) with a stimulus (UCS) that elicits an unlearned response (UCR). As a result of these pairings of the CS and UCS, the CS comes to elicit a response (CR) that is identical or very similar to the UCR.

classical conditioning
A form of learning in which a previously neutral stimulus (CS) is paired with an unconditioned stimulus (UCS) to elicit a conditioned response (CR) that is identical to or very similar to the unconditioned response (UCR).

Note that we consider classical conditioning to be a form of learning not because a new behavior has been acquired, but because an old behavior can be elicited by a new stimulus; behavior is "changed" only in that sense. It's important to notice also (for reasons that will be clear to you later in the chapter) that the process of classical conditioning *does not depend on the behavior of the individual* being conditioned. The metronome and the meat powder were paired whether the dog salivated or not, and the sight of the needle was followed by the stab whether Lester yelped or not. The critical element in classical conditioning is that the CS and UCS be closely associated in time. Our behavior has nothing to do with that fact. As we will see later, if the behavior of the individual can determine whether the stimulus is presented or not, the process is not called classical conditioning.

By the way, are you curious as to why it's called *classical* conditioning? This simply refers to the fact that Pavlov performed the *classic* laboratory studies of learning. For the same reason, classical conditioning is also referred to as *Pavlovian* conditioning.

The Bell and Pad: An Application of Classical Conditioning

A problem that affects many children is **nocturnal enuresis,** or nighttime bed-wetting. Some children do not develop the ability to wake up during the night when they have a full bladder, long after most children have learned to do so; instead, they wet the bed in their sleep. About 15 percent of all 5-year-olds and 2 percent of children over 12 have this problem, especially boys (Doleys, 1977). While this is not a problem of major concern, it's embarrassing for the children and often quite upsetting to the parents.

A simple device, called the *bell and pad,* was developed many years ago (Mowrer & Mowrer, 1938) based on the principle of classical conditioning that deals with the problem of nocturnal enuresis rather successfully. The device consists of two thin metallic sheets that are perforated with small holes and attached separately by wires to a battery-operated alarm. The flexible metallic sheets are laid on top of one another under the child's sheets separated by a sheet of fabric. As soon as the child passes the first drops of urine, the urine closes the electric circuit between the metallic sheets, causing the alarm to wake the child.

In the terminology of classical conditioning, the alarm is a UCS that elicits the UCR of awakening. By repeatedly pairing the alarm with the sensation of a full bladder, these sensations become a CS that elicits the CR of awakening. This process of classical conditioning—which does not hurt, but is not appropriate for the bed training of normal children—has been found to be over 60 percent successful in treating nocturnal enuresis (Doleys, 1977).

Classical Conditioning, Phobias, and Psychosomatic Illness

Lester the beagle and I learned to fear needles through classical conditioning; is it possible that the intense and irrational fears that we call **phobias** are also learned in this way? Suppose, for example, that a child playing in a swimming pool was frightened, and nearly drowned, when he was accidentally knocked down. This one pairing may have been so intense that, even in adulthood, it would leave a conditioned fear of water. Researchers specializing in phobias suggest that many, but probably not all, human phobias are the result of classical conditioning (Marks, 1969). (See *Of Special Interest:* "Little Albert" for more on this topic.)

There is also evidence suggesting that classical conditioning may play a role in the origins of medical conditions believed to be partly or wholly based on psychological causes, commonly referred to as **psychosomatic illnesses.** For example, Dutch researchers have found that they can classically condition asthma attacks to a previously neutral stimulus (Dekker, Pelser, & Groen, 1957). Two asthma patients, one with an allergic sensitivity to grass pollen and the other to house dust, volunteered to be subjects in the study. First, they inhaled the substance (UCS) to which they were allergic through a glass mouthpiece and each suffered a full-blown asthma attack (UCR). This one pairing was so effective that the next time they were brought to the laboratory, the subjects suffered allergy attacks (CR) as soon as the glass mouthpiece (CS) was placed in their mouths, even though it contained only oxygen. This time their asthma attacks were classically conditioned, raising the possibility that asthmatics may learn to have attacks to neutral stimuli outside the laboratory, too. This is not to say that asthma is solely a learned illness—it's clearly caused by physical factors—but, some of the stimuli that elicit it may be classically conditioned.

nocturnal enuresis (nok″tern-el en″u-re′sis) Involuntary urination during sleep among children above age four.

This child's fear may be a conditioned response resulting from the association of dogs and unpleasant experiences.

phobia (fo′be-ah) An intense, irrational fear.

psychosomatic illness (si″ko-so-mat′ik) Bodily illness that is psychological rather than biological in origin (*psycho* = psychological, *soma* = body).

OF SPECIAL INTEREST

Little Albert: Classically Conditioned Fear

In 1920 behaviorist John B. Watson and his associate Rosalie Rayner published what must be the most widely cited example of classical conditioning and stimulus generalization in psychology. Watson was convinced that many of our fears are acquired through classical conditioning and sought to test this idea by teaching a fear to a young child, the now famous little Albert. Albert was first allowed to play with a white laboratory rat to find out if he was afraid of rats: He was not at that time. Then as he played with the white rat, an iron bar was struck loudly with a hammer behind Albert's head. As might be expected, the noise caused Albert to cry fearfully. After seven such pairings, Albert showed a strong fear response when the rat was placed near him. He had learned to fear the rat through classical conditioning. In addition the fear seemed to have generalized to other similar objects. Five days later, Albert reacted fearfully to a white rabbit, a dog, and a sealskin coat. He also showed mildly fearful reactions to balls of cotton and a Santa Claus mask.

For understandable reasons, this experiment would not be considered ethical by today's standards. Although the conditioned fear probably did not persist, Watson and Rayner made no attempt to reverse the conditioning of Albert's fear and they possibly left him with a minor phobia (Watson & Rayner, 1920).

R E V I E W

Your behavior is not a static thing; it will change from day to day and year to year as a result of your experiences. This process of behavior change is called learning. Learning is defined as any relatively permanent change in behavior brought about by experience (rather than by biological causes). The prominence of the study of learning in American psychology can be traced in part to studies of a simple, but important, form of learning launched around the turn of the century by Russian medical researcher Ivan Pavlov. Pavlov was studying salivary reflexes when he noticed that, after a few days in the study, his dogs began salivating before the food was placed in their mouths. He reasoned that they had learned to salivate to the sight of the attendant bringing the food because this stimulus was always associated with (immediately preceded by) the food. Pavlov tested this explanation in a series of studies in which a clicking metronome was repeatedly associated in time with the presentation of meat powder. As a result, the metronome soon came to elicit the response of salivation. In general, when a neutral stimulus is repeatedly paired with a response that elicits an unlearned response, the previously neutral stimulus will begin to elicit the same or a very similar response. We call this form of learning *classical conditioning*.

Operant Conditioning:
Learning from the Consequences of Your Behavior

If you started parking your car in a new parking space marked "For the President Only" and your car was towed away every day as a consequence, you would probably stop parking there after a while. Similarly, if you moved to a new seat in class and suddenly an attractive person started talking with you after class, you would probably choose to sit in that seat for the remaining classes in the semester. To a great extent, people increase or decrease the frequency with which they do things depending on the *consequences* of their actions. We call learning from the consequences of our behavior *operant conditioning*. The term is derived from the word *operate*. When our behavior "operates" on the outside world, it produces consequences for us, and those consequences determine whether we will continue to engage in that behavior. We can define **operant conditioning,** then, as that form of learning in which the consequences of behavior lead to changes in the probability of its occurrence.

In the sections that follow, we examine three major classes of consequences of behavior: positive consequences (*positive reinforcement*), consequences that are positive because something negative ceases or does not occur (*negative reinforcement*), and negative consequences (*punishment*). We look at the effects that these kinds of consequences have on our behavior and at a number of issues and phenomena that are associated with each.

operant conditioning (op′ĕ-rant) Learning in which the consequences of behavior lead to changes in the probability of its occurrence.

Positive Reinforcement

In *positive reinforcement,* the consequences of a behavior are *positive,* so the behavior is engaged in *more frequently.* Simply stated, we define **positive reinforcement** as any consequence of behavior that leads to an increase in its probability of occurrence.

In the early 1960s, a team of preschool teachers helped a young girl overcome her shyness in what has become a widely cited example of the principle of positive reinforcement (Allen, Hart, Buell, Harris, & Wolf, 1964). The teachers were worried because the girl spent little time playing with the other children and too much time with her adult teachers. They decided to encourage peer play through positive reinforcement. They knew that she enjoyed receiving praise from the teachers, so they decided to praise her only when she was playing with another child. This made the consequence of playing with other children a positive one. The results of this use of positive reinforcement are shown in figure 5.4. To be able to evaluate the results of their positive reinforcement program, the teachers first counted the frequency with which the little girl interacted with other children and with adults before anything was done to help her. Then they started to positively reinforce (praise) her for playing with other children, but otherwise they paid very little attention to her (so that she would get positive reinforcement from her teachers only for playing with peers). As can be seen in the second segment of figure 5.4, the little girl's frequency of playing with peers increased markedly when the teachers reinforced her. In order to be sure that the positive reinforcement was responsible for the changes and not some other factor, the teachers stopped reinforcing her for playing with peers in the third segment (the *reversal* phase) of figure 5.4, and then reinforced her again during the fourth

positive reinforcement (re″in-fors′ment) Any consequence of behavior that leads to an increase in the probability of its occurrence.

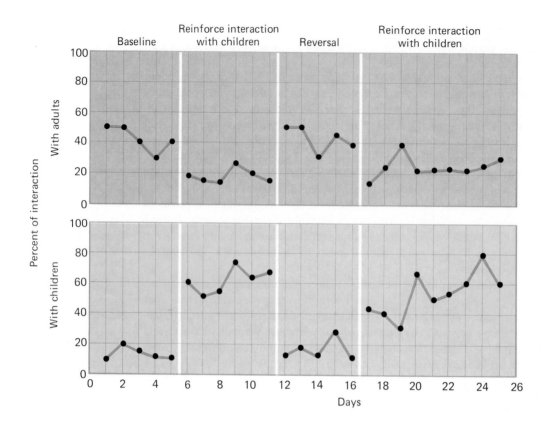

Figure 5.4 Increasing the amount of time that a child spends playing with other children through the use of positive reinforcement (Allen, Hart, Buell, Harris & Wolf, 1964).

phase. As can be seen, the frequency of peer play dropped when the positive reinforcement was discontinued, but increased again when it was resumed in the fourth phase. Thus, the teachers were able to intentionally teach a more adaptive pattern of playing to this child by using positive reinforcement.

Many other applications have been made of this principle, ranging from teaching hospitalized schizophrenic adults more normal patterns of behavior (see *Research Report:* "Learning to Be 'Crazy' ") to teaching employees to reduce the amount of damage sustained when sorting boxes for airfreight delivery (Rimm & Masters, 1979). In each case, the behavior that becomes more frequent is termed the *operant response* and the positive consequence of that response is called the *positive reinforcer*.

Three important issues in the use of positive reinforcement should be noted.

1. *Timing.* The positive reinforcer must be given within a short amount of time following the response, or learning will progress very slowly, if at all. There are some ways to get around this issue of timing (such as immediately telling an employee that she will get a bonus for making an important sale, even though the bonus will not come until the end of the month), but in general the greater the delay between the response and the reinforcer, the slower the learning. This phenomenon has been referred to as the principle of **delay of reinforcement.**

delay of reinforcement
The passage of time between the response and the positive reinforcement that leads to reduced efficiency of learning.

His mother's positive reaction reinforces this child's offer of assistance in making dinner.

2.   *Consistency in the delivery of reinforcement.* In order for learning to take place, the individual providing positive reinforcement must consistently give it after every (or nearly every) response. After some learning has taken place, it's not always necessary, or even desirable, to reinforce every response (as we shall see later in the section "Schedules of positive reinforcement"), but consistency of reinforcement is essential in the beginning of the learning process.

3.   *What we use as a positive reinforcer must, in fact, be reinforcing.* I remember very well making a mistake of this sort. I was working with a child who had a number of problems, among which was the fact that at six years of age he still did not speak or even make spontaneous speech sounds. To begin a language-training program with this child, I decided to use positive reinforcement to increase the rate of spontaneous speech sounds. I spent a number of fruitless days, however, trying to reinforce his vocalizations with M&Ms. When no increases occurred at all, I asked his mother, who had watched every session without making any comment, what she thought the problem might be. She responded that she thought the candy might have something to do with it—her son hated candy! Indeed, the candy did seem to have something to do with it, because when I switched to a positive reinforcer that he liked, raw

RESEARCH REPORT

Learning to Be "Crazy": The Role of Positive Reinforcement

One of the most impressive demonstrations of the power of positive reinforcement in shaping our behavior was a series of studies conducted at Anna State Hospital in Illinois by Teodoro Ayllon. In these studies, Ayllon showed that the abnormal behavior of hospitalized individuals with the severe psychological disorder of schizophrenia could be rather easily modified using positive reinforcement. For example, these patients frequently made delusional statements such as, "I'm the queen; the queen wants a smoke; How's King George, have you seen him?" (Ayllon & Haughton, 1964). Ayllon noticed that these statements frequently got the attention of the attendants on the ward who would try to explain to the patient that she was not the queen. When the patients spoke normally, however, the attendants often ignored them and went on with their duties.

Ayllon suspected that the attention the patients got for their "crazy" statements was reinforcing them and he decided to test this hypothesis in a clinical experiment (Ayllon & Haughton, 1964). Three schizophrenic women who made a high frequency of delusional statements were used as subjects. The first step of the study was simply to measure the total frequency of delusional statements in the three women (labeled as baseline in fig. 5.5). Next, an attempt was made to increase the frequency of delusional statements by reinforcing them more systematically. That is, the attendants were told to pay attention to the women every time they made a delusional statement but to ignore them totally whenever they made normal statements. As can be seen, this more systematic reinforcement of the delusional statements produced a dramatic increase in their frequency. In the third and therapeutic phase of the study, the attendants were asked to reverse the manner in which they paid attention to the women: They were to pay attention to every normal statement but completely ignore every delusional statement. This produced a drop in the frequency of delusional statements to well below the level in baseline and a corresponding increase in the frequency of normal statements.

carrots, his rate of vocalizations rose rapidly. In any intentional use of positive reinforcement, we must be sure that we are actually using a consequence that is reinforcing. Heaping praise on your college roommate for finally cleaning that bathroom may annoy your roommate rather than reinforce the cleaning up. Not all that we intend as a reinforcer actually is.

RESEARCH REPORT

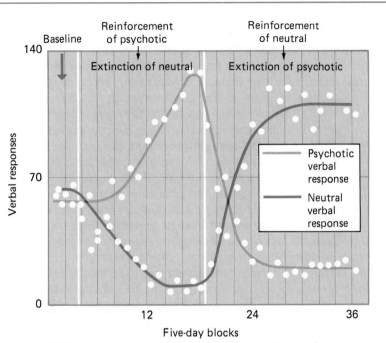

Figure 5.5 The results of Ayllon and Haughton's study of the role of reinforcement from ward attendants in maintaining the delusional statements of schizophrenic women. The rate of delusional statements rises when they are reinforced only for making them, and decreases when they are reinforced for making only normal statements (Ayllon & Haughton, 1964).

These findings were an important breakthrough in the treatment of schizophrenia. It's clear that schizophrenic individuals will act more or less normally depending on the reinforcement that the people around them provide. Schizophrenia cannot be eliminated using only positive reinforcement for normal behavior; but appropriately arranged consequences can sometimes make a dramatic difference. The implications are no less dramatic for those of us who are not schizophrenic, however. Ayllon's findings make it obvious that our behavior can be influenced to a rather astounding degree by subtle reinforcers like the amount of attention that we receive. Have you learned to be polite (rowdy, funny, shy) because of the attention you receive for it?

I do not want to give the impression through this discussion that positive reinforcement is something that only occurs when it's intentionally arranged. For example, we learn that some ways of interacting with our friends or supervisors naturally lead to better relationships than others. We are always affected by the consequences of our behavior and hence are always in the process of learning to adjust to our world through positive reinforcement.

superstitious reinforcement
Reinforcing stimuli that
follow a response
accidentally.

OF SPECIAL INTEREST

Superstitions: How Are They Learned?

Did you ever wonder where our superstitions come from? Most of them are probably learned from others. We see our parents toss a pinch of salt over their shoulder or avoid stepping on cracks in the sidewalk and we learn to do the same thing. Psychologist B. F. Skinner of Harvard University has made the interesting suggestion, however, that some of our superstitions are directly learned through what he calls **superstitious reinforcement.** Skinner uses this term to refer to reinforcing stimuli that follow a response *accidentally,* but seem to the individual to be the natural consequence of that response. Skinner first noticed this phenomenon while working with pigeons who were reinforced for pecking at a small disk. Sometimes a pigeon would engage in some unrelated behavior, such as turning around just before pecking the disk. The consequent reinforcer would reinforce the pigeon both for pecking and the irrelevant response of turning. If the pigeon then happened to turn around again before another reinforced response, he would probably begin turning before every peck, even though turning has nothing to do with the delivery of the food. The food would come after the peck whether the pigeon turned or not. In Skinner's terms the pigeon had learned a *superstition.* And like all superstitions, the pigeon will stubbornly keep engaging in this act even though it serves no real purpose.

Another easy place to spot superstitious behavior that was acquired in this way is by carefully watching a discus thrower just before he or she starts to throw. Many of them go through odd little rituals. Each time the discus thrower steps in the ring, the exact same pattern of behavior is engaged in. As odd as it looks, it's probably just another form of superstitious behavior. This is how it might have been acquired: When the discus thrower is first learning to throw, the behaviors that occur before starting to throw are pretty much random. But when the thrower uncorks a really good throw (a big reinforcer for a discus thrower), any of these random behaviors that were occurring just before the throw will be reinforced through superstitious reinforcement. This is called superstitious because the reinforcement of the good throw had nothing to do with some behavior like touching the shoulder before beginning to throw. In this way, a whole series of irrelevant behaviors may become the superstitions of the discus thrower without him or her ever actually noticing what has happened. Many other superstitions are probably learned in much the same way.

The medal, applause, and recognition that come from winning are strong secondary reinforcers for athletes.

Primary and Secondary Reinforcement

Where do positive reinforcers come from? Are they inborn or do we have to acquire them through learning? Actually, it turns out that some are inborn and some are learned.

There are two types of positive reinforcement, **primary** and **secondary reinforcement.** Primary reinforcers are ones that are innately reinforcing and do not have to be acquired through learning. Food, water, warmth, novel stimulation, physical activity, and sexual gratification are all examples of primary reinforcers.

Secondary reinforcers, in contrast, are learned reinforcers. Interestingly, secondary reinforcers (which play an important part in operant conditioning) are learned through classical conditioning. Remember that classical conditioning involves the association of two stimuli: A neutral stimulus can be turned into a secondary reinforcer by pairing it repeatedly with a primary reinforcer. Consider an example from dog training. In teaching dogs to perform complex acts, such as those required of Seeing Eye dogs, primary reinforcers such as pieces of food are used extensively. It's much more convenient, however, to reinforce the dog for good behavior simply by saying "good dog!" instead of always lugging around a pocketful of dog biscuits. Unfortunately, dogs do not know what you are saying when you praise them and would not care much if they did—that is, not until you *teach* them to care. So, how would you go about making praise into a secondary reinforcer? Actually, it's quite simple. You would only need to say "good dog" to the dog every time you give the dog a biscuit. After enough pairings of these two stimuli, the praise will become a secondary reinforcer and will be effective in reinforcing the dog's behavior.

primary reinforcement
Reinforcement from innate positive reinforcers that do not have to be acquired through learning.

secondary reinforcement
Reinforcement from learned positive reinforcers.

R E S E A R C H   R E P O R T

Learning to Have High Blood Pressure

Rockefeller University psychologist Neal Miller was one of the first researchers to demonstrate that bodily processes controlled by the autonomic nervous system—such as blood pressure—could be controlled through positive reinforcement. He was able to "teach" laboratory animals to have high blood pressure by reinforcing them whenever their blood pressure fluctuated upwards (Miller, 1978). More recently, Miller has used a recent discovery about the effects of high blood pressure on the brain to propose an explanation for the common and serious medical condition known as *essential hypertension* (chronic high blood pressure without apparent medical cause).

Miller's (1980) theory of the origin of hypertension goes as follows: Stress generally produces sympathetic autonomic arousal that leads to increased blood pressure in many individuals. When the blood pressure increases, specialized neurons in the brain called *baroreceptors* are stimulated. Stimulation of the baroreceptors, in turn, inhibits the *reticular activating system* (see chapter 2, p. 67), causing a *calming* effect like that produced by sedative drugs. Miller reasons that this sedative effect strongly reinforces some individuals for responding even to minor stress with high blood pressure. If this reinforcement is frequent enough, the individual may have high blood pressure most of the time. While Miller's theory is speculative, it is promising enough to demand serious attention from researchers (Holroyd & Lazarus, 1982).

intracranial stimulation
(in″trah-kra′ne-al)
Electrical stimulation of the internal structures of the brain.

Dogs are not the only creatures that learn secondary reinforcers, however. People do it, too. How many of the things that motivate us—such as school grades, prize ribbons, money, applause—were acquired through pairing with primary reinforcers? No one can be sure of the answer to that question, but it does appear that learning plays a key role in the fact that these things are reinforcers to many of us.

An interesting sidelight on the nature of reinforcement has been provided by research on the *pleasure centers* of the brain. You may recall from chapter 2 that there are areas in and near the hypothalamus where direct electrical stimulation, known as **intracranial stimulation,** is pleasurable. Stimulation of these areas is highly reinforcing to animals. When caged rats are given an opportunity to press a lever for brief electrical stimulation of a pleasure center, they will press it thousands of times at very high rates until they drop from exhaustion. Hungry rats will even choose intracranial stimulation of the pleasure centers over food. Perhaps this stimulation directly taps into the mechanism that operates during all forms of reinforcement (Olds & Milner, 1954). For more on an important implication of operant conditioning, see *Research Report:* "Learning to Have High Blood Pressure."

Casino operators may not claim to use variable ratio schedules or reinforcement, but they know that an occasional jackpot will keep players at the slot machines.

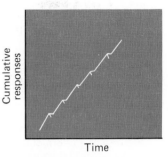

Figure 5.6 Pattern of behavior typically produced by a fixed ratio schedule of reinforcement. The hash marks show the delivery of reinforcement. In figures 5.6 to 5.9, steeper slopes indicate higher rates of responding.

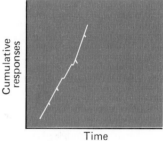

Figure 5.7 Pattern of behavior typically produced by a variable ratio schedule of reinforcement.

fixed ratio schedule
A reinforcement schedule in which the reinforcer is given only after a specified number of responses.

variable ratio schedule
A reinforcement schedule in which the reinforcer is given after a varying number of responses have been made.

Schedules of Positive Reinforcement

Up to this point, we have talked about positive reinforcement as if every response were always followed by a reinforcer. The world is not constructed in such a regular and simple way, however. So what happens when reinforcement follows behavior on some other schedule? Psychologists have distinguished four different schedules of reinforcement and have shown us the effects of each on behavior (Ferster & Skinner, 1957).

1. *Fixed ratio.* On a **fixed ratio schedule** of reinforcement, the reinforcer is given only after a specified number of responses. If sewing machine operators were given a pay slip (to be exchanged for money later) for every six dresses that were sewn, the schedule of reinforcement would be called a fixed ratio schedule. This schedule produces a high rate of response, because many responses need to be made to get the reinforcer, but there is typically a pause after each reinforcer is obtained (see fig. 5.6).

2. *Variable ratio.* On a **variable ratio schedule** of reinforcement, the reinforcer is obtained only after a varying number of responses have been made. For example, in large classrooms you generally have to raise your hand many times before you are called upon by the instructor. Since the number of times it takes to be called on varies, it's a variable ratio schedule. These schedules produce very high rates of responding and the learning is quite permanent. However, if the reinforcement is too infrequent, the response cannot be learned in the first place through variable ratio reinforcement. Usually the response must be reinforced almost every time it occurs in the beginning of the learning process. But once learned, a response can be maintained at very high rates with only infrequent variable reinforcement (see fig. 5.7).

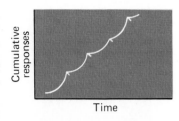

Figure 5.8 Pattern of behavior typically produced by a fixed interval schedule of reinforcement.

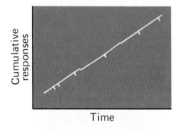

Figure 5.9 Pattern of behavior typically produced by a variable interval pattern of reinforcement.

fixed interval schedule
A reinforcement schedule in which the reinforcer is given following the first response occurring after a predetermined period of time.

variable interval schedule
A reinforcement schedule in which the reinforcer is given following the first response occurring after a variable amount of time.

Skinner box
A cage for animals equipped with a response lever and a food tray dispenser used in research on operant conditioning.

3. *Fixed interval.* In other cases, the schedule of reinforcement is not based on the *number* of responses, but on the passage of *time*. The term **fixed interval schedule** is used when the first response that occurs after a predetermined period of time is reinforced. This produces a pattern of behavior in which very few responses are made until the fixed interval of time is approaching and then the rate of responding increases rapidly (see fig. 5.8). Members of Congress are on a fixed interval schedule for the response of visiting with the voters in their districts. Making a visit back home to talk to the people is of little value to the politicians until the fixed two-year interval between elections starts to elapse. Then visits back home are reinforced by the campaign for votes, so the rate of visits rises dramatically.

4. *Variable interval.* Finally, there is the schedule of reinforcement in which the first response made after a variable amount of time is reinforced. This **variable interval schedule** produces high rates of steady responding like the variable ratio schedule (see fig. 5.9). Like the variable ratio schedule, too, it's not a good schedule for initial learning, but it produces highly stable learning when the response has already been partially learned through more continuous reinforcement. After you learn to say "please" and "thank you" through consistent reinforcement from a parent, it requires only an occasional smile or pat on the back to keep you doing it for a lifetime.

Shaping

In discussing the principle of positive reinforcement, we mentioned some examples of the usefulness of the concept in childrearing, industry, education, and other settings. The concept of *shaping* adds considerably to the usefulness of the principle of positive reinforcement in these applied settings by allowing us to reinforce behaviors that have not occurred yet.

But, before considering the practical applications of this concept, let's go back to the animal learning laboratory where so many of the principles of learning that are useful to humans were first carefully researched. Suppose you wanted to teach a rat to press a lever in the special kind of learning apparatus called the **Skinner box,** named after its creator B. F. Skinner of Harvard University (see fig. 5.10). If you continue to take psychology courses you may in fact be given this assignment in a lab course: "Here's a rat and here's a Skinner box; do not come back until you have taught him to press the lever!" What do you do? If you have not read the section on shaping in your textbook, you might program the Skinner box to drop a little pellet of rat food into the food tray every time the lever is pressed and then wait—and wait and wait—for the rat to press the bar. This strategy might work in time—the rat *might* accidentally press the lever enough times to get reinforced by the food pellets enough to make this a frequent response—but I wouldn't bet on it. Rats generally do not go around pressing levers. When placed in a Skinner box they groom themselves, bite the Plexiglas walls, urinate, defecate, and sniff a lot, but they do not press levers. How then do you teach this uncooperative rodent to press the lever?

Figure 5.10 The "Skinner box" is an apparatus often used in research on operant conditioning. It's named after its designer, B. F. Skinner of Harvard University.

This is where the concept of shaping comes in. In many situations, the response that we want to reinforce never occurs. The thing to do in this case is to reinforce responses that are progressively more similar to the response that you want finally to reinforce (the *target* response). In doing so, you will gradually increase the probability of the target response and can then reinforce it when it occurs. This is called **shaping** or the *method of successive approximations,* because we "shape" the target response out of behaviors that successively approximate it.

Let's return again to where you and the rat sit in the lab. This is what you do: First, whenever the rat (we'll call him "B. F." in honor of B. F. Skinner) gets up and *moves toward the lever,* give him a food pellet. After you do that a few times, the rat ought to be moving toward the lever quite a bit. Then you can wait until B. F. *touches* the lever in some way to reinforce him. Do that a few times and then wait until he *touches it with a downward pushing movement* (if at any time you should have failed to reinforce him enough, you can go back a step). Then after he is reliably touching the bar in a downward motion, B. F. should have quite a high probability of *pushing it down* enough to activate the automatic feeder, which will reinforce him for the complete response of lever pressing.

The principle of shaping has considerable importance outside of the rat lab, too. For example, most beginning skiers cannot be reinforced for making perfect post turns because they just are not able to do them yet. But they can be reinforced for successive approximations to good turns and thereby shaped into good skiing. Similarly, parents should not wait until their three-year-olds do a "good" job of cleaning their rooms; at first you have to reinforce them for an "approximately" clean room. In programs for the mentally retarded, shaping is used to teach them to brush their teeth, perform useful jobs, and to use public transportation.

Reinforcement of successive approximations by an instructor who understands shaping will help this skier become more skilled.

shaping
A strategy of positively reinforcing behaviors that are successively more similar to desired behaviors.

Negative Reinforcement

Reinforcers are not always positive events; sometimes the reinforcing consequence is the *removal or avoidance of a negative event.* Suppose the fellow in the apartment next door plays his stereo so loud that it has kept you awake every night this week. If you assertively ask him to turn it down and the loud music stops, that consequence will reinforce your assertive behavior. There are two types of operant learning based on **negative reinforcement,** escape conditioning and avoidance conditioning, both of which play an important, but often unnoticed, role in influencing our behavior.

negative reinforcement
Reinforcement that comes about from the removal or avoidance of a negative event as the consequence of behavior.

Escape Conditioning

escape conditioning
Operant conditioning in which the behavior is reinforced because it causes a negative event to cease (a form of negative reinforcement).

In **escape conditioning,** the behavior causes the negative event to *stop*. For example, if a young boy has been confined to his room for an hour, that is probably a pretty negative situation to him. If he starts to cry softly and pitifully murmur that no one loves him, and if this causes his parent to relent in a few minutes and let him out of his room, then negative reinforcement has occurred. Which behavior has been strengthened? Probably he will be much more likely to act pitiful the next time he is sent to his room because it had the beneficial consequence of making something negative—the confinement—stop. Escape conditioning, therefore, is a form of negative reinforcement because something negative is removed. It's called escape conditioning because the individual *escapes* from something negative (in the sense of causing it to stop).

Avoidance Conditioning

avoidance conditioning
Operant conditioning in which the behavior is reinforced because it prevents something negative from happening (a form of negative reinforcement).

The other form of negative reinforcement is called **avoidance conditioning.** In it the behavior has the consequence of causing something negative *not to happen* when it otherwise would have happened. Suppose you are terrified of gorillas, but the route that you walk to campus takes you past a yard where a particularly vicious pet gorilla is loosely penned up. If you find a new route to school that does not take you past a single pet gorilla, you will probably continue to take this route because it causes the negative event of passing the gorilla not to occur. Even if it does make you feel a bit like a coward, finding a new route is a highly reinforcing consequence. This is an example of avoidance conditioning, because the behavior of taking a new route was reinforced by avoiding something negative.

The negative things that we avoid in our daily lives are rarely as obvious as gorillas, and the ways we avoid them generally are not as clear-cut as changing routes to avoid a beast of the jungle. For example, Donald Meichenbaum (1966) of the University of Toronto reported a case study of an unusual and subtle form of avoidance conditioning. A 43-year-old man was admitted to a hospital because he could not keep his eyes open. When it was determined that there was nothing physically wrong with his eyelids, he was referred to a psychologist for an evaluation. The psychologist noted that the man's marriage was very unhappy and that his wife dominated him. This suggested the possibility that the man's eyes closed involuntarily as a way of *avoiding* normal interactions with his wife. Indeed, it appeared that the man was able to successfully avoid following his wife's orders because he could not keep his eyes open. The target of the counseling then became the negative marriage. When improvements were made in the ways the husband and wife interacted with each other, the problem with his eyes went away entirely, probably because the man no longer had anything negative to avoid.

Most of the examples we have given here for negative reinforcement have involved learning undesirable patterns of behavior. That is one of the upsetting aspects of negative reinforcement. It's a very powerful method of reinforcement, so we learn patterns of behavior quickly and easily from it. Unfortunately, what we learn are often immature ways of dealing with unpleasant situations rather than mature ways of facing them directly. The child in our first example would have been better off taking his punishment and learning how not to get into trouble next time; the college student would have been better off getting over the fear of the gorilla; and the man whose eyes closed involuntarily obviously needed to deal directly with his marital problems. It's often too easy to learn a quick and easy inappropriate solution through negative reinforcement.

R E S E A R C H   R E P O R T

Learned Helplessness: A Cause of Depression?

Depression is a psychological disorder that affects some 8–10 percent of the people in the United States (Coleman, Butcher, & Carson, 1984). Depressed individuals experience an extreme sadness, lack of energy, negative self-evaluation, and a pervasive sense of *hopelessness and helplessness.* Life is miserable for individuals who are depressed, the future looks bleak, and they feel helpless to do anything to improve their lives. Psychologist Martin Seligman (1975) believes that the depressed individual's helplessness (a pattern of no longer trying to avoid negative events) is a primary cause of depression and is itself a *learned* pattern of behavior. He calls it **learned helplessness.**

Seligman and his colleagues have conducted a number of studies designed to show that a helpless pattern of behavior can be learned. The original experiment involved placing dogs in a box where they received a series of inescapable electric shocks. Seligman felt that these shocks were analogous to stressful events that humans sometimes experience over which they have no control.

In the next part of the experiment, the dogs were placed in an apparatus called a shuttle box. This is a box divided into two compartments by a low hurdle over which the dogs can easily jump. The dogs are again shocked in the shuttle box, but this time the shock is *escapable;* the dogs can easily jump to the safe side of the shuttle box and escape the shock. Normally, dogs learn to escape the shock very easily (they are reinforced through negative reinforcement), but Seligman's dogs who had been exposed to the previous inescapable shocks seemed helpless in this situation. They crouched, whined, and endured the shocks, but they did not learn to escape them.

Outside of the shuttle box, the helpless dogs showed many signs of "depression": They moved listlessly, ate poorly, lost weight, interacted little with other dogs, and showed diminished interest in sex. There is reason to believe that inescapable negative events may also make humans depressed and helpless to control their lives, but more research is needed before we can conclude that this is a cause of depression.

learned helplessness
A pattern of learned behavior characterized by a lack of effort to avoid negative events; caused by previous exposure to unavoidable negative events.

Incidentally, when the parent let the child who was acting pitifully out of his room, the parent was probably reinforced for that lapse in discipline, too. Through what principle of operant conditioning was the parent reinforced? Since the act of letting the child out of his room caused the child's unpleasant whining to stop, the parent was reinforced through escape conditioning. Negative reinforcement of inappropriate behavior is a frequent occurrence that we need to avoid. (See *Research Report:* "Learned Helplessness" for more on negative patterns of reinforcement that are learned.)

Punishment

Sometimes the consequence of behavior is negative, and as a result, the frequency of that behavior will decrease. In other words, the behavior has been *punished*. For example, if you buy a new set of pots and pans with metal handles and pick up a hot pan without a pot holder, a negative consequence will surely occur! And you will probably not try to pick up your new pans in that way again. **Punishment** is a negative consequence that leads to a reduction in the frequency of the behavior that produced it (Church, 1969; Tarpy & Mayer, 1978). When appropriately used, punishment can be an ethical and valuable tool for encouraging appropriate behavior and discouraging inappropriate behavior. In our society, painful forms of punishment are commonly used with children by parents, teachers, and others in authority. Spankings and the like are common features of childrearing. But in addition to the obvious ethical issues, there are serious dangers inherent in the use of punishment that must be weighed against its potential benefits.

punishment
A negative consequence of a behavior that leads to a decrease in the frequency of the behavior.

Dangers of Punishment

The dangers inherent in punishment are as follows:

1. The use of punishment is often *reinforcing to the punisher*. For example, if a parent spanks a child who has been whining and the spanking stops the child from whining, *the parent will be reinforced* for spanking through negative reinforcement. This, unfortunately, may mean that the frequency of spankings, and perhaps their intensity, will increase, thereby increasing not only the amount of physical pain the child endures but even the dangers of child abuse.

2. Punishment often has a *generalized inhibiting effect* on the individual. Repeatedly spanking a child for "talking back" to you may lead the child to quit talking to you altogether. Similarly, criticizing your bridge partner for mistakes may lead him or her to give up playing the game altogether, or at least stop playing with *you*.

3. Punishment is often painful. Thus individuals commonly react to pain by *learning to dislike that person who* inflicts the pain, and by *reacting aggressively* toward that person. Sometimes, an individual takes out his or her resentment on someone else if it's not possible to react directly against the person who gave the pain. Thus, punishment may solve one problem only to increase the chances of another, perhaps worse problem, namely, aggression.

4. What we think is punishment is not always effective in punishing the behavior. In particular, most teachers and parents (and many supervisors, karate instructors, roommates, etc.) think that *criticism* will punish the behavior it's aimed at. However, in many settings, especially homes and classrooms filled with young

children, it has been demonstrated that criticism is often actually a *positive reinforcer* that increases the rate of whatever behavior the criticism follows. This has been called the **criticism trap** (Becker, Engelmann, & Thomas, 1975). For example, some teachers or parents see a behavior they do not like and criticize to get rid of it. But children are often reinforced by the attention they receive when criticized. In this way the criticism reinforces, rather than punishes, the behavior, and it increases in frequency. This leads the adult to use more criticism in an effort to quell this misbehavior. This again reinforces the behavior more and increases its rate in a spiraling upward course.

criticism trap
An increase in the frequency of a negative behavior that often follows the use of criticism that reinforces the behavior it is intended to punish.

5. Even when punishment is effective in suppressing an inappropriate behavior, it does not teach the individual how to act more appropriately instead. Punishment used by itself may be self-defeating; it may suppress one inappropriate behavior only to be replaced by another one. It's not until appropriate behaviors are taught to the individual to replace the inappropriate ones that any progress has been made.

Guidelines for the Use of Punishment

The list above is an indictment of punishment as a method of changing behavior in childrearing, industry, education, or any other setting. It should not be considered to be a total condemnation of punishment, however. In some instances, punishment may be a morally justifiable method of changing behavior. For example, in teaching a young child not to run out into a busy street, it may be the only method that makes sense. In these instances, however, every effort should be made to minimize the negative side effects of punishment by following some guidelines for the use of punishment.

1. Use the least painful punishment possible to avoid negative reactions to the pain by the punished person. Taking away TV time from a 10-year-old or placing a 4-year-old in a chair in the corner for three minutes is at least as effective as spankings, and more humane. But if you are going to use punishment, make sure it's strong enough to be effective.

2. Make sure that you reinforce appropriate behavior to take the place of the inappropriate behavior you are trying to eliminate. Punishment will not be effective in the long run unless you are also reinforcing appropriate behavior.

3. Make it clear to the individual what behavior you are punishing and remove all threat of punishment as soon as that behavior stops. In other words, it might be okay to punish a certain behavior, but it does more harm than good to become generally angry at another person for doing something inappropriate and to hold a grudge against him or her for having done it. Do not punish people; punish specific behaviors instead. And stop punishing when that behavior ceases.

4. Do not give punishment mixed with rewards. For example, do not apologize for what you are doing. Do not hug and kiss the person you have just punished. Mixtures of this sort are confusing and lead to inefficient learning.

5. Once you have begun to punish, do not back out. In other words, do not reinforce begging, pleading, or other inappropriate behavior by letting the individual out of the punishment. It both nullifies the punishment and reinforces the begging and pleading through negative reinforcement.

Distinction between Punishment and Negative Reinforcement

Be wary of a common confusion often made in learning the terminology of operant conditioning. It's tempting to think that punishment and negative reinforcement are synonyms (that they are two terms that mean the same thing). They are not! Negative reinforcement is a form of reinforcement in that it *increases* the probability of the response, because the response causes something negative to cease or not to occur. Punishment, in contrast, results in a *decrease* in the probability of the response, because the response causes something negative to occur.

Contrasting Classical and Operant Conditioning

We have just talked about a number of different forms of "conditioning." This blitz of new concepts can be confusing. If you can get the distinction between classical and operant conditioning firmly in mind, however, the rest of the fine-grain distinctions between these types of learning come easily.

There are two primary ways in which classical and operant conditioning differ from each other:

1. Classical conditioning usually involves reflexive, involuntary behavior that is controlled by the spinal cord or autonomic nervous system. These include fear responses, salivation, and other involuntary behaviors. Operant conditioning, on the other hand, usually involves more complicated spontaneous behaviors that are mediated by the voluntary nervous system.

2. The most important difference, however, concerns the way in which the stimulus that makes conditioning "happen" is presented (the unconditioned stimulus or UCS in classical conditioning and the reinforcing stimulus in operant conditioning). In classical conditioning, the UCS is paired with the conditioned stimulus (CS) *independent* of the individual's behavior. The individual does not have to *do* anything for either the CS or UCS to be presented. In operant conditioning, however, the reinforcing consequence occurs *only if* the response being conditioned has just been emitted; that is, the reinforcing consequence is *contingent* upon the occurrence of the response.

Stimulus Discrimination

As an essential part of adapting to one's world through learning, most responses do not have an equal probability of occurring in any situation. They are more likely to occur in some circumstances than others. For example, schoolchildren are more likely to behave well when the teacher is in the room than when the teacher is not. Similarly, you are more likely to clean up your apartment when your girlfriend or boyfriend says "I'll be over after class" than when no one is coming. Most responses are more likely to occur in the presence of some stimuli than in the presence of others. We call this phenomenon **stimulus discrimination,** meaning that we discriminate between appropriate and inappropriate occasions for a response.

stimulus discrimination
The tendency for responses to occur more often in the presence of one stimulus than others.

Let's go back to the rat lab and see one way in which stimulus discrimination might be learned. The last time you were in the lab, you taught your rat B. F. to press the lever through shaping and positive reinforcement for lever pressing. Let's suppose that you (or your lab instructor) want him to press the bar only in the presence of a specific stimulus such as a light; that is, you want B. F. to learn a stimulus discrimination. We would start by turning on a light over the lever and letting B. F. press the lever and receive the reinforcer several times. Then we turn off the light for a little while and we do *not* reinforce lever presses during this time. Then we turn the light back on and reinforce responses, turn it off and do not reinforce responses, and so on many times. The stimulus in which the response is reinforced is called s^d (short for *discriminative stimulus*) and the stimulus in which the response is never reinforced is called S^Δ. Soon, if we followed the teaching program outlined above, B. F. would begin pressing the lever almost every time the light came on, and almost never press it when the light is off. He would have learned a stimulus discrimination. (See *Of Special Interest:* "Programmed Instruction and Teaching Machines.")

Humans have to learn stimulus discriminations, too—lots of them. We have to learn to say "car" only to the stimulus of a car and not to a toy wagon; we have to learn to say "dog" to the stimulus of the printed letters *D-O-G* and not to other letters; and so on. Many of the stimulus discriminations that we learn are much more subtle than that, however. For example, we must learn to introduce ourselves to others at a party when they are showing interest in us (rather than disinterest), and so on. We have to learn to express sympathy when a sad thing has been told to us. Responses made during the presence of S^ds for that behavior will lead to favorable consequences, while the same behavior made during S^Δ will often lead to unfavorable consequences. Introducing yourself to a person showing interest in you will lead to a pleasant conversation; introducing yourself to a person showing disinterest can make you feel like a jerk.

Stimulus discrimination does not occur only in operant conditioning, however. Let's say that your lab instructor wants you to use classical conditioning to teach B. F. to be afraid of a slow-ringing bell but not a fast-ringing bell. We would start classical conditioning in the normal way, by pairing the slow ring with a UCS for the response of fear (such as a very loud noise). After several pairings, B. F. should be showing a fear response (freezing, crouching, etc.) whenever the slow-ringing bell is sounded. If we now begin presenting the fast ring sometimes, B. F. will respond to that with the fear response, too. But if we continue to present both the slow and fast rings, *but only pair the loud noise with the slow ring,* B. F. would soon only respond with the fear response to the slow ring and not the fast one; he will have learned a stimulus discrimination through classical conditioning.

OF SPECIAL INTEREST

Programmed Instruction and Teaching Machines

The principles of operant conditioning give psychologists powerful tools for influencing behavior. We discussed some simple ways that the behavior of a hypothetical laboratory rat could be changed using

Figure 5.11 A page from a programmed reading text. The student slides a cardboard strip down after every response and views the correct answer on the left. Correct answers are positive reinforcers for accurate reading for most students (Sullivan Associates, 1973).

OF SPECIAL INTEREST

these principles; if you ever take a laboratory course in learning, you will probably be even more impressed by your ability to influence your rat's behavior.

Psychologists who study operant conditioning have been equally impressed with the power of these principles of learning and have sought to apply them to the solution of human needs. B. F. Skinner of Harvard University has not only been a leader in basic animal research on operant conditioning but also in applications of operant conditioning. One of his most significant contributions has been to the development of **programmed instruction.** This is a simple and now widely used method of designing textbooks that incorporates several concepts of operant conditioning. Figure 5.11 shows sample pages from a first-grade programmed reading book. Note that the child reads the words (S^{d}s) and then makes responses. The answers to the questions are on the left covered by a strip of cardboard. As the child makes each response, he or she uncovers the answer to provide immediate positive reinforcement for correct responses.

Programmed instruction has been found to be a successful method of instruction at every age level from first grade through college. Today, it's often automated in *teaching machines* (see fig. 5.12) or through computer terminals.

programmed instruction
Educational materials that incorporate the concepts of operant conditioning, especially positive reinforcement.

Figure 5.12 A child learning from a teaching machine.

Figure 5.13 Stimulus generalization means that the more similar stimuli are, the more likely they will be responded to as if they are the same. In this case, the more similar the wavelength of light to the original stimulus, the more frequent the responding of a pigeon who had been reinforced for pecking when a light measuring 550 nanometers in wavelength was present (Guttman & Kalish, unpublished).

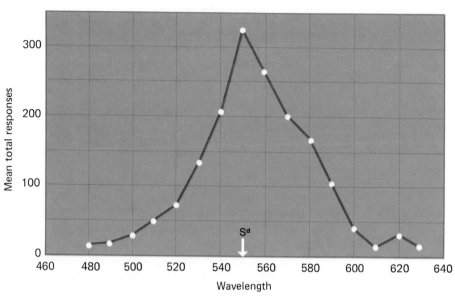

Stimulus Generalization

stimulus generalization
The tendency for similar stimuli to elicit the same response.

The opposite of stimulus discrimination is **stimulus generalization.** This term refers to the fact that people (as well as rats and other creatures) do not always discriminate between stimuli that are similar to one another. Stated another way, the more similar two stimuli are, the more likely the individual is to respond to them as if they were the same stimulus. We call a 1984 Buick "Buick" and call a 1985 Buick by the same name because they are very similar in appearance. Similarly, we call beagles and basset hounds "dogs" because they look, act, sound, and smell a lot alike. And the person who is deathly afraid of cats is afraid of Siamese, tabby, and alley cats alike.

As with everything else, let's go back to the lab to demonstrate it, but this time we will use a pigeon because rats are color blind and pigeons are not. We will reinforce the pigeon only for responding in the presence of a light whose wavelength is, for example, 550 nanometers (a unit used to measure the wavelength of light). In a while, the pigeon will only emit lever presses when the S^d of the light is present. In this part of our study of his learning, however, the fact that he presses the lever only in the presence of the light is important to us only because it gives us a tool for carefully studying stimulus generalization. If we begin changing the wavelength of the light stimulus, we will be able to see that the more we change the wavelength the less likely the pigeon will be to respond to it. If we carefully change the wavelength many times in small gradations, we will be able to make a graph that shows us this fact about stimulus generalization. We have drawn the results of such a study in figure 5.13. Notice that the more similar two stimuli are, the more likely the pigeon is to respond to them as if they are the same; and the less similar they are, the less likely they are to be responded to as the same.

R E V I E W

We learn from the consequences of our behavior. If our behavior leads to a positive consequence, we will be more likely to engage in that behavior again, with the specific pattern of behavior depending in part on the schedule with which reinforcement is delivered. The events that serve as positive reinforcers are both inborn (primary reinforcers) and learned (secondary reinforcers). Positive reinforcement can influence behavior in the first place because it's possible to increase the probability of behaviors that initially never occur by reinforcing successive approximations to that behavior (shaping).

Behavior can be reinforced not only when the consequence is positive, but also when the behavior removes or avoids a negative consequence (negative reinforcement). Actually, two slightly different forms of learning are based on negative reinforcement: (1) escape conditioning in which the behavior removes a negative event, and (2) avoidance conditioning in which behavior causes the negative event not to occur. Punishment, which is not negative reinforcement, is a negative consequence of behavior that reduces the probability of its future occurrence.

Behavior that is reinforced only in the presence of a specific stimulus will tend to occur only in the presence of that stimulus (stimulus discrimination). On the other hand, there is a strong tendency to respond to similar stimuli as if they were the same (stimulus generalization). The phenomena of stimulus generalization and discrimination also occur in classical conditioning.

Extinction: The Process of Unlearning

The process of learning is essential to human life. Through it we learn to cope with the demands of the environment. But the world is apt to change at any time. If we were only able to learn once, we might not be able to survive a change in the environment. If we were Stone Age people who were fond of oranges and we learned to shake the oranges down and eat them, we would do fine until the oranges were all gone. At that point, we would need to "unlearn" the behavior of shaking orange trees and learn to dig for potatoes. The process of unlearning a learned response because of a change in part of the environment that originally caused the learning is termed **extinction.**

extinction (eks-ting'shun) The process of unlearning a learned response because of the removal of the original source of learning.

Removing the Source of Learning

Extinction (unlearning) occurs because the original source of the learning has been removed. In classical conditioning, learning takes place because two stimuli are repeatedly paired together. If, for example, you are hurt a couple of times when you are in the dentist's chair, the dentist's chair will come to elicit the autonomic response of fear (from the pairing of pain with the previously neutral chair). Let's suppose, however, that the clumsy dentist sells his practice to a new,

Cleaning one's room is learned behavior that can be extinguished if all reinforcement for doing a good job ceases.

truly painless dentist and you do not get hurt anymore in that chair. In this case, the cause of learning to fear the dentist's chair is removed. Eventually (classically conditioned fears are difficult to extinguish, unfortunately) the fact that the dentist's chair is never again paired with pain will lead to the extinction of the response of fear to the dentist's chair.

In the case of operant conditioning, extinction results from a change in the consequences of behavior. If a response is no longer reinforced, then that response will eventually decline in frequency. When there are no longer any oranges in the tree, the response of shaking it will no longer be reinforced and shaking will eventually stop. Unlike the extinction of classically conditioned responses, however, frustration is often experienced during the first part of the extinction process of a previously reinforced response. This often leads to a brief burst of the response at a high frequency before the process of extinction begins. When you first discover that there are no more oranges left in the tree, you might shake the tree angrily for a while.

The schedule of reinforcement and the type of reinforcement have a great deal to do with the speed with which the extinction of operant conditioning takes place. Responses that have been continuously reinforced are extinguished more quickly than responses that have been reinforced on variable ratio or variable interval schedules. Perhaps this is so because it's easier to see that the reinforcement is not going to come again if it used to come after every response. It may not be a bad thing that parents, employers, teachers, and others are often too busy to reinforce every good response; an irregular pattern of reinforcement makes the good response more resistant to extinction.

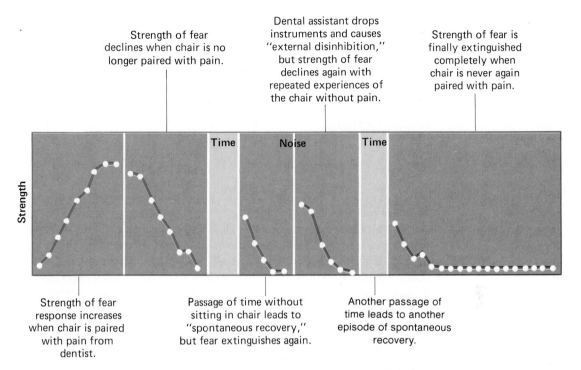

Strength of fear
declines when chair is no
longer paired with pain.

Dental assistant drops
instruments and causes
"external disinhibition,"
but strength of fear
declines again with
repeated experiences of
the chair without pain.

Strength of fear is
finally extinguished
completely when
chair is never again
paired with pain.

Strength of fear
response increases
when chair is paired
with pain from
dentist.

Passage of time without
sitting in chair leads to
"spontaneous recovery,"
but fear extinguishes again.

Another passage of
time leads to another
episode of spontaneous
recovery.

The most difficult responses of all to extinguish, however, are responses learned through avoidance learning. Apparently the individual making the avoidance response never knows whether the negative stimulus has been removed. The individual keeps making the avoidance response because he or she believes that the negative consequence would come if it were not avoided. In this way, an avoidance response continually reinforces itself. If the owner of the gorilla (that you had learned to avoid by taking a long route to school) moved away taking the gorilla, you would never know it if you kept taking the long route, so your avoidance behavior would never be extinguished.

Figure 5.14 The course of extinction of a classically conditioned fear of dental chairs.

Spontaneous Recovery and External Disinhibition

The course of extinction is not always smooth. Normally, the learned response occurs many times before extinction is complete. Consider again the fear of the dental chair: The strength of the response gradually decreases because the CS (chair) is never again paired with the UCS (pain). If, however, there is a long period of time between presentations of the CS (such as a year between visits to the dentist), the fear can reappear the next time the CS is presented (see fig. 5.14). This is termed **spontaneous recovery.** It may occur several times during the course of extinction, but as long as the stimulus continues to be presented alone, the recovered response will be extinguished more quickly each time until the response no longer recovers.

In some cases, the strength of the extinguished response returns for a reason other than spontaneous recovery. If some intense but unrelated stimulus event occurs, it may cause the strength of the extinguished response to return temporarily. For example, if the dentist's assistant dropped a tray of dental instruments while you were sitting in the chair, your fear response might come back

spontaneous recovery
A temporary increase in the strength of a conditioned response that is likely to occur during extinction after the passage of time.

external disinhibition
(dis"in-hi-bish'un)
A temporary increase in the strength of an extinguished response caused by an unrelated stimulus event.

for a while. This phenomenon is called **external disinhibition.** That term will not seem to fit the phenomenon unless you understand that Pavlov, for theoretical reasons of his own, thought that no response was ever really unlearned, just "inhibited" by another part of the brain. He termed this temporary increase in the strength of the response *external disinhibition* because he felt that noise temporarily reduced the inhibition of the response. Both spontaneous recovery and external disinhibition occur during the course of operant as well as classical extinction.

R E V I E W

To adapt fully to a changing world, we must be able to unlearn as well as learn. The process of unlearning (extinction) begins as soon as the source of the original learning is removed. In classical conditioning, this means that no longer pairing the UCS with the CS will produce extinction of the CR; and in operant learning, no longer reinforcing the response will extinguish the response. The course of extinction is often irregular, with the strength of the response often spontaneously recovering after long periods of time or when a strong disinhibiting stimulus occurs.

Theoretical Interpretations of Learning

What is learned? When an individual's behavior changes as the result of classical or operant conditioning, what exactly has happened to the individual? One view that dates back at least to the time of Pavlov is that neural *connections* between brain regions associated with specific stimuli and specific responses are acquired during the learning process. For example, when a rat is reinforced for pressing a lever in the presence of a light, a connection is believed to be automatically created between brain regions associated with the light and the specific pattern of muscle movements of the lever press. The next time the light is turned on, the neural connections will cause the lever press to occur.

Another popular interpretation of learning suggests that learning is best thought of as a change in *cognition* rather than in specific neural connections. As noted earlier in the text, the term cognition refers to the intellectual processes of thinking, expecting, believing, perceiving, and so on. Adherents to this view consider that the individual (rat or human) changes his or her cognitions about a given situation during the learning process. You flinch when a light comes on that has previously been paired with an electric shock, because you *expect* it to be followed by a shock. A rat turns left in a maze because he *knows* that the food was down that way the last ten times he ran through the maze.

This young woman has learned that good grooming usually elicits compliments from her dates. Is this learned behavior involving a stimulus-response connection or is it a behavior based on expectations?

Cognition or Connection?

A considerable amount of research has been conducted through the years to evaluate the connection and cognition theories of learning. Although most of it has been carried out using animals as subjects, what has been learned about the nature of learning is relevant to us human animals, too.

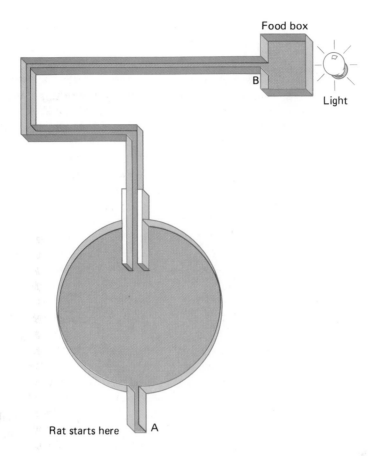

Food box

B

Light

Rat starts here   A

Figure 5.15 The initial part of the apparatus used in Tolman's study of cognitive aspects of learning in rats. The rat begins at point A and receives food when point B is reached (Tolman, Ritchie & Kalish, 1946).

Place Learning

An ingenious experiment to test the cognitive view of learning was designed by the late Edward C. Tolman of the University of California at Berkeley (Tolman, Ritchie, & Kalish, 1946). Rats were initially trained to run down the elevated path shown in figure 5.15. They started at point A, made a series of turns (left, right, right), and ran to point B where food was provided. In the connection view of learning, the rats learned to do this by learning connections between the stimuli of the alley and the particular muscle movements of running and turning. Tolman took a cognitive view, however. He believed that the rats had learned a **cognitive map** of where the food was located relative to the starting place. They did not acquire a fixed pattern of muscle movements; they acquired knowledge of the location of the food.

How can we distinguish between the cognitive and connectionist interpretations? Tolman's experimental test was ingenious. Suppose we give the rats a chance to take a shortcut directly to the food, will they take it? Or will they be unable to recognize it as a better path, since all they had learned was connections between maze stimuli and patterns of muscle movements? Tolman and his colleagues answered this question by blocking the old path (as shown in fig. 5.16) and providing a variety of new choices. Interestingly, the greatest number of rats chose the path that led directly to the food. Tolman interpreted this as meaning that they had learned a new cognition, knowledge of the location of the food.

cognitive map (kog′ni-tiv) An inferred mental awareness of the structure of a physical space or related elements.

Figure 5.16 The modified apparatus used in the second part of Tolman's study of cognitive aspects of learning in rats (Tolman, Ritchie & Kalish, 1946).

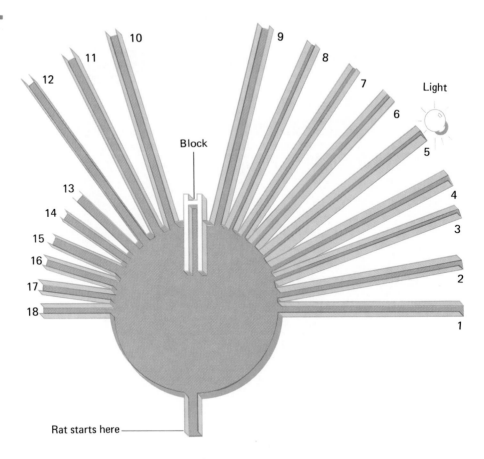

Latent Learning

Tolman conducted another informative experiment that evaluated the cognitive interpretation of learning in a rather different way (Tolman & Honzik, 1930). Suppose we allowed a rat to run around in a complex maze of alleys like the one shown in figure 5.17. Would the rat learn anything? The connectionist view would say no: learning would only occur if reinforcement were delivered at the end of the maze to "stamp in" a connection between the stimuli of the maze and a specific series of movements leading from the starting box to the box containing the food. Tolman, on the other hand, felt that the rat would learn a cognitive map of the maze, but we would not be able to see that he had learned it until the rat was given a good reason (like food) to run to the food box.

In Tolman's experiment, three groups of hungry rats were placed in the maze and timed to see how long it took them to reach the food box. One group was reinforced each time they reached the food box, so they learned to run to it quickly. A second group was never reinforced, so they wandered aimlessly in the maze (never decreasing the time it took to reach the food box). The third group of rats was the interesting one, though. This group was not reinforced for going to the food box for the first 10 days, but was reinforced from then on. Look at figure 5.18 to see what happened. This group showed a sudden decrease in the

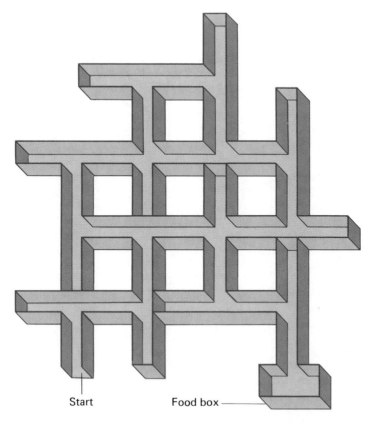

Figure 5.17 The maze used in Tolman's study of latent learning in rats (Tolman & Honzik, 1930).

Start   Food box

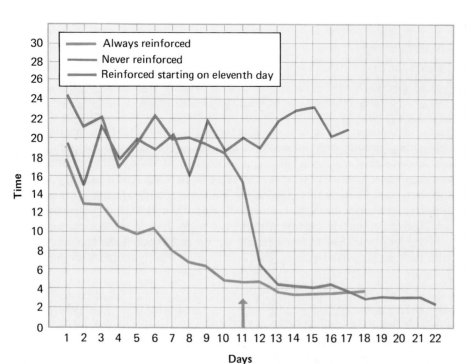

Figure 5.18 The results of Tolman's study of latent learning in rats. A group of rats that was never reinforced for reaching the food box did not improve in the amount of time required to reach it. But a group of rats that was reinforced each time gradually improved. A third group of rats was not reinforced for the first 10 days, but was reinforced from then on. Their rapid improvement indicated that they had latently learned about the maze cognitively before they were reinforced (Tolman & Honzik, 1930).

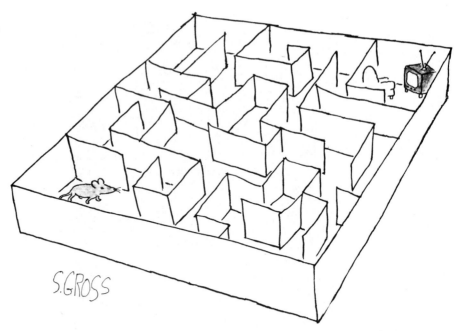

amount of time it took them to reach the goal, catching up almost immediately to the group that had been reinforced every time. Tolman interpreted these results as showing that the unreinforced rats had learned just as much about the location of the food box as the reinforced group, but they only showed their learning when given a reason to do so (the food). If learning were a matter of reinforcement strengthening connections between stimuli and responses, no learning would have been expected prior to the introduction of reinforcement.

Insight Learning

Perhaps the most striking evidence for the cognitive view of learning comes from a series of experiments conducted by a German Gestalt psychologist during World War I. Wolfgang Köhler was visiting the island of Tenerife (in the Canary Islands) when the war broke out and he found himself interned there for the duration of the war. He took good advantage of a poor situation, however, by conducting learning experiments with apes that were native to the island. His best-known study was carried out using an ape named *Sultan*. Köhler put Sultan in a cage where a bunch of bananas and two bamboo sticks (which could be fitted together) were hanging from the ceiling. Sultan originally spent a great deal of time trying to knock down the bananas with one of the sticks, but eventually gave up. Then as he was fiddling idly with the two sticks, he joined the sticks together into one long pole. Sultan immediately got up and knocked the bananas down with the long pole. And every subsequent time he was presented with the same problem, he immediately solved it in the same way.

Köhler repeated this basic experiment many times with other problems, such as providing several boxes that had to be stacked to reach the bananas. Each time, the ape would fail to make any progress and then suddenly learn how to reach the bananas. Köhler said that Sultan learned because of a *cognitive*

This ape can be said to have experienced a cognitive change when it discovered that the stick can be used to pry open the box. Köhler described the phenomenon as insight learning.

change—a new **insight** that he had developed about the problem. As soon as he figured out the solution, the learning process was over. But, see *Research Report:* "Learning Sets" for another perspective on insightful learning. Connection theorists have great difficulty explaining this type of sudden, insightful learning, yet they have contributed much to the understanding of learning, and the theoretical debate is hardly over.

insight (in'sīt)
A form of cognitive change that involves recognition of previously unseen relationships.

Modeling: Learning by Watching Others

Stanford University psychologist Albert Bandura is one of the most influential contemporary proponents of the cognitive view of learning. Perhaps his most important contribution has been to emphasize that people not only learn through classical and operant conditioning, but by observing the behavior of others as well. Bandura calls this **modeling.** In Egypt, for example, where grasshoppers are considered to be a delicacy, people learn to eat them partly by watching other people enjoy themselves while eating grasshoppers. In the United States, in contrast, we learn to think of grasshoppers as disgusting creatures largely by seeing other people's negative reactions to them ("Get the sprayer, Mabel, there's a grasshopper in the kitchen!"). There is nothing inherently good or bad about grasshoppers, but we learn that they are either a delicacy or disgusting by seeing how others feel about them. Similarly, patterns of speech, style of dress, patterns of energy consumption, methods of rearing children, and myriad other patterns of behavior are taught to us through modeling.

modeling
Learning based on observation of the behavior of another.

Bandura considers modeling to be an important demonstration of the role of cognition in learning. A child who watches his older sister play baseball for several years will be able to come pretty close to playing the game properly (that is, know how to hold the bat, how to swing, where to run if he hits the ball) the very first time he is allowed to play. In Bandura's view, a great deal of cognitive

R E S E A R C H   R E P O R T

Learning Sets: Learning to Learn Insightfully

Wolfgang Köhler's studies of insightful learning in apes provided key evidence to support the cognitive view of learning. An important "footnote" to Köhler's observation was provided by Harry Harlow of the University of Wisconsin (1949), which takes some of the mystery out of the insightful behavior of the apes. Harlow showed that the ability to solve problems insightfully is itself at least partially learned.

The apparatus shown in figure 5.19 was used in the study. A tray was presented to the monkey with two objects on it. Although the objects differed from problem to problem, food was always located under one of the objects. The monkeys had six chances to solve each problem. The monkeys in Harlow's experiments solved a total of 312 different problems because Harlow's interest was in whether the ability of the monkeys to solve the problems improved with experience. As can be seen in figure 5.20, their problem-solving ability improved dramatically. Look first at their performance on the first group of problems (problems 1 through 8). While their percentage of correct performance improved gradually over the six trials, they

Figure 5.19 The apparatus used by Harlow to study learning sets (learning to learn insightfully) in monkeys (Harlow, 1949).

RESEARCH REPORT

were still only choosing the correct object about 75 percent of the time by the sixth trial. In contrast, look at their performance on problems 257 through 312. On the first trial, they had to guess which object the food was under, so they were only correct 50 percent of the time. But note that if they did not get it right the first time, they "insightfully knew" that it must be under the other object and made the correct choice from the second trial on.

In Harlow's terms, the monkeys had acquired a **learning set;** that is, they had learned to learn insightfully. Harlow's point was that the insightful performance of Köhler's apes is not characteristic of all learning; rather one must *learn* how to solve a particular class of problems insightfully. Further supporting Harlow's contention is a follow-up study of Köhler's banana-and-stick problem (Birch, 1945). Chimpanzees who had no previous experience playing with sticks could not solve the problem. However, after these chimps had been allowed to play with the sticks for only three days, they were able to solve the banana-and-stick problem easily. Evidently, they had learned something in their play that enabled them to learn insightfully.

learning set
Improvement in the rate of learning to solve new problems through practice solving similar problems.

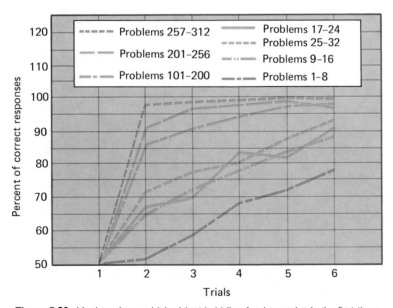

Figure 5.20 Monkeys learn which object is hiding food very slowly the first times they are given this type of problem (problems 1–8). But they learn quickly (insightfully) after they have had a great deal of experience with such problems (problems 257–312) (Harlow, 1949).

Albert Bandura's views about modeling predict that this toddler can push a carriage because of previously watching an adult do it.

learning takes place through watching, *before* there is any chance for the behavior to occur and be reinforced. But, we can learn more through modeling than skills. Bandura has suggested that modeling can also remind us of appropriate behavior in a given situation, reduce our inhibitions concerning certain behaviors that we see others engaging in, or suggest to us what behaviors will lead to reinforcement. This latter point has been particularly well demonstrated through research.

In Bandura's ground-breaking laboratory studies of modeling, children learned to be more aggressive or less fearful as a result of simply observing the behavior of models in films. In one study (Bandura, Ross, & Ross, 1963), one group of children saw an adult kick, hit, and sit on a blow-up Bobo doll. When these children were placed in a playroom (then frustrated by having all toys except the Bobo doll taken away), they were significantly more aggressive toward the Bobo doll than a group of children who had not seen the film—they learned to act more aggressively through modeling. In a similar study with a more uplifting conclusion, research participants who were initially strongly afraid of snakes gradually learned to be less fearful by imitating a series of actions of the model, ranging from looking at a caged snake to holding it (Bandura, Blanchard, & Ritter, 1969). Modeling can be an important and powerful form of learning.

vicarious reinforcement
(vi-kar′e-us)
Observed reinforcement of the behavior of a model that also increases the probability of the same behavior in the observer.

vicarious punishment
Observed punishment of the behavior of a model that also decreases the probability of the same behavior in the observer.

We are not equally likely to imitate all behavior of all models, however. We are considerably more likely to imitate a model whose behavior we see reinforced (**vicarious reinforcement**) than when we see that behavior punished in the model (**vicarious punishment**). In the absence of direct knowledge of vicarious reinforcement and punishment, we are more likely to imitate the behavior of models that are high in status, attractive, likeable, and successful, perhaps because we assume that their behavior often leads to reinforcement (Bandura, 1977).

In recent years, a great deal of debate has centered on the types of models that are presented to our children through the medium of television. Unfortunately, there is solid experimental evidence that seems to confirm these fears. It appears that television does teach children to prefer sugary foods, encourages

Bandura found that children who observed adult models play aggressively with a Bobo doll played more aggressively themselves.

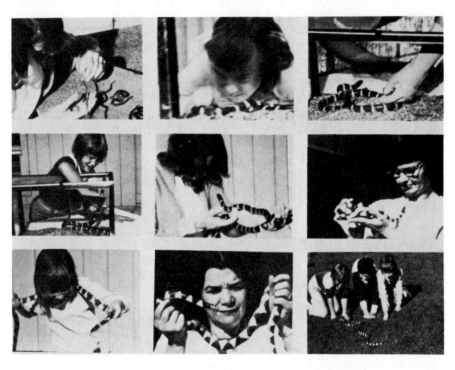

Children who were initially afraid of snakes were less fearful after imitating adult models' approach to and handling of a harmless snake.

sex-stereotyped roles, and perhaps most disturbingly, teaches violence. Although not all psychologists accept their conclusions (e.g., Freedman, 1984), a number of studies have found that the high rate of violent behavior shown on television, from cartoons to westerns, does encourage aggressive behavior in children and adolescents (Berkowitz, 1984; Eron & Huesmann, 1984; Liebert, Neale, & Davidson, 1983; Rubenstein, 1983). In recent years, the television networks have made some strides in improving the amount of prosocial and healthful behavior and attitudes that are modeled on television, but there is still much room for improvement.

Even one experience of overindulgence will be enough for some people to acquire a learned taste aversion.

learned taste aversion
(ah-ver'shun)
Negative reaction to a particular taste that has been associated with nausea or other illness.

Biological Factors in Learning

Learning is a powerful process that quite literally shapes our lives. But we must not overstate the importance of any psychological process, even learning. We must keep in mind that our ability to learn from experience is not limitless; it's influenced in a number of ways by biological factors. We know that it's impossible to teach goldfish to fly and owls to swim, but has it ever occurred to you that our biological nature influences what people can learn?

For example, it appears that people are biologically prepared to learn some kinds of fears more readily than others. It's far easier to classically condition a fear of things that have some intrinsic association with danger (snakes, heights, blood, etc.) using electric shock as the UCS than it is to condition a fear of truly neutral things (such as lunch boxes and skate keys) (Ohman, Erixon, & Löfberg, 1975). A quick look at a textbook of abnormal psychology will tell you, too, that people do have phobias of heights, snakes, and blood, but that almost no one is afraid of lunch boxes or skate keys. Apparently the process of evolution has prepared us to learn potentially useful fears more readily than useless ones.

John Garcia and his associates have discussed another form of learning that exemplifies the role of biological factors in learning (Garcia, Hankins, & Rusiniak, 1974). An example of their experiments can be shown through one of my own experiences as a child. On one fateful evening I ate eight hot dogs. Two hours later I became more than just a little nauseous. As a result it was many years until I ate another hot dog.

This experience of learning to fear hot dogs is an example of a **learned taste aversion.** Learned taste aversions have been the subject of much study by psychologists because they provide another good example of the role of biological factors in learning. Note that I learned to fear the hot dogs through classical conditioning: The hot dogs were the CS and the nausea was the UCS. But think about two facts: The two stimuli were only paired *once,* but I learned a fear that lasted for years. Moreover, there was a time interval between the conditioned and unconditioned stimuli of two hours. Normally a gap of more than a couple of seconds is enough to make classical conditioning impossible. In order for learning to take place under these conditions, we must be highly "prepared" for such learning. Indeed, this makes good sense from an evolutionary perspective; animal species that quickly learn to avoid foods that make them sick (and hence may be poisonous) are species that are more likely to survive. A species that does not quickly learn to avoid poisonous foods is likely to perish.

A particularly sad outcome of our readiness to acquire classically conditioned taste aversions can be seen in the treatment of cancer. Some effective forms of chemotherapy and abdominal radiation therapy have the side effect of causing the patient to be nauseous for a while after treatment. Individuals undergoing these types of treatment are not only quite uncomfortable, but also tend to lose their appetite, causing weight loss that complicates their health problems. Ilene Bernstein (1978) of the University of Washington reasoned that the loss of appetite may be caused in part by learned taste aversions produced by the frequent nausea. To test her hypothesis, a group of children with cancer were given an unusual flavor of ice cream (mapletoff—a mixture of maple and black walnut flavorings) immediately before their regular chemotherapy treatment. Later they were offered the ice cream again. Compared to a group of children who were given the ice cream just before a different kind of treatment that does not produce nausea, far fewer of the first group of children (who had become nauseous after eating the ice cream) wanted the ice cream again. Similarly a group of children who underwent the same nausea-inducing chemotherapy, but had not been given the ice cream just before the treatment, showed no aversion to it. Apparently nausea from the chemotherapy can create learned taste aversions for the foods that are eaten prior to therapy and, over a period of time, can lead cancer patients to avoid many foods.

On a more positive note, a creative and useful application of our knowledge of learned taste aversions has been made by John Garcia and his colleagues in the area of wildlife preservation (Gustavson, Garcia, Hankins, & Rusiniak, 1974). A serious conflict exists in some western states between the interests of sheep ranchers and wildlife preservationists. Because coyotes kill many of the ranchers' sheep, the ranchers kill so many coyotes every year that they endanger their survival as a species. Garcia's research group has developed an alternative plan that keeps the coyotes from killing sheep without being killed themselves. These researchers have demonstrated that if the sheep ranchers place on the range sheep meat containing a chemical that will make the coyotes nauseous, the coyotes will sometimes develop an aversion to the taste of sheep so that they will no longer hunt them. Through this method, sheep and coyotes can peacefully coexist.

Many other biological limits on the learning process have been identified by psychologists. Keller and Marian Breland (1961), a husband-and-wife team of psychologists, tell a revealing story about their experiences in training animals to do tricks for circus sideshows. In one case, they taught a raccoon to deposit tokens in a metal box in order to obtain food. They had no trouble when they gave the raccoon just one token, but when they gave her two, a strange thing happened. She started rubbing the tokens together and "dipped" them into the slot repeatedly, only to pull them out and rub them again. Apparently, the raccoon was engaging in the kind of "food-washing" behavior that is natural for the species. Moreover, this tendency to wash food was so strong that it overrode her hunger. The raccoon washed her "food" so long that she hardly ever deposited it in the slot to get the real food.

These stories about raccoons, phobias, and learned taste aversions are not important in themselves, but they make an important point about the biological limits on learning. We are not able to learn everything equally well. Learning is a powerful process, and humans are good learners, but even people are not capable of learning everything.

R E V I E W

Some psychologists believe that learning is based on the strengthening of neural connections between stimuli and specific patterns of muscle movements. Others suggest that learning involves changes in cognition (knowing what to do, where food is located, what to expect next, and so on). Research on place learning, latent learning, and insight learning provide strong support for the cognitive view of learning. Perhaps the most important learning phenomenon thought to be based on cognitive change is modeling. A great deal of our behavior is learned simply by observing the behavior of others. Regardless of what the nature of learning is, our biological nature places limits on it, making us better prepared to learn some things than others.

S U M M A R Y

Chapter 5 is about the psychological study of learning. Emphasis is on classical conditioning, operant conditioning, and extinction. The last section of the chapter explores theoretical interpretations of learning.

I. *Learning* refers to any relatively permanent change in behavior brought about through experience.

II. *Classical conditioning* is a form of learning in which a previously neutral stimulus *(conditioned stimulus, CS)* is paired with an *unconditioned stimulus (UCS)* that elicits an unlearned or *unconditioned response (UCR)*. As a result, the CS comes to elicit a *conditioned response (CR)* that is identical or very similar to the UCR.

    A. Classical conditioning occurs because of the *association in time* of a neutral stimulus and a stimulus that already elicits the response.

III. *Operant conditioning* is a form of learning in which the *consequences* of behavior lead to changes in the probability of its occurrence.

    A. In *positive reinforcement,* a positive consequence of behavior leads to an increase in the probability of the occurrence of the response. Three issues in the use of positive reinforcement are *timing, consistency,* and *selection of an appropriate positive reinforcer.*

    B. *Primary reinforcers* are innately reinforcing; *secondary reinforcers* are learned.

    C. Four different schedules of reinforcement that result in different patterns of behavior are *fixed ratio, variable ratio, fixed interval,* and *variable interval.*

    D. *Shaping* involves the reinforcement of behaviors that are progressively more similar to the response that is wanted.

    E. *Negative reinforcement* occurs when the reinforcing consequence is the removal or avoidance of a negative event. Two types of negative reinforcement are *escape conditioning* and *avoidance conditioning.*

    F. *Punishment* is a negative consequence of behavior that reduces the frequency of a behavior.

    G. We say that a *stimulus discrimination* has been made when a response is more likely to occur in the presence of a specific stimulus than in its absence. *Stimulus generalization* has occurred when an individual responds to similar but different stimuli.

IV. The process of unlearning a learned response because of the removal of the aspect of the environment that originally caused the learning is termed *extinction.*

    A. Extinction is often slowed because of *spontaneous recovery* and *external disinhibition.*

V. Psychologists disagree about whether learning results from neural *connections* between specific stimuli and specific responses or whether learning is a change in *cognition.*

    A. Research that supports the cognitive view includes Tolman's studies of *place learning* and *latent learning,* Köhler's studies of *insight learning,* and Bandura's work on *modeling.*

    B. The ability of humans to learn from experience is not limitless; it is influenced in a number of ways by *biological factors.*

Suggested Readings

1. For an in-depth study of learning:

    Logan, F. A., & Gordon, W. C. (1981). *Fundamentals of learning and motivation,* 3rd ed. Dubuque, IA: Wm. C. Brown Publishers.

    Tarpy, R. M., & Mayer, R. E. (1978). *Foundations of learning and memory.* Glenview, IL: Scott, Foresman.

2. For more on modeling:

    Bandura, A. (1977). *Social learning theory.* Englewood Cliffs, NJ: Prentice-Hall.

3. For B. F. Skinner's views of operant conditioning and the science of psychology in general:

    Skinner, B. F. (1974). *About behaviorism.* New York: Knopf.

    Skinner, B. F. (1971). *Beyond freedom and dignity.* New York: Knopf.

4. For a firsthand account of early research on classical conditioning:

    Pavlov, I. P. (1927). *Conditioned reflexes.* Gloucester, MA: Peter Smith.

5. A still cogent and controversial novel describing the utopia that one psychologist believes could result from our using the principles of learning to design society is:

    Skinner, B. F. (1948). *Walden two.* New York: Macmillan.

Memory

OUTLINE

KEY TERMS

PROLOGUE

Alexander Luria was a prominent Russian physician who was widely known for his research on higher mental capacities and the brain. One day, a young man (referred to as *S*) came to his hospital office complaining that his memory was *too good*. He often recalled experiences in such vivid detail that he could not shake them from his consciousness; they lingered in a distracting, haunting way that impaired his ability to concentrate on his current circumstances. Because the man was clearly distraught, Luria agreed to study his problem.

Over many years, Luria tested S's memory in a number of different ways. The best known of these tests involved showing S a sheet of paper containing four columns of 12 or 13 numbers each. After viewing the numbers for several minutes, S was asked to reproduce it, which he was able to do without error. Moreover, without looking at the numbers again, he was able to refer to a mental image of it and tell Luria the numbers in any sequence that he was asked. He could "read" a mental image of the numbers across the rows, down the columns, across diagonals with apparent ease. Months later, S was still able to reproduce the table of numbers with few errors. In one series of experiments he was even able to recall complex verbal material after more than 15 years had elapsed.

Although Luria was able to develop a detailed understanding of S's memory ability, he was unable to help him. Ironically, however, S himself found an unusual way to make his life more comfortable. After losing many jobs, he decided to go on stage as a "memory expert." He was able to astound audiences with his ability to recall information and was at least able to earn a comfortable living.

S possessed an extreme degree of *eidetic imagery*—an ability to maintain "visual photographs" of things that he had seen far longer than the fraction of a second that most of us can. Eidetic imagery is fairly common in children, but is much less common in adults. One study of 150 school children found 12 children who possessed this ability to some extent (Haber & Haber, 1964). After looking at a complex picture from *Alice in Wonderland* for 30 seconds, these children were able to answer questions about the content of the picture over four minutes later by referring to a complete mental image of it. Fortunately for them, they did not possess nearly as much of this ability as S did.

P R E V I E W

If we are to benefit from our experiences, we must be able to remember today what happened to us yesterday. New information can be thought of as passing through three stages of memory storage. One stage holds information for very brief intervals; the next for up to half a minute; and the third stage appears to be able to hold information indefinitely. These three memories operate differently and serve different functions, but because information must pass through each one to reach the most permanent memory store, they function as three linked stages in the memory process. Newer conceptions of memory, however, suggest that it's the way in which memories are processed that determines how long they will stay in memory, not the existence of entirely separate memory stores.

Forgetting appears to occur for four reasons. Memory traces in the two stages of memory that briefly hold information appear to fade because of the simple passage of time. Information in the second and third stages also appears to be lost or become irretrievable because of interference from similar memories. We also appear to forget unpleasant or threatening memories in the second and third stage. The third and most permanent memory store is subject to a fourth type of forgetting. Because it primarily holds meaningful information rather than isolated facts, memories become lost because they tend to change over time, sometimes to the extent that the information becomes unrecognizable. Forgetting of information in the most permanent memory store differs from the other two stages in yet another way. Information in this stage is believed to be stored permanently. Forgetting occurs not because the information is lost, but because it becomes difficult or impossible to retrieve.

It's not yet known how the memory trace is stored in the brain, although several theories have been proposed. Theorists have suggested that it involves changes in patterns of electrical activity in groups of neurons, changes in the synapses of the neurons, or changes in molecules within the nucleus of the neuron. It's known, however, that memory traces do not become permanent for about a half an hour after learning and can be disrupted by seizures, blows to the head, or other extraordinary circumstances. Other insights into the biological basis of memory have come from the analysis of cases of severe memory loss called amnesia.

Three Stages of Memory: An Information-Processing View

In recent years, most of the major theories of memory have been written in the language and concepts of *information processing (IP)*, the model used by engineers in the design of computers. These theories of memory posit an analogy between the way the human brain processes information and the way computers do. This is not to say that psychologists believe that brains and computers operate in exactly the same way. Clearly they do not. But, enough general similarity exists to make the IP model a useful model for memory. Before looking at specific theories, let's look briefly at the general IP model and its terminology.

Traders on the stock market need a good memory. According to the IP model, memory is a process involving attention, encoding, and transfer to permanent storage from which information can be retrieved.

The IP model tracks information as it enters a system (such as the brain); is transferred between stages; is controlled, changed, stored, and retrieved for use by a variety of *control mechanisms;* and perhaps passes out of the system. In one IP model of memory, information enters the memory system through the sensory receptors in largely unprocessed form. Attention—an early control mechanism of memory—operates at this level to select information for further processing. The raw sensory information that is selected is represented—**encoded**—in some form (sound, visual image, meaning) that can be used in the next stages of memory. Control processes continue to govern the fate of the information, for example, by mentally repeating some information so that it will not be lost from memory. Other control mechanisms transfer selected information into a more permanent memory storage. As information is needed, it's *retrieved* from memory; but for various reasons, some of it's lost from memory entirely or becomes unretrievable.

encode (en'cōd)
To represent information in some form in the memory system.

When we look at a cookbook to see how much wine to add to the chicken cacciatore, we only need to remember that bit of information for a few seconds. However, you must remember your social security number or your sister's name for your entire lifetime. Some information needs to be stored in memory for only brief periods of time, while other information must be tucked away permanently. The **stage theory of memory** (Atkinson & Shiffrin, 1968) assumes that we humans have a three-stage memory that meets our need to store information for different lengths of time. We seem to have one memory store that holds information for exceedingly brief intervals, a second memory store that holds information for no more than 30 seconds unless it's "renewed," and a third, more permanent memory store. Each of these memories operates according to different rules and serves somewhat different purposes. But because information must pass through each memory to get to the next more permanent one, they are best thought of as three closely linked "stages" of memory, rather than three separate memories. These three stages are known as the sensory register, short-term memory,

stage theory of memory
A model of memory based on the idea that we store information in three separate but linked memories.

Figure 6.1 Stage model of memory.

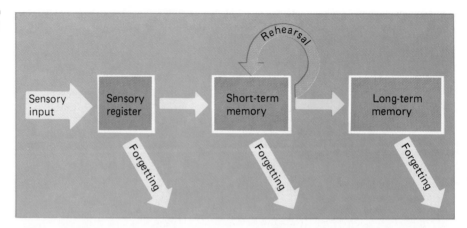

and long-term memory (see fig. 6.1). As you read about the stage theory of memory, keep in mind that it's only a theory. It's an extremely helpful model for making sense of the complex process of memory, but more recent theories have been suggested that the stage theory may be an oversimplification in some ways. Still, a discussion of this theory is an excellent place to begin our study of memory.

Sensory Register

sensory register
The first stage of memory that briefly holds an exact image of each sensory experience until it can be processed.

Figure 6.2 Array of letters like those used in the sensory register experiments conducted by Sperling (1960).

The first stage in memory—the **sensory register**—is a very brief one, designed to hold an exact image of each sensory experience until it can be fully processed. We apparently retain a copy of each sensory experience in the sensory register long enough to locate and focus on relevant bits of information and transfer them into the next stage of memory. For visual information, this "snapshot" fades very quickly, probably lasting about a quarter of a second in most cases. For auditory information, we are able to retain an "echo" of what we heard somewhat longer, probably for as long as four seconds (Tarpy & Mayer, 1978). The information stored in the sensory register does not last long, but it's apparently a complete replica of the sensory experience. This fact has been demonstrated in an important experiment by George Sperling (1960). Sperling presented subjects with an array of 12 letters arranged in three horizontal rows of four letters each (see fig. 6.2). He showed the subjects these letters for 1/20 of a second and then asked them to recall all of the letters in one of the three rows. He did not tell them which row he would ask them to recall ahead of time but signaled to them using a tone. A high-pitched tone indicated the first row, a medium tone the second row, and a low tone indicated the third row. If the tone was presented very soon after the presentation of the array of letters, the subjects could recall most of the letters in the indicated row. But, if the delay was more than a quarter of a second, the subjects recalled an average of just over one letter per row, indicating how quickly information is lost in the sensory register.

Visual information in the sensory register is lost and replaced so rapidly with new information that we seldom are aware we even have such a memory store. Sometimes the longer-lasting echolike traces of auditory information can be noticed, though. Most of us have had the experience of being absorbed in reading when a friend speaks. If we divert our attention from the book quickly enough, we can "hear again" what was said to us, by referring to the echo of the auditory sensation stored in the sensory register.

When we dial a number from the telephone book, we are generally using information that has been stored only in short-term memory.

Short-term Memory

When a bit of information needs storing longer than is possible in the sensory register, it's transferred into **short-term memory,** or **STM.** It's not necessary to intentionally transfer information to STM; generally, just paying attention to the information is enough to transfer it. You transfer a new friend's telephone number into STM because you intentionally memorize it. But you can also remember the amount you just paid for dinner 20 seconds later when you discover you have been given the wrong change even though you did not try to memorize the price of the dinner.

Rehearsal in Short-term Memory

As the name implies, STM is good for only temporary storage of information. In general, information fades from STM in less than half a minute unless it's "renewed," and it often fades in only a few seconds (Ellis & Hunt, 1983). Fortunately, information can be renewed in STM by mental repetition, or **rehearsal,** of the information. When a grocery list is rehearsed regularly in this way, it can be held in STM for relatively long periods of time. If the list is not rehearsed, however, it's soon lost. Rehearsing the information stored in STM has been compared to juggling eggs: The eggs stay in perfect condition as long as you keep juggling them, but as soon as you stop juggling, they are lost.

Our first reliable estimate of the limited life span of information in STM was provided by an experiment conducted by Lloyd and Margaret Peterson (1959). The subjects were shown a single combination of three consonants (such as LRP) and asked to remember it as they counted backward by threes to keep them from rehearsing the letters. The subjects counted backward for brief intervals (0 through 18 seconds) and then were asked to recall the letters. As shown in figure 6.3, the subjects were able to remember fewer than 20 percent of the three-consonant groupings after only 12 seconds had passed. These findings make it clear that memories are quite impermanent in STM unless kept alive by rehearsal.

short-term memory (STM)
The second stage of memory, in which five to nine bits of information can be stored for brief periods of time.

rehearsal
Mental repetition of information in order to retain it in short-term memory.

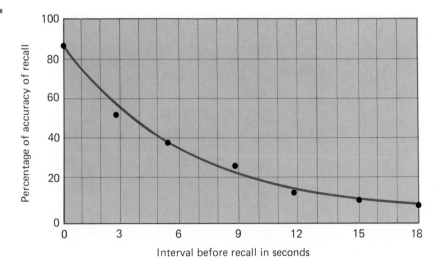

Figure 6.3 The accuracy of recall for a single three-consonant grouping of letters declines rapidly when subjects are prevented from rehearsing by being asked to count backwards (Peterson & Peterson, 1959).

The information stored in STM can be of many different types: memories of the smell of a perfume, the notes of a melody, the taste of a fruit, the shape of a nose, the finger positions in a guitar chord, or a list of names. But we humans have a preference for transforming information into *words* whenever possible for storage in STM. If I asked you to memorize a list of letters (*B, P, V, R, M, L*), you would most likely memorize them by their "names" (bee, pee, vee, etc.) rather than by the shape of the letters. We know this because most people say they do it this way, and because the errors people make are most likely to be confusions of similar sounds (recalling zee instead of bee), rather than confusions of similar shapes (recalling *O* instead of *Q*, or *R* instead of *P*) (Reynolds & Flagg, 1983). We probably use sounds in STM as much as possible because it's easier to rehearse them by mentally talking to ourselves than to rehearse the images of sights, smells, and movements. Nonetheless, STM can store essentially any form of information that can enter the brain through the senses.

Capacity of Short-term Memory

Perhaps the most important thing to know about STM is that it has quite a limited capacity. The exact capacity does differ slightly for different kinds of information, but as psychologist George Miller (1956) put it, it's constant enough to call it the "*magic number 7 plus or minus* ($\pm$) *2.*" Estimates of the span of STM are obtained by asking subjects to memorize simple lists (of randomly ordered numbers, letters, and unrelated words) of different lengths. The length of the list that the subjects can recall half the time is considered to represent the capacity of STM (Miller, 1956). Rarely are we able to hold more than five to nine bits of information in STM, regardless of the nature of that information. This is a very limited capacity, indeed.

The importance of the small capacity of STM is magnified by the fact that it serves more purposes than just temporarily storing information. Space in STM is used when old memories are temporarily brought out of long-term memory to be used or updated. Space in STM is also used when we think. This is why you cannot remember the telephone number of the hardware store that you just looked up if you begin thinking about your purchase before you dial—thinking takes up space in STM and forces out the numbers. The fact that thinking utilizes STM

OF SPECIAL INTEREST

Recall, Recognition, and Relearning: Three Measures of Remembering

What does it mean to remember something? Psychologists have distinguished three different ways of measuring memory that differ from one another in important ways. In the **recall** method, you are asked to recall information with few, if any, cues: Who did Jimmy Carter defeat for the presidency of the United States in 1976? That is a recall method of assessing your memory for that fact.

In the **recognition** method, you are asked to recognize the correct information from among alternatives. The same question above could be asked as a recognition question.

In 1976, Jimmy Carter defeated _____ for the presidency of the United States.

a. Abraham Lincoln
b. Gerald Ford
c. Ben Lahey

Generally, we can "remember" more when tested by the recognition rather than the recall method, because the recognition provides more cues for retrieving information from long-term memory.

The **relearning** (or *savings*) method is the most sensitive of all three of the methods of evaluating memory. Even when you can neither recall nor recognize information, it may be possible to measure some memory of it using the relearning method. In this method, you relearn previously memorized information. If the relearning takes less time than the original learning, then some of the information has been "remembered" in this sense.

recall
The ability to retrieve information from long-term memory with few cues.

recognition
A measure of memory based on the ability to select correct information from among the options provided.

relearning
A measure of memory based on the length of time it takes to relearn forgotten material.

also explains why it's difficult to think about problems that involve more than 7 ± 2 issues. We keep forgetting some of the aspects of the problem because they exceed the limited capacity of STM. In such situations, writing out all the issues on paper helps to keep them straight while you are thinking.

One advantage of the small storage capacity of STM is that it's easy to "search" through it. When we try to remember something in STM, we apparently examine every item that is stored there. Experiments conducted by Saul Sternberg (1969) confirm that we exhaustively search STM every time we try to recall something. Sternberg's experiments even give us an estimate of how long it takes us to examine each bit of stored information. Subjects were asked to memorize lists of numbers of different lengths. They were then shown a number and asked if it was in the list they had just memorized. When subjects had just memorized a long list of numbers it took them longer to respond than when they had memorized a short list. In fact, the amount of time required to respond increased by a rather constant .04 of a second for each item in STM. Apparently that's how long it takes to examine each item.

George Miller says the STM will hold 7 ± 2 bits of information. This shopper probably needs a written list.

fate theory memory.

Chunking

Fortunately, there are some effective ways to get around the limited capacity of STM. One way is to learn the information well enough to transfer it into long-term memory, which as we shall see shortly has no real space limitation. Another way is to put more information into the 7 ± 2 units of STM.

George Miller (1956) calls the units of memory **chunks.** While it's true that we can hold only five to nine chunks in STM, we can often put more than one bit of information into each chunk. If you were to quickly read this list of 12 words once,

chunks
Units of memory.

east
spring
fall
dorsal
west
medial
winter
lateral
north
ventral
summer
south

you probably would not be able to recall it perfectly 10 seconds later since 12 chunks normally exceed the capacity of STM. But if you reorganized the words into *three* chunks (points of a compass, seasons, anatomical directions) and memorized those, the list could be remembered quite easily. This strategy would only work for you if you could regroup the list into meaningful chunks, however. If you did not know the four anatomical directions, it would do you no good to memorize these terms because you could not generate the four directions when you recalled them.

Other chunking strategies can also be used to expand the amount of information that can be stored in STM. It's no accident that social security numbers (as well as bank account numbers and telephone numbers) are broken up by hyphens. Most people find it easier to remember numbers in chunks (319-582-0642) than as a string of single digits.

To sum up what we have just said: STM is a stage of memory of limited capacity in which information—often stored in verbal form—is lost rapidly unless it's rehearsed. The capacity of STM can be increased by increasing the amount of information in each chunk. But no matter how good a job we do of chunking and rehearsing, STM is not a good place to store important information for long periods of time. Such information must be transferred to long-term memory for more permanent storage. (See *Research Report:* "Hermann Ebbinghaus" for more on memory experiments.)

Long-term Memory

Long-term memory, or **LTM,** is the storehouse for information that must be kept for long periods of time. LTM is not just a more durable version of STM; it's a different kind of memory altogether. LTM differs from STM in terms of how information is recalled, why forgetting occurs, and the form in which information is stored.

Because the amount of information stored in LTM is so vast, we cannot scan everything in LTM when we are looking for a bit of information like we do in STM. Instead, LTM has to be *indexed*. We retrieve information from LTM using *cues* much like we use a call number to locate a book in the library. This retrieval can be an intentional act (such as, "What was the name of the secretary in Accounts Receivable?") or an unintentional one, as when hearing a particular song brings back memories of a lost love. In either case, only information relevant to the cue is retrieved rather than the entire contents of LTM.

long-term memory (LTM)
The third stage of memory, involving the storage of information that is kept for long periods of time.

Long-term memory appears to be permanent. It differs from short-term memory in the way information is retrieved, in the way forgetting occurs, and in the kind of information stored there.

RESEARCH REPORT

Hermann Ebbinghaus: The Experimental Psychology of Remembering Nonsense

In 1885, German psychologist Hermann Ebbinghaus published a book entitled *Memory*. In it he described a series of experiments spanning six years in which he served both as the experimenter and only subject. Ebbinghaus's research was an important step in the development of a scientific approach to the study of complex human processes such as memory.

Ebbinghaus was interested in carefully measuring a number of dimensions of human memory, particularly the rate of forgetting over time. In his most famous study, Ebbinghaus memorized lists of information and measured his memory for them after different intervals of time. To be sure that the material he was learning was not affected by his prior experience with it, Ebbinghaus invented an entirely new, meaningless set of items called *nonsense syllables*. During the course of his studies, he memorized hundreds of lists of three-letter combinations (SOV, TIS, YAB).

Ebbinghaus sat in his study looking at one nonsense syllable at a time for a fixed period of time until he had finished the list. He then immediately tested his ability to recall the syllables, and if he could not recall them all in order, he studied the list again until he could. Then after a predetermined interval, he measured his memory for the list. His way of measuring his memory was to relearn the list and measure how much more quickly he was able to do it the second time. Later, he learned another list and tested his memory for it over a different interval of time.

LTM differs also from STM in the way forgetting occurs. There is reason to believe that information stored in LTM is not just durable, but is actually *permanent*. What goes into LTM seems to stay there for good. Psychologists are not completely in agreement on this issue (Loftus & Loftus, 1980), but it seems likely. If memories in LTM are indeed permanent, this means that "forgetting" occurs in LTM not because the memory is gone, but because we are unable to retrieve it for some reason (Matlin, 1983; Reynolds & Flagg, 1983).

The third and most important way in which LTM differs from STM lies in the kind of information that is most easily stored in LTM. You recall that information is usually stored in STM in terms of the physical qualities of the experience (what we saw, did, tasted, touched, or heard), especially sounds. In contrast, LTM primarily stores information in terms of its *meaning*. That is not to say that we cannot recall what fog looked like the first time we saw it pour over the hills near Palo Alto or the taste of fried chicken in our favorite restaurant. But LTM is primarily for storing meanings rather than sensory images. More on this topic in the next section.

RESEARCH REPORT

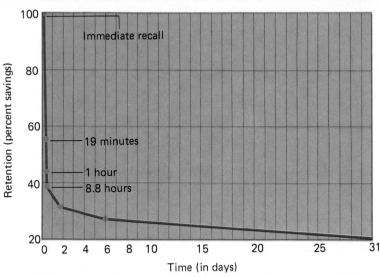

Figure 6.4 The results of Ebbinghaus's study of memory for nonsense syllables (Tarpy & Mayer, 1978).

The results of his research are shown in figure 6.4. Note that Ebbinghaus retained some memory for the lists even after long periods of time. Note also that forgetting is very rapid at first, but proceeds slowly thereafter. Almost half of the original learning was lost within 20 minutes, and almost all of the forgetting that was going to occur had occurred within about nine hours.

It was through studies like these that Ebbinghaus helped lay the foundations for an experimental psychology of complex human processes.

Episodic vs. Semantic Memory

A high school student spends 10 minutes memorizing a list of "birds common to the Southeast" for a test. The next afternoon, he cannot remember one of the words, *vulture*. Does that mean that *vulture* is not in LTM? Or at least, is not retrievable from LTM? In one sense this is true: Obviously the student forgot that vultures were one of the Southeastern birds on the list he tried to memorize. But, in another sense, *vulture* obviously *is* stored in LTM. If you asked the student if vultures have wings, eat dead animals, and are large, he could answer yes to all three questions; that is, he could show you that he remembers what a vulture is.

This distinction between two meanings of the term *remember* has been termed *episodic* versus *semantic* memory by psychologist Endel Tulving (1972). **Episodic memory** refers to memory for specific experiences that can be defined in terms of time and space. **Semantic memory,** in contrast, refers to memory for meaning without reference to the time and place of learning. The recollection

episodic memory
(ep'i-sod-ik)
Memory for specific experiences that can be defined in terms of time and space.

semantic memory
(se-man'tik)
Memory for meaning without reference to the time and place of learning.

OF SPECIAL INTEREST

Serial Position Effect

serial position effect

The finding that immediate recall of items in a list of fixed order is often better for items at the beginning and end of the list than for those in the middle.

Sometimes the order in which we memorize a list is as important as the items in the list itself. It would be useless to memorize the steps in defusing a bomb if you did not remember them in the right order! When psychologists have studied memory for serial lists (lists of words, numbers, and the like that must be recalled in a certain order) a surprisingly consistent finding has emerged. The recall of items in the serial lists is better for items at the *beginning* and *end* of the list than in the middle. This is called the **serial position effect.** Many explanations have been suggested for this effect over the years, but it's perhaps best explained in terms of the differences between short-term and long-term memory. Probably the last items in a list are remembered well because they are still in STM, whereas the first items in a list are remembered well because they can be rehearsed enough times to transfer them firmly into LTM.

This explanation has received strong experimental support (Glanzer & Cunitz, 1966). Subjects attempted to memorize a list of 15 items in serial order. As shown in figure 6.5, the customary serial position effect was clearly found when the subjects were asked to recall the list immediately after learning it. Recall was better for items at both the beginning and the end of the list. But when the subjects were asked to recall the list after a delay of 30 seconds—just beyond the limits of STM—the serial position effect was only half there. Recall was better at the beginning of the list—presumably because those items were best stored in LTM—but not at the end of the

Charlie

"I'm sorry, sir, I can't play 'Red Sails in the Sunset.' It brings back too many memories. 'Stardust?' Nope, that too brings back painful memories. Same for 'Isle of Capri.' Oh, 'Arrivederci Roma?' Oh, yeah, that one also."

that I was surprised yesterday to see a skunk ambling down a sidewalk of a residential street is an episodic memory; but my ability to tell you that a skunk is a black animal with a white stripe that can create a stink (even though I do not remember where or when I learned that information) comes from a semantic memory for the term *skunk.* Although both kinds of memory certainly exist in LTM, semantic memories are generally far more durable than episodic ones.

Another example of LTM's greater facility to store meaning has been shown in a study of the memorization of sentences conducted by J. D. S. Sachs (1967). The experimenter had subjects listen to passages containing a number of different sentences. After intervals of different lengths, she asked the subjects to listen to more sentences and tell her whether they were exactly the same as one of the sentences in the passage. Some of the test sentences were the same, but some were changed either in physical form or in meaning. For example, an original sentence in the passage such as "Jenny chased Melissa" might be changed to "Melissa was chased by Jenny" (change in physical structure, but not meaning) or to "Melissa chased Jenny" (change in both physical structure and meaning). Sachs found that her subjects could tell quite well if a sentence had been changed in either way as long as the test interval was within the span of STM (about 30

OF SPECIAL INTEREST

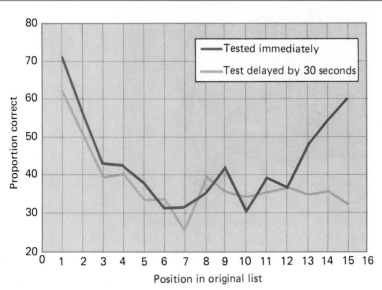

Figure 6.5 When recall of a serial list of 15 items is tested immediately after the presentation of the last item, subjects recall the first and last items better than the middle items. But, when the test is delayed by 30 seconds, fewer of the last items are recalled, suggesting that this part of the "serial position effect" is based on short-term memory (Glanzer & Cunitz, 1966).

list—probably because the subjects could not hold the last items in STM that long. The serial position effects shows that we are simultaneously using both STM and LTM in an attempt to soak up and retain as much of what's going on as possible.

seconds). However, they were only accurate in detecting changes in meaning at longer intervals. Apparently, the meaning of the sentences was held in LTM while details about their physical structure were forgotten when they were lost from STM.

Organization in Long-term Memory

We noted earlier that it's possible to make more efficient use of the limited capacity of STM by organizing information into larger chunks (Miller, 1956). Organization of information is also important for LTM, but it's probably not related to a need to save capacity, since LTM presumably has unlimited capacity. Rather, organization helps to facilitate the retrieval of information from the vast amount stored in LTM. The retrieval task in LTM is vastly different from STM: instead of 7 ± 2 items that can be easily searched, LTM stores such an extensive amount of information that it almost certainly must be organized in some fashion. It's sometimes inconvenient that the 60-odd books in my office are not organized on my bookshelves, but I can still find what I am looking for by searching long enough.

LTM does not use the Dewey Decimal System, but like a library, LTM organizes information to facilitate retrieval.

It would be impossible, on the other hand, to find the same book in the university library if their books were as unorganized and randomly placed on the shelves as mine. Like LTM, the library needs an organized way of storing and retrieving a huge amount of information.

Evidence for the organization of LTM has been available for some time. As long ago as 1944, when subjects were asked to recall items from categories (such as makes of automobiles or animals) that they had learned before the study, they recalled them in bursts of related items, paused, and then recalled another group of items, and so on (Bousfield & Sedgewick, 1944). Seemingly, the bursts of items that were recalled reflected the way they were organized in LTM. Furthermore, when subjects memorized new lists of items that could be categorized, they tended to recall them in related groups. For example, Weston Bousfield (1953) asked subjects to memorize a list of 60 words that could be conceptually grouped into four categories: animals, vegetables, names, and professions (muskrat, blacksmith, panther, baker, wildcat, howard, jason, printer, and so on). Even though the words were presented in random order and could also be read in any order, subjects recalled them in categorical groupings significantly more often than would be expected by chance. Apparently, the words were stored in LTM according to organized categories.

The exact nature of the organization of information in LTM is currently very much a matter of debate. It appears, though, that information is organized primarily in terms of categories of related meaning, but also according to how frequently events have been associated in our experience (Collins & Loftus, 1975; Dodd & White, 1980). It also seems that more links exist between items of information in memory than would be logically necessary to retrieve any item of information. These extra links use additional space in LTM, but make the retrieval of information more efficient. Given the theoretically unlimited capacity of LTM, this would seem to be a good trade-off.

The next time you make a mistake in retrieving information from LTM, examine it to see if you can discern evidence of LTM's organization. If I ate chicken salad the first time I had lunch with Lucille, I might mistakenly remember having eaten tuna salad, but not a pizza. Information is stored primarily in terms of related meaning in LTM.

Levels of Processing: An Alternative to the Stage Model

The model that suggests there are three separate stages of memory (sensory register, STM, and LTM) has been enormously helpful in making sense of the complex phenomenon of memory. More recent research, however, suggests that, at least for technical purposes, this view may be too simplistic. Fergus Craik and Robert Lockhart (1972) have proposed a **levels of processing model** suggesting that the distinction between short-term and long-term memory is a matter of *degree* rather than separate stages. In brief, Craik and Lockhart believe that there is only one memory store beyond the sensory register. The durability of stored information depends on how well it is processed as it is being encoded for memory. Information will be kept only briefly if it's processed at a *shallow* level, but will be kept much longer if it's processed at a *deeper* level. Thus, the differences that we have just described between STM and LTM are not, in this view, differences between two different memory systems operating according to different principles, but between different levels of processing during the encoding process. Furthermore, according to Craik and Lockhart, there is a continuum of levels of processing ranging from very shallow to very deep, rather than just two types of storage (short and long).

levels of processing model
An alternative to the stage theory of memory that states that the distinction between short-term and long-term memory is a matter of degree rather than different kinds of memory and is based on how incoming information is processed.

What is the difference between deep and shallow processing? One way of putting it is to say that shallow processing involves the encoding of superficial perceptual information, while deep processing encodes meaning. Consider the following list of adjectives.

soft
swift
warm
sharp
witty
bright
clean
beautiful

If you asked 10 acquaintances to process this list in a superficial way ("Look at each word for five seconds then circle the adjectives containing the letter *i*.") and asked 10 other acquaintances to process it in a deep way ("Look at each word for five seconds then tell me if it's an adjective that is descriptive of you."), which group do you think would remember more of the words if, without warning, you asked them to recall the list 10 minutes later? Craik and Lockhart's levels of processing view would predict that the subjects who processed the words deeply (the second group) would recall more of the words—not because they had stored the words in a different memory (LTM vs. STM), but because information processed deeply is stored more permanently.

elaboration
(e-lab″o-ra′shun)
The process of creating associations between a new memory and existing memories.

A more recent view suggests that the difference between levels of processing is more general than the distinction between encoding in terms of perceptual characteristics or meaning. Deep processing involves greater **elaboration** of memories during the encoding phase than shallow processing. Elaboration, in this sense, means creating more associations between the new memory and existing memories (Ellis & Hunt, 1983). For example, if you read a paragraph in a textbook and spend a few minutes relating its contents to what you had learned in the previous chapters or to your own life, you will be elaborating the memory—linking it to existing memories. Deeply processing the new information in this way will improve your memory of the paragraph. The interesting thing about this newer view of deep processing is that even superficial perceptual information can be richly elaborated, such as by relating a new telephone number to existing memories about the person you are calling.

It's not yet clear whether the levels of processing view will entirely replace the STM/LTM stage model, or simply modify it by making clear that the "shortness" or "longness" of memory storage is a matter of degree related to how deeply the material is processed. In this text, I have assumed that the stage model and the highly useful concepts of STM and LTM will not be dropped, but will be modified. This is not to underemphasize the importance of the levels of processing view of memory, however. It serves the highly useful purpose of reminding us that information that is learned in a shallow, rote manner will not be around in our memories as long as information that we take the time and effort to understand and elaborate as we learn it. If you have not yet read the section at the front of this book entitled *Before You Begin: The Psychology of Study Skills,* you may want to turn to it now for hints on some simple ways to make memorization more meaningful by processing information more deeply during the encoding process. Also see *Research Report:* "Memory for Rote vs. Meaningful Learning" for practical advice on deeply processing information to be memorized in college courses.

R E V I E W

We can think of human memory as being composed of three different, but related, stages of memory. The sensory register holds a replica of the visual, auditory, or other sensory input for a very brief interval while relevant information is extracted from it. Short-term memory holds information, generally as sounds, for about a half minute unless it's renewed through rehearsal. The capacity of short-term memory is quite limited unless information is organized into larger chunks. Long-term memory stores information primarily in terms of its meaning. Its capacity is very large and memories stored there seem to be permanent. Forgetting occurs because information can no longer be retrieved rather than because it's lost from the long-term memory store. The store of information in LTM is so vast that it must be organized in some way to facilitate retrieval of information. One current theory suggests that the organization is primarily in terms of categories of meaning.

The division of memory into a distinct STM and LTM has been questioned recently. It has been suggested, instead, that the duration that information can be held in memory depends on the depth at which it's processed, not the stage of memory in which it's held. Information that is processed deeply during the encoding process—more richly elaborated—is stored more permanently than information that is processed in a shallow way. If this distinction is kept in mind, however, it still may be useful to think of memory in terms of the STM/LTM stage model.

RESEARCH REPORT

Memory for Rote vs. Meaningful Learning

There are many reasons for not being able to remember something. One of the most common reasons is that the information was never stored properly in memory in the first place. Because long-term memory is far more efficient at storing meaning than isolated facts, it's considerably better to memorize material that you want to store for long periods in a meaningful way than to memorize it in a meaningless rote fashion. The following experiment conducted by Stanford University psychologist Richard Atkinson and his associates (Raugh & Atkinson, 1975) not only makes this point very well but gives you a practical method for making your memorization more meaningful, and hence more effective.

Some of the things that you need to memorize for a college course are inherently meaningful to you, but sometimes you will have to take an active role in *creating* a greater meaningfulness for the material being learned, that is, you have to process it deeply. Raugh and Atkinson (1975) demonstrated the value of teaching students to do this in memorizing Spanish vocabulary words, using what they called the *keyword* method. They asked one group of students to memorize English translations in the standard role way of rotely associating the English word with the unknown Spanish word. Another group was taught to increase the meaningfulness of the association between the English and Spanish word pairs. As shown

Table 6.1 Vocabulary items and keywords used in teaching a foreign language.

Spanish	Keyword	Translation
Charco	[charcoal]	Puddle
Arena	[rain]	Sand
Gusano	[goose]	Worm
Lagartija	[log]	Lizard
Rodilla	[road]	Knee
Prado	[prod]	Meadow
Cebolla	[boy]	Onion
Nabo	[knob]	Turnip
Payaso	[pie]	Clown
Trigo	[tree]	Wheat
Postre	[post]	Dessert
Chispa	[cheese]	Spark
Butaca	[boot]	Armchair
Cardo	[card]	Thistle
Carpa	[carp]	Tent

From Raugh, M. R. and R. C. Atkinson, "A mnemonic method for learning a second language vocabulary." Journal of Educational Psychology, 67, 1–16. Copyright 1975 American Psychological Association. Reprinted by permission of the author.

[*Continued on page 236*]

R E S E A R C H   R E P O R T

[Continued from page 235]

in table 6.1, they were told to think of an English word that sounded like the Spanish word (like "charcoal" for the Spanish word for puddle, "charco") and form a mental image of the English sound-alike word and the actual English translation (a bag of charcoal sitting in a puddle).

Students who learned the Spanish vocabulary in this more meaningful fashion were able to recall an average of 88 percent of the words, while the students who used rote memorization were only able to recall an average of 28 percent when tested later. By actively enhancing the meaningfulness of what was learned, the students were able to greatly improve its storage in LTM. One practical implication of this finding is clear: When faced with a rote memorization task, we should create as much meaning for the task as possible to improve memory for it over long periods of time.

We also should not fail to catch the more subtle implication of Raugh and Atkinson's study. We are all often guilty of doing the opposite of Raugh and Atkinson's efficient memorizers. We often do not take the time to understand the meaning in inherently meaningful material. Instead, we try to memorize it in rote fashion. This rote learning cannot be effectively stored in LTM, so it's difficult to learn and even more difficult to remember.

Why Forgetting Occurs

So far we have talked about remembering and forgetting in terms of the three stages of memory. We have noted that forgetting is different in STM and LTM, but we have skirted the issue of the causes of forgetting. Why do some memories become lost or irretrievable? What causes forgetting to occur? There are four major theories of forgetting that should be discussed in some detail: *decay theory,* which states that time alone causes memory traces to fade; *interference theory,* which suggests that other memories interfere with remembering; *reconstruction theory,* which proposes that memory traces become distorted with time, sometimes to the point of becoming unrecognizable; and the *theory of motivated forgetting,* which suggests that we forget information that is unpleasant or threatening.

Decay Theory

decay theory
The theory that states that forgetting occurs as the memory trace fades over time.

According to **decay theory,** some form of physiological change, called the "memory trace," remains in the brain after learning, and gradually fades over time unless it's reactivated by being recalled from time to time. According to this theory, forgetting occurs simply because time passes. This theory has been around for a long time and fits our commonsense understanding of forgetting. It had been discarded by psychologists as being wholly incorrect until recent years. As we shall see in a moment, forgetting is more complicated than the mere fading of memory traces and involves factors other than time. But the acceptance by most

psychologists of some version of the three-stage conception of memory has brought decay theory back at least into limited favor. It appears that the simple passage of time is a cause of forgetting both in the sensory register and in STM. It does not appear that decay due to the passage of time is a cause of forgetting in LTM, however. Memory "traces" appear to be "permanent" once they make it into LTM. Forgetting does not seem to happen in LTM because of time, but because other factors make memories irretrievable.

Interference Theory

Interference theory is based on considerable evidence that forgetting in LTM does not occur because of the passage of time, but because other memories interfere with the retrieval of what you are trying to recall, particularly if the other memories are similar to the one you are trying to remember. Suppose you take an interest in French impressionist painters and you read a book about the painting techniques of Degas, Monet, and Matisse. It would be no great feat to memorize each painter's techniques and keep them straight, but suppose you then learn about the techniques of three more French impressionists, and then three more. Pretty soon, recall becomes difficult, probably because the similar memories interfere with the retrieval of one another. The same thing happens when you try to remember a lot of telephone numbers, grocery-list items, or math formulas.

    The fact that the other memories must be similar to the one you are trying to recall in order to interfere with its retrieval has been shown in a simple experiment by Delos Wickens and his associates (Wickens, Born, & Allen, 1963). Wickens asked one group of subjects to memorize six lists of three-digit combinations (632, 785, 877). As can be seen in figure 6.6, these subjects got progressively worse at recall as they memorized more and more lists. The previously memorized lists interfered with the recall of each new list. A second group of subjects was asked to memorize five lists of combinations of three letters, and then to memorize a list of three-digit combinations like that used in the first group. As can also be seen in figure 6.6, these subjects became progressively less successful at recalling the letter combinations due to the buildup of interference. But when they memorized the list of digit combinations instead of a sixth list of letters, their memory performance shot up showing that the letters were too dissimilar to the digits to interfere with their recall. Interference only comes from similar memories.

(left)
Forget the combination? According to the decay theory, forgetting occurs because time passes.

(right)
If you cannot remember the name of the restaurant where you had the great wonton soup, it may be because similar memories are interfering with the one you want.

interference theory
The theory that states that forgetting occurs because similar memories interfere with the storage or retrieval of information.

Figure 6.6 As two groups of subjects memorized additional lists of letter combinations (L) or number combinations (N), proactive inhibition built up from the similar lists, and memory declined. When one group shifted from memorizing letters to memorizing numbers, their recall improved dramatically. The proactive inhibition only affects memory for very similar material; the previously learned letters do not affect memory for numbers (Wickens, Born & Allen, 1963).

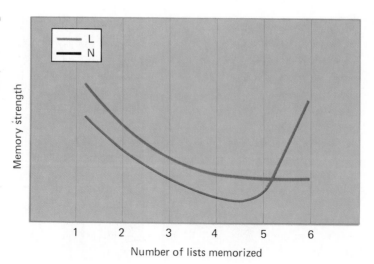

In the experiment by Wickens, the interference came from memories that were formed *before* learning the list; the prior memorization of similar material caused interference with the recall of newly learned material. Interference can also come from memories that are formed *after* memorizing the material in question. If the subjects in the Wickens study had tried to recall the first digits they had learned after memorizing five additional lists, they would have found that a great deal of interference had been created.

Psychologists refer to the interference built up by *prior* learning as *proactive interference* and to interference created by *later* learning as *retroactive interference*. These two forms of interference have been frequently studied in a number of experiments that use the same format or **paradigm.**

paradigm (pār′a-dīm) A pattern or format for conducting research.

Proactive Interference

In the **proactive interference** paradigm, the subjects memorize two sets of related material, such as memorizing two similar lists of words, and then are tested later on their memory for the *second* list. Their memory for the second list is compared to another group of subjects (the control group, see p. 30) who engage in an unrelated task (such as finding and underlining the number 7 in a table of numbers) instead of learning the first task. These procedures are sequenced as follows.

proactive interference (pro-ak′tĭv in″ter-fēr′ens) Interference created by memories from prior learning.

Proactive interference group	Learn list A	Learn list B	Later test on list B
Control group	Perform unrelated task	Learn list B	Later test on list B

If the proactive interference group performs less well than the control group, then it can be concluded that the memories from list A interfered with the recall of list B.

Retroactive Interference

In the **retroactive interference** paradigm, the subjects learn lists A and B and are later tested on their recall of list A. The control group also learns list A, but performs an unrelated task instead of learning list B. The sequence of procedures in this paradigm is as follows.

retroactive interference
(ret″ro-ak′tiv)
Interference created by memories from later learning.

Retroactive interference group	Learn list A	Learn list B	Later test on list A
Control group	Learn list A	Perform unrelated task	Later test on list A

If the subjects in the retroactive interference group are less able to recall list A than the control group, it would be reasonable to conclude that the later learning of list B interfered with the recall of list A. Using these two paradigms, researchers have been able to carefully study the properties of interference in memory and to demonstrate that it's a powerful cause of forgetting.

Up to this point, we have talked about interference as a cause of forgetting, or retrieval failure, in LTM. Interference is also a cause of forgetting in STM, but it may operate in a different way to disrupt memory. Whereas interference appears to confuse the process of retrieval in LTM, interfering memories seem to disrupt STM either by overloading its capacity or by weakening or completely knocking an item out of storage (Klatzky, 1980). If you look up the telephone number 689–2354 and someone says "I think it's 698–5423" before you can dial, you may experience interference in STM.

While there is much evidence to support the interference theory of forgetting in both STM and LTM, we should not be too quick in deciding that it's the only factor involved in forgetting. For one thing, nearly all of the research evidence we have on interference in LTM concerns memory for isolated facts, even though LTM is better suited for storing meaning. Tulving (1972) reminds us that it may be a very different matter to forget in a memory experiment that we were supposed to remember a list including the word "frog" than to forget what a frog is. (See *Of Special Interest:* "It's on the Tip of My Tongue.")

Reconstruction Theory

First stated in 1932 by Sir Frederic Bartlett, **reconstruction theory** suggests that some memory traces become so distorted over time that they are unrecognizable. Memories change with time in such a way as to become less complex, more consistent, and more congruent with what the individual already knows and believes. For example, if you hear a long story about Max (whom you dislike) that is favorable to him on some points and slightly negative on other points, your recollection of that story might be somewhat different a week later when you retell it to a friend. In general, the story would tend to become shorter and less detailed. But because your preconceived view of Max was negative, the most obvious changes would be a forgetting of positive facts, an exaggeration of negative facts, and maybe even the addition of a few fictional facts more in line with your feelings about him. Am I right? Have you ever passed on a slightly distorted tale? Would you trust someone who does not like you to recall accurately a story about you?

reconstruction theory
The theory that states that forgetting is due to changes in the structure of a memory that make it inaccurate when retrieved.

OF SPECIAL INTEREST

It's on the Tip of My Tongue . . .

We have all had the maddening experience of trying to recall a fact that we can *almost* remember. This "tip of the tongue" phenomenon was investigated by Harvard University psychologists Roger Brown and David McNeill (1966) by giving definitions of uncommon words to college students and asking them to recall the word. For example, they might be read the definition of *sampan* ("a small boat used in shallow water in the Orient that is rowed from behind using a single oar"). Often the students could recall the word sampan. Sometimes, though, they felt that they simply did not know the word, and the researchers were able to create the tip of the tongue sensation in these subjects. When this happened, the students found that they were able to recall some information about the word ("It starts with s." or "It sounds like Siam."), or about the thing the word referred to ("It looks a little like a junk."), even when they could not retrieve the word. And then moments later, the word would pop into memory for some subjects, proving that it was there all the time but just could not be retrieved for the moment.

Perhaps all information stored on long-term memory is still there, but just cannot always be retrieved. Have you ever had the experience of being reminded of a past event that you thought was long forgotten ("Remember the time in second grade . . .") only to find that you could remember a rich set of details that you had not thought about in years? Perhaps these memories were irretrievable only until the right cue was used to call them out of storage. Do you remember the experiment conducted by Wilder Penfield that was described in chapter 2? Does it help to give you the cue that he was a brain surgeon? Can you recall information about him now? What happened when he touched electric current to the brain of surgery patients? They experienced vivid flashbacks, sometimes from childhood. Were these memories that could not have been otherwise retrieved?

The distortion of memories has been demonstrated in a classic experiment (Carmichael, Hogan, & Walter, 1932). Researchers showed their subjects ambiguous line drawings as shown in the middle column of figure 6.7, (labeled "stimulus figures"). The subjects were given verbal labels telling them what each figure represented, but two different groups of subjects were given different labels for each figure (shown in the figure as "word list I" and "word list II"). For example, half of the subjects were told that the second figure in figure 6.7 was a "bottle" while the other half were told that it was a "stirrup." Later the subjects were asked to draw figures that they had seen from memory. As predicted by reconstruction theory, the drawings were distorted to fit the labels that they had been given for the ambiguous figures.

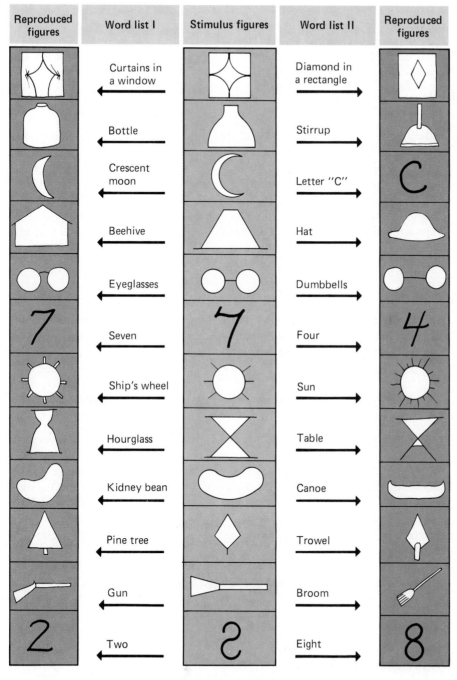

Reproduced figures	Word list I	Stimulus figures	Word list II	Reproduced figures
	Curtains in a window		Diamond in a rectangle	
	Bottle		Stirrup	
	Crescent moon		Letter "C"	
	Beehive		Hat	
	Eyeglasses		Dumbbells	
	Seven		Four	
	Ship's wheel		Sun	
	Hourglass		Table	
	Kidney bean		Canoe	
	Pine tree		Trowel	
	Gun		Broom	
	Two		Eight	

Figure 6.7 Subjects were shown the list of stimulus figures presented in the middle column along with one of the two word lists. As can be seen in the left and right columns, the figures they drew later were reconstructed to fit the labels they had learned for them (Carmichael, Hogan & Walter, 1932).

Several experiments make it clear that the distortions of memories hypothesized by Bartlett do not occur gradually over time, but occur during the process of retrieval itself (Reynolds & Flagg, 1983). First, when the Carmichael, Hogan, and Walter (1932) study was repeated by Prentice (1954), no differences were found among the three groups when the subjects were asked to *recognize* the original visual stimuli (instead of drawing them). Apparently, the verbal labels did not alter what was stored in memory or how well it was retained. More convincing is the fact that the distorting effect of the visual labels is even more dramatic when the subjects are given the labels (*bottle, stirrup,* etc.) *just before* they are asked to draw the shapes (Hanawalt & Demarest, 1939; Ranken, 1963). It seems likely that reconstructive forgetting is a type that occurs during the process of remembering (retrieval).

Reconstruction theory provides an interesting view of forgetting affecting LTM that is intuitively appealing. But until recent years this theory has had little impact on the research on memory, perhaps because Bartlett (1932) stated it in rather vague terms in the first place. Recent versions of reconstruction theory make use of the distinction made by Tulving (1972) between episodic and semantic memory. For example, John Bransford and Jeffrey Franks (1971) have suggested that we tend to distort, or reconstruct memories, because in LTM we store the meaning of events better than the episodic details. If we try to recall an event later, we will be more likely to remember its meaning than the details. Thus without being aware that we are doing so, we make up details that are consistent with the meaning we have remembered.

Bransford and his associates tested this version of reconstruction theory in the following experiment (Johnson, Bransford, & Solomon, 1973). Subjects listened to passages such as the following.

> It was late at night when the phone rang and a voice gave a frantic cry. The spy threw the secret document into the fireplace just 30 seconds before it would have been too late.

Later, the subjects were asked if they had heard the following sentence.

> The spy burned the secret document 30 seconds before it would have been too late.

Notice that this is not a sentence that they had previously heard; the original sentence said nothing about actually burning the document (there might not have been a fire in the fireplace). Most subjects, however, said that they had heard the second sentence. According to Bransford and colleagues, the meaning of the sentence, which strongly implies the document was burned, was retrieved from LTM, but the details were reconstructed to fit this meaning rather than directly remembered. As Bartlett (1932) said, memory is partly an "imaginative reconstruction" of experience.

We saw in chapter 3 that the human brain must construct full perceptions out of the often inadequate sensory information given to it, such as filling in the blind spot in our visual perception. The reconstruction theory and its supporting evidence suggest that we also construct our memories from minimal information at times.

Motivated Forgetting

motivated forgetting
Forgetting that is believed to be based on the upsetting or threatening nature of the information that is forgotten.

repression
Sigmund Freud's theory that forgetting occurs because the conscious mind often deals with unpleasant information by pushing it into unconsciousness.

Many years ago, Sigmund Freud suggested that we forget information because it's threatening to us in some way. We have much more to say about the theory of **motivated forgetting** in chapter 11 on personality, but Freud believed that the conscious mind often deals with unpleasant or dangerous information by pushing it into unconsciousness, by an act of **repression.** This theory of forgetting has not been extensively tested in the laboratory, but support has come from a number of clinical case studies. Although it's a rare condition, there are many well-documented cases of memory loss for highly stressful events, such as auto accidents, crimes, and the like (Lahey & Ciminero, 1980).

According to Freud, motivated forgetting can occur as a result of repressing details of stressful events.

This type of evidence is not strongly supportive of the theory, however, for three reasons. First, because case histories do not involve careful experimental control, other causes of memory loss are often possible, such as a blow to the head in an automobile accident. Second, as we see in a later section, it may be that the effect of the stressful event is to disrupt the biological process of consolidating the memory trace in LTM rather than to cause the memory to be repressed. And third, this type of evidence makes motivated forgetting seem like something that is not a part of ordinary lives, but only related to unusually stressful events.

The results of a fascinating study of memory for everyday events show us a side of motivated forgetting that is certainly more relevant to our lives. While this study is not immune to criticism for lack of experimental control, it offers intriguing, if not scientifically solid, support for the concept of motivated forgetting. University of Utah psychologist Marigold Linton (1979) was interested in our memory for day-to-day events and decided to study it extensively using one highly motivated subject—herself. Every day from 1972 to 1977 she wrote a brief description of each major event in her day on a separate card (e.g., "landed at Orly Airport in Paris"). During the six-year period, she wrote more than 5,000 descriptions of everyday events.

Each month, Linton spent from 8 to 12 hours testing her memory for the events; she randomly pulled 150 cards from her file, read the brief description, and tried to recall a mental image of the event. If she could form a clear image, she counted the event as remembered. Overall, she found that her memory for these day-to-day events was quite good. She could remember 95 percent of the events that happened two years ago, and about 70 percent of the events of five years ago.

Most interesting from the standpoint of motivated forgetting, however, was a pattern that Linton noticed in what was forgotten. Before each test session, Linton "warmed up" her memory by thinking over the major events of the past year. These were often pleasant memories that were enjoyable to think about.

RESEARCH REPORT

Mood and Memory

Stanford University psychologist Gordon Bower is interested in how our moods influence our memory (Bower, 1981). When we are in happy or sad moods, do we tend to remember events that are consistent with our moods? Are we better able to remember information that was learned when we were in the same mood as when we try to recall it?

To investigate the influence of mood on memory, Bower and his colleagues asked subjects to memorize two lists of words: one after they had been put in a sad mood through hypnosis and another after they had been put in a happy mood. Later they attempted to recall the lists when they were put in the same or different mood. The subjects were able to recall about 80 percent of the words that they had learned in the *same* mood in which they were attempting to recall it, but less than 50 percent of the words learned in *different* moods.

Bower interpreted these results as meaning that when memories are stored, the mood that we are in when they are stored is one of the cues that we use to index the memory. When we search for the memory, the mood that we are in at the time is one of the cues that we use to look for the stored memory. If we are in the wrong mood, it will be like trying to look for a book in the library with part of the call number incorrect. Like the book, the memory will be much harder to find.

However, recent work by Bower himself (Bower & Mayer, 1985) has raised doubts about Bower's theory of the relationship between mood and memory. Although several other researchers had repeated Bower's experiment and found the same result—known as

But as she had her memory jogged by reading the cards, she found that she had been forgetting many of the annoying, upsetting, and tension-filled events in her life. As a result, she often found that the testing sessions left her feeling quite depressed about her life. Perhaps there is some truth, then, to the idea that we tend to forget what we do not want to remember. Before this theory can be taken seriously in scientific terms, however, it must be tested in adequately controlled studies. Even at that, it's clear that motivated forgetting can never be a general theory of forgetting, for much of what we forget is either positive or neutral in nature. (See *Research Report*: "Mood and Memory" for other influences on memory.)

R E S E A R C H   R E P O R T

replication in science—two other researchers had not been able to replicate Bower's study. This led Bower to attempt to replicate his own results, which he was not able to do. Much to his credit as a scientist, Bower has taken pains not only to publish findings that contradicted his own theory, but to notify textbook authors so that incorrect information would not be given to students. This is an example of science at its best.

But, we must not make the mistake of assuming that mood and memory are not related at all. Other experiments suggest that it is, at least in some ways. For example, Snyder and White (1982) have shown that persons are able to recall far more happy events that have recently happened in their lives when they are happy than when they are sad. Conversely, it is easier to recall sad events than happy events when sad. In many ways this finding is of greater importance than Bower's unreliable finding concerning the memorization of lists. Snyder and White's finding helps explain why sad moods sometimes last so long. When we are sad we tend to recall and think about mostly unpleasant events and have a hard time remembering anything pleasant. Since our moods are strongly influenced by the happy or unhappy things that we think about (Velten, 1968), our memories can create a cycle of continuing unhappiness. Something happens to make us unhappy, which makes us remember other unhappy things, which makes us feel more unhappy, which makes us remember other unhappy things, and so on. Fortunately, something pleasant usually creeps into our lives to get us out of the cycle. The overall message of these studies is clear: While it's easy to think of mood and memory as separate processes, they are inextricably intertwined.

R E V I E W

There are four major causes of forgetting, each with different relevance to the three stages of memory. Forgetting in the sensory register seems to occur primarily because of simple decay of the memory over time. Forgetting in short-term memory can be attributed to decay over time, but also to interference from other similar information stored in memory. Interference from other memories may explain some forgetting in long-term memory, but much forgetting also seems to be caused by the reconstruction of memories to the point that they are inaccurate or unretrievable. Memories may also be lost from LTM because they are unpleasant or threatening to us in some way.

The study this student does in preparation for an exam may be more effective if it's followed by a night of sleeping and dreaming.

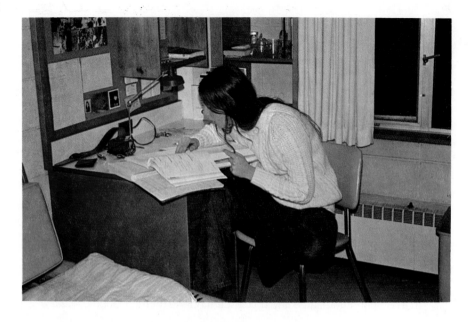

Biological Basis of Memory: The Search for the Engram

engram (en'gram)
The as yet unidentified memory trace in the brain that is the biological basis of memory.

It's obvious that some physical change must take place in the nervous system when we learn something new (McGaugh, 1983; Rosenzweig, 1984). If something did not stay in the individual, how would we be able to recall the new learning at a later time? The "something" that remains after learning—the "memory trace" or **engram** as psychologists often call it—is the biological basis of memory. While the engram has long been searched for, there is no consensus among psychologists as to what or where it is. We do know some interesting facts about the memory trace, such as how long it takes to form and how it can be disturbed. But we only have controversial theories about its physical nature at present. In this section, we will study the biological basis of long-term memory. First, we look at theories and research on the nature of the so-called engram. Second, we then examine the effects of biological damage to the brain to see what it reveals about memory. Much less is known about the biological basis of short-term memory.

Consolidation: Forming the Engram

consolidation
The process through which a long-term memory becomes stable.

It takes about 30 minutes for an engram to become stable, or to **consolidate.** If we do not know what an engram is in physical terms, then how do we know how long it takes to form? The answer comes from the fact that we know some effective, if crude, ways to block their consolidation. If laboratory rats are taught to perform a simple task (such as turning left in an alley that forks to the left and right), and then convulsive seizures are induced by chemicals or passing an electric shock through the brain within about 30 minutes, the animals will later show no memory for the task. If the seizures are induced after this 30-minute time period, in contrast, there will be no loss of memory. What is happening here? Apparently the seizure is so disruptive to the operation of the nervous system that it interferes with the physical consolidation of the memory, but only if it occurs before the memory has become fully consolidated. A hard blow to the head, or even a highly stressful event such as witnessing a crime, can similarly disrupt the consolidation process and erase the still fragile memory trace. In these cases, the memory loss covers the period of approximately 30 minutes that immediately preceded the accident or event. Thus, from extensive research and the analysis of clinical cases of memory loss, it has been possible to estimate the time required for the consolidation process at about 30 minutes.

Engram Theories: What Is a Memory Trace?

A number of theories have been proposed to explain the biological nature of long-term memory. None has been widely accepted, but there is growing evidence supporting two general types of biological theories.

Neuronal Theories of Memory

One view of the engram is that it's a change in either the electrical activity of neurons or in the pattern of synaptic linkages between them. Donald Hebb (1949) suggested, for example, that each experience sends a different pattern of electrical signals through the neurons of the nervous system. This pattern repeats itself by "reverberating" for awhile after the experience, thus allowing the experience to be recalled. Under some circumstances, the reverberating pattern of electrical impulses causes physical changes in the synapses of the neurons that makes the memory more permanent. Research based on this theory has largely supported the notion that experience causes physical changes in neurons and their synapses, but no progress has been made in locating specific memories (Rosenzweig, 1984).

Molecular Theories of Memory

Another popular biological theory of memory suggests that memory traces are based on changes in some of the *molecules* that make up the neurons rather than in the gross structure of the whole neuron or the synapse. One such molecular theory suggests that memories are stored by *proteins* that are produced by the brain during learning experiences. It's not known which proteins are involved in memory or how they operate, but there is strong experimental evidence that proteins play an important role in long-term memory. In a typical experiment, laboratory mice are trained in a simple, stimulus discrimination task (such as reinforcing the mice for turning into the black alley of a T-maze but not for turning into the white alley). Just before the training begins, half of the mice are given a drug that blocks the creation of brain proteins and half are given an injection of saline (a weak saltwater solution that has no effect on the brain). Both groups of mice are able to learn the simple task equally well, but when they are tested a few hours later, the group given the drug that blocks the formation of brain proteins shows no memory for the discrimination task. The mice that were not given the drug, in contrast, still turn into the black alley more than the white one. The results of many similar studies suggest two tentative conclusions.

1. Proteins produced by the brain during learning appear to play a role in long-term memory since the group given the drug that blocked protein synthesis did not "remember" the task several hours later.

2. These proteins do not appear to be involved in short-term memory since the mice were able to learn the task during training—which almost necessarily requires short-term memory for what occurred during the immediately previous learning trials (Davis & Squire, 1984).

Another molecular theory suggests that long-term memories are stored in the complex molecules called *RNA* (*ribonucleic acid*) that are found in the nucleus of all body cells, including neurons (McConnell & Malin, 1973). These molecules are closely related to *DNA* (*deoxyribonucleic acid*), the key molecules in genes and the carriers of heredity. Evidence supporting the RNA theory of memory comes from varied sources; it's all controversial at present, but still interesting.

The most direct tests of the RNA theory of memory have been provided by James McConnell and his colleagues (e.g., McConnell & Malin, 1973). McConnell conducted a number of experiments on the possibility of extracting memories from one animal's brain and transferring them to the brain of another animal. He used inch-long animals called *flatworms,* or *planaria,* with simple brains as the subjects for his study. He first classically conditioned the planaria to respond to a dim light by violent twisting. A dim light was turned on shortly before an electric shock was delivered, which is an unconditioned stimulus for violent twisting in planaria. Then, he minced the conditioned planaria and fed them to other untrained planaria who, like good cannibals, ate them. In other studies, the brains of conditioned planaria were liquified and injected into unconditioned ones. If the memory trace for the conditioning were transferred to the brains of the new planaria, they should twist when a dim light is presented without being conditioned, and they did. In general, the evidence supporting the protein theory is stronger than the evidence for the RNA theory, but the evidence is not conclusive for either theory (Sokolov, 1977).

The search for the engram continues. If it does turn out to be a molecule, it's remotely possible that someday future students will be able to take a pill containing memories for an entire college course or all of Shakespeare's sonnets.

Amnesia: Disorders of Memory

Two major disorders of memory deserve our attention, both because they are important conditions in their own right and because of what they tell us about the biological basis of memory. We begin with a clinical case history describing an individual who suffers from severe memory loss, known as anterograde amnesia, as a result of brain surgery. His tragic case tells us much about memory disorders and vividly shows us how important an intact memory is for the normal experience of life.

Anterograde Amnesia

Anterograde amnesia is a disorder of memory characterized by an inability to store and/or retrieve new information in LTM that is well exemplified in the case history of *H. M.* (Milner, Corkin, & Teuber, 1978). H. M. began suffering major epileptic seizures at the age of 10. These increased in frequency despite the use of antiseizure medications to about once a week by age 27, leading his neurosurgeon to conclude that surgery must be performed to stop the seizures. The surgery destroyed several forebrain structures including the hippocampus. The procedure dramatically reduced the incidence of the seizures but left him with severe anterograde amnesia. He retained his above-average intelligence and had nearly normal memory for anything that he had learned *prior* to the surgery, but had severe memory deficits for events that occurred *after* the surgery.

H. M.'s short-term memory was generally normal after the surgery; he could retain verbal information in STM for about 15 seconds without rehearsal and could retain it for longer intervals if he was allowed to rehearse it. However, H. M. either could not transfer information into LTM or if he could, he could not retrieve it. He had almost no knowledge of current events because he forgot the news almost as soon as he had read about it; he could read the same magazine or work the same crossword puzzle over and over because they were "new" to him each time; he had no idea what time of day it was unless he had just looked at a clock; and generally he could not remember that his father had died since H. M.'s operation.

The most dramatic disruption caused by his memory problems, however, was to his social life. Although he could recognize friends, tell you their names, and relate stories about them, he could only do so if he knew them before the surgery. People that H. M. met after the surgery remained, in effect, permanent strangers to him. Each time a person came to his house, he had to learn the person's name again, and he could remember it for more than 15 seconds or so only if he continued to rehearse it. This effectively meant that H. M. was incapable of forming new social relationships—a poignant, but dramatic lesson in how important a basic cognitive function like memory is to our social lives.

H. M.'s inability to make new use of LTM was not total, however. He retained reasonably good ability to learn and retain perceptual and motor skills, and thus was able to learn to perform employable skills under supervision. However, he had to be reminded each day what skill it was that he knew how to perform; if he left his job for a short while, he could not remember what kind of work it was that he did. Similarly, when other individuals with anterograde amnesia have been taught to play a simple tune on the piano, they have been able to still play it the next day, but are surprised by their ability to do so because they have no recollection of being taught to play the tune on the day before (Hirst, 1982). Thus, the difficulties in using LTM are highly selective: some kinds of memories are affected while others are not.

Causes of Anterograde Amnesia

What caused H. M. to have this peculiar and sadly debilitating form of memory disorder? What happened to him during the surgery that damaged his ability to make new use of LTM? For one thing, it's clear that whatever happened to H. M. does not only occur during brain surgery to halt epilepsy, but also can be caused by brain tumors, lack of oxygen to the brain, damage to blood vessels in the brain, senility, and severe nutritional deficiencies. Hard blows to the head can also cause anterograde amnesia, although it's quite often only a temporary condition (Hirst, 1982).

anterograde amnesia
(an'ter-o-grād)
Disorder of memory characterized by an inability to store and/or retrieve new information in long-term memory.

It has been speculated that the key biological damage in anterograde amnesia is to the hippocampus (Scoville & Milner, 1957). This forebrain structure has been thought to govern the consolidation of memories from STM to LTM. Indeed, destruction of the hippocampus has been commonly, but not universally, found to have occurred in cases of anterograde amnesia. Other theorists, however, have suggested that nearby connections between the cortex and subcortical structures, or even parts of the cortex, are more important to the normal functioning of LTM (Hirst, 1982). A full answer will have to await additional research, but it does not seem unreasonable at the present time to assume that more than one brain structure is involved, since different forms of brain damage produce slightly different patterns of anterograde amnesia (Hirst, 1982).

Theoretical Implications of Anterograde Amnesia

The study of individuals with anterograde amnesia has led both to a better understanding of amnesia itself and of the basic processes of normal memory. The case of H. M. and others like him were originally presented as evidence for a distinction between STM and LTM as separate memory systems (Atkinson & Shiffrin, 1968; Milner et al., 1968). The fact that STM is apparently intact in cases of anterograde amnesia, but that LTM for newly acquired information is seriously impaired (although LTM for old information may not be disturbed), suggests that the brain damage destroyed the mechanism for *transferring* information from STM to LTM. Information from in-depth studies of patients with this memory disorder suggests that this is probably not an adequate explanation, however, and that an explanation of anterograde amnesia based on the levels of processing view (Craik & Lockhart, 1972) of short-term and long-term information storage might be more successful.

Specifically, two kinds of data suggest that individuals with anterograde amnesia can *store* new verbal information on a long-term basis. First, proactive inhibition is a much stronger source of forgetting in patients with anterograde amnesia than in normal individuals. For example, if amnesiac individuals memorize two lists of words, many of their errors in attempting to recall the second list will be words from the first list (Warrington & Weiskrantz, 1968). This means that the first list is in LTM since words from the first list could not cause proactive inhibition if they were not stored in memory on a long-term basis. Second, when amnesics are provided with additional cues to help them recall new long-term memories, they are able to do so, again suggesting that information is stored in LTM (Warrington & Weiskrantz, 1978).

Thus, these studies of individuals with anterograde amnesia suggest that new information can be stored in LTM but the amnesic has difficulty retrieving it. It would not be reasonable to assume that their brain mechanism for retrieval is destroyed, however, since old long-term memories can be retrieved with little difficulty by H. M. and some other individuals with anterograde amnesia. The difficulty appears to be in *encoding* new long-term memories so they can be retrieved. This view of anterograde amnesia is more consistent with the levels of processing view of memory. That is, the amnesic may not be able to process most kinds of new information deeply enough for retrieval from LTM but can process it deeply enough for retrieval from STM.

Retrograde Amnesia

Some individuals are unable to recall old information from the past; that is, they cannot retrieve old long-term memories. **Retrograde amnesia** is just the opposite of anterograde amnesia, then, in that it's old rather than new long-term memories that cannot be recalled. As in anterograde amnesia, however, there is typically little or no disruption of STM. Generally, the period of memory loss is not for the individual's entire lifetime. Rather, it extends back in time from the beginning of the disorder. Memory might be lost for a period of minutes, days, or even years.

Retrograde amnesia can be caused by seizures (as we saw earlier in our discussion of consolidation), brain damage of various sorts, a blow to the head, or by highly stressful events. When retrograde amnesia has been caused by seizures or by stress, it generally occurs alone. When it has been caused by brain damage or a blow to the head, however, it generally occurs along with anterograde amnesia. H. M. was actually an exception in that most brain-damaged individuals with anterograde amnesia also experience retrograde amnesia for the period of a few days or weeks prior to the onset of their amnesia (Hirst, 1982).

Both anterograde and retrograde amnesia are experienced by individuals with **Korsakoff's syndrome,** a disorder caused by prolonged loss of the vitamin thiamine from the diet of chronic alcoholics. Because of their extreme degree of memory loss, individuals with Korsakoff's syndrome often engage in *confabulation*—when they cannot remember something that is needed to complete a statement, they make it up. Generally, they are not being knowingly dishonest, but are engaging in an exaggerated version of normal reconstructive distortion.

retrograde amnesia
(ret′ro-grād)
Disorder of memory characterized by an inability to retrieve old long-term memories, generally for a specific period of time extending back from the beginning of the disorder.

Korsakoff's syndrome
(Kor-sak′ofs)
A disorder involving both anterograde and retrograde amnesia caused by excessive use of alcohol.

R E V I E W

The memory trace, or engram, must be stored in the brain in some form after learning; otherwise, recall at a later time would not be possible. The biological nature of the engram is still a matter of speculation, but some of its properties can now be reasonably inferred. For example, seizures, blows to the head, and stress can block the consolidation of long-term memories if the "erasing" event occurs within about 30 minutes of the learning. This suggests that it takes about that long for the engram to become permanent. Several theories have been proposed about the specific nature of the engram, suggesting that it's a pattern of electrical activity, a change in neuronal synapses, or a change in the RNA in the nuclei of neurons. However, conclusive evidence has not yet been provided to support any of these theories.

A group of disorders involving memory loss, known as amnesia, are instructive to study. Anterograde amnesia is characterized by a normal STM, normal memory for information that was in LTM prior to the onset of the amnesia, but an inability to retrieve new information from LTM. This condition is almost always caused by brain damage, generally involving the hippocampus. The memory disorder known as retrograde amnesia involves a loss of memory for old long-term memories, usually for a specific period of time extending back from the cause of the amnesia, such as a blow to the head, stressful event, seizure, and so on. Chronic alcoholics sometimes experience such extensive brain damage due to nutritional deficiencies that they develop Korsakoff's syndrome, which is marked by both anterograde and retrograde amnesia.

S U M M A R Y

Chapter 6 examines how we process information and how we remember or forget that information.

I. Human memory is composed of three stages of memory.
  A. The *sensory register* holds an exact image of each sensory experience for a very brief interval until it can be fully processed.
  B. *Short-term memory* holds information for about a half minute.
    1. Information fades from short-term memory unless it is renewed by *rehearsal*.
    2. Short-term memory has a limited capacity of 7 ± 2 items.
    3. The capacity of STM can be increased by organizing information into larger *chunks*.
  C. *Long-term memory* stores information primarily in terms of its meaning. Information is organized in LTM primarily in categories of related meanings and according to how frequently events have been associated in our experience.
    1. *Episodic memory* refers to memory for specific experiences that can be defined in terms of time and space.
    2. *Semantic memory* refers to memory for meaning.
  D. The *levels of processing* model views the distinction between short-term and long-term memory in terms of degree rather than separate stages.
II. There are four major causes of forgetting, each with different relevance to the three stages of memory.
  A. *Decay theory* states that forgetting occurs simply because time passes.
  B. *Interference theory* states that forgetting occurs when other memories interfere with retrieval. Interference can occur from memories that were formed by prior learning (*proactive interference*) or from memories that were formed by later learning (*retroactive interference*).
  C. *Reconstruction theory* states that memory traces of retrieval from LTM become partially distorted or totally unrecognizable during the process.
  D. Memories may be lost from long-term memory through *repression* because they are unpleasant or threatening.
III. The biological basis of memory is the *memory trace* or *engram*.
  A. Engrams *consolidate* or become permanent in about 30 minutes.
  B. A number of theories propose to explain the biological nature of memories. *Neuronal theories* view the engram as a change in the electrical activity of neurons or in the pattern of synaptic linkages between them. *Molecular theories* suggest that memory traces are based on changes in some of the molecules that make up the neurons.
  C. Amnesia is a major disorder of memory.
    1. An inability to store and/or retrieve new information in LTM is *anterograde amnesia*. Damage in anterograde amnesia occurs in the hippocampus.
    2. The inability to retrieve old, rather than new, long-term memories is known as *retrograde amnesia*.

Suggested Readings

1. A scholarly, yet very readable analysis of cognition and memory:

   Ellis, H. C., & Hunt, R. R. (1983). *Fundamentals of human memory and cognition* (3rd ed.). Dubuque, IA: Wm. C. Brown Publishers.

2. A fascinating discussion of memory that is solidly based on research evidence:

   Loftus, E. (1980). *Memory: Surprising new insights into how we remember and why we forget.* Reading, MA: Addison-Wesley.

3. For a detailed look at the relationship between mood and memory:

   Bower, G. H. (1981). Mood and memory. *American Psychologist, 36*, 129–148.

4. For more information on the biological basis of memory:

   Deutsch, J. A. (1973). *The physiological basis of memory.* New York: Academic Press.

SEVEN

Cognition, Language, and Intelligence

O U T L I N E

K E Y   T E R M S

P R O L O G U E

Perhaps the most important reason that the human race has survived for over 1.5 million years is that we are *intelligent*. Compared to other animal species, we are extremely good at solving problems. We survive cold weather by building shelters and making warm clothing; we invent wheels to move heavy objects; and we develop antibiotics when threatened by disease.

But, we speak of human intelligence here not to praise it, but to marvel at its quirks, foibles, and flaws! If human intelligence is a miracle of evolution, it's an amazingly flawed miracle. When our intellectual processes are examined carefully, it's sometimes amazing that we soft-skinned and slow-moving humans have been able to survive by our wits.

To help us understand the sometimes peculiar properties of human reasoning, Daniel Kahneman and Amos Tversky conducted a fascinating series of experiments. In one study, a group of physicians were presented with the following problem.

> Imagine that the United States is preparing for the outbreak of a rare Asian disease, which is expected to kill 600 people. Two alternative programs to combat the disease have been proposed. Assume that the exact scientific estimates of the consequences of the programs are as follows: If Program *A* is adopted, 200 people will be saved. If Program *B* is adopted, there is a ⅓ probability that 600 people will be saved and a ⅔ probability that no people will be saved. Which of the two programs would you favor? (Kahneman & Tversky, 1982, p. 163)

What decision would you have made? The majority of physicians polled by Kahneman and Tversky chose Program *A*. But, a fascinating thing happened when the researchers presented exactly the same problem in a different way. A second group of physicians was presented with the following version of the same problem.

> If Program *A* is adopted, 400 people will die. If Program *B* is adopted, there is a ⅓ probability that nobody will die and a ⅔ probability that 600 people will die. (pp. 163–164)

Would framing the problem in this different manner have influenced your decision? It did influence the physicians. When presented in the latter way, the majority chose *B*. The sure death of 400 people was too difficult to accept when stated this way. Although there is no logical difference (stated either way, 200 people would live and 400 people would die if Program *A* were adopted), our decision making is irrationally influenced by the way the question is framed.

Another study by Kahneman and Tversky makes the same point in a different way.

> Imagine yourself on your way to a Broadway play with a pair of tickets for which you have paid $40. On entering the theater you discover that you have lost the tickets. Would you pay $40 for another pair of tickets? Now imagine you are on your way to the same play without having bought tickets. On entering the theater you realize that you have lost $40 in cash. Would you now buy tickets to the play? (p. 160)

Logically, the two situations are identical (in both cases you are out $40 and have to decide whether or not to buy new tickets), but most subjects said they would be more likely to buy new tickets if they had lost the money rather than the tickets. Cold logic goes out the window again. So, how intelligent do you think we are now? Perhaps the best way to view human intelligence is to recognize its amazing capacity and extreme importance to our survival, yet to try to understand its shortcomings and compensate for them.

```
P R E V I E W
```

Cognition is a broad term referring to the intellectual processes through which we obtain, change, store, and use information. Cognition is involved in nearly every aspect of psychology, but is almost interchangeable with the topics of this chapter—thinking, language, and intelligence. The basic units of thinking are concepts; these categories of things or qualities allow us to reason in general rather than specific ways. Perhaps the most important form of thinking is productive thinking or problem solving. In this cognitive process, we must be able to formulate problems correctly, flexibly evaluate the information and tools available to us, and generate and evaluate alternative solutions if we are to be able to use information to reach our goals.

Language is the symbolic code used to communicate meaning from one person to another. Humans are not the only species to use languages, but our languages are more flexible than animal languages. We can communicate an unlimited number of meanings using a limited set of elements and rules for combining them into utterances, while animal languages are more limited. Language is intimately involved in much thinking, but thinking is not the same thing as silent language and there is little convincing evidence to believe that our thinking is limited by the elements and structure of language.

Intelligence can be thought of as the sum total of all of our useful cognitive abilities. The term *intelligence* is important in psychology today primarily because of the IQ tests that have been developed to measure it. These are useful in predicting with fair accuracy an individual's performance in many school and job situations. Like most human characteristics, intelligence seems to be strongly influenced both by heredity and experience.

Definition of Cognition

cognition
The intellectual processes through which information is obtained, transformed, stored, retrieved, and otherwise used.

Cognition can be defined as those intellectual processes (such as perception, memory, thinking, and language) through which information is obtained, transformed, stored, retrieved, and used. Let's take this complicated definition apart and see that it has three primary facets:

1. *Cognition processes information. Information* is the stuff of cognition: the stuff that is obtained, transformed, kept, and used. Much of this information is dealt with in the form of categories or concepts, the subject of the next section.
2. *Cognition is active.* The information that the world gives us is actively changed, kept, and used in the process of cognition. In cognition, information is
   a. *Obtained* through the senses,
   b. *Transformed* through the interpretive processes of perception and thinking, and
   c. *Stored and retrieved* through the processes of memory,
   d. *Used* in the processes of problem solving and language.
3. *Cognition is useful.* It serves a purpose. We think because there is something we do not understand. We use language when there is something that we need to communicate to others. We create when we need something that does not exist. Humans use cognition to survive physically and to live in a social world.

Cognition involves intellectual processes through which information is obtained, transformed, stored and retrieved, and put to use.

Much has been learned about cognition in the past 50 years. In this chapter we will survey those findings for problem solving, concept formation, language, and general intelligence. Other important aspects of cognition have already been discussed in the chapters on perception, consciousness, learning, and memory. And more aspects of cognition will be mentioned in later chapters on development, emotion, personality, stress, abnormal behavior, and social psychology. Cognition is more than a topic in the science of psychology; it's a theme that cuts across many diverse topics.

Concepts: The Basic Units of Thinking

The incredibly sweet, juicy pear that I ate last night while sitting on my deck was a specific object; but *pears* in general are a concept. When my good friend called to tell me her new phone number, that was a thoughtful act; but *thoughtfulness* in general is a concept. **Concepts** are categories of things, events, or qualities that are linked together by some common feature or features in spite of their differences. Each generous act is different from each other one, but they can be grouped together because they share the common quality of generousness. Write a definition for the term *generous* and you will have defined it as a concept. Your definition would be a statement that includes all cases of generous acts and excludes all nongenerous acts.

Nearly all productive thinking would be impossible were it not for concepts. Consider the following syllogism.

All human beings are mortal.

I am a human being.

Therefore, I am mortal.

When I reason in that way, I am using the general concepts of human beings and mortality. Without concepts we would only be able to think in terms of specific things and acts. Concepts allow us to process information in more general, efficient ways. In this way, concepts are the basic units of logical thinking.

concepts (kon′septs)
Categories of things, events, or qualities that are linked together by some common feature or features in spite of their differences.

Simple and Complex Concepts

Some concepts are based on a single common feature, such as the concept "red." If a thing is red, it belongs to the concept of red regardless of its other characteristics. Red apples, red balls, and red T-shirts are all examples of the concept of red, in spite of the other ways in which these objects differ. Other concepts are more complex. **Conjunctive concepts** are defined by the simultaneous presence of two or more common characteristics. The concept of "maiden aunt" is an example of a conjunctive concept as it has three simultaneous defining characteristics (female, unmarried, and sister of one of your parents). To be considered a maiden aunt, a person must have all three characteristics. **Disjunctive concepts** are defined by the presence of one common characteristic *or* another one, *or both*. For example, a person might be considered to be schizophrenic if he persistently has distorted perceptual experiences (such as hearing strange voices that are not there) *or* persistently holds distorted false beliefs (such as believing he is a king or a CIA agent), *or both*. The concept of "schizophrenic person" is a disjunctive concept because it is defined by the presence of either of two characteristics or both of them.

Concept Formation: Learning New Concepts

As interesting as concepts are, the way they are learned is perhaps even more interesting to study. For both the child learning basic concepts (each child must learn from scratch all of the concepts like "bigger," "dogs," and "red" that we adults take for granted) and for adults learning more complex concepts, concept formation is a fascinating process.

conjunctive concepts
(kon''junk-tiv')
Concepts defined by the simultaneous presence of two or more common characteristics.

disjunctive concepts
(dis''-junk-tiv')
Concepts defined by the presence of one of two common characteristics or both.

Adults take for granted that all these animals belong to the concept "shell."

Suppose you were a psychiatrist working for the U.S. Army during World War I and were trying to determine the best way to treat "combat fatigue," a psychological reaction to the stress of combat that sometimes renders soldiers unfit for further combat. Note that you are trying to learn a new concept. The "best way to treat combat fatigue" is a category of ways of handling soldiers that would differ somewhat from case to case but would have one or more common characteristics.

How would you go about learning this new concept? How would you identify the common feature or features that distinguish effective from ineffective treatment? You might start by looking at the records of 100 cases of combat fatigue victims and dividing them into piles of those who responded well to treatment and those who did not. Then you would look for features that distinguished the two groups. Being a psychiatrist, your first hypothesis might be that those soldiers suffering from combat fatigue who were given medications responded better than those who were not. If you tested this hypothesis by looking to see if most of the soldiers who were given drugs improved, while those who were not given drugs did not improve, however, you would see that this was not the key to effective treatment. Soldiers given medications were not more likely to improve than soldiers who were not given drugs.

You might also test out, and then reject, hypotheses about the type of professional giving the treatment (psychiatrist, nurse, or medical assistant), or the diet given the soldier, and so on. Eventually, you would discover, as did Dr. T. W. Salmon who actually went through this exercise, the following conjunctive concept. The effective treatment of combat fatigue: (1) consisted of simple rest and talking about combat, (2) was given immediately, and (3) was provided near the front lines. When treatment was handled this way, combat fatigue was a relatively minor reaction to stress that passed quickly. When the individual was removed from the front lines and taken to a hospital in a safe area, however, the reactions were generally more severe and long-lasting, perhaps because these reactions served the purpose of keeping the soldier out of further combat. That is

Figure 7.1 Cards like those used in laboratory studies of concept formation.

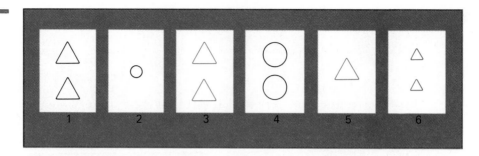

not to say that the soldiers were intentionally faking, but if we apply a concept that you learned in chapter 5 to this situation it becomes clear that severe symptoms were negatively reinforced by avoiding further combat for the soldier.

Let's not miss the forest for the trees. The purpose of this story was not to teach you about combat fatigue, but to give you an example of concept formation in practice. Concept formation is a special kind of thinking in which hypotheses about the defining characteristics of the concept are tested by examining positive and negative instances of the concept. In the example just discussed, those cases that were successfully treated were positive instances and those cases that were unsuccessfully treated were negative instances.

The formation of concepts has been extensively studied in the psychology laboratory using arbitrary concepts. For example, a subject was shown cards that each contained a geometric figure. As shown in figure 7.1, the figures can be either a circle or a triangle, can be colored either blue or magenta, can be presented singly or in pairs, and can be either large or small. The cards were shown to the subject with the information that some of the cards belonged to the concept and the others did not. The subject then had to learn what the concept was. Each time the subject saw a card, she guessed whether it was a member or nonmember of the concept, and the experimenter told her whether she was right or wrong. Suppose the six cards in figure 7.1 were presented to you in the order shown (left to right). The odd-numbered cards are members of the concept and the even-numbered cards are not. What is the concept?[1] Research on concept formation using such a procedure has revealed much about this aspect of cognition. For example, concepts with more irrelevant dimensions (number and color are irrelevant in the example in fig. 7.1) are more difficult to learn (Bourne, 1966). (See *Research Report:* "Strategies of Concept Formation.")

Natural Concepts

Eleanor Rosch (1973) has suggested that all concepts are not equally easy for us to learn; some are more "natural" than others. This idea is an extension of the notion (discussed in chapter 5) that we are biologically prepared to learn some things more readily than others. Rosch suggests that, by virtue of being born human beings, we are more prepared to learn some concepts than others.

One characteristic of concepts that makes them easier or more difficult to learn is their *inclusiveness*—that is, how many members there are of the concept. Three levels of inclusiveness are distinguished—somewhat arbitrarily at this stage of research:

1. *Superordinate concepts* are very inclusive, and therefore, contain a great many members. For example, "vehicles" is a superordinate concept that contains all of the many cars, boats, planes, wagons, and so on that carry loads.

1. The concept illustrated in this example is large triangles.

2. *Basic concepts* are of a medium degree of inclusiveness, and are the easiest to learn according to Rosch (1973). "Cars" would be an example of a basic concept as it is less inclusive than the superordinate concept "vehicles," yet there are still many members of this category.

3. *Subordinate concepts* are the least inclusive level of concepts. For example, there are far fewer members of the subordinate concept "Porsches" than the basic concept "cars" or the superordinate concept "vehicles."

Medium degree inclusive concepts such as "cars" are called basic concepts; the broader concept of "vehicle" is a superordinate concept; and the narrower concept of "Mercedes Benz" is a subordinate concept.

Rosch offers an observation on the way young children learn concepts as evidence that basic concepts are the easiest level of concept to learn. Children generally learn basic concepts, such as "cars," before they learn superordinate or subordinate concepts, such as "vehicles" or "Porsches."

Why should this be so? Why should basic concepts be easier to learn than either superordinate or subordinate concepts? Rosch suggests that the explanation lies in several characteristics of basic concepts (Matlin, 1983; Rosch, Mervis, Gray, Johnson, & Boyes-Braem, 1976). Members of basic concepts:

1. *Have many common attributes.* For example, the members of the basic concept "screwdriver" are all used to set screws, have a metal protrusion, have a handle, are usually 4 to 10 inches long, and so on. Members of the superordinate category of "tools" have far fewer characteristics in common. And while the members of the subordinate category of chrome-plated screwdrivers have many common characteristics, only a few of them are not common also to the concept of screwdrivers (technically, this issue is considerably more complex, but this statement is accurate enough for our purposes [Jones, 1983]).

2. *Have similar shapes.* All screwdrivers (a basic concept) are shaped about the same, but the same cannot be said about all tools (a superordinate concept). The shapes of all chrome-plated screwdrivers (a subordinate concept) are also similar, but they are distinguishable from other screwdrivers on the basis of only one difference—the chrome plating.

3. *Share motor movements.* The motor movements that are associated with members of basic level concepts are similar (turning screwdrivers), but the same cannot be said for superordinate concepts (the motor movements for using different kinds of tools are very different). Members of subordinate concepts like chrome-plated screwdrivers also share motor movements, but they are generally the same or similar to the basic concept to which they belong.

4. *Are easily named.* If you were asked to name 10 of the objects in your dorm room, chances are that most of the words that you would use would refer to the basic concepts to which the objects belong. People tend to say "screwdriver" instead of "tool" or "chrome-plated screwdriver" and to say "pen" instead of "writing instrument" or "Bic."

R E S E A R C H   R E P O R T

Strategies of Concept Formation

Jerome Bruner is a psychologist now teaching at Columbia University. One of the topics of his research concerns differences among the strategies that different people use to test hypotheses in concept formation. He studied these strategies in a now classic experiment (Bruner, Goodnow, & Austin, 1956) by watching subjects form concepts using cards that could be sorted into two piles on the basis of unstated concepts. For instance, say the unstated concept was that all black triangles go in pile A, while everything else goes in pile B. After a series of experiments, Bruner concluded that people generally test hypotheses using one of four major strategies.

1. *Simultaneous scanning.* In this strategy the individual simultaneously tests several different hypotheses at the same time. "If it was wrong to put this card in pile A, then it must not be circles, red, or borders around the card that are important, but it could be black or triangles or both." This is an efficient strategy for gathering a lot of information each time a card is seen, but it puts a heavy load on short-term memory and often leads to errors.
2. *Successive scanning.* In the successive scanning strategy the individual tests one hypothesis at a time. This is a simpler strategy, but unless one of the first hypotheses is correct, it is very time-consuming.

Rosch believes that these special characteristics of basic concepts make them more "natural"—easier to learn and use in the human information-processing system.

Other strong evidence for Rosch's theory of natural concepts comes from her research with the Dani tribe of New Guinea (Rosch, 1973). This tribe, which possesses a very limited technology, has only two color concepts in its vocabulary: *mola* for light colors and *mili* for dark colors. Hence, these people are ideal subjects for research on learning new color concepts. Rosch taught her Dani subjects new color concepts in much the same way that artificial concepts are taught in laboratory studies (just described above). When the subjects were taught to give a label to members of a color category that corresponded to a "pure" primary color (wavelengths that are near the middle of the range described as red or blue, for example) the concept was easier to learn than when the color was an intermediate one (such as bluish-green). Perhaps because of the nature of the color transducers in the eye (the cones), some color concepts are more natural than others. Interestingly, this conclusion is supported by the fact that names for the relatively pure hues of red, blue, green, and yellow are the most universally named in the world's languages (Berlin & Kay, 1969).

R E S E A R C H   R E P O R T

3. *Conservative focusing.* This is an efficient strategy that tests hypotheses through a process of elimination. The individual begins by assuming that every characteristic of the first card correctly placed in pile A is a defining characteristic. Remember that in this example the concept is black triangles and that all other aspects of the cards are irrelevant. If the first card correctly placed has three large black triangles, then the individual using the conservative focusing strategy would assume that the defining characteristics of the concept were three, large, black, and triangle. If the next correctly placed card contained three small black triangles, largeness could be eliminated as a potential defining characteristic, and so on until this concept had been identified.

4. *Focus gambling.* Focus gambling is very much like conservative focusing, except that the individual changes his or her hypothesis by more than one characteristic at a time. In this way the individual gambles on guessing correctly more quickly, but is using a less sure and systematic method of testing hypotheses.

As would be expected, some of Bruner's subjects used no systematic strategy at all, but guessed wildly. These were the least successful learners of all.

R E V I E W

Concepts are the basic units of thinking. They allow us to reason because they permit us to think in terms of general categories. Concepts are categories that have one or more features in common in spite of differences among members of that concept. All red things belong to the concept of "red" even though apples, fire trucks, and red balls differ from one another in many ways. Some concepts are defined in terms of a single characteristic while others are defined in terms of multiple characteristics in complex ways. The learning of new concepts has been compared to the testing of hypotheses: The individual examines members and nonmembers of the concept until the common feature or features have been identified. All concepts are not equally easy to learn, however; apparently some concepts are more "natural" than others.

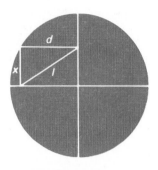

Figure 7.2 If you know the length of the radius of the circle, what is the length of line *l*? This problem shows the importance of formulating a problem in the correct way (Köhler, 1969).

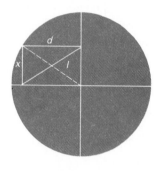

Figure 7.3 The problem given in figure 7.2 can be easily solved if it's viewed in the right way. Its solution requires you to think of line *l* as one of two diagonals of a rectangle rather than as part of a triangle. Line *l* is equal to the other diagonal (dotted line), which is the radius of the circle (Köhler, 1969).

problem solving
The cognitive process through which information is used to reach a goal that is blocked by some obstacle.

Problem Solving: Using Information to Reach Goals

Without concepts, sophisticated thinking would be impossible. The most useful forms of human thinking are in terms of concepts. Let's look now at one such useful kind of thinking—solving specific problems.

What should you do when you think you have upset your boss with the hotly political statement that you made at last night's cocktail party? Do you tell her you were just joking? Do you talk to her again tomorrow in the hope that you can agree to disagree without animosity? Do you forget about it on the assumption that she will not let politics interfere with her evaluation of your job performance? Do you wait and see if she acts as if you really did offend her— remember you only *think* you upset her—before you do anything further? What do you do?

Fortunately, no one really expects textbook writers to be able to answer such knotty questions but merely to discuss the general process through which we solve problems. **Problem solving** can be defined as the cognitive process through which information is used to reach a goal that is blocked by some kind of obstacle. Let's examine that process.

Cognitive Operations in Problem Solving

The focus of much current research is on the cognitive *operations* of problem solving. Operations remove obstacles to goals. What cognitive operations do we take in trying to solve problems and reach our goals?

There are three major types of cognitive operations involved in problem solving that apparently must be performed in sequence. First, we have to perceive and formulate the problem to decide what kind of problem we face. Second, we need to evaluate the elements of the problem to decide what information and tools we have to work with. Finally, we often need to generate a list of solutions and evaluate them.

Formulating the Problem

Before we begin to solve a problem, we must be able to define it. Sometimes the problem we face is obvious. For example, I want to drive to Florida, but I do not have enough cash to buy gas; what do I do? Other times, the nature of the problem is not at all clear. For example, you may know that the goal of being promoted in your job is not being reached, but you may not know what is preventing you from being promoted. Do I need to perform my job better? Do I need to get along with my superiors better? Do I need to be more assertive in requesting a promotion? To solve a problem, *you have to know what the problem is.*

As Michael Posner (1973) has pointed out, the key to effective problem solving is often our initial formulation of the problem. Take the problem illustrated in figure 7.2, for example. If you know the radius of the circle, what is the length of line *l*? See if you can figure it out. The trick is in *not* thinking of it as a problem involving the triangle *l, d, x*. Formulating the problem in *that* way blocks our being able to see what solution is called for. As can be seen in figure 7.3, the problem can be easily solved by thinking of *l* as the diagonal of the rectangle with sides *x* and *d*. The radius of the circle, then, is the other diagonal of the rectangle (dashed line in figure 7.3), and since we know that the two diagonals of a rectangle are equal, it's easy to determine that line *l* is the same length as the radius.

If you take the Quantitative Abilities section of the Scholastic Aptitude Test (SAT) or the Graduate Record Examination (GRE), you'll face a number of problems whose mathematical solutions are probably well known to you, but they are difficult because they require you to formulate the problem in a way that is not immediately obvious. The trick is in being able to shift from one formulation to another until the correct one is found, but your *first* formulation is often difficult to leave behind even when it's incorrect (Posner, 1973).

Understanding the Elements of the Problem

After formulating the problem, we must make an inventory of the elements of the problem—the information and other resources available to us. Often, effective problem solving requires that we *flexibly* interpret the meaning and utility of these elements. Many of life's problems require an insightful reorganization of the elements of the problem: When you lock your keys in your car, a bent coat hanger becomes a door opener. But, one of the ways in which human problem solving is rather predictably fallible is that we are often *not* flexible enough in evaluating the elements in problems. Consider the following situation. Karl Duncker (1945) has provided a problem for you to solve. See in figure 7.4 that you are given three candles, some matches, and a box of thumbtacks. Your problem is to find a way to put the candle on the wall such that it will not drip wax on the floor or table when burning. Turn to figure 7.5 when you have come up with an answer and check it out.

Figure 7.4 The Duncker candle problem: How can you mount the candle on the wall so that it will not drip wax on the table or floor when it's burning? See figure 7.5 for the solution (Bourne, Ekstrand & Dominowski, 1971).

The dilemma most of us have in evaluating the elements of problems is that we get stuck in "mental ruts," or in psychological terms, we get stuck in **sets.** The term **set** refers to an habitual way of approaching or perceiving a problem. Because problems often require a novel or flexible use of their elements, a habitual way of looking at the elements of a problem can interfere with finding a solution. If you had trouble with the Duncker candle problem, it was probably because you—like most people—thought of the box in the habitual way; the box is not immediately thought of as part of the solution as it is merely seen as an incidental item that holds the thumbtacks.

set

A habitual way of approaching or perceiving a problem.

Let's look at another famous problem that was developed to illustrate the interference of set. Psychologist Karl Luchins (1942) asked college students to imagine that they had three jars of different sizes and were asked how they would measure out an amount of water that was different from that held by any single jar. For example, they might be asked to measure five quarts when the three jars held the following quantities:

Jar A   Jar B   Jar C

How would you solve this problem? Five quarts can be measured by filling jar B, then pouring water from it until jar A is filled, leaving 25 quarts in jar B. Then jar C is filled twice from jar B, leaving five quarts in jar B. It's simple when you catch on to the method. In algebraic terms, the solution can be expressed as $B - A - 2C$.

Figure 7.5 The solution to the Duncker candle problem: The candle problem requires a new perception of the function of the box in which the tacks came. Tacked to the wall, the box becomes a candle holder (Bourne, Ekstrand & Dominowski, 1971).

Perhaps we do not always consciously consider the operations involved in solving a problem, but the sequence appears to remain the same: We perceive and formulate the problem; we evaluate the elements; and we generate a list of possible solutions.

After solving five more problems using jars of different sizes, but all of which could be solved using the equation B — A — 2C, the subjects were given a problem like this: Measure 20 quarts when jar A contains 24 quarts; jar B contains 52 quarts, and jar C contains 4 quarts. This problem could be solved using the equation B — A — 2C, but did you solve it that way? Or did you see that it could be solved more simply by subtracting one jar C from jar A (A — C)? In Luchins's study, over three-fourths of his subjects solved the problem the long way.

Why did Luchins's subjects make a difficult problem out of a simple one? Do people just have a tendency to do everything the hard way? Luchins ruled out that unlikely possibility in his experiment by having another group of subjects skip the first six B — A — 2C problems and solve the seventh problem *first*. These subjects *all* used the simple A — C solution. The subjects who took the long solution to the seventh problem simply fell into a "mental rut" or set.

Are you becoming convinced that human problem solving is rather predictably fallible? If not, try your intellect on one last example of the interfering effects of set:

> A small boy and his father were out together for a bicycle ride when a runaway truck hit them. They were both seriously injured and were rushed, unconscious, to the nearest hospital. While the more critically injured father was taken directly to an operating room, the boy was wheeled to the emergency ward for examination. A doctor on call was summoned; the doctor entered the emergency ward and exclaimed in surprise, "Oh heavens, that's my son!"
> (Reynolds & Flagg, 1983, p. 253)

How can this story be correct? Need a hint to break the effect of set? Are you being sexist? That's right; the doctor is the boy's mother. None of us should fall victim to that kind of prejudicial set, but many of us do. (See *Of Special Interest:* "Functional Fixedness" for additional information on the problem of set.)

Generating and Evaluating Alternative Solutions

Very often there is more than one solution to a problem. Our task then is to generate a list of possible solutions, evaluate each one by attempting to foresee what effects or consequences it would produce, choose the best solution, and then develop an effective way of implementing it.

Recall from the opening of this section the problem of thinking you had offended your supervisor with a political statement. Life is chock-full of similar situations. Clinical psychologist Marvin Goldfried has written extensively about the need for all of us to learn to solve such problems effectively (Goldfried & Davison, 1976). No one is going to solve all problems well, but we could all stand a little improvement. A simple flowchart outline based on Goldfried's approach that clinical psychologists Ira Turkat and Jim Calhoun (1980) give to clients who are trying to improve their problem-solving skills follows.

1. Identify problem (what is the problem situation?)
   a. Be as specific as possible.
2. Generate all possible options (what choices do I have?)
   a. Do not judge any option.
   b. Wild ideas are welcome.
   c. Produce as many options as possible.
   d. Combining options is acceptable.

OF SPECIAL INTEREST

Functional Fixedness

As discussed in the text, *set* is one of the most common barriers to effective problem solving. Sometimes we must break out of our habitual ways of viewing the elements of the problem to discover a solution. One of the most troublesome of these sets has been referred to as **functional fixedness.** Before we define this term, let's look at a problem where it's encountered. Consider the Maier (1931) *string problem.* Figure 7.6 shows that you are in a room where two strings are hanging from the ceiling. Your job is to tie the strings together. The problem is that when holding onto one string, you cannot reach the other. The only other thing in the room with you is a pair of pliers, but even holding onto one string with the pliers, you cannot reach the other string. What do you do? Turn the page and look at figure 7.7 for the solution. The difficulty that most people have in solving this problem is similar to the one in Duncker's candle problem. We are simply not accustomed to using pliers as a pendulum to move a string, just as we wouldn't ordinarily use a tack box as a candle holder. Karl Duncker (1945) referred to the difficulty we have in seeing new uses for objects as *functional fixedness.* It's a kind of set that interferes with problem solving by focusing our thinking about the elements in a problem on their habitual uses. Often the key to effective problem solving is being able to break out of functional fixedness and other interfering sets when appropriate.

functional fixedness
A set that interferes with problem solving by focusing thinking on the habitual uses of the elements in a problem.

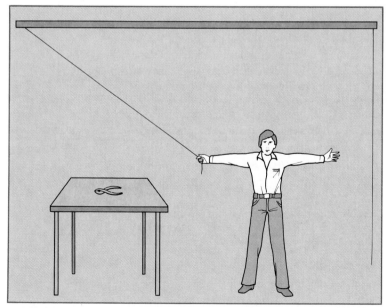

Figure 7.6 The Maier string problem. How do you tie the two strings together if you cannot reach them both at the same time? See figure 7.7 for the solution.

[Continued on page 268]

OF SPECIAL INTEREST

[Continued from page 267]

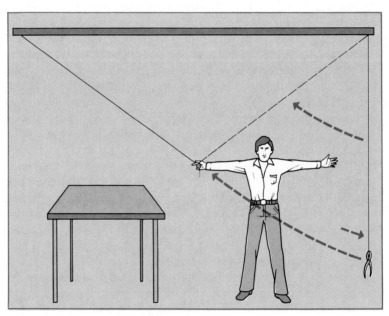

Figure 7.7   The solution to the Maier string problem is to use the pliers as a pendulum to get the second string closer to you.

3. Eliminate any obviously poor choices.
4. Examine the remaining options one at a time.
   a. List all possible negative consequences of this option.
   b. List all possible positive consequences of this option.
   c. Eliminate option if it's generally negative.
   d. Go on to next option (steps a–c).
   e. Compare all remaining options.
   f. Select most positive option.
5. Generate all possible ways to implement option (How can I best do this?)
   a. Use steps 2–4.
6. Implement strategy to solve the problem.

Excellent chess players can generally beat computers at chess because heuristic computer programs, which look for shortcuts, fail to consider all of the long-range consequences of each move.

Algorithmic and Heuristic Operations

The cognitive strategies to carry out the steps in the problem-solving operations just described can be of two general types. **Algorithms** are systematic patterns of reasoning that (if followed) guarantee a correct solution. Generally, computers use algorithms. Indeed they are especially suited for them, since they can quickly consider the many alternatives required by complex algorithms. Computers do not always use algorithms, however. For extremely complex problems, computers are sometimes programmed to use shortcuts known as **heuristics.** Heuristics are strategies that maximize the probabilities of finding a correct solution. But since they do not systematically evaluate every possible solution, heuristics do not guarantee finding the correct one.

The concept of heuristic reasoning comes in part from research that attempts to simulate human intelligence using computers. Efforts to program computers to play the game of chess, for example, were originally frustrated by the enormous number of possible solutions that would have to be considered before making each move. To avoid such extensive algorithmic programs, heuristic programs were written. For example, the program is written to maximize protection of the queen or to control the center of the board. Moves that meet these goals are executed, but the long-range consequences of each move are not considered by the artificial intelligence program. That is why excellent chess players can generally beat computers at chess.

The concept of heuristic reasoning is an important one because there is reason to believe that humans operate using heuristics more than algorithms. This is so either because algorithms require so much cognitive capacity and effort or because we simply do not possess algorithms for most of the problems we face in life.

algorithm (al'go-rith'm)
A systematic pattern of reasoning that guarantees finding a correct solution to a problem.

heuristics (hu-ris'tiks)
A pattern of reasoning that increases the probability of finding a correct solution to a problem.

Suppose you are presented with the following problem: What occupation should Steve pursue in college? You are told that Steve is shy, helpful, good with figures, and has a passion for detail. You are also told that you can ask and receive additional information to use in solving the problem. How would you solve this problem?

Amos Tversky (Tversky & Kahneman, 1973) has identified two heuristics that are frequently used in human problem solving—representativeness and availability. The *representativeness* heuristic makes predictions based on the similarity between the information you have and the outcome you want to predict, regardless of the availability of other information. We have a tendency to use this heuristic to predict Steve's best choice of an occupation on the basis of which occupation we believe his personality is most representative (accountant, pharmacist, etc.). This might be a good strategy, but it leads us not to seek out and evaluate other information that might be helpful (such as Steve's preferences, his previous school grades, or the availability of employment in different occupations).

The *availability* heuristic bases decisions on the availability of relevant information in memory. Rather than seeking additional information, we take another shortcut and use the information we can remember. In the case of predicting Steve's best occupation, we might recommend that he become an attorney based on our recollection of an attorney to whom Steve bears a striking resemblance in ability and temperament. These cognitive shortcuts are obviously efficient in terms of effort, but certainly will not always lead to effective problem solving. However, humans frequently think heuristically.

Creative Problem Solving: Convergent and Divergent Thinking

Creativity is highly valued in our culture but is a difficult concept to define. No specific scientific definition has been widely accepted among researchers, and a wide gulf exists between the ways in which scientists define creativity and the way it's thought of by those in the arts. We can define **creativity** in general terms, however, as the ability to produce "products" (such as plays, solutions to social problems, poems, sources of energy, symphonies) that are both novel and socially valued (useful, aesthetically beautiful, informative, and so on).

To a considerable extent, there is an overlap between creativity and general intelligence. Most of the individuals that we think of as being highly creative are also highly intelligent (Butcher, 1968). But most researchers in the area of creativity believe that creative thinking is separate to some extent from general intelligence. There are some highly creative people, in other words, who are not highly intelligent and vice versa.

This distinction between intelligence and creativity is closely related to the distinction between convergent and divergent thinking. **Convergent thinking** is logical, conventional, and focused on a problem until a solution is found. **Divergent thinking** is loosely organized, only partially directed, and unconventional (Guilford, 1950). To make the definition of divergent thinking more concrete, a measure of divergent thinking that is commonly used in psychological research asks the individual to list as many novel uses as possible for common objects.

creativity
The ability to make human products and ideas (such as symphonies or solutions to social problems) that are both novel and valued by others.

convergent thinking
Thinking that is logical, conventional, and that focuses on a problem.

divergent thinking
Thinking that is loosely organized, only partially directed, and unconventional.

The contractor of this house needs to use divergent thinking when creating the design and convergent thinking to be sure the building is structurally sound.

Those individuals who list the most novel uses, whether they are "sensible" uses or not, are considered to be the most divergent thinkers. Divergent thinkers, in other words, more easily break out of sets that limit our thinking. In our culture, people who are good divergent thinkers tend to be thought of as creative (Butcher, 1968). But as just noted, a good many highly intelligent individuals are talented in both divergent and convergent thinking. This may be the ideal combination as it would seem to allow for problem solving that is both creative and practical.

R E V I E W

Problem solving is the process of using information to reach a goal that has been blocked by some obstacle. We use cognitive operations to solve problems. Key steps in this process are the initial formulation of the problem, the understanding of the elements of the problem (the information and resources available for problem solving), and the generation and evaluation of alternative strategies. Problem solving can fail at any of these levels: We can be unsuccessful because we define the problem incorrectly, because we get stuck in sets in our perception of the elements of the problem, or because we fail to fully evaluate the consequences of alternative solutions. Creative problem solving requires the ability to think in flexible and unusual ways (divergent thinking), but the most useful creative solutions are ones that have also been thought out logically (convergent thinking). Fortunately, many intelligent people excel in both divergent and convergent thinking.

Language: Symbolic Communication

Next to thinking on the trophy shelf that displays the greatest cognitive achievements of the human species is *language*. Without language, human beings and human civilization would be a pale shadow of what they are. **Language** is a symbolic code used in communication. Without an efficient means of communication, it would not be possible to coordinate the efforts of many people in a division of labor, to regulate their behavior for the common good through laws, or to amass the wisdom learned through experience by previous generations and pass it on through education. And perhaps the most keenly felt loss of all is that psychology textbooks could neither be written nor read.

Semantics: The Meaning of What Is Said

The function of language is to say something to someone. The "something" is the meaning (the *semantic content*) that is communicated through language. Suppose you want to communicate to your child that *the peanut butter is on the top shelf.* That idea must be translated into the language code and expressed to your child who must receive and comprehend it by translating it back into the same idea. Thus, meaningful ideas are sent from person to person via the system of symbols that we call language.

The fact that **semantic content** and language codes are not the same thing can easily be seen in a number of ways. For one thing, it is possible to express the same meaning in more than one way. *The peanut butter is on the top shelf* and *it's on the top shelf that the peanut butter is located* are physically very different patterns of sounds, but they express exactly the same meaning. Furthermore, it would be possible to express the same proposition in Chinese, Latin, French, or sign language. This distinction was made by linguist Noam Chomsky (1957), who called the superficial spoken or written structure of a statement its **surface structure** and the underlying structure that holds the statement's meaning its **deep structure.**

While humans have the most flexible and symbolic language for communicating propositions, we are not the only species that uses a language. Bees, for example, use a simple but elegant language to communicate messages such as *flowers containing a nectar supply are about 200 meters away on a line that is 20 degrees south of the angle of the sun.* The bee who has made this discovery tells the other bees about it not through speech or written memos, but through a symbolic dance.

If the nectar is within about a hundred meters of the hive, the bee does a *round dance* (see fig. 7.8), first turning a tight circle in one direction, and then reversing and circling in the opposite direction. This dance does not communicate the direction of the nectar find, so it sends swarms of bees flying out in all directions within 100 meters of the hive looking for the nectar. If the nectar is 200 to 300 meters from the hive, the "speaker" bee gives better directions to his attentive audience. The bee does a *tail-wagging dance.* This dance is in the form of a tight figure eight. The direction of the nectar is communicated through the angle of the middle part of the dance relative to the sun. The distance is communicated by the rate of turning, the rate of tail wagging, and the sound made

language
A symbolic code used in communication.

semantic content
(se-man'tik)
The meaning in symbols, such as language.

surface structure
The superficial spoken or written structure of a statement.

deep structure
The underlying structure of a statement that holds its meaning.

Round dance   Tail-wagging dance

Figure 7.8 The language dances of honeybees. The round dance indicates that nectar is within 100 meters of the hive. The tail wagging dance points in the direction of the nectar when it's over 200 meters away. Distances between 100 and 200 meters are signaled by a third dance. (Von Frisch, 1974)

by the vibration of the wings. Distances between 100 and 200 meters are communicated through much looser figure-eight patterns in the tail-wagging dance (von Frisch, 1967).

Using these dances, bees are able to communicate rather complex messages very efficiently. Unlike humans, however, they have a limited vocabulary and can only communicate in a way that is firmly limited by inheritance. Human language, in contrast, is far more flexible.

Generative Property of Language: Elements and Rules

Human language is a highly *efficient* system. It's particularly efficient in accomplishing so much while putting so little demand on our memories. Stop for a second and think about the sheer magnitude of language. Consider how many different things you have said in your lifetime. If we could accurately estimate the number, it would be staggering. Now, let's imagine that human language were not an efficient system. Imagine that we had to learn and remember a different utterance for everything we wanted to say. While it would be theoretically possible to store that many utterances in long-term memory, we would have to spend every waking hour of our lives doing nothing but memorizing utterances. Obviously we do not spend anywhere near that amount of time learning language. More importantly, humans do not speak using a fixed stock of utterances. We could get by in a crude and uninteresting way talking like that, but fortunately we do not. Everyday, you say utterances that no one has ever said before.

If we do not memorize our utterances, where do they come from? The fact is that we make them up as we go along. In more precise terms, we "generate" language from a set of elements and a set of rules for combining them into speech. When we say that language is **generative,** we mean that an infinite set of utterances can be made using a finite set of elements and rules (Chomsky, 1957). What are these elements and rules?

generative property of language
(jen'ĕ-ra''tiv)
The ability to create an infinite set of utterances using a finite set of elements and rules.

Human language is generative. That means an infinite set of utterances can be made using a finite set of elements and rules.

phoneme (fo′nēm)
The smallest unit of sound in a language.

morpheme (mor′fēm)
The smallest unit of meaning in a language.

syntax (sin′-taks)
The grammatical rules of a language.

Phonemes

One way of looking at the elements of language is to consider its individual sounds. The **phoneme** is the smallest unit of sound in a language. In English, everything we say, and everything that we will ever say, is made up of only 44 phonemes (there are more phonemes than letters of the alphabet in English, because some letter combinations such as *ch* and *th* stand for separate phonemes). Different languages have different numbers of phonemes, but the principle is the same in every language: Every utterance is generated from a surprisingly small number of sounds.

Morphemes

When most people think about the individual building blocks of language, they have in mind something like morphemes. **Morphemes** are the smallest units of meaning in a language. Morphemes are closely related to but are not the same as words. Some morphemes stand alone as words. *Word, stand,* and *fast* are each single freestanding morphemes. Other morphemes can only exist bound to other morphemes. Examples are the morpheme for past tense in push*ed,* the plural morpheme in car*s,* and the prefix morpheme *anti* meaning "against" in the word *antibiotic.* The average person knows thousands of morphemes, but can speak an infinite number of utterances using a finite set of morphemes and rules for combining them.

Syntax

The rules of a language that allow an infinite number of understandable utterances to be generated are called **syntax.** There are rules for the ways in which phonemic sounds can be combined in morphemes and rules for how morphemes can be combined in utterances. These rules are the heart of generative language, for without them, only a finite number of things could be said with the finite set of morphemes.

We discuss the way that language develops in the next chapter on child development, but it's interesting to note that children develop language in the order of learning phonemes first, then morphemes, then syntax. Children first learn to babble in the speech sounds of their language, then they use some freestanding morphemes by themselves (mamma, milk, bye-bye), and then they begin to acquire syntactic rules for combining morphemes into longer and more complex utterances.

Language and Thought

When you think, do you talk to yourself? Is that all thinking is, silently talking to yourself? Thinking cannot *just* be talking to yourself since we can obviously think in visual images, sounds, and images of movements—and some thinking may not be in conscious images at all. In any case, however, a great deal of thinking is in verbal form. For this reason, psychologists have long been interested in the relationship between language and thought. Two key questions have been asked by psychologists: (1) Is verbal thinking just talking subvocally (silently) to yourself? and (2) Does the structure of different languages influence thinking?

Peripheralism: Thinking as Subvocal Speech

Behaviorist John B. Watson believed that what we experience as verbal thinking is no more than the sensations produced by tiny movements of the speech apparatus that are too small to produce audible sounds. In this view, thinking is literally no more than talking to yourself, but at a volume that no one but you can hear. Watson's theory is known as **peripheralism**, the belief that thinking occurs not in the brain, but in the voice box (that is peripheral to, or outside of, the brain).

peripheralism
(pĕ-rif′er-al-izm)
The theory that thinking is a matter of talking silently to oneself.

Peripheralism has been refuted in a number of ways, but the most dramatically convincing evidence comes from two sources. First, Hans Furth (1966) studied the thinking of individuals who had been deaf and mute (could not speak any language including sign language) from birth. As adults, these individuals were essentially average in thinking and intelligence. They suffered some deficits due to the restrictions that a lack of language places on learning, but even though they could not speak, they were not incapable of thinking as Watson would have predicted.

Even more dramatic evidence against peripheralism comes from a classic study in which Dr. Edward Smith served as his own subject (Smith, Brown, Toman, & Goodman, 1947). It will be immediately obvious why no one else would have volunteered to be the subject. Smith took *curare,* a drug used by South American Indians on blow darts that temporarily paralyzes its victim. The drug paralyzed all of the skeletal muscles in Smith's body, including those involved in speaking. It even paralyzed the muscles involved in breathing so that he had to be artificially respirated during the experiment. After the effects of the drug had worn off and the paralysis dissipated, Smith reported that he had been able to think in words as clearly as ever. This fact casts an unremovable shadow on the theory that verbal thought is no more than talking subvocally to yourself.

Whorfian Hypothesis: The Influence of Language on Thought

Even if language and thought are not synonymous, the fact that much thinking is in the form of language raises the possibility that the structure of language could influence thinking in some way. This hypothesis has been stated by Benjamin Whorf (1956) and is known as the *Whorfian* or **linguistic relativity hypothesis.** Although Whorf was most concerned with the impact of different languages on the thinking of people from different cultures, his concrete examples of how this might happen generally concerned the relationship between language and perception. For example, Eskimos have several different words for

linguistic relativity hypothesis
The idea that the structure of a language may influence the way individuals think.

RESEARCH REPORT

Can Apes Learn Human Language?

As the discussion of the language of bees in the text makes clear, humans are not the only animals who possess the tool of language. Nor are bees. But, there are significant differences between human language and any known animal language, however. Animal languages appear to be inherited and are not dependent on learning for their development. Human languages, in contrast, must be learned through interactions with fluent speakers. In addition, human languages are more generative (see p. 273). Animals possess a limited stock of fixed utterances that can be varied little, while humans can generate an infinite number of unique utterances.

These differences between human and animal languages have led some psychologists to assume that only humans can ever acquire a human language because we alone have the mental abilities needed for a generative language (Lenneberg, 1967). Until recently, this was an assumption that was difficult to challenge. A few attempts had been made to teach human language to animals, but they had failed. Two husband-and-wife teams of psychologists had even taken infant chimpanzees into their homes and raised them like their own children, specifically giving them intensive tutoring in language. However, the better of the two chimps only learned to say four words crudely (Hayes & Hayes, 1951; Kellogg & Kellogg, 1933).

If humankind's nearest cousins, the apes, could not learn human language, then it seemed a safe bet at one time that human abilities were required to learn a human language.

However, another wife-and-husband team of psychologists, Beatrice and Allen Gardner (1971), have dramatically reopened the question. They reasoned that chimpanzees have not been able to learn to speak English because they simply possess a *mouth and throat* that is not well suited for spoken language rather than having inadequate mental abilities. To prove their point, the Gardners raised a young chimp, Washoe, to whom they taught American Sign Language (ASL), a language made up of hand signals used by the deaf. Washoe has acquired a limited, but real command of the ASL version of English. She uses over 200 signs and uses them in combinations like *gimme sweet drink*. Impressively, Washoe has even taught sign language to her adopted chimpanzee son and regularly converses with him.

Washoe is not the only ape to learn a human language, either. Stanford University's Penny Patterson (1977) has taught over 600 signs to Koko, a gorilla who may be showing even more spontaneous and generative use of language than Washoe. Koko signs "That Koko" when she sees herself in the mirror; she once called a ring, a sign she had not been taught, a "finger bracelet"; and she

RESEARCH REPORT

Washoe uses over 200 ASL signs, many in combinations. Here Washoe signs *sweet* in response to the lollipop.

once replied to the question "How are you feeling?" by signing "I was sad and cried this morning." Perhaps most impressively, Koko knows enough sign language to have been given an intelligence test and to score only slightly below the average for humans of her age.

The fact that we can now have two-way conversations with apes is an unsettling reality that will rightly force many of us to rethink our views of "dumb animals." These findings should be kept in proper perspective, however. So far, apes use language almost exclusively as a tool to get food, to ask the trainer to play a tickling game, and the like. They rarely just comment on their world or ask questions to gain information (Rumbaugh & Gill, 1976; Slobin, 1979).

Furthermore, a challenge to the conclusion that apes are capable of learning human language has come from the research of Columbia University psychologist Herbert Terrace (1980). Terrace has also taught ASL to a chimp (named Nim Chimpsky) but concluded that Nim was unable to master true human language. At issue are two primary questions: (1) Do the chimps use language spontaneously? And (2) do they exhibit an understanding of syntax; that is, can they generate novel, meaningful sentences in which the order of the signs conveys the intended meaning?

Terrace suggests that the answer to both questions is no. None of the chimps uses language spontaneously very much. For example, only about 10 percent of Nim's statements were spontaneous; the rest were in response to a statement by a human. (But the question arises: How many spontaneous utterances must one make before being considered speaking like a human? Is 10 percent enough?)

[*Continued on page 278*]

RESEARCH REPORT

[Continued from page 277]

If the chimps have failed to master sign language in the way humans do, it will be on the issue of syntax that this conclusion will be most likely reached. Terrace found no evidence that Nim was able to generate novel combinations of signs that were syntactically correct. When he reviewed the transcripts from Washoe and other chimps, he reached the same conclusion. This conclusion is hotly debated by those who believe that Washoe does possess true human language, and the final conclusion certainly is not in yet. At present, it appears that apes may have learned to use language at the level of a two-year-old human, but they have not progressed beyond that point (Reynolds & Flagg, 1983). Still, the apes's elementary use of language is more evidence of "humanity" than was once thought possible for apes. And the apes's progress has done much to "talk" at least some scientists out of their belief that only humans can learn human languages.

snow and can discriminate between different kinds of snow better than, say, residents of Florida. Does the fact that Eskimos have more words to describe different kinds of snow—and can notice small differences between different kinds of snow—mean that their additional words improve their perception of snow? Whorf proposed that the presence of these words in the Eskimo vocabulary improves visual perception. It seems at least as plausible to assume that the Eskimos first learned to perceive slight differences among different kinds of snow and *then* invented a vocabulary for talking about them to others.

An interesting experimental test of the Whorfian hypothesis was conducted by Eleanor Rosch with the same Dani tribe from New Guinea used in her research on learning natural color concepts (Heider & Oliver, 1972). She compared the memory for colors of the Dani, who have only two color names, with that of American college students whose language contains many color names. The subjects were briefly shown single color chips and asked to find the same color 30 seconds later among 40 color chips. The logic behind the experiment was as follows: If the Whorfian hypothesis is right, then a person's language should influence memory for colors. Specifically, colors with the same name should be confused in memory more easily than color with different names, so the Dani were expected to remember less than the English speakers. The results did not support Whorf's theory. Neither Dani nor American subjects confused colors that were equally different in wavelength more often when they had the same color names rather than different color names, in spite of the large differences in the number of color names in the two languages.

The idea that the structure of languages can influence thought has also been a hotly debated issue with strong political implications in the United States. Many American blacks speak a version, or dialect, of English that differs substantially from standard English in phonemes, morphemes, and syntax (Lahey, 1973). Thus speakers of Black English are not making grammatical "errors"

These people from different cultures have different words to describe water. According to Benjamin Whorf, the vocabulary of a language can influence the way speakers of that language think.

when they speak; they are correctly speaking a separate dialect of English. Sociologist Basil Bernstein (1970) has suggested that Black English is a *"restricted"* code by which it's impossible to express some complex logical propositions. As a result, Bernstein suggested that speakers of Black English are less able to think logically than speakers of standard English. William Labov (1970), however, has convincingly demonstrated that Black English is just as logically complete as standard English. According to Labov, Bernstein heard a limited version of Black English in his studies because many of the low-income black children he studied simply would not speak comfortably in their full language around whites.

In short, there has been very little evidence to prove that language restricts thinking, even that part of thinking that is in the form of language. As Dan Slobin (1979) pointed out, however, it still has not yet been firmly established that language *does not* influence thinking, either. Thus, it remains an open question that begs for experimental study.

R E V I E W

Language is the efficient symbolic code used in human communication. It utilizes a finite set of sounds, units of meaning, and rules for combining them to convey a limitless set of meanings. Although much of our thinking is in the form of language, it has been conclusively demonstrated that thinking is not simply subvocal (inaudible) speech. The question of whether the structure of our language limits our ability to think has not been satisfactorily answered, but current evidence suggests that it probably does not.

Sir Francis Galton
(1822–1911)

intelligence (in-tel′ĭ-jens)
The cognitive ability of an
individual to learn from
experience, to reason well,
and to cope with the
demands of daily living.

g
A broad general factor of
intelligence, a concept
endorsed by some
investigators of intelligence.

Intelligence: The Sum Total of Cognition

In the sense used in this book, **intelligence** refers to the cognitive ability of an individual to learn from experience, to reason well, and generally cope effectively with the demands of daily living. In short, intelligence has to do with how well a person is able to use cognition in coping with the world.

The term *intelligence* was not in widespread use until it was popularized in the late 1800s by the writings of Sir Francis Galton. Galton was a cousin of Charles Darwin, the scientist given credit for developing the theory of evolution based on natural selection of inherited characteristics. Galton believed that intellectual ability was inherited and he tried unsuccessfully to develop an intelligence test to use in his research. Although he was unsuccessful in his own research, Galton gave psychology the concept of intelligence.

Differing Views of Intelligence

Since Galton's time, intelligence has been the subject of intensive research, theoretical pronouncements, and often heated debate. After nearly 100 years of scrutiny, however, psychologists still cannot agree on several basic issues. There are differing opinions on how many kinds or dimensions of intellectual ability exist, but a promising new approach suggests that instead of trying to answer that question, we should work to identify the basic cognitive components of intelligence.

Intelligence: General or Specific Abilities?

In Galton's view, intelligence is a single *general factor* that provides the basis for the more specific abilities that each of us possesses. According to this conception, if we are generally intelligent, we will be more likely to develop strong mechanical, musical, artistic, and other kinds of ability. This view that a general factor of intelligence underlies each of our more specific abilities has been advocated in more modern times by psychologist Charles Spearman (Spearman & Wynn-Jones, 1950), who uses the term **g** to refer to the general factor of intelligence. Spearman based his opinion on complex mathematical analyses of intelligence test scores that support, but do not prove, his theory of general intelligence. The concept of a *g* factor of intelligence is also held by David Wechsler, who is the author of the most widely used intelligence tests for children and adults in the United States today (Wechsler, 1955).

Other psychologists have argued that intelligence is not a single general factor, but a collection of many separate specific abilities. These psychologists make a great deal of the fact that most of us are much better in some cognitive skills than others, rather than being generally good at everything. Louis Thurstone (1938), for example, developed an alternative to tests of general intelligence, called the *Primary Mental Abilities Test,* that measures seven different intellectual abilities. J. P. Guilford (1967), taking an even more extreme position than Thurstone, suggested that some 120 different abilities make up what we call intelligence.

This issue remains unsettled today. As a result, it's common practice when measuring the intelligence of individuals to provide estimates of both general and more specific facets of intelligence.

Cognitive Components of Intelligence

A promising new way of conceptualizing and studying intelligence has recently been proposed by psychologist Robert Sternberg (Sternberg, 1979, 1981; Sternberg & Gardner, 1982) and others. This approach suggests that the basic nature of intelligence can be illuminated by applying what we have learned in research on cognition, particularly research carried out using an information-processing model of cognition.

Sternberg has proposed a tentative theory of intelligence that specifies the cognitive steps that a person must use in reasoning and solving some kinds of problems—or in simple terms, the cognitive components of intelligence. For example, consider the following analogy problem (Sternberg, 1979).

> LAWYER is to CLIENT as DOCTOR is to?
> a. MEDICINE
> b. PATIENT

To solve this problem, Sternberg believes that we must go through a number of cognitive steps. Among these steps, the person must:

1. *Encode* (mentally represent in the memory system in some usable form) all relevant information about the problem. In this case, the person might encode information related to the term lawyer that includes: knows the law, represents others before the courts, is paid fees for providing services, etc. For the term client, the information that this is an individual who obtains professional assistance and pays a fee for those services would need to be encoded, and so on for all of the attributes of all of the terms in the problem.

2. *Infer* the nature of the relationships between the terms in the problem. In this case, it is essential to see that lawyer and client are related because a lawyer provides a service for a fee and a client obtains a service by paying a fee.

3. *Map* or identify common characteristics in relevant pairs of elements. In this case, the person must see that both lawyers and doctors provide services for fees and that both clients and patients obtain services by paying fees.

4. *Apply* the relationship identified between lawyer and client to the relationship between doctor and patient.

5. *Compare* the alternative answers, and

6. *Respond* with an answer; in this case, "patient."

Sternberg suggests that this way of looking at intelligence does more than provide us with a convenient way of describing the steps in intelligent reasoning. It gives us a framework for discovering which components are most important in determining whether one person is "more intelligent" than another. For example, several initial studies have provided a finding that is, at least at first glance, rather surprising (Sternberg, 1979). Better reasoners are *slower* to complete the encoding component than poor reasoners even though they are faster at all of the other stages. Sternberg explains this finding by drawing a parallel to a lending library. A library that invests more time in carefully cataloging books (like the encoding component) will be more than repaid for this investment of time in terms of more rapid access to and lending of the books (like the rest of the components of the solution). Supporting this interpretation is the finding of Chase and Simon (1973) that the critical difference between expert and beginning chess players is that experts encode the board positions more effectively.

Another finding of early studies using this new model of intelligence is that almost all errors in analogy problems occur because the process of identifying or comparing the attributes of the elements is stopped prematurely. In this light, it is important that one key difference between the way adults and children solve analogy problems is that adults process information more exhaustively. Such findings hold promise in identifying the key cognitive elements in effective intelligence, and even may allow us to improve intelligence in the future by training people to carry out those key components more effectively (Sternberg, 1981).

Measures of Intelligence: The IQ Test

Intelligence would be too vague a concept to be of much use to psychologists if it were not for the fact that reasonably accurate and meaningful tests have been developed to measure it. A measure of intelligence makes it possible to use the concept of intelligence in both research and clinical practice. As noted in chapter 1, the first person to develop a useful measure of intelligence was Alfred Binet. About 1900 he developed a test that helped distinguish intellectually normal from subnormal Parisian schoolchildren. In the United States Binet's test was refined by Lewis Terman of Stanford University, as the still widely used *Stanford-Binet Intelligence Scale*. Rather similar tests were also developed by David Wechsler, known as the *Wechsler Intelligence Scale for Children, Revised* or *WISC–R* and the *Wechsler Adult Intelligence Scale, Revised* or *WAIS–R*. Items similar to those on the WISC–R are as follows:

Information	Which president signed the Emancipation Proclamation?
Similarities	How are a bell and a violin alike?
Arithmetic	If you buy five pieces of gum for 18 cents each, how much change would you get back from a dollar?
Vocabulary	What does *dissipate* mean?
Comprehension	What should you do if you see another child bitten by a dog?
Picture completion	Show me the part that is missing in this picture (wheel of a car).
Picture arrangement	Arrange the pictures on these cards so they tell a story that makes sense.
Block design	Arrange these blocks so they look like the design in this picture.
Object assembly	Put this puzzle together as quickly as you can (jigsaw puzzle of a dog).
Coding	Use this key that matches numbers with geometric shapes to write the shape that goes with each number in the block below it.

"WHAT WITH THE PRIMARY MENTAL ABILITY TEST AND THE DIFFERENTIAL APTITUDE TEST AND THE READING READINESS TEST AND THE BASIC SKILLS TEST AND THE I.Q. TEST AND THE SEQUENTIAL TESTS OF EDUCATIONAL PROGRESS AND THE MENTAL MATURITY TEST, WE HAVEN'T BEEN LEARNING <u>ANYTHING</u> AT SCHOOL."

How is it possible to develop a test that measures intelligence when psychologists cannot decide what intelligence is? Intelligence tests are no more than a small sample of *some* of the cognitive abilities that constitute intelligence. These tests are considered useful not because we are sure they measure the right things, but because they do a fairly good job of *predicting* how people will perform in situations that seem to require intelligence, such as in school or on the job. This state of affairs has led some psychologists to say—only slightly in jest—that intelligence should be defined as what intelligence tests measure. We cannot be very confident that intelligence tests are very good at measuring "intelligence," whatever that turns out to be. But intelligence tests are fairly good at picking out those individuals who perform well on tasks that seem to require intelligence.

Construction of Intelligence Tests

We can perhaps better understand the nature of intelligence tests, and the meaning of the related term *IQ,* by taking a brief look at how intelligence tests are constructed. Binet constructed his test by looking for a large number of items related to cognitive efficiency that differentiated children of different ages. That is, he looked for items that about half the children of one age could answer, but that nearly all older children and very few younger children could answer. He did this based on the assumption that intellectual abilities improve with age during childhood.

Once Binet had compiled a list of items, he gave them to a large number of children of different ages to determine how many children at each age level could answer each question. Then he arranged the order of the questions in the test from the least to the most difficult.

In simplified terms, the score obtained on Binet's intelligence test is equal to the number of questions you answer correctly, but it's expressed in terms of the age of the children for which your score is the *average.* For example, if you correctly answer 18 items, and the average number of items answered by children 8 years and 6 months in age was 18, then your score on the test would be expressed as "8 years 6 months." Binet called this score the *mental age.* If your mental age is higher than your actual age (*chronological age*), then you would

Albert Einstein had uncommon intelligence. Only about 2 percent of the general population have IQs above 130.

intelligence quotient (IQ)

A numerical value of intelligence derived from the results of an intelligence test.

normal distribution

The symmetrical pattern of scores on a scale in which a majority of the scores are clustered near the center and a minority are at either extreme.

be considered bright because you answered the average number of items for older children. If your mental age is lower than your chronological age, then you would be considered below average in intelligence because you could only answer the average number of questions answered by younger children. This is all that an intelligence test is: a measure that compares your performance on items believed to reflect intelligence with the performance of individuals of different ages.

Is a child with a mental age of 9 years 4 months and a chronological age of 7 years 2 months brighter than a child with a chronological age of 8 years 5 months and a mental age of 10 years 3 months? Because it's difficult to compare the mental ages of children of different chronological ages, and for other technical reasons that we need not consider here, a more easily used score than the mental age was later developed for intelligence tests called the **intelligence quotient** or **IQ.** The intelligence quotient is obtained by dividing the mental age (MA) by the chronological age (CA) so that children of different chronological ages can be directly compared. To remove the decimal point, the result is multiplied by 100. Thus, *IQ = MA/CA × 100.* For example, if a child's MA is 6 years 6 months and his chronological age is also 6 years 6 months, then his IQ would be 100.

IQs that are over 100 indicate that the person is more intelligent than average (the MA is greater than the CA). For example, if a child obtains an MA of 10 years 0 months, but her CA is only 8 years 0 months, then her IQ would be 10/8 × 100 = 125. Conversely, IQs less than 100 indicate that the individual is less intelligent than average. A child who is 10 years 0 months in CA, but obtains an MA of only 7 years 0 months would have an IQ of 7/10 × 100 = 70. Although IQs are calculated in a mathematically different way for most modern intelligence tests, they still have the same meaning. They tell us what the ratio is between an individual's mental and chronological ages.

As figure 7.9 shows, IQ scores tend to resemble a **normal distribution.** This means that in the general population most people obtain average IQ scores or scores that are very close to 100. As scores deviate from 100 in either direction (higher or lower than 100), the scores become progressively less common. Thus, scores of 90 or 110 are common, but scores of 50 or 150 are quite uncommon. Only about 2 percent of the general population have IQs above 130, and a similar percentage have IQs below 70.

Figure 7.9 The normal distribution of IQ test scores.

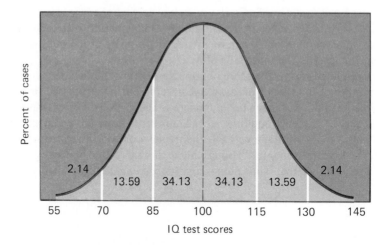

Characteristics of Good Intelligence Tests

When you measure the size of a window with a yardstick before buying drapes, you don't have to ask how good yardsticks are for measuring length. For the purpose you are using it, yardsticks are good measuring instruments. For something as important, yet difficult to define, as intelligence, however, it makes sense for us to ask how accurate the measuring instrument is. The following is a list of criteria that an intelligence test must meet before we accept it as an adequate measuring instrument. In chapter 11 on personality tests, you will see how these criteria apply equally to all psychological tests.

1. **Standardization.** Since intelligence tests are designed to compare the performance of one person with others, the test must be given in the same way to every person. If this were not so, differences in performance might be due to differences in the way the test is administered rather than to true differences in ability. For this reason, properly designed psychological tests contain detailed instructions telling the examiner how to administer the test to each person in the same *standardized* way.

   standardization
   Administering a test in the same way to all individuals.

2. **Norms.** In order to compare the individual's score with that of others, the developer of the test must give the test to a large sample of people who are believed to represent the general population. For example, you could not develop an intelligence test for adults by only giving the test to college students, since they are a brighter sample of individuals than the general population. The sample used in evaluating the performance of individuals given the test is called the *normative sample*. It must be large enough to validly represent the general population and it must contain approximately the same proportion of each subgroup in the general population to be a valid standard of comparison for anyone taking the test. For example, a normative sample that contained no Chicano children could not be validly used to evaluate young Chicanos.

   norms
   Standards (created by the scores of a large group of individuals) used as the basis of comparison for scores on a test.

3. **Objectivity.** An intelligence test must be constructed so that there is little or no ambiguity as to what constitutes a correct answer to each item. If there is ambiguity, and the scoring is subjective rather than *objective,* then factors other than the individual's performance might influence the scoring, such as the examiner's mood or prejudices.

   objectivity
   Lack of subjectivity in a test question so that the same score is produced regardless of who does the scoring.

4. **Reliability.** To be useful, an intelligence test must be *reliable.* This means that the scores obtained would be approximately the same if administered on two different occasions or by two different examiners. If the scores change a great deal from one testing to the next, no faith can be put in the scores.

   reliability
   A test's ability to produce similar scores if the test is administered on different occasions or by different examiners.

RESEARCH REPORT

Is It Good to Be Intellectually Gifted?

In recent years, public school systems across the United States have begun to provide special educational programs for "gifted" children. "Gifted" is usually defined in terms of high IQ scores, but with some attention being paid to creativity. These programs are funded on two grounds: (1) that the nation needs to enrich the education of its brightest future leaders, and (2) that these children are so bright that they sometimes need help to avoid developing psychological problems. This latter argument—that being more intelligent than one's peers causes problems—is not universally accepted. Is it true that being intelligent is generally a handicap or is it an advantage like we have heretofore assumed?

The best answer to this question comes from the research of Lewis Terman (1925), creator of the Stanford-Binet Intelligence Scale and expert on high intelligence. In the early 1920s Terman identified more than 1,500 highly intelligent boys and girls living in California. They were mostly between the ages of 8 and 12 when identified and had IQs that averaged about 150. Terman studied these geniuses both as children and later as adults. Follow-up evaluations of Terman's subjects, now in their 60s and 70s, have been reported by Richard Herrnstein (1971) and Daniel Goleman (1980).

As children, the gifted group was found to be functioning very well in every evaluated area of life. They were making better grades in school, were considered more honest and trustworthy, and were taller and stronger than their peers of average IQ. In their middle 40s, the gifted group was still found to be highly successful. About 70 percent had graduated from college (compared to about 8 percent of their generation), 40 percent of the male graduates had earned law degrees, medical degrees, or Ph.D. degrees, and 85 percent were working as professionals or as managers in business. Their total family incomes were more than double the average for white families from the same socioeconomic status. Physically, the gifted group was still considered superior to their peers, in that their death rate was one-third less than the national average. The gifted group experienced no fewer minor emotional problems than average, but showed lower rates of alcoholism and criminal convictions. The latest reports suggest that this group of highly intelligent individuals is still doing far better than average in many ways near the end of their working years. Clearly, these results suggest that high intelligence is generally a good thing to possess.

5. **Validity.** Most importantly, an intelligence scale must be *valid,* that is, it must measure what it's supposed to measure. Validity can be evaluated in a number of different ways, but for intelligence tests, the most important issue is the degree to which it *predicts* performance on other tasks that most people agree require intelligence. This is referred to as *predictive validity.* For example, the Wechsler and Stanford-Binet intelligence tests are considered valid in part because they are fairly good predictors of performance in school. About 25 percent of the differences in school performance among a group of students can be predicted from IQ scores. This is not a high level of predictability because for one thing it indicates that many factors besides intelligence contribute to school performance. But intelligence test scores are better predictors of school performance than any other measure that psychologists or educators now possess. So, in this sense, intelligence tests are valid.

validity
The extent to which a test measures what it's supposed to measure.

Contributing Factors: Causes of High and Low IQ

Why is one person highly intelligent while another person is less so? Is it heredity; do we inherit high or low IQs? Or is it the intellectually stimulating or impoverished environment in which we grow up that determines our IQ? Until recent years, most psychologists believed that only the learning environment in which the child was reared was important, but considerable evidence now exists that shows that Sir Francis Galton was at least partially correct: Intelligence is partly determined by heredity.

In chapter 2 we mentioned that the two main sources of information about heredity in humans are twin studies and adoption studies. Both have been conducted with intelligence test scores, and both clearly point to the influence of heredity. The IQ scores of genetically identical monozygotic (identical) twins are considerably more similar than the scores of dizygotic twins even though both kinds of twins are reared in essentially the same intellectual environment. Dizygotic twins, who are no more alike genetically than siblings born at different times, are, in fact, no more similar in IQ than any other siblings. Furthermore, it makes little difference whether monozygotic twins grew up in the same home or were adopted and raised in *separate* homes. In both cases, their IQs are nearly identical (Erlenmeyer-Kimling & Jarvik, 1963; Lewontin, 1982).

Adoption studies have similarly indicated that heredity is one of the more important factors determining IQ. A large number of studies have shown that the IQs of adopted children are more similar to the IQs of their biological parents with whom they never lived than their adoptive parents who raised them. Taken together, the twin and adoption studies make a strong case that heredity is one of the determinants of IQ. So, if you are as smart as you think you are, your parents are probably smarter than you thought they were!

OF SPECIAL INTEREST

The Stability of IQ Scores in Young Children

There has been a recent trend toward beginning children's education earlier. While in the 1940s starting kindergarten at age five was considered "early" by most parents, many children today begin structured learning activities at age three. And it's not uncommon to hear about "educational" programs for infants. Along with this trend toward earlier education, there has also been a trend to attempt earlier identification of children who will have problems in school. While this is definitely a worthwhile goal, we must be careful not to put too much faith in IQ scores obtained at early ages.

This caution against early IQ testing is based on results of the important Berkeley Growth Study. This study followed a large number of individuals from birth to age 25. One major interest of the researchers was the stability of IQ scores at different ages (Bayley, 1965). Are IQ scores constant across every age or are they subject to change? The results of this study showed that there was virtually no relationship between IQ scores taken at age 2 and age 18. Other evidence suggests that the relationship is slightly stronger, but not strong enough to meaningfully predict an individual's adult IQ from early childhood (Jensen, 1980). It's not possible to predict what an individual's IQ will be at age 18 from an IQ score obtained at age two. Prediction from scores obtained at age 6 is fairly good, but IQ scores don't become truly stable until about age 7 to 10. We must not be in too big a rush to measure a child's IQ—it might change considerably between ages 2 and 10.

The intellectual environment in which a child is reared is also an important factor in intelligence, however. The exposure that children have to the world of adult intelligence through interactions with their caregivers seems essential to normal intellectual development. Children who have been so severely neglected by their parents as to be deprived of this stimulation show very little intellectual development, but usually develop rapidly when placed in good foster homes (Clarke & Clarke, 1976).

But while the role of the environment in intellectual development is an important one, there appear to be broad limits on the nature of the needed environmental stimulation. This is perhaps best shown by the classic study of Skeels (1966). Skeels was a psychologist who worked with orphans who were reared in a state institution in Iowa in the 1930s. At that time, the amount and quality of the care that the adult attendants provided was very poor, with ratios of 10 infants to 1 caretaker not being unusual. Many of the children who grew up in this institution were tested to be mentally retarded, but Skeels noted that some infants who were reared in a ward for mentally retarded adult women due to lack

OF SPECIAL INTEREST

The Question of Racial Differences in Intelligence

It has long been known that American blacks score an average of 10 or more points less than whites on IQ tests. This fact is accepted by most psychologists, but the *interpretation* of the meaning of this finding has been the subject of heated debate. Most psychologists (e.g., Kamin, 1974) believe that these differences mean very little about the real intellectual potential of blacks. They point to two issues. First, most intelligence tests are based on items that are common to the white culture and are standardized mostly on whites. Because blacks come from a somewhat different culture from whites, they are at a disadvantage compared to whites in answering IQ test items. Therefore, this group argues that intelligence tests are not valid for use with blacks and that the differences in test scores reflect cultural rather than intellectual differences. To bolster this point, psychologist Robert L. Williams (1972) has shown that when an intelligence test was constructed using items common to the black culture, whites scored lower than blacks on the average.

Second, Leon Kamin and others point to the fact that, although some real improvement has been made in recent years, most living American blacks grew up in a distinctly prejudiced environment where economic and educational disadvantages have influenced their intellectual development. The differences in IQ scores may be a measure of the discrimination blacks have suffered rather than true differences in intellectual capacity.

Arthur Jensen (1973) of the University of California at Berkeley, on the other hand, originally argued that the differences in IQ scores not only reflected actual differences in intellectual ability, but also that these differences were genetically based. That is to say, Jensen stated that blacks are innately inferior to whites. His most recent statement confirms his belief that blacks and whites differ in intelligence, but he no longer explains these differences in genetic terms (Jensen, 1980).

As long as we live in a prejudiced society that places blacks at a disadvantage and encourages the maintenance of separate black and white cultures, we probably will not be able to decide whether the differences between the two come from biased tests or true differences in intelligence. But there is certainly no evidence to support the belief that blacks are genetically inferior. Furthermore, one well-designed experiment that evaluated the IQs of black children who were adopted as infants by white families showed IQs that were average for white children. Apparently the experience of growing up in advantaged white homes was the crucial factor for these children (Kamin, 1974). This may mean that environmental factors are responsible for all racial differences in IQ, perhaps because individuals who grow up in a white environment are better able to perform on intelligence tests based on the white culture.

The child's exposure to the world of adult intelligence through interaction with caregivers seems essential to normal intellectual development.

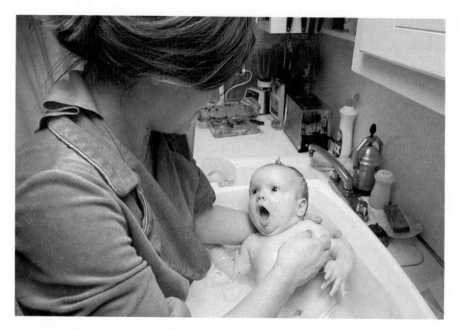

of space showed unexpected improvements in IQ. Skeels reasoned that the stimulation provided by the retarded women was sufficiently better than the almost nonexistent stimulation provided in the orphanage. To test this idea, he had 13 low IQ orphans placed in the adult's ward for 18 months. These children showed an increase in IQ of an average of over 25 points, placing them in the normal range of intelligence! In sharp contrast, a group of orphans who were left in the orphanage showed an average *drop* in IQ of 25 points. Although it is unlikely that the quality of intellectual stimulation provided by the mentally retarded "foster parents" was very good, it was enough to allow the intelligence of these children to develop normally. Clearly both heredity and environment are important in determining intelligence.

R E V I E W

The term *intelligence* refers to our ability to use cognitive processes to cope with the demands of daily life. This vague concept has found an important place in contemporary psychology because tests have been developed that predict with reasonable accuracy performance on tasks that require intelligence, particularly school and job performance. Scores on these intelligence (IQ) tests indicate whether an individual has correctly answered as many questions as the average person of his or her own age. Higher IQs indicate that the person has scored the same number of points as the average person of an older age; lower IQs indicate the opposite. Useful IQ tests must be standardized, evaluated against proper norms, objective, reliable, and valid.

It's not yet clear whether intelligence should be thought of as a single general factor or as many independent facets of intellectual ability. Consequently, some widely used IQ tests report both a general score and several more specific scores. Regardless of how they are conceptualized, both heredity and environmental factors help determine an individual's level of intelligence.

S U M M A R Y

Chapter 7 discusses our intellectual processes, how we use language, and how human intelligence is measured.

I. In the process of *cognition,* information is obtained through the senses, transformed through the interpretive processes of perception and thinking, stored and retrieved through the processes of memory, and used in the processes of problem solving and language.

II. *Concepts,* the basic units of thinking, are categories of things, events, or qualities linked together by some common feature or features.

    A. Some concepts are categories based on a single common feature; others are more complex.

        1. Members of categories defined by *conjunctive concepts* have two or more common characteristics.

        2. Members of *disjunctive concepts* have one common characteristic or another one, or both.

    B. *Concept formation* is a special kind of learning in which hypotheses about the defining characteristics of a concept are tested by examining positive and negative instances of the concept.

    C. All concepts are not equally easy for us to learn; some are more natural than others.

III. In *problem solving,* information is used to reach a goal that is blocked by an obstacle.

    A. Cognitive operations are used to solve problems. After we decide what kind of problem we face, we evaluate the elements of the problem and decide what information and tools we have to work with. Then we generate a list of solutions and evaluate them.

    B. *Algorithmic* and *heuristic* operations are two types of cognitive strategies used in solving problems.

    C. Creative problem solving requires the ability to think in flexible and unusual ways (*divergent thinking*); the most useful solutions are thought out logically (*convergent thinking*).

IV. *Language* is a symbolic code used in human communication.

    A. *Semantic content* is the meaning communicated through language.

    B. We generate language from a set of elements and a set of rules for combining them into speech.

        1. The *phoneme* is the smallest unit of sound in a language. The English language has only 44 phonemes.

        2. *Morphemes* are the smallest units of meaning in a language.

        3. *Syntax* is the rules of a language through which an infinite number of understandable utterances are generated.

    C. Much of our thinking is in the form of language.

        1. *Peripheralism* is a theory that states that thinking is no more than silent speech occurring in the peripheral voice box and not in the central brain.

        2. The *Whorfian* or *linguistic relativity hypothesis* states that the structure of language influences how people think.

V. *Intelligence* refers to the cognitive abilities of an individual to learn from experience, to reason well, and to cope effectively with the demands of daily living.
   A. Intelligence is viewed as a single *general factor* by some psychologists and as many independent kinds of intellectual ability by others.
   B. Intelligence tests measure a small sample of the cognitive abilities that constitute intelligence.
      1. The *intelligence quotient* is obtained by dividing the *mental age* by the *chronological age*.
      2. Useful IQ tests must be *standardized, objective, reliable, valid,* and evaluated against proper *norms*.
   C. Both heredity and environmental factors help determine an individual's level of intelligence.

Suggested Readings

1. A scholarly statement on the psychology of language is provided by:
   Slobin, D. I. (1979). *Psycholinguistics*. Glenview, IL: Scott, Foresman.

2. An up-to-date, scholarly, and readable overview of cognition:
   Ellis, H. C., & Hunt, R. R. (1983). *Fundamentals of human memory and cognition* (3rd ed.). Dubuque, IA: Wm. C. Brown Publishers.

3. For a first-hand account of Penny Patterson's attempt to teach language to a gorilla and of Herbert Terrace's experiences with the chimpanzee Nim Chimpsky:
   Patterson, F. (1977). The gestures of a gorilla: Language acquisition in another primate species. In J. Hamburg, J. Goodall, & L. McCown (Eds.), *Perspectives in human evolution* (Vol. 4). Menlo Park: Benjamin Press.
   Terrace, H. S. (1980). *Nim*. New York: Knopf.

4. For opposing views on the topic of racial differences in intelligence:
   Jensen, A. R. (1980). *Bias in mental testing*. New York: Free Press.
   Kamin, L. J. (1974). *The science and politics of IQ*. Potomac, MD: Lawrence Earlbaum.

The Life Span

Infant and Child Development

OUTLINE

KEY TERMS

P R O L O G U E

Jean Piaget was a Swiss researcher who, until his death in 1980, studied the development of cognition in children. In many ways, it can be said that his pioneering work gave adults a very different understanding of children. Perhaps Piaget's most important contribution was to show us that children of different ages understand the world in ways that are often very different from adults.

To illustrate this point, let's first look at an adult ability and then compare it to the child's. Imagine that you drop by your instructor's office for a visit and sit down on the opposite side of his desk. Would the objects on top of the desk look the same to you and your instructor? Of course not. The paper clip that you can see sitting in front of his coffee cup is hidden from his view, and you can't see the wad of bubble gum that is stuck to his side of the pencil sharpener. We adults have so little trouble understanding that our perception of things depends on our *perspective* that we take this ability for granted. However, we are not born with the ability to take another person's perspective—it *develops*. One reason that the cognition of young children is so fascinatingly different from adults is that they cannot understand any perspective but their own.

A classic experiment by Piaget and his frequent collaborator Barbel Inhelder (1963) makes this point very well. Children of different ages were shown three small three-dimensional replicas of "mountains" arranged on a table top. On the other side of the table, a doll was seated. The children were asked to look at the mountains and then were asked to indicate which picture from several showed the mountains as the *doll* would see them. Six-year-olds could not do it at all, some seven- and eight-year-olds could, and children nine to eleven years of age had no more trouble with the task than an adult would.

What does this study tell us? Piaget and Inhelder interpreted it to mean that young children have a great deal of difficulty understanding the world from any perspective but their own. Think about that for a second—it's a tremendous limitation to be unable to see the world as others see it. Have you ever tried explaining to a young child that the moon does not *really* follow her around or that it's possible for his mommy to also be your sister? The inability of young children to take another's perspective is very much related to their difficulties in understanding such adult ideas. Incidentally, more recent studies have shown that younger children (as young as four) can take another's perspective on some easier tasks (Borke, 1975), but the gist of Piaget and Inhelder's conclusion remains the same: Young children understand their worlds in ways that are so different from adults that it is sometimes like trying to communicate with a creature from Mars. To relate to children better and more effectively serve their needs, we must understand how they differ from us as they develop.

development
The more-or-less predictable changes in behavior associated with increasing age.

━━━━━━━━━━━━━━━━━━━━━━━━━━━━━━━━
P R E V I E W
━━━━━━━━━━━━━━━━━━━━━━━━━━━━━━━━━

Life doesn't stand still. We are in a state of constant change throughout our lives. When we ask ourselves who we are, we think of ourselves in terms of who we are *now.* But we have been and will be many different people in our lifetime: an infant, a child, a teenager, a young adult, a mature person, and an aged person. The thread of continuity that runs through our lives is very real, but we change more than we realize. To understand ourselves fully, we must understand the process of **development,** the more-or-less predictable changes in behavior associated with increasing age.

Psychologists differ on the question of how much our development is biologically determined or shaped by the learning environment. In the past, some psychologists viewed developmental changes as "unfolding" according to a predetermined biological plan much as an oak tree grows from an acorn. Others saw the environment "molding" our development like clay in the hands of a potter. Most psychologists today, however, believe that development is the product of the *combined* forces of "nature" (biology) and "nurture" (environment). Toilet training, for example, clearly involves a process of learning for the child, but it will not be successful until the child has reached an appropriate level of biological maturation. The timing of learning experiences may be important in other ways as well. Experience during early critical periods has long-lasting effects on animal behavior. The effects of early experience may be important for humans as well, but they appear to be less permanent.

Psychologists are also in disagreement as to whether development proceeds as a continuous process of gradual change or as a series of distinct "stages." It's probably appropriate to view development in terms of stages, but as ones that blend somewhat gradually from one to another. Regardless of how development is conceptualized, however, variations in the rate of development clearly are normal within broad ranges.

In this chapter, we trace the normal course of development from the moment of conception through childhood. Twenty years ago, this chapter would have ended our discussion of development, but today it's recognized that developmental changes continue throughout the life span. Consequently, the next chapter will continue to trace the course of normal development through adolescence, adulthood, and later life.

Nature, Nurture, and Maturation: Molding or Unfolding?

As we discussed in chapter 2, our behavior is the product of a rich *blend* of both biological factors (our inheritance, biological structure, glandular functioning, disease) and psychological aspects of the environment (our experiences and current situation). Not long ago, however, psychological development was the major battleground for the "nature-nurture controversy."

Human children are born with the biological mechanisms for learning language. But the language they learn is determined by the environment in which they are reared.

Nature or Nurture?

In the past, some psychological theorists asserted that nearly all important developmental changes are controlled by biological factors (nature): that is, our behavior "unfolds" over time, like a plant growing from seed to flower. Other theorists asserted that the psychological environment (nurture) is the master of our development: Our behavior is "molded" by experiences, like clay in the hands of a sculptor. Radical behaviorist John B. Watson (1925) even went so far as to say:

> Give me a dozen healthy infants, well-formed and my own specified world to bring them up in and I'll guarantee to take any one at random and train him to become any type of specialist I might select—doctor, lawyer, artist, merchant chief and, yes, even beggar-man and thief, regardless of his talents, penchants, tendencies, abilities, vocations, and race of his ancestors (p. 82).

Current thinking asserts that both nature and nurture combine to influence our actions, thoughts, and feelings, but contemporary theorists are still divided in their opinions and tend to lean more toward either the molding or unfolding view of development (Kagan, 1984).

Language provides a good example of the interplay of nature and nurture in our lives. There can be no question that experience is important in language development. Children will only learn to use language if they are exposed to language, and will learn to speak whatever language to which they are exposed. For example, a French child adopted by a Chinese-speaking family will grow up speaking Chinese, not French. But neither goldfish nor marmosets will learn to speak a human language when given the same amount of experience required by a human child to learn language. One must have a human brain (or as discussed in chapter 7, an ape brain might be sufficient) to learn a human language. In the absence of the right nature, nurture can accomplish nothing.

Other examples of the blending of nature and nurture abound in child development. Few children will learn to use a baseball glove unless taught to do so (or without at least seeing others play ball). But you cannot effectively teach children to do much with a glove until considerable physical development has taken place (after age four or so). Twin and adoption studies show that intelligence is influenced by heredity, but research on enriched intellectual stimulation shows that experience is also an important factor. A child with severe mental retardation due to brain damage can be taught some intellectual and social skills with intensive training, but because of the limits imposed by his biological damage, he can never be made fully "normal." We are creatures of complex combinations of both our nature and nurture.

Maturation

maturation
(mach″u-ra′shun)
Systematic physical growth
of the body, including the
nervous system.

When we think of biological factors in the development of behavior, we think primarily of genetics. But in the study of development, the most important biological factor to consider is **maturation.** This term refers to systematic physical growth of the nervous system and other bodily structures. A primary question for the psychologist who specializes in the study of development is, "How much of the changes that we see occurring with age are the result of physical maturation rather than increased experience?"

As you have probably come to expect, the answer is that *both* experience and maturation play an important role in most areas of behavior, but maturation is a surprisingly powerful factor in many ways. For example, experience obviously plays an important role in toilet training—children must be taught to use the toilet—but maturation also plays a key role. According to research, successful toilet training is difficult for most children before the age of 24 months. They are simply not maturationally ready to learn that task. After 24 months of age, however, most children learn rapidly.

An experiment using identical twin boys illustrates the idea of maturational readiness beautifully. Toilet training was begun for one boy, Hugh, when he was only 50 days old. Training for Hilton, the other twin, did not begin until 700 days of age (almost two years). As shown in figure 8.1, Hugh made no real progress until about 18 months of age, while Hilton's progress was rapid from the beginning. Both children learned, but only when they reached the proper level of maturation (McGraw, 1940).

Much research also suggests that maturation plays a prominent role in other aspects of physical development. For example, *swaddling,* the practice of wrapping cloth around infants to bind them to a board that runs along their backs so that they can be propped up while parents work, is common among the Hopi and Apache Indians and some Eastern European cultures. One study shows that such swaddling does not seriously delay the onset of walking (Dennis & Dennis, 1940). Swaddled infants have less motor experience during the first months of life than children in other cultures, but they still begin to walk at about the same age. But another study by Wayne Dennis (1973) indicates that *extreme* variations in experience can affect even aspects of development that are under strong maturational control. Infants raised in extremely impoverished orphanages in the Middle

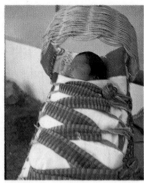

An infant bound in
swaddling

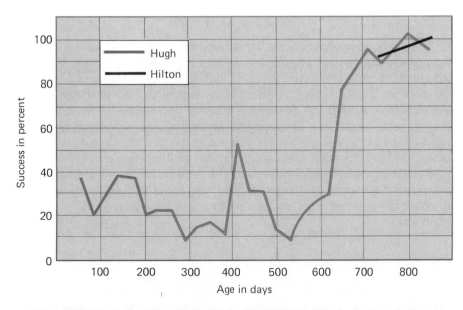

Figure 8.1 The importance of maturational readiness is shown in McGraw's (1940) study of toilet training twin boys named Hugh and Hilton. Although Hugh's training was begun at 50 days of age, no progress was achieved until he was about 650 days of age. In contrast, Hilton's progress was rapid because training was begun when he was maturationally ready (McGraw, 1940).

Toilet training, typical of many human behaviors, is learned more quickly when the child is maturationally ready.

East during the 1930s were given *no* opportunities to leave their small cribs and virtually *no* social interaction. As a result, they were slow in walking and other areas of physical, social, and intellectual development.

Interestingly, we shall see shortly that maturation functions in much the same way in social, intellectual, and other areas of development. For example, it's unlikely that we could teach an 18-month-old to play cooperatively with other children, or teach a four-year-old the concept of physical mass, or teach the concept of "justice" to a six-year-old. These behaviors and concepts generally cannot be learned until later, suggesting again that maturation is involved.

R E V I E W

Children change dramatically but rather predictably from birth to adulthood—from a nearly helpless infant to a competent adult. This fact has led some theorists in the past to assert that developmental changes in behavior are biologically programmed to "unfold" with increasing age. Other theorists have argued that changes in behavior occur because the learning environment "molds" our development. Today it's generally believed, however, that development results from a blend of both biological and environmental influences. Maturation provides an important example of this interaction between biology and environment: Some forms of learning (that are clearly dependent on the environment) can occur efficiently only when the child has reached a certain level of readiness through physical maturation.

Critical Periods and Early Experience

When the Puritans came to America in the 1600s, they brought with them a belief about children that most of us still hold today—namely, that early childhood is the "formative period" for our personalities. We believe that the experiences that we have as a young child powerfully, and permanently, shape our adult behavior. We believe that if we are built of fragile glass in our early years, we will be fragile all our lives; but if we are built of steel in the formative years, we will have lifelong strength. This is not just a belief held by laypeople; many psychologists hold it, too. But, is it true that early experiences irreversibly form our personalities?

Imprinting

Supporting this view that our early experiences are of prime importance is a large body of research on nonhuman animals. German biologist Konrad Lorenz (1937), for example, has extensively studied the behavior and development of the graylag goose. During one phase of his investigations, he wanted to know why young goslings followed their mothers in the little single-file parades that are the joy of farmers and park-visiting children everywhere. Do they follow the mother goose because of an *inborn* tendency or instinct (nature) or do they *learn* to follow (nurture) their mother? Lorenz found that goslings do have an inborn tendency to follow, but that they will follow *any* moving, noisy object that they are exposed to after hatching, not just mother geese. Furthermore, once they begin following something, they generally will not follow anything else but that object. If their mother is out to lunch when they hatch and a rooster should happen to strut by, they will follow him until they are mature geese—presumably much to his embarrassment.

   Lorenz called this special kind of early learning **imprinting.** He thought of it as a true form of learning—perhaps the goslings are negatively reinforced for following by a reduction of fear of being alone—but a kind of learning that was highly constrained by biological factors. The goslings will only follow the first, moving, noisy object they see and will usually learn to follow no other object after they have been imprinted. The maturational control of this learning is seen even more clearly in the fact that imprinting can occur only (or at least most readily)

imprinting
(im'print-ing)
A form of early learning that occurs in some animals during a critical period.

Konrad Lorenz followed by some of his goslings.

during a brief period of the bird's life called the **critical period.** If imprinting does not occur during the sensitive critical period, it will probably never occur. Still, the fact that imprinting is a kind of learning—part of nurture—is obvious from the fact that the birds will learn to follow anything that meets the biological requirements. Goslings have been imprinted on quacking duck decoys and footballs pulled by squeaking pulleys. In addition, a famous *Life* magazine photo shows Konrad Lorenz being followed by a flock of goslings who had imprinted on him. It's not clear, however, that anything comparable to imprinting occurs in humans, although we do form attachments to our caregivers through prolonged experience with them.

critical period
A biologically determined period in the life of some animals during which certain forms of learning can take place most easily.

Early Social Deprivation

Studies conducted with monkeys, who are close to humans on the evolutionary ladder, also show the long-lasting effects of early experience in a way that seems more relevant to the human condition than imprinting. Harry Harlow (Harlow & Novak, 1973) carried out a number of studies of the role of early social experiences in development. Are our earliest social experiences especially important to the development of social behavior in childhood and adulthood? Sigmund Freud would have us believe that these early experiences are of the greatest significance, but until Harlow, few researchers had experimentally tested Freud's claims.

Harlow's best-known experiment occurred as an afterthought, a brilliant afterthought, to another experiment. Harlow was originally interested in the factors influencing the attachments of infant monkeys to their mothers. Specifically he wanted to determine the relative importance of the mother's warmth and softness compared to the fact that she provided nourishment through nursing. To find out, Harlow raised a group of infant monkeys without real mothers. They were raised in cages with two dolls made of wire shaped to look like mother monkeys. One doll was left bare while the other was padded with terry cloth to duplicate the feel of the mother's body. At times, a nursing bottle was placed in the wire mother; at other times, it was placed in the cloth mother.

Harry Harlow (1905–1981)

Harlow's studies of early
social deprivation in
monkeys revealed that
abnormal experiences
during the first six months
of life have a detrimental
effect on the social
behavior of adult monkeys.

The results of the experiment were clear-cut. The infant monkeys spent most of their time on the soft cloth mother, leaving it only long enough to nurse when the bottle was on the wire monkey; warmth and softness are clearly the more important determinants of attachment in this case. Perhaps the more significant findings came from the afterthought experiment, however.

After the initial experiment, Harlow returned the monkeys, who had never lived with a real mother, to regular group cages with other monkeys. When they reached adulthood (about three years of age for these monkeys), they were placed in breeding cages with another monkey of the opposite sex. It was then that Harlow noticed that the social, sexual, and emotional behavior of these monkeys was distinctly abnormal. Females raised without early experience with a mother appeared fearful and viciously attacked the male when a sexual advance was made. The males, on the other hand, alternated between fearfulness and overenthusiastic, clumsy sexual advances.

Although they had normal social experiences for two and a half years, these monkeys' abnormal experiences during the first six months of life had a continuing detrimental effect on their social behavior. Moreover, when a few of the females finally became pregnant and had offspring, the lasting effects of the early social deprivation were made more clear. When the mother-deprived monkeys became mothers themselves, they rejected and even attacked their own infants. Some of the mother-deprived mothers even killed their own infants and the rest had to be removed from the cage to prevent their deaths.

These findings are consistent with other facts that are known about the social development of animals. For example, lambs who are removed from the flock and bottle-fed by humans will never return to the flock, even as adults. They show an interest in other sheep, but vacillate between approaching and avoiding them. If artificially impregnated, they allow their young to nurse from them, but they are indifferent mothers.

Studies by Jerome Kagan and by Ann and A. B. D. Clarke suggest that many of the effects of abnormal early experiences in human children can be reversed, but only if they are offset by positive, appropriate experiences at later ages.

Much less is known about the effects of abnormal early experiences in humans, and, as a result, opinion is deeply divided among psychologists. Some believe that abnormal experiences produce irreversible damage (e.g., Bruner, 1974), while others believe that under favorable conditions the early effects may not be permanent. Jerome Kagan (1978) and Ann Clarke and A. B. D. Clarke (1976) have followed the development of children who had been abused and neglected as infants to evaluate the long-term effects of the most abnormal kind of early experience a child can have.

One such child was locked in a small bedroom by her parents for her first two and a half years and given only minimal care. At age two and a half, she was discovered and permanently adopted by a stable, loving family. Although she had no language and was severely undernourished at the time of adoption, she was found to be normal by age 14 (Kagan, 1978). Similar stories about other abused and socially isolated children and large-scale investigations of children who had been adopted from very impoverished orphanages (Dennis, 1973) paint a similar picture, provided they are placed in favorable environments well before adolescence (Pines, 1981). While the immediate effects of abnormal early experiences can be profound, they can often be reversed by positive, appropriate experiences at later ages. The human infant, then, may be a highly resilient creature that can recover from most traumatic early experiences (Kagan, 1984).

Obviously, this evidence should *not* be used to justify or excuse child abuse or neglect in any way. For one thing, we are not yet sure that the effects of abnormal early experiences are, in fact, reversible. Furthermore, the hope of future recovery can in no way excuse the misery of a child. But this new evidence should encourage us not to give up hope for victims of abnormal early experiences. By providing them with the most favorable environments that we can arrange, we *may* be able to reverse their deficits.

Thus, drastically altering the early experience of nonhuman animals seems to produce long-lasting effects at times, but the evidence is more optimistic for humans. Early experience, even distinctly abnormal early experience, may not *irreversibly* form our personalities. Humans appear to be more open to the effects of experience throughout the life span. Still, this conclusion comes from only a handful of studies of children with abnormal early experiences who were placed in good homes at an early age and showed marked improvement. Children with abnormal early experiences who live in marginally stable families might be less able to recover.

R E V I E W

Are our personalities irreversibly formed by our experiences in early childhood? Research on the phenomenon of imprinting in animals shows that experiences during critical periods of early development can have life-long effects on animal behavior. And Harlow's experiments with social deprivation during the infancy of monkeys also show long-lasting effects of abnormal early experiences. Studies of human infants who have had abnormal early experiences, but who were adopted by normal families when still children, however, suggest that humans may be less permanently influenced by early experience than other animals and are more open to environmental influences throughout the entire life span.

Ages and Stages of Development

While nearly all psychologists agree that behavior changes over time, there is considerable disagreement over how to conceptualize those changes. One group sees behavior as changing *gradually* with age, while the other school of thought sees behavior as going through a series of *abrupt* changes from one **stage** to the next. To relate this difference in opinion to our previous discussion, those who see gradual changes generally lean more toward a "molding" view by which they interpret behavior as gradually changing, mostly due to increasing experience. Those who see stages in development typically lean toward a view of behavior that "unfolds" over time, largely due to biological maturation.

stage
One of several time periods in development that is qualitatively distinct from the periods that come before and after.

Stage theorists believe that the changes occurring from one stage to the next make children *qualitatively* different (different in "kind") rather than *quantitatively* different (different in amount) from what they were at a previous stage. When a child learns to use simple words to express herself, she has changed qualitatively—that is, she has become different from the kind of child she was when she could not use language. This is not a change in the amount of some behavior, but a qualitative change that opens up new experiences and possibilities. Although stage theorists believe that changes *between* stages are qualitative, they believe that children change quantitatively *during* each stage. For example, once the child has mastered some simple words, she will progress for a while by simply learning *more* simple words before the next qualitative change takes place (combining words syntactically).

Stage theorists also believe that all children must pass through the *same* qualitatively different stages in the *same* order. Stages are believed to be biologically programmed to unfold in a fixed sequence in all normal persons. In addition, they believe that a child cannot progress to the next stage until the current one has been mastered.

One notable critic of stage theory has been British psychologist T. G. R. Bower (1971). He has pointed out in a variety of studies that the transition from one "stage" to another is often quite gradual and variable. A close examination of the writings of even the staunchest stage theorists, however, shows that they recognize that the transition from one stage to the next is a gradual blending. In other words, a child may master one part of a new stage while still struggling with part of a previous stage. One gifted professor of psychology suggested to me that the stages of child development are like a rainbow: We can see that there are different colors in a rainbow, but it's not possible to see exactly where one color stops and the next one begins; the colors blend together.

In the sections that follow, we discuss three major stage theories: Jean Piaget's theory of cognitive development, Lawrence Kohlberg's theory of the development of moral judgments, and Erik Erikson's theory of personality development. By taking a close look at each of these theories, we will gain a better appreciation of stage theories in general and learn a little about the development of children in each of these three important areas. Later in the chapter, however, we discuss the normal sequence of development of many behavioral systems together. The purpose is to show the *coordinated* nature of development in different aspects of behavior. Marked changes in perception, language, cognition, emotions, and social behavior tend to occur at about the same ages in children. If we discussed the development of these systems separately, this linkage and interdependence might be missed.

Jean Piaget (1896–1980)

Piaget's Stage Theory of Cognitive Development

Perhaps the best-known stage theory in psychology is that of Jean Piaget. Piaget was a Swiss biologist and psychologist who wrote extensively about the development of cognition in children. He believed that children pass through a series of four qualitatively different stages of cognitive development from infancy to adulthood. Each of these stages is broken down into substages as well. For example, Piaget distinguishes six infant substages within the first stage of development.

Let's attempt to understand Piaget's complex theory in three steps: First, we look at the *processes* of cognitive development—that is, the characteristics of the child's mind that cause cognitive abilities to change. Second, we briefly look at the four major stages that Piaget distinguishes in cognitive development. And, third, as we discuss the normal course of development later in the chapter, we examine in some detail the developmental changes that characterize each stage.

Processes of Cognitive Development

schema (ske′mah)
A term used by Piaget to refer to concepts in children's thinking.

Each person, whether an infant, child, or adult, strives to make sense out of the confusing jumble of experiences that life provides. The person does so by organizing the world into concepts, or **schemas** to use Piaget's term. These schemas give the child a general way of categorizing perceptions, thoughts, and behaviors that simplifies the world's complexities. For example, one of the earliest schemas is sucking. The child at first sucks reflexively, but soon seems to organize the world into suckable objects: breasts, fingers, bottles, pacifiers, and so on. Each object looks and tastes a little different and must be sucked slightly differently, but they all fit within the same general sucking schema.

assimilation
(ah-sim″i-la′shun)
The process of adding new information to existing schemas.

Piaget calls the process through which the child learns that new objects or events can be added to an existing schema **assimilation.** When the infant discovers that his thumb can be included in the schema of suckable objects, he is assimilating new information into an existing schema. In the terms of our previous discussion, assimilation can be thought of as quantitative changes in the child's cognitions.

equilibrium
(e″kwi-lib′re-um)
A state of balance when the knowledge of a child fits existing schemas.

accommodation
(ah-kom″o-da′shun)
The process of adding new information that forces a child to modify existing schemas.

As long as the child is able to deal with all new experiences by incorporating them into existing schemas, he is in a comfortable state of balance, or **equilibrium.** But when new experiences cannot be successfully understood and dealt with in terms of existing schemas, the child is pushed into an uncomfortable state of disequilibrium, and he will change his schemas to again make sense of the world. Piaget calls the process of changing schemas to incorporate new experiences **accommodation.** For example, the child's initial sucking schema might classify *all* objects as things that can be sucked. Parents are very careful to keep objects out of the reach of infants that would not be safe to suck, so the child does not run into anything that is not pleasurable to suck at first. Later, however, the child will try to suck fuzzy teddy bears or shoes coated with bitter shoe polish. In this way, he will discover that his schema must be modified—accommodated—to fit this new information. The child now sees the world as composed of some objects that are pleasurable to suck and others that are distinctly unpleasant to suck. As the child matures and accumulates experiences, it becomes increasingly necessary to change old schemas through accommodation. At several points in development, the changes are dramatic enough to say that the child has entered a qualitatively different stage.

Awareness that objects still exist after they are removed from view (object permanence) occurs between the ages of six and nine months.

Four Stages of Cognitive Development

Piaget distinguishes between four primary stages of cognitive development. Notice that although changes take place within each stage, children change dramatically from one stage to the next in terms of the ways they understand and deal with reality. The following age ranges are only approximate, since different children pass through the stages at different rates. But they are helpful in organizing this information.

1. **Sensorimotor stage** *(birth to two years)*. During this stage, the infant conceptualizes the world in terms of schemas that incorporate sensory information and motor activities, hence the term *sensorimotor*. The child develops schemas for sucking and grasping, and learns to coordinate them, as in grasping an object and placing it in the mouth for sucking. Late in this stage, the child develops the ability to represent objects from the real world in her mind as an image. For example, by six to nine months of age, the child begins to understand that objects exist even when they are out of sight. This is called **object permanence.** Before that time, if an object that the infant is looking at is hidden from sight by a cloth, the infant will not push aside the cloth to look for it. It's as if the infant does not know that the object is still there—a variation of "out of sight out of mind." After six to nine months of age, however, the infant will search for the object behind the cloth, suggesting that she knows that it's back there somewhere. But although the child can represent parts of the world in mental images, she cannot yet use those images to reason. That is part of the dramatic change that brings us to the next stage.

2. **Preoperational stage** *(two to seven years)*. By about two years of age most children are capable of thinking in mental images. The young child's ability to think is quite different from that of adults,

sensorimotor stage
In Piaget's theory, the period of cognitive development from birth to two years.

object permanence
The understanding that objects continue to exist after they have been removed from view.

preoperational stage
In Piaget's theory, the period of cognitive development from ages two to seven.

egocentrism
(e″go-sen′trizm)
The self-oriented quality in the thinking of preoperational children.

animism (an′i-mizm)
The egocentric belief of preoperational children that inanimate objects are alive, like the children are.

however. For one thing, the child's thought is **egocentric,** or self-centered. Piaget does not mean by this term that the child is selfish, but that the child is simply not able to understand that she is not the center of the universe. For example, egocentrism leads young children to believe that inanimate objects are alive just as they are (known as **animism**). It's common for children of this age to believe that the moon is alive and actually follows them around when they are walking or riding in a car at night. The child's imagination is often very active at this stage and because of her egocentrism, it's difficult for the child to distinguish real from imaginary at times. That's why imaginary friends that seem very real to the child are relatively common during this stage. As we see later, other errors of logic are quite common, too, giving young children a special kind of logic all of their own, such as "Grandma, he's not your son; he's my dad!"

concrete operational stage
In Piaget's theory, the period of cognitive development from ages seven to eleven.

3. **Concrete operational stage** *(seven to eleven years)*. The dramatic change in cognition that marks the beginning of the concrete operational stage is the increased ability to reason logically. The child's thinking becomes less egocentric, more logical, and more complex. The child still cannot fully understand or reason with abstract concepts, however. The child can deal with concrete concepts such as animals, pollution, and sharpness, but cannot deal with abstractions such as justice, infinity, or the meaning of life.

formal operational stage
In Piaget's theory, the period of intellectual development usually reached about age 11, and characterized by the ability to use abstract concepts.

4. **Formal operational stage** *(eleven years on)*. From adolescence on, the individual is able to use full adult logic, including the understanding of abstract concepts. The youth is able for the first time to understand the abstractions that underlie many aspects of science, mathematics, politics, and ethics.

We will have more to say about each of these stages later in the chapter. For now, it's enough to understand Piaget's fundamental insight: The cognition of a single individual at age one, then at age 5, age 9, and age 17 is so different that it sometimes appears that they are persons from different planets.

Kohlberg's Stage Theory of Moral Development

Lawrence Kohlberg (1969) has provided us with another important stage theory of development that is in many ways similar to, and originally inspired by, the developmental theory of Jean Piaget. Kohlberg's theory encompasses only a small part of cognitive development and deals primarily with the development of moral (ethical) reasoning.

To collect the data upon which to base his stage theory of moral development, Kohlberg presented children and adolescents with moral dilemmas and asked for evaluations of the people and actions involved. The following is an example of the type of dilemma used by Kohlberg in his research.

Lawrence Kohlberg

In Europe, a lady was dying because she was very sick. There was one drug that the doctors said might save her. This medicine was discovered by a man living in the same town. It cost him $200 to make it, but he charged $2,000 for just a little of it. The sick lady's husband, Heinz, tried to borrow enough money to buy the drug. He went to everyone he knew to borrow the money. He told the man who made the drug that his wife was dying, and asked him to sell the medicine cheaper or let him pay later. But the man said, "No, I made the drug and I'm going to make money from it." So Heinz broke into the store and stole the drug.

Did Heinz do the right thing? Kohlberg was interested in the logical process through which people arrived at their answers to moral dilemmas. Based on his analysis of the process, Kohlberg concluded that moral development could be understood as having three levels, with two stages at each level—a total of six stages. The percentage of children of different ages making ethical judgments about these moral dilemmas at each of the three levels is shown in figure 8.2.

1. *The premoral level.* At this level, the child has no sense of *morality* as adults understand that term. At stage 1, the child bases moral judgments simply on the desire to avoid punishment. At stage 2, the child bases moral judgments on the desire to obtain rewards. The rewards can be as simple as candy or as complex as reciprocal favors ("You help me reach those apples, and I'll share them with you.")

2. *The conventional level.* At stage 3, the child's moral universe expands to include intangible factors, such as approval or disapproval, liking or disliking. The child's moral view is based on what others will think of him or her. At stage 4, the opinion of others is still the key, but the child has a firmer idea of which "others" are important—namely, parents, teachers, and other authorities. Obedience to "legitimate" authority is the keynote.

3. *The principled level.* At stages 5 and 6, the individual judges the rightness or wrongness of actions according to ethical principles rather than according to their consequences. At stage 5, the principles are those generally accepted in the community. At stage 6, the individual acts according to his or her own personal principles, which may have been carefully and passionately thought out and which may or may not coincide with the principles generally accepted in the community. Mahatma Gandhi, Martin Luther King, and Eleanor Roosevelt are often cited as examples of people who operated at the stage 6 level.

Kohlberg found that most children in the preoperational stage of cognitive development—that is, up to about age 7—function at the premoral level. By age 13, most children base most of their decisions on factors related to the conventional level. Many people, he suggested, remain at the conventional level throughout life. Only some adults advance to stage 5, and still fewer advance to stage 6.

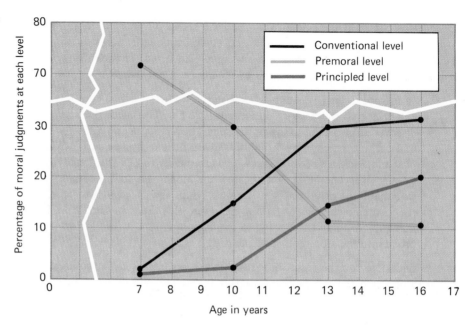

By the way, how did you evaluate Heinz's act of theft? Was it moral? Judging from a stage 6 perspective, it could be argued Heinz did the right thing. After trying to obtain the drug legally, he ignored the consequences of his action (imprisonment), disregarded the community's standards (the laws against theft), and followed what he probably thought was the higher moral principle of saving his wife's life. Does that evaluation bother you? Not everyone would agree that this use of the stage 6 reasoning is correct, since it tends to place the individual above the law. Indeed, an individual could provide an explanation for why Heinz was *wrong* that was in terms of stage 6 of moral development. For example, an individual's personal principles might say that it is better for society as a whole to always respect the property rights of others and allow Heinz's wife to die. It is not the particular decision that differs at the different levels of moral development, but the nature of moral reasoning involved.

Erikson's Stage Theory of Personality Development

Erik Erikson provides us with a very different example of a stage theory of development. His focus is on the person's developing relationships with the people in his social world. But, although Erikson, Piaget, and Kohlberg are interested in very different aspects of development, their theories share the common assumptions of stage theory: Each person will pass through a series of qualitatively different stages in a fixed order.

Erikson's stages are conceived of somewhat differently from Piaget's or Kohlberg's. They are not periods in which a particular pattern of cognition or moral reason prevails; Erikson's stages are turning points, or *crises,* the outcome of which will partly determine the course of future personality development. In using the term *crises,* Erikson is not suggesting that these turning points are always experienced as emotionally difficult periods, although they certainly can be for some individuals. Rather, Erikson chose this term to emphasize their far-reaching implications.

Erik H. Erikson (1902–   )

Table 8.1 Erik Erikson's stages of personality development

Age	Name of Stage	Developmental Accomplishments
0–1 year	Basic trust vs. mistrust	Learns to feel comfortable and trusts parents' care; or develops a deep distrust of a world that is perceived to be unsafe.
1–3 years	Autonomy vs. shame and doubt	Learns sense of competence by learning to feed self, use toilet, play alone; or feels ashamed and doubts own abilities.
3–5 years	Initiative vs. guilt	Gains ability to use own initiative in planning and carrying out plans; or if cannot live within parents' limits, develops a sense of guilt over misbehavior.
5–11 years	Industry vs. inferiority	Learns to meet the demands imposed by school and home responsibilities; or comes to believe that he or she is inferior to others.
11–18 years	Identity vs. role confusion	Acquires sense of own identity; or is confused about role in life.
18–40 years	Intimacy vs. isolation	Develops couple relationship and joint identity with partner; or becomes isolated from meaningful relationships with others.
40–65 years	Generativity vs. stagnation	Concerned with helping others, leaving children, products, and ideas to future generations; or becomes self-centered and stagnant.
65 years on	Integrity vs. despair	Reaps benefits of earlier stages and understands and accepts meaning of a temporary life; or despairs over ever being able to find meaning in life.

The eight stages of Erikson's theory of personality development, which contain the crises or turning points, are presented in table 8.1. The name given to each stage by Erikson reflects the two possible outcomes of the stage. To a great extent, particularly in infancy and childhood, the outcome is influenced by actions of the child's parents and other significant people in the individual's life. For example, if the infant's parents provide consistent, warm, and adequate care during the child's first year (stage of Basic Trust vs. Mistrust), he will learn to trust the world as a basically safe place. If the child is cared for inconsistently or is physically or emotionally abused, he will consider the world an unsafe place that cannot be trusted. Erikson believes that this basic sense of trust or mistrust is usually carried with the individual throughout life.

To take another example, the challenge of the fourth stage (Industry vs. Inferiority) is learning to meet the demands placed on the child by parents (to clean her room in a way that pleases her parents), by teachers (to read, write, and calculate), and peers (to ride a bike, to take turns). If the child masters these demands, he develops a belief that effort (industry) leads to success. If the child fails to meet the demands of this stage, Erikson believes that a lifelong feeling of inferiority develops.

At this point in our discussion of development, the content of these three stage theories is less important than the fact that they illustrate the concept of stages in child development very well. However, we discuss the first three of Piaget's stages more fully as we describe the normal course of infant and child development later in this chapter. A discussion of the formal operational stage, which covers adolescent and adult development, is covered in the next chapter. Because of the importance of Erikson's ideas to contemporary views of adolescent and adult development, we discuss his theory in more detail in the next chapter, too. One last comment is needed before moving on to other issues: Piaget, Kohlberg, and Erikson certainly do not exhaust the list of important stage theorists. There are many other interesting and significant theories of this type. In fact, Sigmund Freud provided us with a stage theory of personality development that is discussed in chapter 11.

Variation in Development: Getting There at Different Times

We have been laying the groundwork so far for a description of normal developmental changes in childhood. Before we do that, however, we should discuss one more key concept, that of *variation* in child development. Anyone who deals with children—whether as a parent, teacher, or other professional—must understand that it's normal for development to be highly variable. This is true in two senses: (1) there are differences between children in development; (2) and children vary in the rate of their own development from one period to the next.

Individual Differences

Different children develop at different rates. It's normal for one child to walk or talk several months before another child. When we look at charts of the *normal age* at which children sit, walk, speak in sentences, and so on, we must remember that large variations from those norms may mean nothing at all. Deviations from average are not unusual: Variation is the rule, not the exception in child development. Any large variation in development should be discussed with a pediatrician or child psychologist, but small variations should not be a cause of concern.

Discontinuities in Development

It's also normal for children to be variable and irregular in their own development. Children who are shorter than their age-mates often shoot up suddenly to become taller than most. A fussy baby can become a calm, happy child. And it's not unusual for a child who was above average on an IQ test at age four to be just average at age nine or vice versa. Discontinuities in development, again, are the rule rather than the exception.

Psychologists Jerome Kagan and Howard Moss (1962) have provided some informative data on variation in normal development. They followed a large group of children from the state of Ohio over a period of 14 years. In general, they found that it was difficult to predict how a child would behave from one age to the next because their development was too variable. Moreover, it was impossible until about age 10 to predict with any accuracy how children would behave as young adults. Even then the predictions were only moderately accurate. The personality of a young child is not a good forecast of adult personality.

Both of these children are the same age. A considerable amount of variation in human development is normal.

R E V I E W

Psychologists who lean toward a view that developmental changes "unfold" largely through maturation also see those developmental changes as occurring in distinct steps or "stages," which all children pass through in the same order. Those psychologists who lean toward a view of developmental changes as being "molded" by learning experiences tend to perceive these changes as being more gradual in nature and not marked by clear-cut stages. It's useful to think of development as occurring in something like stages, but ones that are not clearly separable from one another.

Regardless of which position one takes on the issue of stages, children clearly do not all develop at the same rate. Normally, the rate of development for different children differs considerably. In addition, a given child develops irregularly, progressing slowly during one period and spurting forward during another period. See table 8.2 for a summary of developmental milestones from birth to adolescence.

Table 8.2 Summary of developmental milestones from birth to adolescence

Ages	Physical	Perceptual
Neonate (birth to 2 weeks)	Grasping, rooting, and other reflexes, but otherwise little motor control.	Hearing good; smell and taste fair; skin senses appear poor; color vision; fuzzy visual perception to about 12 inches, blurred beyond that.
2 months	Can raise head and chest on arms when lying face down; can grasp object placed in front of face.	Visual discrimination good up to 12 feet; can perceive depth; can distinguish faces.
6–9 months	Can roll over from back to front at 6 months; can sit alone; can crawl.	Vision is 20/20 by 6 months.
12 months	Walks alone; can grasp with fingers and thumbs.	
18 months		
2–7 years	Improvements in gross and fine motor coordination (rarely reverses letters by age 6); growth still steady, but much less rapid than infancy; very active.	Attention span growing but short; mature perception.
7–11 years	Slowed rate of physical growth and development; gradual improvements in coordination.	Lengthened attention span; mature perception.
11 years and up	"Adolescent growth spurt" at puberty, then virtual cessation of growth.	Mature attention and perception.

Cognitive and Linguistic	Social and Emotional
Can imitate mother sticking out tongue; makes cooing sounds.	Shows active signs of discomfort in activity, crying, or passive state.
Cooing.	Smiles to human face or high-pitched voice.
Babbles clear syllable sounds; understands that objects have a permanent existence; begins to be aware of ''self'' as independent from objects; intentionally manipulates environment; can understand some nouns; responds to ''bye-bye'' and gestures.	Emergence of anger and fear: fear of heights, strangers, separation from parent; fearfully anticipates injection from nurse; emergence of shyness.
Says first words.	
Understands prohibitions; can respond to ''show me your nose;'' has speaking vocabulary of 20 words.	
Speaking vocabulary of 250 words by age 2; uses word combinations by age 2; rapid transition to adultlike language by age 4; improvements in articulation; thinking still ''egocentric'' (i.e., cannot see things from another's perspective); has trouble with cause-and-effect and quantitative concepts; obeys rules to avoid punishment, i.e., no developed sense of morality (preconventional morality); emergence of symbolic thought.	Shows guilt after misbehavior and shame after failure by age 2; close relationship with parents and teachers; emergence of peer friendships; shift from ''solitary'' and ''parallel'' play to ''cooperative play''; emergence of fears of unexperienced events: fire, drowning, traffic accidents, etc.; ''selfishness'' common; clear emergence of sex differences.
Marked improvements in logical thinking: acquires concept of *conservation* (e.g., when liquid poured from low, wide glass into tall, thin glass, it does not increase in volume) and *reversibility* (e.g., that $3 \times 5 = 15$ means that $5 \times 3 = 15$ also); improved understanding of time and space; thinking still limited to concrete ideas; more understanding of moral rules, with shift to concern over approval rather than personal gain.	Strong peer friendships and cliques; few friends of opposite sex; peer approval as important as adult approval; sex typing of behavior distinct.
Emergence of abstract logical thinking: can understand concepts of peace, injustice, eternity, etc.; thinking no longer egocentric; evaluates actions according to intentions rather than consequences of the action; adherence to moral rules because of their inherent importance.	Opposite-sex and same-sex friendships; nonconformity to adult standards, but peer approval more important to most than adult approval; at end of period, shift to less intense same-sex friendships.

Normal Course of Development

We now turn to a summary of normal development from conception through late childhood. As we do so, we talk about the *average ages* at which various changes take place. These average ages are of little importance; they are used primarily to portray the *pattern* of age-related changes. Except for the first (prenatal) section, we describe the typical course of physical, perceptual, cognitive, linguistic, social, and emotional development plus the relationship among these behavioral systems.

Prenatal Period: Pregnancy

Development begins from the moment of conception, that is, the moment the ovum (egg) of the female is fertilized by the sperm of the male. At that point, a process that is nothing less than magical begins: the growth of a single cell weighing one five-millionth of an ounce into a marvelously complex human infant in nine months time.

    The course of prenatal development is fascinating and important to understand (fig. 8.3). The single cell subdivides into two cells during the process of **mitosis**; these two cells each divide again producing a clump of four cells, which by continuous division become 8, 16, 32, and so on. Very soon, however, this group of cells begins to differentiate. First, it becomes the **blastocyst**—a hollow ball with a lump of cells on the outside and fluid in the middle. Gradually, the lump of cells moves into the center of the hollow ball, attached to the side by a stalk. As the hollow ball grows, part of it becomes part of the **placenta**—the blood-rich structure connected to the uterine wall that provides a source of oxygen and nourishment to the **embryo**. Also from the lump of cells another sac soon grows that surrounds the lump. This is known as the **amniotic sac** in which the embryo grows suspended in the **amniotic fluid.** This is the fluid that often "breaks" through the membrane of the amniotic sac just before birth and that obstetricians sometimes test to monitor the health of the developing fetus.

    In a short time the embryo becomes a recognizable peanut-shaped **fetus** and the stalk becomes the hollow **umbilical cord** that carries gases and nutrition from the mother's placenta. By 60 days from conception, the amniotic sac has expanded to fill the placenta and the embryo looks like an infant, with arms, legs, and ears, even though it is less than one-fourth the size of the palm of your hand. From this point on, development is a process of rapid growth and differentiation of the nervous system, sense organs, circulatory system, and so on, until the infant is delivered.

    Aside from the unfolding of the infant from a single cell, the most impressive aspect of this process of prenatal development is the *isolation* of the growing fetus from the outside world. Throughout the prenatal growth, except for the first few days, no cell of the infant is exposed. At first, the lump of cells is enclosed within the placenta that it creates for itself. Later, it envelops itself in the amniotic sac—a kind of sac within a sac. Inside these sacs, the growing infant is cushioned in fluid from all but the most potent physical trauma.

    That is not to say, however, that the growing infant is entirely protected. Unfortunately, a variety of factors can disrupt the course of prenatal development. Excessive X rays can damage the embryo, for example. But the most common threats to the embryo enter through the umbilical cord from the mother.

mitosis (mi-to′sis)
Cell division resulting in two identical cells.

blastocyst (blas′to-sist)
The cluster within the hollow ball of cells that develops early in pregnancy and later becomes the fetus.

placenta (plah-sen′tah)
The structure that holds the fetus against the uterine wall and nourishes it.

embryo (em′bre-o)
The early stage of prenatal life lasting from the second to the seventh week of pregnancy.

amniotic sac (am″ne-ot′ik)
The protective covering for the developing embryo.

amniotic fluid
The fluid within the amniotic sac in which the embryo is immersed.

fetus (fe′tus)
The stage of prenatal life lasting from the seventh week of pregnancy until birth.

umbilical cord (um-bil′i-kal)
The structure that connects the fetus to the placenta, and through which nutrients pass to the fetus.

Figure 8.3 The unfolding of the human embryo from a single fertilized cell during pregnancy.

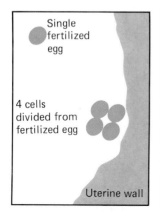
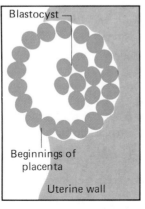
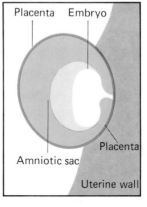
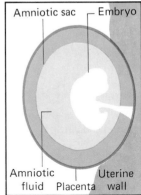

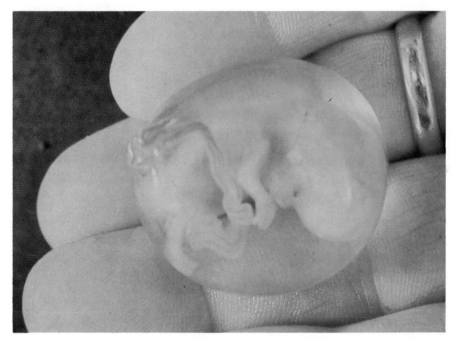

A human embryo at eight weeks of age.

Excessive alcohol consumption, tobacco use, narcotic drug abuse, use of some prescription drugs, some illnesses such as rubella (German measles), nutritional deficits, and other practices of the expectant mother can influence the embryo, causing physical malformation or mental retardation in some cases.

The most vulnerable time for exposure to such damaging agents is the first **trimester** (the first three months) of pregnancy. Unfortunately women usually are not aware that they are pregnant for the first month or two. During this time, the infant develops most rapidly and is most vulnerable. Therefore, sensible precautions should be taken whenever a woman thinks she *might* be pregnant.

trimesters
The three 3-month stages of pregnancy.

OF SPECIAL INTEREST

Natural Childbirth

Since the early 1960s some important changes have occurred in the way that most neonates enter the world. Prior to this time, nearly all children were born while their mothers were under general anesthesia and their father paced nervously in the waiting room outside. Since the 1960s, however, more and more parents have used the Lamaze method of **natural childbirth.** Today, training programs are available in nearly all urban areas to teach this type of natural childbirth to parents.

In the first part of the training program, parents are given educational information about the birth process. The pregnant mother and the father learn what to expect during pregnancy and childbirth and how to prepare for it. The second part consists of a training program in relaxation, pain control, and active participation in childbirth. The expectant mother is taught to relax and diminish pain in a variety of ways. The expectant father learns to provide physical and emotional support both before and during the birth process.

The Lamaze method enables most women to deliver children while fully awake and with little or no medication. This provides an added safety factor for both the mother and child, and allows the mother to experience the birth process. In addition, the father is included in the delivery room in an active supportive role so that he too can experience the birth of his child. The great satisfaction and added safety provided by this method is responsible for its rapid and wide adoption in the United States and other countries today.

In recent years, a variation on the natural childbirth method has been proposed by a French obstetrician, Fredrick Leboyer (1975). The rationale of the Leboyer method is to avoid making the birth process "traumatic" for the neonate. The neonate is, therefore, eased into a dimly lit, quiet delivery room without the traditional slap on the bottom. The infant is gently massaged by the mother and the doctor and placed on the mother's stomach for up to five minutes before the umbilical cord is cut. The neonate is then gently washed in a basin of warm water resembling the amniotic fluid of pregnancy. The Leboyer method has been enthusiastically received in many areas of the United States at this time. While a few early studies suggest that the Leboyer birth process may enhance the attachment between mother and infant, there is little current evidence to evaluate it positively or negatively from either a psychological or medical standpoint.

natural childbirth
Birth in which the mother is alert, takes an active role, and is not highly anesthetized.

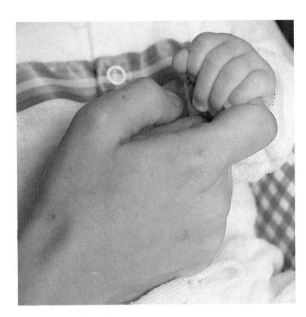

A neonate will reflexively grasp anything that is placed in its hand.

Neonatal Period: The Newborn

The first two weeks of life are termed the **neonatal period** and mark the transition from the womb to independent life. What is the world of the neonate like? In answer to this question, let's look at several interrelated aspects of the neonate's behavior.

neonatal period
(ne″o-na′tal)
The first two weeks of life following birth.

Physical Development

Physically, the neonate is weak and dependent on adults. It cannot raise its head or roll over by itself. It does have a repertoire of a few useful reflexive behaviors, however. When stimulated on one side of the mouth, for example, the neonate turns its head toward the stimulation and begins searching and sucking until something is in its mouth. This **rooting reflex** enables the baby to take its mother's nipple in its mouth and nurse. Similarly, the neonate will reflexively grasp anything that is placed in its hand and hold on, usually with enough strength to support its weight if grasping with both hands.

rooting reflex
An automatic response in which an infant turns its head toward stimulation on the cheek.

Perceptual Development

The perceptual abilities of neonates are surprisingly well developed. Their hearing is fairly good, and they can tell the difference between some odors and tastes. However, they are distinctly nearsighted little people! They can see fairly well (but probably fuzzily) up to about 12 inches from their eyes, but the world is probably a blur to them beyond that (Salapatek, 1977). See *Research Report:* "The Pattern Vision of Neonates and Infants" to see how the sensory abilities of neonates are studied. Little is known about their skin senses, but they are believed to be relatively insensitive at first (McCall, 1979).

RESEARCH REPORT

The Pattern Vision of Neonates and Infants

A great deal has been learned about the perceptual abilities of neonates and infants over the past 25 years. How is this possible? How can you ask infants what they are seeing, hearing, and tasting? Obviously you cannot, but developmental psychologists have developed some ingenious ways to infer what infants are perceiving from subtle changes in their behavior. The pioneering studies of pattern vision in infants by Robert Fantz (1961) are an excellent example of this type of research.

Using an apparatus (fig. 8.4) that painlessly records the amount of time infants spend looking at each of two stimuli, Fantz has demonstrated, for example, that infants prefer to look at vertical stripes rather than a solid gray stimulus. This finding has been usefully applied in hospital settings in recent years to test the vision of infants believed to have visual defects. By gradually narrowing the width of the stripes until the infant no longer prefers to look at it (until it presumably "looks gray" to the infant), the infant's visual acuity can be measured accurately (Dobson, Teller, Lee, & Wade, 1978).

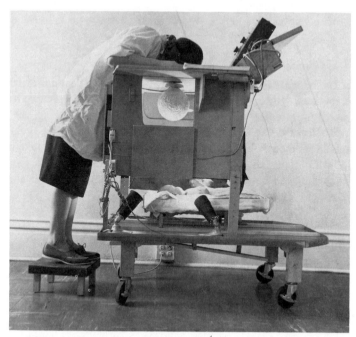

Figure 8.4 The apparatus used by Robert Fantz to measure the length of time infants spent looking at different kinds of visual stimuli.

Cognitive and Linguistic Development

Little is known about the neonate's cognitive abilities, but clearly some are already developed at birth. Even a two-week-old neonate can show some memory for a visual form and can react to different faces as if they are members of the same conceptual class (Cohen, 1979; McCall, 1979). The latter is a surprisingly complex event requiring a considerable degree of awareness. The neonate has no language, of course, but can vocalize in crying.

Emotional and Social Development

The emotions of the neonate are quite diffuse. It's believed that only five basic emotional states can reliably be distinguished in the neonate: surprise, happiness, discomfort, distress, and interest (Izard, 1978). A sixth state, sleep, is very common at this stage, occupying about 16 hours per day (Roffwarg, Muzio, & Dement, 1966). The neonate also engages in little of what could be called social behavior, except the intimate contact between neonate and parent in cuddling and nursing. At first, the neonate is a passive participant, but as we see in a moment, it soon becomes an active partner in social interactions.

Infancy: Two Weeks to Two Years

At two weeks of age, the baby acquires the official title of infant. Much is going on developmentally during this period of rapid change. According to Piaget, infancy is the *sensorimotor stage* of life, a period in which much progress occurs in physical and perceptual development.

Physical Development

Physical development and growth is more rapid during the first year than at any other time in life. By two months, many infants can raise their head and chest on their arms and can grasp an object that is held directly in front of their head and shoulders. By six months, many can roll over from back to front, sit, and soon begin to crawl. By one year, many can walk alone and grasp small objects with their fingers and thumbs. By two years, they are "getting into everything" and walking well, but with the peculiar gait that earns them the nickname of "toddlers."

Perceptual Development

From two weeks to two months, rapid change takes place in all senses. Clear vision increases to 12 feet during this period. Young infants amuse themselves, and their families, by staring at interesting visual stimuli. They prefer to look at patterned stimuli with sharp contours (Banks & Salapatek, 1981). Fortunately for parents, human faces fall into this category (Santrock & Yussen, 1984).

By carefully monitoring changes in the behavior of infants, researchers have learned that young infants not only prefer the human voice (i.e., they orient to it rather than to other sounds), but they can tell the difference between similar speech sounds such as "pah" and "bah" by their second month (Kagan, 1978). Infants are also capable of distinguishing between liquids of slightly different levels of sweetness (McCall, 1979).

During the sensorimotor stage, infants will stare at interesting visual stimuli, including human faces.

By five months the infant looks at the face as a whole (a "gestalt") in the way adults do, instead of focusing on the contours of the eye, mouth, and hair as they did at two months (Cohen, 1979). By six months their vision is 20/20 (normal adult vision). By two years, the infant's visual perception is very similar to that of the adult, but attention span is quite short. Similar developments have taken place in the other senses as well.

From about two months on, the infant begins to interact actively with its environment. It no longer passively stares at objects, but takes great pleasure in pushing, pulling, and mouthing them. This kind of experience, in which the infant actively changes the sensations it receives by using its hands and feet to alter the environment (sensorimotor experience), is believed to be important in the development of motor behaviors such as crawling (Held & Hein, 1963).

Cognitive and Linguistic Development (Piaget's Sensorimotor Stage)

Less is known about cognitive development in the first six months of life than other periods. But clearly infants can learn during this period, as any mother who has tried to shift a two-month-old from a three-hour to a four-hour feeding schedule knows. Infants who are used to four-hour schedules show little distress during the fourth hour, while infants who have been on three-hour schedules give cries of loud distress when not fed until the fourth hour (Marquis, 1941). Clearly, they had learned when to expect their next feeding. Similarly Kenneth Kaye (1967) of the University of Chicago has made an interesting finding about the learning of young infants. When infants pause during nursing, mothers often encourage them to drink again by bouncing them gently and talking to them. Because most infants enjoy this treatment, some infants will learn to pause for long periods in order to get mom to reinforce them (McCall, 1979)!

Around six to nine months of age, however, infants appear to have become quite different in cognitive functioning. Apparently for the first time, they appear to intentionally manipulate things in the environment, to understand that their individual "selves" are different from the rest of the world, and to acquire the

Strong attachments are formed between infants and caregivers during the first two years of life.

concept of *object permanence* (understand that objects have a permanent existence). This is both a happy and a sad development for parents. Now that the nine-month-old knows that spoons still exist when thrown on the floor, the infant quickly masters the game of "dropsies" (McCall, 1979). They joyously fill their mealtimes with the game of throwing their spoons on the floor while dad or mom picks them up, muttering all the while.

By nine months, too, infants begin to understand some noun words like "ball" and "cookie" and can respond to "bye-bye" and other gestures. These changes mark the beginnings of a far more complex level of cognitive functioning. By 12 months, most infants can say some words, and by 18 months the infant has a speaking vocabulary of 20 words. By 18 months the average infant can also understand prohibitions ("No, no . . . don't touch!") and can respond correctly to "Show me your nose (ear, toe, mouth, etc.)." By age two, the infant has a speaking vocabulary of 250 words and speaks in word combinations that fascinate adults for accomplishing so much by saying so little. It has often been referred to as **telegraphic speech** as it leaves out the same words one would leave out of a brief telegram. Sentences like "milk all gone" and "Daddy silly" say all that needs to be said.

telegraphic speech
The abbreviated speech of two-year-olds.

Emotional and Social Development

At about two months of age, the infant shows the first true social behavior: smiling to a human face. By this time, also, parents can reliably distinguish between cries of pain, "angry-frustrated" cries, and hunger cries (Schaffer, 1971), showing that the infant's emotions are beginning to differentiate.

The development of emotions takes an even more dramatic turn at about six to nine months of age. At the same time that the infant makes rapid progress in crawling, cognition, and the comprehension of language, the infant first begins to show fear of strangers, fear of separation from parents, and fear of heights. Infants also first learn to fear the sight of a nurse preparing a hypodermic needle for injection at about six to nine months (Izard, 1978; Sroufe, 1978).

RESEARCH REPORT

Fear of Heights and the Visual Cliff

The interrelationship between physical, perceptual, cognitive, and emotional development is particularly clear in the case of the fear of heights. Cornell University psychologist Eleanor Gibson developed an interesting method of studying *depth perception* in infants in the late 1950s (Gibson & Walk, 1960) that has been used more recently to study fear of heights. Gibson found that when nine-month-old infants were placed on the "visual cliff" (see fig. 8.5) they showed fear and avoidance of the high side. The visual cliff is made using a clear sheet of Plexiglas. Under one side, a patterned floor is right under the glass. On the other side, the pattern is several feet below the glass. When lighted properly, it appears to be a cliff off which the infant could fall.

It's interesting to note that infants can *perceive* the depth of the visual cliff several months before they show any fear of it. They look puzzled when placed on the deep side of the visual cliff at four months, but do not show fear until after they can crawl at six to nine months and have experienced stumbling and falling first hand (Lewis & Rosenblum, 1978; Scarr & Salapatek, 1970).

Figure 8.5 The "visual cliff" apparatus used by Eleanor Gibson to study depth perception in infants.

By two years, emotions grow more complex. By this time, many infants act guilty after misbehavior and seem to feel ashamed after failure. Two-year-old infants are richly social creatures, who have formed strong **attachments** to their parents or other caregivers (Lewis & Rosenblum, 1978). The strength of this attachment can be seen in three ways. First, infants will often cling, grasp, grab, and do whatever else they can to stay close to their parents. Nothing short of the parent's physical closeness and undivided attention will suffice at times. Second, when infants six to nine months or older are separated from their parents, they often show intense **separation anxiety**—the crying, fussing, and screaming that babysitters know so well. Third, infants of this age sometimes also exhibit fear of strangers; no one but the adults to whom they are attached (parents, day-care workers, grandparents) have the same soothing effect.

attachment
The psychological bond between infants and caregivers.

separation anxiety
The distress experienced by infants when they are separated from their caregivers.

Early Childhood: Two to Seven Years

According to Piaget, a dramatic change occurs as the child reaches the preoperational stage at about two years of age. Notice how different the young child is from the infant.

Physical Development

Early childhood is still a period of rapid growth, but growth is far less explosive than in infancy and is declining in rate annually. Great improvements in the coordination of small and large muscle groups take place during this period, which sees the emergence of hopping, skipping, throwing, and the other motor behaviors that are so much a part of early childhood.

Perceptual Development

Perceptual development is essentially completed by the end of the sensorimotor period of infancy. This is fortunate since the now mobile and rambunctious child needs the protection of good sensory and perceptual systems. Large improvements occur, however, in attention span and the child's ability to use perceptual abilities intentionally.

Cognitive and Linguistic Development (Piaget's Preoperational Stage)

Perhaps the most impressive developmental change during the *preoperational stage* is the growth in language. From a speaking vocabulary of 250 words at age two, the child reaches a vocabulary of over 1,500 words by age four, learning an average of two new words per day during the third year! From simple two- or three-word combinations at age two, the child masters much of adult syntax during the same time period. Seemingly, the child has finally achieved the maturational capacity to learn language and so proceeds to do so without hesitation.

The age of two also marks some important cognitive changes. For the first time, symbolic thought is occurring. But as Piaget puts it, the reasoning of the young child differs *qualitatively* from that of the adult. Piaget refers to the period from two to seven years as the *preoperational stage* due to the lack of mastery of logical operations (logical thinking). For example, as we discussed earlier, the

"He has some teeth, but his words haven't come in yet."

OF SPECIAL INTEREST

Where Do Babies Come From?

The beliefs of children that so often amuse adults are a rich source of information about their cognitive development. A case in point is children's beliefs about the origins of babies. Developmental psychologist Kathleen Stassen Berger (1980) has summarized information on this topic in a way that is both amusing and informative. Many children three to four years of age believe that babies are purchased, that their parents buy them at hospitals or stores. One child of this age approached his parents with all of his saved money and asked them to buy him a little brother or sister.

Other children in this age range understand that children grow inside their mothers, but have their own special understanding of this process. One four-year-old thought that his mother had eaten a rabbit or duck and that it had turned into a baby. Another preschooler asked his mother to grow him either a baby or a puppy, whichever she preferred. Another, after hearing a full explanation of sexual reproduction from his mother, responded, "That's the silliest story I ever heard."

The egocentrism and lack of logic displayed by these conceptions of the origins of babies reflect the child's overall level of cognitive development. While the ways that they make sense out of the mysteries of reproduction are not accurate, they are satisfying to the children and an unending source of amusement to their parents.

transductive reasoning
(trans-duk′tiv)
Errors in understanding cause-and-effect relationships that are commonly made by preoperational children.

preoperational child tends to be *egocentric,* or self-oriented, in thinking. **Transductive reasoning**—errors in inferring cause-and-effect relationships—is also common in the preoperational child. For example, a preoperational child might conclude that spiders cause the basement to be cold. Indeed, the basement *is* cold and there *are* spiders in it, but young children often confuse the cause-and-effect relationships among such facts.

By the end of this period the preoperational child begins to grasp logical operations and makes fewer cause-and-effect errors. The child may be able to pick out all the blue marbles from a jar or all the big marbles at age five, but thinking about two concepts at one time is still difficult. Picking out all the big, blue marbles may still be too much.

Emotional and Social Development

Both positive and negative emotions are fairly well developed by age two, but they become considerably richer and more intricate during the preoperational stage. Most of this elaboration of emotion seems to be linked to cognitive development. For example, children do not develop fears of unexperienced things such as fires, drowning, and traffic accidents until well into the preoperational period when they are capable of understanding the concepts behind the fears.

Between the ages of two and five, play activities of young children gradually shift from solitary play to parallel play to cooperative play.

The most notable social changes during this period are in relationships with peers. At age two, most children engage in **solitary play.** That is to say, they play by themselves, even if there are other children present. This type of play rapidly decreases in frequency from ages two to five. At first, solitary play is replaced by **parallel play,** in which children play *near* one another in similar activities, but not *with* one another. By the end of the preoperational stage, **cooperative play,** which involves a cooperative give-and-take, has become the predominant type of play (Barnes, 1971).

The shifting pattern of play seems to parallel cognitive development. In the early part of the preoperational stage when thinking is highly "egocentric," it's not surprising that "selfishness" and lack of cooperation should prevail. Young children may not be able to understand any other type of play. As they reach the end of the stage, however, egocentric thinking declines and cooperative play increases.

There is a similar shift in emotional outbursts from the beginning to the end of the preoperational stage. Two- and three-year-olds typically engage in temper tantrums that are directed at no one, while four- to seven-year-olds direct their aggression at others (Sheppard & Willoughby, 1975). Although this kind of behavior is hardly "sociable," it's a more social, less egocentric form of emotion.

By the age of two, most boys and girls have begun to act in sex-typed ways. Males tend to play with trucks, airplanes, and blocks; girls play mostly with dolls, stuffed animals, and dress-up clothes (Fagot, 1974). They seem to have a conscious awareness by this early age of their own sex (McConaghy, 1979) and understand the sex stereotypes of the culture concerning clothing, occupations, and recreation (Ruble & Ruble, 1980). For more on this topic, see *Of Special Interest:* "Sex-Role Development."

solitary play
Playing alone.

parallel play
Playing near but not with another child.

cooperative play
Play that involves cooperation between two or more children.

OF SPECIAL INTEREST

Sex-Role Development

Currently, the equality of women and men is an important issue in the United States and other countries. What role can psychology play in this important legal, political, and ethical issue? For one thing psychology can help to define and measure *differences* in behavior between the average American male and female. For another, psychology can help to illuminate the causes and development of those differences.

It would not be reasonable in our culture to make the claim that men and women should be considered equal because there are no differences between them. Considerable evidence suggests that there are at least some well-defined differences between typical male and female behavior (Maccoby & Jacklin, 1974). For example, after age 10 or so, girls on the average exceed boys in verbal ability, while boys on the average exceed girls in visual-spatial ability.

How do these sex differences develop? Some differences in behavior between the sexes may have a biological basis. For example, male neonates are more active and fussy, on the average, than female neonates. Since these gender differences appear before parents have had much opportunity to treat male and female newborns differently, it appears to be a biological difference. It also has been well documented that young male monkeys engage in more rough-and-tumble play and more aggression than young female monkeys (Harlow & Harlow, 1965). Furthermore, female monkeys will exhibit typically male play patterns if they are injected with the male hormone testosterone at a critical time in brain development. A great many of the differences in behavior between the sexes, however, appears to be based on the children's learning environment. Boys are taught to act masculine, girls to act feminine.

Middle Childhood: Seven to Eleven Years

These are the elementary school years. It's no accident that formal education begins in earnest during this period, because most children are then intellectually and socially ready for the demands of school.

Physical Development

Physical growth proceeds at a slow pace in middle childhood, but it's a healthy period in which most children experience little illness. Continued improvements in strength and coordination are the only notable advances.

Perceptual Development

Mature perception has been the child's possession for some time. An increase in attention span enabling the child to cope with the challenges of elementary school is the only important change.

OF SPECIAL INTEREST

Lisa Serbin (1980) of Montreal's Concordia University has summarized much of the available evidence on how adults appear to unintentionally, but powerfully, teach male and female children to behave differently. In general, more attention and more discipline is given to males than females. Through modeling, reinforcement, and suggestions, teachers and parents encourage children to engage in what is considered to be appropriate behavior for their sex. The media, television, and books also tend to portray males and females in a way consistent with sexual stereotypes, despite efforts in recent years to eliminate such stereotyping. Finally, peers can often serve a socialization role in the development of gender differences. It's often noted that children whose sex-role behavior differs from the norm are shunned or subtly corrected by other children.

What about you? Would you give a 9-year-old girl a baseball mitt? Would you be more likely to let a 10-year-old boy or a 10-year-old girl carry a 20-pound suitcase? If a child in your care cut herself or himself, would your behavior differ depending on whether the child was a boy or a girl? Most of us do treat male and female children differently. There is substantial reason to believe that at least some sex differences develop partially or wholly because of different learning experiences for boys and girls.

Freud overstated his case when he proclaimed that "anatomy is destiny." Biologically based sex differences probably do exist, but we do not yet have enough solid evidence to know how significant biological sex differences are, if indeed they exist. In any case, differences in behavior never justify prejudice and discrimination.

Cognitive and Linguistic Development (Piaget's Concrete Operational Stage)

The opening of the *concrete operational stage* is marked by important cognitive changes. Children emerge as capable thinkers who use most adult concepts except for abstract concepts. They can order objects (seriation) according to size, weight, and other dimensions. They understand the **reversibility** of logical operations: having added together $7 + 2 = 9$, they have little trouble reversing the operation to see that $9 - 2 = 7$.

One of the most fascinating acquisitions of the concrete operational child is the concept of **conservation.** When children younger than seven are shown two wide beakers containing equal amounts of water, they have no trouble seeing that they contain the "same amount" of water. But when the water from one beaker is poured into a tall, narrow beaker right in front of their eyes, they usually think the tall beaker contains "more" water because it's higher. Children over the age of seven who are in the concrete operational period are not fooled by appearances

reversibility
(re-ver-si'-bil-i-te)
The concept understood by concrete operational children that logical propositions can be reversed (if $2 + 3 = 5$, then $5 - 3 = 2$).

conservation
(kon-ser'vā-shun)
The concept understood by concrete operational children that quantity (number, mass, and so on) does not change just because its shape or other superficial features have changed.

In the concrete operational stage, children learn to recognize that the volume of a liquid does not change when it is poured into a beaker of a different shape.

decenter (de-sen'ter)
To think about more than one characteristic of a thing at a time; a capacity of concrete operational children.

in this way. According to Piaget, the concrete operational children are able to deal with conservation problems because their thought is more **decentered,** which means that they can think of more than one thing at a time. Consequently, the concrete operational child no longer has trouble picking out the big, blue marbles from a jar; he or she can deal with both concepts at the same time.

Emotional and Social Development

Little changes of note occur in the expression of emotions during the concrete operational stage, but social relationships are markedly different than before. Children enter this period with close ties to their parents. While these continue to be important, relationships with peers become increasingly significant during this period. Before age seven, children have friendships, but they generally are not enduring, and typically are not close. After seven, peer friendships become more important to children and tend to last longer. Friendship groups, or *cliques,* also emerge during the concrete operational stage. Most friendships are with members of the same sex, and those cross-sex friendships that do exist are generally "just friends." While the terms *boyfriend* and *girlfriend* are freely used, they have little meaning in the adult sense.

RESEARCH REPORT

Twenty Questions

One simple and interesting way to see the developmental changes taking place in cognition is to play logical games with children. Psychological researchers played the game "Twenty questions" with children who were 6, 8, and 11 years of age. The game is played by one person thinking of an object and giving only the clue that it's either "vegetable, animal, or mineral." The other participants can ask any question they wish in attempting to discover the identity of the object, but only 20 questions. The questions of the preoperational children (age six) were entirely *blind guesses.* They made no attempt to narrow down the alternatives with logical *constraint* questions ("Is it living?" "Is it smaller than a bread box?"). As figure 8.6 shows, the percentage of blind guesses declined during the concrete operational stage (ages 8 and 11), while the percentage of logical constraint questions increased (Mosher & Hornsby, 1966). Even in this simple game, we can see the dramatic changes in the ways children deal with the world using logical thinking.

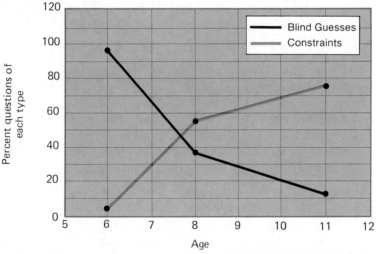

Figure 8.6 The percentage of constraint questions and blind-guess questions asked by children of different ages in a game of 20 questions (Mosher & Hornsby, 1966).

REVIEW

When we look back over the explosive growth of a simple cell into a child, it appears that there may be some utility in discussing development in terms of "stages." Interrelated changes in several behavioral systems do occur that may be dramatic enough to justify the phrase "qualitatively different stage." However, the entrance to a new stage is not marked by abrupt changes. Developmental changes are gradual, inconsistent, and take place both within and between stages. There is value, then, in thinking of human development in terms of stages, but there are limits on that value. Human growth is both a series of landmark steps and a continuous, flowing process. There are no shortcuts to describing the marvelous complexities of human development.

S U M M A R Y

Chapter 8 traces the normal course of development from the moment of conception through late childhood.

I. Some psychologists believe that developmental changes in behavior are biologically programmed to "unfold" with increasing age while others believe that changes in behavior are "molded" by the environment that we experience.

    A. *Maturation,* the systematic physical growth of the nervous system and other parts of the body, is a key concept to "unfolding" theorists, while learning is the key concept to "molding" theorists.

    B. Today, most psychologists believe that both *nature* (biological factors) and *nurture* (environment) *combine* to influence our actions, thoughts, and feelings.

II. Some theorists believe that early childhood is the "formative period" for our personalities.

    A. Research on *imprinting* in animals shows that experiences during *critical periods* of early development can have long-lasting effects on animal behavior, but there may not be such clear-cut critical periods in human development.

    B. Harlow's experiments with social deprivation during the infancy of monkeys show long-lasting effects of abnormal early experiences, but human infants seem capable of recovering to a great extent from early abnormal experience.

III. *Stage theorists* believe all children must pass through the same *qualitatively different* stages in the same order.

    A. Piaget identified four stages of *cognitive development* from infancy to adulthood.

        1. *Assimilation* is the process of adding new information to existing concepts, or schemas, that results in quantitative changes in a child's cognition. The process of changing schemas in qualitative ways to incorporate new experiences is known as *accommodation.*

        2. During the *sensorimotor stage* (birth to two years) an infant conceptualizes the world in terms of schemas that incorporate sensory information and motor activities.

        3. In the *preoperational stage* (two to seven years), children can think in mental images, but exhibit *egocentric* thinking.

        4. The *concrete operational stage* (seven to eleven years) is marked by increased ability to reason logically.

        5. In the *formal operational stage* (eleven years on) an individual uses full adult logic and understands abstract concepts.

    B. Kohlberg's theory of *moral development* is concerned with the logical process of arriving at answers to moral dilemmas.

        1. At the *premoral level* a child has no sense of morality as adults understand that term.

        2. A child's moral view is based on what others will think of him or her at the *conventional level.*

        3. At the *principled level* individuals judge right and wrong according to ethical principles rather than by the consequences of actions.

    C. Erikson's theory of *personality development* focuses on a person's developing relationships with others in the social world.

    D. There are broad/normal differences in development between different children of the same age and differences in the rate of development of the same child from one period to the next.

IV. *Average ages* at which changes in development take place are used to portray the *pattern* of age-related changes.

    A. During the *prenatal period,* development is a process of rapid growth and differentiation of the major systems and organs of the body.

    B. The *neonatal period* is the first two weeks of life, and marks the transition from the womb to independent life.

    C. *Infancy* (two weeks to two years) is a time of rapid changes in physical, perceptual, cognitive, linguistic, social, and emotional development.

    D. During *early childhood* (two to seven years) growth is less explosive and rapid than during infancy.

    E. *Middle childhood* (seven to eleven years) is characterized by slow physical growth, but important cognitive changes occur, such as the emergence of *conservation.*

Suggested Readings

1. An in-depth analysis of child development is provided by:
   Santrock, J. W., & Yussen, S. R. (1984). *Children and adolescents: A developmental perspective.* Dubuque, IA: Wm. C. Brown Publishers.

2. For a closer look at the development of cognition in children:
   Flavell, J. H. (1977). *Cognitive development.* Englewood Cliffs, NJ: Prentice-Hall.

3. For more on the development of social behavior in children:
   Shaffer, D. (1980). *Social development.* Belmont, CA: Wadsworth.

4. An overview of infant development is provided by:
   Bower, T. G. R. (1974). *Development in infancy.* San Francisco: W. H. Freeman.

5. An analysis of the role of early experience in human development is given by:
   Clarke, A. M., & Clarke, A. B. D. (1976). *Early experience: Myth and evidence.* New York: Free Press.

6. Perhaps the most sophisticated and informative book ever written for laypeople about child development is:
   Kagan, J. (1984). *The nature of the child.* New York: Basic Books.

Adolescence, Adulthood, and Aging

OUTLINE

KEY TERMS

What kind of things upset you? What are the most troublesome stresses and strains that you face in daily living? Think about it for a moment and see if you can mentally write a list of the 10 "most difficult" areas of your life. Now consider this: Do you think that your list would have been significantly different if you were 10, 20, or 30 years older or younger? Do people of different ages face different challenges in their daily lives?

In one study hundreds of individuals at four stages of life (high school seniors, young newlyweds, middle-aged parents, and older adults about to retire) were asked about the stresses that they most commonly faced (Lowenthal, Thurnher, & Chiriboga, 1975). These investigators found that there were marked differences in the stresses encountered at each stage of life. Older adults experienced fewer stressful events overall, and there were clear-cut differences in the kinds of stresses encountered. For example, 76 percent of the younger adults felt stress because of educational demands, while only 6 percent of the older adults were stressed in this way. Housing was a source of stress for six times as many younger adults than older ones, and stress from dating and marriage was more than four times as common in the younger age groups. Work, on the other hand, was a source of stress to almost twice as many older adults than younger ones.

These results clearly point to one conclusion: The experience of life is *different* for people of different ages. But life is different at each of its stages in a multitude of ways, not just in the stressors we face. That's the theme of this chapter. The process of development does not end with the close of childhood; rather, predictable changes continue to occur across the full life span.

Life is a process of continuing change. The child becomes an adolescent; the adolescent becomes a young adult; the young adult gradually becomes an aged adult. While it's true that changes in adulthood do not come as quickly or dramatically as during infancy and childhood, the life span from adolescence through old age is marked by developmental changes that, in their own way, are just as significant as earlier ones.

Adolescence is ushered in by the monumental physical changes through which the person who was a child only yesterday becomes sexually capable of being the parent of a child. The adolescent period is marked by rapid physical growth and change, and by a heightening of sexual and social interest in the opposite sex. It's a time in which peers are more important than parents in terms of attachment and influence, and a period of increased emotionality for some, but not most, adolescents. The adolescent is capable for the first time of reasoning in abstractions. Partly for this reason he or she may spend a great deal of time contemplating such abstract issues as justice and equality.

There is no clear-cut demarcation of the shift from adolescence to adulthood. Rather than at any specific age, individuals pass from adolescence to adulthood when they establish adult social relationships and adult patterns of work. It's clear that adults continue to change in somewhat predictable ways throughout the life span, but there is less agreement on the causes of those changes. Some feel that adults pass through a series of biologically programmed and timed stages, while others feel that the changes are responses to major life events such as marriage, childbearing, retirement, and so on. Of all aspects of the adult, intelligence seems to be the least changeable psychological characteristic, but some changes occur even there.

Partly through a process of biological change and partly for psychological reasons, most of us will eventually reach the stage of old age. For most individuals, old age is surprisingly full of life if meaningful involvement with life continues and the many negative myths about old age are not believed. Usually, older individuals come to terms with their own mortality during this period and accept the final "stage" of life, their own death.

Adolescence: Passage into Adulthood

adolescence
The period from the onset of puberty until the beginning of adulthood.

puberty (pu'ber-te)
The point in development at which the individual is physically capable of sexual reproduction.

Adolescence is the time of transition from childhood to adulthood. It's defined as the period from the onset of **puberty** until the beginning of adulthood. Puberty covers the time that the primary and secondary sex characteristics of the body emerge, indicating that the individual is physically capable of sexual reproduction. Adulthood has no clear point of beginning in American culture, but it's a period during which the individual focuses on "adult" concerns: on work, on forming marital or other serious relationships, and perhaps on rearing a family.

The fact that the beginning point of adulthood is marked by a change in behavior (acting like an adult in your work, your relationships, etc.), rather than a physical change (like puberty) or a cognitive change (like Piaget's stages of childhood), has important implications. The age at which adulthood is generally thought to begin is, in an important sense, arbitrary. In different cultures, adolescence differs dramatically in duration since young people typically adopt adult

Activation of sexual desire occurs during adolescence.

roles at different ages. Indeed, adolescence does not "exist" at all in some non-industrialized cultures—puberty marks the transition directly from childhood to adulthood, with no period of adolescence in between. Similarly, adolescence was brief or nonexistent for youths in nineteenth-century Europe and the United States. Today, however, the period of adolescence is quite long, perhaps in part because of the current emphasis on prolonged education before entering the job market.

Neither scientists nor artists are quite sure how to conceptualize adolescence. It's frequently portrayed as a time of storm and stress, but it's just as frequently portrayed as the happy days of carefree youth. This confusion probably stems from the fact that for different people, and for all people at different times, the experience of adolescence can be either very happy or exceedingly tormented. In any case, one thing is certain: Adolescence is a period of dramatic change.

Physical Development: Growing Up in Spurts

A number of psychologically important physical changes occur during adolescence, particularly during puberty, the event that opens the adolescent period. These changes alter physical appearance so much that—in what seems like a moment—girls come to look like women and boys like men. Height and weight increase sharply, pushing adolescents suddenly to adult size. A look in the mirror forever changes the adolescent's image of himself or herself.

Primary and Secondary Sexual Characteristics

Puberty begins with the production of sex hormones by the ovaries in females and the testes in males. These hormones trigger a series of physiological changes that lead to ovulation and menstruation in females and the production of sperm cells in males. These are the **primary sex characteristics** that indicate that the adolescent has the ability to reproduce. These physical changes are accompanied by activation of sexual desire and corresponding increases in dating, kissing, petting, masturbation, and other sexual activities.

primary sex characteristics
Ovulation and menstruation in females and production of sperm in males.

OF SPECIAL INTEREST

Sex Differences in Adolescent Sexuality

The advent of the capacity to reproduce sexually during puberty is accompanied by increased sexual interest for most adolescents. This new and often potent sex drive is expressed in many ways: kissing, petting, intercourse, and masturbation. While there are many similarities in the sexuality of male and female adolescents—and the similarities seem to be growing each decade as new studies are conducted—there are still some noteworthy differences between the sexes. For males, the first orgasm is almost always achieved through masturbation. At least 80 percent of all adolescent boys masturbate, compared to about 60 percent of girls. Surprisingly, boys are also more likely to feel guilty, abnormal, or embarrassed about their masturbation than girls do. Thankfully, though, few modern youths still believe in the myths that masturbation causes blindness, insanity, or hairy palms (Berger, 1980).

Boys are more likely to have experienced intercourse at every age than females, but the difference has been shrinking for many years. For example, Alfred Kinsey (Kinsey, Pomeroy, Martin, & Gebhard, 1953) found that by graduation from college in the early 1950s, 25 percent of females and 50 percent of males had experienced intercourse. By the early 1970s, studies were generally finding that 40 percent of females and 60 percent of males were no longer virgins. At some colleges, however, over 80 percent of both male and female seniors reported that they were not virgins (Jessor & Jessor, 1975). The "double standard" that "boys do, but nice girls don't" is apparently on the wane.

Males are still more likely to have sex with females with whom they are not seriously involved and to have more sexual partners than females, however (Sorensen, 1973). In general, males are more likely to experience sex as a distinct and powerful drive that must find an outlet, and to feel that sexual experience will make them more masculine and admired by their male peers. For females, sexuality is often a less distinct drive, blended with feelings of love and commitment (Berger, 1980). However, in a survey of adolescents conducted in the 1970s, a majority of both sexes felt that sexual relationships should be part of a committed relationship, rather than a casual matter (Sorensen, 1973).

Drawing by D. Reilly; © 1973
The New Yorker Magazine, Inc.

"Well, whatever it is we change into, it can't come soon enough for me."

Menarche, or the first menstrual period, occurs on the average at about 12 years, 6 months in American females, and the production of sperm begins about two years later in males (Tanner, 1970). Interestingly, the age of menarche is younger today than in the past and younger here than in many foreign countries. In 1900 the average age of menarche in the United States was about 14 years, and even today, the average age in one New Zealand tribe is over 17 years (Tanner, 1970). Researchers believe that these differences are due to improved nutrition and health care in the United States over the years and that menarche will not begin much younger in the future as the natural limit appears to have been about reached (Petersen, 1979).

menarche (mĕ-nar'ke)
The first menstrual period.

The more obvious changes occurring during puberty are the development of the **secondary sex characteristics.** In females, the first change is an accumulation of fat in the breasts that results in a slight "budding," followed by a gradual enlargement of the breasts over a period of several years. There is also a growing accumulation of fat around the hips resulting in a broadening that further gives the appearance of the adult female body shape. Finally, about the time of menarche, pubic hair begins to grow.

secondary sex characteristics
Development of the breasts and hips in females; growth of the testes, broadening of the shoulders, lowered voice, growth of the penis, and facial hair in males; and growth of pubic and other body hair in both sexes.

In males, the first secondary sexual change is the growth of the testes, followed by a broadening of the shoulders, lowering of the voice, and growth of the penis. Soon, pubic and facial hair grow, thus creating the physical image of an adult male.

Adolescent Growth Spurt

Another outwardly obvious sign of puberty is the rapid increase in weight and height known as the **adolescent growth spurt.** Just before puberty, rapid weight gain is common, mostly in the form of fat. This can be a source of concern to both the adolescent and his or her parents, but soon most of this weight is redistributed or shed. At about the onset of puberty, the adolescent suddenly shoots up in height. As shown in figure 9.1, the rate of growth in height steadily declines from infancy, but rises sharply for a little over a year in early adolescence. During the year of most rapid growth, many boys gain as much as 4 inches and 26 pounds,

adolescent growth spurt
The rapid increase in weight and height that occurs around the onset of puberty.

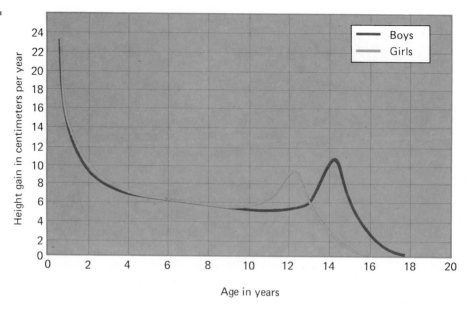

Figure 9.1 The adolescent growth spurt can be seen by the rapid increase in height that occurs in males and females at the beginning of puberty (Tanner, Whitehouse & Takaishi, 1966).

and many girls add as much as 3½ inches and 20 pounds. There is little accumulation of fat during this period; there is usually even a lowering of the proportion of body fat. About a year after the spurt in height, the body sees its most rapid growth in muscle, giving the average adolescent a leaner, stronger, more mature appearance.

In late adolescence, weight gain in the form of excess fat is common. This is largely due to a rapid decline in the **basal metabolism rate**—the rate at which the body burns calories—during adolescence. From age 11 to age 25, there is a 20 to 25 percent decrease in metabolism. This means that weight gain is inevitable if the teenager's calorie consumption and activity level remain the same. If the individual starts eating more or becomes less active during late adolescence—as is common for college students—the accumulation of unwanted fat can be surprisingly rapid.

The rapid changes in height and weight during the adolescent growth spurt and late adolescence can be devastating to parents who must foot the bills for their suddenly clothes-conscious adolescents who seem to grow out of clothes on a weekly basis. For a number of more serious reasons, physical changes of adolescence can be of even greater concern to the adolescents themselves. This is a period of newly emerging awareness of one's sexuality and of romantic attraction to others. Any factor that creates concern in the adolescent's mind about his or her physical appearance and attractiveness may be very disturbing indeed.

Some aspects of adolescent physical development that frequently upset adolescents are the following:

1. *Sex differences in growth rates.* While males and females grow at about the same rates during childhood, females experience puberty and the adolescent growth spurt about two years earlier than males. This means that girls are frequently taller and more mature in appearance than boys from ages 12 to 14. This can be a minor catastrophe to some adolescents who associate "masculinity" with physical stature and measure "femininity" in petite dress sizes.

basal metabolism rate
(ba'sal mĕ-tab'o-lizm)
The rate at which the body converts calories into energy.

2. *Different growth rates of body parts.* One of the most disconcerting aspects of adolescent growth is the fact that different body parts grow at different rates. Hands and feet grow before arms and legs, and arms and legs grow before the torso. Noses, ears, and jaws can outpace the growth of the rest of the face, and it's even common for the body to temporarily grow in lopsided fashion (one breast or ear before the other). Naturally, most adolescents are unaware that these distortions are only temporary, and often have a tough time being patient while the body catches up with itself. It can be pretty upsetting to most adolescents to look in the mirror and see gangly arms, lopsided breasts, and a nose that seems to grow like Pinocchio's.

3. *Irregular changes in weight and physique.* The rapid gains in height, the shifts in body fat (gain of fat in early adolescence, loss and redistribution of fat during the growth spurt, and tendency to gain fat again during late adolescence), and the late development of muscle tissue often cause the adolescent's physique to change dramatically. Because adolescents are often newly and intensely concerned about physique, these changes can be both perplexing and upsetting. Sometimes these changes can be wonderful, however, as for the chubby 12-year-old who spurts into a tall, slim 16-year-old.

4. *Troublesome skin changes.* The skin undergoes a number of changes during puberty that are unwelcome to the adolescent. Sweat and odor glands step up their activity, producing body odor and the need for frequent bathing. Even more distressing is the fact that greatly increased output of oil glands means that half of all girls and two-thirds of all boys have problems with acne during adolescence.

5. *Variation in age of puberty.* Within each sex, there is wide variation in the age of puberty. Sexual maturation and the growth spurt can begin anytime within a six-year range for both sexes (Faust, 1977; Tanner, 1970). These differences in the timing of puberty can be of considerable significance to the individuals concerned. Early growth in height and muscle is generally advantageous to boys, particularly in sports and other activities requiring physical prowess so important to prestige among male peers. The boy who lags behind in size, strength, and mature appearance is at a definite disadvantage until his late growth spurt. The blessings of early maturation for girls seem to be more mixed. Girls who develop sexually early may be the object of attention of older boys; but they are often embarrassed by their height and budding sexuality until their slower maturing age-mates catch up and they are less conspicuous. See *Research Report:* "Early and Late Maturation" for more on this topic.

Early puberty and its
associated growth spurt is
generally advantageous to
adolescent boys; the
results with girls appear to
be mixed.

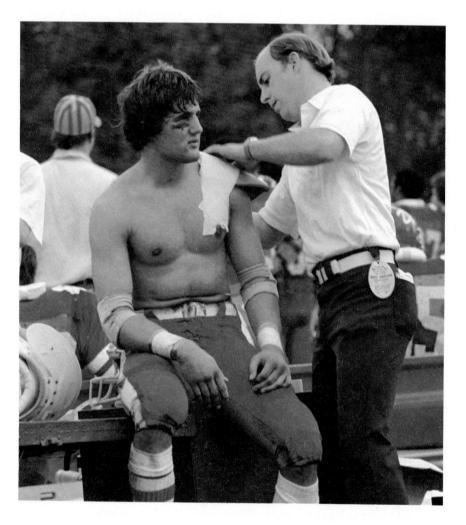

Cognitive Development: Piaget's Formal Operational Stage

formal operational stage
In Piaget's theory, the
period of intellectual
development usually
reached about age 11, and
characterized by the ability
to use abstract concepts.

At about age 11, the shift from the concrete operational stage to formal operational thought begins first in some adolescents, and then in others. Many individuals do not reach this advanced level of thinking until early adulthood, and
some never reach it at all (Berger, 1980; Piaget, 1972). The **formal operational
stage** is characterized by an ability to use abstract concepts. The logic of formal
operational thinking goes beyond the concrete details of each incident or problem
to the underlying abstract principles involved.

In a classic experiment conducted by Swiss developmental psychologists
Barbel Inhelder and Jean Piaget (1958), children and adolescents of different
ages were given two weights that could be hooked at different places on the arms
of a scale; their job was to make the scale balance. Seven-year-old children—
who were at the beginning of the concrete operational stage—were generally unable to balance the scale at all. They could understand that the two weights must
be placed on opposite arms of the scale, but did not seem to understand the importance of where the weights were hooked on the arms. By the end of the concrete operational stage, age 10, most children were able to balance the scale
through trial and error, but were not able to explain in words how it worked.

RESEARCH REPORT

Early and Late Maturation

There is a great deal of variation in the age at which puberty begins; some individuals reach puberty much earlier than others. Is it better to mature earlier or later? The blessings and pitfalls of early and late maturation have been extensively studied by developmental psychologists Nancy Bayley, Mary Cover Jones, and their associates (Faust, 1960; Jones, 1965; Jones & Bayley, 1950; Jones & Mussen, 1958). Their analyses of the data from the large-scale Berkeley Growth Study described in chapter 7 show that the effects of early versus late maturation are complex, but significant.

To be precise in their measurements, these researchers defined maturation in terms of rate of bone growth as measured by X rays. Bone maturation is highly correlated with age of puberty, however, making the data relevant to our discussion. Jones, Bayley, and associates found that early maturation had some benefits for males, but some possible costs as well. As teenagers, the early maturing boys were more popular, more attractive, and more sophisticated than their late maturing male peers, but were also rated as less playful, less creative, and less flexible. When studied again in their late 30s, similar differences were still found. The men who had matured earlier tended to hold positions of greater leadership in their jobs and were more dominant, controlled, and independent. On the other hand, the early maturing males were found to be more rigid in their approach to life. There were, however, many exceptions to these findings, as with any finding based on group averages.

Early and late maturing females have not been studied as extensively, but Faust (1960) has examined their popularity during the elementary and junior high school years. The early maturing girls were somewhat less popular with female peers in elementary school when their advanced development separated them from other girls, although they were more popular with adults and older peers than were late maturing girls. By junior high school, however, the early maturing girls were found to be more popular with their age-mates of both sexes than later maturers.

By about age 14, many of the subjects had reached the stage of formal operational thinking and were able to explain that the farther a weight is placed from the center (fulcrum) of the scale, the more downward force it exerts. These children were able, without trial and error, to place a 5-kilogram weight twice as far from the fulcrum as a 10-kilogram weight on the other side. They could also easily deduce from this principle that weights of 3 and 6 or 2 and 4 kilograms would balance on the same hooks used by the 5- and 10-kilogram weights. They understood, in other words, the *abstract* principle that it's the *ratio* of weights and distances that matters, not the specific weights involved in any one example. They were able to think in abstract logical terms.

The ability to understand abstract concepts is a characteristic of formal operational thought.

The abstract quality of formal operational thinking can also be seen in the individual's ability to evaluate logical propositions (Berger, 1980). For example, adolescents who have reached the formal operational stage of cognitive development are able to decide that the statement, "The single-colored poker chip in my hand is green and it is not green" is false without additional information. Younger children are more likely to ask to see the chip before answering, thus showing that their thinking is still based on concrete facts rather than abstract principles (Osherson & Markman, 1974).

Individuals who have achieved formal operational thinking are able to use it in many areas of their lives. Piaget suggests, for example, that adolescents often seem preoccupied by concepts such as truth, justice, and the meaning of life partly because the capacity to think in such abstract terms is so new to them.

Although most adolescents have reached the level of formal operational reasoning, their cognition often retains an immature quality at times. David Elkind (1967, 1981; Elkind & Bowen, 1979) has pointed out that adolescents often possess a form of egocentrism that, while different from the egocentrism of young children, similarly distorts their perception of reality. There are four primary features of **adolescent egocentrism.** As you will readily notice, the thinking of fully mature adults is not always free of these characteristics. However, the four reality-distorting qualities described by Elkind are more characteristic of the adolescent stage than any other—and help explain why conversations between adolescents and adults are sometimes so frustrating to both parties.

adolescent egocentrism
The quality of thinking that leads some adolescents to believe that they are the focus of attention in social situations, to believe that their problems are unique, to be unusually hypocritical, and to be "pseudostupid."

1. The primary characteristic of adolescent egocentrism has been termed the *imaginary audience* by Elkind. The adolescent often feels that the focus of everyone's attention is on him. If he stumbles or stammers, *everyone* will notice, talk about, and never forget the event. Of course, the crowd is no more interested in what that particular adolescent does than anyone else and is far less interested in his minor tragedies than in their own. The audience that the adolescent believes detects his every flaw does not really exist—it's imaginary.

2. Adolescent egocentrism also manifests itself in what Elkind calls
    the *personal fable*. The adolescent often feels that her problems—
    over school, complexion, friends—are totally unique, having
    never been experienced by anyone else in a remotely similar way.
    Understandably, this form of egocentric thinking can heighten the
    adjustments that are a normal part of adolescence and can lead
    to a sense of isolation in some adolescents.

3. Adolescent egocentrism is typified by an unusual degree of
    hypocrisy. Adolescents are even more likely than adults to
    condemn in others the same actions and traits that they find
    acceptable in themselves. The adolescent is outraged when she
    learns that her mother claimed a luncheon with a friend as a
    business expense on her income taxes, but excuses herself for
    cheating on her social science test because the teacher "is a jerk for
    making us learn such boring junk."

4. Finally, adolescent egocentrism is characterized by what Elkind
    (1981) colorfully calls *pseudostupidity*. Often this involves an
    overreliance on the power of logic. The adolescent might say, "If
    alcoholics know they're going to die from cirrhosis of the liver, why
    don't they just stop drinking?" The cold logic of their argument
    makes it difficult for them to consider that it's difficult for
    alcoholics to stop their consciousness-numbing addiction for many
    psychological and physical reasons. At other times, however, this
    pseudostupidity takes the form of using unnecessarily convoluted
    and complex logic when simpler thinking will suffice. These
    unusual patterns of logic also tend to make reasoning with
    adolescents a notable challenge.

Emotional and Social Development

The shift from childhood to adolescence, and then from adolescence to adulthood, is marked by changes in the emotional and social spheres of our lives. Until
relatively recently, however, these changes have been more the subject of speculation than of research.

Adolescent Emotions

Since 1904 when the first American text on adolescent psychology was published
by G. Stanley Hall, a debate has continued unabated about the nature of adolescent emotions. Is it a carefree period of happiness, or as Hall would have it,
a time of "storm and stress"? Actually, Hall was just adding his opinion to a
debate that has gone on at least since the time of Plato. Like many philosophical
debates that are eventually settled by scientific evidence, the truth lies somewhere between the extreme viewpoints.

Current research suggests that about a quarter of all adolescents do experience a difficult, tumultuous adolescence. This may seem like a high percentage, but it is about the same as the percentage of adults who are estimated
to be experiencing marked emotional distress. Another 25 percent experience an
easy, carefree adolescence marked by happy relationships with both peers and

identity crisis
The difficulty encountered
by some adolescents in
achieving an adult identity.

parents. The experience of the remaining half falls somewhere in between (Offer, 1969; Offer & Offer, 1975; Offer, Ostrov, & Howard, 1981). The reasons for these differences in the experience of adolescence are largely unknown; but an adolescent who is attractive, intelligent, athletic, popular, affluent, and healthy probably has an easier time going through this period.

Adolescence can be a particularly unhappy time for those individuals who experience a difficult **identity crisis.** If you look back to table 8.1, page 313, you will see that, according to Erik Erikson, the challenge of the adolescent period is to develop a sense of identity. I am comfortable with my current adult identity as a psychologist and teacher, but when I was a freshman in college I was far from certain who I was. At times, I was a premedicine student, at other times an artist, and for a brief time I was even a diffident economist. A substantial number of adolescents have great difficulty achieving an adult identity. Until one emerges, they are left with little direction and often experience a great deal of anguish in the process.

One possible indicator of the difficulties experienced by many adolescents as they cope with physical changes and develop an adult identity is the temporary drop in self-esteem that occurs during this period. One survey asked 2,000 girls aged 8 to 18 questions about their self-esteem (Simmons, Rosenberg, & Rosenberg, 1973). The 8-year-olds were pretty happy with themselves. From age 11 to 14 the girls' self-esteem was less positive, but then began improving at around 16 years, and was even more positive than for the 8-year-olds by age 18. Adolescence can be rough on your opinion of yourself, but the damage is only temporary in most cases.

What do these facts tell us about adolescence? Is it a time of emotional turmoil? Perhaps it depends on your standard of comparison. Adolescence does not appear to be a period that is much unhappier than adulthood, but it does appear to be a more emotionally difficult time than childhood. One particularly sad index of this difference is the increase in the rates of mental illness and suicide that occur about the time of puberty. From age 10 (before puberty for most children) to age 14 (after puberty for most adolescents), severe periods of depression, the disorder known as schizophrenia, the eating disorder called anorexia nervosa, several kinds of anxiety (nervous) conditions, and suicide increase *tenfold* (Hawton & Osborn, 1984; Lahey & Ciminero, 1980). It is not currently known why these tragically dramatic increases occur, but they are clearly associated in some way with the occurrence of puberty. Thus, even if adolescence is not a more problematic period than adulthood, it is a far more difficult time than childhood for a small proportion of adolescents.

Sadly, too, there appears to have been an increase in recent years in the frequency of adolescent suicides. The rate of suicide has probably not increased in younger adolescents, but probably has increased in older adolescents. Recent statistics indicate that approximately 7 adolescents aged 15 to 19 commit suicide for every 100,000 persons of that age (Hawton & Osborn, 1984). That rate of suicide is still lower than the rate for adults, but is significantly higher than for the same age group in the United States in the 1950s. There is no widely accepted explanation for this increase in suicide rates. It is tempting to blame it on the pressures of contemporary life, but that explanation may not be correct. Long-term statistics suggest that suicide rates among older adolescents were high during the first 10 years of this century, then dropped dramatically, and have recently risen again to the older, higher level (Hawton & Osborn, 1984). It is not yet clear why these fluctuations in the rate of teenage suicide have occurred, but it is the topic of much current study.

Peer influence is at its height during adolescence.

Adolescent Social Development

Adolescents also show marked changes in the area of social relationships. Adolescence is a time of drifting and sometimes of breaking away from the family unit. While relationships with peers become increasingly important through late childhood, by adolescence peers have become the most important people in the individual's life. This shift in orientation toward peers can be seen in the dramatic increase in conformity to the ideas and judgments of the peer group that occurs at the beginning of puberty (ages 11 to 13), but declines from age 15 on (Costanzo & Shaw, 1966). It's probably no accident, incidentally, that the peak of conformity to the crowd occurs at the same time as the low ebb of self-esteem just noted on the previous page. When we are feeling the least good about ourselves, we may be the most vulnerable to others' opinions of us.

At the same time that friendships and romantic relationships become more intense, the adolescent becomes less interested in family activities, may begin to reject some family values, and may rebel against parental authority. While most adolescents do not go through a stormy period of rebelliousness (Adelson, 1979), nearly all distance themselves somewhat from their parents during this period. One study found that even on weekends, young adolescents spend more than twice as much time with peers as with parents (Condry, Simon, & Bronfenbrenner, 1968).

If we think of adolescence as a *transition* phase between childhood and adulthood, distancing and even a certain amount of rebelliousness can be thought of as positive steps toward the development of an independent adult life-style. These changes are not always viewed in a positive light by the parents and teenagers involved, however. As peer influence becomes more powerful than parental influence, adolescents begin to adopt the values, attitudes, style of dress, and language of their peers. Sometimes peer influence is in direct opposition to the wishes of the parents, resulting in painful conflict—which reaches its height at about the ninth grade (Santrock, 1981)—as parents attempt to reassert their authority.

Surprisingly, though, most adolescents remain remarkably close to their parents in terms of values and attitudes. Surveys conducted by Daniel Yankelovich (1974) have found that adolescents differ very little from their parents on most basic values relating to work, self-control, saving money, competition, private property, compromise, and legal authority. Prejudices, attitudes, and beliefs of adolescents tend to be similar to those of their parents. Some differences do exist, however. Adolescents generally view religion as less important, are more accepting of sex and living together outside of marriage, and favor less traditional roles for women.

Researcher Joseph Adelson (1979) illustrates the similarity between parent and adolescent values by noting the presidential election results of 1972. Eighteen-year-olds had just been given the right to vote and the conventional wisdom was that because of their feverish commitment to politics and their intense opposition to the Vietnam War, they would sweep George McGovern to victory over Richard Nixon. It turned out that the conventional "wisdom" was an inaccurate stereotype based on the publicized liberal views of a small proportion of adolescents. When the votes were in, the adolescent vote was small and only slightly more liberal than that of their parents.

Thus, the popular view of adolescence as a period of universal turmoil does not hold up to scientific scrutiny. Adolescents are not all in a constant state of conflict with their parents or within themselves. Adolescence is a decade of transition: many changes occur and many challenges are met between the ages of 11 and 21. For a sizable minority of adolescents, this transition is very difficult indeed, and for the great majority of adolescents, it's difficult some of the time.

R E V I E W

In the span of about a decade, each individual passes from childhood to adulthood. This adolescent period of transition begins with the adolescent growth spurt and the emergence of primary and secondary sex characteristics (puberty), and ends with the assumption of adult patterns of work, living, and relationships. It's a period of dramatic physical changes. Considerable gains are made in height, weight, and strength; body fat is redistributed; and boys and girls come to look like men and women. These physical changes are often of considerable concern to self-conscious adolescents, particularly when irregularities and sex differences in physical development are obvious. Cognitively, most adolescents develop formal operational thinking, which gives them the ability to reason abstractly, but they experience an adolescent form of egocentrism. Socially, they complete the shift from a focus on parents to a focus on peer relationships. In spite of these changes, adolescents generally remain surprisingly close to their parents in most fundamental values and attitudes. Adolescence can be a period of mostly stormy emotions for some adolescents. But most adolescents experience emotional difficulties only some of the time.

Sigmund Freud believed that a happy adulthood is a mixture of love and work, and his follower Erik Erikson has pointed out the importance of play.

Adulthood: Loving, Working, and Playing

When Freud was asked what the secret to a long and happy adult life was, he answered "lieben und arbeiten"—love and work. Few adult men or women are completely content without a meaningful, loving relationship with another or without meaningful, satisfying work in or out of the home. Indeed, psychologists define adulthood not in terms of age, but as the time at which individuals seek a lasting marital (or other similar) relationship and begin to work to support themselves and/or assume the responsibility of caring for a home.

If Freud were alive today, he might add another item, play, to his list. Many contemporary psychologists, such as Freud's follower Erik Erikson, believe that in addition to love and work, people must have a satisfying amount of hobbies, sports, exercise, and adventure in their lives to be healthy, relaxed, and happy. The challenge of adulthood for each of us, then, is to create a life with a happy blend of love, work, and play. (See *Of Special Interest:* "Playing Around.")

But adulthood is not a single phase of life. The challenges of love, work, and play change considerably during adulthood. The demands of maintaining a marriage are very different for newlyweds, parents of infants, parents of teenagers, or a couple in their 70s. Similar changes occur in the demands of work and play. In other words, adulthood is not the end of the process of development. Developmental changes *continue* throughout adulthood.

Stability and Change in Adulthood

The study of adult development is only a recent part of psychology. Previously, psychologists thought of the individual's personality as being formed in childhood and then lived out in adulthood. Because of this view of adulthood, most of the early research that was conducted on adult development were studies designed to find out how stable intelligence and personality were across the adult years.

OF SPECIAL INTEREST

Playing Around

Erik Erikson (1963) has revised Freud's view that love and work are the cornerstones of a happy life by adding a third element, play. Living as we do in a society that is still influenced by Puritan thinking that equates leisure with wasted time, however, it's difficult for us to take the subject of play seriously. But there are signs that this state of affairs is changing: Growing numbers of Americans are coming to view leisure activities as not only morally acceptable, but an essential part of a psychologically and physically healthy life. Americans now work an average of 1,200 fewer hours per year than their grandfathers, and unions are finding that their younger members value leisure time as much or more than income in contract bargaining (Jones, 1977; Kreps & Spengler, 1973).

The American commitment to leisure can be further seen in the facts that in 1976 alone we spent 2 billion dollars on golf, 1.3 billion on skiing, 50 million on tennis; we owned 4 million campers, 2 million snowmobiles, and 1.5 million surfboards (Jones, 1977). Leisure is important throughout the life span, but it changes in form across time. Adolescents spend most of their time in peer-related leisure activities; young married adults spend most of their free time in activities around the home; while older adults travel, go out to dinner, and develop more individual sports and leisure interests (Rogers, 1980).

But, is play as important as Erikson and others believe that it is? Are adults who find time to play happier adults? The value of one type of play, vigorous sports and exercise, has been studied for the first time in recent years. For example, Blumenthal, Sanders, Williams, Needels, and Wallace (1982) evaluated the psychological benefits of an exercise program (stretching and running or walking) for adults aged 25 to 61. After 10 weeks of three medically supervised 45-minute workouts per week, the participants were less tense, tired, anxious, and depressed than a similar group of adults who did not exercise. Similarly, a study of over 500 college men and women found that men who participated in sports to a considerable extent reported more life satisfaction than men with little or no sports participation; this was true both during college and five years after graduation. For women, however, the amount of participation in sports was not related to life satisfaction (Varca, Shaffer, & Saunders, 1984). The evidence is not all in by any means, but exercise appears to have psychological benefits for both sexes, while sports participation seems to be a psychologically useful form of play for men. However, we should be careful not to conclude that vigorous forms of play are the only beneficial ones; we do not yet know if more sedentary hobbies are psychologically beneficial, but there is no reason to expect that they are not.

Some research has shown that healthy older adults experience no significant declines in intelligence.

Stability of Intelligence during Adulthood

Developmental psychologist Werner Schaie and his colleagues have studied the intelligence test performance of several groups of individuals across their adult years. They asked the question: Is intelligence an unchanging characteristic of the adult or does it decline with aging? Their studies showed that there is decline in only some facets of intelligence before the age of about 75. The few declines that begin in the 50s and 60s tend to be in aspects of intelligence that put a premium on speed, such as timed measures of manual dexterity or verbal fluency. No declines occur before about age 75 in fundamental aspects of intelligence such as knowledge of word meanings, ability to reason, understanding of mathematical concepts, or the ability to profit from education (Schaie & Parham, 1977).

Other research suggests that Schaie's research exaggerates the declines in adult intelligence. His findings reflect declines in the *average* IQ scores of large groups of subjects. Not all subjects in the group show these declines, however. Healthy older adults show no significant declines in IQ. Declines occur only for individuals who have experienced some kind of damage to the brain such as cerebral arteriosclerosis—"hardening" of the arteries that carry oxygen to the brain, resulting in the death of brain cells (Birren, Butler, Greenhouse, Sokoloff, & Yarrow, 1963). Declines occur in the *average* IQ of older adults because disorders such as arteriosclerosis are increasingly more common in the aged. If we can stay healthy and keep blood pumping to the brain, we all may have a few good years left. (But read *Research Report:* "Cross-sectional and Longitudinal Studies of Development" to see how our conclusions about intelligence and aging have changed.)

A noticeable decline in intellectual functioning in some older adults that may also have a biological basis is the deterioration of memory. Initially, the changes occur for memory of recent events. The older adult who has suffered intellectual decline may not be able to remember what she had for breakfast, why he walked to a friend's house, or where she left her purse, but he generally can recall events that happened long ago quite well. It's only in the advanced stage of physiological deterioration of brain functioning known as **senility** that the individual begins to experience difficulties in retrieving information that was learned long ago—such as the periodic inability to recall the names of close friends or grandchildren.

senility (sĕ-nil′ĭ-te)
The physiological deterioration of brain functioning that occurs in some older adults.

RESEARCH REPORT

Cross-sectional and Longitudinal Studies of Development: Intelligence as a Case in Point

Research on the stability of intelligence test scores (IQ) has been important both for what it tells us about IQ and aging, and also for the lesson it taught psychologists about how to conduct research on adult development. The earliest studies of the stability of IQ during adulthood compared the IQs of individuals of different ages who were all tested during the same year. For example, in 1955 a study might have tested the IQs of people who were then 30, 50, and 70 and compared their IQ scores. This strategy for conducting developmental research is called a **cross-sectional design.** It compares individuals who are of different ages at one point in time.

These early cross-sectional studies of intelligence suggested that IQ was not very stable during the later adult years; it declined considerably from about age 50 on. The problem with this type of research strategy is that the individuals who are of different ages were born and grew up at different times. For example, a person who was 20 in 1955 was born in 1935, while a person who was 60 in 1955 was born in 1895, a very different era in the United States in terms of health care, nutrition, education, travel, communication, and so on. Tests on individuals of the same age who were born in different years, have shown that those born more recently are significantly more intelligent than those born longer ago (Schaie & Labouvie-Vief, 1973). Apparently, the changes in our way of life have had a beneficial impact on intelligence.

While the finding that individuals born during different eras have different IQs when they reach the same age is important and interesting in its own right, it also has important implications for how psychologists should study the development of intelligence during adulthood. Cross-sectional studies are not valid since they use subjects who were born and grew up in different eras.

The alternative to cross-sectional research is the **longitudinal design** in which the same individuals are measured as they reach different ages. For example, the IQ of a group of people might be measured when they are all 30, later when they reach 50, and again at 70. Because all of the subjects in longitudinal studies were born in the same year, the problems associated with cross-sectional studies of development are eliminated. However, longitudinal studies are obviously much more time-consuming to conduct.

It's particularly important that longitudinal studies have been conducted on the stability of intelligence in adulthood, however, since they paint a very different picture of adult intelligence. As discussed in the text, longitudinal studies of IQ find declines in very few aspects of intelligence in healthy adults throughout their life span.

cross-sectional design
A research design that compares individuals who are of different ages at one point in time.

longitudinal design
A research design in which changes in the same individuals are studied as they reach different ages.

This characteristic pattern of deterioration of memory suggests that short-term memory declines before long-term memory. Actually, this is not the case. Studies show that the ability of older adults with memory problems to recall information, such as a series of digits, for brief periods of time is not impaired. Their short-term memory is fine. They only show deficits when they have to *transfer* information from short-term memory to long-term memory and/or retrieve it again. Thus, when an older adult consistently is unable to remember her new telephone number over a period of months, it's probably because she cannot transfer it to and from long-term memory. This fact has led to speculation that physiological deterioration in some older adults damages the brain structure required for the transfer between short- and long-term memory before damaging other structures involved in memory (Ford & Roth, 1977).

Another intriguing but as yet unexplained aspect of intellectual decline in the aged has been noted in a few studies. Subjects in studies of intelligence have often shown substantial declines in IQ scores in the year or two prior to their death. It is not known whether this decline, known as the *terminal drop,* is due to deterioration in health or a marked psychological disengagement and apathy prior to death (Riegel & Riegel, 1972).

Stability of Personality during Adulthood

Is our personality as stable across the span of adulthood as our intellectual abilities? **Personality** is defined as the sum total of our typical ways of responding. Part of one person's personality may involve being kind to children, being anxious in social situations, and being impulsive in making decisions, while another person may characteristically act in just the opposite ways. Obviously, personality has many facets, and current evidence suggests that some facets change more across the adult life span than others (Moss & Susman, 1980).

personality
The sum total of the typical ways of acting, thinking, and feeling that makes each person unique.

Traits such as enjoyment of being with other people, enjoyment of excitement, high general level of activity, anxiousness, self-consciousness, and openness to feelings are fairly stable throughout adulthood (Costa & McCrae, 1976). Other traits such as desire for power, aggressiveness, and need for achievement change much more (Skolnick, 1966).

There is growing evidence of a few predictable personality changes that most adults can expect to go through in their middle and later adult years. Adults often become more insightful, dependable, comfortable, candid, and more accepting of life's hardships (Haan, 1976; Neugarten, 1964). Men also become more aware of their need for affection and their aesthetic needs, while women tend to become more assertive in middle adulthood (Gutmann, 1977; Neugarten, 1968). Although life certainly becomes more difficult for some older adults, it becomes easier and more enjoyable for most. Evidence from the Berkeley Growth Study (Maas & Kuypers, 1974) suggests that a key factor determining which adults will age happily is the extent to which their earlier adult lives are *centered* on something. Women whose lives were centered on either their husbands or their own careers were happier in later adult life than women who had no real commitment earlier in life.

Researchers are trying to determine if changes in adult behavior are the result of a change from one biological stage to another or if such changes in behavior are triggered by important events.

Adult Development: Biological Stages or Environmental Events?

While it's clear that adults continue to change in some ways through the years of the adult period, there is presently little agreement among psychologists as to the best way to conceptualize those changes. Psychologists have reached far fewer firm conclusions about adults than children. Are there biologically timed *stages* in adult development that are nearly as distinct as those in childhood? Or are the changes of adulthood related to *events* that commonly take place during this period rather than to stages that are tied to biological aging? For example, if a change in adult behavior typically takes place around the age of 50, is that because people change from one biological stage to another when they reach that age or because an important event usually happens around age 50 (such as the last child leaving home)? Or both?

There is no firm answer to these questions because there is a great deal of consistency in the ages at which people experience important events in their adult lives. These events tend to occur at about the same time for a surprising proportion of people. Figure 9.2, for example, shows the age at which 50 percent of women (the median age) of four different economic classes experienced important events in the family cycle (Olsen, 1969). Note the striking degree of similarity among these different groups. Furthermore, there is striking similarity in the median age at which major events were experienced by women born in different decades from 1900 to 1939 (Norton, 1974). When we discuss the possible existence of stages of adult life later in this chapter, we must remember that separating age and events is difficult. But the prevailing view is that events trigger developmental changes in adulthood—the so-called **social clock** (Rogers, 1980).

social clock
The roughly predictable sequence of important events in the adult life span.

The idea that there is a social clock—a roughly predictable sequence of important life events—that influences our adult development is important in a second way. Individuals who experience events at times other than the usual time for that event often react differently to them. For example, retiring earlier than age 65 is generally more difficult to adjust to than retiring at the typical age. On the other hand, fathers who decide to have children later in life are generally more comfortable and effective in that role (Bourque & Back, 1977; Nydegger, 1973). (See *Research Report:* "The Social Clock.")

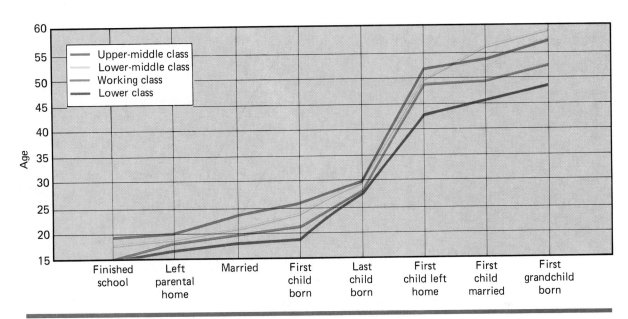

Figure 9.2 The "social clock" can be seen in the median age at which women of four different socioeconomic classes experience significant life events (Olsen, 1969).

Men who become fathers later in life are generally more comfortable in that role.

R E S E A R C H   R E P O R T

The Social Clock: Having Children and Marital Satisfaction

Studies of marital satisfaction show a clear cycle of changes in happiness that is related to the social clock—the normal sequence of events in adult life. Figure 9.3 shows that, on the average, marital satisfaction drops sharply after the birth of the first child and does not rise again until after the children have left the home (Rollins & Feldman, 1970). This strong U-shaped relationship has also been found in other independent research studies (Gould, 1978).

While the satisfactions of having children are both obvious and well documented (Gould, 1978), children create considerable stress as well. They restrict social, occupational, and leisure time; require a great deal of physical labor (laundry, food preparation); and can be maddening at times because of the "childish" behavior that is normal for youngsters. These demands can leave both parents (but particularly the one who most cares for the child) tense, tired, and cross at the end of the day—a stark contrast to the happy, romantic, energetic partner of the courtship and early marriage.

If these changes in the behavior of the spouse are incorrectly attributed by either partner to a loss of love or decreased sexual attraction, painful problems can be precipitated that may erode marital satisfaction. But even if the changes are correctly attributed to the normal stresses and strains of family life, the middle period of the family cycle is a less relaxed and enjoyable time of life for many men and women. The only remedies are love, patience, and a clear belief in the value of the family.

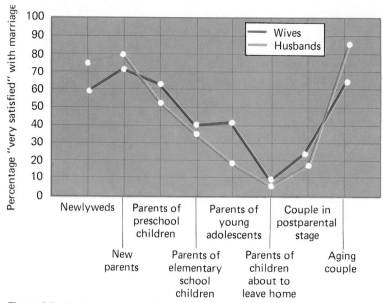

Figure 9.3 On the average, marital satisfaction drops for both men and women after their children are born and does not rise again until after their children have left home (Rollins & Feldman, 1970).

Developmental Stages of Adulthood

A number of psychologists have suggested that enough is now known about adult development to sketch a tentative picture of the stages of adulthood. There is sure to be considerable disagreement among psychologists about this issue until more data are available. At present, opinion seems to be about equally divided among psychologists as to whether or not adults go through a series of stages.

Erik Erikson (1963) and Daniel Levinson (1978) have each proposed a set of stages of adult life. These stages are somewhat different from the stages of infant and child development in that (1) not every adult is believed to go through every stage; (2) the order of the stages can vary for some individuals; and (3) the timing of the stages is not controlled by biological maturation. Although physical aging can be a contributing factor, timing of adult stages is primarily caused by the social clock events in the life cycle that tend to occur at about the same time for most individuals. Although Erikson proposes three stages of adulthood and Levinson proposes nine stages, Levinson's theory is based on Erikson's and can be thought of as an elaboration of Erikson's views. For this reason, we will discuss both stage theories together. Notice that both theorists see adulthood as a series of alternating periods of stability and transition.

Early Adulthood: Intimacy vs. Isolation

Erikson (1963) discusses his proposed stages of adult life in terms of the challenges, or crises, faced at each stage and the consequences of successfully or unsuccessfully meeting those challenges. If you refer again to table 8.1, page 313, you can see that these adult stages are the continuation of the stages of development Erikson believes begin in infancy. He refers to early adulthood as the stage of *intimacy versus isolation*. The challenge of this stage is to enter into committed, loving relationships with others that partially replace the bonds with parents. If we are successful in this task, we will have the intimacy needed to progress in adult life; if not, we will become isolated and less capable of full emotional development according to Erikson.

Levinson (1978) sees the early adulthood phase as being composed of three briefer stages. The *entering adulthood* stage stretches from the early to the late 20s. The individual is primarily occupied with the choice of a mate, beginning a career, and, for many, the birth of children.

The *age 30 transition* is a stage occurring anytime from the late 20s to the early 30s. It's a time of reassessment of one's mate, job, and other circumstances. The individual often feels that if changes are to be made in his or her life, they must be made now "before it's too late." Changes in jobs, divorces, and moves to new cities (sometimes back to one's hometown) are relatively common during this period. This questioning only leads other individuals to reaffirm the choices they made in the earlier periods.

The *settling down* stage is a time of working hard toward one's goals. It extends roughly from the early 30s to about age 40. In this phase adults sometimes join the PTA Executive Board to improve the quality of their child's school, plant trees in the lawn, and work long hours for promotion to a senior position at work. The individual is often aware of feeling like a full member of the adult generation at this time.

OF SPECIAL INTEREST

The Climacteric and Menopause

As discussed in the text, most psychologists believe that the more or less predictable changes that characterize adult development are timed by the social clock rather than biological aging. In other words, events in the social world of the person are believed to be more responsible for psychological changes during adulthood than is biological aging. One biological event in the aging process that does appear to have some impact on adult development—but far less than many of us believe that it does—is the **climacteric.** The climacteric is a roughly 15-year period between the ages of about 45 and 60 in which there is a loss of the capacity to sexually reproduce in women and a decline in the reproductive capacity of men.

In women, the decrease in the level of sex hormones during this period eventually leads to the end of menstruation, or **menopause.** This event, which takes place at 46 to 48 years of age on the average (but can normally take place between the ages of 36 and 60) is sometimes an uncomfortable time for the woman. It's often accompanied by "hot flashes," anxiety, and depression, although most women do not find it to be as difficult as they were led to expect (Hultsch & Deutsch, 1981). Although 50 percent of women experience some discomfort during menopause, only 10 percent go through severe distress (McKinlay & Jeffreys, 1974).

Many women expect that menopause and the loss of the ability to reproduce as well as the accelerated aging of physical appearance that can occur with menopause will be accompanied by a loss of sexual interest. But this is definitely not a necessary outcome. Women who enjoy and regularly engage in intercourse before menopause experience no sexual difficulties or loss of sexual interest after menopause (Masters & Johnson, 1966). Many women, in fact, report increased sexual interest because the risk of pregnancy has passed. These findings suggest that the difficulties experienced by some women after menopause may be caused, in part at least, by the expectation that it will be difficult.

The changes that accompany the male climacteric are generally less notable than in women. There is a decline in the number of sperm cells produced (but men of all ages produce live sperm cells), and there are slight changes in the pattern of sexual arousal, but the decrease in sex hormones that occur during the climacteric appear to have no major psychological or sexual effects.

climacteric (kli-mak'ter-ik) The period between about ages 45 and 60 in which there is a loss of capacity to sexually reproduce in women and a decline in the reproductive capacity of men.

menopause (men'o-pawz) The cessation of menstruation and the capacity to reproduce in women.

The challenge of the middle years, according to Erikson, is to find meaning in life and work, other than selfish gains. This is the stage of generativity versus stagnation.

Middle Adulthood: Generativity vs. Stagnation

During this stage from about age 40 to 65, the individual must come to grips with what his or her life is really going to be like. By this time the adult usually realizes that the ambitious dreams of early adulthood cannot all be fulfilled. Few of us who dreamed of becoming famous scientists, wealthy business executives, community leaders, or the like are still able to cling to these dreams in middle adulthood. Too many promotions have been missed, too many investments have gone bad, and too many elections have been lost to believe that we can be the unqualified successes we once dreamed of being. The challenge of this stage then, which Erikson refers to as the stage of *generativity versus stagnation,* is to find meaning in the things that we *can* do in our work and family lives and continue to be productive (*generative*). If not, many individuals will compare what they are so unfavorably to what they wish they were that they will give up entirely and stagnate.

The importance of being generative, or productive, during middle adulthood is not just a matter of mere work to Erikson. The person who successfully navigates middle adulthood develops a devotion to endeavors that live beyond one's own life span. This might take the form of building a family business, guiding one's children or grandchildren, or training and taking younger coworkers under one's wing as a mentor. Generativity is a matter of "reaching out" rather than being self-centered. A person who merely works hard may be meeting his or her own selfish needs only. According to Erikson, this person is self-absorbed or stagnant and will find that life loses much of its meaning during middle adulthood.

For many women who spent their earlier adult lives as homemakers rearing children, work may be a more important part of the challenge of remaining generative than for men. The woman who faces an "empty nest" during middle adulthood may feel suddenly useless. She has spent the last 25 years or so giving to others, but now finds that her role as the mother of grown children requires little from her. At this point, she may maximize her generativity by returning to the work force and taking a job that she has previously put off to meet the needs of others. For some women, then, the move back into the work force to maintain generativity can be seen as the opposite of the move of men, who have long been employed and shift toward doing more for others (Lowenthal, Thurnher, & Chiriboga, 1975). But this move may accomplish the same purpose in avoiding stagnation.

Levinson describes four brief stages of middle adulthood. Middle adulthood opens with the *midlife transition*. This transitional stage spans four to six years, reaching a peak in the early 40s. For some individuals, this transition is quite easy, but for others it's a period of anguish and turmoil. The majority of a sample of 40 men studied by Levinson—10 executives, 10 biologists, 10 factory workers, and 10 novelists—experienced at least some turmoil during their early 40s. Erikson described this stage as the early peak of the struggle between generativity and stagnation—can I find meaning in my life the way it's turning out? It's also a time to face growing evidence of biological aging and to accept or agonize over one's wrinkles and gray hair.

The *entering middle adulthood* stage, from about 45 to 50, is a period of calm and stability for most people that emerges from the mid-life crisis. It's sometimes marked by career changes, new health fitness programs, geographical moves, or divorce. But more often this stage is a continuation of the life that preceded it. Individuals who are happy with themselves following the mid-life transition often find this period to be one of the most productive and creative times of their lives. The illusory ambitions that were shattered during the midlife transition have often been replaced with more attainable goals that are pursued with vigor. Individuals often feel that the painful process of reassessment of the early 40s led to changes that left them a better person.

The *age 50 transition* is a stage that is similar to the age 30 transition. For most adults this is a time to reassess the goals and life-style chosen during midlife and the entering middle adulthood stages. Another stable period from about age 55 to 65 follows the age 50 transition. Levinson refers to this stage as the *culmination of middle adulthood.*

The Berkeley Growth Study found that a key factor in the happiness of older adults is the extent to which they were committed to something during their earlier adult lives.

R E V I E W

Like all of the periods of life, adulthood is a time of change. Intelligence remains relatively constant throughout the adult years in most healthy adults, but personality is subject to more change. There is disagreement among psychologists as to whether the changes in adulthood are the result of biologically programmed stages of development or simply reactions to significant events in adulthood, such as marriage and the birth of children. The prevailing view, however, is that most adults will undergo changes and challenges at roughly the same ages, because through a process known as the social clock we experience significant events at approximately the same ages. Erikson and Levinson have outlined a series of stages of adult life, but until more research evidence is available, these should be considered tentative.

Again, it's important to remember that not all developmental psychologists believe that adulthood can be thought of as a series of stages or at least that the idea of stages has been exaggerated in recent years. Rossi (1980), for example, argues that the inevitability and negative impact of the mid-life transition has been dangerously exaggerated—not all individuals experience a "transition" at this point in life, and it is certainly not a "crisis" for everyone. Furthermore, he urges caution in interpreting current research findings on this topic. Because all of our current studies of adult "stages" have been based on people who were children during the years of the Great Depression, the stages identified may not turn out to be characteristic of individuals born during different time periods. While the concept of adult stages is a provocative idea that may offer us new insights, the scientific jury is still out on the question.

Aging and Late Adulthood: Integrity vs. Despair

Erikson refers to the late 60s and beyond as the stage of *integrity versus despair.* Levinson devotes little of his theory to the later adult years and adds little to Erikson's ideas. The older adult who sees meaning in his or her life when considered as a whole continues to live a satisfying existence instead of merely staying alive. The person who sees life as a collection of unmet goals and unanswered riddles may despair of ever achieving a meaningful life and will often withdraw and live out the remaining years like a prison sentence.

But far more older Americans find meaning rather than despair in their lives. This may come as a surprise to you. Just as most of us once thought that the process of development ended in childhood, most of us *still* think that there is little real life after age 65. Too often we think of older adults as leading colorless, joyless, passionless lives. It's surprising to learn that real *living* can continue until death.

Biological Aspects of Aging

Aging is partly a biological process. Over the years, the body deteriorates—skin sags and wrinkles, artery walls become less flexible, muscular strength is lost, and so on. A major cause of this biological deterioration is the slowing and eventual loss of the ability of cells to divide and replace themselves in old age. (See *Of Special Interest:* "Life Expectancy.") Biological aging, although closely related to chronological age, is not synonymous with it. Some individuals age slower than others, due to differences in exercise, diet, stress, illness, heredity, and other factors. Some children, in fact, who have the rare disease called **progeria,** which speeds up aging, go through the entire biological process of aging by 13 years of age.

progeria (pro-je're-ah) A rare disease in which children go through the entire biological process of aging by about 13 years of age.

Psychological Aspects of Aging

Aging is not only a biological process; it involves many psychological aspects as well. Older people are different from younger people because they have experienced more, lived through eras that younger individuals have not, have often retired from their jobs, no longer have living parents, often have children who are adults, and a host of other factors. Just as people experience biological aging at different rates, the psychological experience of aging also differs from person to person.

The key psychological variables that seem to be associated with happy aging are (1) whether one stays "engaged" in life's activities and (2) whether one believes myths about old age. Considerable research suggests that older individuals who continue to be actively engaged in meaningful activities are the happiest as older adults (Maddox, 1964; Neugarten & Hagestad, 1976). These activities can involve family, hobbies, volunteer service, or continued employment. All that matters is that they be activities that are meaningful to the individual.

In the stage of integrity versus despair, older adults who see meaning in their lives when considered as a whole will continue to find life satisfying.

Factors such as exercise, diet, stress, illness, and heredity affect the rate of aging in humans.

OF SPECIAL INTEREST

Life Expectancy: The Limit of Fifty Cell Divisions

The average life expectancy has increased dramatically in modern times. The average Roman in the year 1 A.D. lived to about age 22. During the Middle Ages, the life expectancy was about 35 years. As late as the year 1900, the average life span in the United States was only 47.3 years, but increased to 72.8 years by 1976 (Hultsch & Deutsch, 1981). These increases in life expectancy raise the question of how long we can prolong life. Will our children match Methuselah's reported 969 years?

Actually, there are two reasons to believe that, unless we have the major breakthrough in the ability to retard biological aging that some scientists expect in the near future, we have stretched the life expectancy about as far as it can go. For one thing, the figures on increases in life expectancy are misleading. Most of the increases in the average life expectancy have come from medical improvements that have reduced the frequency of *premature* deaths, particularly in infancy, that greatly reduced the *average* span of life in former times. There has been little increase in the span of life for individuals who have lived until old age. In 1900 the average American who had survived until age 20 could expect to live 42.8 more years. By 1976 the average 20-year-old could expect to live 47.3 more years—an increase of only 4.5 years even though the overall life expectancy had gone up 25.5 years during the same period (Hultsch & Deutsch, 1981).

The second reason why we may have pushed the maximum life span to its limits is even more compelling. Many scientists believe that the key process that allows the body to renew and maintain itself, cell division, is genetically programmed to go on for a fixed period and then stop. Evidence for this theory comes from studies in which separate living human cells are placed in special environments or "cultures" and allowed to divide at a rapid rate. Under these ideal conditions, human cells should be able to continue dividing indefinitely, but instead they divide approximately *50* times and then stop. Furthermore, cells taken from older people (cells that have already divided many times) divide fewer times than cells from younger people. Apparently they have already used up many of their allotted cell divisions (Hayflick, 1965). Unless some way is found to alter this preprogrammed limit on cell division, there is little hope of any real extension of the span of human life.

*"I was grinding out barnyards and farmhouses and cows in the meadow,
and then, suddenly, I figured to hell with it."*

The other key to a satisfactory older adulthood seems to be in ignoring the restrictive myths and stereotypes of old age so prevalent in our society. Many older adults are active in sports and creative in the arts and sciences. They sometimes attend college, throw exciting parties, and in general they do not behave like passive, irritable "old people" of the stereotype. Philosopher Bertrand Russell, artists Marc Chagall and Pablo Picasso, political leaders Golda Meir and Mao Tse-tung, and psychologist Jean Piaget continued to be productive into their 80s.

Sexuality provides another prime example of the effects of myths on the aged. Most of us think of the aged as sexless and may even be appalled to think that many lead vigorous sex lives. The fact of the matter is that 80 percent of healthy married men in their 70s continue to have intercourse (Kinsey, Pomeroy, & Martin, 1948). In addition, there is reason to believe that today unmarried men in their 70s and 80s have intercourse even more frequently than married men of the same age (Long, 1976). While there are some changes in the amount of time necessary to obtain a full erection in males and in vaginal lubrication in females that occur in the 70s and 80s, loving couples can easily have satisfying sex lives. The problem is that many older people believe that these age changes mark the end of their sexuality and retreat from further attempts. They then become victims more of their own myths about old age than of old age itself (Rogers, 1980).

One key to happy aging is not believing the myths about old age. Many people, such as author Isaac Bashevis Singer, are quite productive in later years.

Death and Dying: The Final "Stage"

Everything has an end, including each of our lives. The life cycle begins with the life of a single cell and ends with the death of the person that unfolded from that cell. In recent years, the topic of death and dying has finally received some long overdue scientific attention with interesting results.

Psychological Causes of Death

Psychological factors can contribute to the time of death in important ways. Stressful events, for example, can precipitate death in individuals who have serious health problems. Men whose wives have recently died are somewhat more likely to suffer fatal heart attacks than men of the same age whose wives are living (Parkes, 1972). The same thing has been found for recently widowed women, particularly if they are under the age of 65 at the time of their husbands' deaths (Rowland, 1977). Do not be frightened by these findings, however, if you or someone close to you has recently suffered the loss of a spouse. While this loss is a devastatingly traumatic one, the increase in deaths following the death of a spouse is small.

Other psychological factors also seem to be involved in the timing of death. For example, deaths are more common in older individuals in the period immediately following a birthday than in the months just preceding it. Apparently birthdays serve as a landmark; we hold on until we get another year of age under our belt and then seem to let go until another birthday seems to be within reach (see figure 9.4.) (Phillips & Feldman, 1973).

Fear of Death

Thoughts of death are an important part of the last stages of life for many individuals. Older adults spend more time thinking about death than younger adults. Contemplating and planning for one's death is a normal part of old age (Kalish & Reynolds, 1976). Happily, older adults tend to be less frightened by death than younger adults. Older adults usually come to accept its inevitability with little anguish.

One's fear of death is related to other variables besides age, however. One significant factor is religious belief. Highly religious individuals experience the least fear of death. Nonreligious individuals experience moderate levels of anxiety about death, while religious people who do not consistently practice their faith experience the greatest fear of dying (Nelson & Nelson, 1973).

Acceptance of Impending Death

Psychiatrist Elizabeth Kübler-Ross (1969; 1974) provided us with new and important insights on the process of dying through her interviews of hundreds of terminally ill patients at the University of Chicago teaching and research hospital. From these interviews, she developed a theory that people who learn of their impending death (and sometimes their loved ones) tend to pass through five rather distinct stages:

1. *Denial*. At first, the individual strongly resists the idea of death by denying the validity of the information about his terminal illness. It's common at this stage for the terminally ill person to accuse his or her doctor of being incompetent, to seek a more favorable diagnosis, or to look for a "miracle cure." Sometimes the denial is more subtle, however. The individual may simply act like the news of impending death had never been revealed, and proceed like nothing is wrong for a while.

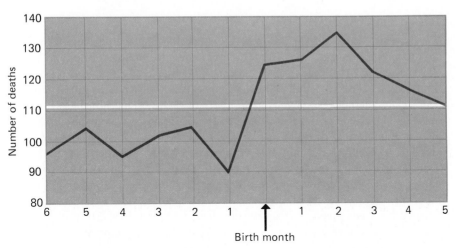

Figure 9.4 The number of deaths before and after the month of birth (Phillips & Feldman, 1973).

2. *Anger.* After the initial denial, the terminally ill person reacts to the fact of his or her impending death with anger: Why me? It's not fair that this should be happening to me! There is much hostility, envy of others, and resentment during this stage. As a result, the terminally ill person is often highly irritable and frequently quarrels with nurses, doctors, and loved ones.

3. *Bargaining.* The anger and denial of the impending death is largely gone by this third stage, and the terminally ill person fully realizes that death is coming. But death still is not accepted as inevitable. Instead, the person tries to strike bargains to prolong his or her life. These bargains may be in the form of willingness to undergo painful treatments to extend life, but they are more often silent deals with God, such as "I'll leave most of my money to the church if I can have six more months?" Interestingly, if the person does live past this bargaining stage, the bargain is usually broken—the church does not get the money.

4. *Depression.* Eventually, the reality of impending death leads to a loss of hope. Bargains no longer seem possible; death is coming no matter what. Often the person begins to feel guilty about leaving loved ones behind, incapable of facing death with dignity, and quite depressed.

5. *Acceptance.* In time, the depression lifts and the person finally achieves an acceptance of death. This generally is not a happy feeling of acceptance, but a state of emotional exhaustion that leaves the individual peacefully free of negative emotions.

Kübler-Ross (1974) points out herself that not every terminally ill person passes through these same stages. Reactions to impending death are highly individual. If we go through the process of dying with a loved one, we must be careful not to impose on him or her our views of how the process of accepting death should proceed. Still, much important information has come from the studies of Kübler-Ross.

The Moment of Death

What does it feel like to die? How would a psychologist even attempt to gather data to answer this question? Surprisingly, some information is available on the experience of dying. Recent developments in medicine have made it possible to bring people who are "clinically dead" back to life in some instances. Stopped hearts can sometimes be started again. Interviews have been conducted with these individuals by psychiatrist Raymond Moody (1976) to gain an understanding of what the moment of death feels like. His findings are impressive because these individuals, even though they had no contact with one another and had never heard of another person's experience with death, reported similar experiences. It must be kept in mind, however, that they were not "dead" at all in the sense that their brains ceased to function, and it is difficult to know how much they were affected by drugs given to them during their medical crises. But even if these interviews only give us tentative information about the moment just *before* death—and therefore can shed no light on the existence of an afterlife—they are still fascinating.

The individuals who had "died" typically reported the following sequence of events. First, their heads were filled with a pleasant, sometimes musical ringing or buzzing sound. Next, they sensed that their minds or "spirits" separated from their bodies. Sometimes they were able to watch the physician trying to revive them, but more often they felt that they were being transported quickly away from their bodies. This was experienced as moving through what felt like a long tunnel. At first, the experience of dying was an unpleasant one as the individual fearfully fought death. But a sense of peace soon settled over them. Many individuals reported seeing the spirits of dead loved ones while passing through the tunnel and in time, the tunnel brightened and a shining Godlike spirit of love was felt at the end of the tunnel. But at this point all of the interviewed individuals returned to normal "living" as their hearts were restarted.

More recently, nationally known pollster George Gallup reported the results of a survey of individuals who had nearly died, but had been revived following sudden accidents (Gallup & Proctor, 1982). The near-death experiences reported by these individuals were considerably less similar to one another than the ones described by Moody (1976), but quite a number of Gallup's interviewees did report experiences like the ones described above. What do you think? Did these individuals experience death, or did they just have an hallucination when their hearts stopped beating?

R E V I E W

Although some older adults despair of ever achieving a meaningful pattern of living, many others achieve a sense of integrity and continue to find life meaningful and joyful until death. Aging is partly a biological process of physical deterioration that appears to be limited by the ability of the body's cells to divide and replace themselves. But aging is also a psychological process that can be slowed to some degree by staying engaged in meaningful activities and by not believing many of the negative myths about old age so prevalent in our society. Regardless of how the individual lives out the later adult years, the final "stage" of life is always death. Older adults tend to be accepting of their impending deaths, especially religious adults, but individuals who must face the knowledge of their impending death earlier in the life span generally go through several stages of anguish before reaching a state of acceptance. Interviews with individuals who had been pronounced clinically dead and then revived may give some insights as to the experience of death. However, these individuals probably were only close to death so we cannot be confident of their reports.

S U M M A R Y

Chapter 9 is the second chapter on the process of human development. It discusses adolescence, adulthood, aging, and death.

I. *Adolescence* is the developmental period from the onset of *puberty* until the beginning of adulthood.
   A. The production of sex hormones in puberty trigger biological changes known as the *primary sex characteristics.*
      1. *Menarche,* the first menstrual period, occurs at about 12 years and 6 months in American females.
      2. Production of sperm begins about two years later in males.
   B. *Secondary sex characteristics* appear in both sexes during puberty.
   C. The *adolescent growth spurt* lasts for a little over a year in early adolescence. In late adolescence weight gain is common due to a decline in the *basal metabolism rate.*
   D. Girls tend to experience puberty about two years earlier than boys.
      1. For both sexes different parts of the body grow at different rates, weight and physique change in irregular ways, and many adolescents experience skin problems.
      2. Within each sex, there is wide variation in the age at which puberty begins.
   E. Piaget's *formal operational stage*—the ability to use abstract concepts—occurs in some individuals by about age 11.
   F. Many adolescents go through what Erikson calls an *identity crisis,* but for most adolescents the period is not particularly stormy.
   G. Peers replace the family as the most important influence on the adolescent. However, most adolescents remain relatively close to their parents in terms of values and attitudes.
II. Adulthood is not a single phase of life. Changes involving love, work, and play continue throughout adulthood.
   A. Intelligence appears stable throughout adulthood in healthy adults. Memory loss among some older adults will occur if they have experienced damage to the brain due to aging (*senility*).
   B. Some relatively predictable personality changes that occur for many people during adulthood include becoming more insightful, dependable, and candid. A key factor in happy aging is the extent to which an individual's life was *centered* on something during earlier adult years.

    C. Most psychologists say that changes during adulthood are related to events that occur at relatively fixed times of life, which are called the *social clock.*

    D. Developmental stages of adulthood appear different from those of childhood in that not every adult goes through each stage, the order of the stages can vary, and the timing of the stages is not controlled by biological maturation.

    E. Erikson calls early adulthood the stage of *intimacy versus isolation,* during which many individuals enter committed, loving relationships.

    F. Erikson calls middle adulthood the stage of *generativity versus stagnation,* during which many individuals find meaning in work and family lives.

III. Erikson calls the period from the late 60s on the stage of *integrity versus despair;* older adults who see meaning in their lives when considered as a whole continue to live a satisfying existence.

    A. A major cause of biological aging is the slowing of the ability of cells to divide and replace themselves.

    B. Psychological variables associated with happy aging are whether one stays ''engaged'' in life's activities and whether one believes the myths about old age.

    C. Older adults tend to be less frightened by death than do younger adults. Studies by Kübler-Ross suggest that people who learn of their impending death tend to pass through five distinct stages: *denial, anger, bargaining, depression,* and *acceptance.*

Suggested Readings

1. For more on the psychology of adolescence:

    Santrock, J. W. (1981). *Adolescence.* Dubuque, IA: Wm. C. Brown Publishers.

2. For a view of adolescence by adolescents themselves:

    Offer, D., Ostrov, E., & Howard, K. I. (1981). *The adolescent: A psychological self-portrait.* New York: Basic Books.

3. For several perspectives on stages of adult life:

    Levinson, D. J. (1978). *The seasons of a man's life.* New York: Knopf.

    Lowenthal, M. F., Thurnher, M., & Chiriboga, D. (1975). *Four stages of life: A comparative study of women and men facing transitions.* San Francisco: Jossey-Bass.

    Rollins, B. C., & Feldman, M. (1970, February). Marital satisfaction over the family life cycle. *Journal of marriage and the family,* p. 26.

4. A closer look at the psychology of aging is provided by:

    Maas, H. S., & Kuypers, J. A. (1974). *From thirty to seventy.* San Francisco: Jossey-Bass.

5. An excellent overview of development across the adult life span is provided by:

    Hultsch, D. F., & Deutsch, F. (1981). *Adult development and aging: A life-span perspective.* New York: McGraw-Hill.

The Self

TEN

Motivation and Emotion

OUTLINE

KEY TERMS

P R O L O G U E

One of the most consistently enjoyable parts of my career is the opportunity to conduct research. Even if I never contribute anything significant to our knowledge of human behavior through research, each study is an intriguing puzzle and each finding another clue in a mystery that puts any spy novel to shame. Still, for all my enthusiasm, for all my love of research, I wonder if the great researcher Walter Cannon could have talked me into doing for science what he persuaded his colleague A. L. Washburn to do to understand the motive of hunger.

Cannon and Washburn (1912) were trying to isolate the biological mechanism of hunger. They believed that the feeling of hunger was caused by contractions of the stomach wall. To determine if this idea was correct, Cannon convinced Washburn to swallow a balloon that was attached to a long tube connected to an air pump. The balloon was then inflated to fill Washburn's stomach. In this way, stomach contractions could be mechanically detected because they squeezed the balloon and increased the air pressure in the tube (see fig. 10.1). While the intermittent contractions were being measured, Washburn, who could not talk because of the tube gagging his mouth and throat, indicated when he felt a conscious sensation of hunger by pressing a key connected to a recording instrument. (History does not tell us, however, whether Washburn used his other hand to signal more negative feelings to Cannon during this unpleasant experiment.)

The question of interest to these researchers was the relationship between stomach contractions and feelings of hunger. As predicted, Washburn generally *did* feel hungry during the contractions, leading them to conclude that hunger was no more than the rumbling contractions of an empty stomach. As we shall see later in the chapter, such contractions are still believed to be part of the feeling of hunger for many people, but many more important factors are also involved. This conclusion is clearly demonstrated by the fact that patients who have had their stomachs surgically removed, or have had the sensory nerves cut from that area as part of treatment for some types of ulcers, still feel hungry in the same way they always have, including the experience of hunger pangs in that region (Cofer, 1972). If contractions were the only biological factor involved in the conscious experience of hunger, these patients would have lost all desire for food. In spite of Washburn's selfless contribution to science, it turns out that stomach contractions are only one factor in hunger, and one of the least important factors at that.

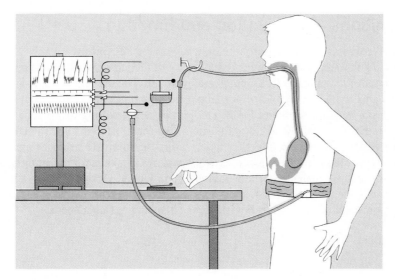

Figure 10.1 Diagram of the device used in the experiment by Cannon and Washburn (1912) to find out if stomach contractions cause a conscious feeling of hunger. Note the balloon swallowed by Washburn to measure the contractions (Murchison, 1929).

P R E V I E W

When we ask why a person is behaving in a particular way, we are often asking about motivation. Motives are factors that make us active rather than inactive and lead us to do one thing rather than another. If I have just eaten, I may take a nap or quietly read the newspaper; but if I am hungry, I will get up and get busy fixing food. The motive of hunger activates and directs my behavior. Some motives are based on the survival needs of the body for food, water, and warmth. When a bodily need exists, we are driven in a sense to find a way to restore the body to its proper balance of nutrients, fluids, and temperature. These biological motives are regulated by intricate and sensitive mechanisms under the control of the hypothalamus that detect the body's needs.

Other motives—the so-called psychological motives—are not directly related to the survival needs of the body. The motive to maintain a moderate level of novel stimulation and activity, the motive to achieve and be successful, and the motive to have friendly relationships with others are examples of psychological motives. Often these motives are strongly influenced by learning experiences and therefore differ from individual to individual and culture to culture.

Emotions are complex reactions that involve a positive or negative conscious experience accompanied by autonomic arousal and related behavior. When you see a car driving toward you, you feel a negative conscious experience; your autonomic nervous system churns you up, and you run. Psychologists generally agree on this description of the elements involved in emotions, but they disagree considerably on how these elements work together to create the full emotional experience. Some aspects of emotions appear to be inborn and not dependent on learning, while other aspects are clearly influenced by our learning experiences.

Aggression is an important topic that is related to both the topics of motivation and emotion. Unfortunately, psychologists disagree about the causes of aggression. This is a key point since psychologists differ greatly in their prescriptions for reducing violence in society.

Definitions of Motivation and Emotion

To people who are interested in human behavior, the key question is *why?* Carol wants to know why she continues to have sex with Michael when she knows she does not love him and is afraid of getting pregnant. The manager of the packing plant wants to know why two of her employees do not seem to care about doing a good job. A father wants to know why his son is not willing to work hard for good grades in school. Answers to questions like these often involve the concept of motivation. **Motivation** refers to those factors that activate behavior and give it direction. Meg is in the kitchen actively cooking. If she were not hungry, she might be inactive instead, perhaps taking a nap. Unmet motives lead to activity rather than inactivity. The fact that she is hungry also helps explain why she is cooking instead of calling her boyfriend or balancing her checkbook.

motivation
Internal state or condition that activates behavior and gives it direction.

Hungry grocery shoppers are motivated shoppers who are likely to buy more food than nonhungry shoppers.

Motivation is closely related to the topic of emotions. **Emotions** are positive or negative feelings that are generally reactions to stimulus situations that are accompanied by physiological arousal and characteristic behavior. When we are afraid, for example, we experience an acutely unpleasant feeling: the sympathetic division of our autonomic nervous system is aroused and the fear generally shows in our behavior. The emotion of passion, on the other hand, is a conglomeration of very different feelings, biological changes, and behavior.

Motivations and emotion are closely linked concepts for three reasons: (1) The arousal of emotions activates behavior as motives do. (2) Motives are often accompanied by emotions. For example, the motive to perform well on a test is often accompanied by anxiety; sexual motivation is generally blended with the emotions of passion and love. (3) Emotions typically have motivational properties of their own. Because you are in love, you are motivated to be with your special person; because you are angry you want to strike out at the object of your anger. We begin this chapter with a discussion of basic motives necessary for the biological survival of the person, then move to a discussion of more "psychological" motives, and end with a discussion of human emotions.

emotion
Positive or negative feelings generally in reaction to stimuli that are accompanied by physiological arousal and related behavior.

Primary Motives: Biological Needs

Many human motives stem from the *need* for things that keep an organism alive: food, water, warmth, sleep, avoidance of pain, and so on. We consider these **primary motives** because we must meet these biological needs or die. The sexual motive is also considered to be a primary motive, not because we would die if it were not fulfilled, but because the species could not reproduce and survive if the sexual motive were not satisfied.

This chapter focuses on the biological motives of hunger and thirst, partly because they are the best understood of the primary motives. Information is also provided elsewhere in the book on the primary motives of avoidance of pain in chapter 3 and need for sleep in chapter 4.

primary motives
Human motives for things that are necessary for survival, such as food, water, and warmth.

Homeostasis: Biological Thermostats

Most of the primary drives are based on the body's need to maintain a certain level of essential life elements: adequate sugar in the blood to nourish cells, sufficient water in the body, and so on. These critical levels are regulated by **homeostatic mechanisms.** These mechanisms sense imbalances in the body and stimulate actions that will restore the proper balance. The homeostatic mechanisms of the body are often compared to the thermostats of home heating systems. When the temperature of the house falls below a preset level, the thermostat senses that fact and signals the heater to produce heat until the proper temperature has been restored, then it signals the heater to turn off. Bodily responses to imbalances can involve both internal reactions and overt behavior. For instance, when the water level in body cells falls below a safe level, a signal is sent to the kidneys to reabsorb additional water from the urine. At the same time, a signal is sent to the brain that leads the animal—human or otherwise—to seek out and drink liquids. Similar homeostatic mechanisms are involved in hunger and the maintenance of body temperature.

Hunger: The Regulation of Food Intake

It's 10:30 A.M. and I am not hungry, but sometime in the next two or three hours, I will feel hungry enough to leave my typewriter and eat lunch. How will my body know that I need to eat? What will happen inside to make me feel hungry? And, how does this process regulate my food intake and body weight?

Over the past few years, I have been erratic about exercise. I played racquetball regularly for three months, did not exercise at all for six months, played again for six months, did nothing for a few months, and so on. Recently I have been lifting weights and doing aerobic exercise regularly for about six months, but a good example of how to maintain one's body, I'm not! Consistency is not one of my stronger qualities. But, my point is this: throughout all these changes in activity level—and similar changes in how wisely I ate—my body weight has stayed within a few pounds of 170. How is the body able to maintain its weight so precisely over such a long period of time, especially in view of large changes in activity level? We will answer these questions by taking a close look at the biological and psychological mechanisms of hunger, while making comments about being over or underweight as we go along.

Biological Regulation of Hunger

The biological control center of hunger is not the rumbling stomach but the **hypothalamus.** This small forebrain structure, which was first discussed in chapter 2, is involved in the regulation of a number of motives and emotions. Interestingly, two separate parts of the hypothalamus are involved in the regulation of eating in directly opposing ways. The hypothalamus contains a *feeding center* that initiates eating when food is needed and a *satiety center* that terminates eating when enough food has been consumed. The role of these hypothalamic centers has been dramatically demonstrated in experiments with rats. When the feeding center is electrically stimulated, rats that are too satiated (full) to eat, will begin eating again. If the feeding center is surgically destroyed, rats will stop eating altogether and starve to death if not artificially fed. Conversely, if the satiety center is surgically destroyed, the rats will overeat into a startling state of obesity (excessive fat). Figure 10.2 shows a normal rat and a **hyperphagic** rat whose body weight tripled after surgical destruction of the satiety center. These

homeostatic mechanism
(ho″me-o-stat′ik)
Internal bodily mechanism that senses biological imbalances and stimulates actions to restore the proper balance.

hypothalamus
(hi″po-thal′ah-mus)
The part of the forebrain involved with motives and emotions, and the functions of the autonomic nervous system.

hyperphagia
(hi″per-fa′je-ah)
Excessive overeating that results from the destruction of the satiety center of the hypothalamus.

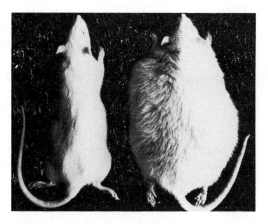

Figure 10.2 Destruction of the satiety center in the hypothalamus causes rats to eat themselves into a state of extreme obesity called hyperphagia. A normal rat is shown on the left.

rats do not eat more times each day than normal rats, but continue eating much longer each time they eat. Apparently the destruction of the satiety center eliminates the homeostatic signal to stop eating when enough food has been consumed.

Alexander Reeves and Fred Plumb (1969) reported a clinical case study of a human with damage to the satiety center in the hypothalamus that bears striking resemblance to hyperphagic laboratory animals. A 20-year-old bookkeeper sought medical help for her suddenly abnormal appetite and weight gain. A tumor was located through X rays in the hypothalamus, but it could not be surgically removed. Prior to her death three years later, she regularly consumed 10,000 calories per day in an endless attempt to satisfy her hunger. This case suggests that the role of the hypothalamus in the regulation of hunger in humans is similar to that of other animals. (See *Research Report:* "Obesity.")

But while the evidence for the dual role of the hypothalamus in the regulation of hunger is strong, recent evidence suggests that the biological mechanism is more complex than was once believed. It now seems likely that other forebrain structures near the hypothalamus also play a part in the regulation of hunger (Groves & Schlesinger, 1979).

What information does the hypothalamus use in regulating eating? Apparently two cues are used to regulate hunger on a daily basis, and a third cue is used to regulate body weight on a long-term basis.

1. *Stomach contractions.* It appears that Cannon and Washburn, whom we discussed at the beginning of the chapter, were partly right about the role of stomach contractions. The most immediate cue in the regulation of hunger really does come from the stomach. Contractions signal the feeding center, while a full stomach activates the satiety center.

2. *Blood sugar levels.* Eating is also regulated on a short-term basis by the amount of sugar (glucose) in the blood. The hypothalamus apparently contains specialized neurons that can detect the level of glucose in the bloodstream. The liver, which is a storehouse for sugar, also seems to be capable of sensing the level of blood glucose. When glucose begins to fall below the level needed to provide energy to the body cells, the feeding center activates the appetite. When eating has raised the concentration of glucose to a sufficient level, this fact is detected by the satiety center, which informs the organism to stop eating.

When the level of glucose in the blood is insufficient to provide energy to body cells, the hypothalamus activates the appetite.

RESEARCH REPORT

Obesity: Fat in Rats and Humans

As discussed in the text, rats whose satiety centers have been surgically destroyed overeat themselves into extreme obesity. Not only do they overeat, but their eating is peculiar in being strongly influenced by *external* factors. They will overeat, for example, only if the foods given to them *taste* good. If the food is made slightly bitter, they will eat less food than normal-weight rats. If the food is sweetened with sugar, on the other hand, they will eat more than normal rats. Taste is not the only external factor that influences the eating of rats with damaged satiety centers. They are also unwilling to exert much *effort* to get their food. If they have to work hard at pressing a lever to obtain food, the obese rats will obtain less than normal rats.

Stanley Schachter (1971) conducted a simple but interesting experiment to see if obese humans are also less willing to work for food than normal-weight people. Groups of obese and nonobese human subjects were asked to perform a routine task as part of a psychology experiment. Almonds were put out on a desk for the subjects to eat as they worked. For half of the subjects, the almonds were shelled and for half they were not shelled. The actual focus of the experiment was not on the task they were performing, but whether or not they ate the almonds. As shown in table 10.1, about half of the normal-weight subjects ate almonds whether they were shelled or not. In contrast, almost all of the obese subjects ate almonds if they were already shelled, but almost none of them were willing to work to shell the almonds. Like obese rats with damaged satiety centers, they were overly sensitive to the external factor of effort.

insulin (in'su-lin)
A hormone produced by the islets of Langerhans that reduces the amount of sugar in the bloodstream.

glucagon (gloo'kah-gon)
A hormone produced by the islets of Langerhans that causes the liver to release sugar into the bloodstream.

The role of blood glucose in the regulation of hunger has been experimentally demonstrated in three major ways. Two of the experimental methods involve the two hormones secreted by the islets of Langerhans. When **insulin** is injected into the bloodstream of a satiated person, it causes a drop in the level of glucose, and the person feels hungry. Conversely, when the hormone **glucagon** is injected into the bloodstream of a hungry person, it produces an increase in blood glucose, and the individual no longer feels hungry. Similarly, if blood from a rat that has recently eaten (and would be high in glucose) is injected into a rat that has been deprived of food, the food-deprived rat will not eat when given food. Blood glucose levels are a key mechanism in the control of hunger.

Since it takes a little time for food to be digested and enter the bloodstream in the form of glucose, dieters are often advised to eat more slowly to reach a level of blood glucose that makes them feel "full" *before* they reach their accustomed level of food intake. The widely sold "diet candies" can sometimes aid diets in much the same way. By eating a small amount of the sugary candy before

R E S E A R C H   R E P O R T

Table 10.1 Number of almonds eaten by overweight and normal-weight subjects when the almonds were shelled or unshelled

Subjects	Kind of Almonds	Number of Subjects Who Ate Almonds	
		Ate	*Did not eat*
Normal-weight	Shelled	11	9
	Unshelled	10	10
Overweight	Shelled	19	1
	Unshelled	1	19

From Schachter, Stanley, "Some extraordinary facts about obese rats and humans," in American Psychologist, 26, *129–144. Copyright 1971 American Psychological Association. Reprinted by permission of the author.*

Research on obese rats has led psychologists to take a new look at obesity in humans and see characteristics that they had not seen before. No one is suggesting that obese humans have suffered hypothalamic damage. They differ from rats with hypothalamic damage in a number of important ways and brain disorders have only been linked to human obesity in rare cases. But this line of research has led to some good diet hints. Obese individuals who are trying to lose weight should only keep low-calorie foods that do not taste especially good around the house. If preferred foods are in the house, dieters will be more likely to eat them. Also, obese individuals on diets should not keep food around that can be eaten without preparation. They should make themselves work hard for their food by preparing and cooking it from scratch. These two techniques often help reduce the intake of food.

each meal, the temporarily increased glucose level of the blood may lead to a feeling of fullness earlier and reduce the overall intake of food, presumably enough to more than compensate for the calories in the candy.

3. *Blood fat levels.* The long-term maintenance of body weight is managed by a different mechanism. It's apparently regulated by the ability of the hypothalamus to detect, in some as yet unknown way, the level of fat in the body. Probably the hypothalamus works by monitoring the level of the fat *glycerol* (Bennett & Gurin, 1982) in the blood. When an individual gains weight, blood glycerol increases. This increase may be detected by the hypothalamus, which could restore long-term body weight by signaling a decrease in eating or an increase in activity level that would burn off calories, or both. Less is known about the specific mechanisms involved in the regulation of long-term body weight, however, than the mechanisms that control daily eating. (See *Research Report:* "Fat and Thin Siamese Twins" for more on the role of blood fat in the regulation of hunger.)

Learning plays a role in eating habits. Many families encourage and model overeating.

Specific Hungers

Did you ever get a craving for a particular kind of food? Did you wonder if your body was trying to tell you something—that it needed a nutrient in that food? Animals who are experimentally deprived of protein, a vitamin, or fat, will tend to eat greater quantities of foods containing that element when later given a choice. For example, rats whose adrenal glands have been surgically removed—producing a fatal deficiency in the body's supply of sodium unless sodium is consumed in the form of salt—show a preference for salty water within 15 seconds of its being offered (Nachman, 1962). Such rats even prefer water containing lithium salts that make them sick afterward (Nachman, 1963). Since human eating is strongly influenced by learning and other psychological factors, it's not known whether we are as good as rats at listening to the nutritional needs of our bodies. But, that craving might be telling you something important.

Psychological Factors in Hunger

Although hunger is clearly a motive that is tied to biological needs, psychological factors are involved in the regulation of food intake as well. Learning plays a considerable role in determining *what* we eat, *when* we eat (we are often ready to eat at our customary times for eating, even if we have just had a snack), and even *how much* we eat (many families encourage and model overeating). Emotions also play a role in eating. People who are anxious often nibble and gorge more than usual, and people who are depressed may lose their appetite for long periods of time (ironically, though, individuals who get depressed in the middle of a diet often lose the will to diet and binge on food).

Perhaps the most troublesome psychological factors to those who are trying to control their eating, however, are **incentives.** How many times have you finished dinner at a restaurant or family gathering, feeling a bit overstuffed, only to be tempted into eating more by a seductive dessert? Incentives are external cues that activate motives. The smell of fresh-baked bread makes you hungry; passing a fast-food joint on your way home from school creates a craving for

incentive
An external cue that activates motivation.

RESEARCH REPORT

Fat and Thin Siamese Twins: Long-term Regulation of Weight

The ability of the hypothalamus to detect the level of fat in the body was demonstrated in a convincing, if unpleasant, experiment in which pairs of rats were surgically joined to create artificial *Siamese twins* (Hervey, 1959). They were joined in such a way that the blood of each animal mixed with that of the other, and the hypothalamic satiety center of *one* of the rats was surgically destroyed. This resulted in the characteristic overeating and obesity in the rat upon whom the operation had been performed. The interesting finding, however, concerned the weight of the other rat. As can be seen in figure 10.3, the rat who had not been operated upon became *thinner* as its Siamese twin became fatter. Something in the blood of the obese rat signaled the satiety center of the normal rat to reduce eating, to the point that it became thinner than normal. Hervey concluded from this research that the normal twin became thinner because it was able to detect the high amount of fat in the other animal through their mixed blood. The satiety center of the fat rat could not respond to the increased fat levels in the blood because it had been destroyed. These results are strong evidence for the ability of the hypothalamus to detect fat levels through the blood, although much remains to be learned about the mechanism involved.

Figure 10.3 "Siamese twin" rats created through surgery to study the long-term regulation of hunger and body weight. The satiety center of the rat on the right had been surgically destroyed (Hervey, 1959).

French fries; and the sight of the dessert creates a desire to eat even when you are way past the point of biological hunger. Incentives have their effect through the same brain mechanisms that regulate the biological aspects of hunger. The sight of food causes neurons in your hypothalamus to fire, particularly if it's a favorite food (Rolls, Burton, & Mora, 1976). The role of incentives in motivation is not limited to hunger; incentives are a factor in thirst, sex, and other motives as well.

Thirst: The Regulation of Water Intake

Just as we must control the intake of food to survive, we must also regulate the intake of water. What is the homeostatic mechanism involved in thirst? Actually, there are several mechanisms as in the case of hunger; like hunger also, the key regulatory centers are in the hypothalamus.

Biological Regulation of Thirst

A *drink center* and a *stop drinking* center are located in different sections of the hypothalamus. Surgical destruction of the drink center causes the animal to refuse water; destruction of the stop drinking center results in excessive drinking. Although the control centers for thirst occupy much of the same space as the centers for hunger, they operate separately by using different neurotransmitter substances (Grossman, 1960).

The hypothalamus uses three principal cues in regulating drinking: mouth dryness, loss of water by cells, and reductions in blood volume.

1. *Mouth dryness.* The thirst cue that we are most consciously aware of is dryness of the mouth. In the 1920s, biologist Walter Cannon studied the role of mouth dryness in thirst, this time using himself as the subject. After drinking large amounts of water to be sure he was not thirsty, he injected himself with a drug that stops the flow of saliva. Very soon, he felt thirsty. Next, he injected his mouth with a local anesthetic that blocked all sensations from his mouth. This quickly eliminated the sensation of being thirsty. Cannon concluded that mouth dryness was the cue that led to the sensation of thirst, but he was only partially correct again. We know today that other factors play more important roles.

2. *Cell fluid levels.* When the total amount of water in the body decreases, the concentration of salts increase in the fluids of the body. Of particular importance to the regulation of thirst are *sodium salts* that exist primarily in the fluids outside the body's cells (because salts cannot pass through the semipermeable membranes of the cells). Decreases in the total body fluids of even 1 to 2 percent produce increases in the sodium concentration that are large enough to draw water out of the cells and *dehydrate* them (Hole, 1978). This happens to cells throughout the body, but when certain specialized cells in the drink center of the hypothalamus dehydrate and shrivel, they send two messages to correct the situation. They chemically signal the **pituitary gland,** which is located just below the hypothalamic drink center, to secrete the **antidiuretic hormone (ADH)** into the bloodstream. When ADH reaches the kidneys, it causes them to conserve water in the body by reabsorbing it from the urine. In addition, the hypothalamic center simultaneously sends a message of thirst to the cerebral cortex, which initiates searching for and drinking liquids.

pituitary (pĭ-tu′ĭ-tār″e)
The body's master gland, located near the bottom of the brain, whose hormones help regulate the activity of the other glands in the endocrine system.

antidiuretic hormone (ADH) (an″ti-di″u-ret′ik)
A hormone produced by the pituitary that causes the kidneys to conserve water in the body by reabsorbing it from the urine.

Homeostatic mechanisms in the body signal the brain when the water level in body cells falls below a safe level.

3. *Total blood volume.* The third cue used by the hypothalamus to regulate thirst is total blood volume. As the volume of water in the body decreases, the volume of blood—which is mostly composed of water—decreases as well. A decreased volume of blood is first sensed by the kidneys. The kidneys react in two ways. First, they cause blood vessels to contract to compensate for the lowered amount of blood. Second, in a series of chemical steps, they cause the creation of the substance **angiotensin** in the blood. When angiotensin reaches the hypothalamus, the drink center sends a thirst message to the cerebral cortex, which eventually leads to drinking.

angiotensin
(an″je-o-ten′sin)
A substance in the blood that signals the hypothalamus that the body needs water.

Psychological Factors in Thirst

Psychological factors also play a role in the regulation of drinking, although overall this role does not appear to be as large as in hunger. Learning influences which beverages we drink (the average citizen of Nepal prefers yak's milk to cow's milk) and when we drink them (an advertising campaign was mounted a few years ago to convince us to drink orange juice at times other than breakfast). Incentives, such as the sight of a glass of beer, may activate thirst in a person who is otherwise not thirsty. But stress and emotions seem to have little effect on drinking compared to eating, except for the drinking of beverages that contain alcohol or stimulants (coffee, tea, colas, and so on) that alter mood.

Sexual Motivation

Without a sexual motive, humans and other animals that depend on sexual reproduction would soon be extinct. While hunger, thirst, and other primary motives are necessary for the survival of the individual, sexual motivation is a primary motive that is essential to the survival of the species. The same basic biological mechanisms are involved in sexual motivation in all mammals, but the biological controls that govern sexual behavior are less significant in humans than in most other animals.

Our hardworking friend the hypothalamus contains a center that functions in the initiating of sexual behavior. This center is the equivalent of the hypothalamic feeding and drinking centers. If it is surgically destroyed, sexual behavior will not be initiated even in the presence of provocative sexual stimuli. Another area of the hypothalamus and related brain structures serve as inhibitors of sexual behavior. If these areas are damaged, animals become hypersexual, that is, they engage in excessive sexual behavior.

In nonhuman mammals, hormones often play a major role in regulating sexual motivation. Female dogs, cats, and rats are receptive to sexual intercourse only when they are ovulating—a time referred to as being "in heat." Males of these species are less influenced by hormones than females and are receptive to sexual stimulation at most times. In some species, however—mice, deer, and goats, for example—males will engage in sexual intercourse only during annual or biannual seasons ("ruts") when they are producing sperm.

The sexual behavior of many species is also regulated by odors, such as those produced by your dog when she's in heat that attract every male dog in the neighborhood. Monkeys, apes, and humans appear to be much less influenced by hormones and odors than lower animals; but a little cologne probably does not hurt in attracting a mate.

In addition to the common brain centers involved, sex resembles the primary motives of hunger and thirst in other ways as well. Individuals who have been deprived of sex for long periods of time are more likely to engage in intercourse than a person who has just completed intercourse, much like a hungry person is more likely to eat than a person who has just eaten. The culmination of sexual acts, the *orgasm,* serves to release sexual tension, much as food and drink relieve hunger and thirst. And much as the incentive of an appealing kind of food will lead a full person to eat more, the sight of an attractive female can stimulate a sexually satisfied male (Wilson, Kuehn, & Beach, 1963). In addition, stress and emotions have a similar effect on sex and eating. Anxiety and depression are generally accompanied by a change in sexual motivation—usually a decrease, but sometimes an increase.

The sexual motive differs from other primary motives, however, in three major ways. First, although orgasms bring a reduction in the individual's "need" to have sex, it's clear that events that *increase* the desire to have sex are also highly reinforcing. The vast amount of money that is spent each year on sexually explicit magazines, movies, and other forms of erotic entertainment testify to this fact.

Second, sexual motivation differs from the other primary motives in the extent to which it's influenced by cognition, learning, and situational factors. Sex can be a physical pleasure, an expression of love, as well as a way to reproduce. For some it's intensely romantic, to others merely pleasurable; for some it's a way to feel masculine or feminine; to others it is evil and disgusting. Some individuals enjoy sex almost daily, while others vow never to engage in it for religious or other personal reasons. Eating and drinking are also influenced by psychological factors, but apparently not to the same extent as sex.

Third, as mentioned before, we do not have to satisfy our sexual motives to survive.

The Concept of Drive Reduction

In psychological terms, how do biological needs, such as dehydration of the body cells or lowered blood glucose levels, motivate our behavior? An answer to this question that was in vogue among psychologists until recent years involves the concept of **drive reduction.** In simple terms, the biological need is said to create an uncomfortable psychological state (called a *drive*) that compels us to act in a way (such as drinking or eating) that reduces the biological need and restores homeostasis. Thus, the drive directly activates and directs our behavior rather than the biological need.

drive reduction
The view that motives are based on the body's need to restore homeostasis when its biological needs are unmet.

The concept of drive reduction was tied by many theorists to the concept of positive reinforcement. It makes good sense to suppose that we would be reinforced by those things that restore homeostatic balance by reducing biological needs.

The concept of drive reduction successfully explains motives such as hunger and thirst. Clearly an imbalance in our body tissues is reduced when we drink or eat; and we have all experienced the conscious desire to eat or drink that corresponds roughly to what is meant by the term drive. The concept of drive is not successful in explaining some other phenomena, however. For example, it's easy to see how sexual arousal creates a drive state (even though there is no biological need involved) that is reduced by orgasm. But the concept of drive reduction cannot easily explain the fact that the opportunity to view sexually *arousing* films (which would presumably increase sexual drive) is reinforcing or the fact that rats will be reinforced by the opportunity to engage in incomplete acts of sexual intercourse that do not lead to orgasm (Sheffield, Wulff, & Backer, 1951). Furthermore, as we see in the next section, a number of motives are important in the regulation of human behavior that do not appear to be tied to biological needs at all. In the absence of biological needs, the concept of drive reduction makes little sense. Consequently, its use in present-day psychology is generally limited to biologically based motives. Unfortunately, no widely accepted general theory of motivation has taken the place of drive reduction.

R E V I E W

The term *primary motivation* refers to states based on biological needs that activate and guide behavior. Examples of primary motives include hunger, thirst, motives for maintaining warmth, and the avoidance of pain. These are motives that must be satisfied if the organism is to survive. Sexual motivation is also considered to be a primary motive, however. It's not necessary to satisfy this motive in order for the individual to survive, but satisfaction of the sexual motive is necessary for the survival of the species. Several of the primary motives are clearly linked to the body's need to maintain a proper level of nutrients, fluids, temperature, and the like, called the need to maintain homeostasis. The concept of drive has been used to explain how a homeostatic need of the body can influence behavior. This concept suggests that homeostatic needs create psychological states (drives) that the individual strives to reduce. Behaviors resulting in the reduction of a drive (and the restoration of homeostatic balance) will be reinforced by the drive reduction. The utility of the concept of drive reduction is limited only to those motives that are based on homeostatic needs, however.

Primary motives are generally based on a complex number of biological factors. For example, the control centers for eating and drinking are located in the hypothalamus. The hypothalamus responds directly or indirectly to a number of bodily signals that food or water is needed. In the case of hunger, stomach contractions, levels of blood glucose, and levels of blood fat are all involved in the regulation of eating. Thirst is similarly regulated by a combination of mouth dryness, level of fluids in the body cells, and the total volume of blood in the body.

Although the primary motives are based on biological survival needs, psychological factors are involved in these motives as well. External stimuli, such as the sight of a highly preferred food or beverage, can act as an incentive that activates eating or drinking, even when the individual is satiated. Learning also influences what, when, and how much we eat and drink.

psychological motives
Motives that are related to the individual's happiness and well-being, but not to survival.

novel stimulation
New or changed experiences.

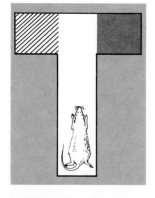

Figure 10.4 T-maze like those used to study stimulus motivation in rats.

Psychological Motives

Psychological motives are motives that are not directly related to the biological survival of the individual or the species. They are "needs" in the sense that the individual's happiness and well-being depend on these motives. Even more than primary motives, psychological motives vary considerably in the degree to which they are influenced by experience. Some psychological motives are found in every normal member of a species and seem to be innate, while others seem to be entirely learned. In this section, we look at three psychological motives: the need for novel stimulation, for affiliation with others, and for achievement.

Stimulus Motivation: Seeking Novel Stimulation

Did you ever come home to an empty house and flip on the radio or television just to kill the silence? Have you ever spent all day Saturday writing a term paper then feel you *have* to get up and take a walk or talk to someone just for sheer diversion? Most people get bored easily if there is little overall stimulation or if the stimulation is unchanging. We, and other animals, have an apparently inborn motive to seek **novel stimulation.**

If you put a rat in a T-maze (see fig. 10.4) in which it must choose between turning right into an alley painted gray or turning left into one painted with complex stripes, the rat will explore the more complex, more "interesting" alley first. But, next time, it will be more likely to turn into the gray alley that it has not seen yet, apparently because it is "curious" about it (Dember, 1965).

The need for novel stimulation motivated this monkey to learn to unlock the window that opens into the room with an electric train.

Figure 10.5 A monkey disassembling mechanical lock puzzles for no reward other than the activity and novel stimulation involved in the process.

Monkeys that are kept in boring cages will similarly work hard pressing a lever to earn a chance to look at other monkeys or even to watch a model train run (Butler, 1953). Monkeys will also work manual puzzles for hours without any reward except finally getting it apart (Harlow, Harlow, & Meyer, 1950) (see fig. 10.5). Watch a human infant play with his crib toys for a few minutes and you will see that humans, too, are motivated to manipulate, investigate, and generally shake up our environments. If you go without physical activity for a while, you will see that we have a need for activity, too.

Optimal Arousal Theory

Although there is no known homeostatic mechanism to account for our need for novel stimulation, we clearly need a certain amount of it in order to feel comfortable. But just as too little stimulation is unpleasant and will motivate us to increase stimulation, *too much* stimulation is unpleasant, too, and will motivate us to find ways to decrease it. Too many people talking at once, too much noise, or a room that contains too many clashing colors and patterns will send a person off in search of a few minutes of peace, quiet, and reduced stimulation. Apparently a desirable level of stimulation does exist; and we feel uncomfortable going either above or below this level (Korman, 1974).

Our apparent "need" for an optimal level of stimulation has led psychologists to suggest that each individual strives to maintain an **optimal level of arousal** in the nervous system. Arousal, as used in this way, is a rather vague term, but it refers to the overall state of alertness and activation of the person. The individual who is sleeping is at a very low level of arousal; the relaxed person is at a somewhat higher level; the active, alert person is functioning at a moderate level; the anxious person is experiencing a high level of arousal; and the person who is in a frenzied panic is at an extremely high level. Arousal is linked to the activity of the **reticular formation** described in chapter 2 and, at higher levels of arousal at least, to the activity of the sympathetic division of the autonomic nervous system. Optimal arousal theory does not suggest, however, that there is a biological need for a moderate or optimal level of arousal. The individual can survive at high or low levels of arousal, but he or she is motivated to achieve a comfortable, optimal level of arousal by acting in ways that increase or decrease stimulation.

Arousal and Performance: The Yerkes–Dodson Law

Not only is arousal an important motivational concept, it's also linked to the efficiency of our performance in various situations. If arousal is too low, performance will be inadequate; if it's too high, performance may become disrupted and disorganized. This simple notion is often referred to as the **Yerkes–Dodson law,** but it's somewhat more complicated than it looks at first. The level of arousal ideal for different kinds of performance differs considerably. Football players "warm up" and "psych up" physically and emotionally to reach high levels of arousal for the game. It would be difficult to exceed the ideal level of arousal needed for highly physical contact sports. On the other hand, the performance of a skilled craftsperson applying pottery glazes by hand would be most efficient at much lower levels of arousal (see fig. 10.6). Too much arousal, as in the form of high levels of anxiety, would tend to disrupt the delicate, skilled performance of the potter.

Affiliation Motivation

Do you usually enjoy being with friends? Do you feel lonely during periods when you do not have many friends? Human beings are social creatures: Given the opportunity, we generally prefer to be with other people. In this sense, it can be said that people have a **motive for affiliation.**

---

optimal level of arousal
The apparent human need for a comfortable level of stimulation, achieved by acting in ways that increase or decrease it.

reticular formation
(re-tik′u-lar)
The system of neural structures spanning parts of the hindbrain, midbrain, and forebrain that play a role in cortical arousal and attention.

Yerkes–Dodson law
A law stating that effective performance is more likely if the level of arousal is suitable for the activity.

motive for affiliation
The need to be with other people and to have personal relationships.

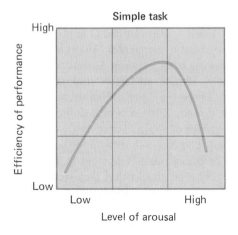

Simple task

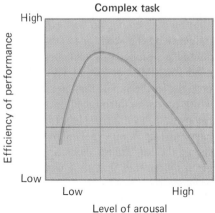

Complex task

Figure 10.6 The Yerkes-Dodson law describes the relationship between the amount of arousal and the efficiency of performance. In general, either insufficient or excessive arousal results in insufficient performance, but the optimal level of arousal is higher for simple, physically active tasks than for complex, highly skilled tasks.

Human beings are social creatures that have a motive for affiliation.

The need for affiliation is presumably present in all normal humans, but most research on this topic concerns differences between individuals who have different levels of this motive. Individuals who are high in the need for affiliation, for example, tend to prefer being with others rather than satisfying other motives. When asked to perform a clerical task with a partner, individuals who are high in the need for affiliation, but low in need for achievement, choose to work with a friend, regardless of how competent the friend is. In contrast, individuals who are low in the need for affiliation, but high in need for achievement, choose the partner that they believe to be most competent (French, 1956).

Some research has looked at factors that influence how much need for affiliation a given person will exhibit at a particular point in time. One important influence on the need for affiliation is anxiety. Stanley Schachter (1959) has conducted a number of experiments on the relationship between anxiety and the need for affiliation. In a typical experiment, female university students were brought to the laboratory in small groups. There they met a man dressed in a white coat who introduced himself as a Dr. Gregor Zilstein, a professor of Neurology and Psychiatry. He told half of the groups of subjects that they would be participating in an experiment involving painful electric shocks—and they were shown the forbidding shock apparatus in the background. The other half of the groups were told that they would receive very mild shocks that they would experience as a mere tickle. Presumably, the first group was made far more anxious than the second group, a presumption that was validated by the student's own ratings of their anxiety. Both groups were given the choice of waiting alone in individual waiting rooms or together in a group waiting room.

As Schachter predicted, almost two-thirds of the subjects who were made to feel anxious chose to wait in groups, indicating a high level of need for affiliation. However, only one-third of the low anxiety group chose to wait together. Apparently, anxiety increases our motive to affiliate— "misery loves company" as the saying goes. Schachter found, however, that the effect of anxiety on the desire to affiliate was strongest for firstborn siblings or only children. Other research has also pointed to the presence of higher need for affiliation in firstborn males and females (Dember, 1964). Perhaps, there is something about the way that firstborns were reared that makes affiliation more important to them.

Achievement Motivation

achievement motivation (n Ach)
The psychological need in humans for success in competitive situations.

Who was voted "most likely to succeed" in your high school class? Was he or she a "go-getter" who was willing to work hard to gain success? Someone who was not afraid to accept responsibility and seemed to perform best in competitive situations? If so, your class probably voted for someone high in **achievement motivation,** abbreviated as **n Ach** (need to achieve). Achievement motivation is the psychological need for success in school, sports, occupation, and other competitive situations. Chances are very good that this person went into an occupation that provides rewards for *individual* achievement, such as sales, engineering, architecture, or law, rather than one that does not single out successful individuals for rewards, such as a government bureaucratic job. Chances are, too, that your high school's most likely to succeed went into an occupation that was realistically matched to his or her abilities. Individuals who are high in *n Ach* generally experience little anxiety or fear of failure, but tend to choose jobs and other challenges (such as college courses) in which they have a realistic chance for success. And when success is achieved, the high *n Ach* individual enjoys the fruits of his or her labors more than the average person (Atkinson, 1964; McClelland, Atkinson, Clark, & Lowell, 1953).

Achievement Motivation and the Type A Personality

The description of the person high in *n Ach* is a positive one of calm, energetic success, and this is a generally accurate portrait. The price that some high achievers pay, however, is substantial. Some individuals high in *n Ach* experience more than the average amount of *somatic* (bodily) tension, manifested as aches, pains, and illnesses. The key to whether or not a high *n Ach* person will experience serious somatic problems seems to be the individual's amount of *hostility.*

Highly motivated achievers who compete in an aggressive, hostile manner may have Type A personality, which is associated with increased risk of heart disease.

Some highly motivated achievers become excessively angry when they are interrupted or, worse still, when they fail. Such individuals compete in an aggressive, hostile manner at all times. They do not play tennis for fun or exercise but to *beat* their opponent, and they become upset if they lose.

Cardiologists Meyer Friedman and Ray Rosenman (1974) have termed this type of hostile, achievement-oriented person the **Type A personality.** Other common characteristics of the Type A personality include directing conversations to topics that interest him or her and loud, explosive speech patterns. In addition, Type A personalities have a pervasive sense of time urgency and a belief that people who act quickly succeed; as a result, they often do two things at once to save time (Diamond, 1982; Matthews, 1982). There is a little Type A personality in most of us, and you should be concerned only if it's excessive. The reason that two heart specialists are interested in Type A behavior is that it takes a serious toll on the body. In one study of 3,400 men age 39 to 49, the frequency of heart disease was 6.5 times higher than normal in Type A men (Friedman & Rosenman, 1974), and in other large-scale study the risk for cardiac disease was twice as high in Type A men and women (Rosenman & Chesney, 1982). It is not clearly known how Type A personality is related to cardiac disease, but across a number of studies, Type A individuals have been shown to respond to frustrating, difficult situations with greater increases in blood pressure, blood cholesterol, and other substances that are related to heart disorders (Haynes, Feinlieb, & Kannel, 1980; Matthews, 1982).

Type A personality
A personality type characterized by high n Ach, a sense of time urgency, and hostility.

Fear of Failure and Fear of Success

There can be great costs of being high in *n Ach* if the person falls into the hostile Type A pattern. And, even more relaxed high achievers must learn to balance the demands of hard success-oriented work with the need for leisure, family, and friends. However, being low in *n Ach* does not guarantee a happy life either. Many low *n Ach* people are not interested in achieving status or material success and are happy to spend their time and energy in other ways. Many other individuals low in *n Ach,* however, are very anxious in competitive situations, such as tests and sales competitions, and greatly fear failure. These emotions may lead some individuals to avoid competitive occupations for which they are otherwise well suited or to experience considerable discomfort if they do enter such jobs (Atkinson, 1964).

Several researchers have shown that not only is a fear of failure common, but so is a fear of *success*. Individuals are said to fear success if they are overly concerned about the pressures and responsibilities that are associated with success or concerned that success would lead to their rejection by others. Psychologist Matina Horner (1969) studied fear of success by asking women to complete sentences that begin like, "After the first term finals, Anne finds herself at the top of her medical school class. . . ." How would you complete that sentence? If you found yourself in that situation, would you enjoy your success, feel pressured to continue to be first, or fear ostracism by jealous classmates? Horner found that fear of success was common in women and felt that it was related to the passive, noncompetitive roles that women have been expected to assume in our society. Because many women have been taught that they should be homemakers and nurses, they fear rejection from men and other women if they become engineers or physicians, Horner believes.

More recent research using Horner's sentence-completion technique, however, suggests that fear of success is no more common in females than in males (Morgan & Mausner, 1973). However, when males and females were placed in direct competition in laboratory tasks, females were less competitive (House, 1974; Morgan & Mausner, 1973). Although we have come a long way toward eliminating prejudicial stereotypes about women's roles, females in our culture still may be less willing than males to take the risks involved in success. Or alternatively, women may accurately perceive that the risks are still greater for females (Jung, 1978).

Origins of Achievement Motivation

Achievement motivation is probably a learned motive. Evidence for this proposition comes from several sources. For example, boys with high *n Ach* tend to have fathers who are in occupations that demand individual achievement (Turner, 1970). Probably these fathers encourage, model, and reinforce achievement in their sons. More strikingly, as first discussed in the Prologue to chapter 5, Ruth Benedict (1934) long ago showed that there are cultures in the world where individual achievement is not only considered undesirable but also repugnant and embarrassing. The Zuñi Indians, who once flourished in the desert southwest of the United States, actively avoid personal achievement or recognition. An individual who found himself in the public spotlight—such as by heroically saving a child from stampeding horses—would be so embarrassed that he would banish himself from the tribe and physically punish himself for months before feeling ready to return quietly. Further evidence along these lines has been provided by David McClelland. He was able to show the influence of learning on *n Ach* by *teaching* it to business leaders from countries that were traditionally low in achievement motivation. The teaching not only raised scores on measures of *n Ach* but also increased their business productivity as well (McClelland & Winter, 1969).

Solomon's Opponent-Process Theory of Acquired Motives

Richard Solomon (1980) of the University of Pennsylvania has proposed a theory that has important implications for our learning of *new* motives, particularly ones that are difficult to understand in any other way. Why do some people love to jog, fight in karate matches, or parachute out of airplanes? How do some people become so "addicted" to their spouses, boyfriends, or girlfriends that they cannot leave them, even when they *do not enjoy* being with them anymore?

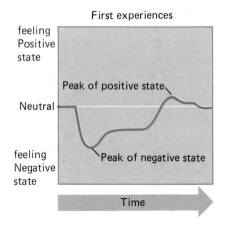

First experiences

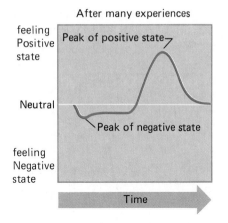

After many experiences

Figure 10.7 General illustration of Solomon's opponent-process theory of acquired motives as it applies to initially negative experiences, such as parachute jumping (Solomon, 1980).

Solomon provides an intriguing answer to these and other questions with his **opponent-process theory of motivation.** (Make a note to yourself not to confuse this with the opponent-process theory of color vision on the final exam!) Solomon explains craving such diverse things as parachute jumping, drugs, and lost lovers by means of two concepts: (1) every state of positive feeling is followed by a *contrasting* negative feeling, and vice versa, and (2) any feeling—either positive or negative—that is experienced many times in succession loses some of its intensity.

The classic example is parachute jumping. Solomon summarizes data (that no one doubts!) that makes it clear that parachute jumping is frightening at first. Novice jumpers show many verbal and nonverbal signs that they are scared (if you consider sweating, screaming, and wetting your pants signs of being scared. . . .). When the novice jumper lands, he or she is generally in a mild state of shock, but soon begins smiling and talking excitedly about the jump. That is, the negative state of fear is followed by the contrasting positive state of euphoria. The shift from negative fear to positive euphoria that reinforces the act of jumping is shown graphically in the left-hand part of figure 10.7. But, after many jumps, the fear becomes less intense. This change is shown in the right side of figure 10.7. There is a lessening in fear from the first experiences with jumping to later jumps. But, note that the amount of reinforcing *contrast* in the two parts of figure 10.7 stays the same. This means that as the fear is reduced the amount of euphoria produced afterward becomes even stronger. This is Solomon's explanation of the learning of new motives like karate, motorcycle racing, and jogging—even using saunas. Not only does the initial negative state diminish due to repetition, but you get hooked by the contrasting shift to increasingly more intense levels of positive feeling.

The process of becoming addicted to things that feel good at first follows the opposite course. The wonderful, druglike feeling that comes from being with that new guy that you have a crush on, for example, is followed by a contrasting feeling of missing him when he is not with you. Not only is being with him positive, but getting him back is doubly reinforcing because it stops the negative feeling of missing him. Furthermore, as the positive feelings diminish, as shown in figure 10.8, the feeling of missing—even needing—the loved one becomes more intense. If you stop seeing him because the positive feeling is gone, it is this negative feeling of missing him that motivates you to go back. This is Solomon's explanation for why it's often so hard to end a loveless relationship. It's not the happiness that holds you—that is long since gone—it's the negative withdrawal

opponent-process theory of motivation
Solomon's theory of the learning of new motives based on changes over time in contrasting feelings.

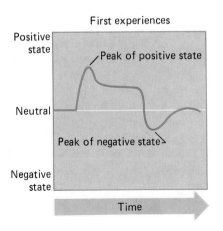

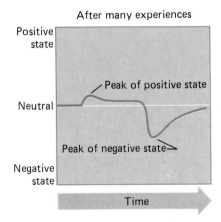

Figure 10.8 General illustration of Solomon's opponent-process theory of acquired motives as it applies to initially positive experiences such as taking euphoric drugs (Solomon, 1980).

symptoms that are so difficult to get through. If this sounds like a drug addiction, it's no accident. Solomon sees addictions to heroin and other drugs as forming in exactly the same way. First comes the pleasurable "rush," followed by the uncomfortable feeling of coming down. After frequent use, the pleasure of using the drug (cocaine, nicotine, etc.) in the same amount is greatly diminished, but the pain of withdrawal is much worse. It's the pain of withdrawal that powerfully motivates the addict to take more of the drug, not the diminished pleasure that the drug brings. Solomon's theory is not relevant to all motives, but may help us understand the learning of some perplexing new ones.

Intrinsic and Extrinsic Motivation

intrinsic motivation
(in-trin′sik)
Human motives stimulated by the inherent nature of the activity or its natural consequences.

extrinsic motivation
(eks-trin′sik)
Human motives stimulated by external rewards.

Psychologists have found it useful to distinguish between intrinsic and extrinsic motivation. We speak of **intrinsic motivation** when the person is motivated by the inherent nature of the activity or its natural consequences or both. For example, the monkeys that we mentioned earlier who will take apart mechanical puzzles for no reward other than getting them apart are intrinsically motivated to solve puzzles. Similarly, people who donate anonymously to charity because they wish to contribute without being recognized are intrinsically motivated. **Extrinsic motivation,** on the other hand, is external to the activity and not an inherent part of it. If a child who hates to do arithmetic homework is encouraged to do so by payment of a nickel for every correct answer, he is extrinsically motivated. That is, he works for the external payment rather than for an intrinsic interest in math.

Perhaps the most interesting and significant issue concerning the distinction between intrinsic and extrinsic motivation is the question of when extrinsic rewards should be supplied by parents, teachers, and employers in an effort to increase motivation. When is it wise to use extrinsic motivation in the form of positive reinforcement to increase the frequency of some behavior (such as completing homework, delivering packages on time, and so on)? There is considerable evidence suggesting that if a behavior occurs infrequently—and its intrinsic motivation can be assumed low for that individual—then extrinsic motivation is successful in increasing the frequency of occurrence of the behavior. Children who hate to do their math homework often will do it diligently if rewarded with additional allowance money. And because of the success they experience, they

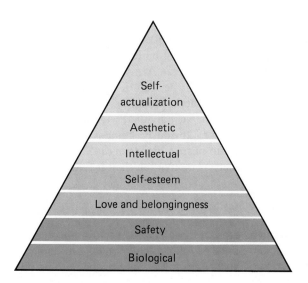

Figure 10.9 Maslow's hierarchy of needs (Maslow, 1970).

will sometimes come to enjoy math (Rimm & Masters, 1979). On the other hand, if the individual is already intrinsically motivated to perform an activity, adding extrinsic motivation will often detract from the intrinsic motivation. For example, when young children who like to draw pictures in school were given certificates for good drawing, they drew pictures less often than children who had not received certificates (Lepper, Greene, & Nisbett, 1973). We must be careful to avoid squelching intrinsic motivation by providing unnecessary extrinsic rewards.

Maslow's Hierarchy of Motives

We have touched on only a few of the human motives, but it's already obvious that we are creatures of many and varied needs. Abraham Maslow (1970) has put forward an interesting theory about our many motives. According to Maslow, we are not a crazy-quilt confusion of motives; rather, our motives are organized in a hierarchy arranged from the most basic to the personal and advanced.

 Maslow's hierarchy of motives (needs) is shown in figure 10.9. If lower needs in the hierarchy are not met for the most part, then higher motives will not operate. Higher needs lie dormant until the individual has a chance to satisfy immediately pressing lower needs like hunger, thirst, and safety. When the lower needs have been met, then motives to develop relationships with others, to achieve a positive self-esteem, and to produce art, philosophy, or to otherwise realize one's full potential (**self-actualization**) become important to the individual.

 Maslow's hierarchy of motives helps to explain such things as why starving peasant farmers are not particularly interested in the political philosophies of rival governments; or why, throughout history, science, art, and philosophy have mostly been produced when a nation could afford to have a privileged class who did not have to work to eat. The concept of the hierarchy of motives also helps us understand why a person would give up a prestigious, but time-consuming, career to try to save a marriage with a much-loved spouse. Higher motives become unimportant when lower motives are unmet.

Maslow's hierarchy of motives
The concept that more basic needs must be met before higher level motives become active.

self-actualization
According to Maslow, the seldomly reached full result of the inner-directed drive of humans to grow, improve, and use their potential to the fullest.

But as helpful as Maslow's hierarchy of motives is, there are some obvious exceptions to it. The hierarchy does not explain why an individual would risk his life to rescue a friend from a burning building. Nor does it explain why imprisoned members of the Irish Republican Army intentionally starved themselves to death in 1981 to gain what might be seen to outsiders as minor changes in the way they were treated as prisoners. Similarly, the hierarchy fails to shed light on the common occurrence of an individual's ignoring spouse and children to pursue self-esteem in a career. Obviously, humans are sometimes willing to endure unmet lower motives to pursue higher ones. Still, Maslow's hierarchy appears to explain more facets of motivation than it fails to explain.

R E V I E W

Psychological motives are not directly linked to the biological survival of the individual or species. Some psychological motives are common to all normal members of a species and seem to be innate, while others appear to be primarily, if not entirely, learned. The stimulus motive—the need to maintain a moderate level of novel stimulation and activity—is an example of an apparently inborn psychological motive. The stimulus motive has led psychologists to speculate that individuals seek to maintain an optimal level of arousal in the nervous system by regulating stimulus input and activity levels.

Motives for achievement and affiliation seem to be more influenced by learning and differ from individual to individual or culture to culture. Competitive males who seek occupations with a high probability of personal success and willingly accept responsibility tend to have fathers with similar traits, suggesting that the men learn this achievement motive from their fathers. Other individuals appear to avoid competitive occupations because they have learned either to fear failure or to fear success. Learning also appears to be an important factor in the need for affiliation—the desire to be with others—because this need is generally stronger in firstborn and only children, who may have been reared differently from later-born children. Increased levels of anxiety also tend to increase the need to affiliate. Some motives are intrinsic; that is, individuals engage in the activity because of its inherent value. Other motives are extrinsic and will only stimulate action if there is an external incentive.

The many human motives do not appear to operate as a disorganized hodgepodge; rather they appear to be organized in a hierarchy. Lower-level motives, particularly the biological motives, must be satisfied before motives higher in the hierarchy become active and important.

Emotions: Feelings, Physiology, and Behavior

What do poets write about? Of all the facets of human existence, which do they choose for their themes? It's not depth perception, neural transmission, or cognitive development; it's not classical conditioning or intelligence. They write mostly about *emotions,* the experiences that give color, meaning, and intensity to our lives. One obvious reason poets focus on emotions is that emotions are interesting. People love to mull over their feelings and passions, and to learn about the real or imagined emotions of others. If not, poems, plays, novels, and soap operas probably would not exist. But there is another reason why poets write about emotions: trying to capture emotions in words is such a *challenge.* Psychologists, too, find it difficult to write about emotions. There is probably more disagreement on how to define the word emotion than any other term in psychology.

In recent books on emotion, Robert Plutchik (1980) quoted 28 different definitions of emotion, and K. T. Strongman (1973) summarized 20. Still there is some agreement among psychologists as to what emotions are. Most definitions distinguish the same four elements to define emotion: (1) there is a *stimulus situation* that provokes the reaction; (2) there is a positively or negatively toned conscious experience—the "emotion" that we feel; (3) there is a bodily state of *physiological arousal* produced by the autonomic nervous system and endocrine glands; and (4) there is related *behavior* that generally accompanies emotions— the animal that is afraid cringes, trembles, then runs.

How many different emotions are there? Do you know? Do not feel bad if you do not, because psychologists do not know either. Even though most of us have probably experienced most emotions, psychologists cannot agree on how many different emotions there are. This really is not too surprising when you consider that a full listing of emotions would have to deal with many subtle distinctions. How is *liking* a person different from *respecting* a person? How does *love* differ for a spouse, a child, a parent, or a lover?

It's more surprising, however, that we have not been able to at least agree on a list of the most basic emotions. Carroll Izard (1972) thinks there are nine basic emotions: interest, joy, surprise, distress, anger, disgust, contempt, shame, and fear. All other emotions are thought to be combinations of these basic ones. For example, anxiety is a mixture of fear with two or more other basic emotions (distress, anger, shame, guilt, or interest). Plutchik (1980) names eight somewhat different, basic emotions and has different ideas as to how they are combined to create complex emotions. But no scientist has yet been fully able to capture emotion in words in a way that would lead even most other psychologists to agree.

Three Theories of Emotion

Perhaps the most important differences among psychologists concern the way they believe the four elements of emotions (stimulus, conscious experience, physiological arousal, and behavior) are related to one another. Three main theories have been proposed to explain the workings of emotions. (Refer to fig. 10.10 as you read the following theories.)

Emotions are experiences that give color, meaning, and intensity to our lives.

1. James–Lange theory

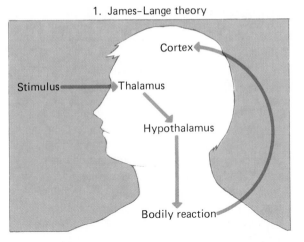

2. Cannon–Bard theory

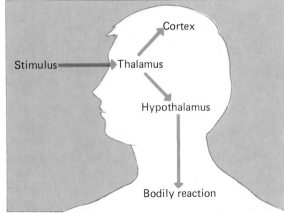

3. Cognitive theories

Arnold–Ellis version

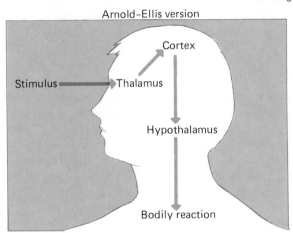

Schachter–Singer version

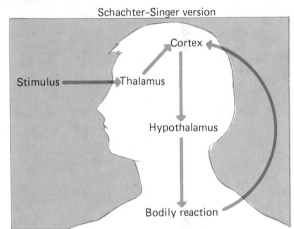

James–Lange Theory

The common sense view of emotions is that the stimulus of seeing a mugger makes one consciously feel afraid and that the conscious fear leads us to tremble and run. William James (1890) suggested that this view is just backward, however. He believed that the emotional stimulus is routed (by the sensory relay center known as the thalamus) directly to the hypothalamus, which produces the bodily reactions of fear. The sensations from this bodily reaction are then sent back to the cortex and produce what we feel in the conscious experience of emotion. According to James, "we feel sorry because we cry, angry because we strike, afraid because we tremble." A number of years later, Danish physiologist Carl Lange (1922) independently proposed the same theory so it's known today as the **James–Lange theory of emotion.**

Figure 10.10 Illustration of the three major theories of emotion: (1) the James–Lange theory, (2) the Cannon–Bard theory, and (3) the cognitive theories of Arnold and Ellis and Schachter and Singer.

OF SPECIAL INTEREST

Lie Detectors:
Can We Measure the Physiology of Guilt?

A common part of police investigations of crimes is the *lie-detector test*. In this test, the individual is asked questions about the crime while physiological measurements are taken that indicate sympathetic arousal of the autonomic nervous system—such as sweating, blood pressure, heart rate, breathing rate, and muscle tension—using a device called a *polygraph*. This test is based on the fairly solid assumption that people react emotionally—autonomically—when they tell lies.

When properly conducted, the lie-detector examination uses a procedure known as the *guilty knowledge test*. In this procedure, the individual is asked questions about information that would be known only by the guilty party. For example, the examiner might ask if the person had stolen a long list of items (e.g., ring, watch, wallet). If the suspect answered ''no'' to most of the items, but showed an emotional response only to those items that were actually stolen, the results would suggest the guilt of the suspect. The guilty knowledge test is necessary because even innocent people often react emotionally to questions like ''Did you rob the Smith's house?''

The idea behind lie-detector tests is a good one, but there are some serious problems with it. First, polygraph operators are not licensed in all states, and many are poorly trained to conduct examinations. Second, some hardened criminals feel little or no guilt about their crimes so do not appear guilty in the examination. Perhaps the most important problem, however, is the fact that lie-detector tests are not completely accurate. They are estimated to be wrong *at least* 5 percent of the time (Lykken, 1979), and may be inaccurate far more often than that (Saxe, Doughterty, & Cross, 1985). Five percent is not a large percentage, but it's a significant one when you consider that it could lead to the release of 5 out of 100 guilty individuals or the conviction of 5 innocent ones.

Since you are not likely to commit a crime, the shortcomings of lie-detector tests may seem like a pretty abstract issue. But it may be directly relevant to you some day. A growing number of large companies use lie-detector tests to screen potential employees or to reevaluate their honesty each year. This means that you might very well have to take a lie-detector test, with a great deal riding on the accuracy of the results. This is particularly troubling when you realize that the chances of error are probably higher than 5 percent when broad questions are asked such as ''Have you ever stolen from your employer?'' or ''Have you ever used illegal drugs?''

OF SPECIAL INTEREST

James–Lange theory of emotion
The theory that conscious emotional experiences are caused by feedback to the cerebral cortex from physiological reactions and behavior.

Because we tend to "feel" emotions throughout our bodies rather than just in our heads, the James–Lange theory makes sense. But several years after the death of William James, Harvard University biologist Walter Cannon (1927) published a set of strong criticisms of the James–Lange theory. His four major points were as follows:

1. Animals whose nerves have been surgically cut to deprive them of feedback from the organs aroused by the autonomic nervous system still seem to experience normal emotional reactions.

2. The physiological reactions that accompany different emotions are so similar that it's hard to see how a person could feel distinctly different emotions like fear and rage simply from the first sensory feedback provided by autonomic arousal.

3. The internal organs respond relatively slowly to the autonomic nervous system—too slowly, according to Cannon, to provide the nearly instantaneous emotional experience involved, for example, in seeing a mugger.

4. Artificially inducing physiological arousal by injecting human subjects with the hormone adrenaline produces a sensation of arousal, but not a feeling of emotion.

Cannon's criticisms did not disprove the James–Lange theory, but they certainly made it seem less plausible.

Interestingly, contemporary psychologist Carroll Izard (1972; 1977) has modified the James–Lange theory in order to get around Cannon's criticisms. Izard believes that the most important sensory feedback in producing the conscious experience of emotion comes from *facial muscles*. Smile for a few seconds, then frown. Did you feel a little happier and then sadder? Most people do a little. Could emotions be that simple? Are they only sensory feedback from facial muscles?

There is some evidence that favors Izard's update of the James–Lange theory of emotion. For one thing, the facial expression of emotions in both Western and non-Western cultures around the world has been found to be surprisingly similar. Five emotional expressions in particular have been found to be almost universal—anger, disgust, happiness, sadness, and a combination of surprise and fear. Even people who have been blind from birth and cannot see facial expressions of emotions in others show the five basic emotional expressions themselves (Ekman & Oster, 1979). This suggests that these patterns of emotional expression are inborn in humans and supports Izard's contention that facial expressions are important in emotions. Furthermore, there is some experimental support for Izard's theory. Subjects who were given electrical shocks reported less pain when they were told to make no facial reactions to the shock than when they let their emotions show in their faces. Perhaps the sensory feedback from their facial expressions made the difference in the amount of pain they experienced (Colby, Lanzetta, & Kleck, 1977).

OF SPECIAL INTEREST

Body Language: Nonverbal Communication of Emotion

In 1970 Julius Fast wrote a best-selling book called *Body Language.* Its message was that people often communicate a lot about their feelings through their posture and movements, sometimes more than they are willing to tell you in words. The book may have overstated its case, but the idea is a sound one. People do express their feelings in nonverbal ways. And it's not just the body that carries meaning. Facial expressions and tone of voice convey a great deal of information about emotion. Most of us are pretty good at reading this "body language." Sneers, flirtatious postures, and angry stances are usually easy to interpret. Still, communication problems do occur with body language. If your date is still and formal in posture, does that reveal a lack of interest in you, or does it reflect so much interest that he or she is scared that you will not return the affection? A great deal of research has been conducted on the nonverbal communication of emotions, but because it's a complex subject, not enough is currently known to offer you a foolproof guide to the accurate reading of bodies.

This evidence from cross-cultural and experimental studies supports Izard's theory but not conclusively. Unfortunately for Izard's theory, people with total paralysis of the facial muscles can still experience normal emotions (Plutchik, 1980). While sensory feedback from face and gut are probably *part* of many emotional experiences, it seems unlikely that that is all there is to the conscious experience of an emotion.

Cannon–Bard Theory

Walter Cannon (1927) did not just criticize the James–Lange theory, he proposed an alternative theory of his own. This theory was later revised by Philip Bard (1934) and is known as the **Cannon–Bard theory of emotion.** Cannon believed that information from the emotional stimulus goes first to the brain relay center called the thalamus. From there, the information is simultaneously relayed *both* to the cerebral cortex, where it produces the emotional experience, and to the hypothalamus and autonomic nervous system, where it produces the physiological arousal that prepares the animal to fight, run away, or react in some other way. To Cannon and Bard, the conscious emotional experience and physiological arousal are two simultaneous and largely independent events.

Cannon–Bard theory of emotion
The theory that conscious emotional experience and physiological reactions and behavior are relatively independent events.

*Drawing by Koren; © 1981 The
New Yorker Magazine, Inc.*

"David, you're denying your feelings again, aren't you?"

Cognitive Theories

A number of individuals have proposed a third theory of emotion in which *cognitive interpretation* of the incoming stimulus in the cerebral cortex is the key event. In our discussion, we distinguish between two versions of cognitive theory, one proposed by Magda Arnold (1960) and Albert Ellis (1962), and a second proposed by Stanley Schachter and Jerome Singer (1962).

Arnold–Ellis Cognitive Theory. The cognitive theory of Arnold and Ellis harkens back to the ancient Greek philosopher Epictetus who said, "People are not affected by events, but by their interpretations of them." For example, if you receive a box in the mail that makes a ticking sound, will you be happy or afraid? If the return address says the box is from Violet, and Violet is your deadly enemy, you might think it contains a time bomb and feel afraid. If Violet is a loving friend, however, you would open the box feeling happy, expecting to find a clock. In this case, the interpretation of the stimulus, not the stimulus itself, causes the emotional reaction. Thus, in the **Arnold–Ellis cognitive theory of emotion,** information from the stimulus travels first to the cerebral cortex where it's both interpreted and experienced, then a message is sent down to the autonomic nervous system that results in physiological arousal. This theory of emotion has been the topic of a rather heated debate between two eminent researchers in recent years (Lazarus, 1982, 1984; Zajonc, 1980, 1984). In spite of their best efforts, however, it is probably safe to say that neither proponents nor few readers' minds were changed.

Arnold–Ellis cognitive theory of emotion
The theory that emotional reactions are dependent on cognitive interpretations of stimulus situations.

R E S E A R C H   R E P O R T

Cognitions and Emotions

Evidence that supports the Arnold–Ellis cognitive theory was provided by an experiment in which four groups of college students were shown an upsetting film showing a number of crude circumcisionlike operations conducted without anesthesia as part of the puberty ceremony of an Australian aborigine tribe (Speisman, Lazarus, Mordkoff, & Davison, 1964). One group of subjects saw the film without a soundtrack. A second group heard a soundtrack that emphasized the agony experienced by the boys. A third group heard a soundtrack that described the operations in a detached intellectual way. And a fourth group heard a soundtrack that ignored the painful operation by talking about irrelevant details. Although all of the subjects saw the same film, the soundtracks apparently had a big effect on their cognitive interpretation of what they saw. The group who heard the soundtrack emphasizing the agony of the operations showed much greater autonomic arousal than the group with no soundtrack. The soundtrack that emphasized the agony led to an interpretation of the film as a more upsetting stimulus. The groups who heard soundtracks that deemphasized the emotional nature of the events, either by intellectualizing or ignoring it, showed less autonomic arousal. The cognitive element (the contents of the soundtrack) considerably altered the emotional meaning of the film.

The Arnold–Ellis cognitive theory of emotion has played an important role in clinical psychology during the past 15 years. It has led to the development of methods of psychotherapy designed to teach depressed and anxious individuals to interpret stimuli in less emotionally disturbing ways (Beck, 1976; Ellis, 1962). (See *Research Report:* "Cognitions and Emotions" for additional evidence that supports the Arnold–Ellis cognitive theory of emotions.)

Schachter–Singer Cognitive Theory. Stanley Schachter and Jerome Singer (1962) have proposed another influential version of cognitive theory that combines the process of cognitive appraisal with the James–Lange theory. In the **Schachter–Singer cognitive theory of emotion,** the conscious experience of emotion arises from three interrelated elements: (1) the cognitive appraisal of a situation as being dangerous, exciting, or emotionally important in some other way (in this sense, it resembles the Arnold–Ellis theory), (2) sensations produced by autonomic arousal (in this way it is like the James–Lange theory), and (3) the cognitive interpretation that the autonomic arousal is the *result* of the emotion-

Schachter–Singer cognitive theory of emotion
The theory that emotional reactions are dependent on cognitive interpretations of both stimulus situations and physiological reactions and behavior.

ally important situation. It is this third element that is the unique contribution of the Schachter–Singer theory (Reisenzein, 1983). Schachter and Singer believe that emotional arousal is diffuse and not specific to the different emotions; it is only through congitive interpretation of its source that arousal plays its important role in emotional experience.

Schachter and Singer's theory helps explain such things as why sexual attraction is often mistaken for love, and why frightened hostages often develop friendly feelings toward their captors if they are treated with even a slight amount of respect. Because the autonomic sensations produced in emotional situations are not distinctive, it's easy to misinterpret their meaning. Sexual arousal can be mistaken for love and fear for friendship if we interpret the arousal incorrectly.

Schachter and Singer (1962) tested their theory in an important experiment. Subjects were brought to a laboratory for what they thought would be a study of the effects of a vitamin on vision. They were given an injection of the supposed vitamin and asked to wait with another subject for the experiment to begin. The other subject was actually a confederate of the experimenters. The injection contained the hormone epinephrine, a substance that causes sympathetic autonomic arousal. Schachter and Singer were interested in how the subjects would cognitively *interpret* this arousal under a number of different circumstances.

With half of the subjects, the confederate acted in a happy, silly manner; with the other half of the subjects, he acted angrily and walked out of the experiment. As predicted by Schachter and Singer, the behavior of the confederate influenced the subjects' cognitive interpretations of their arousal. When they were with a happy confederate they rated themselves as happy; when they were with an angry confederate they interpreted their emotions as anger. Interestingly, this effect was found only when the subjects were not accurately informed about the true effects of the injection. When they were informed, the behavior of the confederate did not influence their emotions—they simply attributed the arousal to the drug.

Rainer Reisenzein (1983) of the Free University of Berlin has recently reviewed the experimental evidence relevant to the Schachter–Singer theory of emotion that has been gathered in the 20 years since it was first stated. He concluded that the most convincing support for this theory has come from studies showing that *misinterpreted* arousal can intensify emotional experiences. Most of this research has used sophisticated laboratory techniques such as the use of epinephrine described above. However, two simple studies that are more relevant to our daily lives illustrate the findings of this research quite well. In the first study, university students were asked to rate their overall happiness with their lives. In general, how happy are you with your life? Do you think that the answer to this question would be influenced by minor aspects of the mood that you are in when asked? Apparently, it can be for most of us. Schwartz and Clare (1983) found that university students rate their overall happiness as greater on sunny days than on rainy days. They concluded that even differences in mood caused by something as insignificant as the weather are often *misinterpreted* and add to (or detract from) ratings of our emotions. Supporting their conclusion was the fact that there were no differences between ratings of general happiness on rainy and sunny days when the students were specifically told to ignore their current moods.

Actually these findings come as no surprise to me; I *hate* rain and have been known to be somewhat less than jolly when the sun doesn't shine. But, if you are still not convinced, see *Research Report:* "On Falling in Love on a Swaying Suspension Bridge" for an even more compelling demonstration. Not all of the evidence surveyed by Reisenzein (1983) supported the Schachter–Singer theory, however. In particular, recent advances in our ability to measure autonomic arousal suggests that different patterns of arousal may be associated with different emotions after all (Ekman, Levenson, & Friesen, 1983). Clearly psychology is in need of a new comprehensive theory of emotion that can clear the air. Our current theories all seem to be correct part of the time, but incorrect or incomplete just as often.

According to the Schachter–Singer cognitive theory of emotions, Patricia Hearst, who was taken hostage in the 1970s by the Symbionese Liberation Army, may have misinterpreted the autonomic arousal of fear when she chose to become an SLA convert.

Role of Learning in Emotions

Most psychologists who specialize in the study of emotions believe that at least the most basic emotions are inborn and do not have to be learned. Cats do not have to be taught how to arch their backs in rage; dogs do not have to be trained to wag their tails; and people probably do not have to learn their emotions. Izard (1978) supplied photos of infants to support his view that emotional reactions appear at such young ages that it seems unlikely that parents have already taught them to their infants. More convincingly, even children who are deprived of most normal learning experiences because of being born deaf and blind show normal emotional reactions (Eibl–Eibesfeldt, 1973).

Comparisons of different cultures, however, make it clear that learning does play an important role in emotions. Some cultures teach people to reveal little of their emotions in public. Other cultures encourage free emotional expression. And families encourage different patterns of emotional expression through modeling and reinforcement (Bandura, 1969). It's also clear that learning has a great deal to do with the stimuli that produce emotional reactions. As described more fully in chapter 5, there is evidence that many individuals with excessive fears (*phobias*) of elevators, water, automobiles, and the like learned their fears through modeling, classical conditioning, or avoidance conditioning (Marks, 1969).

RESEARCH REPORT

On Falling in Love on a Swaying Suspension Bridge

It was mentioned in the text that Schachter and Singer's cognitive theory of emotion was helpful in explaining why people so commonly misinterpret their emotions—such as hostages confusing the emotion of fear for friendly attraction to their captors. Donald Dutton and Arthur Aron (1974) have conducted a clever and interesting experiment to test Schachter and Singer's ideas about the confusion of emotions.

The subjects were unsuspecting males between the ages of 18 and 35 who were visiting the Capilano Canyon in British Columbia, Canada, without a female companion. An attractive female experimenter approached the men and asked them to answer questions as part of a survey that she was supposedly conducting on reactions to scenic attractions. The key item in the study required them to make up a brief story about an ambiguous picture of a woman. Their stories were later scored for the amount of sexual content, which was considered a measure of the amount of sexual attraction that the male subjects felt toward the attractive interviewer. To provide a second measure of interpersonal attraction, the interviewer tore off a piece of paper from the survey and gave her name and phone number to the subject, inviting him to call her if he wanted to talk further.

Have I mentioned where the interviews took place? Half of the interviews were conducted in such a way as to create a high level of arousal (fear) in the male subject, and the other half were conducted to create a low level of arousal. The high-fear interviews were

RESEARCH REPORT

conducted while the subject was *on* a 450-foot-long cable and wood suspension bridge with low handrails that stretched across the Capilano Canyon some 230 feet above rocks and shallow rapids. The authors reported that the bridge had "a tendency to tilt, sway, and wobble, creating the impression that one is about to fall over the side" (p. 511). The low-fear interviews were conducted while on a solid wooden bridge upstream that any coward could cross.

The results strongly supported Schachter and Singer's (1962) theory that the autonomic arousal that accompanies all emotions is similar and that it's our cognitive interpretation of the cause of that arousal that is important. The subjects who were highly aroused (confirmed by their own later reports) while on the swaying suspension bridge made up stories that contained significantly more sexual imagery than the low-fear subjects. The high-fear group was also more than four times as likely to call the female interviewer later. Apparently, the high-fear group interpreted their autonomic arousal as a greater degree of attraction to the interviewer.

Similar enhancement of attraction presumably occurs in other highly arousing situations such as football games, emergency landings while on airplanes, and the like. So, be careful to separate all the possible sources of arousal when you are trying to decide if you are in love. On the other hand, if you really want a blind date to be attracted to you, you might arrange to meet him or her on the Capilano Canyon suspension bridge. Of course, there's always the possibility that your date will interpret the arousal as anger with you for getting him or her up there!

R E V I E W

Emotions are fascinating psychological states that are difficult to describe and define. Most definitions of emotion, however, contain four elements: (1) the stimulus that provokes the emotion; (2) the positively or negatively toned conscious experience; (3) the state of arousal of the body produced by the autonomic nervous system and endocrine glands; and (4) the behavior that characteristically accompanies emotions. Psychologists cannot agree, however, on how these four elements work together during emotions. Three primary theories have been proposed to explain emotions: The James–Lange theory, the Cannon–Bard theory, and two versions of cognitive theory, each viewing a different relationship between stimulus, experience, arousal, and behavior. Many elements of emotions are apparently inborn in all humans, but learning seems to play a role in determining how much emotion will be displayed, how it will be displayed, and which stimuli will evoke emotional reactions.

Aggression: Emotional and Motivational Aspects

Aggression is a topic of paramount importance to the human race. We pride ourselves on being humane creatures who have left the brutal jungle to establish "civilized" societies. But the sad reality is that no other animal species even comes remotely close to our sad record of violent and harmful acts against members of our own species. While fights to the death do sometimes occur over mates and territory in lower mammals and apes do apparently "intentionally murder" other apes on rare occasions, no species rivals the frequency of human aggression. In your lifetime alone, millions of humans have been killed by other humans in wars, revolutions, and acts of terrorism (Julian, 1973). Violent crimes and murder have always been a part of human societies, but in recent years their frequency has reached unprecedented levels in many parts of the world. Perhaps most incomprehensible is the frequency of aggression toward members of one's own family. More than a third of the murders investigated by the FBI have been committed by one family member against another and some 3 percent involve the murder of a child by a parent. Each year in the United States, 4 million husbands and wives violently attack each other, resulting in severe injuries in a quarter million of the cases. Each year, too, 2 million children are kicked, beaten, or punched by their parents (Gelles, 1977; Gelles & Strauss, 1977; Steinmetz & Strauss, 1974).

Why are human beings so aggressive? Can we do anything to curb violence in our society? Aggression is a complex phenomenon with both motivational and emotional aspects that we should carefully examine. Like most important topics in psychology, aggression has been the focus of a great deal of research and theoretical speculation. One view holds that aggression is a natural instinct; another suggests that it's a natural reaction to adverse events such as frustration and pain; while a third viewpoint considers aggression as learned behavior. We look at these theoretical positions one at a time.

Freud's view that watching a professional fight provides a cathartic release of instinctual aggressive energy is not universally accepted by psychologists.

Freud's Instinct Theory: The Release of Aggressive Energy

Sigmund Freud suggested that all animals, humans included, are born with potent aggressive instincts. These instincts create a drive to commit aggressive acts that must be satisfied. In other words, they create an uncomfortable pressure that must be released in some way. Often the aggressive instinct is released in an overt act of aggression. But the key to curbing violence, according to **Freud's instinct theory,** lies in finding nonviolent ways to release aggressive energy such as competing in business or sports, watching aggressive sports, or reading about violent crimes.

Freud's instinct theory
The theory that aggression is caused by an inborn aggressive instinct.

Freud's central point that aggression is instinctual has been echoed in modern times by a number of biologists who suggested that violence is necessary for the "survival of the fittest" (Lorenz, 1967). Author Robert Ardrey (1966) put it this way:

> Man is a predator whose natural instinct is to kill with a weapon.
> The sudden addition of the enlarged brain to the equipment of an
> armed, already successful, predatory animal created not only the
> human being but also the human predicament. (p. 332)

The most controversial aspect of Freud's theory is his belief that instinctual aggressive energy must be released in some way. He calls the process of releasing instinctual energy **catharsis.** Freud's suggestion that societies should encourage the nonviolent catharsis of aggressive energy has been much debated. In particular, some psychologists believe that the ways that Freud and his followers have suggested as safe means of catharsis actually have the effect of increasing aggression. A bit later in this section we look at research bearing on this topic.

catharsis (kah-thar′sis)
In Freud's theory of motivation, the release of instinctual energy.

Frustration-Aggression Theory

Other psychologists believe, like Freud, that aggression is an inborn part of human nature, but they do not agree that it stems from an ever present instinctual need to aggress. Instead, they believe that aggression is a natural reaction to the frustration (blocking) of important motives. This **frustration-aggression theory** (Dollard, Doob, Miller, Mowrer, & Sears, 1939) suggests, for example, that a child who takes a toy from another child may very well get a sock in the nose, or that a nation that frustrates another nation's desire for a seaport might become a target of war. People and nations who are frustrated react with anger and aggression. Later psychologists broadened the frustration-aggression hypothesis by noting that aggression is also a natural reaction to pain, heat, and other aversive events (Berkowitz, 1983).

Social Learning Theory

To Freud, people have a need to aggress that must be relieved; according to the frustration-aggression hypothesis, people only aggress in response to frustrating or other adverse circumstances. According to Albert Bandura (1973) and other social learning theorists, people are aggressive only if they have *learned* in some way that it's to their benefit to be aggressive. Social learning theorists do not deny that frustration can make us more likely to be angry and aggressive, but they state that we will only act aggressively in reaction to frustration if we have learned to do so. We must see others be successful by being aggressive, or we must win victories of our own through aggression (make someone stop bothering us or take away someone else's possession) before we will become aggressive people.

Social learning theorists directly conflict with Freud on the topic of catharsis. Freudian psychologists believe that we must find cathartic outlets for our aggressive energy to keep it from emerging as actual aggression. They recommend such things as yelling when angry and vicariously experiencing aggression by reading violent books or watching violence on television. Social learning theorists argue that these activities will not decrease violence, but instead will *increase* it by teaching violence to the person (Bandura, 1973). The evidence on the practice of yelling or hitting a punching bag instead of hitting the person with whom you are angry is inconsistent, but sometimes, at least, these activities increase violent behavior (Geen & Quanty, 1977).

The evidence against the idea of vicarious catharsis through watching violence on television is quite clear, however. Televised violence does not decrease violence in those who watch it; it *increases* it. The evidence is particularly clear for children. As discussed more completely in chapter 5, there is evidence that watching televised violence increases violent play, increases actual violence, and makes children less likely to intervene in the violent acts of other children (Bandura, 1973; Liebert, Neale, & Davidson, 1983; Thomas & Drabman, 1975). Since 75 percent of the television programs in the United States contain violence (compared, for example, to 10 percent in Sweden), the issue of televised violence is understandably one of national concern (Liebert et al., 1983).

R E V I E W

Aggression is a topic of fear and concern to laypeople, and a difficult pattern of behavior for psychologists to explain. Three major theories have been proposed to explain human aggression. Sigmund Freud proposed that aggression was the result of an inborn motive to aggress that pressed to be released. The frustration–aggression theory suggests that aggression is an inborn reaction to frustration. And social learning theory suggests that aggression is not an inborn behavior, but that people will aggress only if they have learned to do so. The most interesting conflict between these theories concerns Freud's prescription for reducing violence in society. Freudian psychologists suggest that some outlet—catharsis—must be found for the aggressive motive, but that this can be a nonviolent outlet such as hitting a punching bag or watching violence on television. Much research on this topic suggests that Freud was wrong and supports the social learning theory view that such supposed outlets merely teach people to be more violent.

S U M M A R Y

Chapter 10 defines motivation and emotion, discusses primary motives and psychological motives, and explores three theories of emotions. The topic of aggression is included in the chapter to illustrate how emotion and motivation influence our lives.

I. *Motivation* refers to those factors that activate behavior and give it direction. *Emotions* are positive or negative feelings usually accompanied by behavior and physiological arousal that generally are reactions to stimulus situations.

II. *Primary motives* are human motives that stem from the need for things that keep a person alive.

   A. *Homeostatic mechanisms* in the body sense imbalances of essential life elements and stimulate actions that will restore the proper balance.

   B. Hunger is biologically regulated through the *feeding center* and *satiety center* of the *hypothalamus*.

      1. Rats will become *hyperphagic* (obese because of overeating) if the satiety center is destroyed.

      2. Cues for regulating hunger on a daily basis are *stomach contractions* and *blood sugar levels; blood fat* is apparently involved in long-term regulation of hunger.

   C. Learning influences when we eat, what we eat, and how much we eat. Hunger, as well as other motives, is affected by *incentives*—external cues that activate motives.

D. The hypothalamus also controls thirst. Cues used to regulate drinking are mouth dryness, loss of water by cells, and reductions in blood volume.

E. Learning influences drinking behavior and incentives can activate thirst.

F. Sex centers in the hypothalamus function to initiate or inhibit sexual behavior. In many nonhuman mammals, hormones and odors affect sexual behavior.

G. The sexual motive differs from other primary motives in several ways, the most obvious of which is that humans do not have to satisfy the sexual motive in order to survive.

H. The concept of *drive reduction,* which was once applied to many motives, is now restricted to biological motives such as hunger and thirst.

III. Psychological motives are "needs" in the sense that the individual's happiness and well-being, but not survival, depend on these motives.

A. Humans and other animals have an inborn motive to seek *novel stimulation;* humans seek an *optimal level of arousal.* The *Yerkes–Dodson Law* states that if arousal is too low, performance will be inadequate; but if it is too high, performance may become disrupted and disorganized.

B. Individuals high in *affiliation motivation* tend to prefer being with others rather than satisfying other motives.

C. *Achievement motivation (n Ach)* is the psychological need for success.

D. Individuals who usually compete in an aggressive, hostile manner have *Type A personality* and are prone to heart disease.

E. *Intrinsic motivation* refers to motives stimulated by the inherent nature of the activity. *External motivation* is motivation stimulated by external rewards.

F. According to Maslow, motives are organized in a hierarchy arranged from the most basic to the most personal and advanced.

IV. *Emotions* are the experiences that give color, meaning, and intensity to our lives.

A. Theories that attempt to explain emotions include the *James–Lange theory,* the *Cannon–Bard theory,* and the cognitive theories of *Arnold and Ellis,* and *Schachter and Singer.*

B. Most psychologists believe that many basic emotions are primarily inborn, but that learning also plays an important role in emotions.

V. *Aggression* is a complex phenomenon.

A. Freud suggested that all people are born with potent aggressive instincts that are released through *catharsis.*

B. Other psychologists say aggression is a reaction to the frustration (blocking) of important motives (the *frustration-aggression hypothesis*).

C. Social learning theorists explain aggression as *learned behavior.*

Suggested Readings

1. The biological basis of primary motives is reviewed in:

    Groves, P., & Schlesinger, K. (1982). *Biological psychology.* (2nd ed.).
    Dubuque, IA: Wm. C. Brown Publishers.

2. An excellent analysis of higher human motivation is provided by:

    Jung, J. (1978). *Understanding human motivation: A cognitive approach.* New
    York: Macmillan.

3. A new and interesting look at human emotion is given by:

    Plutchik, R. (1980). *Emotion: A psychoevolutionary synthesis.* New York:
    Harper & Row.

4. The relationship between cognition and abnormal emotions is discussed by:

    Ellis, A. (1962). *Reason and emotion in psychotherapy.* New York: Lyle Stuart.
    Beck, A. T. (1976). *Cognitive therapy and the emotional disorders.* New York:
    International Universities Press.

5. For a psychological perspective on human aggression:

    Bandura, A. (1973). *Aggression: A social learning analysis.* Englewood Cliffs,
    NJ: Prentice-Hall.

Personality Theories and Assessment

OUTLINE

KEY TERMS

PROLOGUE

Bertha Pappenheim's unusual problems began at age 21. After six months of caring for her dying father each night, the formerly healthy young woman suddenly became paralyzed in her legs, arms, and neck, and lost the ability to talk except in a meaningless garble. She also had a frequent, deep cough, but her physician could find nothing physically wrong with her. In time, her speech and muscular coordination returned, only to be followed by other strange symptoms. She complained of seeing writhing snakes and grinning skulls; she was deaf for a time; experienced blurred vision; and could not swallow water for six weeks. But, after 18 months of frequent therapy sessions with her physician, Joseph Breuer, she was completely free of these bizarre maladies. Bertha was proud of her progress and happy as she said good-bye to Dr. Breuer, presumably for the last time.

As the young physician sat eating supper with his family that same evening, however, he was summoned back to Bertha's home by her maid. When Breuer arrived, he found Bertha writhing in bed, complaining of painful cramps in her lower abdomen. Suddenly, she shocked Breuer with the words, "Now Dr. Breuer's baby is coming! It is coming!" She was giving birth to a completely imaginary baby! This last symptom so disturbed and confused Dr. Breuer that he decided that it would be best to transfer her to the care of another physician.

The time of these events was 1882–83; the place was Vienna, Austria. We speak of her case now because of the important role it played in the development of one influential theory of personality. Because so little was known at that time about such problems (that we will turn to again in Chapter 12 under the name of *conversion disorders*), Breuer discussed this case with another young Viennese physician by the name of Sigmund Freud. In 1895, Breuer and Freud jointly published an account of Bertha Pappenheim's problems, giving differing interpretations of her symptoms. To protect her identity, she was given the pseudonym of "Anna O." Their detailed description of her now-famous case, and Freud's interpretation of it, laid part of the groundwork of Freud's *psychoanalytic* theory of personality.

Freud believed that six months of being alone with her father while he was sick in bed heightened unconscious sexual desires for her father to the point that they threatened to become conscious. The paralysis and other symptoms, according to Freud, served the purpose of making it impossible for her to express her sexual longings; they held in check her nearly uncontrollable and wholly unacceptable desires. Later, some of these sexual feelings were transferred to Dr. Breuer, by whom she unconsciously wished to become pregnant. It was only after her father died and she left Dr. Breuer's care that her unusual problems cleared up.

While you may or may not find Freud's explanation plausible, the case of Anna O. was of historical importance in helping to launch one of psychology's most influential theories of personality. Bertha Pappenheim's poignant story after her treatment by Breuer, however, was one of torment, triumph, and tragedy that is worthy of study in its own right. Her new physician attempted to treat her with morphine, to which she soon became addicted and had to be placed in a mental institution. But by age 28, she had recovered and moved with her mother to Frankfurt. Although wealthy, Bertha began working in an orphanage for illegitimate children, first as a volunteer and then as its director. Gradually, the scope of her work grew to encompass educating unwed mothers, fighting anti-Semitism, and becoming an important activist for women's rights. In 1904, she founded the Federation of Jewish Women, which was successful in stopping the slave trade that exported impoverished Jewish girls to South America where they were forced into prostitution. She also went against the orthodox religious views of her time and founded a school for Jewish women, the Beth-Jakob Seminary. Bertha Pappenheim's death in 1936 spared her from the worst in the Nazi persecution of Jews, and the ultimate rape of her efforts. In 1938, the Nazis announced that the seminary would become a brothel and its students prostitutes. Rather than suffer this indignity, the 93 young women dressed in their finest clothes and swallowed poison (Freeman, 1972).

P R E V I E W

People are not all alike. There are noticeable differences in the ways that people act, think, and feel. In other words, different people have a variety of different *personalities.* We use the term personality to refer to the typical ways of acting, thinking, and feeling that distinguish one person from another.

Why is my personality the way it is? Why did I not develop a very different personality? Three major theories of personality have been offered as answers to the question *why:* psychoanalytic, humanistic, and social learning theories. The psychoanalytic view was first stated by Sigmund Freud. He saw personality as the result of the interplay of three forces within the mind—roughly speaking, a battle between selfish instincts, moralistic conscience, and realistic thinking. The particular balance that emerges from this three-way interplay of mental forces is the primary determinant of personality, but personality is shaped in other ways, too. The most important instinctual motives are sex and aggression. These motives are too dangerous to be directly expressed in many instances, and the ways in which they are displaced into other areas of life (business competition, love relationships, and so on) have a major impact on personality. Sexual motivation is important to the formation of personality in another way as well. During the course of development from infancy to adulthood, the bodily site of primary sexual gratification shifts from the mouth, to the anus, to the genitals in Freud's conception. If events occur in childhood that cause the sexual motive to become fixated at an immature developmental stage, the personality will be affected throughout adulthood. Finally, our personalities are influenced by the people with whom we identify and pattern our lives after.

The social learning theory of personality takes a less complex view of personality development. From this perspective, personality is simply something that is learned through interactions with other members of society. Personality is no more than patterns of behavior and cognitions, particularly cognitions about oneself.

Humanists see personality as emerging through a process of inner-directed growth toward self-improvement. Each person possesses a positive drive to deal with life's problems and realize one's fullest potential. Only through harmful encounters with society is this process of growth interrupted. To understand a person's personality, humanists believe that one must attempt to view life as that person views it. The primary determinant of personality is each individual's personal view of reality. The most important aspect of this view of reality is his or her view of self; an accurate concept of and a reasonable evaluation of oneself are essential to proper personality functioning.

Psychologists disagree as to the best terms in which to describe an individual's personality. Some prefer to describe personality in terms of relatively unchanging traits, while others believe that a description of how the individual's behavior is influenced by differing situations must be included. Information is gathered by psychologists to use in preparing descriptions of personality through interviews, direct observations of behavior, and a variety of personality tests.

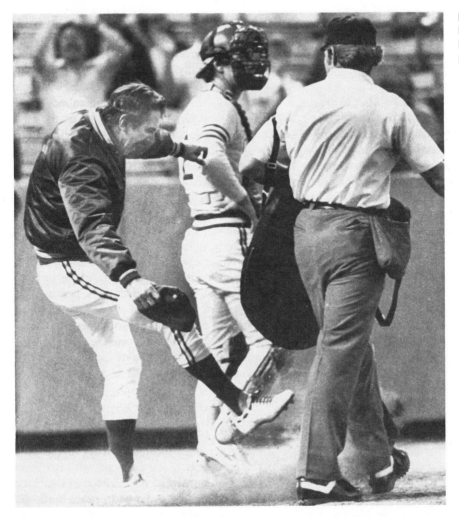

Baseball manager Billy Martin's temper is a well-known aspect of his personality.

Definition of Personality

Who is Ben Lahey anyway? What am I like? You have read thousands of words that I have written by now, but you really do not know very much about me. What would I need to tell you so that you would feel that you had gotten to know me as a person? I would probably start out with a description of my physical appearance—height, weight, eye color, hair color. I would tell you what I like to eat and about my job, but that is pretty superficial stuff. If you saw me eating at the student union, you would pick up most of that information in the first few seconds. But to really get to know me as a person, you need to know something about my thoughts, my feelings, my actions. In other words, I need to describe my personality to you.

But what do we mean when we use the term *personality*? It's no accident that the word *person* is in the word *personality*. Your personality defines you as a person, rather than just a biological conglomeration of organs. One's **personality** is the sum total of all of the ways of acting, thinking, and feeling that are *typical* for that person and make that person *different* from all other individuals.

personality
The sum total of the typical ways of acting, thinking, and feeling that make each person unique.

Notice that the two emphases in this definition are on the terms "typical" and "different." An individual's personality is composed of all the relatively unchanging psychological characteristics that are *typical* for that person. Some people are typically generous; others are typically impulsive; others are typically shy. If people did not have at least some relatively unchanging qualities, we would never know what to expect from them. Each time we encountered an individual, it would be like we were dealing with a stranger. The fact that we do not have to deal with each person as a stranger reflects the fact that each person's personality is made up of some relatively unchanging psychological characteristics.

The second emphasis in the definition of personality is on the term *different*. Each person's unique pattern of typical ways of acting, thinking, and feeling sets him or her apart from each other person. Each of us is a unique person because no one else has exactly our combination of typical psychological qualities. Even if every person were exactly identical in every physical characteristic—eye color, height, weight, tone of voice—we would be able to distinguish one person from another because of their typical ways of acting, thinking, and feeling. Psychologists who specialize in the study of personality want to know *why* each individual develops the unique personality that he or she does. Are personalities learned? Are they inherited? (See *Research Report:* "Do We Inherit Our Personalities?") Or are they formed by critical events that occur during early childhood? Psychologists also want to know how to *assess,* or measure, personalities. The first part of this chapter acquaints you with three major theories of personality development; the second section explores some of the major methods used to measure personality.

Psychoanalytic Theory: Sigmund Freud

Sigmund Freud was a young physician building a medical practice in Vienna in the late 1800s. He was particularly interested in treating patients with emotional problems but felt frustrated by the lack of knowledge that existed at that time. Although he had devoted many years of study in Austria and France to the disorders of the brain and nerves, Freud found what he had learned to be of little help to his patients. Thus, being a man of considerable confidence and intelligence, Sigmund Freud set about to develop his own methods of treatment. In the course of his development of treatment methods, Freud also developed a general theory of personality, an explanation for why people develop their unique patterns of typical behavior. His view is known today as **psychoanalytic theory.**

psychoanalytic theory
Freud's theory that the origin of personality lies in the balance between the id, the ego, and the superego.

Freud's theory of personality began with a very limited question. He wanted to understand the condition known today as *conversion disorder.* In this condition, the individual appears to have a serious medical problem such as paralysis or deafness for which there is no medical cause. As discussed in the Prologue to this chapter, Freud and his colleague Joseph Breuer published a description of Anna O., one of Breuer's cases. Freud was fascinated by this case and wanted to know how and why the mind could create such discomfort for the individual.

As he studied Anna O. and other cases of conversion disorder, Freud became convinced that these individuals had no conscious desire to have their pains, paralysis, or other hysterical symptoms. Indeed, they were coming to Freud for treatment because they wanted to be free of the symptoms. Why, then, did they have the symptoms? To explain this paradox, Freud turned to a concept that was at least as old as the writings of Plato. Freud suggested that part of the human mind exists in such a way that the individual has no awareness of it. In other words, part of the mind is *unconscious.* While the concept of the unconscious

R E S E A R C H   R E P O R T

Do We Inherit Our Personalities?

This chapter describes three major theoretical views of the nature and origins of personality from a psychological perspective. But it has been clear since reading chapter 2 that behavior is influenced by biological as well as psychological factors. Is the same true of personality? Are there biological factors that influence our personalities?

The most carefully studied biological factor in personality is inheritance. A number of twin studies summarized in chapter 2 suggest that genetics are one of the determinants of personality, but a recent study by Yale University researcher Sandra Scarr and her associates (Scarr, Webber, Weinberg, & Wittig, 1981) provides our best set of data on genetic factors in personality to date. Scarr studied 120 families with adolescent children of their own and 115 families with adolescent children who had been adopted in infancy. The focus of the study was on the similarity between the parents and adolescents on personality test scores. On the basis of their experimental test scores, these two types of families were examined to separate the similarities due to parental rearing from the similarities due to genetic relationship (the natural children were genetically related to their parents, while the adopted children had no genetic relationship to their adoptive parents). Thus, if the natural children had personality test scores that were more similar to their parents than did adopted children, it could reasonably be concluded that genetics was one of the factors in determining personality.

The results of Scarr's study did indicate a genetic factor in personality, but a relatively small one. The personality test scores of the adopted children bore no resemblance at all to those of their adoptive parents. The natural children showed greater similarity to their parents, but the degree of relationship was still relatively small. Thus, the role of genetics in the formation of different personalities seems to be a modest one at best. We should remember, though, that there is evidence that genetics may be involved to a somewhat greater extent in the development of some kinds of serious psychological disorders (see chapter 2, pp. 74–85 of this text for further discussion of the topic of genetics).

mind did not originate with Freud, we associate it with him because he gave it such importance in his theory of personality. To Freud, our lives are dominated not by our conscious minds, but by forces that operate in the unconscious. Freud believed that unconscious sexual motives were at the heart of Anna O.'s problems. As he worked with other patients with conversion disorder, Freud became convinced that all such cases were caused by unexpressed sexual motives. And, in time, unconscious sexual urges became the cornerstone of Freud's general theory of personality.

Figure 11.1 A diagram of Freud's concept of three levels of consciousness.

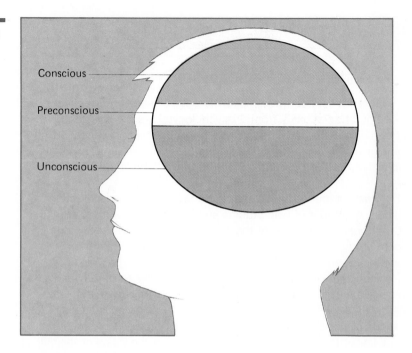

Freud's Mind: Three Levels of Consciousness

Freud distinguished three levels of conscious awareness—the *conscious mind,* the *preconscious mind,* and the *unconscious mind.* We are presently aware of the contents of the first level of the mind, but temporarily unaware of the contents of the second level, and permanently unaware of the contents of the third.

To Freud, the mind is like an iceberg; the **conscious mind** is merely the tip visible above the surface, whereas the bulk of the important workings of the mind lurk mysteriously beneath the surface (see fig. 11.1). Just below the surface is what Freud called the **preconscious mind.** It consists of memories that are not presently conscious, but can be easily brought into consciousness. You are not thinking right now about your last meal, or the name of your psychology instructor, or the taste of your favorite drink, but you could quickly bring those items into conscious awareness if you wanted to. The preconscious mind is the vast storehouse of easily accessible memories. The contents of the preconscious were once conscious and can be returned to consciousness when needed.

Further down from consciousness lies the **unconscious mind.** It's the storehouse for primitive instinctual motives plus memories and emotions that are so threatening to the conscious mind that they have been **repressed,** or unconsciously pushed into the unconscious mind. The contents of the unconscious mind, unlike the preconscious mind, are not normally accessible to consciousness. They can rarely be made fully conscious, and then only with great difficulty.

Freud's Mind: Id, Ego, and Superego

Freud also divided the mind into three parts in a different, but related, way. The best-known aspect of Freud's theory of personality is his view that the mind is composed of three parts, each with a very different function: the *id,* the *ego,* and the *superego* (see fig. 11.2).

conscious mind
That portion of the mind of which one is presently aware.

preconscious mind
That portion of the mind that contains information that is not presently conscious but can be easily brought into consciousness.

unconscious mind
The part of the mind of which we can never be directly aware, that is the storehouse of primitive instinctual motives, and of memories and emotions that have been repressed.

repression
Sigmund Freud's theory that forgetting occurs because the conscious mind often deals with unpleasant information by pushing it into unconsciousness.

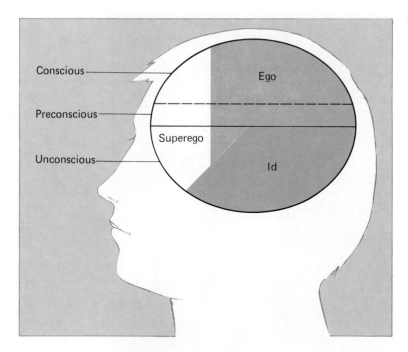

Figure 11.2 A diagram of the relationship between the id, ego, and superego, and the three levels of consciousness.

Id: The Selfish Beast

When the infant is born, the mind has only one part, the **id.** The id is composed primarily of two sets of instincts, *life instincts* and *death instincts*. Freud wrote relatively little about the death instincts, but he believed that aggression and even suicidal urges arose from these instincts. The life instincts give rise to motives that sustain and promote life, such as hunger, self-protection, and sexual desire. To Freud, the sexual and aggressive urges are by far the most important of these motives. As strange as it may seem, sex and aggression are used by Freud to explain a vast range of personality characteristics, from kindness to shyness to cruelty. From birth on, Freud believed that every person's life is dominated by these two motives—the desire to experience sexual pleasure and the desire to harm others. Because the id operates entirely at the unconscious level of the mind, however, we are generally not aware of these motives. Only safe, watered-down versions of our true sexual and aggressive urges ever reach conscious awareness.

Freud's view of the dark side of the human mind is not an easy one for most of us to accept. Freud tells us that there lives within each of us a selfish, cruel beast. The beast—the id—operates according to the **pleasure principle.** The id wants to obtain immediate pleasure and avoid pain regardless of how harmful it might be to others. But the id's selfishness is not its most alien characteristic to most of us. According to Freud, the id seeks to satisfy its desires in ways that are totally out of touch with reality. The id, in fact, has no conception whatsoever of reality. The id attempts to satisfy its needs using what Freud calls **primary process thinking**—by simply forming a wish-fulfilling mental image of the desired object. We use the primary process when we daydream about having sex, or think about eating chocolate fudge cake, or angrily think of how we would like to get revenge on the person who embarrassed us yesterday. Dreams are also a primary process means of fulfilling motives. The primary process satisfies motives through imagination rather than in reality.

id
According to Freud, the inborn part of the unconscious mind that uses the primary process to satisfy its needs and that acts according to the pleasure principle.

pleasure principle
According to Freud, the attempt of the id to seek immediate pleasure and avoid pain regardless of how harmful it might be to others.

primary process thinking
According to Freud, the attempt by the id to satisfy its needs by forming a wish-fulfilling mental image of the desired object.

Were the id supreme, this woman might walk out of the store without paying for the ski suit.

"A penny for your thoughts, hon."

Drawing by Lorenz; © 1980 The New Yorker Magazine, Inc.

ego (e'go)
According to Freud, that part of the mind that uses the reality principle to satisfy the id.

reality principle
According to Freud, the attempt by the ego to find safe, realistic ways of meeting the needs of the id.

But a person could not actually survive for long living by the pleasure principle (eventually you would get hurt if you fulfilled every selfish desire without regard for the feelings of others) or using only the primary process of wish fulfillment (forming a mental image of food will not meet the biological needs of the body for nutrition). Fortunately, during infancy, the period of time in which we have only an id, we have adults around who see to it that our needs are realistically and safely met. As we grow up, our interactions with our parents and other parts of the real world lead us to convert part of the id into two other parts of the mind—the ego and the superego—that help us cope more effectively with the world.

Ego: The Executive of Personality

The **ego** is formed because the id has to develop realistic ways of meeting its needs and avoiding trouble caused by selfish and aggressive behavior. The ego operates according to the **reality principle.** This means that it holds the id in check until a safe and realistic way has been found to satisfy its motives. The id would be happy to form a mental image of a sex object, and when that was not wholly satisfying it would want to immediately rape the object. The ego, on the other hand, holds the id in check long enough to charm and seduce the sex object. The ego's goal is to help the id fulfill its needs. It only opposes the id's wishes long enough to find a realistic way to satisfy them. The ego can be thought of as the *executive of the personality* because it uses its cognitive abilities to manage and control the id and balance its desires against the restrictions of reality and the superego.

OF SPECIAL INTEREST

Psychological Problems: Freud's Perspective

Why do so many people have psychological problems such as depression and anxiety? Freud looked at us and saw a mind fighting against itself. As long as the forces of the id, ego, and superego are fairly well balanced, the personality functions smoothly. But if the delicate balance is lost between the three conflicting forces, psychological problems will develop. If the person develops an excessively strong superego, the id motives will often go unsatisfied and will strain to be released. This straining conflict between the id and superego can produce an uncomfortable level of anxiety. If the superego is too weak, on the other hand, the person will be inappropriately aggressive, sexual in a selfish way, or may commit criminal acts. If the person's ego is weak, he or she may have difficulties controlling impulses and meeting the demands of the real world. Failure to cope with the demands of life can lead to depression.

Problems can also arise out of the psychosexual stages of development. When fixations occur, it means that some part of the mind is sealed off from further development. Every fixation leaves the individual more like an infant and less like an adult.

Because the fixations and conflicts that cause psychological problems are unconscious, we are generally unable to help ourselves through them, according to Freud. He suggests that a form of professional treatment, called *psychoanalysis,* is needed in which the therapist helps the troubled person bring the unconscious causes of his or her problems out into consciousness where they can be dealt with rationally. This and other approaches to therapy for psychological problems will be discussed in chapter 13.

Superego: The Conscience and Ego Ideal

The id and ego have no morals. They seek to satisfy the id's selfish motives without regard for the good of others. The ego tries to be realistic about how those motives are satisfied. But as long as the needs are *safely* met, it does not care if rules are broken, lies are told, or other people are wronged. While each of us wants our desires to be satisfied immediately, if everyone acted in this manner simultaneously, chaos would probably be created in society.

Society places restrictions on the actions of the id and ego by creating the **superego,** the part of the mind that opposes the desires of the id by enforcing moral restrictions and by striving to attain a goal of "ideal" perfection. Parents are the main agents of society in creating the superego. They teach moral principles to their children by punishing transgressions and rewarding proper behavior. These experiences become incorporated into the child's mind as the two

superego (soo″per-e′go) According to Freud, that part of the mind that opposes the desires of the id by enforcing moral restrictions and by striving to attain a goal of perfection.

conscience (kon'shens)
According to Freud, the moral inhibitions of the superego.

ego ideal
According to Freud, the standard of perfect conduct of the superego.

displacement
(dis-plās'ment)
A defense mechanism in which the individual directs aggressive or sexual feelings away from the primary object to someone or something safe.

sublimation
(sub''lĭ-ma'shun)
According to Freud, a form of displacement in which a socially desirable goal is substituted for a socially harmful goal; the best form of displacement for society as a whole.

identification
The tendency to base one's identity on, and model one's actions after, individuals who are successful in gaining satisfaction from life.

parts of the superego. According to Freud, parental punishment creates the set of moral inhibitions known as the **conscience,** while their rewards set up a standard of perfect conduct in the superego called the **ego ideal.** These two parts of the superego work together by punishing behavior that breaks the moral code through guilt and rewarding good behavior through pride. As the superego develops strength, children are able to control themselves and behave in ways that allow society to function smoothly. According to Freud's view, most of us do not steal, murder, and rape not because we do not want to, or because our egos could not find relatively safe ways to do so, but because our superegos hold these desires in check.

Displacement and Identification: Becoming a Member of Society

The ego is not always able to find ways to satisfy id motives that avoid trouble and stay within the moral boundaries of the superego. Sometimes the ego must settle for a *substitute* for the goal of the id. A child who would really like to kick his father may have to settle for slugging his little brother instead. Or if his superego prohibits hurting his brother, he may have to kick his teddy bear. The process of substituting a more acceptable goal is called **displacement.**

In terms of the interests of society, the best kind of displacement is called **sublimation.** In this form of displacement, a socially desirable goal is substituted for a socially harmful goal. Competing in school is a sublimation of aggressive motives; painting nude portraits is a sublimation of sexual motives, and so on. Indeed, Freud believed that all of the cultural and economic achievements of society were the result of sublimation. Thus, the individual who sublimates id energy is not only able to fit into society, but contributes to its advancement as well.

Another process that allows individuals to learn to operate in society without friction is **identification.** This term refers to the fact that we tend to model our actions after individuals who are successful in gaining satisfactions from life. According to Freud, this is more than just a superficial act of imitation; we incorporate the model person's goals, actions, and values into our personalities. Thus, children come to behave more like the adults they identify with. In this way, identification serves an important role in socializing children.

Competing in the classroom is an example of a result of the Freudian concept of sublimation.

Growing Up: The Stages of Psychosexual Development

Freud's theory of personality is a *developmental* theory. He believes that our personalities are formed as we pass through a series of developmental stages from infancy to adulthood. Events that happen as the individual passes through these stages can be critical in the formation of personality. Excessive punishment or reward from parents, or traumatically stressful events experienced during a period of development, can leave the person's personality "stuck" or *fixated* at that stage. This fixation of personality development will, according to Freud, leave a lifelong mark on the personality.

To Freud, the developmental stages represent a shifting of the primary outlet of id energy, particularly sexual energy, from one part of the body to another. For this reason, they are called **psychosexual stages.** The five stages of psychosexual development are as follows.

Oral Stage (birth to one year)

The infant's earliest source of id gratification is the mouth. During the **oral stage,** the infant gets pleasure from sucking and swallowing. Later when he has teeth, the infant enjoys the aggressive pleasure of biting and chewing. If the infant enjoys swallowing too much, however, she may fixate on this stage and become an **oral receptive personality** who continues to seek pleasure through the mouth by overeating and smoking and by being a gullible person who "swallows" ideas too easily.

If the infant's oral pleasures are frustrated, on the other hand, such as by a mother who sticks rigidly to a feeding schedule regardless of the infant's desire to eat, he may grow up to be a fixated **oral aggressive personality** who seeks aggressive pleasure through the mouth, for instance, by being verbally hostile to others. Similar fixations are possible at every stage of development.

Anal Stage (one to three years)

When parents decide to toilet train their children during the **anal stage,** the children learn how much *control* they can exert over others with their anal sphincter muscles. Children can have the immediate pleasure of expelling feces, but that may cause their parents to punish them. If they delay gratification until they are on the toilet, children can gain the approval of their parents. According to Freud, excessive punishment of failures during toilet training may create a fixated personality that is either stingy, obstinate, and compulsive (**anal retentive**) or cruel, messy, and disorderly (**anal expulsive**).

Phallic Stage (three to six years)

During the **phallic stage,** the genitals become the primary source of pleasure. According to Freud, the child begins to enjoy touching his or her own genitals and develops a sexual attraction to the parent of the opposite sex. Freud believed that the shift to genital pleasure goes on in the unconscious mind, so we are not consciously aware of the touching or the incestuous urges. Instead, the child merely feels an intense love for the opposite sex parent: Daughters become "daddy's girl" and sons become "mommy's boy." These sexual attractions bring about the intense unconscious conflict that Freud calls the *Oedipus complex* for boys and the *Electra complex* for girls.

---

psychosexual stages
Developmental periods in the personality theory of Sigmund Freud during which the sexual energy of the id finds different sources of satisfaction.

oral stage
According to Freud, the first psychosexual stage (from birth to one year), in which id gratification is focused on the mouth.

oral receptive personality
A personality type in which the person seeks pleasure through overeating, smoking, and other oral means.

oral aggressive personality
A personality type in which the person seeks pleasure by being verbally hostile to others.

anal stage
According to Freud, the second psychosexual stage (from one to three years), in which gratification is focused on the anus.

anal retentive personality
A personality type based on anal fixation in which the person is stingy, obstinate, and compulsive.

anal expulsive personality
A personality type based on anal fixation in which the person is cruel, messy, and disorderly.

phallic stage (fal'ik)
According to Freud, the third psychosexual stage (from three to six years), in which gratification is focused on the genitals.

Oedipus complex
(ed'i-pus)
According to Freud, the unconscious wish of all male children to kill their fathers and sexually possess their mothers.

castration anxiety
(kas-tra'shun)
According to Freud, the fear of a young boy that his father will punish his sexual desire for his mother by removing his genitals.

Electra complex
(e-lek'-trah)
According to Freud, the transfer of a young girl's sexual desires from her mother to her father after she discovers she has no penis.

penis envy
The desire of a young girl to possess a penis.

latency stage
According to Freud, the fourth psychosexual stage (from about 6 to 11 years), during which sexual energy is sublimated and converted into socially valued activities.

The latency stage (ages about 6 to 11) of Freud's theory of psychosexual development is a time when sexual energy is sublimated and converted into interest in schoolwork, sports, and other activities.

Freud borrowed the term **Oedipus complex** from the ancient Greek play *Oedipus Rex* by Sophocles. It tells the mythical story of an infant who was abandoned by the King and Queen of Thebes and grew up in a rival city. As a young man, not knowing who his parents are, Oedipus returns to Thebes, kills his father, and marries his mother. Freud believes that the play reveals a wish that is in all of us during the phallic stage of development.

According to Freud, all males unconsciously want to kill their fathers and sexually possess their mothers. Because such desires are unacceptable, they are blocked from consciousness. But the incestuous desires remain in the unconscious id where they cause considerable discomfort. The child unconsciously senses that if these hidden impulses ever become unleashed, he will enrage his father. A fear arises in the immature mind of the boy that his father will punish his sexual desires toward his mother by removing his genitals—a fear called **castration anxiety.** This fear eventually leads the boy to repress desires for his mother and to avoid angering his father by identifying more strongly with him.

The **Electra complex** of female children is more complicated, but it's the counterpart of the male Oedipus complex. In recent years, this has been one of Freud's most controversial doctrines since most contemporary readers find that it portrays women in a negative light. The Electra complex begins with the girl's "upsetting" discovery that she does not have a penis like a man, but has an empty space instead. According to Freud, the girl unconsciously concludes that she has already been castrated and blames the mother for letting this happen to her. As a result she transfers her love and sexual desire from her mother to her father. In doing so, she hopes to share with him the valued penis that she has lost. The desire to possess a penis is termed **penis envy** by Freud. This sexual attachment to the father must be transformed into wholesome affection because of the demands of society, but Freud believes that the attachment persists with less repression than in the male Oedipus complex (Hall & Lindzey, 1978). Still, after a brief period of primary attachment to the father, the girl begins again to identify with her mother.

Latency Stage (six to eleven years)

The **latency stage** is that period of life from about age 6 to 11 in which sexual interest is relatively inactive. Sexual desire has been strongly repressed through the resolution of the Oedipal or Electra complexes and is not a source of trouble at this time. Instead, sexual energy is going through the process of sublimation and is being converted into interest in schoolwork, riding bicycles, playing house, and sports. To pass successfully through this developmental period, the child must develop a certain degree of competence in these areas.

Genital Stage (eleven years on)

With the arrival of puberty and the **genital stage,** there is renewed interest in obtaining sexual pleasure through the genitals. Masturbation often becomes frequent and leads to orgasm for the first time. Sexual and romantic interest in others also becomes a central motive. But because the parents have been successfully ruled out as sex objects through the Oedipus and Electra complexes, the new sex objects are peers of about the same age.

While some interpersonal relationships are entered into merely to obtain selfish genital pleasure, the individual who has reached the genital state is able to care about the welfare of the loved one as much or more than herself. This forms the basis for the more or less lasting relationships that characterize the genital stage and extend throughout adulthood. Sublimation continues to be important during this period as sexual and aggressive id motives become transformed into energy for marriage, occupations, and childrearing.

genital stage (jen′ĭ-tal) According to Freud, the psychosexual stage (from 11 years through adulthood) in which sexual and romantic interest is directed toward one's peers.

Theories Derived from Psychoanalysis

Psychoanalytic thinking continues to be important in contemporary psychology, although mostly through revised versions of Freud's theory of personality. Some modern psychologists adhere to an orthodox version of psychoanalysis, but far more endorse somewhat newer versions that grew out of Freudian thinking but differ on several major points. These revisions of psychoanalysis each differ from one another in some ways, but they share a common view that Freud placed too much emphasis on unconscious sexual motivation and aggression and gave too little importance to positive aspects of personality.

The revisions of Freud's thinking began in a storm that took place during his own lifetime. As Freud's fame spread throughout Europe, he developed a group of followers. But when two of these followers, Carl Jung and Alfred Adler, disagreed with Freud on the issue of sexual motivation, they were angrily dismissed from the loyal fold. Freud was an authoritarian individual who tolerated little disagreement from others.

Carl Jung

Carl Jung was a physician who had just begun his career working in a psychiatric hospital in Switzerland when he read Freud's most influential early work, *The Interpretation of Dreams*. He began to correspond with Freud and travel to Vienna for meetings. As Jung and Freud became friends, Jung joined the inner circle of Freud's disciples as an influential member. Jung published a number of works that used Freud's ideas to explain aspects of severe mental illness, but gradually Jung came to question Freud's emphasis on sexual motivation. Within seven years of their first meeting, these differences in opinion led to a severing of their personal and professional relationship.

Jung felt that Freud took a one-sided negative view of the human condition. While he thought that the unconscious mind did contain selfish and hostile forces, Jung believed that it also contained positive, even spiritual, motives. In fact, a fundamental characteristic of the human mind to Jung was that all important elements came in the form of *opposites*. We possess the potential to be both good and evil, masculine and feminine, mother and father.

One of Jung's most original and lasting contributions to the understanding of personality is the pair of opposite personality traits known as *extroversion* and *introversion*. Each of us possesses a desire to be friendly, open to the things happening in the world, and concerned about others (**extroversion**); but each also possesses a tendency to focus our attention on ourselves, to be shy, and to meet our own needs (**introversion**). As with all of the polar opposites, Jung felt that it was important to allow a balance of these two opposing tendencies. We should not be too much of an introvert or too much of an extrovert.

extroversion (eks″trah-ver′zhun) According to Jung, the tendency of some individuals to be friendly and open to the world.

introversion (in-tro-ver′zhun) According to Jung, the tendency of some individuals to be shy and to focus their attention on themselves.

Each of us, according to Jung, is a blend of introvert and extrovert. Jung felt that a balance of these two opposing tendencies is desirable.

personal unconscious
According to Jung, the motives, conflicts, and information that are repressed by a person because they are threatening to that individual.

collective unconscious
According to Jung, the content of the unconscious mind with which all humans are born.

Jung also modified Freud's view of the unconscious. He felt that we each possess both a *personal unconscious* and a *collective unconscious*. The **personal unconscious** contains those motives, conflicts, and information that we have repressed into unconsciousness because they are threatening to us. The **collective unconscious** is the unconscious mind with which all humans are born. He used the term collective to emphasize the fact that its contents are the same for all humans. Much of his later career was devoted to blending his interest in psychology with his childhood interest in cultures from the past. He assembled many sorts of evidence to suggest that every culture expresses the same sorts of unconscious motives in very much the same symbolic ways. For example, the sexual symbol of the phallus (the penis) has appeared in many cultures throughout history in the form of totem poles, scepters held by kings to symbolize authority, and structures such as the Washington Monument.

Alfred Adler

Alfred Adler was a young physician practicing medicine in Vienna when he was invited to join the Vienna Psychoanalytic Association. He soon became a favorite of Freud and was asked to be the second president of the society succeeding Freud himself. In time, however, the two argued over the publication policies of the association's journal and parted company. Differences between the psychological views of the two men had already become apparent, but they became increasingly obvious after the personal dispute.

Adler agreed with Freud that the struggle to come to grips with one's sexual and hostile impulses was important to the development of personality, but he did not feel it was the most important factor. In his early career, Adler felt that the primary struggle in personality development was the effort to overcome *feelings of inferiority* in social relationships and to develop feelings of superiority. At first, he limited this view to individuals who were born with physical defects, as was Adler himself, but later he expanded this view to include physically normal individuals as well. Because we are all small and dependent on the protection of adults as children, we all begin life with feelings of inferiority. The task of personality development, according to Adler, is to outgrow the inferiority of childhood and to see ourselves as competent adults. So important did he feel that the role of parents and other caretakers was in this crucial process that Adler devoted much of his time to the development of a preschool program that he thought fostered proper personality development. Even today, "Adlerian" preschools are popular in many parts of Europe and the United States.

Later in his career, Adler deemphasized the importance of struggling to outgrow childhood feelings of inferiority. In fact, he felt that the effort to achieve feelings of superiority over other individuals was an essentially unhealthy motive. Instead, he focused on two other factors as the most important elements in personality development. First, Adler felt that all human beings are born with a positive motive, *social interest,* to establish loving, helpful relationships with other people. The full development of a healthy personality requires that the individual learn to express this motive fully in his or her relationships with others. This contrasted with Freud's belief that only selfish motives are inborn. Second, Adler felt that people's lives are governed by their *goals.* Often these goals are not realistic at all, but they regulate our actions anyway as we strive to achieve them. Adler's emphasis on goals, by giving such importance to a cognitive ego function, was also a sharp contrast to Freud.

More contemporary psychoanalytic psychologists have continued to revise the theories of Freud in much the same directions as initiated by Adler. Writers such as Karen Horney, Erich Fromm, Harry Stack Sullivan, and Erik Erikson (the latter theorist's views were presented in chapters 8 and 9 because of their relevance to development across the life span) have continued to develop the neo-Freudian view of personality. Like Adler, they deemphasize the importance of sexual and aggressive motives, emphasize positive aspects of personality, maintain that the conscious cognitive functions of the ego are of greater significance than the unconscious forces of the id, and assert the importance of developing adequate social relationships.

R E V I E W

Sigmund Freud's theory of personality grew out of his early interest in the cause of the hysterical symptoms of some of his patients. He decided that, since they had no conscious reason to have such symptoms, the cause must be unconscious, specifically repressed sexual or aggressive desires. Through the course of many years of treating patients with a variety of psychological problems, Freud came to believe that unconscious motives, particularly sexual and aggressive ones, were the source of most aspects of our personalities. Freud divided the mind into three levels of consciousness (conscious, preconscious, and unconscious) and into three parts with different functions (id, ego, and superego). The id is the storehouse of the unconscious life and death instincts, and the inborn, selfish part of the mind that operates according to the pleasure principle. The id seeks immediate satisfaction of its needs without concern for the welfare of others. The ego is the executive of the personality that controls the id through adherence to the reality principle; it seeks to satisfy the needs of the id in ways that are both realistic and safe. The superego represents society's rules of right and wrong that often hold the id in check, not on the basis of what is realistic but on what is moral.

OF SPECIAL INTEREST

Freud's Myth of the Vaginal Orgasm

Although Sigmund Freud devoted much of his writing to the topic of sex, he discussed it primarily as a cause of neurosis rather than as an important topic in its own right. When he did specifically address the issue of sexual behavior, it was generally within the context of his theory of the *stages of psychosexual development.* As discussed in this chapter, Freud believed that the id's sexual energy shifted from one bodily outlet to another during the course of development (from mouth, to anus, to genitals). A relatively minor point made by Freud concerning the female orgasm in this discussion has caused considerable trouble for women ever since, however.

During the *phallic stage* of development (ages three to six), the source of sexual pleasure for the child is the male penis or female clitoris. During this immature stage of sexuality, the focus is on self-centered forms of stimulation and the child may learn that touching the penis or clitoris is pleasurable. Later, in the *genital stage* (11 years of age and on), the site of sexual pleasure for the male is again the penis, but this time the focus of sexuality is on a more "mature" form of pleasure, sexual intercourse that leads to reproduction. Freud believed that, during the genital stage, the female's sexuality shifts from the clitoris to the vagina. Because the vagina is involved in intercourse, Freud considered pleasure from vaginal orgasms to be mature, while orgasms from clitoral stimulation were "immature" and evidence that the woman had become fixated at the infantile phallic stage.

The process of becoming an acceptable member of society is aided by the psychological processes of displacement and identification. When it's too dangerous to directly satisfy an id motive, the motive is displaced on a safer, substitute goal. The most desirable form of displacement from society's perspective is sublimation, in which dangerous motives are transformed into socially desirable motives. The process of identification with social models further aids the individual's acceptance as a member of society.

Sexual energy is transformed during the life span in yet another way. As the individual matures from infancy to adulthood, the principal means of obtaining sexual pleasure shifts from one part of the body to another. Pleasure shifts from the mouth to the anus and then to the genitals; it

OF SPECIAL INTEREST

Freud's view of clitoral orgasm led psychoanalysts—and other physicians and counselors who were influenced by them—to advise women to avoid clitoral stimulation so that they could progress to a more mature level of sexuality. The relatively recent studies by William Masters and Virginia Johnson (1966) laid the myth of the vaginal orgasm to rest. They showed that all orgasms, whether from intercourse or masturbatory stimulation of the clitoris, are biologically identical and that even in intercourse a primary source of pleasure is indirect stimulation of the clitoris through movement of the fold of tissues that covers it. More importantly, they found that the clitoris is the primary source of pleasure for most women and that it's far easier for most women to reach orgasm with some form of relatively direct stimulation of the clitoris. This means the advice that has been given to women to avoid clitoral stimulation has led many of them to be unable to achieve orgasm or to feel "immature" if they did so through clitoral stimulation.

In some ways, however, Freud's condemnation of stimulation of the clitoris must be considered mild in contrast to the prevailing opinions in his time. Female masturbation was so thoroughly condemned as a threat to morals and health in Europe during the late 1800s that it was not uncommon to have the clitoris surgically removed during childhood, in a *clitoridectomy.* Furthermore, this operation is still practiced in some parts of Africa and the Middle East (Hosken, 1979).

passes through a period where it lies more or less dormant and then reemerges as genital sexuality. Abnormal experiences at any of these stages can lead to fixations that hinder the full development of an effective personality.

Following the lead of Jung and Adler who broke away from orthodox psychoanalytic views during Freud's lifetime, contemporary psychoanalysts generally deemphasize the importance of sexual and aggressive motives. They believe that conscious ego functions are more important than unconscious id functions in guiding behavior and emphasize the importance of social relationships in personality formation.

CATHY   **by Cathy Guisewite**

Social Learning Theory: Albert Bandura

The social learning view of personality is vastly different from that of the psychoanalysts. Little or no attention is paid to topics such as instincts, the unconscious mind, or the developmental stages that are of primary importance to psychoanalysis. Instead, social learning theorists focus on a psychological process that is largely ignored by psychoanalysts, *learning*. To a social learning theorist, personality is simply something that is learned; it's the sum total of all the ways we have learned to act, think, and feel. Because personality is learned from other people in society, the term *social learning* is used.

social learning theory
The theory that our personalities are formed primarily through learning from other members of society.

    Social learning theory had its origins in the behavioral writings of Ivan Pavlov, John B. Watson, and B. F. Skinner. Each of these theorists has argued that personality is no more than learned behavior and that the way to understand personality is simply to understand the processes of learning. To social learning theorists, the key concepts in the study of personality are not id, ego, and superego, but classical conditioning, operant conditioning, and modeling, which were discussed in chapter 5. We will not repeat our discussion of these principles here, but it may be helpful for you to glance back over this material.

    In the social learning theory view, a person will develop an adequate personality only if he or she is exposed to good models and is reinforced for appropriate behavior. An inadequate learning environment, on the other hand, will result in inadequate personality development.

    A recent study of the origins of fear provides a good example of the social learning position. This was a study of the learning of snake fears in rhesus monkeys (because researchers cannot ethically expose human children to social situations that may transmit fears), but the results probably apply to humans as well. Psychologist Susan Mineka and colleagues (Mineka, Davidson, Cook, & Keir, 1984) found that young monkeys who had been raised in a laboratory—and had never seen a snake—could learn to fear snakes through modeling. Although none of the monkeys showed fear of snakes when initially tested, they showed a strong and lasting fear after observing older monkeys (who had been raised in the wild and feared snakes) react fearfully to live or toy snakes. Simply seeing an adult react fearfully transmitted the fear to the younger monkeys and changed the monkey's "personality" in this specific way. To the social learning theorist, personality is formed through many such learning experiences.

The leading figure in social learning theory today, and the person who gave the theory its name, is Stanford University psychologist Albert Bandura (1977). In one sense, Bandura is very much a behaviorist. He agrees with the view that personality is the sum total of learned behavior. But he broke with traditional behaviorism in two main ways: (1) he emphasized the importance of cognition in personality, and (2) he portrayed people as playing an active role in determining their own actions, rather than being passively acted upon by the learning environment.

According to Bandura, our cognitions are a prime determinant of our behavior. A person who believes that helping others makes them less self-reliant will be stingy; and a person who thinks that other people find her boring will act quiet and shy. Bandura (1982) places particular emphasis on our cognitions about our ability to handle the demands of life. In his terms, **self-efficacy** is the perception that one is capable of doing what is necessary to reach one's goals—both in the sense of knowing what to do and being emotionally able to do it. People who perceive themselves as self-efficacious accept greater challenges, expend more effort, and may be more successful in reaching their goals as a result. A person with a poor sense of self-efficacy about social poise may not accept a promotion at work because it would involve giving many speeches and having to negotiate with dignitaries. Although our perceptions of self-efficacy are learned from what others say about us, our direct experiences of success and failure, and other sources, these cognitions continue to influence our behavior "from the inside out."

Bandura (1977) also places emphasis on the learning of personal standards of reward and punishment by which we judge our own behavior. We learn our personal standards from observing the personal standards that other people model and from the standards that others use when rewarding or punishing us. But, although we are the passive recipients of these standards in a sense, we then actively use them to govern our own behavior in the process that Bandura calls **self-regulation.** When we behave in ways that meet our personal standards, we cognitively pat ourselves on the back—we reinforce ourselves. We generally do not actually say to ourselves, "Good going, fellow, you did okay!" Rather, we feel a self-reinforcing sense of pride or happiness when we have met our standards. Conversely, we punish ourselves (feel guilty, disappointed) when we fail to meet our personal standards. The process of self-regulation is particularly helpful in explaining why we often act in ways that appear to provide no reinforcement from others, such as the writer who works for years on the novel that no one has read yet.

Bandura (1977) also portrays us as playing an active role in our lives by stating that social learning is **reciprocally determined.** This means that not only is a person's behavior learned, but also that the social learning environment is altered by the person's behavior. The environment that we learn from, after all, is made up of people. If we behave toward them in a timid way, or a friendly way, or a hostile way, those people will react in very different ways to us—and will hence be teaching us very different things about social relationships. The aggressive, overconfident person will learn that the world is a cold, rejecting place; the friendly person will learn that the world is warm and loving. Personality is learned behavior, but it is also behavior that influences future learning experiences.

Albert Bandura
(1925–   )

self-efficacy
According to Bandura, the perception of being capable of achieving one's goals.

self-regulation
According to Bandura, the process of cognitively reinforcing and punishing our own behavior, depending on whether or not it meets our personal standards.

reciprocal determination
(re-sip″ro-kal)
Bandura's observation that the individual's behavior and the social learning environment continually influence one another.

Like the most recent neo-Freudian versions of psychoanalytic theory, social learning theorists view the primary challenge of personality development as the development of adequate social relationships. To do this, the person must *learn* both appropriate ways to relate to other people and appropriate *cognitions* (beliefs, expectations) about himself or herself and about relationships with others. Adequate social relationships are important because few people are happy without them, but also because they influence the process of social learning.

R E V I E W

The leading proponent of social learning theory is Albert Bandura. While this approach to personality theory grew out of the behaviorism of Pavlov, Watson, and Skinner, Bandura expanded behavioral thinking by emphasizing the importance of cognition in personality and the active role played by individuals in the social learning process. To the social learning theorist, the process of learning is of central importance to personality development. The relatively consistent pattern of acting, thinking, and feeling that we refer to as personality is the result of learning from our experiences with other members of society and the cognitions we learn in that process that influence future behavior.

Humanistic Theory: Maslow and Rogers

humanistic theory
The psychological view that human beings possess an innate tendency to improve and determine their lives by the decisions they make.

The **humanistic theory** of psychology is often referred to as the *third force* in psychology. Although it has deep historical roots in philosophy, it has only been since the 1950s that humanism has become an influential movement in psychology. As influential as this approach to personality is, however, it's the least unified and well-defined of the three major viewpoints. This lack of unity probably is due less to the newness of humanistic psychology than to its origins. The two other schools of thought began with ideas of a single person. Although the views of the original leaders were subsequently revised by later followers, the original writings of Pavlov and Freud gave a certain unity to the theories that followed. Humanistic theory, on the other hand, emerged from the writings of a number of figures who shared a few basic concepts.

The founders of humanistic psychology include Carl Rogers, Abraham Maslow, Victor Frankl, Virginia Satir, Fritz Perls, Thomas Szasz, and Rollo May, to name only a few. It's impossible, therefore, to write a single statement that adequately summarizes the humanistic approach to personality. For this reason, we focus on the views of Carl Rogers, emphasizing those parts of his theory that are consistent with the views of humanists in general.

Inner-Directedness and Subjectivity

inner-directedness
A force that humanists believe all people possess that internally leads them to grow and improve.

Humanists believe that humans possess an internal force, an **inner-directedness,** that pushes them to grow, to improve, and to become the best individuals they are capable of being. People have the freedom to make choices, and they are generally pretty good at making intelligent choices that further their personal growth. This inner-directedness is the primary force behind the development of personality.

Obviously, humanists have a positive view of the human species, but they are not blind to the fact that life is a struggle for everyone at some point and that many people consistently make a mess of their lives. We lose our ability to grow and to make good choices when we live with critical, rejecting people or when society tries to force us to be something that we are not. And, as Maslow has pointed out, the transition to higher motives is stunted when more basic motives are unsatisfied (see Maslow's hierarchy of needs in chapter 10, p. 399, and *Of Special Interest:* Self-actualized Personalities).

The personality that develops through the positive push of inner-directness can only be understood "from the inside out," that is, from the perspective of the individual. To the humanist, reality is inherently *subjective.* Everyone views life in somewhat different, highly personal terms. What is real for you may not be real for me. You may see people as basically immoral, while I see them as basically moral. Each person's personality is a direct reflection of the individual's subjective view of reality. Our consistent ways of acting, thinking, and feeling reflect our unique perceptions of what life is all about. And, as we will see in the next section, no subjective view of reality is more important to humanistic theorists than our subjective view of ourselves.

The Self-Concept

The concept of the "self" is central to the personality theory of Carl Rogers and other humanists. Our **self-concept** is our subjective perception of who we are and what we are like. Of all of our subjective views of life, our view of ourself is most important to our personalities. The concept of self is learned from our interactions with others: You might learn that you are a good athlete by seeing that you run faster than most other people or by your parents telling you that you are a good athlete.

Rogers distinguishes between two self-concepts. There is the **self**—the person that I think I am—and the **ideal self**—the person that I wish I were. For example, I am pretty sure I can never be better than a "C" class racquetball player (self), but I would *love* to win tournaments in the "A" class (ideal self). On a higher plane, I see myself as a fairly nice person, but I wish I could learn to be less selfish at times. Rogers' concept of the ideal self is very similar to Freud's ego ideal.

self-concept
Our subjective perceptions of who we are and what we are like.

self
According to humanists, the person one thinks he or she is.

ideal self
According to humanists, the person one wishes he or she were.

Self-concept (our perception of who we are and what we are like) is learned from our interactions with others.

self-actualization
According to Maslow, the seldomly reached full result of the inner-directed drive of humans to grow, improve, and use their potential to the fullest.

OF SPECIAL INTEREST

Self-actualized Personalities

A major belief of humanistic psychologists is that humans possess an inner drive to grow, improve, and use their potential to the fullest. Abraham Maslow calls the ultimate in completed growth **self-actualization.** According to Maslow, the self-actualized person has reached the highest level of personal development and has fully realized his or her potential as a human being. What is a self-actualized person like? Maslow (1967, 1970) gives the following description.

1. The self-actualized person has reached a high level of moral development and is more concerned about the welfare of friends, loved ones, and humanity than self.

2. The self-actualized person is usually committed to some cause or task, rather than working for fame or money.

3. Life is experienced in intense, vivid, absorbing ways, often with a sense of unity with nature.

4. Self-actualized people are open and honest and have the courage to act on their convictions even if it means being unpopular.

5. Self-actualized individuals are not particularly interested in fads, fashion, and social customs, often appearing unorthodox.

6. Self-actualized individuals enjoy friends but are not dependent on their company or approval; they enjoy privacy and independence. On the other hand, their feelings for their close friends are intensely positive and caring.

7. Life is always challenging and fresh to the self-actualized person.

8. They have an accurate, rather than a romanticized, view of people and life, yet they are positive about life.

9. Self-actualized individuals are spontaneous and natural in their actions and feelings.

Both self-concepts are so important that if there are problems in either one, the person will be affected. For one thing, excessive discrepancies between the self and the ideal self can be uncomfortable. It's okay for the ideal self to be slightly out of reach—that is one of the things that stimulates us to improve ourselves. But if the ideal self is so unrealistically perfect that we know it can never be reached, then we feel like failures.

OF SPECIAL INTEREST

Albert Einstein
(1879–1955)

Eleanor Roosevelt
(1884–1962)

Ludwig van Beethoven
(1770–1827)

Do not despair if you do not compare too well against Maslow's list. For one thing, self-actualization is at the end of a lifelong process of improvement according to Maslow. You just may not have gotten there yet! Remember, too, from the chapter on motivation that *all* lower-level motives must be satisfied before a person can proceed toward self-actualization. If you are like most of us, you still have an unmet motive or two that is blocking your full development. Maslow felt that there are really very few self-actualized individuals in the world. He identified a few that he thought probably were and studied them. His list included Albert Einstein, Eleanor Roosevelt, and Ludwig van Beethoven.

Maslow believed that we partially actualized souls get an occasional glimpse of what it is like to be self-actualized in what he calls **peak experiences.** These are intensely moving, pleasurable, beautiful experiences when a person is fully absorbed in the experience, forgetting his or her selfish interests and feeling a sense of unity with the world. These experiences can occur when looking at the stars, watching the birth of a baby, making love with your beloved, or even during something mundane like taking a shower. Most of us will experience some peak experiences in our lifetime, but Maslow tells us that they are more common for self-actualized individuals.

peak experience
An intensely moving experience in which the individual feels a sense of unity with the world.

An inaccurate self-concept can also cause problems. If our view of our "selves" is not reasonably *congruent* (similar to the way we actually act, think, and feel), then we will develop an obscured view of ourselves. For example, if I see myself as free from prejudice, but I feel resentment when someone from a minority group gets preference over me in a job promotion, then my feelings of resentment would not "fit" my self-concept. According to Rogers, I might deny

symbolization
In Rogers' theory, the process of representing experience, thoughts, or feelings in mental symbols of which we possess awareness.

conditions of worth
The standards used by others or ourselves in judging our worth.

those feelings that are incongruent with my self-concept by not admitting them to awareness. In Rogers' terms, we are aware of feelings and information only when they are mentally **symbolized.** The failure to symbolize parts of our experience is harmful not only because it leads to inaccurate concepts of self, but also because feelings can continue to influence us, often in conflicting or anxiety-provoking ways, even when we are not aware of them.

We begin to deny awareness to some of our feelings and experiences as a result of our parents' reactions to our behavior. By reacting with warmth and praise to some of our actions (sharing a toy with little sister), but with coldness and punishment to others (hitting little sister with the toy), our parents create **conditions of worth.** They let us know that they find us "worthy" under some conditions and "unworthy" under other conditions. We internalize many of these and perceive ourselves as worthwhile only when we act and feel in accordance with those conditions. Furthermore, we often deny feelings that are inconsistent with the internalized conditions of worth. The child, for example, may not symbolize her hostile feelings toward her sister, robbing herself of a valuable bit of self-awareness.

Rogers' concept of unsymbolized feelings is similar in some ways to Freud's view of repressed feelings. Both can continue to influence the person, often in a harmful manner. But Freud views some repression as a necessary part of life, while Rogers believes that lack of awareness is always harmful. If we are to allow full expression to our inner-directed tendency to grow, we must be fully aware of (symbolize) all of our feelings and experiences. It is only in this way that we can accurately understand and accept ourselves for exactly what we are (while always striving to do better).

Humanism Compared to Psychoanalysis and Social Learning Theory

Humanism, psychoanalysis, and social learning theory all differ from one another in their views of the basic nature of human beings and of society. In psychoanalytic theory, people are seen as selfish and hostile at birth; they are nothing but id. Society is seen as a good force that instills the ego and superego into children thus enabling them to behave realistically and morally enough to live in the social world.

To the humanist, the psychoanalytic view is exactly wrong. People possess a positive inborn drive to grow and improve. Instead of being born evil, the human is born basically good. Society, on the other hand, is seen by the humanist as a frequently destructive force that leads people to deny their true feelings (of jealousy, insecurity, passion), and creates unattainable ideal self-concepts (for example, American society tells us that we should all be attractive, athletic, sexy, famous, and rich).

Social learning theorists differ from both psychoanalytic and humanistic theorists in their evaluation of the basic nature of humans and society. Social learning theorists see humans as neutral at birth, having the potential to learn to be either good or bad. Similarly, society can be either destructive or constructive. A part of society that teaches inappropriate behavior to its children is destructive, while a part of society that teaches appropriate behavior is constructive.

In short, the three major contemporary theories of personality differ in many fundamental ways. Psychology was born in a state of disagreement—remember there were many different "founders"—and we may always have to live with disagreements. When you are dealing with a subject as complicated and emotionally compelling as human beings, disagreements are to be expected.

R E V I E W

Humanism is the recent and influential third force in personality theory. While it's the least unified of the three movements, a number of basic concepts about personality are shared by nearly all humanists. The most significant factor in the development of personality is the positive inner-directed drive to grow and improve. Unless our experiences with society interfere with this drive, it can be counted on to direct personal growth in positive directions. The personality that develops from this growth only can be understood from the point of view of the individual. Personality is seen as reflecting each person's subjective view of reality. We act, think, and feel in accordance with how we view reality. And the most important aspect of that view of reality is our subjective concept of self. The ways I view both the self that I think I am and the self I would like to be are powerful determinants of my personality. If my ideal self is unattainably perfect, I will always fall painfully short of my standards. If my concept of myself is inaccurate, I will not be able to deal with information about myself that is not congruent with my self-concept. Incongruent information is not admitted to consciousness, a state of affairs that humanists view as unhealthy for the personality.

Humanists, psychoanalysts, and social learning theorists take very different views of the basic nature of people and society. Psychoanalysts view humans as wholly selfish and hostile ids at birth. Society, in contrast, is seen as a positive force providing experiences that create the ego and superego that allow humans to function effectively in society. Humanists view people as essentially good, but see society as a negative force that often interferes with the individual's inner-directed growth. Social learning theorists see people as having the potential to develop in either positive or negative ways depending on whether their personality was learned from positive or negative aspects of society.

Traits and Situations: Describing the Consistencies of Personality

Psychologists of all three theoretical persuasions are often called upon to *describe* an individual's personality. What is the best way to do this? How can an individual's entire personality be reduced to a few words? Typically, we use terms like friendly, aggressive, flirtatious, and fearful. We are so fond of describing people in such terms, in fact, that there are more than 17,000 words for them in the English language (Allport & Odbert, 1936). In psychological terms, these words refer to **traits.** Traits are defined as relatively enduring and consistent ways of behaving. When we say that a person has the trait of friendliness, for example, we mean that she is friendly to most people in most situations, and that her friendliness does not change much as time goes by.

traits
Relatively enduring and consistent ways of thinking, acting, and feeling that are believed by some theorists to be the basic units of personality.

Social learning theorists argue that behavior is influenced by a combination of characteristics of the person (traits) and the situation. This is known as interactionism.

Trait Theories of Personality

Some psychologists have developed their ideas about traits to the extent that they are considered to be theories of personality, but these are not theories in the same sense as the psychoanalytic, social learning, and humanistic theories of personality just discussed. Trait theories are more concerned with *describing* the nature and operation of traits than *explaining* their origins. For example, Freud postulated that stinginess had its origins in the anal stage of psychosexual development (explanation). Trait theorists, in contrast, would be more concerned with whether stinginess actually was a trait, how it relates to other traits, and the like (description). Although there are many important trait theories of personality, the best known are those of Gordon Allport and Raymond B. Cattell.

Allport's Trait Theory

Allport (1937, 1961) believed that the most important traits were those motivational traits related to our *values*. Allport tells us that the best way to understand people and predict how they will behave in the future is to find out what they value—the things that they will strive to attain. A person who values money more than family life, for example, can be expected to accept a promotion that would mean greater pay, but require spending more time away from home. A person who values family life over money, in contrast, could be predicted to make the opposite decision.

An important topic to all trait theorists is the ways that traits are related to one another and are organized. Because humans distinguish so many different traits in one another, each trait theorist has tried to reduce this confusing complexity by showing that some traits are more important than others. Allport (1961) believed that traits could be ranked in terms of their importance as *cardinal, central,* or *secondary.* Cardinal traits are those that dominate a person's life. The quest for knowledge could be said to be one of the cardinal traits that dominated Albert Einstein's life, while the desire for social justice dominated Mahatma Gandhi's behavior. Allport felt that relatively few people possess such cardinal traits. Much more common, however, are the central traits. These are important traits that influence and organize much of our behavior. For example, much of Bob's behavior might be seen to serve the purpose of obtaining sexual gratification, while his brother Bill may be relatively uninterested in sex but many of his actions reflect his strong desire for power and prestige. Secondary traits are much more specific (such as being rude to door-to-door salespeople) and much less important to a comprehensive description of a person's personality.

Allport's distinction between cardinal, central, and secondary traits helps us sift through the many possible ways of describing and understanding an individual's personality. Unfortunately, there can be no fixed list of cardinal or central traits because they differ from person to person. One individual may have no cardinal traits at all, while another person does, and what is a central trait in me may be a secondary trait in you. Furthermore, Allport believes that although some traits can be found in all people (the *common traits*), other traits are only found in some individuals (the *personal dispositions*).

Cattell's Trait Theory

Another influential trait theory of personality is the more recent theory of Raymond B. Cattell (1950, 1966, 1982). Cattell has made extensive use of sophisticated statistical techniques to identify traits; as a result his theory aspires to much greater mathematical precision than Allport's. Like Allport, he believes that motivational traits related to values (which Cattell calls *dynamic* traits) are important in understanding personality, but he also emphasizes two other types of traits. *Ability* traits relate to our effectiveness in satisfying motives, such as intelligence, social skills, and the like. *Temperament* traits describe largely inherited aspects of our behavior, such as energy level, speed of action, and emotional reactivity.

Like Allport, Cattell attempts to reduce the confusion inherent in the description of traits by specifying some as more important than others. *Surface* traits are relatively unimportant clusters of behaviors that appear to go together, whereas *source* traits are the more important underlying traits on which the surface traits are based. Cattell has identified 16 source traits and has developed a personality test to measure them (Cattell, Saunders, & Stice, 1950).

Situationism and Interactionism

Skinner (1953), Mischel (1968), and others have argued strongly against the concept of traits, however. They suggest that behavior is determined by the situations people find themselves in, not traits inside the person. This viewpoint, known as **situationism,** suggests that our behavior is consistent only as long as our situations remain consistent. Generally these situations involve other people. A person might be friendly most of the time to her husband and nice neighbors, but cold and distant to her spiteful and gossipy coworkers, and stiff and formal with her boss. A man might be conventional and hardworking for years, but become carefree and eccentric after his divorce. According to the situational view, people behave in ways that suit their situations, so their behavior cannot be consistent enough to be adequately described in terms of traits.

situationism
(sit″u-a′shun-izm)
The view that behavior is consistent only as long as situations remain consistent.

interactionism
(in″ter-ak′shun-izm)
The view that behavior is
influenced by a combination
of the characteristics of
both the person and the
situation.

More recently, social learning theorists have suggested a compromise between the trait and situationism positions (Bandura, 1977; Mischel, 1981, 1984). Not only is it a logical compromise, but considerable evidence supports the validity of this view (Bowers, 1973). The compromise view, known as **interactionism,** suggests that our behavior is influenced by a combination of characteristics of the person and the situation. You might know somebody who is friendly and even fairly dominant in a one-to-one conversation, but painfully shy in a group. Or you might know somebody who is fairly quiet and dull in a one-to-one conversation but a witty, vibrant conversationalist at crowded parties. The important point about these two people is that although the situations changed them both (the one-to-one conversation versus the crowded party), it changed them in *different* ways. People are influenced by situations, it's true, but different individuals are affected by situations in different ways. That is the point of interactionism. The only way to fully describe a person's personality is to describe both the person's personal characteristics and how the person behaves in different situations.

Darryl Bem (Bem & Allen, 1974) has added an interesting and important footnote to the concept of interactionism. He reminds us that one of the important ways in which individuals differ from one another is that some people are influenced more by situations than others. Some people are grumpy with everybody all the time, while other people are friendly with some people, grumpy with others, and in-between with the rest. With this in mind, a complete description of personality must also indicate the degree to which the person is influenced by different situations.

Bem's footnote about interactionism also raises an interesting question: Is it better to be a person who is strongly or weakly influenced by situations? While it certainly would not be good to be wishy-washy and change your behavior every time the wind blows, Bem suggests that it's also not good to be too unchanging. Only individuals with serious psychological problems are rigidly insensitive to their surroundings. It's probably best to respond to changing situations to a moderate degree.

R E V I E W

Psychologists typically describe the consistencies in personality by using trait descriptions. A number of psychologists have developed their ideas about traits to the extent that they can be considered theories of personality, but ones that describe personality more than explain it. Situationists have suggested that trait descriptions are inadequate because people do not behave as consistently across different situations as the concept of trait implies; they behave differently in different situations. Social learning theorists have recently suggested that the most adequate description of personality must include both a description of traitlike consistencies in behavior and a description of how the individual's behavior is influenced by different situations. (See *Research Report:* ''Situational Influences on Personality.'')

Personality Assessment: Taking a Measure of the Person

Psychologists who work in business, schools, prisons, and clinics are frequently called upon to make important decisions about people. Which employee should be promoted to sales manager? Should this person receive a parole from prison? What should be done to help this person out of a state of depression? Such questions can be answered with confidence only when the psychologist knows what the person is like—that is, how the person typically behaves in ways that distinguish him or her from other individuals. In other words, the psychologist must know a great deal about the person's personality.

You could probably describe the personality of your best friend, your brother or sister, or your parent fairly well. You have seen them in a variety of situations and know how they typically behave. But psychologists usually do not have the luxury of getting to know their clients over long periods of time. They must come up with a picture of their client's personality in short order. To do this, a number of ways of quickly assessing personality have been developed. These include interviews, structured observations of behavior, psychoanalytically inspired projective tests, and personality tests.

Interviews and Observational Methods

The most universally used method of personality assessment is the **interview.** Although few psychologists use it by itself, nearly every psychologist interviews the client by asking questions designed to reveal his or her personality. These interviews can range from the highly structured and formal to the very unstructured. Interviews are an essential part of getting to know the client, but they have serious limitations. For one thing they are inherently subjective; different psychologists may evaluate the same behavior of the client during the interview in different ways. Second, interviews are artificial situations that bring into question the validity of the information obtained from them. Interviews are stressful events that may bring out atypical behavior. A person may feel very anxious when interviewing for a job but might ordinarily be a calm person when at work. In this way, interviews can be misleading. They are often supplemented by other methods to ensure a more complete and accurate view of the person's personality.

One alternative to interviewing is *observing* the person's actual behavior in a natural or simulated situation. **Observational methods** are particularly popular in business. For example, psychologists who consult with businesses on employee promotion often observe the employees being considered for promotion in situations that simulate actual managerial situations. Several employees might be given the problem of dividing up a limited budget for an employee health plan and then be observed as they negotiate a solution to the simulated problem.

In an attempt to make observational methods more objective, a variety of observational *rating scales* have been developed. In these scales, the observer responds to specific items in describing the behavior observed. For example, the rating scale might include the item "Was friendly" and ask the observer to circle

interview
A subjective method of personality assessment that involves questioning techniques designed to reveal the personality of the client.

observational method
A method of personality assessment that involves watching a person's actual behavior in a natural or simulated situation.

R E S E A R C H   R E P O R T

Situational Influences on Personality: Ten Cents Can Make You a Better Person

The school of thought referred to in the text as *situationism* suggests that it's impossible to describe people in terms of traits because situations influence behavior so strongly. Take the trait of helpfulness. Are you a helpful person? Do you know people who you would describe as being very helpful or not at all helpful? Most of us think of helpfulness as a characteristic that some people have and some people do not have—that is, we think of it as a trait. Like other traits, we generally think of helpfulness as something that comes from within our personality rather than something that is determined by the situations we are in. But let's see if that common-sense understanding of helpfulness stands up under experimental scrutiny.

One study (Isen & Levin, 1972) that sheds light on the effects of even subtle aspects of situations on traits went like this: A male experimenter went to a pay telephone in a covered shopping mall and attempted to make a call. He acted as if there was no answer, hung up, and left. Sometimes he left the dime in the coin return and sometimes he took it. A female experimenter was window-shopping nearby, waiting for the next person to use the phone. The person could be male or female, but was a subject in the experiment only if he or she was alone and not carrying anything.

As the person—who had no idea that he or she was a subject in a psychology experiment—left the telephone booth, the female experimenter walked in front of his or her path and dropped a folder full of papers. Was the subject helpful? Did the subject stop and help the experimenter pick up her scattered papers? More to the point of this experiment, would a subtle situational event such as finding a dime in the telephone influence a person's tendency to be helpful?

Figure 11.3 shows the surprising results of this study. One hundred percent of the female subjects and 75 percent of the male subjects who had found a dime were helpful, but almost none of

one of the following responses: "strongly agree," "agree," "disagree," or "strongly disagree." Most rating scales provide a comprehensive assessment of the person by using many such items. A commonly used type of rating scale takes advantage of the fact that teachers have learned a great deal about the children in their classrooms by observing them in the normal course of teaching. School psychologists who are assessing the personality of children frequently ask teachers to fill out rating scales on their students.

R E S E A R C H   R E P O R T

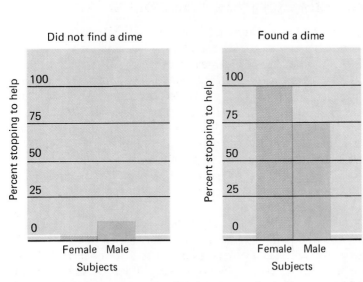

Figure 11.3 The percentage of subjects who stopped to help a person pick up scattered papers after finding or not finding a dime in a pay telephone coin return (Isen & Levin, 1972).

the subjects who had not found a dime stopped to help pick up papers. Now what do you think about helpfulness: is it a trait within the person or simply behavior that is determined by the situation? Even the small windfall of finding a dime influenced helpfulness to an amazing extent. As stated in the text, few psychologists presently believe that it's sufficient to think of personality as only being influenced by situations—different people react to the same situations differently—but this experiment may help you understand why many psychologists feel that just describing personality in terms of fixed traits is inadequate as well. Both a description of characteristics of the person and how these personal characteristics interact with changing situations is needed for a full description of personality.

Projective Personality Tests

Next to interviews, the most widely used method of personality assessment is the **projective test.** These tests are based on the belief of psychoanalysts that it's the unconscious mind that contains the important roots of personality. But since the ego works fervently to keep the contents of the unconscious mind out of awareness, a way must be found to slip past the censor of the ego. Psychoanalysts believe that the motives and conflicts of the unconscious mind can be revealed by projective tests.

projective test
A test that uses ambiguous stimuli designed to reveal the contents of the client's unconscious mind.

Figure 11.4 The Thematic Apperception Test uses pictures like this to evaluate personality. The person is asked to make up a story based on such ambiguous pictures to allow the contents of the unconscious mind to be projected into the story (Murray, 1943).

Projective tests ask the individual to interpret ambiguous stimuli so that the contents of the unconscious mind can be "projected" into the interpretation, much like a slide projector projects an image on a blank screen. For example, the *Thematic Apperception Test* (TAT) asks the individual to make up a story about ambiguous pictures like the one in figure 11.4. What do you see in this picture? Is it an old woman happily remembering her youth? Is it a picture of the evil side of a young woman who is plotting the murder of her father? Psychoanalysts believe that because the stimuli are ambiguous the ego is not able to fully censor the unconscious thoughts and motives that are projected into the story made up about the picture.

Even more ambiguous stimuli are used in the *Rorschach Inkblot Test*. The test consists of 10 symmetrical inkblots like the ones in figure 11.5. The individuals tell what the inkblots look like and what parts of the inkblot they are focusing on. Do you see a vagina surrounded by a menacing spider? Are you projecting a fear of sex? Complex scoring systems are often used with the Rorschach inkblots, but many users interpret the responses subjectively.

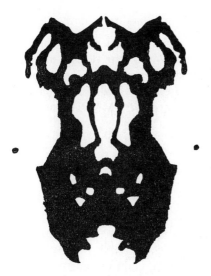

Figure 11.5 In the Rorschach inkblot test, the individual is asked to explain what he or she sees in ambiguous stimuli such as these.

"It looks as if someone spilled ink on a piece of paper and then folded it in half."

Thomas Cheney

Objective Personality Tests

A more recent development in personality assessment is the objective personality test. These tests have only been widely used since World War II in an attempt to get away from the subjectivity of interviews and projective tests. The objective personality test consists of a number of written questions about the person. For example, the *Minnesota Multiphasic Personality Inventory* (MMPI) consists of 566 true/false questions like the following.

1. I get along well with others.

2. Sometimes I hear voices telling me to do bad things.

3. At times I am full of energy.

4. I am afraid of losing my mind.

5. Everyone hates me.

The MMPI is an objective test in the sense that no attempt is made to subjectively understand what the person meant by the answer to each question. Rather, the person's answers are compared to the answers of other individuals with known personality characteristics who have taken the test.

The items on the MMPI are divided into 10 "scales," each designed to measure a different aspect of personality. The items were selected for each scale on the basis of the response of individuals known to have that characteristic in extreme form. For example, one scale is designed to measure the extent to which a person is prone to experience depression. The scale was developed by administering a large number of questions to a group of people who were seeking treatment for depression and a group of individuals who were not depressed. The items that were selected for the depression scale were those that the depressed people consistently answered in one way, and the others answered in the *opposite* way. For example, the depressed group would tend to answer "true" to a question like "Life often doesn't seem worth living," while the other group would tend to answer "false."

This method of test construction allows for the objective interpretation of scores. A person's score on the depression scale is simply determined by the number of questions answered in the same way as the depressed group, not a selective interpretation of the person's answers. Many other objective personality tests have been developed in the same or similar ways.

In recent years the ultimate in objective interpretation of the MMPI has been made possible by companies that provide computerized interpretations of MMPI test results. An example of a computer interpretation is provided in figure 11.6. Such computer interpretations have stirred quite a controversy. The criticism raised is that they are *too* objective. Because they do not take into account any information other than the test responses (such as the person's educational level, history of psychological adjustment, behavior during the interview, and so on), the interpretations are sometimes partially or wholly incorrect. This would not be a problem if the user of the computer interpretation service were knowledgeable about personality assessment. But unfortunately some of the users of this service are not psychologists and they use the computer because they cannot make their own interpretations. (See *Research Report:* "Are Personality Tests Too Believable?")

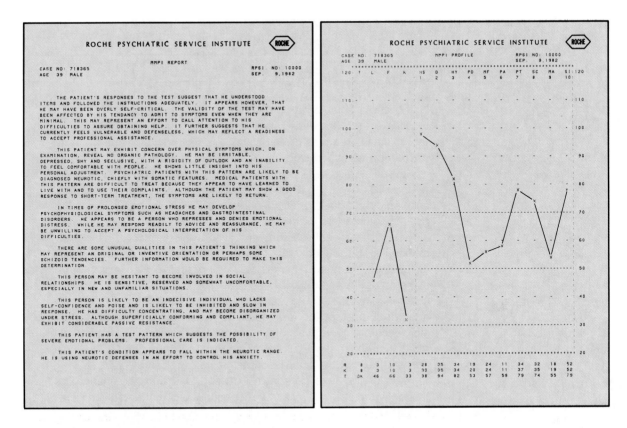

Evaluation of Personality Tests

It's obviously helpful for psychologists to be able to assess the personalities of the individuals with whom they are working. Not all psychologists agree, however, that personality tests are accurate enough to use for that purpose. A great deal of research has been done (but often with disappointing results) to determine whether personality tests are good at measuring what they are supposed to measure.

Research on the Rorschach, TAT, and other projective techniques suggests that these tests generally are not successful in distinguishing between individuals with and without psychological problems; they are even less successful in predicting behavior (Mischel, 1968). The objective personality tests fare somewhat better but much is still left to be desired. In spite of the fact that they were developed using groups that differ on personality characteristics, many studies have shown that the tests are unable to distinguish between groups that differ on these same characteristics (Mischel, 1968). Even in the most successful demonstrations the tests are not always accurate. For example, chronic marijuana users can be distinguished from nonusers with 80 percent accuracy using objective personality tests (Hogan, Mankin, Conway, & Fox, 1970). Even so, the test is inaccurate 20 percent of the time.

These results suggest that we should be cautious, at least, in interpreting the results of personality tests. Some psychologists even argue that we should not use personality tests at all. Advocates of personality testing point out, however, that an understanding of the personality of the people with whom we are working

Figure 11.6 A computer interpretation of the results of an MMPI testing (Roche Psychiatric Service Institute—Hoffman LaRoche).

RESEARCH REPORT

Are Personality Tests Too Believable?

One of the problems with personality tests is that we are so prone to *believe* their findings. There is something mystical about tests that makes it seem as if they have a special power to see the real us, particularly when we are not sure who the "real" us is.

Several studies have demonstrated the power of personality tests to be believable, even when the results are a complete hoax. In one such study (Stagner, 1958), 68 personnel managers—who work with psychological tests in their jobs—were given a published personality test. Later, each person was given a description of his or her personality. Supposedly, the description was based on the results of the test, but the managers were all actually given exactly the same made-up personality description.

As in previous studies, an astounding 50 percent of the managers thought that the fake personality descriptions were "amazingly accurate" portrayals of their actual personalities. Forty percent more thought that the descriptions were "rather good." Only 10 percent thought that the descriptions were inaccurate.

Parts of the fake personality descriptions that the managers thought were particularly accurate descriptions of themselves were as follows.

You have a tendency to be critical of yourself.

You prefer a certain amount of change and variety and become dissatisfied when hemmed in by restrictions and limitations.

You pride yourself as an independent thinker and do not accept others' statements without satisfactory proof.

At times you are extroverted, affable, sociable, while at other times you are introverted, wary, reserved.

The success of this deception was due in part to the fact that the descriptions were vague and referred to the kinds of things that most people believe about themselves. Indeed, the descriptions were taken from popular astrology charts. Still, we should keep these findings in mind when interpreting the results of valid personality tests.

is so important that we must try to assess personality in the best way that we can. They further point out that the studies that show poor accuracy in personality tests use only raw test scores. They do not allow the psychologist to use other information about the person to reach an overall evaluation. It's only in this way, they argue, that personality tests are valid.

R E V I E W

Because psychologists usually do not have an opportunity to assess each client's personality by getting to know the person over a long period of time, they have had to develop methods of quickly learning about a person's personality. The most widely used method of personality assessment is the interview in which questions are asked that probe the nature of the individual's personality. Personality is also often assessed by directly observing the individual in natural or simulated settings, or by having people such as teachers or employers who have observed the person's behavior over a long period of time fill out checklists describing the pattern of behavior that they have observed. Psychoanalytically oriented psychologists often rely on projective tests to learn about the unconscious roots of personality. These tests ask the person to respond to ambiguous stimuli in the hope that the person will project important features of his or her unconscious mind into the interpretation of the stimuli. Psychologists who prefer less subjective methods of personality assessment often use objective tests. These utilize items that were objectively selected for the test by comparing the answers of groups of individuals who do or do not possess the personality characteristics in question. In general, objective personality tests have been shown to be more effective in distinguishing among groups with various personality traits, but some psychologists question whether even these tests are accurate enough to use in making decisions that affect people's lives.

S U M M A R Y

Chapter 11 defines personality, explores three major perspectives on personality—psychoanalytic, social learning, and humanistic—describes traits, and discusses several approaches to personality assessment.

I. *Personality* is the sum total of all the ways of acting, thinking, and feeling that are typical for that person and make that person unique.

II. Psychoanalytic theory was developed by Sigmund Freud in the late nineteenth century.

    A. Freud distinguished three levels of conscious awareness—the *conscious mind,* the *preconscious mind,* and the *unconscious mind.* In his view, the mind is composed of three parts—id, ego, and superego.

        1. The *id* operates on the *pleasure principle.* It seeks to obtain immediate pleasure and avoid pain.

        2. The *ego* operates on the *reality principle.* It seeks safe and realistic ways to satisfy the id.

        3. The *superego* opposes the id by imposing moral restrictions and by striving for perfection.

    B. When the ego cannot find ways to satisfy the id, it seeks a substitute.

        1. The substitution of a more acceptable goal is *displacement,* and displacement of a socially desirable goal is called *sublimation.*

        2. *Identification* is the tendency to model our actions and identity after individuals who are successful in gaining satisfactions from life.

C. Freud's theory is *developmental* in that it distinguishes five stages in the development of personality: the *oral stage,* the *anal stage,* the *phallic stage,* the *latency stage,* and the *genital stage.* During the phallic stage, boys experience the *Oedipus complex,* and girls experience the *Electra complex.*

D. Alfred Adler and Carl Jung broke away from Freud primarily over the issues of sexual motivation and the presence of positive aspects of personality.

E. Contemporary psychoanalysts generally deemphasize unconscious sexual and aggressive motives. They believe that conscious ego functions are more important than unconscious id functions in guiding behavior, emphasize positive aspects of personality, and assert the importance of developing adequate social relationships.

III. To *social learning theorists,* the key concepts in the study of personality are classical conditioning, operant conditioning, and modeling.

A. Albert Bandura says that social learning is *reciprocally determined* by the actions of behavior on the environment, and vice versa.

B. Behavior is self-regulated by our internalized cognitive standards for self-reward and limited by our perception of our own self-efficacy.

IV. *Humanistic theory* is based on a belief that humans possess an *inner-directedness* that pushes them to grow. To the humanist, reality is *subjective.*

A. *Self-concept* is our subjective perception of who we are and what we are like. Carl Rogers distinguishes between the *self* (the person I think I am) and the *ideal self* (the person I wish I were).

B. Problems result when feelings and information that are congruent with a person's self-concept are denied conscious awareness.

V. Some psychologists believe that one's personality can be described in terms of traits. *Traits* are defined as relatively enduring and consistent ways of behaving.

A. Other psychologists believe that situations determine behavior. This is known as *situationism.*

B. Social learning theorists have suggested a compromise—*interactionism*—which says that behavior is influenced by a combination of traits and the situation.

VI. Personality assessment is the use of psychological methods to learn about a person's personality.

A. The most widely used method is the *interview.*

B. Personality is also assessed by *observing* the person's behavior in a natural or simulated situation. *Rating scales* help make observational methods more objective.

C. The second most widely used method of personality assessment is the *projective test,* which psychoanalysts believe reveals the motives and conflicts of the unconscious mind.

D. Objective personality tests, such as the *MMPI,* consist of questions that measure different aspects of personality. Objective personality tests are generally better at assessing personality than projective techniques, but all personality tests are only partly accurate.

Suggested Readings

1. For in-depth discussions of the major theories of personality:

   Cartwright, D. S. (1979). *Theories and models of personality.* Dubuque, IA: Wm. C. Brown Publishers.

   Hall, C. S., & Lindsey, G. (1978). *Theories of personality.* (3rd ed.). New York: Wiley.

2. For a readable, detailed summary of Sigmund Freud's basic concepts:

   Hall, C. S. (1954). *A primer of Freudian psychology.* Cleveland: World Publishing.

3. A readable summary of Carl Jung's theory of personality is presented in:

   Hall C. S., & Nordby, V. J. (1973). *A primer of Jungian psychology.* New York: Taplinger.

4. Interviews with leading humanists Carl Rogers, Abraham Maslow, and others are presented in:

   Frick, W. B. (1971). *Humanistic psychology.* Columbus, OH: Merrill.

5. An excellent statement of the social learning view of personality is presented by:

   Bandura, A. (1977). *Social learning theory.* Englewood Cliffs, NJ: Prentice-Hall.

6. No one presents Carl Rogers' views on healthy living like Carl Rogers does:

   Rogers, C. R. (1980). *A way of being.* Boston, MA: Houghton Mifflin.

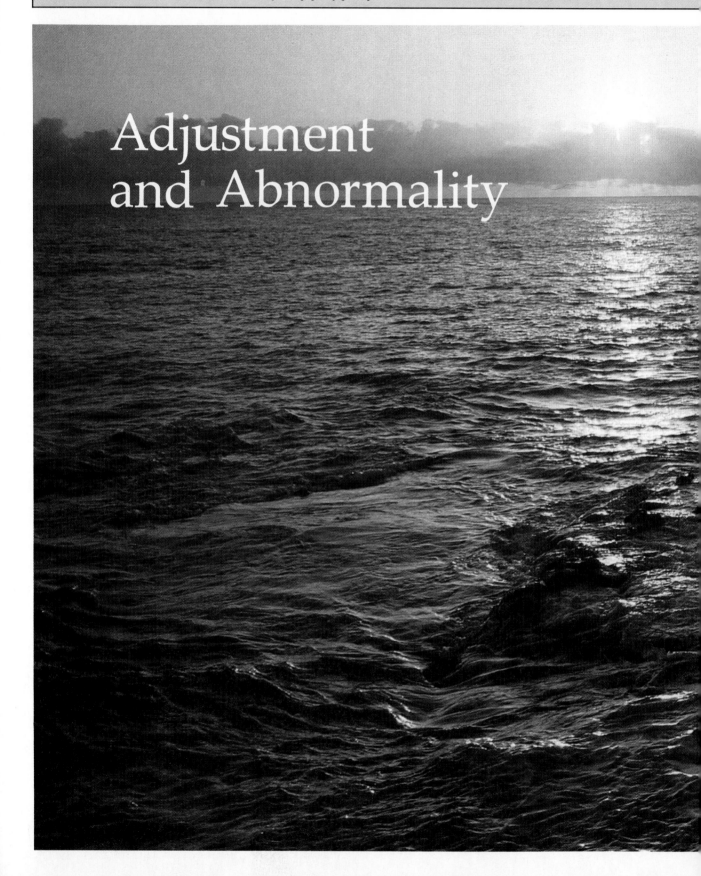

PART

Adjustment
and Abnormality

Stress and Abnormal Behavior

OUTLINE

KEY TERMS

Although the last American soldiers returned from Vietnam a decade ago, thousands of former servicemen and women continue to "fight" that tragic war in a psychological sense. They cannot seem to leave the stress of the war behind: Extremely upsetting recollections of their combat experiences involuntarily intrude upon their awareness; they experience recurrent, horrible combat dreams that rob them of sleep; they feel guilt that they survived while others did not; they feel a pervasive tenseness and sense of disgust; and they often feel alienated from the very society for which they fought. Their agony has been given the unwieldy name of combat-related posttraumatic stress disorder—in simple terms, they are suffering delayed reactions to the stress of war.

Such reactions to the stress of war are not unique to the Vietnam War—Sigmund Freud wrote about "war neurosis" in survivors of World War I—but the Vietnam War appears to have produced unprecedented numbers of posttraumatic stress disorders. It has been estimated that 500,000 Vietnam veterans experience at least some mild problems of this sort (Egendorf, Kaduschin, Rothbart, & Sloan, 1981). Fortunately, an unprecedented amount of research is currently under way concerning the nature and best treatment of posttraumatic stress disorder. For example, a group of veterans seeking psychological help for these problems at the Los Angeles Veterans Administration Medical Center were studied to determine what kinds of stressful military experiences most commonly precipitated the reaction (Foy, Sipprelle, Rueger, & Carroll, 1984). Compared to veterans with other types of psychological problems, posttraumatic stress reactions were most common in soldiers who had the most prolonged and distressing combat experiences, such as being wounded in combat or being responsible for the death of a civilian.

War is not the only kind of stress, of course—civilians can experience intensely stressful events, too. Psychologists Paul and Gerald Adams of Utah State University have provided us with an eye-opening picture of human reactions to the 1980 Mount Saint Helens' eruption (Adams & Adams, 1984). These researchers studied the residents of the nearby town of Othello, Washington, during the seven-month period following the eruption. Compared to the same seven months of the preceding year, the residents of Othello were diagnosed by the town's physicians and mental health workers as having 200 percent more stress-related physical illnesses and psychological disorders, and the town police responded to 45 percent more reports of family violence. Apparently, the stress of the volcanic ashfall took a heavy human toll on the residents of Othello.

Most of us will never be exposed to the stressors of combat or volcanic eruptions, but we will undergo other forms of stress—divorce, death of a family member, loss of employment, being a victim of violent crime, high-pressure jobs, and so on. Most of us will feel the effects of stress for at least brief periods of time in our lives. In fact, stress is so prevalent and stress reactions are so understandable, it's a wonder that we are as well adjusted as most of us are. What determines how well we will cope with stress? Why is one person well adjusted while another is not? These are enormously important questions that psychology is finally beginning to answer.

P R E V I E W

A happy person is one who can enjoy the good times and cope with the bad. Stress hits our emotions, our motivations, our ability to think clearly, and our bodies; it comes from the frustrations, conflicts, pressures, and changes in our lives. Generally, we are better able to cope with stress when we have had previous experience with it, can predict it, and can control it to some extent. Sometimes we cope with stress effectively by removing its source or by managing its effects on us, but at other times we react ineffectively with aggression, withdrawal, or other defenses that distort reality.

Coping with stress, sometimes well and sometimes badly, is a normal part of life. But sometimes people develop abnormal ways of acting, thinking, and feeling in response to stress, sometimes even in the face of only minimal stress. Abnormal behavior is behavior that is harmful to the individual or to others. But although it's easy to conclude that a person who behaves in harmful ways needs help, it's often difficult to make the subjective judgment that a specific person's behavior is abnormal. How harmful must it be? And by whose standards should we judge the harmfulness?

What causes abnormal behavior? Many answers have been given to this question throughout history. The earliest answer was that evil spirits caused it, but other views of the causes of abnormal behavior have also been taken throughout history. Some have felt that it comes from disturbances of the biological functioning of the body; others believe that it has psychological causes such as stress or faulty cognitions about self or others. Currently, both psychological and biological theories are popular, and there is a move toward explanations combining both kinds of factors.

Abnormal behavior takes many forms. In its modern meaning, the term *neurotic* does not refer to a specific kind of psychological problem; rather it refers to a broad range of disorders that are relatively mild, do not seriously impair the individual's ability to meet the requirements of independent daily living, and do not involve gross distortions of reality. Specific types of disorders of the neurotic sort include excessive anxiety and fear: conditions in which symptoms of health problems have psychological rather than physical causes; disturbances in memory, temporary alterations of perception, and sudden changes in personality and identity; and relatively mild depression.

In contrast, *psychotic* disorders are ones that seriously impair the individual's daily functioning and involve marked distortions of reality. Psychotic conditions include schizophrenia and severe forms of depression that sometimes alternate with periods of unrealistic euphoria. Both disorders involve false beliefs and perceptions that result in the individual's being "out of touch with reality." Schizophrenia is also characterized by distorted emotions and withdrawal from social relationships. In general, neurotic and psychotic disorders are thought to result from the breakdown of a normal personality. Personality disorders, on the other hand, are a third broad class of problems that are thought to result from the faulty development of personality in childhood.

Stress and Coping

Life is not all smooth sailing; all of us must face difficult and painful times in our lives. Whether it be failing a course, losing a job, experiencing conflicts about how to care for an aged parent, enduring a divorce, or dealing with a pressure-packed job, we must face and cope with stress. **Stress** *can be thought of as any event that strains or exceeds an individual's ability to cope* (Lazarus & Launier, 1978). Stress can produce a variety of psychological and physiological reactions, generally ones that are based on activation of the sympathetic division of the autonomic nervous system (refer back to chapter 2, p. 52).

The study of stress often provides a new perspective on our own feelings and behavior. Most of us are not used to thinking, "I'm feeling this way because it's a natural reaction to the stress I'm under." But in many cases, stress is the cause for our most puzzling feelings and behavior.

Frustration results when we are unable to satisfy a motive.

stress
Any event or circumstance that strains or exceeds an individual's ability to cope.

Sources of Stress

What are the events and circumstances that cause stress? Most sources of stress are obvious to us all—they rip and tear at our lives—but other sources of stress are quite surprising. Unless we know what to look for, the sources of stress can cause a great deal of trouble while remaining hidden from view. The major sources of stress are included here.

Frustration

When we are not able to satisfy a motive, **frustration** results. You see frustration in the face of a child who cannot reach the candy she's dropped, or in the exasperation of the college senior who finds that he cannot register for the one class that he needs to graduate. When frustrations are serious, as in the case of the woman who has been denied a deserved and hoped for promotion, or when they are prolonged, as when individuals living in poverty cannot obtain proper food or medical care, they can be a major source of stress.

frustration
The result of being unable to satisfy a motive.

Conflict

Conflicts are closely related to the concept of frustration. **Conflict** occurs when two or more motives cannot be satisfied because they interfere with one another. Suppose you have been invited to spend a week with friends at the beach, and then your car breaks down. You check your budget and find that you can afford *either* to fix your car *or* go to the beach—that is a conflict! There are four major kinds of conflicts (Lewin, 1931; Miller, 1944):

conflict
The state in which two or more motives cannot be satisfied because they interfere with one another.

1. *Approach-approach conflicts.* In **approach-approach conflicts,** the individual must choose between two positive goals of approximately equal value. Suppose that when you finish school you are offered two very attractive jobs. Both seem to offer good working conditions, high prestige, and excellent salary. If both jobs are so good, why do you feel so anxious? Why are you having stomachaches and trouble sleeping? Even though both goals are positive ones—you would be happy with either job—the choice between these two goals can be very stressful. This is an example of a hidden source of stress. Because everything looks so positive, it's often difficult to see that you are in a serious conflict. The choice between two colleges, two boyfriends, or two ways to spend the summer can be similarly stressful.

approach-approach conflict
Conflict in which the individual must choose between two positive goals of approximately equal value.

In an avoidance-avoidance conflict, the individual must choose between two or more negative outcomes, such as the pain of the tooth and the expected pain of going to the dentist.

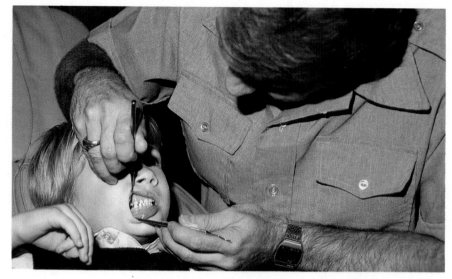

avoidance-avoidance conflict
Conflict in which the individual must choose between two negative outcomes of approximately equal value.

2. *Avoidance-avoidance conflicts.* This type of conflict involves more obvious sources of stress. In **avoidance-avoidance conflicts,** the individual must choose between two or more negative outcomes. The person with a toothache must choose between the pain of the tooth and the pain of going to the dentist. The teenage boy who is challenged to a fight by the school bully must choose between getting hurt in the fight or suffering embarrassment in front of his friends for cowardice if he does not fight.

approach-avoidance conflict
Conflict in which achieving a positive goal will produce a negative outcome as well.

3. *Approach-avoidance conflicts.* **Approach-avoidance conflicts** arise when obtaining a positive goal necessitates a negative outcome as well. A student who is accepted to a prestigious medical school in another state will be in a stressful conflict if she knows that it will mean being separated from her fiancee who is a law student at her present university. Attending the medical school will have both positive and negative consequences, so the student may begin experiencing considerable stress as the time grows nearer for beginning school.

Notice that I said the student would begin to experience stress as the time grew *nearer* for her to attend medical school. There is an important and interesting fact about approach–avoidance conflicts behind that statement. As the positive and negative outcomes grow nearer, either in distance or time, the relative strength of the motives to approach and avoid them changes. This change has been described graphically in terms of the *gradients of approach and avoidance.* Notice in figure 12.1 that the strength of the motive to avoid the negative consequence increases quickly (has a steep gradient) as distance (or time) from the goal decreases. Strength of the motive to approach the goal, on the other hand, increases slowly (has a gradual gradient). At any particular distance from the goal, the effective amount of motive to approach or avoid is the remainder when the motive to avoid is subtracted from the motive to approach.

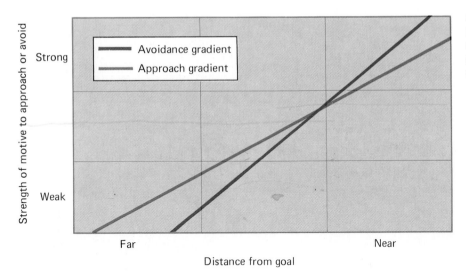

Figure 12.1 Gradients of approach and avoidance in an approach-avoidance conflict.

At greater distances, there is a stronger motive to approach than avoid, so the net motive is to approach. At shorter distances, the motive to avoid is stronger than the motive to approach, so there is a net motive to avoid. Let's look at what this means in terms of our example.

The student who had been accepted to medical school began to experience a high level of stress about the time that the strength of the approach and avoidance motives were about equal. If the motives to approach and avoid were actually about equal in strength as diagramed in figure 12.1, she might even change her mind and give up her admission to medical school as the time to attend became near and the net motive had switched strongly in favor of avoidance. After turning down her admission, however, she would again be at a great "distance" from the medical school. She might again feel a motive to approach and wish she had not decided against going.

Have you ever found yourself in such a conflict? Did you find yourself going back and forth on the decision? If so, you have had a very common human experience. The actual outcome of such a conflict depends on many factors, but particularly the relative strength of the two motives.

4. *Double approach-avoidance conflicts.* Sometimes the conflicts that we face are complex combinations of approach and avoidance conflicts. A **double approach-avoidance conflict** requires the individual to choose between alternatives that contain both positive and negative consequences. Imagine that you are a promising high school athlete and you have been offered athletic scholarships to two colleges. One is from a strong school that won its conference championship in basketball last season, but you strongly dislike the coach and several of the other players on the team. The other is from a weaker school that has an embarrassing record of performance in recent years, but you like the coach and players. What do you do? Do you go to the stronger college where there are

double approach-avoidance conflict
Conflict that requires the individual to choose between two alternatives that each contain both positive and negative consequences.

Figure 12.2 The amount of sympathetic autonomic arousal (as measured by changes in the electrical conductance of the skin caused by changes in skin sweat) in inexperienced parachutists at different ''distances'' from the approach-avoidance goal of jumping (Epstein & Fenz, 1965).

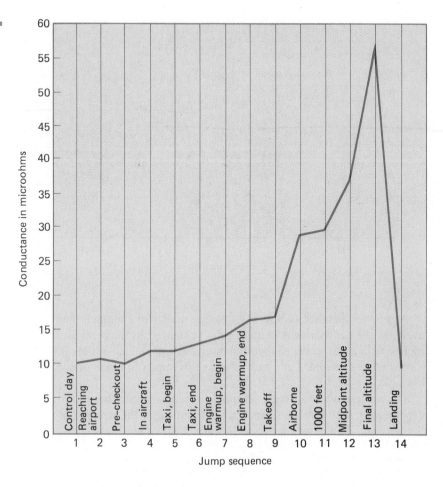

people you do not like, or do you go to the embarrassing school where you like the people with whom you will be playing? This is a double approach-avoidance conflict since both choices involve both positive and negative outcomes.

Researcher Seymour Epstein has vividly demonstrated the stressfulness of conflicts in his studies of parachute jumpers (Epstein, 1982). Epstein views parachute jumping as involving an approach-avoidance conflict because the jump entails both dangerous risks and exhilarating thrills. In one part of his research program, inexperienced jumpers were rigged with devices to measure the amount of sympathetic autonomic arousal by monitoring changes in skin sweat. As shown in figure 12.2, the autonomic reaction of the jumpers mounted dramatically to a peak at the moment of the jump, then returned to normal levels immediately after landing. While few of us face such obvious stressors, the more subtle conflicts in our lives apparently affect our bodies in similar ways.

Pressure

Does the pressure of working for good grades ever get to you? If you have been employed, was it a high-pressure job? The term **pressure** is used to describe the stress that arises from threats of negative events. In school, there is always the possibility that you will not perform well and you will fail. Some jobs are loaded with possibilities for making a mess of things and getting fired. Some marriages

pressure
Stress that arises from the threat of negative events.

The term *pressure* is used to describe the stress that arises from threats such as the possibility of poor performance on an exam.

are sources of pressure because one spouse always seems to displease the other, no matter how hard he or she tries not to. The pressure of trying to avoid these negative events can sometimes be more stressful than the negative events themselves.

Life Events

In recent years, a great deal of research has focused on the stressful nature of important events in life. Negative life events are clearly a source of stress; death of a family member, learning that one has a life-threatening illness, and loss of a job are potent sources of stress. There is also reason to believe that positive life changes can be stressful under some circumstances (Sarason, Johnson, & Siegel, 1978). Marriage, birth of a child, job promotion, and buying a house are examples of events that most people think of as positive, but they may also require stressful adjustments in patterns of living. Hence, positive life changes can be another source of stress of which we are typically unaware.

The relationship between stressful life events and physical illness has been the subject of a great deal of research (Holmes & Rahe, 1967; Rabkin & Streuning, 1976). United States Navy physicians Thomas Holmes and Richard Rahe have developed a scale to measure the amount of stress from life events in terms of *life change units (LCUs)*. Table 12.1 shows this scale of stress of events and the amount of stressful impact that Holmes and Rahe believe each event has on our lives. The individual taking the test indicates which events have happened to him or her during the last year and adds up the units of impact. Holmes and Rahe (1967) have found that Navy personnel who had experienced unusually high levels of life stress during the past year were more likely to develop a wide range of medical problems while on sea duty than individuals with lower life change units. Other evidence also suggests that high levels of life stress lead to depression and anxiety (Habif & Lahey, 1980). The moral of the story: Space out your life change units when you can (Lloyd, Alexander, Rice, & Greenfield, 1980). Do not graduate from college, move to a new city, take a new job, buy a new house, get married, and have a baby all in one year. If you do, do not be surprised if you are tense, moody, and have stomachaches.

Table 12.1 The social readjustment rating scale

Life Event	Mean Value
Death of spouse	100
Divorce	73
Marital separation	65
Jail term	63
Death of close family member	63
Personal injury or illness	53
Marriage	50
Fired at work	47
Marital reconciliation	45
Retirement	45
Change in health of family member	44
Pregnancy	40
Sex difficulties	39
Gain of new family member	39
Business readjustment	39
Change in financial state	38
Death of close friend	37
Change to different line of work	36
Change in number of arguments with spouse	35
Mortgage or loan for major purchase (home, etc.)	31
Foreclosure on mortgage or loan	30
Change in responsibilities at work	29
Son or daughter leaving home	29
Trouble with in-laws	29
Outstanding personal achievement	28
Spouse begins or stops work	26
Begin or end school	26
Change in living conditions	25
Revision of personal habits	24
Trouble with boss	23
Change in work hours or conditions	20
Change in residence	20
Change in schools	20
Change in recreation	19
Change in church activities	19
Change in social activities	18
Mortgage or loan for lesser purchase (car, TV, etc.)	17
Change in sleeping habits	16
Change in number of family get-togethers	15
Change in eating habits	15
Vacation	13
Christmas	12
Minor violations of the law	11

"I left for work this morning and took a cab. When I got out, the driver said, 'Looks like a super day.' I walked into my office and my secretary offered me a Danish, 'Try one,' she said. 'They're super!' We had a staff meeting on the Brinton matter, which the chairman of the board characterized as 'super.' Roy Damon took me to lunch at what he called a 'super' little French place. I rode home with Bill Johnson and Ron McGruddy, who kept talking about some 'super' new film. As I came in, the doorman complimented me on my 'super' tie, and the elevator operator asked me if I didn't think we were having 'super' weather. My wife greeted me as I entered the apartment and said she had prepared a 'super' treat for dinner. I don't remember anything after that."

Environmental Conditions

There is growing evidence that aspects of the environments in which we live (temperature, air pollution, noise, humidity, etc.) can be sources of stress. For example, urban riots have occurred much more frequently on hot than cool days (mid-80s Fahrenheit), although they have been rare on extremely hot days (perhaps because extreme heat leads to lethargic lack of energy) (Baron & Ramsberger, 1978). Similarly, visits to the psychiatric emergency room of California's Sacramento Medical Center were found to be related to environmental conditions (Briere, Downes, & Spensley, 1983). Visits for all types of psychological problems were higher during periods of high air pollution and there were more emergency visits for depression during cloudy, humid days. These environmental sources of stress do not appear to be as potent as other stressors, but apparently contribute to our overall stress levels.

Stress Reactions and Coping

When we are under stress, we feel it. The specific reaction differs greatly from individual to individual, but stress is never pleasant. These reactions include both psychological and physiological components.

Figure 12.3 Changes in resistance to stress during the three stages of the general adaptation syndrome (Selye, 1976).

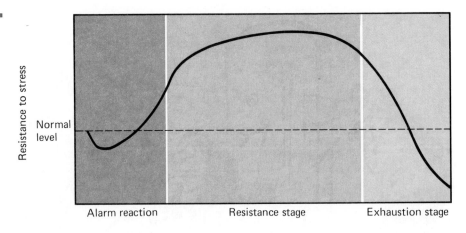

Resistance to stress

Normal level

Alarm reaction   Resistance stage   Exhaustion stage

Physiological Reactions: The General Adaptation Syndrome

In a lifelong program of research, physician Hans Selye (1976) has demonstrated that the body reacts in essentially the same way to any threat, whether the threat is in the form of an infection, injury, a tumor, or a psychological stress. The body mobilizes its defenses to ward off the threat in a pattern referred to by Selye as the **general adaptation syndrome (GAS).** Three stages can be distinguished in this syndrome (see fig. 12.3).

general adaptation syndrome (GAS)
According to Selye, the mobilization of the body to ward off threats, characterized by a three-stage pattern of the alarm reaction, the resistance stage, and the exhaustion stage.

1. *Alarm reaction.* The body's initial response to threat or other stress is to mobilize its stored resources. The sympathetic division of the autonomic nervous system increases heart rate and blood pressure, diverts blood away from digestion and into the skeletal muscles, increases perspiration, and in other ways prepares the body for a physical struggle. The endocrine glands pump adrenaline and other hormones into the bloodstream that aid the actions of the autonomic nervous system and increase levels of blood sugar.

   When intense or prolonged, these bodily changes give rise to conscious feelings of general muscle tension, stomachaches, headaches, and other feelings of "sickness." In the early stages of the general adaptation syndrome, it's often difficult to distinguish between the feelings associated with catching a cold, being under psychological stress, or even falling in love. Because anything that causes an alarm reaction produces essentially the same response from the body, the differences are often relatively subtle.

   During the alarm reaction stage, the rapid mobilization of resources leaves the individual temporarily less resistant to the stress than originally. This state of affairs is quickly changed as the next stage is entered.

2. *Resistance stage.* During the second stage of the GAS, the body's resources have been fully mobilized, and resistance to the stress is at a high level. This resistance is costly in terms of resources, however. If new stress (psychological or physical) is encountered, the body will be less able to deal with it. In this way, psychological stress can leave the person more vulnerable to physical stress (disease), and vice versa. Moreover, if the stress continues, the individual's resources will eventually become depleted, leading to the third stage of the GAS.

3. *Exhaustion stage.* Finally, the individual's resources have become exhausted, and resistance to the stress is lowered. In cases of prolonged exposure to severe physical stress (such as intense cold), death can occur during the exhaustion stage. Psychological stress rarely is able to precipitate death, but it can severely disrupt bodily functioning. Ulcers, chronic high blood pressure, and even heart attacks can be brought about by prolonged psychological stress (Selye, 1976).

Psychological Reactions to Stress

The physiological reactions to stress are accompanied by psychological reactions, as well. These changes primarily involve emotions, motivations, and cognitions. Under stress, we feel anxious, depressed, and irritable. We experience changes in our appetite for food and may gain or lose large amounts of weight. Our interest in sex often decreases, but it may increase. Cognitive changes occur as well: We have difficulty concentrating, lose our ability to think clearly, and find that our thoughts keep returning to the source of the stress.

But we do not just passively *react* to stress; we respond with efforts to cope with it. The term **coping** refers to attempts to deal with the source of the stress or control our reactions to it, or both. As we see in the next two sections, some of our attempts to cope are more effective than others. (See *Research Report:* "Psychological Aftermath of the Stress of Rape.")

coping
Attempts by individuals to deal with the source of stress and/or control their reactions to it.

Effective Coping

Effective methods of coping remove the source of stress or control our reactions to it.

1. *Removing stress.* One effective way of dealing with stress is to remove the source of stress from our life. If an employee holds a job that is stressful, discussions could be held with the employer that might lead to a reduction in the pressures of the job, or the employee could simply resign. If the stress stems from an unhappy marriage, either marriage counseling could be sought or the marriage could be terminated. In a variety of ways, coping with stress can take the form of locating its source and eliminating it. Unfortunately, this is not always possible. It's not always feasible or appropriate to quit a job or leave a marriage, and some sources of stress, such as the death of a spouse, just cannot be removed.

2. *Managing stress reactions.* When the source of stress cannot realistically be removed or changed, an effective option is to manage the *reaction* to the stress. For example, an individual may decide to start a new business knowing full well that the first year or two will be hectic. She would be unwilling, then, to remove the source of the stress (the new business), but could learn to control the reactions to the stress. One strategy might be to schedule as much time as possible for relaxing activities such as exercise, hobbies, or time with friends. Another would be to seek special training from a psychologist in controlling the bodily reactions to stress by learning to deeply relax the large body muscles (relaxation training is discussed more in chapter 13).

R E S E A R C H   R E P O R T

Psychological Aftermath of the Stress of Rape

Rape is a terrifying, demeaning event that is acutely stressful for the victim. Extensive research has been conducted in recent years by Karen Calhoun and her associates on the psychological effects of this violent act (Atkeson, Calhoun, Resick, & Ellis, 1982; Calhoun, Atkeson, & Resick, 1982; Resick, Calhoun, Atkeson, & Ellis, 1981). Calhoun studied 115 women who had been raped, comparing them to a group who had not been raped. As expected, she found that the experience produced strong negative reactions in the women immediately after the rape. As a group, the raped women were more depressed, more fearful, and experienced more disturbances in personal relationships than the nonraped women. These stress-induced reactions gradually dissipated, however, so that there were no significant differences between the two groups by the time four months had elapsed since the rape. Similar temporary increases in general anxiety and decreases in sexual interest have been reported by other researchers, although general anxiety has been found to be elevated as long as one year after the rape (Kilpatrick, Resick, & Veronen, 1981). Fortunately, even though the stress of rape is traumatic, the recovery is complete for most women.

Ineffective Coping

Unfortunately, many of our efforts to cope with stress are ineffective. They may provide temporary relief from the discomfort produced by stress, but do little to provide a long-term solution and may even make matters worse. Three common, but ineffective, coping strategies are as follows.

1. *Withdrawal.* Sometimes we deal with stress by withdrawing from it. Many students encounter courses in college that are far more difficult than anything they had experienced in high school. Attempting to study difficult material can be highly stressful and can lead to a withdrawal from studying—by playing electronic games, shooting baskets in the gym, partying, and the like. Similarly, a husband may ineffectively cope with the stress of his unhappy marriage by withdrawing to the refuge of a bar every day after work.

2. *Aggression.* As we discussed in chapter 10, a common reaction to frustration and other stressful situations is aggression. The woman who has tried unsuccessfully to create romantic interest in a man may suddenly become hostile toward him. The man who cannot get a screw to fit into a curtain rod may throw a temper tantrum and hurl the rod to the floor in disgust.

An ineffective method of coping with stress from an unhappy marriage is to withdraw to the refuge of a bar.

3. *Defense mechanisms.* According to Freud, one of the key functions of the ego is to "defend" the person from a buildup of uncomfortable tension. When something stressful occurs (such as frustration or embarrassment) or when conflict arises because the superego blocks an id desire, tension is created that must be discharged somehow. Freud believed that the ego possesses a small arsenal of **defense mechanisms** that are unconsciously used to discharge tension. The major defense mechanisms are as follows.

Displacement: When it's unsafe or immoral to express aggressive or sexual feelings toward the person who is creating stress (such as a boss who pressures you), that feeling can be directed toward someone safe (such as yelling at your spouse when you are really angry with your boss).

Sublimation: Stressful conflicts over dangerous id impulses are reduced by converting the impulses into socially approved activities such as schoolwork, literature, sports, and so on.

Projection: One's own dangerous or unacceptable id desires are seen not as one's own, but as the desires of others. A person who has stressful conflicts about sex might perceive himself as having little sexual desire but view other people as being obsessed with sex.

Reaction formation: Conflicts over dangerous id impulses are avoided by unconsciously transforming them into the opposite desire. A married man with strong desires for extramarital sex might start on a campaign to rid his city of massage parlors and prostitutes. A woman who wishes her hateful mother would die might devote herself to finding ways to protect her mother's health.

defense mechanisms
According to Freud, the unrealistic strategies used by the ego to discharge tension.

displacement
(dis-plās′ment)
A defense mechanism in which the individual directs aggressive or sexual feelings away from the primary object to someone or something safe.

sublimation
(sub″lĭ-ma′shun)
According to Freud, a form of displacement in which a socially desirable goal is substituted for a socially harmful goal.

projection (pro-jek′shun)
According to Freud, a defense mechanism in which unacceptable id desires are viewed as the desires of others and not as one's own.

reaction formation
According to Freud, a defense mechanism in which unacceptable id desires are avoided by transforming them into the opposite desires.

regression
According to Freud, a defense mechanism in which tension is reduced by returning to an infantile pattern of behavior.

rationalization
(rash"un-al-i-za'shun) According to Freud, a defense mechanism in which stress is reduced by "explaining" events in ways that reduce their stressful qualities.

repression
Sigmund Freud's theory that forgetting occurs because the conscious mind often deals with unpleasant information by pushing it into unconsciousness.

suppression
According to Freud, a defense mechanism in which the ego consciously prevents unacceptable information or feelings from entering the conscious mind.

Regression: Stress may be reduced by returning to an infantile pattern of behavior, such as a business executive who has a stomping, screaming temper tantrum when his or her company suffers a major setback.

Rationalization: Stress is reduced by "explaining it away" in ways that sound logical and socially acceptable. A man who is rejected by his lover may decide that he is glad because she had so many faults or because he really did not want to give up the single life.

Repression: Potentially stressful, unacceptable desires are kept out of consciousness without the conscious mind's being aware that the repression is occurring.

Suppression: The ego consciously keeps potentially threatening information, feelings, and desires out of awareness by intentionally not thinking about them.

Freud suggests that such defensive coping is effective in the short run by helping us feel better, but inhibits long-term solutions to stress by *distorting reality*. For example, suppose that a woman copes with the loss of a boyfriend by deciding that he was a jerk (rationalization). There might be something that she needs to change in herself to avoid losing another boyfriend. But she will never understand the need for change if she decides that the only reason her boyfriend left was because he was a jerk. The other defense mechanisms can be harmful in similar reality-distorting ways.

Factors That Influence Reactions to Stress

Different people are affected by stress in different ways. The loss of a job may be devastating to one person, mildly upsetting to another, and viewed as an opportunity to find a better career by a third person. Similarly, the same person may handle stress easily one time and be very upset by it the next. Why are there such differences in the ways people handle stress? Much remains to be learned about this topic, but enough is presently known to outline some of the factors that seem related to individual differences in reactions to stress. In addition to the sheer amount of stress (or stresses), what determines how we will react to stress?

Prior Experience with the Stress

Stress reactions are generally less severe when the individual has had some prior experience with the stress event. For example, a soldier who is going into combat for the fourth time will usually be less stressed by it than a soldier facing combat for the first time.

Predictability and Control

In general, stress events are less stressful when they are predictable than when they are not; and they are less stressful when the individual perceives that he or she can exert some degree of control over the stress. For example, mild electric shocks are unpleasant stressful events that are often used in laboratory studies of stress. Let's look at two experiments using this stress that address the related issues of predictability and control. In one study, three groups of subjects listened to a voice counting. At the count of 10, one group of subjects received an electric shock 95 percent of the time, a second group received a shock 50 percent of the time, while the third group received a shock only 5 percent of the time. A measure of sympathetic autonomic arousal was taken during the counting (a measure of the amount of skin sweat). Which group do you think showed the strongest reaction to the threat of shock? The shocks were least predictable for the group that received shocks only 5 percent of the time. Even though they received the fewest shocks, the high degree of uncertainty made their experience more stressful than for the other two groups (Epstein & Roupenian, 1970). However, when the stress continues over long periods of time, predictable stress appears to become more stressful than unpredictable stress (Abbott, Schoen, & Badia, 1984).

A second study focused on personal control over stress events. Two groups of subjects participated in a difficult cognitive task in which errors were punished by electric shocks. One group could exercise some control over this stressful situation by taking breaks whenever they wished, but the other group could take breaks only when told to do so. The amount of autonomic stress reaction (as measured in this case by elevations in blood pressure) was significantly greater for the group that had no personal control over the stress (Hokanson, DeGood, Forrest, & Brittain, 1963). Stress events that come up in our daily lives that are not predictable or controllable are generally all the more stressful.

Social Support

The magnitude of reactions to stress is considerably less for individuals with good social support from close friends and family members than for individuals with inadequate social support. It's not yet clear how social support functions to buffer us against stress, but having someone to talk to, receive advice from, and be reassured by is an important factor determining our reactions to stress. Valerie Habif and her colleague (Habif & Lahey, 1980) found a strong relationship between the amount of depression experienced by college students and the amount of life stress if the students had inadequate social support, but there was little relationship between stress and depression for students with good social support. This is a particularly important finding since many college students find themselves away from home and without adequate social support for the first time in their lives.

Medical researchers have also found, for example, that 90 percent of pregnant women who had experienced severe stress and had poor social support had some form of birth complication, but that only 33 percent of severely stressed women with adequate social support experienced complications (Nuckolls, Cassel, & Kaplan, 1972). Furthermore, individuals who live alone—and are, therefore, more likely to have inadequate social support—are more likely to have both psychological and medical problems than individuals who live with others (Webb & Collette, 1975).

Social support is also helpful in making and sticking with stressful decisions. Yale University psychologist Irving Janis developed a program to help cigarette smokers stop smoking—and not resume smoking. Some clients were given "buddies" who were also in the program and were instructed to keep in close contact during the first crucial weeks (they met weekly and spoke daily on the telephone for five weeks). Ten years later, almost all of these high social support clients were still total nonsmokers. In contrast, clients who were not given buddies or who contacted their buddies infrequently were averaging over a pack of cigarettes a day. Similar positive effects of buddies were found in a weight-loss program by Janis (Janis, 1983; Janis & Hoffman, 1982). A little help from our friends can bring out the best in us under stress in a great many ways.

Person Variables

As noted in chapter 11, many contemporary personality theorists believe that our behavior is caused by the interaction—joint effect—of both the situations in which we find ourselves and our personal characteristics (see p. 447). This *person × situation interactional* view is very much related to the issue of the magnitude of stress reactions. Considerable evidence now indicates that some individuals react more strongly than other individuals to the situational variable of stress because of their personal characteristics. For example, there appear to be inherited differences in reactivity to stress (Farber, 1982) and differences among individuals based on different ways in which they cognitively interpret stress (Beck, 1976; Ellis, 1962; Holroyd & Lazarus, 1982). Considerable research is currently under way in an effort to better understand the nature of these personal differences in stress reactions.

R E V I E W

We all must face stressful events that require some form of coping. The most common sources of stress are frustration, the many forms of conflicts, pressure, and positive and negative life events. At times, we cope effectively with stress either by finding ways to remove the source of stress or by managing the stress reaction. At other times, however, we cope ineffectively through withdrawal, aggression, and defense mechanisms. The magnitude of the emotional, cognitive, and bodily toll that stress takes on us varies from individual to individual and from time to time for the same individual. The factors that seem to be related to the magnitude of stress reactions are prior experience with the stress, predictability and control over the stress, social support, and genetic and other person variables.

Abnormal Behavior

As we have just seen, there is a wide range of normal reactions to stress. All of us are going to experience some emotional discomfort, cognitive inefficiency, and bodily reactions to stress and all of us will cope ineffectively with stress at least part of the time. Some individuals cope so poorly with stress, however, that their reactions must be considered abnormal. Others act, think, and feel in abnormal ways even in the face of what would appear to be little or no stress. In this and the following sections of this chapter we discuss abnormal behavior in its many forms.

Definition of Abnormal Behavior

The term *abnormal* is one of the most elusive terms in psychology. It's not a difficult term to define in words, but it's often difficult to apply to specific individuals because the definition involves so much *subjectivity*. **Abnormal behavior** is defined as those actions, thoughts, and feelings that are harmful to the person or to others.

abnormal behavior
Actions, thoughts, and feelings that are harmful to the person or to others.

This harm may take many forms, ranging from personal discomfort (as in feeling depressed) to physical damage (as in assaulting another person). Notice that abnormality is defined only in terms of harm. It's not enough that a pattern of behavior be *unusual* (statistically uncommon for that group of people) to be considered abnormal. Extreme intelligence and honesty are unusual, but they would hardly be considered abnormal. On the other hand, some patterns of behavior that are not uncommon are clearly harmful. The intense prejudice against Jews that was so prevalent during the days of Hitler's Germany was common, but abnormal. Some psychologists think that cigarette smoking, which is common in our culture today, could be considered abnormal because of the health problems that it causes.

This definition of abnormality requires subjective judgments in two ways. First, even though abnormality is defined in terms of harm rather than unusualness, it must be decided whether an individual's problems are *severe enough* to be considered "harmful." For example, almost everyone suffers some discomfort at times from shyness. How shy does a person have to be to be considered abnormally shy? Shier than 90 percent of other people? More than 95 percent of others? Clearly, psychologists must make largely arbitrary decisions about it in different ways.

Second, subjectivity is also a problem in the definition of what is *harmful*. That decision reflects the values of the person making the determination, and values differ greatly from one culture to another. For example, the Zuñi Indians of the southwestern United States believed it was good to be able to have hallucinations without taking drugs, for it meant that the gods were blessing you with visits. Some sects of the Moslem faith in Iran and India believe that it's holy to mutilate oneself during religious ceremonies. Nearly all psychologists in the United States would consider hallucinations and self-mutilation harmful, but differences of opinion exist on other issues such as the normality or abnormality of homosexuality or cigarette smoking in our culture. There is probably no complete solution to the problem of subjectivity. The best we can do is to be aware of the problem and try to minimize the role played by our own personal values in making subjective judgments about the behavior of others.

Advocates of the continuity hypothesis believe that abnormal behavior is just a more severe form of normal psychological problems.

continuity hypothesis
(kon″ti-nu′i-te)
The view that abnormal behavior is just a more severe form of normal psychological problems.

discontinuity hypothesis
(dis-kon″ti-nu′i-te)
The view that abnormal behavior is fundamentally different from normal psychological problems.

The concept of abnormal behavior is difficult to use not only because of its inherent subjectivity, but also because psychologists have not been able to agree on how abnormal behavior differs from normal behavior. The **continuity hypothesis** of abnormal behavior states that abnormal behavior is just a more severe form of normal psychological problems. This hypothesis is held by many humanists and social learning theorists. The **discontinuity hypothesis,** on the other hand, suggests that abnormal behavior is entirely different from normal psychological problems. Advocates of the continuity hypothesis argue that terms like *insanity* and *mental illness* should not be used because they imply that the individuals have *sick minds* that separate them from the rest of society. Advocates of the discontinuity hypothesis (primarily psychoanalytic psychologists) believe that only such strong terms can accurately portray the true nature of abnormal behavior.

Historical Views of Abnormal Behavior

Before we discuss contemporary views of the causes of abnormal behavior, it's instructive to look back at beliefs about its cause through history. This historical perspective will make the point that our ideas about the causes of abnormal behavior determine what we do to help those who experience it.

Supernatural Theories

The oldest writings about behavior, including those of Plato, the Bible, and the tablets of Babylonian King Hammurabi (1750 B.C.), indicate that, in our earliest belief, abnormal behavior was thought to be caused by evil spirits. Although there have been some who disagreed with this notion during every period in history, the idea that people with psychological problems are possessed by evil spirits was the most influential view during the entire 3,500-year period of history stretching from Hammurabi to shortly before the American Revolution.

During most of the time that the supernatural theory held sway, the consequences for those with psychological problems were not too severe. Treatment mostly took the form of prayer and chanting, with the most unpleasant treatment being purgatives—foul liquids that were supposed to help the person vomit out the evil spirit. During the Middle Ages (500–1500), however, these supernatural beliefs were translated into far more harmful forms of "treatment."

In medieval Europe, the Catholic church published an official document called the *Malleus Maleficarum,* or the *Witches' Hammer.* It gave detailed descriptions of the methods of treatment, or *exorcism,* for those people acting in the abnormal ways that "revealed" possession by the devil. Treatment began with prayers and other treatments, but for those whose behavior did not improve, the *Malleus* recommended torture to drive out the devil. If that did not work, the body of the "witch" had to be destroyed to save its soul from the devil. (See *Of Special Interest:* "Exorcisms and Witch Trials" for more on this subject.)

Biological Theories

One of the ancient voices that argued against the supernatural theory of abnormal behavior was the fifth century B.C. Greek physician Hippocrates. He believed that biological disorders of the body caused abnormal behavior. According to Hippocrates's view, the body contains four important fluids, or *humors:* blood, phlegm, black bile, and yellow bile. If these fluids get out of balance, abnormal behavior is the result. An excess of black bile, for example, leads to depression; an excess of yellow bile causes irritability.

Hippocrates's theory was inaccurate, of course, and so he was not able to punch much of a hole in the supernatural approach. But he set the stage for later developments by suggesting that abnormal behavior might have *natural* rather than supernatural causes. During the 2,000 years after Hippocrates, a number of scientists who had been influenced by Hippocrates's idea searched in vain for a biological cause of abnormal behavior. Finally, in the 1800s medical researchers such as German physician Richard von Krafft–Ebing made discoveries that led to resurgence of biological theory and the eventual birth of psychiatry as a discipline.

Richard Von Krafft–Ebing
(1840–1902)

Krafft–Ebing was working with a now rare form of severe psychological disturbance called *paresis.* He and a number of independent researchers discovered that paresis was actually an advanced stage of the venereal disease *syphilis.* Syphilis is a bacterial infection that begins with a sore, or chancre, on the genitals or on another point of entry, that is later followed by a copper-colored skin rash. The untreated disease then goes through a long "invisible" period that eventually leads to the destruction of important bodily organs. If the bacteria destroy brain cells, paresis is the result. Because of the long period of time between the original infection and the later paresis, it was not known that the two conditions were related until Krafft–Ebing demonstrated through inoculation tests that all individuals with paresis also had syphilis.

The discovery that paresis had a biological cause sent shock waves through the medical community. Soon physicians—who up to this time had little to do with people with abnormal behavior—were placed in charge of mental institutions, and the medical speciality of psychiatry was formed. There were high expectations that the biological causes for all the other forms of abnormal behavior would soon be discovered. But although the discovery of penicillin and its use in

OF SPECIAL INTEREST

Exorcisms and Witch Trials: Abnormal Psychology during the Dark Ages and Today

Psychology has changed a lot during the past 500 years, particularly in the way we deal with abnormal behavior. Consider the medieval period (500–1500 A.D.), for example, a time in history that is often aptly referred to as the Dark Ages. During this period in Western Europe, it was widely believed that the best cure for abnormal behavior was *exorcism,* a stiff regimen of prayer, fasting, and drinking foul concoctions that caused vomiting. When it became clear that exorcism was ineffective in "treating" abnormal behavior, stronger methods came into vogue. People who behaved in deviant ways and could not stop doing so after exorcism were considered to be witches or warlocks (male witches). It was believed that the only way to save the souls of these creatures was to burn their bodies to drive out Satan. As a result, thousands of "witches" were burned in the United States and Europe during this period in the name of salvation. Even as late as 1692, 20 individuals were put to death as witches in Salem, Massachusetts. Nineteen were hung for "witchcraft" while the twentieth victim died as a result of heavy rocks being placed on him in an effort to force him to confess (Phillips, 1933).

Fortunately, much has changed in our conceptions of abnormal behavior since then. But have we completely gotten over the supernatural beliefs of the Dark Ages? Consider the following news report from the 8 May 1978 issue of *Time* magazine:

> When Anneliese Michel died at the age of 23 in Klingenberg, West Germany, in the summer of 1976, she was little more than a skeleton, weighing a mere 68 lbs. Yet shortly before

the treatment of syphilis almost totally eradicated paresis, few other biological causes of abnormal behavior were discovered. In recent years, major advances in the treatment of some severe forms of abnormal behavior have been made possible by the development of effective drug therapies, however.

Psychological Theories

Hippocrates was not the only ancient Greek suggesting a *natural* explanation for abnormal behavior. Pythagoras, who also gave us geometry, was very active in the treatment of psychological problems. He held the then radical belief that psychological problems are caused by *psychological* factors such as stress. He placed individuals with problems in "temples" in which they received rest, exercise, a good diet, an understanding person to talk to, and practical advice on

OF SPECIAL INTEREST

she died, her parents said Anneliese performed an astonishing 500 deep knee-bends in one day. The source of her power, her parents believed, was nothing less than the devil himself. Anneliese's release from evil spirits came only with death, after she starved herself during a nightmarish ten-month series of Roman Catholic exorcism rituals. Two weeks ago, a court in Aschaffenburg found two priests and Anneliese's parents, wealthy mill-owner Josef Michel, 60, and his wife Anna, 57, guilty of negligent homicide in her death. The four, who last week appealed their conviction, drew six-month suspended prison sentences.

Anneliese's parents had agreed to the exorcism with the local bishop's approval after doctors failed to rid her of epileptic-like convulsions. The prosecution took no issue with the rite of exorcism, which Fathers Wilhelm Renz and Ernst Alt conducted according to a Catholic ritual promulgated in 1614. But prosecutor Karl Stenger argued that calling a doctor to examine the girl "would not have compromised the defendants' religious convictions." Churchmen seemed to agree. Munich's Joseph Cardinal Katzinger said that the 1614 ritual "must be thoroughly revised," and the German Bishops' Conference ruled last week that no more exorcisms would be permitted unless a doctor was called in.

Reprinted by permission from Time.

how to straighten out their lives. Records from his temples suggest that Pythagoras's methods were highly successful. But unfortunately, the psychological ideas of Pythagoras were not able to compete with the supernaturalists until modern times.

Although there were many important advocates of psychological theory, not until Sigmund Freud published his influential views was psychological theory able to compete with the supernatural and biological approaches. Although Freud's model of unconscious conflicts was quite different from the ideas of Pythagoras, Freud became the modern champion of the view that psychological problems had psychological causes.

OF SPECIAL INTEREST

Insanity and the Law

What does it mean to be *insane?* Actually insanity is not a psychological or psychiatric term but a legal term. And to make matters more complex, insanity has not one, but three, different legal meanings, depending on whether it's used as a criminal defense, in a hearing on competency to stand trial, or in a hearing on involuntary commitment to a mental institution.

1. *Not guilty by reason of insanity.* In some states, a person cannot be convicted of a crime if he or she were legally "insane" at the time the crime was committed. There are many definitions of the term "insane" in this context, but perhaps the most influential formula was proposed by the American Law Institute and adopted by many state and federal courts in the 1970s. It states, "A person is not responsible for criminal conduct if at the time of such conduct, as a result of mental disease or defect, he lacks substantial capacity either to appreciate the wrongfulness of his conduct or to conform his conduct to the requirements of the law." This definition means that people committing crimes are considered "not guilty by reason of insanity" if they had little ability to tell right from wrong, or had little ability to control their actions at the time of the crime, because of serious psychological problems. Generally, juries will only consider severely psychotic or severely mentally retarded persons to be insane according to this rule, and since individuals with these problems rarely commit crimes, it's rarely a successful defense.

   The controversial nature of this use of the term insanity in the courtroom was made clear in the public reaction to the trial of John W. Hinckley, Jr. in 1982. Hinckley admitted to having shot Ronald Reagan and others in an unsuccessful attempt to assassinate the President. The jurors

Contemporary Views of Abnormal Behavior

Today, abnormal behavior is believed to be a natural phenomenon with natural causes. While there are still many people in our era who believe that psychological disturbances are supernatural in origin, this kind of thinking has no place in modern psychology and psychiatry. Overall, the psychological approach is the dominant viewpoint today, but the biological approach is influential as well.

OF SPECIAL INTEREST

found Hinckley not guilty because they believed that he was insane. As a result, Hinckley received no prison sentence for his actions, but was committed to St. Elizabeth's Psychiatric Hospital in Washington, D.C. If he convinces his doctors that he is sane at some point in the future, he could be released at any time. The public dissatisfaction with this verdict was intense and was partly responsible for changes in the law concerning the insanity defense. Juries in a number of states now can find defendants "guilty but mentally ill." In this case the person receives a prison sentence, but is also given psychiatric treatment.

2. *Competence to stand trial.* The term *insanity* is also used in hearings to determine whether the individual is competent to stand trial. In this sense, the question of insanity is whether the people are able to understand the proceedings of the trial sufficiently to aid in their own defense. Again, it's primarily severely psychotic and mentally retarded individuals who are considered incompetent according to this definition.

3. *Involuntary commitment.* A third meaning of the term insanity arises in hearings on the involuntary commitment of individuals to mental institutions. It's legal in most states to commit people to an institution against their will if a court finds them to be insane. Generally, the courts interpret this as meaning that the individuals are a direct danger to themselves or to others, usually meaning a physical danger. Behaving in strange ways is not enough to justify involuntary commitment. There must be an element of danger.

As research evidence has accumulated, it has become increasingly clear that both biological and psychological factors are involved in the origins of many psychological disorders. Some disorders are solely biological in origin (such as those caused by brain injuries), and some are solely psychological in origin (such as acute grief reactions to the death of a loved one in normal individuals). But many other disorders appear to involve both kinds of causes. Inherited predispositions to certain kinds of problems, abnormal amounts of specific neurotransmitter substances in the brain, and tendencies to react autonomically to stress in

OF SPECIAL INTEREST

Psychological Theories of Abnormal Behavior

What causes abnormal behavior? In most instances, we have no firm answer but a lot of guesses. Each of the major theories of personality discussed in chapter 11 offers explanations for most of the major forms of abnormal behavior. Let's look at major depression as an example of how these theoretical explanations differ. Keep in mind that each theory is presented in greatly simplifed form. Complete theories of depression fill books.

To the psychoanalyst, depression is the result of the loss of an important person. When an individual suffers the death of a father or the loss of a girlfriend, the mind vainly tries to hold onto the lost person by identifying with him or her, unconsciously thinking that I *am* my lost father or girlfriend. Because Freud believes that our ids make us want to hurt the people that we love, he feels that this aggression toward the lost love is now turned inward on ourselves resulting in our depression. This self-aggression is made worse if we feel guilty for things we feel we did to hurt the loved one (the superego wants you to be nice to everybody at the same time your id wants you to hurt the person), or if we feel that we did things to drive the person away.

an abnormal way are some of the biological factors believed to be partially responsible for a variety of psychological disorders. The psychological factors involved in these same disorders include stress, abnormal social learning histories, ineffective coping strategies, and inadequate social support. Apparently, the biological and psychological factors work together to determine whether a person will experience psychological problems. For example, individuals whose autonomic nervous systems have a tendency to react excessively to stress will only have problems if their lives are filled with considerable stress and if they have poor social support. If present trends continue, we will probably see a fusion of the biological and psychological approaches into a single, naturalistic viewpoint. (See *Research Report:* "Is Abnormal Behavior Inherited?")

OF SPECIAL INTEREST

Humanistic theories view depression as resulting from distortions of the self-concept. If the standards of my ideal self are unreachable, I will feel anxiety as I strive fruitlessly to attain them, then I will experience depression when I give up.

Social learning theories see depression as the result of our learning experiences. If we have had a long history of being unable to avoid negative experiences and have not learned effective ways of obtaining positive consequences from life, depression will result. If the depression causes others to treat us nicely (positive reinforcement), it will last longer. Also, if we have learned faulty cognitive strategies that lead us to exaggerate the negative side of life, we will be more likely to become depressed.

Obviously, these three theories take very different views of depression. It's not possible to decide at the present time which, if any, is the correct view, although each seems to offer insights at times. In general, depression is a complex phenomenon that will probably require more complicated and complete explanations than offered by any of these theories. It seems especially likely that future theories will need to incorporate both psychological and biological variables.

REVIEW

Actions, thoughts, and feelings that are harmful to the individual or to others are considered to be abnormal. This definition is a difficult one to implement because of the subjectivity involved. How severe must an individual's problem be before he or she is considered harmful? And by whose cultural standards should harmfulness be defined? Moreover, psychologists have not been able to agree on how abnormal behavior differs from normal psychological problems. Is abnormal behavior just a more severe version of normal problems, or is it fundamentally different in nature? Advocates of the continuity hypothesis take the former view, while advocates of the discontinuity hypothesis take the latter view.

Differences in perspectives among contemporary psychologists seem minor, however, when compared to differing views that have been taken of abnormal behavior throughout history. Abnormal behavior has been thought to result from supernatural causes or from biological abnormalities, as well as from psychological causes. The supernatural theory is of little importance in today's psychology, but both biological and psychological factors are currently thought to be involved in the origins of abnormal behavior.

RESEARCH REPORT

Is Abnormal Behavior Inherited?

Since before the time of Plato, it has been suspected that psychological disorders are inherited, but no one has been able to prove or disprove this hypothesis. Suppose you were a scientist interested in the causes of abnormal behavior. What kinds of evidence would you collect to investigate this question?

You might first gather data to see if abnormal behavior "runs in families" like many people believe that it does. For example, you might study the offspring of people with schizophrenia to see if the offspring also develop the disorder. If you did, you would find that 10 percent of the children of one schizophrenic parent also develop schizophrenia during their lifetime (Hanson, Gottesman, & Heston, 1976). That is not a very large percentage, but it's 12 times higher than the percentage for nonschizophrenic parents, and it's high enough to indicate that schizophrenia *could* be inherited as a recessive trait.

But we cannot conclude that schizophrenia is inherited solely on the basis of information that its occurrence is more common in the offspring of schizophrenic parents. Using this information alone, we cannot rule out the equally plausible explanation that 10 percent of the offspring of schizophrenics develop schizophrenia because the psychological problems of the parents led them to rear their children in abnormal ways. It might not be genetics that causes schizophrenia at all, but the environment in which the child grows up. We need some way of separating the effects of inheritance from environment.

One strategy that researchers have used involves studying children of schizophrenic parents who were not reared by their natural parents but were adopted and reared by normal parents. The results of these studies still show that 10 percent of the offspring of schizophrenic parents developed schizophrenia, even when they were raised by normal adoptive parents (Heston, 1966). Again, these findings suggest that schizophrenia might be partially inherited.

RESEARCH REPORT

Monozygotic and dizygotic twins (see chapter 2, p. 80) have also been used in a number of studies of the inheritance of schizophrenia. Schizophrenic individuals are located who have a twin sibling who is also tested for schizophrenia. If inheritance plays a part in causing schizophrenia, then monozygotic twins with identical genetic inheritance should have more twin siblings who are also schizophrenic than genetically dissimilar dizygotic twins. A number of studies suggest that this is, in fact, the case. On the average, 24 percent of the monozygotic twin siblings are also schizophrenic, while only 6 percent of the dizygotic twin siblings have schizophrenia (Lahey & Ciminero, 1980).

The results of twin studies clearly support the hypothesis that inheritance is involved in the cause of schizophrenia, but one important fact should be noted. Some *76 percent* of the monozygotic twins of schizophrenics did *not* exhibit schizophrenia, in spite of the fact that they had *identical inheritance.* If schizophrenia were inherited in the simple sense that eye color is inherited—even if it were a recessive trait—both members of monozygotic twin pairs would develop schizophrenia if one twin did. Thus if one of the monozygotic twins had the gene or genes for schizophrenia, the other would too.

The fact that far fewer than 100 percent of the monozygotic twins of schizophrenics also are schizophrenic has led to today's view that schizophrenia is not inherited *per se,* but that a predisposition or tendency to develop schizophrenia is inherited. It's obviously a weak predisposition since only 10 percent of the offspring of schizophrenic parents develop the disorder, but it does appear to be *one* of the causes. Other causes are thought to be stress, abnormal learning experiences, and maladaptive personal relationships.

No other psychological disorder has been studied as extensively as schizophrenia. It appears at present, however, that at least a few other disorders have an inherited genetic predisposition, while other disorders do not. But it's at least clear that abnormal behavior is not inherited in the sense that we usually use that term.

...ncepts of "Neurosis" and "Psychosis"

...**neurosis** has been important in psychology and psychiatry since the ...)s when physician William Cullen first used it to refer to a broad range ...vely mild psychological problems that he thought were caused by "weak ...in the literal sense of weak neurons. In more recent times, however, the ...g of the term *neurosis* has been changed to refer simply to relatively mild ...ers in which the individual does not "lose contact with reality." The term ...ued to be a widely used diagnostic label until the third edition of the *Di-tic and Statistical Manual (DSM-III)* of the American Psychiatric Association dropped the term as a diagnostic category. If you were neurotic in 1979, you no longer were when the DSM-III was published in 1980. The term was officially dropped because it was considered to refer to a too wide range of disorders to be a meaningful diagnostic term. The term is still in use, however. But today, the term *neurotic* is used as an adjective to refer to a broad range of disorders rather than as the name of a single diagnostic category. In the following sections we discuss three categories of neurotic conditions from the DSM-III—anxiety disorders, somatoform disorders, and dissociative disorders. In addition, mild major depression would be considered to be a neurotic condition.

The term *neurosis* needs to be contrasted with the term **psychosis.** This term also does not refer to a specific disorder, but refers to a broad type of disorders. Psychotic disorders are relatively incapacitating ones in which the individual has lost contact with reality. In simple terms, this means that the person's thinking or perceptions are so distorted that he or she is "living in a different world" from other people. For example, the psychotic person may hear voices that are not there or may believe that he is from another planet. This characteristic will become clearer to you when we discuss psychotic disorders later in the chapter. Schizophrenia, severe major depression, and bipolar affective disorders are considered to be psychotic conditions.

psychosis (si-ko'sis)
Psychological disorders that are relatively disabling and involve "loss of contact with reality."

Anxiety Disorders

Every life is a mixture of positive and negative emotions. But many people experience excessive levels of the kinds of negative emotions that we identify as being *nervous, tense, worried, scared,* and *anxious.* These terms all refer to anxiety. Ten to fifteen million Americans experience such uncomfortable and disruptive levels of anxiety that they are said to have **anxiety disorders.** Anxiety disorders take a variety of different forms as described below.

anxiety disorders
(ang-zi'ē-te)
Psychological disorders that involve excessive levels of negative emotions such as nervousness, tension, worry, fright, and anxiety.

Phobias

A **phobia** is an intense, unrealistic fear. In this case, the anxiety is focused so intensely on some object or situation that the individual is acutely uncomfortable around it and will often go to great pains to avoid it. There are three types of phobias: (1) *simple phobia,* (2) *social phobia,* and (3) *agoraphobia.*

Simple phobia is the most specific and least disruptive of the phobias. Examples include intense fear of heights, dogs, blood, public speaking, and closed spaces. Generally, individuals with specific phobias have no other psychological problems and their lives are disrupted only if the phobia creates a direct problem in daily living. For example, a fear of elevators would be highly disruptive for a person who works in a skyscraper, but it probably would not be for a vegetable farmer.

phobia (fo'be-ah)
An intense, irrational fear.

simple phobia
A phobic fear of one relatively specific thing.

People who experience excessive levels of negative emotions—referred to as being *nervous, tense, worried, scared,* and *anxious*—are said to have anxiety disorders.

Other forms of phobia, by their very nature, always cause serious problems for the individual. **Social phobia** involves extreme fears of social interactions, particularly those with strangers and those in which the person might be evaluated negatively, such as a job interview or a first date. Because this kind of phobia severely limits social interactions, it disrupts an individual's life.

Agoraphobia is the most damaging of all of the phobias. Literally meaning "fear of open spaces," agoraphobia involves an intense fear of leaving one's home or other familiar places. In extreme cases, the agoraphobic individual is totally bound to his or her home, finding a trip to the mailbox an almost intolerable experience. Other agoraphobic individuals are able to travel freely in their neighborhood, but cannot venture beyond it.

A 30-year-old German man recounts his experience with agoraphobia in the following passage.

> The brief trips to Bonn filled me with a surging sense of the impossible and the far . . . a feeling, especially as to distance, that could convert a half mile, or even five blocks from home, in terms of subjective need and cowardice, into an infinity of remoteness. . . . I start a little walk down the street about a hundred feet from the house, I am compelled to rush back, in horror of being so far away . . . a hundred feet away . . . from home and security. I have never walked or ridden, alone or with others, as a normal man, since that day. . . .
>
> At times this emotional effect remains merely a diffuse state of terror, an intensity running the whole scale from vague anxiety to intensest feel of impending death; . . . I am in terror of the seizure of terror; and I fear seizure at a given distance; there are then perfectly rational subterrors lest I may panic and make a public spectacle of myself, or I am in front of an automobile, or actually collapse from nervous exhaustion as soon as I get a certain distance from home—a distance varying back and forth from yards to miles—for the past 15 years I am overwhelmed with the feeling of insecurity, or terror that I can't hit back. (Leonard, 1928, pp. 238, 278, 302, 319)

social phobia
A phobic fear of social interactions, particularly those with strangers and those in which the person might be viewed negatively.

agoraphobia
(ag''o-rah-fo'be-ah)
An intense fear of leaving one's home or other familiar places.

Generalized and Panic Anxiety Disorders

generalized anxiety disorder
An uneasy sense of general tension and apprehension that makes the individual highly uncomfortable because of its prolonged presence.

panic anxiety disorder
A pattern of anxiety in which long periods of calm are broken by an intensely uncomfortable attack of anxiety.

While phobias are linked to specific stimulus situations, the other anxiety disorders involve a kind of anxiety that is independent of environmental triggers. Individuals with **generalized anxiety disorder** experience a vague, uneasy sense of tension and apprehension, sometimes referred to as *free-floating anxiety*. Generalized anxiety makes the individual highly uncomfortable not because it's an intense kind of anxiety—it's generally relatively mild—but because of its relentless, almost unending presence. The person with generalized anxiety disorder does experience periods of calm, but they are often few and far between.

The individual with **panic anxiety disorder** experiences a pattern of anxiety that is almost the exact opposite of generalized anxiety. There may be long periods without anxiety, but that calm is suddenly broken without warning and without obvious cause. The individual is seized by a sharp, intensely uncomfortable attack of anxiety. Respiration increases and suddenly rapid heartbeats can be felt pounding with such intensity that the individual often feels that he or she is having a heart attack, or at the very least is going crazy. These frightening events are fairly common experiences for normal individuals who are under stress. These anxiety attacks are considered abnormal only when they recur frequently.

The fact that panic attacks involve a sudden and intense increase in sympathetic autonomic arousal was demonstrated by British psychiatrist Michael Lader (Lader & Matthews, 1970). While he was studying the autonomic activity of a woman who was prone to panic attacks, she spontaneously experienced an attack in his laboratory. Figure 12.4 graphically shows the sudden changes in three measures of autonomic arousal that took place during the panic attack.

Figure 12.4 Changes in three measures of sympathetic autonomic arousal that occurred when an individual experienced a panic attack while being studied in a laboratory (Lader & Matthews, 1970).

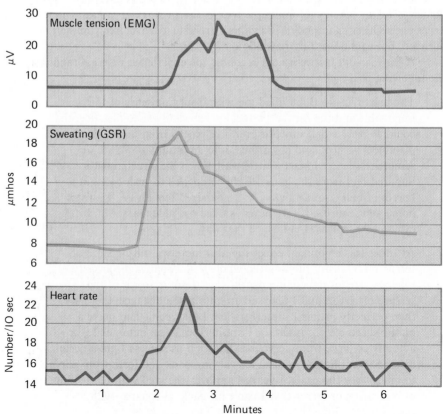

The case of Richard Benson further illustrates the experience of panic anxiety disorder.

> Richard Benson, age 38, applied to a psychiatrist for therapy because he was suffering from severe and overwhelming anxiety which sometimes escalated to a panic attack. He had been treated for this problem in a private psychiatric hospital, but several weeks after his release, the severe anxiety symptoms recurred and he decided to seek outpatient therapy. During the times when he was experiencing intense anxiety, it often seemed as if he were having a heart seizure. He experienced chest pains and heart palpitations, numbness, shortness of breath, and he felt a strong need to breathe in air. He reported that in the midst of the anxiety attack, he developed a feeling of tightness over his eyes and he could only see objects directly in front of him (tunnel vision). He further stated that he feared that he would not be able to swallow.

> Mr. Benson indicated that he had been anxious most of his life, but it was only since his promotion at work six months ago that the feelings of anxiety became a severe problem. The intensity of the anxiety symptoms was frightening to him and on two occasions his wife had rushed him to a local hospital because he was in a state of panic, sure that his heart was going to stop beating and he would die. (Leon, 1977, p. 113)

Charlie

Reprinted by permission: Tribune Media Services.

Obsessive-Compulsive Disorders

Also classified with anxiety disorders are the **obsessive-compulsive disorders.** Obsessions and compulsions are two separate problems, but they often occur together in the same individuals. *Obsessions* are anxiety-provoking thoughts that will not go away. They seem uncontrollable and even alien, as if they do not belong to the individual's mind. Thoughts such as a recurrent fear of losing control and killing someone or about having an incestuous sexual relationship can cause extreme anxiety.

obsessive-compulsive disorders
Disorders that involve obsessions (anxiety-provoking thoughts that will not go away) and/or compulsions (irresistible urges to engage in specific irrational behaviors).

A person suffering from obsessive-compulsive disorder may have recurrent thoughts of being contaminated by germs that lead to irresistable compulsions to wash his hands repeatedly.

Compulsions are irresistible urges to engage in behaviors such as repeatedly touching a spot on one's shoulder, washing one's hands, or checking the locks on doors. If the individual tries to stop engaging in the behavior, he or she experiences an urgent anxiety until the behavior is resumed. Obsessions and compulsions are often found in the same person, like the person who compulsively washes his hands because he is obsessed with thoughts about germs. About 70 percent of all people with obsessive–compulsive disorder have both obsessions and compulsions, while 25 percent have only obsessions, and only 5 percent have only compulsions (Wilner, Reich, Robins, Fishman, & van Doren, 1976).

Somatoform Disorders

somatoform disorders
(so''mah-to-form)
Disorders in which the individual experiences the symptoms of physical health problems that have psychological rather than physical causes.

Somatoform disorders are conditions in which the individual experiences the symptoms of physical health problems that have psychological rather than physical causes. *Soma* is the Latin word for body, hence somatoform disorders are thought to be disorders in which psychological problems "take the form" of bodily problems. But while these symptoms of health problems are not physically caused, they are very real and uncomfortable to the individual. In other words, they are not faked. There are four types of somatoform disorders: *somatization disorder, hypochondriasis, conversion disorder,* and *psychogenic pain disorder.* Because of similarities among them, we discuss these four disorders in pairs.

Somatization Disorders and Hypochondriasis

somatization disorders
(so''mah-ti-za'shun)
Intensely and chronically uncomfortable psychological conditions that involve numerous symptoms of somatic (bodily) illnesses without physical cause.

Somatization disorders are intensely and chronically uncomfortable conditions that indirectly create a high risk of medical complications. They take the form of chronic and recurrent aches, pains, fever, tiredness, and other symptoms of somatic (bodily) illness. In addition, these individuals frequently experience memory difficulties, problems with walking, numbness, blackout spells, nausea, menstrual problems, and a lack of pleasure from sex. These complaints are often expressed in dramatic ways that increase the probability of sympathy and special treatment from others.

Individuals with somatization problems also typically experience other psychological difficulties as well, particularly anxiety and depression. They frequently have problems with their jobs, schoolwork, or in meeting household responsibilities. The most dangerous aspect of somatization disorders, however, concerns the measures the affected individuals take to find relief from their discomfort. They frequently become addicted to alcohol or tranquilizers, and often take medications prescribed by many different physicians whom they are seeing simultaneously (without telling the other physicians), thus increasing the risk of dangerous chemical interactions among the drugs. Worse still, because of their frequent complaints to physicians, they are often eventually the recipients of unnecessary surgery, especially unnecessary hysterectomies (removal of the uterus in women).

hypochondriasis
(hi''po-kon-dri'ah-sis)
A mild form of somatization disorder characterized by excessive concern about one's health.

Hypochondriasis can be thought of as a milder form of somatization disorder with some special features of its own. The hypochondriac experiences somatic symptoms, but they are not as pervasive or as intense as in somatization disorders. Hypochondriacs also do not experience most of the serious side effects such as depression, drug addiction, and unnecessary operations. Their lives, however, are dominated by their concerns about their health. They show a preoccupation with health, overreact with concern to minor coughs and pains, and go to unreasonable lengths to avoid germs, cancer-causing agents, and the like.

Conversion Disorders and Psychogenic Pain Disorders

Conversion disorders are the most dramatic of the somatoform disorders. The name comes from the Freudian theory that anxiety has been "converted" into serious somatic symptoms in this condition rather than being directly experienced as anxiety. Individuals with this problem experience functional blindness, deafness, paralysis, fainting, seizures, inability to speak, or other serious impairments in the absence of any physical cause. In addition, these individuals appear to be generally ineffective and dependent upon others. These symptoms understandably impair the individuals' lives, particularly their ability to hold a job or to do housework. Conversion disorders can usually be distinguished from medical problems without great difficulty. In most cases, the symptoms are not medically possible. For example, in conversion disorders the areas of paralysis and loss of sensation are not shaped in the way they would be if there were actual nerve damage (see fig. 12.5). Similarly, people with conversion paralysis of the legs can be observed to move their legs normally when sleeping.

Perhaps the most interesting characteristic of conversion disorders is known as *la belle indifference,* "the beautiful indifference." Individuals with conversion disorders often, but not always, *are not upset* by their condition. The individual with conversion disorder who wakes up paralyzed one morning may show some emotional response, but not nearly to the extent as a person who is physically paralyzed, for example, in an automobile accident. Some psychologists believe that the conversion symptoms are welcome, in a sense, as they serve to get these people out of responsibilities or to force others to let them be dependent.

Consider the following case:

> A 22-year-old man . . . was referred with complaints of night blindness and failing vision. His visual acuity had deteriorated rapidly and he was found to have tubular fields of vision and a gross abnormality of dark adaptation. . . .
>
> The onset of his symptoms seemed closely related to his difficulties with a girlfriend who lived some miles away from his home. In order to visit her he would have to drive at night which was made impossible by his night blindness. Soon after the relationship was broken and the girl became engaged to another man the symptoms cleared up. Visual acuity improved . . . and the visual fields showed only slight contraction. (Behrman & Levy, 1970, p. 193)

Conversion disorders usually begin during acute stress and generally provide some kind of benefit (i.e., reinforcement) to the individual. In the case of the 22-year-old man described above, the benefit was in not having to admit that he did not want to visit his girlfriend.

Psychogenic pain disorders are very similar to conversion disorders except that the primary symptom is *pain* that has no physical cause. Sometimes psychogenic pain can be distinguished from physically caused pain because it does not follow nerve pathways. But in the case of low back pain, joint pains, and chest pains, a diagnosis of psychogenic pain disorder can be made only after all possible physical causes have been carefully ruled out. Like conversion disorders, psychogenic pain usually occurs at times of high stress and generally is beneficial to the individual in some way, as in getting the person out of a dull job and onto disability payments.

conversion disorders
(kon-ver′zhun)
Somatoform disorders in which individuals experience serious somatic symptoms such as functional blindness, deafness, and paralysis.

psychogenic pain disorders
(si″ko-jen′ik)
Somatoform disorders in which the individual experiences a relatively specific and chronic pain that has a psychological rather than physical cause.

Figure 12.5 Because of the pattern in which the sensory nerves serve the skin surface, it would be medically possible to experience anesthesia within any of the lines shown on the bodies. Typical conversion anesthesias do not conform to these patterns, however (Van De Graaff, 1984).

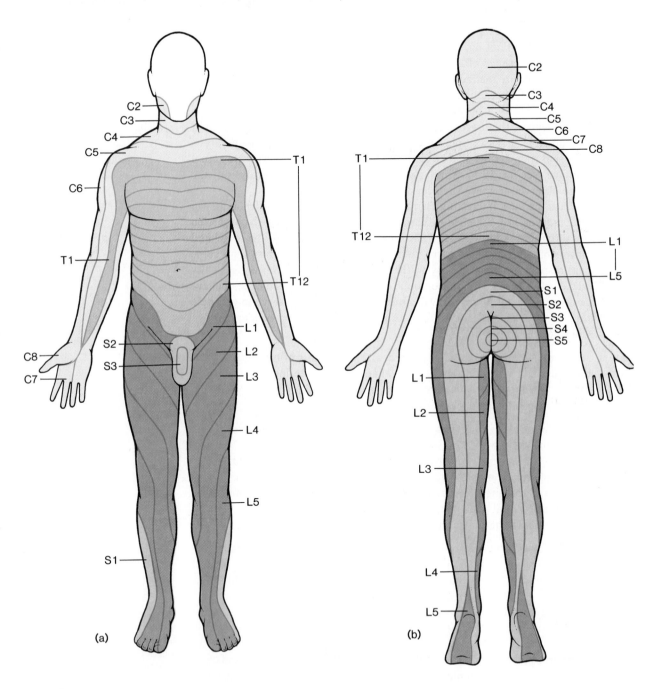

(a)

(b)

Dissociative Disorders

Dissociative disorders cover a broad category of loosely related rare conditions involving sudden alterations in cognition. In the various types of dissociative disorders there is a change in memory, perception, or "identity." There are four kinds of dissociative disorders: *amnesia, fugue, depersonalization,* and *multiple personality.*

Amnesia and Fugue

As described in chapter 6, amnesia is a loss of memory that can have either a physical or psychological cause. **Dissociative amnesia** is psychologically caused; it most often occurs after a period of intense stress and involves loss of memory for all or part of the stressful experience itself, such as loss of memory for an automobile accident in which the individual was responsible for the death of another person. Individuals who suffer amnesia as a result of stress generally have no other psychological problems and typically recover their memories in time.

Fugue states resemble amnesia in that there is a loss of memory, but the loss is so complete that the individual cannot remember his or her identity or previous life. The fugue episode is also typified by a period of semiconscious "wandering" that may take the individual around the corner or across the continent. In many instances, the individual takes on a new personality during the fugue episode, usually one that is more sociable, more fun-loving, and less conventional than the previous one. Generally these changes are transient. Consider the following case:

> When Mrs. Y. was brought to the hospital by her husband, she was dazed, confused, and weeping. Apparently aware of her surroundings and able to answer brief questions in filling out the admitting form, she could not, at the time, discuss any of her problems with the admitting physician. Her husband reported that she had left their home two weeks previously while he was at work. All the effort of her husband and the police to trace her had failed until approximately 24 hours prior to her admission to the hospital when Mr. Y. received a report that a woman of her description had been arrested in a nearby city. When he arrived and identified her, she did not at first recognize him, did not know her own name, and could not remember what had happened to her or anything about her past. The police informed Mr. Y. that she had been arrested for "resorting" after a motel owner had called the police to complain that several different men had visited the motel room she had rented three days before in the company of a sailor. Mrs. Y. seemed unable to remember any of these alleged events. Gradually she came to recognize her husband as he talked anxiously with her whereupon she began to weep and requested to be brought home. . . .

dissociative disorders (dis-so''she-a-tiv) A category of conditions involving sudden cognitive changes, such as a change in memory, perception, or identity.

dissociative amnesia A dissociative disorder that involves a loss of memory and that has a psychological rather than a physical cause.

fugue (fūg) A period of "wandering" that involves a loss of memory and a change in identity.

Mrs. Y. was very fatigued, and for the next three days she slept a great deal of the time. . . . On the fourth day she became much more alert, joked with the other patients, watched TV, and joined in a card game. Her doctor attempted to interview her and she seemed eager to cooperate, but soon after entering the room she burst into tears and fled back to her bed. Her condition continued to improve, and two days later she was able to talk at length with her doctor about her marriage and her childhood, but remained amnesic about the events immediately preceding her hospitalization.

Only much later in treatment did the patient have any recollection at all of what had occurred during the previous two weeks and even then her memories were spotty. (Goldstein & Palmer, 1963, pp. 71–72)

Depersonalization

depersonalization
(de-per″sun-al-i-za′shun)
The perceptual experience of one's body or surroundings becoming distorted or unreal in some way.

The term **depersonalization** refers to experiences in which the individual feels that he or she has become distorted or "unreal," or that distortions have occurred in one's surroundings. The individual might feel that his hands have become enlarged, numb, or out of control. Or she might feel that she has become a robot—even though she knows she is a real person—or that her room is not real or that her parents are not real people. The individual generally knows that these feelings are not accurate, although they have an eerie reality to them. One of the more common experiences of depersonalization is the sense of leaving one's body and being able to look back at it from the ceiling.

As was mentioned when we discussed depersonalization as an altered state of consciousness in chapter 4, experiences of depersonalization are rather common, especially in young adults. Unless they are accompanied by other problems or become recurrent to the point of being uncomfortable, these depersonalized experiences are not considered abnormal. Generally, they are nothing more than an unsettling experience that makes one question one's sanity for a few days.

Multiple Personality

multiple personality
A dissociative disorder in which the individual shifts abruptly and repeatedly from one "personality" to another.

Individuals who exhibit the kind of dissociative disorder known as **multiple personality** shift abruptly and repeatedly from one "personality" to another as if more than one person were inhabiting the same body. This disorder, commonly known as "split personality," is quite rare, but it has been described in detail enough times now that most clinical psychologists admit such a syndrome exists. Generally, the two or more personalities are quite different from one another. The original one is typically conventional, moralistic, and unhappy, while the other personalities tend to be quite the opposite. At least one other personality is usually sensual, uninhibited, and rebellious. In most cases, the individual is not aware of the other personalities when they are "in" their original personality, but the other personalities know about their rival personalities and are often antagonistic toward the original one.

In 1977 Chris Sizemore published an autobiography revealing that she was the case of multiple personality made famous in the 1950s movie, *The Three Faces of Eve*. Initially, she experienced two distinctly different personalities, referred to in the movie as Eve White and Eve Black. Eve White was depressed, anxious, conventional, and inhibited, while Eve Black was seductive, uninhibited, and wild. In her autobiography, Chris Sizemore reveals that she eventually went through 22 separate personalities, but that in recent years she feels she has a single well-adjusted personality. A similar pattern was reported for the case of "Sybil," a woman who developed 16 personalities during the course of 42 years (Schreiber, 1973).

R E V I E W

The term *neurosis* is no longer used to refer to a category of psychological problems but as an adjective that describes a wide range of disorders. Neurotic disorders are relatively mild and do not involve gross distortions of reality. Psychotic disorders, on the other hand, are generally severe and do involve gross distortions of reality.

Anxiety disorders are common problems characterized by anxiety that is experienced either as a low and relatively constant level of generalized anxiety, as sharp and intense attacks of anxiety, as focalized phobias of various sorts, or as linked to obsessive thoughts or compulsive actions.

In somatoform disorders, the individual experiences the symptoms of medical conditions that have psychological rather than physical causes. In some types of somatoform disorders the symptoms are dramatic and clear-cut such as blindness, paralysis, or chronic pain. In other cases, the individual experiences multiple vague aches, pains, and maladies or is just excessively concerned with health.

Dissociative disorders are uncommon psychological problems involving sudden alterations in cognition. These may take the form of memory losses, change of identity, or feelings of unreality. In rare cases, the alteration of identity is so dramatic that the individual appears to possess more than a single personality.

Affective Disorders

Affective disorders are disturbances of mood. There are two primary forms of such mood disturbances, depression and mania. Depression can occur alone (a condition known as *major depression*), but mania seems to always alternate with depression (*bipolar affective disorder*). Both conditions produce great misery for the individual.

affective disorders
(ah-fek′tiv)
Psychological disorders involving disturbances of mood.

Affective disorders are disturbances of mood. When depression occurs alone it's known as major depression. If the depression alternates with mania, it's known as bipolar affective disorder.

Major Depression

major depression
An affective disorder characterized by episodes of deep unhappiness, loss of interest in life, and other symptoms.

The individual experiencing **major depression** is deeply unhappy and finds little pleasure in life. In addition, the depressed person has little hope for the future, a negative opinion of self and others, is frequently lethargic, and often sees no reason to live. This state is often accompanied by anxiety, sleep problems, changes in appetite, loss of interest in sex, and sometimes suicide attempts. Many individuals who experience depression will experience it only once, but others will be depressed many times during their lifetime if not properly treated. In these cases, the depression comes in episodes that last from several days to several months, followed by periods of normal moods.

Major depression is quite common, affecting 10 or more million Americans. Generally it's mild and accompanied by anxiety and is considered to be a neurotic type of disorder. Like other neurotic individuals, people with mild depression are very uncomfortable, but they are generally able to cope with the demands of daily living. Severe major depression is less common, but far more disabling. Often this is accompanied by bizarre beliefs and perceptions that represent a psychotic distortion of reality. The following excerpt describes a case of severe (psychotic) depression that required the individual to be hospitalized during treatment because of his suicidal tendencies and distortions of reality (e.g., he believed that his stomach was rotting away). (See also *Research Report:* "Cognitive Distortions in Depression?")

> E. D., aged 60, was admitted to the hospital because he was depressed, ate insufficiently, and believed that his stomach was "rotting away." At 51 the patient suffered from a depression and was obliged to resign his position. This depression continued for about nine months, after which he apparently fully recovered. He resumed his work but after two years suffered from a second depression. Again he recovered after several months and returned to a similar position and held it until two months before his

R E S E A R C H   R E P O R T

Cognitive Distortions in Depression?

As discussed in chapter 10, Albert Ellis, Aaron T. Beck, and others believe that our *cognitions* can create emotional problems. If we think in ways that exaggerate the importance of stressful events in our lives, then we will experience more uncomfortable emotions than most other people. The research of Peter Lewinsohn, Walter Mischel, and their associates (1980), however, suggests that at least one of the "distorted" cognitions that was believed characteristic of depressed individuals is not a distortion at all.

Lewinsohn asked individuals who were experiencing major depression to participate in a group discussion for approximately 20 minutes. During this time, they were rated by a group of judges on their friendliness, assertiveness, warmth, and other social qualities. After the group discussion, each participant also rated himself or herself on the same dimensions. Another group of people who were not depressed went through exactly the same procedure.

As would have been predicted by Beck and Ellis, the depressed group rated their social skills as being less adequate than did the nondepressed subjects. Is this evidence that depressed individuals distort their view of themselves? Actually, it turns out that the self-ratings of the depressed group were *quite accurate* when compared to the ratings of the judges. It was the normal subjects whose view of themselves was distorted! They rated themselves as being significantly more socially skilled than the judges did. Furthermore, when the depressed individuals were given treatment and became less depressed, their self-perceptions became more like the normal group: they, too, began to rate themselves in unrealistically positive terms. Perhaps having this kind of "distorted" perception of ourselves is a good thing. Maybe we would all be depressed if we saw ourselves in the realistic terms in which others see us!

admission. At this time he began to worry lest he was not doing his work well, talked much of his lack of fitness for his duties, and finally resigned. He spent Thanksgiving Day at his son's in a neighboring city, but while there he was sure that the water pipes in his own house would freeze during his absence and that he and his family would be "turned out into the street." A few days later he was found standing by a pond, evidently contemplating suicide. He soon began to remain in bed and sometimes wrapped his head in the bed clothing to shut out the external world. He declared that he was "rotting away inside" and that if he ate, the food would kill him. He urged the family not to touch the glasses or towels he used lest they become contaminated. (Kolb, 1977, p. 455)

bipolar affective disorder
(bi-po'lar)
A condition in which the individual experiences periods of mania that alternate irregularly with periods of severe depression.

mania (ma'ne-ah)
A disturbance of mood in which the individual experiences a euphoria characterized by unrealistic optimism and heightened sensory pleasures.

Bipolar Affective Disorder

In the condition known as **bipolar affective disorder,** periods of mania alternate irregularly with periods of severe depression. **Mania** is a disturbance of mood that can be quite enjoyable to the individual in the short run, but is usually damaging both to the person and to others in the long run. During the manic episode, the individual experiences a remarkable "high"—an intense euphoria in which sensory pleasures are heightened, one's self-esteem is very high, thoughts race, little sleep is needed, and unrealistic optimism prevails. Grandiose and financially damaging schemes and buying sprees are common during these periods, as are quitting jobs, divorce, and sexual promiscuity. Psychotic distortions of reality in beliefs and perceptions are also common during manic periods. When well-meaning friends and family members try to control the manic individual, they are often rebuffed in sharp anger. Although an intensely pleasurable state, mania can be quite harmful to the person's finances and personal relationships. This harm can be clearly seen in the case of "Mrs. M."

> At 17 she suffered from a depression that rendered her unable to work for several months, although she was not hospitalized. At 33, shortly before the birth of her first child, the patient was greatly depressed. For a period of four days she appeared in coma. About a month after the birth of the baby she "became excited" and was entered as a patient in an institution for neurotic and mildly psychotic patients. As she began to improve, she was sent to a shore hotel for a brief vacation. The patient remained at the hotel for one night and on the following day signed a year's lease on an apartment, bought furniture, and became heavily involved in debt. Shortly thereafter Mrs. M. became depressed and returned to the hospital in which she had previously been a patient. After several months she recovered and, except for relatively mild fluctuations of mood, remained well for approximately two years.

> She then became overactive and exuberant in spirits and visited her friends, to whom she outlined her plans for reestablishing different forms of lucrative business. She purchased many clothes, bought furniture, pawned her rings, and wrote checks without funds. She was returned to a hospital. Gradually her manic symptoms subsided, and after four months she was discharged. For a period thereafter she was mildly depressed. In a little less than a year Mrs. M. again became overactive, played her radio until late in the night, smoked excessively, took out insurance on a car that she had not yet bought. Contrary to her usual habits, she swore frequently and loudly, created a disturbance in a club to which she did not belong, and instituted divorce proceedings. On the day prior to her second admission to the hospital, she purchased 57 hats. (Kolb, 1977, pp. 455–456)

Mania may occur only once, but often returns in multiple episodes. When mania is recurrent, it alternates irregularly with episodes of severe depression. This alternating disorder was formerly known as *manic-depressive psychosis* and is now known as bipolar affective disorder. Bipolar affective disorders are rela-

RESEARCH REPORT

Depression and the Stress of Childbirth

In recent years, a great deal of research has been devoted to the topic of **postpartum depression**—depression that is precipitated in women by the birth of an infant. This type of depression has received close attention because of its obvious importance to the mother and her infant, because it is a prevalent problem—affecting approximately 20 percent of all mothers—and because it provides a unique opportunity to study the psychological effects of a specific stressful life event (Hopkins, Marcus, & Campbell, 1984). It has been found that postpartum depression does not differ significantly from depression that occurs at other points in the lives of females and males. Perhaps more importantly, it now appears that the role of the stress of childbirth operates much like any other stressor. Postpartum depression is a more common reaction in individuals who have shown a previous tendency to be depressed (Paykel, Emms, Fletcher, & Rassaby, 1980), who have experienced greater amounts of total life stress of all types (Paykel et al., 1980), and who have less social support because they have few friends, unsupportive relatives, unhappy marriages, or are not married (O'Hara, 1980).

For some individuals, then, even the positive event of childbirth can lead to a period of depression serious enough to require professional help. Postpartum depression is not to be confused with the milder (but, still uncomfortable) "maternity blues," however. More than half of all women go through a brief period of tearfulness, tension, and irritability for the first day or two, and it is not uncommon for these feelings to continue for some time after birth along with changes in appetite, sleep disturbances, and lack of sexual interest (Hopkins et al., 1984).

postpartum depression
Major depression that begins immediately following childbirth.

tively uncommon problems; only 15 percent of individuals with affective disorders show this alternating pattern of intense highs and lows. Fortunately, bipolar affective disorder is a disorder that generally can be treated somewhat effectively with medication.

REVIEW

Affective disorders are disturbances of mood. Major depression involves one or more episodes of this negative mood state. These episodes range from mild to severe, with severe episodes sometimes being accompanied by bizarre perceptions and beliefs that distort reality. In bipolar affective disorder, the episodes of depression alternate irregularly with periods of the mood disturbance known as mania. Although this is an intensely pleasurable state, it's harmful in that it can lead to financial difficulties, destroy personal relationships, and is often accompanied by reality-distorting perceptions and beliefs.

Schizophrenia

Psychologist: "Why do you think people believe in God?"
Patient: Uh, let's, I don't know why, let's see, balloon travel. He holds it up for you, the balloon. He don't let you fall out, your little legs sticking out down through the clouds. He's down to the smokestack, looking through the smoke trying to get the balloon gassed up you know. Way they're flying on top that way, legs sticking out, I don't know, looking down on the ground, heck, that'd make you so dizzy you just stay and sleep you know, hold down and sleep there. The balloon's His home you know up there. I used to be sleep outdoors, you know, sleep outdoors instead of going home. He's had a home but His not tell where it's at you know. (Chapman & Chapman, 1973, p. 3)

The person giving this confused and confusing answer has a serious problem known as **schizophrenia.** It's a rare disorder, affecting less than 1 percent of the general population. However, it's a dramatic form of abnormality that, unless successfully treated, renders normal patterns of living impossible. Schizophrenia involves three major areas of abnormality: cognitive disorders, emotional disturbance, and social withdrawal.

1. *Cognitive disorders.* The central feature of schizophrenia is a pervasive disturbance of cognition that renders the individual "out of touch with reality." The individual often holds strange and inaccurate beliefs, has distorted or false perceptual experiences, and exhibits fragmented and illogical thinking and language.

2. *Emotional disturbance.* Emotions are also distinctly distorted in schizophrenia. They may appear to be inappropriate to the situation (as when an individual laughs upon hearing sad news) or may change so rapidly and illogically as to appear "fragmented." On the other hand, the individual may display no emotion at all, known as "blunted" emotions.

3. *Social withdrawal.* Schizophrenia is also typified by withdrawal from social relationships. In some cases, the individual may seem to want intimate ties but fears them, or in other cases he or she may simply show little real interest in relating to others.

Schizophrenia is a broad class of psychotic disorders that is broken down into three major subtypes in the DSM-III: *paranoid, disorganized,* and *catatonic schizophrenia.* A fourth category, *undifferentiated schizophrenia,* is used to classify individuals who do not fit into the other three categories. (See *Research Report:* "Piecing Together Evidence to Support a Biochemical Theory of Schizophrenia.")

Paranoid Schizophrenia

The **paranoid schizophrenic** holds *false beliefs,* or **delusions,** that seriously distort reality. Most often, these are beliefs in the exceptional importance of oneself, so-called *delusions of grandeur*—such as being Jesus Christ, a CIA agent, the inventor of a cure for war. These are often accompanied by delusions that, because one is so important, others are "out to get me" in attempts to thwart the individual's important mission, known as *delusions of persecution.*

If I were schizophrenic and believed that I were an agent of the CIA who alone had the ability to save the president from assassination by the Russians, I might also believe that my students were Russian spies who were trying to confuse and poison me. Think for a moment how bizarre I would seem to others who learned of my paranoid delusions, especially since I would express them in disorganized, incoherent language. Think, too, about the terrifying, bewildering existence I would live if I believed those things. It would be small wonder that my emotions would seem unpredictable and strange, and that I would withdraw from social contact.

schizophrenia
(skiz″o-fren′e-ah)
A psychological disorder involving cognitive disturbance, emotional disturbance, and social withdrawal.

paranoid schizophrenia
(par′ah-noid skiz″o-fre′ne-ah)
A subtype of schizophrenia in which the individual holds false beliefs or delusions—often delusions of persecution and grandeur—that seriously distort reality.

delusion
A false belief that distorts reality.

R E S E A R C H R E P O R T

Piecing Together Evidence to Support a Biochemical Theory of Schizophrenia

Theories do not always come from the laboratory; sometimes they are generated from observations made while treating people with psychological disorders in the clinic. An excellent example of this kind of theory is the *dopamine hypothesis* of schizophrenia. Dopamine is a neurotransmitter substance that functions in parts of the brain (including the hypothalamus and limbic system) that play a role in emotions and attention. The dopamine hypothesis suggests that schizophrenia develops in individuals whose neurons are unusually sensitive to dopamine. Interestingly, this is probably the most widely endorsed theory of schizophrenia among psychiatrists even though it has never received strong support from direct experimental tests (Neale & Oltmanns, 1980; Uhr, Stahl, & Berger, 1984). The route by which informal evidence has been assembled to support the dopamine hypothesis tells an interesting story of Sherlock Holmes-like observation and deduction in the clinic.

Great strides were made in the treatment of schizophrenia in the 1950s with the introduction of the *phenothiazine* drugs, but it was not known for some time how these drugs worked. The first clue was that phenothiazines often produce a serious side effect when not used properly, for example, muscular control problems like those found in Parkinson's disease. Since Parkinson's disease is caused by a deterioration of the ability of parts of the brain that use the neurotransmitter dopamine to transmit neural messages, it was hypothesized that the phenothiazine drugs operate by interfering in

hallucination
A false perceptual experience that distorts reality.

Unfortunately, the cognitive disturbances of the paranoid schizophrenic does not stop with delusions. Many individuals with this disorder also experience false perceptual experiences or **hallucinations.** Their perceptions are either strangely distorted or they may even hear, see, or feel things that are not there. These bizarre experiences further add to the terrifying, perplexing unreality of the paranoid schizophrenic's existence. (See *Of Special Interest:* "Paranoia and the Reverend Jim Jones" to compare paranoid schizophrenia to the disorder known simply as paranoia.)

RESEARCH REPORT

some way with dopamine. Subsequent research has shown that these drugs diminish the effectiveness of dopamine by blocking the sites on the dendrites of neurons that are stimulated by dopamine. Thus, if drugs that produce improvements reduce dopamine transmission, it makes sense to theorize that schizophrenia is caused by excessive dopamine transmission.

Another sort of clinical evidence that further supports the dopamine hypothesis comes from experience with the side effects of the stimulant drugs called *amphetamines*. These drugs, such as *dextroamphetamine* or "speed," are widely used as diet pills because they suppress appetite. They are also widely abused because of the intense high and feelings of energy they produce. Excessive use of amphetamines, however, can lead to a condition called *amphetamine psychosis* that closely resembles paranoid schizophrenia. The fact that this condition resembles schizophrenia is important since amphetamines produce this psychotic reaction by stimulating dopamine transmission (Snyder, 1974). Furthermore, the best treatment for amphetamine psychosis is phenothiazine medication, which is also the best treatment for schizophrenia. The dopamine hypothesis is still speculative as much remains to be learned about the biochemical basis of schizophrenia (Uhr et al., 1984). It provides an interesting glimpse at scientific sleuthing in the clinic, however.

Disorganized Schizophrenia

Disorganized schizophrenia resembles paranoid schizophrenia in that delusions and hallucinations are present, but the cognitive processes of the disorganized schizophrenic, as the name implies, are so disorganized and fragmented that the delusions and hallucinations have little recognizable theme or meaning. The central features of this type of schizophrenia are extreme withdrawal from normal human contact and a shallow "silliness" of emotion. The disorganized schizophrenic acts in childlike ways, reacts inappropriately to both happy and sad events, and generally presents a highly bizarre picture to others.

disorganized schizophrenia (skiz''o-fre'ne-ah) A subtype of schizophrenia characterized by shallow silliness, extreme social withdrawal, and fragmented delusions and hallucinations.

OF SPECIAL INTEREST

Paranoia and the Reverend Jim Jones

paranoia (par''ah-noi'ah)
A nonschizophrenic
disorder characterized
by delusions of grandeur
and persecution that are
more logical than those of
paranoid schizophrenics
in the absence of
hallucinations.

Paranoia is a rare disorder that is characterized by delusions of grandeur and persecution. It's not a form of schizophrenia, however, and can be distinguished from paranoid schizophrenia because the delusions in paranoia are less illogical and have no hallucinations. The paranoid schizophrenic might think that he is Napoleon and that he is currently working as a disc jockey for the CIA. The paranoiac, on the other hand, might believe that she can see a truth that no one else has seen and that it's essential that she lead Americans away from reliance on machines. The delusions are more subtle and more believable.

Often it's the believability of the paranoiac's delusions that makes them so dangerous. The Reverend Jim Jones is a frightening case in point. Jones was a minister who had an impressive record of working for the poor when he came to believe that he was a prophet of God, perhaps even a new Messiah. He convinced a large number of people of the truth of his delusion and founded a new religious sect. When he began to feel that his sect was being persecuted by the government, he took his followers to the South American country of Guyana and founded the People's Temple Jonestown Settlement. There, he ruled as an absolute master over his flock, at one point decreeing that only he was fit to have sex with and impregnate the women of Jonestown. When a task force from the United States flew to Jonestown to investigate rumors of human rights violations, his followers killed members of that group. Realizing that trouble was ahead and believing that he had the wisdom of God, Jones ordered all of his followers to commit suicide by drinking a poison that was always on hand for just such a situation. Believing that they were told to take their lives by the new Messiah, hundreds of men, women, and children drank the poison and died. Individuals with paranoia are not always dangerous, but they can be when they act on their delusions.

Catatonic Schizophrenia

catatonic schizophrenia
(kat''ah-ton'ik
skiz''o-fre'ne-ah)
A subtype of schizophrenia
in which the individual
spends long periods in an
inactive, statuelike state.

Catatonic schizophrenia is quite different in appearance from the other forms of schizophrenia. While catatonics sometimes experience delusions and hallucinations, their most obvious abnormalities are in social interaction and posture and body movement. There are long periods of catatonic stupor, an inactive statuelike state in which the individuals seem locked into a posture. Catatonic schizophrenics are often said to exhibit "waxy flexibility" during these stupors—they will passively let themselves be placed into any posture and maintain it. Often the individual ceases to talk, appears not to hear what is spoken to him or her, and may no longer eat without being fed.

Frequently, however, the stupor is abruptly broken by periods of agitation. The person may pace and fidget nervously, or may angrily attack others. Both of these patterns may alternate with periods of relative normality.

Catatonic individuals sometimes exhibit a state of catatonic stupor during which they may maintain a single posture for several hours.

R E V I E W

Schizophrenia is a broad range of psychotic disorders characterized by disturbances of cognition that grossly distort reality, by distortions of emotions, and by withdrawal from social relationships. The DSM-III distinguishes three major subtypes of schizophrenia. Paranoid schizophrenia is characterized by delusions of grandeur and persecution, often accompanied by hallucinations. Disorganized schizophrenia resembles paranoid schizophrenia but is typified by even more fragmented cognition and by shallow, silly emotions. Catatonic schizophrenia is quite different in appearance from the other types, being marked by stupors in which the individual may maintain postures for long periods of time.

Kinds of Personality Disorders

As described in the text, personality disorders are relatively consistent patterns of abnormal behavior that begin in childhood and persist through all or most of adulthood. The following are brief descriptions of all of the types of personality disorders listed in the third edition of the American Psychiatric Association's Diagnostic and Statistical Manual of Mental Disorders (DSM-III). Two of these personality disorders are described in more detail in the text as examples.

Be careful not to diagnose yourself or your friends while reading this list. The pattern must be extreme and consistent to qualify for a diagnosis.

1. *Schizoid Personality Disorder:* Lack of interest in social relationships, emotional coldness, absence of affection for others, may live solitary life-style.
2. *Schizotypal Personality Disorder:* Few friendships, suspiciousness, strange ideas, such as belief that his or her mind can be read by others and that messages are being received in strange ways.
3. *Paranoid Personality Disorder:* High degree of suspiciousness and mistrust of others, extreme irritability and sensitivity, coldness and lack of tender feelings.
4. *Histrionic Personality Disorder:* Self-centered, frequently seeking to be the center of attention, manipulating others through exaggerated expression of emotions and difficulties, superficially charming but lacking genuine concern for others, frequent angry outbursts.

Personality Disorders

personality disorders
Psychological disorders that are believed to result from personalities that developed improperly during childhood.

To this point, we have been talking about psychological problems that develop in individuals who were once considered to be normal. To oversimplify the case, neurotic and psychotic disorders are considered to result from "breakdowns" in relatively normal personalities. In contrast, the **personality disorders** discussed in this section are believed to result from personalities that developed improperly in the first place.

There are a number of different personality disorders that differ widely from one another but share several common characteristics: (1) all personality disorders begin early in life; (2) they are disturbing to the person or to others; and (3) they are very difficult to treat. We look at two very different personality disorders to provide examples of this type of problem. See also *Of Special Interest:* "Kinds of Personality Disorders" for a brief description of these and other personality disorders.

5. *Narcissitic Personality Disorder:* Unrealistic sense of self-importance, preoccupied with fantasies of future success, requires constant attention and praise, reacts very negatively to criticism or is indifferent to criticism, exploits others, feels entitled to special consideration, lack of genuine concern for others.

6. *Antisocial Personality Disorder:* Superficially charming but experiences great difficulties in maintaining intimate social relationships, dishonest, often violent, experiences little guilt about breaking social conventions or the law.

7. *Borderline Personality Disorder:* Impulsive and unpredictable, unstable personal relationships, angry, almost constantly needs to be with others, lack of clear identity, feelings of emptiness.

8. *Avoidant Personality Disorder:* Extreme shyness or social withdrawal in spite of a desire for friendships, extremely sensitive to rejection, very low self-esteem.

9. *Dependent Personality Disorder:* Passively dependent on others for support and decisions, low self-esteem, puts needs of others before self.

10. *Compulsive Personality Disorder:* Perfectionistic, dominating, poor ability to express affection, excessive devotion to work, indecisive when faced with major decisions.

11. *Passive-Aggressive Personality Disorder:* Does not act in overtly aggressive ways, but resists demands of others by intentionally forgetting, procrastinating, or being stubborn.

Schizoid Personality Disorder

The suffix *-oid* means "like," hence schiz*oid* personality disorder is like schizophrenia, particularly in exhibiting blunted emotions and social withdrawal. Unlike true schizophrenia, however, this condition is not characterized by serious cognitive disturbances.

Individuals with **schizoid personality disorder** have little or no desire to have friends, and indeed are not interested in even casual social contact. They are classic "loners." Usually they are very shy as children, but are not abnormally withdrawn until later childhood or adolescence. Gradually, they seem to lose interest in friends, family and social activities, and retreat more and more into a solitary existence.

They display little emotion, and appear cold and aloof. Later in life, people with schizoid personality disorder often lose interest in personal appearance, hygiene, and other polite social conventions. Often they do not work and may even fall into the life of a drifting hobo or work as a streetwalking prostitute.

schizoid personality disorder
(skiz'oid)
A personality disorder characterized by blunted emotions, lack of interest in social relationships, and withdrawal into a solitary existence.

antisocial personality disorder
A personality disorder characterized by smooth social skills and a lack of guilt about violating social rules and laws and taking advantage of others.

Antisocial Personality Disorder

Individuals with **antisocial personality disorder** have a personality disorder quite different from the schizoid group. They frequently violate social rules and laws, take advantage of others, and feel little guilt about it. These individuals often have smooth social skills: They are sweet-talking con artists who are very likable at first. But they experience great difficulties in maintaining close personal relationships. They enter into marriages and other intimate relationships easily, but they tend to break up quickly.

Antisocial personalities have a low tolerance for frustration. They act on impulse, lose their temper quickly, and lie easily and skillfully. They are often hardened, violent criminals, but in other cases successfully assume false identities as physicians, attorneys, and the like by faking their credentials.

In childhood, antisocial personalities are very difficult children. They are often bullies, who fight, lie, cheat, steal, and are truant from school. They blame others for their misdeeds, feel picked on by their parents and teachers, and never seem to learn from their mistakes.

Individuals with antisocial personality disorder rarely feel anxious or guilty—they are calm, cool characters. They are highly uncomfortable, however, when they are kept from excitement. They have an abnormal need for stimulation, novelty, and thrills. Because they often turn to alcohol and drugs for excitement, they frequently become addicts. The primary harmfulness of the antisocial personality disorder is in the damage that is done to others. They often leave a trail of victims—victims of their lies, their crimes, their violent outbursts, and their broken intimate relationships.

The following case of antisocial personality disorder illustrates these problems well:

> Donald's misbehavior as a child took many forms including lying, cheating, petty theft, and the bullying of smaller children. As he grew older he became more and more interested in sex, gambling, and alcohol. When he was 14 he made crude sexual advances toward a younger girl, and when she threatened to tell her parents he locked her in a shed. It was about 16 hours before she was found. Donald at first denied knowledge of the incident, later stating that she had seduced him and that the door must have locked itself. He expressed no concern for the anguish experienced by the girl and her parents, nor did he give any indication that he felt morally culpable for what he had done.
>
> When he was 17, Donald left the boarding school, forged his father's name to a large check, and spent about a year traveling around the world. He apparently lived well, using a combination of charm, physical attractiveness, and false pretenses to finance his way. During subsequent years he held a succession of jobs, never staying at any one for more than a few months. Throughout this period he was charged with a variety of crimes, including theft, drunkenness in a public place, assault, and many traffic violations. In most cases he was either fined or given a light sentence.

His sexual experiences were frequent, casual, and callous. When he was 22 he married a 41-year-old woman whom he had met in a bar. Several other marriages followed, all bigamous. In each case the pattern was the same: he would marry someone on impulse, let her support him for several months, and then leave. . . .
(Lahey & Ciminero, 1980, pp. 326–327)

R E V I E W

While other kinds of psychological disorders are thought to result from the "breakdown" of a normal personality, personality disorders are thought to result from faulty personality development during childhood. These disorders begin early in life, are disturbing to the individual or to others, and are difficult to treat. For example, individuals with schizoid personality disorder were very shy children who increasingly lost interest in social relationships as they grew older. Eventually, they lose interest in proper dress and social conditions, display little emotion, and rarely hold regular jobs. Antisocial personality disorders are characterized by rule-violating behavior as a child that develops into a disregard for the customs of society as adults. Such individuals are dishonest con artists who are smooth and likable at first, but who have great difficulties maintaining normal relationships. They also have an abnormal need for stimulation, are prone to violence, and do not seem to learn from punishment.

Atypical Sexual Behavior and Sexual Deviance

Human beings differ widely in their sexual preferences and practices, and vary in their ability to successfully perform their preferred sexual practices. In the sections that follow, we look at the range of unusual or **atypical sexual behavior.** Attention is given to the fact that some atypical patterns of sexual behavior are considered normal even though they are unusual, some forms are considered to be abnormal under some circumstances, and some forms of atypical sexual behavior are always considered abnormal. We also look at the most common **sexual dysfunctions**—difficulties in performing preferred sexual practices. All sexual dysfunctions are considered abnormal in the sense that they are upsetting to the people involved and are therefore harmful. Describing these problems as abnormal may seem improper to you, however, because they are rather common—most of us will experience some sexual dysfunction at least briefly in our lives—and because they are experienced by people who generally are otherwise quite normal.

atypical sexual behavior
Sexual practice that differs considerably from the norm.

sexual dysfunction
An inability to engage successfully or comfortably in normal sexual activities.

Normal Atypical Sexuality

In the sections that follow, we discuss unusual patterns of sexual behavior. In the first two sections, atypical patterns of sexuality are described that are only considered abnormal if the individuals who engage in the sexual practices consider them abnormal for themselves. Remember, a pattern of behavior cannot be considered abnormal solely on the basis of being unusual; there must be a demonstrable element of harm involved.

homosexual
An individual who prefers to form intimate and sexual relationships with members of his or her own sex.

Homosexuality

Homosexuals are individuals who prefer to form intimate relationships and to engage in sexual behavior with members of their own sex. Approximately 4 percent of males are exclusively homosexual, but 10 percent have engaged in homosexual relations for at least three years of their adult life. Furthermore, 37 percent of all males have had at least one homosexual experience, generally in adolescence. In women, the percentages are somewhat lower: 2 to 3 percent are mostly or exclusively homosexual, and 19 percent have had at least one homosexual experience (Kinsey, Pomeroy, & Martin, 1948; Kinsey, Pomeroy, Martin, & Gebhard, 1953; Masters, Johnson, & Kolodny, 1982). Exclusive homosexuality is an uncommon sexual pattern, therefore, but transient homosexual experiences are not.

Until the publication of the third edition of the Diagnostic and Statistical Manual of the American Psychiatric Association (DSM-III), homosexuality was considered to be abnormal and a form of psychological disorder. It was eliminated from the DSM-III, however, and is presently considered to be a problem only if the homosexual person considers it to be abnormal (known as **ego-dystonic homosexuality**). This decision was based on two primary considerations: (1) homosexuality is not inherently harmful to the person or to others; and (2) homosexuals as a group are as well adjusted psychologically as heterosexuals (Reiss, 1980). Furthermore, there has also been a failure to consistently identify any psychological or biological (e.g., hormonal) factors that cause homosexuality (Masters, Johnson, & Kolodny, 1982). There is evidence that public acceptance of homosexuality as a normal variant is growing, but many individuals and religious groups still consider it to be abnormal and immoral.

ego-dystonic homosexuality
(e'go-dis-ton'ik)
Homosexuality that creates discomfort because the homosexual personally considers his or her sexual preferences abnormal.

Notable differences in the sexual behavior between homosexual men and women have been documented in recent research (Bell & Weinberg, 1978). In general, homosexual men are more sexually active than lesbians, but there are even more striking differences in the numbers of sexual partners that males and females have. Homosexual men are much more likely to have brief, emotionally uncommitted sexual encounters than are homosexual women. One study of over 900 homosexuals of both sexes found that fewer than 40 percent of lesbians had experienced a sexual encounter with a stranger, while almost all homosexual males had done so. Fewer than 50 percent of lesbians had had sexual relationships with more than nine partners in their lifetime, while more than half of male homosexuals estimated that they had had sexual encounters or relationships with at least 250 partners. Twenty-five percent of homosexual men reported 1,000 or more sexual partners (Bell & Weinberg, 1978).

Transvestism and Transsexualism

transvestism
(trans-ves'tizm)
The practice of obtaining sexual pleasure by dressing in the clothes of the opposite sex.

These two superficially similar patterns of sexuality are often confused because they both involve dressing in the clothing of the "opposite sex." But, they have little else in common except that they are rarely harmful to anyone. **Transvestism** refers to the practice of obtaining sexual pleasure by dressing in the clothes of the opposite sex. Transvestites are almost always males who have relatively well-adjusted heterosexual lives, but engage in cross-sex dressing for stimulation. A few transvestites are homosexual males who cross-sex dress to pick up heterosexual males for sex without undressing and revealing their male identity.

Transsexualism, a condition in which the person feels trapped in a body of the wrong sex, leads some individuals to undergo surgery that will change their sex organs to those of their desired sex. The professional tennis player Renee Richards underwent a sex-change operation to create female sex organs.

    Transsexualism, on the other hand, refers to a condition in which the individual feels trapped in a body of the wrong sex. For example, a person who is anatomically male feels that he is actually a woman who somehow was given the wrong body. Often the transsexual will occasionally or permanently dress in clothes of the opposite sex (opposite to the anatomical sex), but this cross-sex dressing has nothing to do with sexual arousal. The person merely feels that he or she is dressing in the clothes of their true sex. In some instances, the person will undergo hormone injections and plastic surgery to change his or her sex organs to those of the desired sex. Male-to-female sex change operations are much more common than the opposite, probably in part because surgically created penises are less satisfactory than surgically created vaginas (specifically, erections and sexual pleasure are not possible).

transsexualism
(trans-seks'u-ah-lizm)
A condition in which an individual feels trapped in the body of the wrong sex.

The sex-change clinic at Johns Hopkins Medical Center stopped doing sex-change operations during the 1970s because follow-up studies showed that their patients were no happier with their lives after surgery than before. Follow-up studies of patients from other centers, however, have shown that the patients were generally happy with their new bodies if properly selected for surgery and counseled on what to expect from it (Baker, 1969; Pauly, 1968).

Abnormal Patterns of Atypical Sexual Behavior

While many authorities consider the unusual patterns of sexual behavior just described to be normal under most circumstances, the following patterns range from ones that are *usually* considered to be abnormal to ones that are *always* considered to be abnormal because of the harm caused to the individual and/or others.

Voyeurism and Exhibitionism

voyeurism (voi′yer-izm)
The practice of obtaining sexual pleasure by watching members of the opposite sex undressing or engaging in sexual activities.

Voyeurism is the practice of obtaining sexual pleasure by watching members of the opposite sex undressing or engaging in sexual activities. Voyeurs generally find this exciting only when the person they are watching is unaware of their presence and when there is an element of danger involved. They are no more aroused than the average person at a nudist camp or watching a stripper, but become very excited peeping into windows (Tollison & Adams, 1979). Because they often frighten the person they are watching, and because the activity is illegal, voyeurism is considered to be abnormal. Generally the voyeur is a male who has trouble establishing normal heterosexual relationships; sometimes they commit rape and other crimes, but they are generally not considered dangerous.

exhibitionism (ek″si-bish′ŭ-nizm″)
The practice of obtaining sexual pleasure by exposing one's genitals to others.

Exhibitionists are individuals who obtain sexual pleasure from exposing their genitals to others. Almost all exhibitionists are heterosexual males who typically are married, but who are shy and have inhibited sex lives. Exhibitionists generally want to shock their victims, but rarely are dangerous in other ways (Tollison & Adams, 1979). Because such behavior is illegal and frightening, however, exhibitionism is considered abnormal.

Fetishism

fetishism (fet′ish-izm)
The practice of obtaining sexual arousal primarily or exclusively from specific objects.

Fetishism refers to the fact that some individuals are primarily or exclusively aroused by specific objects. In some cases, the fetish is only an exaggeration of normal interest in specific body parts. For example, some individuals are only or primarily aroused by breasts, buttocks, blue eyes, and so on. But the term fetish is usually reserved for cases involving inanimate objects such as panties, shoes, or stockings. Often, the fetishist (who is usually a male) is aroused only by "used" articles and is sexually aroused by the act of stealing them from an unknowing woman. Because this can be frightening and is illegal, fetishism is considered abnormal when practiced in this manner.

Sexual Sadism and Masochism

sexual sadism (sad′izm)
The practice of obtaining sexual pleasure by inflicting pain on others.

sexual masochism (mas′-o-kizm)
A condition in which receiving pain is sexually exciting.

Sexual sadism is the practice of receiving sexual pleasure from inflicting pain on others. **Sexual masochism** is the condition in which receiving pain is sexually exciting. Sometimes verbal abuse or "degradation" is substituted for physical pain. Approximately 5 to 10 percent of men and women find giving or receiving pain to be sexually exciting at times, but this is the preferred or only method of sexual arousal for very few individuals. Many individuals who practice sadism and masochism, or *S&M,* do so with a consenting partner who also enjoys the practice, and they do not inflict pain that is severe or medically dangerous—for example, mild spankings, pinching, and so on. In such cases, S&M may be considered normal if care is taken to avoid accidental harm and one's partner is *truly* willing. In other cases, however, S&M involves intense pain (such as whipping, burning, and kicking) that is inflicted on an unwilling participant. In rare cases, the sadist mutilates or even murders the victim to receive pleasure. Such practices are unquestionably abnormal.

Forced Sexual Behavior

Several other forms of deviant sexual patterns are clearly abnormal because they involve actual, threatened, or implied force to the victim if sex is not engaged in. These acts include rape, pedophilia, and incest. In **rape,** an individual forces another person to engage in a sexual act. In the vast majority of cases, the rapist is a male and the victim is a female. In some prison environments, however, it's not unusual for men to be victims of homosexual rapes by other men. In both cases, violence is involved and depression and other psychological reactions are common in the victim for a long time after the rape.

rape
The act of forcing sexual activity on an unwilling person.

    Pedophilia is the practice of obtaining pleasure from sexual contact with children. Generally overt force is not employed, and often the child is not aware of the sexual nature of what is occurring. In any case, pedophilia is forced sexual behavior in the sense that it occurs without the individual's consent. The child molester is typically a male heterosexual and the victim is usually a young girl. In some cases, the molester is a female or a male homosexual and the victim is a young boy. In a surprising 90 percent of cases, the molester is a neighbor or someone else who knows the child before the incident (Mohr, Turner, & Jerry, 1964).

pedophilia (pe″do-fil′e-ah)
The practice of obtaining pleasure from sexual contact with children.

    Incest refers to sexual relations between relatives. Morton Hunt (1975) found that 15 percent of the individuals he surveyed reported sexual activities with relatives. When incest occurs between similar-aged family members, force generally is not involved. However, incest is potentially harmful even in these cases because of the guilt it may create, the possibility of producing an abnormal offspring, and the tensions it may create within the family.

incest (in′sest)
Sexual relations between relatives.

    Implicit or explicit force is usually involved, however, when adult family members—generally a stepfather, uncle, or father—have sexual relations with children. These encounters are often confusing, upsetting, and guilt-producing in the children and should be considered a form of child abuse.

Sexual Dysfunction

Several types of problems can interfere with successful and pleasurable sexual intercourse. As mentioned earlier, these problems are common and considered abnormal only when they are prolonged. Even when prolonged, however, they do not indicate that the individual has other kinds of psychological problems. Sexual problems can and do occur in perfectly normal individuals. For example, one study found that women with sexual dysfunctions were essentially identical on psychological tests to women without dysfunctions (Munjack & Staples, 1977).

impotence (im'po-tens)
The inability of some males to achieve or maintain an erection of the penis long enough to have satisfactory sexual intercourse.

ejaculatory disorder (e-jak'u-lah-to''re)
Male sexual dysfunction in which the individual either reaches orgasm and ejaculates sperm too early or not at all.

premature ejaculation
A male sexual dysfunction in which the individual reaches orgasm and ejaculates sperm too early.

retarded ejaculation
A male sexual dysfunction in which the individual is unable to experience orgasm and ejaculation.

orgasmic dysfunction (or-gaz''mik dis-funk'shun)
A female sexual dysfunction in which the individual is unable to experience orgasm.

vaginismus (vaj''i-niz'mus)
A female sexual dysfunction in which the individual experiences involuntary contractions of the vaginal walls, making the vagina too narrow to allow the penis to enter comfortably.

dyspareunia (dis''pah-roo'ne-ah)
A sexual dysfunction in which the individual experiences pain during intercourse.

Male Dysfunctions

The most common sexual dysfunctions in males are impotence and ejaculatory disorders. **Impotence** refers to the inability to have or maintain an erection of the penis long enough to have satisfactory sexual intercourse. In rare cases, the individual has never been able to have an erection, but usually impotence occurs in men who have been successful previously in having intercourse. Almost all men experience this problem for brief periods at least once during their life as the result of anxiety, fatigue, alcohol, or illness, but some men experience this problem for prolonged periods of time.

In the **ejaculatory disorders,** the individual either reaches orgasm and ejaculates sperm too early or not at all. Ejaculating too early to allow the female to reach orgasm, **premature ejaculation,** is by far the most common ejaculatory disorder. This, too, is commonly experienced by most males, especially sexually inexperienced men. But it's easily treated by professional counseling. The inability to experience orgasm and ejaculation, **retarded ejaculation,** is a far less common problem and may require more involved treatment.

Female Dysfunctions

The most common female sexual dysfunction is **orgasmic dysfunction,** or the inability to experience orgasm. Many women are unable to experience orgasm for brief periods or with some partners, but some have never been able to have orgasm and some lose the ability for long periods of time. Other less common female dysfunctions are vaginismus and dyspareunia. **Vaginismus** refers to involuntary contractions of the walls of the vagina that make it too narrow to allow the penis to enter in sexual intercourse. In **dyspareunia,** the woman experiences pain during intercourse. Often, but not always, these conditions are accompanied by orgasmic dysfunction and anxiety associated with sex. Like the male dysfunctions, the female dysfunctions can usually be eliminated with professional help.

R E V I E W

A number of less common patterns of sexual behavior involve no harm to the individual or others and are considered to be normal even though they are unusual and perceived as immoral by some members of society. Other forms of deviant sexual behavior are considered abnormal only if they are practiced in a way that is harmful, while other forms of sexual behavior are inherently abnormal because of the harm involved. Homosexuality refers to preference for sexual partners of the same sex. The transvestite obtains sexual pleasure from dressing in clothing of the opposite sex. Transsexualism is the condition in which individuals consider themselves to be trapped within bodies of the opposite sex. Unless the individual is troubled by the condition, homosexuality, transvestism, and transsexualism are generally not harmful to anyone. Fetishism—obtaining sexual pleasure from specific objects—need not be harmful, but can be if the objects are stolen or the preference causes trouble in some other way. Sadism—sexual arousal from inflicting pain—may be harmless if practiced in a mild way with a completely willing partner, but is generally considered abnormal because of the pain and medical risk involved. Masochism—sexual arousal from receiving pain—is generally considered abnormal for the same reason.

Voyeurism refers to the practice of obtaining sexual pleasure by peeping at nude or sexually involved individuals. Exhibitionism is the practice of obtaining sexual excitement by exposing one's genitals to an unwilling person. Because of the frightening nature and illegality of these activities, both exhibitionism and voyeurism are considered abnormal. Forced sexual behaviors, including rape, pedophilia, and incest, are always considered abnormal because of the psychological discomfort and physical harm that may occur.

A number of sexual dysfunctions interfere with pleasurable and successful heterosexual intercourse. The most common include the inability to have or maintain erections and the inability to properly time orgasm in males. In females, the most common dysfunction is the inability to have orgasms. Some women experience involuntary contractions of the walls of the vagina that prevent intercourse or cause intense pain during intercourse.

S U M M A R Y

Chapter 12 introduces us to the common sources and reactions to *stress,* and to the wide range of abnormal thoughts, feelings, and actions that humans experience.

I. Stress is any event or circumstance that strains or exceeds the individual's ability to cope.
   A. *Frustration, conflict, pressure, life events,* and *environmental conditions* are five major sources of stress.
   B. Coping reactions to stress include both psychological and physiological components.
      1. The *general adaptation syndrome* is a physiological reaction that includes the *alarm reaction,* the *resistance stage,* and the *exhaustion stage.*
      2. Psychological reactions to stress primarily involve changes in emotions, motivations, and cognitions.
      3. *Effective methods* of coping remove the source of stress or control our reactions to it.
      4. *Withdrawal, aggression,* and *defense mechanisms* are *ineffective* methods of coping.
   C. Prior experience with stress, predictability and control over stress, social support, and person variables are factors that are related to the magnitude of stress reactions.
II. Abnormal behavior includes those actions, thoughts, and feelings that are harmful to the person and/or others.
   A. Our ideas about the causes of abnormal behavior determine what we do to help those who experience it.
   B. Abnormal behavior is viewed today as a *natural,* rather than a *supernatural,* phenomenon.
III. The term *neurosis* refers to mild disorders without gross distortions of reality; *psychosis* refers to severe conditions that involve distortion of reality.

IV. Anxiety disorders are characterized by excessive anxiety.
    A. Intense, unrealistic fears are called *phobias.*
    B. *General anxiety disorders* are characterized by free-floating anxiety.
    C. *Panic anxiety disorders* involve attacks of intense anxiety.
    D. *Obsessions* are anxiety-provoking thoughts that will not go away; *compulsions* are urges to repeatedly engage in a behavior.

V. *Somatoform disorders* are conditions in which an individual experiences symptoms of health problems that are psychological rather than physical in origin.
    A. *Somatization disorders* are a type of somatoform disorder that involves multiple minor symptoms of illness that indirectly create a high risk of medical complications; *hypochondriasis* is characterized by excessive concern with health.
    B. *Conversion disorders* are a type of somatoform disorder that involves serious specific somatic symptoms in the absence of any physical cause; *psychogenic pain disorders* involve pain without physical cause.

VI. In the various types of *dissociative disorders,* there is a change in memory, perception, or identity.
    A. *Dissociative amnesia* and *fugue states* involve memory loss that has psychological rather than physical causes.
    B. In *depersonalization,* individuals feel that they or their surroundings have become distorted or unreal.
    C. Individuals who exhibit *multiple personalities* appear to possess more than one personality in the same body.

VII. *Affective disorders* are disturbances of mood.
    A. The individual experiencing *major depression* is deeply unhappy and lethargic.
    B. In the condition known as *bipolar affective disorder,* periods of *mania* alternate irregularly with periods of severe depression.

VIII. Schizophrenia involves three major areas of abnormality: *cognitive disorders, emotional disturbances,* and *social withdrawal.*
    A. The *paranoid schizophrenic* holds false beliefs or delusions—usually of grandeur and persecution—that seriously distort reality.
    B. *Disorganized schizophrenia* is characterized by extreme withdrawal from normal human contact, fragmented delusions and hallucinations, and a shallow "silliness" of emotion.
    C. *Catatonic schizophrenia* is marked by stupors in which the individual may maintain postures for long periods of time.

IX. *Personality disorders* are thought to result from personalities that developed improperly during childhood rather than from breakdowns under stress.
    A. *Schizoid personality disorders* are characterized by a loss of interest in proper dress and social contact, a lack of emotion, and an inability to hold regular jobs.
    B. The *antisocial personality* frequently violates social rules and laws, is often violent, takes advantage of others, and feels little guilt about it.

X. A number of less common patterns of sexual behavior are considered to be normal even though they are unusual. *Homosexuality, transvestism,* and *transsexualism* are atypical sexual patterns that deviate considerably from the norm, but are not considered to be abnormal unless the individual is unhappy with his or her sexual pattern.

XI. Abnormal patterns of atypical sexual behavior include *voyeurism, exhibitionism, fetishism, sadism, masochism, rape, incest,* and *pedophilia. Sexual dysfunctions* are problems that can interfere with successful and pleasurable sexual intercourse.

Suggested Readings

1. A sophisticated but readable discussion of stress by the father of the concept:
   Selye, H. (1976). *The stress of life.* New York: Knopf.

2. An overview of coping and abnormal behavior is provided by Tony Ciminero and friend:
   Lahey, B. B., & Ciminero, A. R. (1980). *Maladaptive behavior: An introduction to abnormal psychology.* Glenview, IL: Scott, Foresman.

3. Issues of concern to our own personal adjustment are addressed in:
   Coleman, J. C. (1984). *Contemporary psychology and effective behavior* (7th ed.). Glenview, IL: Scott, Foresman.

4. A personal account of the experience of schizophrenia is found in the classic book:
   Sechehaye, M. (1951). *Reality lost and regained: Autobiography of a schizophrenic girl.* New York: Grune & Stratton.

T H I R T E E N

Therapies

OUTLINE

KEY TERMS

PROLOGUE

In the Prologue to chapter 12, we discussed those veterans who were experiencing painful delayed reactions to the stress of combat in the Vietnam War. What can be done to help these individuals finally leave the pain of the war behind? At the Jackson, Mississippi, Veterans Administration Medical Center and elsewhere a therapy technique called *flooding* is being used with apparent success in posttraumatic stress disorder (Keane & Kaloupek, 1982). Flooding is an unpleasant procedure that can only be used with clients who are highly motivated to find a solution to their problems. One such individual was a 36-year-old veteran of combat in Vietnam who came to the Medical Center seeking help for his many problems. He was chronically anxious, slept very little, had intense paniclike attacks of anxiety two to three times per week, and had catastrophic nightmares and daytime "flashbacks," in which he vividly relived traumatic war events in his imagination. In addition, he had been attempting unsuccessfully to drown his problems in a quart of gin each day for the past five years.

The veteran's psychologist began treatment by asking him to imagine a particularly upsetting scene in which a buddy was accidentally shot and killed in the mess hall while a gun was being cleaned. The therapist helped him remember the details of the situation in vivid detail to make the image as realistic and as upsetting as possible. He asked the veteran to recall the location, the weather, the terrain, his companions, and how he was feeling just before the shooting. Then he was asked to imagine every detail of the shooting itself. When the veteran became visibly shaken by this memory, he was urged to continue to imagine the scene in vivid detail until he was emotionally exhausted. After eight daily sessions of "flooding" himself with the emotions associated with this memory, the veteran was asked to begin imagining a second traumatic event in which another buddy was killed in front of him in an ambush attack.

After 20 such daily sessions, dramatic improvements had occurred. The veteran was sleeping normally, had virtually no more flashback recollections or nightmares, and was no longer feeling anxious. When contacted a year later to check on his progress, he was virtually free of the problems that had led him to seek treatment.

In this case, the technique of flooding was apparently quite successful. Would all psychologists take this same approach to therapy? Would a physician have felt that some form of medical therapy might have been more appropriate? After reading the diversity of opinions about the nature of personality expressed in chapter 12, it will come as no surprise to you that there are a diverse variety of opinions and theories about therapy for psychololgical problems as well. As you read on, you will learn that flooding is a technique of *behavior therapy,* the form of psychotherapy associated with the social learning theory of personality. As you read about the other forms of psychotherapy and medical therapy, try to imagine how each would attempt to help this veteran who was reliving the horrors of the Vietnam War.

P R E V I E W

Psychotherapy is a process of people helping people. In this process, a trained professional seeks to help a person with a psychological problem by using methods based on psychological theories of the nature of the problem. These therapy methods include everyday activities such as asking questions, making suggestions, and demonstrating alternative ways of behaving, but psychotherapy differs from commonsense attempts to help because of the theories that determine *what* is asked, *what* is suggested, and so on. There are many different forms of psychotherapy that are associated with the different theories of personality that we studied in chapter 12.

Psychoanalysts see abnormal behavior as the result of unconscious conflicts among the id, ego, and superego. These conflicts remain hidden from consciousness because the ego and superego see them as dangerous and block them out. The process of psychoanalysis, then, is a process of relaxing the censorship exerted by the conscious mind and bringing unconscious conflicts into awareness where they can be intelligently resolved. Because the contents of the unconscious are revealed only in disguised, symbolic ways, however, the psychoanalyst must help the individual interpret these glimpses of the hidden side of the mind.

Humanistic psychologists also believe that the goal of psychotherapy is to help the person achieve greater self-awareness, but in ways that differ from psychoanalysts. Carl Rogers and other humanists believe that feelings and information that differ too much from a person's concept of self—both the person we think we are and the self we would like to be—are often denied conscious awareness. The humanistic psychotherapist seeks to help the person to allow this information into his or her consciousness and to achieve fuller self-awareness. Some forms of humanistic psychotherapy attempt to do this by providing a warm and safe emotional environment in which the individual feels safe to explore feelings that have been denied awareness. Other forms of humanistic psychotherapy use techniques such as directly pointing out discrepancies in behavior that are believed to reveal unsymbolized feelings.

Behavior therapy is the approach to psychotherapy that is associated with the social learning view of personality. Because psychological problems are believed to be the result of unfortunate learning experiences—the individual simply *learned* his or her problems—the behavior therapist plays the role of a teacher helping the person unlearn abnormal ways of behaving and learn more effective patterns of behavior to replace them. Cognitive therapy is a recent approach to psychotherapy that has strongly influenced the behavior therapy movement and has largely been incorporated into it. Cognitive therapists suggest that illogical beliefs and ways of thinking are the cause of abnormal behavior. They attempt to talk people out of these faulty cognitions by pointing out their irrationality.

Help for abnormal behavior is not only delivered in one-to-one psychotherapy, however. It's sometimes provided in the form of group or family therapy, as services delivered in the community to prevent psychological problems and assist those who have them, and often takes the form of medication and other kinds of medical treatment.

Definition of Psychotherapy

Generally, people with the serious kinds of psychological problems described in chapter 12 need professional help. There are many different forms of help available for psychological disorders from psychologists, psychiatrists, and other professionals (psychiatric social workers, marriage counselors, and so on). In this chapter, we will describe the major forms of therapy and relate them to differing theories of personality (chapter 11) and differing views of abnormal behavior (chapter 12).

In general terms, **psychotherapy** can be defined as a specialized process in which a trained professional uses psychological methods to help a person with psychological problems. The term psychological methods can refer to almost any kind of human interaction (such as talking, demonstrating, or reinforcing) that is based on a psychological theory of the problem, but it does not include medical treatment methods such as medications or surgery.

Different forms of psychotherapy that are associated with psychoanalytic, humanistic, and social learning theories of personality involve very different psychological methods. The approach to psychotherapy associated with social learning theory, known as *behavior therapy*, views the process of helping as a form of teaching. The therapist helps the person learn not to engage in harmful behaviors and to learn adaptive behaviors to take their place. The approaches to psychotherapy associated with psychoanalytic and humanistic views of personality see their goal as providing *insight*, that is, bringing feelings (or conflicts or information) of which the person is unaware into conscious awareness. Although the methods of psychoanalysis and humanistic therapy differ greatly, they both view the therapist not as a teacher but as a *catalyst*, an agent who makes change possible but does not actually cause or enter into the change. Therapies that strive for increased awareness view the person with problems as the agent of his or her own improvement.

Defining psychotherapy as a psychological process of helping people with psychological problems is correct, but limited in an important way. Many individuals legitimately enter into psychotherapy to improve their daily lives rather than to rid themselves of abnormal behavior. Individuals often seek therapy because they feel that they simply are not getting full enjoyment from their careers or are not approaching intimate personal relationships in appropriate ways. Psychotherapy is also often used to enhance sexual and marital relationships, to learn to manage normal reactions to stress better, and so on. Often this use of psychotherapy is called **personal growth therapy.**

Psychoanalysis

Psychoanalysis is the approach to psychotherapy founded by Sigmund Freud. It's based on Freud's belief that the root of all psychological problems is unconscious conflicts among the id, ego, and superego. Conflicts inevitably exist among these three competing forces, but they can cause problems if they get out of hand. If too much of the energy of the superego and ego is devoted to holding the selfish desires of the id in check, or if these prohibitions are weak and the id threatens to break free, psychological disturbances are the result. According to Freud, these problems must be brought into consciousness if they are to be solved.

Charlie

"Nonsense—there are *lots* of famous men who were *short!* Tommy O'Hara the famous jockey was *short!* Billy Howard the famous jockey was *short!* Joe Velasquez the famous jockey was *short!* Bobby Van Dam the famous jockey was *short!* . . ."

Reprinted by permission: Tribune Media Services

psychotherapy
(si-ko-ther′ah-pe)
A form of therapy in which a trained professional uses methods based on psychological theories to help a person with psychological problems.

personal growth therapy
Psychotherapy for normal individuals who want to enhance their personal adjustment, improve interpersonal relationships, learn to react better to stress, and so on.

psychoanalysis
(si″ko-ah-nal′i-sis)
A method of psychotherapy developed by Freud based on his belief that the root of all psychological problems is unconscious conflicts between the id, the ego, and the superego.

OF SPECIAL INTEREST

Ethical Considerations in the Use of Psychotherapy

The relationship between client and psychotherapist is a unique one. The patient divulges large amounts of personal information and places his or her future in the hands of the psychotherapist. For these reasons, it's essential that the highest ethical standards be followed in the practice of psychotherapy. The following set of guidelines have been issued by the Association for Advancement of Behavior Therapy (1978) to help ensure ethical practice.

A. Have the goals of treatment been adequately considered?
 1. To ensure that the goals are explicit, are they written?
 2. Has the client's understanding of the goals been assured by having the client restate them orally or in writing?
 3. Have the therapist and client agreed on the goals of therapy?
 4. Will serving the client's interests be contrary to the interests of other persons?
 5. Will serving the client's immediate interests be contrary to the client's long-term interest?

B. Has the choice of treatment methods been adequately considered?
 1. Does the published literature show the procedure to be the best one available for that problem?
 2. If no literature exists regarding the treatment method, is the method consistent with generally accepted practice?
 3. Has the client been told of alternative procedures that might be preferred by the client on the basis of significant differences in discomfort, treatment time, cost, or degree of demonstrated effectiveness?
 4. If a treatment procedure is publicly, legally, or professionally controversial, has formal professional consultation been obtained, has the reaction of the affected segment of the public been adequately considered, and have the alternative treatment methods been more closely reexamined and reconsidered?

C. Is the client's participation voluntary?
 1. Have possible sources of coercion on the client's participation been considered?
 2. If treatment is legally mandated, has the available range of treatments and therapists been offered?
 3. Can the client withdraw from treatment without a penalty or financial loss that exceeds actual clinical costs?

D. When another person or an agency is empowered to arrange for therapy, have the interests of the subordinated client been sufficiently considered?
  1. Has the subordinated client been informed of the treatment objectives and participated in the choice of treatment procedures?
  2. Where the subordinated client's competence to decide is limited, have the client as well as the guardian participated in the treatment discussions to the extent that the client's abilities permit?
  3. If the interests of the subordinated person and the superordinate persons or agency conflict, have attempts been made to reduce the conflict by dealing with both interests?
E. Has the adequacy of treatment been evaluated?
  1. Have quantitative measures of the problem and its progress been obtained?
  2. Have the measures of the problem and its progress been made available to the client during treatment?
F. Has the confidentiality of the treatment relationship been protected?
  1. Has the client been told who has access to the records?
  2. Are records available only to authorized persons?
G. Does the therapist refer the clients to other therapists when necessary?
  1. If treatment is unsuccessful, is the client referred to other therapists?
  2. Has the client been told that if dissatisfied with the treatment, referral will be made?
H. Is the therapist qualified to provide treatment?
  1. Has the therapist had training or experience in treating problems like the client's?
  2. If deficits exist in the therapist's qualifications, has the client been informed?
  3. If the therapist is not adequately qualified, is the client referred to other therapists, or has supervision by a qualified therapist been provided? Is the client informed of the supervisory relation?
  4. If the treatment is administered by mediators, have the mediators been adequately supervised by a qualified therapist?

From Association for Advancement of Behavior Therapy. Ethical issues for human services *(pamphlet). New York: AABT, 1978. Reprinted by permission.*

A patient and her therapist
in a session of
psychoanalysis.

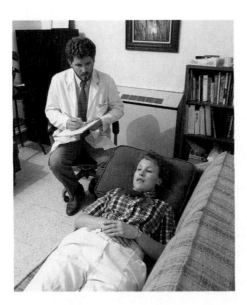

Bringing unconscious conflicts into consciousness is not an easy matter, though. Recall from chapter 11 that the id is completely unconscious. Even the sexual and aggressive motives that we consciously experience have been transformed by the ego into safe and socially acceptable versions of the id's true desires. According to Freud, the ego operates as if the raw, selfish desires of the id are too dangerous to allow into consciousness, so it works diligently to dam up the id in the recesses of our unconscious mind. Special therapy methods must be used, therefore, to allow information about unconscious id conflicts to slip past the censorship of the ego.

Generally it's possible to bring information out of the unconscious only when the ego's guard is temporarily relaxed, and even then, the id is only able to reveal itself in disguised symbolic forms. Thus, the job of the psychoanalyst is to: (1) create conditions in which the censorship of the ego is relaxed; and (2) to *interpret* the disguised symbolic revelations of the unconscious mind to the patient.

Most contemporary psychoanalysts do not practice an orthodox version of psychoanalysis, but rather practice versions based on the revisions of Jung, Adler, and more contemporary psychoanalysts. Still, many of the specific methods of therapy used by Freud are still in use today. These include free association, dream interpretation, interpretation of resistance, the interpretation of transference, and catharsis.

free association
A tool used by Freud in which the patient is encouraged to talk about whatever comes to mind, allowing the contents of the unconscious mind to slip past the censorship of the ego.

Free Association

Freud's primary tool of therapy was the method of **free association.** In this method, the individual talks in a loose and undirected way about whatever comes to mind. No thought or feeling is to be withheld, no matter how illogical, trivial, unpleasant, or silly it might seem. Freud hoped that this technique would lead to a "turning off" of the intellectual control of the ego and allow for glimpses of the unconscious. Occasionally, as the mind wanders, the id slips out. To make

In traditional psychoanalysis, the therapist sits out of the patient's sight. Freud had his patients lie on a couch while he sat in a chair to the left.

this more likely to happen, Freud had his patients lie on a couch facing the ceiling. He sat out of sight behind them so they would feel that they were talking to themselves rather than revealing forbidden information to another.

Incidentally, contemporary research suggests that Freud's choice of a reclining position for his patients may have had an important effect on his approach to psychotherapy. After working with many patients, Freud came to believe that he must help the patient achieve insight primarily about events that happened in childhood. Interestingly, Pope (1978) found that when individuals are asked to let their "mind wander" aloud, reclining people speak significantly more about the *past* than people who are sitting. Freud's choice of a reclining posture for his patients may have led them to focus on the past and led him to think of the past as being of prime importance in therapy.

The "glimpses of the unconscious" revealed during free association have hidden, symbolic meaning that must be translated or *interpreted* to the patient by the psychoanalyst. For example, the patient might mention during the course of free association that he wanted to go hunting with his father, but that he never asked him to go hunting because he was afraid that his father was too old and might get hurt. To the psychoanalyst, this statement might be a statement about phallic symbols (guns) and the son's unresolved Oedipal conflict (see chapter 11, p. 432) that has left him with an unacceptable desire to shoot his father. When properly interpreted to the patient, Freud believed that this information about the unconscious would help the person consciously solve his or her problems.

Dream Interpretation

Dream interpretation was used by Freud in much the same manner as free association. As we mentioned in chapter 4, the obvious or *manifest content* of dreams is believed by psychoanalysts to symbolically mask the true or *latent content* of dreams. By asking patients to recall dreams, Freud believed he had obtained another "window" on the unconscious.

dream interpretation
A method developed by Freud in which the symbols of the manifest content of dreams that are recalled by the patient are interpreted to reveal their latent content.

For example, a recurrent dream of an adolescent boy in which he was drifting through a slimy swamp on a raft, reaching down repeatedly into the dirty water, and pulling up shoes might have no meaning at all to the adolescent. The psychoanalyst might translate it to mean that the boy was experiencing conflicts over his heterosexual desires. Shoes are commonly taken to symbolize vaginas in psychoanalytic thinking, and the dirty, forbidding water from which he was attempting to possess these vaginas might represent his guilt feelings about sex.

Interpretation of Resistance

resistance
Any form of patient opposition to the process of psychoanalysis.

Freud also placed heavy emphasis on the interpretation of what he called **resistance** in therapy. Resistance is any form of opposition of the patient to the process of psychoanalysis. Resistance can occur in two ways. It might take vague forms such as missing appointments with the therapist or questioning the value of psychoanalysis. Or, it might be a specific resistance to the interpretations of the therapist. In either case, resistance meant to Freud that he had located a conflict in the patient that was so laden with anxiety that the patient wanted to avoid talking about it. This avoidance of the topic made Freud all the more interested in pursuing it.

Angrily telling a psychoanalyst that he's wrong for suggesting that you ever wanted to have casual sex with a person you did not love may convince your therapist that this is something that you actually want to do but that you consider morally unacceptable. In order to give you better insight into your own motives, your psychoanalyst might interpret this resistance to you. If you erroneously continue to think you do not want casual sex, you will not be able to understand and deal with the anxiety that you experience. If, on the other hand, you become aware that you do want casual sex, but that you feel that it would be immoral to do so, you can make more rational, informed choices about your behavior.

Interpretation of Transference

The relationship that forms between patient and therapist can also be a source of information about the unconscious to the psychoanalyst. Because the patient comes to the therapist in need of help, reveals a great deal of private information, and receives acceptance and support, it's not surprising that a rather intense relationship often develops. This relationship is not like the one you have with your dentist, but more, like a close parent-child relationship.

transference
(trans-fer′ens)
The phenomenon in psychoanalysis in which the patient comes to feel and act toward the therapist in ways that resemble how he or she feels and acts toward other significant adults.

Because of the intensity of the relationship in therapy, psychoanalysts believe that the kind of relationship the patient has with the therapist reveals a great deal about the way the patient relates to his or her parents and other significant authority figures. Psychoanalysts call this phenomenon **transference.** When patients repeatedly ask for reassurance that they will not be dropped as clients, or argue about fees, or make sexual advances, they are believed to be transferring to the therapist feelings that they have for other significant adults in their lives. That is, they are feeling and acting toward the therapist in the same basic ways that they feel and act toward their parents, employers, and so on. When interpreted to the patients, psychoanalysts believe that transference can serve as another valuable source of insight.

"*Mr. Prentice is not your father. Alex Binster is not your brother. The anxiety you feel is not genuine. Dr. Froelich will return from vacation September 15th. Hang on.*"

Catharsis

In addition to the interpretation of symbolic revelations of unconscious conflicts, psychoanalysis allows the patient to release some of the emotion that is pent up with unconscious conflicts. All forms of psychotherapy can be very emotional experiences that at times involve talking about highly upsetting topics. Letting these emotions out—a process psychoanalysts call **catharsis**—provides a temporary relief from discomfort.

This relief does not solve problems in and of itself, but does make the patient feel better. Catharsis also may help the process of psychoanalysis, however, because a patient who feels better will generally be better able to make intelligent decisions about discoveries from the unconscious.

catharsis
The release of emotional energy related to unconscious conflicts.

R E V I E W

Psychoanalysis is the method of psychotherapy based on Freud's theory of personality. The therapist attempts to help the patient by bringing unconscious conflicts into consciousness so they can be intelligently resolved. Because the ego works to block from consciousness the contents of the unconscious mind (including conflicts among the id, ego, and superego), the psychoanalyst must create conditions to relax the censorship of the ego. Even when the unconscious mind reveals itself at these times, however, it does so in disguised, symbolic ways. This means that a second function of the psychoanalyst is to interpret the disguised information revealed during psychoanalysis to the patient. The specific method most commonly used by the psychoanalyst to relax the ego's censorship is free association. Comments made by the patient during these wandering, unguided conversations are believed to symbolically reveal hidden conflicts. In addition, the psychoanalyst interprets information from dreams, resistance to the process of therapy, and the way the patient acts toward the psychoanalyst (transference) to reveal further the unconscious mind to the patient. Finally, psychoanalysis is believed to provide temporary relief by allowing the patient to vent some of the emotion tied up in unconscious conflicts (catharsis).

Humanistic therapy, like
psychoanalytic therapy,
attempts to bring what is
unconscious into conscious
awareness.

Humanistic Psychotherapy

The humanistic and psychoanalytic schools of thought both believe that the primary goal of therapy is the bringing forth of feelings of which the individual is unaware into conscious awareness. Recall from chapter 11 that Carl Rogers gives us an alternative way of thinking about feelings and information of which we are not consciously aware. Unlike Freud, Rogers does not believe that we are born with an unconscious mind. Rather, we deny awareness to information and feelings that differ too much from our concepts of self and ideal self (by not symbolizing them).

Using the same example that we used to illustrate Freud's concept of the unconscious, suppose you were a person who wanted casual sex. If your ideal self (the one you thought you should ideally be) were the kind of person who would never have casual sex, you might deny conscious awareness to that desire. The desire for casual sex did not arise from an unconscious id according to Rogers, but the end result is the same: When a feeling is denied awareness, it can create anxiety until it's brought into the open. That is, it creates trouble until the individual achieves full awareness of his or her feelings. Because humanists view full self-awareness as necessary for the complete realization of our inner-directed potential, they speak of the process of therapy in terms of "growth in awareness" rather than in insight.

The methods used by humanistic therapists differ considerably from those used in psychoanalytic psychotherapy. A description of methods of humanistic therapy is complicated by the fact that there are actually a number of different approaches grouped together under the name of humanism. We can get a perspective on these therapies by looking at the methods of two leaders of the humanistic psychotherapy movement, Carl Rogers and Fritz Perls.

OF SPECIAL INTEREST

An Excerpt from Psychoanalytic Psychotherapy

Client: We had a salesmen's meeting, and a large group of us were cramped together in a small room and they turned out the lights to show some slides, and I got so jumpy and anxious I couldn't stand it.

Therapist: So what happened? [Question]

C: I just couldn't stand it. I was sweating and shaking, so I got up and left, and I know I'll be called on the carpet for walking out.

T: You became so anxious and upset that you couldn't stand being in the room even though you knew that walking out would get you into trouble. [Clarification]

C: Yeah. . . . What could have bothered me so much to make me do a dumb thing like that?

T: You know, we've talked about other times in your life when you've become upset in close quarters with other men, once when you were in the army and again in your dormitory at college. [Confrontation]

C: That's right, and it was the same kind of thing again.

T: And if I'm correct, this has never happened to you in a group of men and women together, no matter how closely you've been cramped together. [Further confrontation]

C: Uh. . . . Yes, that's right.

T: So it appears that something especially about being physically close to other men, and especially in the dark, makes you anxious, as if you're afraid bad might happen in that kind of situation. [Interpretation]

C: (Pause): I think you're right about that . . . and I know I'm not physically afraid of other men. Do you think I might get worried about something homosexual taking place?

From I. B. Weiner (1975), Principles of psychotherapy. *New York: Wiley. Copyright 1975 by John Wiley & Sons, Inc.*

Client-Centered Psychotherapy

Rogers refers to his humanistic approach as **client-centered psychotherapy** (he prefers the term *client* to the more medically oriented term *patient*) because the client is at the *center* of the process of psychotherapy, not the therapist (Rogers, 1951). A sample of this approach is provided in *Of Special Interest:* "An Excerpt from Client-Centered Therapy." The emphasis is on the ability of clients to help themselves rather than on the ability of the therapist to help the clients. The job

client-centered psychotherapy
Carl Rogers' approach to humanistic psychotherapy in which the therapist creates an atmosphere that encourages clients to discover feelings of which they are unaware.

OF SPECIAL INTEREST

An Excerpt from Client-Centered Therapy

The following is an excerpt from a conversation between humanistic psychologist Carl Rogers (R) and a client (C), a depressed young man:

Rogers: Everything's lousy, huh? You feel lousy? (Silence of 39 seconds)

R: Want to come in Friday at 12 at the usual time?

Client: [Yawns and mutters something unintelligible.] (Silence of 48 seconds)

R: Just kind of feel sunk way down deep in these lousy, lousy feelings, hm? Is that something like it?

C: No.

R: No? (Silence of 20 seconds)

C: No. I just ain't no good to nobody, never was, and never will be.

R: Feeling that now, hm? That you're just no good to yourself, no good to anybody. Just that you're completely worthless, huh? Those really are lousy feelings. Just feel that you're no good at all, hm?
[From a session three days later]

C: I just want to run away and die.

R: M-hm, m-hm, m-hm. It isn't even that you want to get away from here to something. You just want to leave here and go away and die in a corner, hm? (Silence of 30 seconds)

---

of the therapist in client-centered therapy is not to employ specific therapy techniques or to interpret the client's behavior, but to create an atmosphere that is so emotionally safe for the clients that they will feel free to express to the therapist (and to themselves) the feelings they have denied awareness. Growth in awareness comes not from interpretations, but from the client's feeling safe enough to explore hidden emotions in the therapy sessions. Rogers believes that the creation of this safe atmosphere requires three elements from the therapist. The therapist must be (1) warm, (2) genuinely able to like the clients and unconditionally accept everything they think, feel, or do without criticism, and (3) must have *empathy,* an accurate understanding and sharing of the emotions of the client.

The closest thing to a specific "technique" in client-centered therapy is the process of **reflection.** The therapist helps the clients clarify the feelings expressed in their statements by reflecting back the emotions of the client. Sometimes the therapists ask questions, but other than reflections, client-centered therapists say relatively little in therapy. In particular, they strictly avoid giving advice to clients. They feel that clients can easily learn to solve their own problems after they have gained awareness, but that they will remain dependent on the therapist if the therapist solves their problems for them.

reflection (re-flek'shun)
A technique in humanistic psychotherapy in which the therapist reflects the emotions of the client in order to help clients clarify their feelings.

OF SPECIAL INTEREST

R: I guess as I let that soak in I really do sense how, how deep that feeling sounds, that you—I guess the image that comes to my mind is sort of a—wounded animal that wants to crawl away and die. It sounds as though that's kind of the way you feel that you just want to get away from here and, and vanish. Perish. Not exist. (Silence of 1 minute)

C: [almost inaudibly] All day yesterday and all morning I wished I were dead. I even prayed last night that I could die.

R: I think I caught all of that, that for a couple of days now you've just wished you could be dead and you've even prayed for that, I guess that. One way this strikes me is that to live is such an awful thing to you, you just wish you could die, and not live. (Silence of 1 minute, 12 seconds)

R: So that you've been just wishing and wishing that you were not living. You wish that life would pass away from you. (Silence of 30 seconds)

C: I wish it more'n anything else I've ever wished around here.

R: M-hm, m-hm, m-hm. I guess you've wished for lots of things but boy! It seems as though this wish to not live is deeper and stronger than anything you ever wished before. (Silence of 1 minute, 36 seconds)

Reproduced from Person-centered therapy by B. D. Meador & C. R. Rogers (1979) in Raymond J. Corsini's Current Psychotherapies, *2d ed., pp. 155–158.*

Gestalt Psychotherapy

Humanistic psychologist Fredrick (Fritz) Perls named his approach to humanistic psychotherapy **Gestalt therapy** (Perls, Hefferline, & Goodman, 1951). The term *Gestalt* was chosen to emphasize a point first made by the Gestalt psychologists (whom we initially encountered in chapter 1). Writing in the early 1900s, this group pointed out that sensations have no meaning unless they are organized into "whole" perceptions. In an analogous way, Fritz Perls wanted to help his clients perceive themselves in a whole way by admitting conflicting information into awareness.

The goal of Gestalt therapy is essentially the same as that of client-centered therapy, namely, creating a therapeutic experience that will help the client achieve greater self-awareness. But the kinds of therapeutic experiences created by Gestalt and client-centered psychotherapists are as different as night and day.

Gestalt psychologists are actively involved in the conversations of therapy sessions. In particular, they challenge their client's statements when they think the statements do not reflect their client's true feelings, and they point out revealing inconsistencies in the present. For example, if a client claimed to *never*

Gestalt therapy
A humanistic therapy in which the therapist takes an active role (questioning and challenging the client) to help the client become more aware of his or her feelings.

Fritz Perls (1893–1970)

feel anxious about her performance on the job, she might get a reply like "Oh, come now Mary, everyone gets anxious about job performance sometime. And what do you think it means that you start nervously tapping your fingers and squirming in your seat every time I bring up the subject? I think your denials of anxiousness cover up your true feelings."

The emotional atmosphere of Gestalt therapy is also quite different from client-centered therapy. While Gestalt therapists show concern for their clients, they often deal with them in a confrontive, challenging manner. They are far from warm and accepting in their pushing, prodding, and questioning. Perls refers to this confrontation as a "safe emergency": While it's upsetting to the clients, it occurs in the safe environment of therapy. He feels that the safe emergency of confrontation with the therapist is necessary to shake loose the client's repressions.

R E V I E W

Humanistic psychotherapy strives to help clients achieve fuller self-awareness. Humanists believe that information about individuals that differs too much from their concept of self—both the self they think they are and the self they think they should be—will be denied awareness. This lack of awareness is harmful both because it keeps the individual from having an accurate view of self to use in making decisions and because the unsymbolized information threatens the person's inaccurate self-image and creates anxiety. Different approaches to humanistic psychotherapy use different methods to bring unsymbolized information out into the open and give the person self-awareness. Client-centered psychotherapists (who prefer the term client to the medical term patient) create a safe emotional environment in therapy that they believe will allow clients to grow in self-awareness. This is accomplished through the therapist's warmth, empathy, and unconditional acceptance. In addition, the therapist uses the technique of reflection; the humanistic therapist repeats the message that she hears in the client's statements to help the client clarify what he is feeling. Gestalt therapists take a very different approach to humanistic therapy. They actively confront clients about inconsistencies in their statements, as well as between their statements and nonverbal behavior, that they feel reveal conflicting information and feelings. By pointing out these inconsistencies they hope to help the clients achieve greater self-awareness.

Behavior Therapy

behavior therapy
Psychotherapy based on social learning theory in which the therapist helps the client unlearn abnormal ways of behaving and learn more adaptive ways to take their place.

Behavior therapy is the approach to psychotherapy that is associated with the social learning theory of personality. Recall from chapter 11 that abnormal behavior is viewed by social learning theorists as *learned behavior*. Rather than the product of unconscious conflicts, abnormal behavior simply is learned from inappropriate experiences of classical conditioning, operant conditioning, and modeling. In other words, the individual is abnormal because his environment taught him to be. For example, a young man who was frightened by social encounters might be reinforced for social withdrawal by the reduction in anxiety (negative reinforcement) that it produced. If so, social learning theorists would predict that this individual would learn to be increasingly withdrawn.

Because of this view of the origins of abnormal behavior, it's natural that behavior therapists would see the process of learning as central to the process of therapy as well. As mentioned earlier in the chapter, the behavior therapist plays the role of a *teacher,* a person who helps the client unlearn abnormal ways of behaving and learn more adaptive ways to take their place. The behavior therapist would attempt to help the socially withdrawn young man mentioned on the previous page to unlearn his fear of social interaction, and then teach him appropriate ways of interacting socially.

A number of different therapy methods have been derived from the basic principles of learning for use in behavior therapy. We survey a few of the major techniques used to reduce abnormal fears, teach new skills, and break abnormal habits. As you read about each of them, notice the innovative ways in which they teach adaptive behavior.

Fear Reduction Methods

Several behavior therapy methods are used for the treatment of the abnormal fears that we call phobias. In different ways, each attempts to extinguish the fear response to the phobic stimulus and replace it with a relaxation response. Two of the most widely used methods are *systematic desensitization* and *flooding.*

Systematic Desensitization

Systematic desensitization was developed by psychiatrist Joseph Wolpe (1958). It's a complex procedure that involves a number of steps. Initially, the therapist interviews the client to get a thorough knowledge of all aspects of the phobic stimulus ranked in order from least feared to most feared. For example, a medical student who is phobic of blood might react with a slight amount of fear to watching a patient's finger being pricked but with intense fear to watching open-heart surgery. A number of such fear-provoking stimuli are arranged in a *hierarchy* of phobic stimuli that will be used later in therapy. The second step in systematic desensitization is to teach the client a method of deeply relaxing the muscles of the body called **progressive relaxation training.** The purpose of this training is to put the client into a deep state of relaxation that can be conditioned to the phobic stimulus in place of the fear response.

Once the client has mastered deep muscle relaxation, the heart of the desensitization procedure is begun. The client is placed in a state of deep relaxation and asked to vividly imagine the weakest phobic stimulus on the hierarchy (in our example of the medical student, the weakest stimulus is watching a finger being pricked). If imagining that scene causes any fear at all, the individual is asked to raise a finger as a signal and stop imagining the scene. If the client can imagine the scene without fear, however, the therapist asks her to imagine the next scene. If that is too fear provoking, the client returns to the first scene for a while, and later attempts to imagine the more intense scene without fear. When this can be done, she moves up the hierarchy. Over a number of sessions, the client is often able to imagine even the most feared scene without disturbing her relaxed state. This repeated pairing of the phobic scenes with relaxation conditions relaxation to the phobic stimuli and inhibits further fear.

systematic desensitization
A behavior therapy method in which the client is taught not to fear phobic stimuli by learning to relax in the presence of successively more threatening stimuli.

progressive relaxation training
A method of learning to deeply relax the muscles of the body.

O F   S P E C I A L   I N T E R E S T

An Excerpt from Behavior Therapy

(Statements in brackets are comments of the therapist that were not stated during the therapy session.)

Client: The basic problem is that I have the tendency to let people step all over me. I don't know why, but I just have difficulty in speaking my mind.

Therapist: [My immediate tendency here is to reflect and clarify what the client said, adding a behavioral twist. In paraphrasing what she has already said, I can cast it within a behavioral framework by introducing such terms as "situation," "respond," and "learn."] So you find yourself in a number of different situations where you don't respond the way you would really like to. And if I understand correctly, you would like to learn how to behave differently.

C: Yes. But you know, I have tried to handle certain situations differently, but I just don't seem to be able to do so.

T: [Not a complete acceptance of my conceptualization, seemingly because she has tried to behave differently in the past and nothing has happened. What I should do, then, is somehow provide some explanation of why previous attempts may have failed, and use this to draw a contrast with a potentially more effective treatment strategy that we'll be using in our sessions.] It's almost as if there is a big gap between the way you react and the way you would like to react.

C: It seems that way, and I don't know how to overcome it.

T: Well, maybe you've tried to do too much too fast in the past, and consequently weren't very successful. Maybe a good way to look at the situation is to imagine yourself at the bottom of a staircase, wanting to get to the top. It's probably too much to ask to get there in one gigantic leap. Perhaps a better way to go about changing your reaction in these situations is to take it one step at a time.

C: That would seem to make sense, but I'm not sure if I see how that could be done.

T: Well, there are probably certain situations in which it would be less difficult for you to assert yourself such as telling your boss that he forgot to pay you for the past four weeks.

OF SPECIAL INTEREST

C: (Laughing.) I guess in that situation, I would say something. Although I must admit, I would feel uneasy about it.

T: But not as uneasy as if you went in and asked him for a raise.

C: No. Certainly not.

T: So, the first situation would be low on the staircase, whereas the second would be higher up. If you can learn to handle easier situations, then the more difficult ones would present less of a problem. And the only way you can really learn to change your reactions is through practice.

C: In other words, I really have to go out and actually force myself to speak up more, but taking it a little bit at a time?

T: [This seems like an appropriate time to introduce the function of behavior rehearsal. I won't say anything about the specific procedure yet, but instead will talk about it in general terms and maybe increase its appeal by explaining that any failures will not really "count." If the client goes along with the general description of the treatment strategy, she should be more likely to accept the details as I spell them out.] Exactly. And as a way of helping you carry it off in the real-life situation, I think it would be helpful if we reviewed some of these situations and your reactions to them beforehand. In a sense, going through a dry run. It's safer to run through some of these situations here, in that it really doesn't "count" if you don't handle them exactly as you would like to. Also, it can provide you an excellent opportunity to practice different ways of reacting to these situations, until you finally hit on one which you think would be best.

C: That seems to make sense.

T: In fact, we could arrange things so that you can actually rehearse exactly what you would say, and how you would say it.

C: That sounds like a good idea.

A behavior therapist working with a client who is afraid of snakes might use *Raiders of the Lost Ark* as part of an intense session of flooding the client with images of the phobic stimulus.

Flooding

flooding
A method of behavior therapy in which the client is confronted with high levels of the phobic stimulus until the fear response is extinguished.

An alternative to systematic desensitization is **flooding.** This procedure takes less time to implement and can be used even with clients who cannot master deep muscle relaxation, but it involves considerably more discomfort for the client. While systematic desensitization can be completed with the client's experiencing no more than a slight degree of fear, flooding requires the client to be "flooded" with high levels of the fear for prolonged periods of time. The procedure is generally conducted in a single session that lasts from two to eight hours. The session is not terminated until the fear response is extinguished and the phobic stimulus is no longer capable of eliciting the fear response.

Flooding is often conducted by having the client imagine the phobic stimulus, but the most effective fear reduction method of all is *in vivo flooding,* flooding that is conducted in the presence of the actual phobic stimulus. For example, if the client is afraid of crowds, the therapist would take him to shopping malls, for rides on crowded buses, for walks on crowded sidewalks, and so on until the fear response had been exhausted in a wide variety of crowded situations.

Operant Skills Training

A major emphasis of behavior therapy is on the teaching of new, adaptive skills using methods derived from operant conditioning. The particular skills that are taught vary widely depending on the kind of problems experienced by the individual, so we look at two areas of skill training to provide examples of this approach.

Social Skills Training

People with severe anxiety disorders, affective disorders, and schizophrenia frequently have difficulties interacting with other people. They tend to appear shy, awkward, "odd," and have difficulties expressing their feelings. Most of us experience similar difficulties in interacting with others in some situations (such as first dates and job interviews), but for some people this is a pervasive experience coloring nearly all of their social encounters. (See *Research Report:* "Practice dating.")

R E S E A R C H   R E P O R T

"Practice Dating": An Effective Treatment for Social Anxiety

Many of us are "shy," particularly in situations in which we know we are being evaluated and could experience rejection. Dating is a prime example: Meeting, asking out, and interacting with new acquaintances is highly anxiety-provoking for most of us, and devastating for many. Anxiety about dating and the resulting loneliness are one of the most common reasons that college and university students seek help from their campus counseling centers, in fact. One counseling center has responded to this need by developing a program that is not only effective, but very easy to implement (Christensen & Arkowitz, 1974).

Male and female college students who sought help for their dating anxiety were paired for "practice dates." Each student went on six dates with six different students of the opposite sex who were matched with them for age, height, race, and distance from the campus. At the end of each practice date, the students gave each other written feedback (through the therapist). They noted four positive aspects of their date's behavior and one aspect that needed improving. The only role of the therapist was to arrange the dates and serve as a consultant when needed. The dating experiences and the feedback were the active ingredients in this innovative form of therapy. An evaluation of students who participated in the project showed that they experienced large decreases in anxiety and marked increases in the frequency of later dating. Perhaps your counseling center has a similar program available.

These people with social deficiencies are taught to speak more often in social situations, to speak in a voice that is loud enough to hear, to make appropriate eye contact, and to make fewer odd comments. This is usually accomplished by **role playing** whereby the therapist and clients act as if they are people in problematic social situations. For example, if the client has great difficulties on job interviews and will soon be seeking a job, the therapist might role-play hypothetical job interviews. The therapist might first take the role of the client and *model* appropriate social behavior. Then, the client would play the role of herself in the next hypothetical job interview. The therapist would then provide *positive reinforcement* in the form of praise for the good aspects of the client's social behavior and suggest ways of improving the inappropriate aspects. Over a number of role-play sessions, enough improvement is usually obtained to allow the client to try role-played job interviews with other people and eventually to take a crack at the real thing.

Particular attention has been paid by behavior therapists to the widespread social skills problem of *unassertiveness*. Many people—both "normal" individuals and people with problems—have a difficult time expressing their true feelings, asking questions, disagreeing, and standing up for their rights. Sometimes

role playing
A therapeutic technique in which the therapist and client act as if they are people in problematic situations.

these individuals continuously hold their feelings in and let others take advantage of them, partly because other people do not know what they want. In most cases, however, unassertive people keep their feelings inside until they become so angry that they pour them out in an aggressive tantrum.

assertiveness training
A method of behavior therapy that teaches individuals assertive rather than passive or aggressive ways of dealing with problematic situations.

Assertiveness training is used to develop assertive rather than aggressive ways of expressing feelings to others. Usually this is done by role playing like other forms of social skills training. For example, the client might initially take the role of a friend who asks the therapist for a loan of 50 dollars in spite of the fact that he knows that the therapist is short on money and that he has owed the therapist 60 dollars for the past three months. The therapist would model an assertive way of handling the request ("I wish I could help you, but I don't have enough money to do it, and I really don't think it would be a good idea for me to lend you more money until you're able to pay me back what you already owe me."). Then they would reverse roles and let the client try to handle a similarly difficult situation. After considerable practice with the therapist, the client should possess enough skills and feel comfortable enough to handle real-life situations in an assertive way.

Developmental Skills Training

Skills training programs based on modeling and positive reinforcement have been used extensively in training children with mental retardation and other delays in development. Because these children do not learn as quickly as other children, the training procedure must be precisely implemented. Even learning to tie a shoelace can be a challenging task to a mentally retarded child. This skill is taught by first having a therapist slowly model each of the steps involved in shoe tying (pulling the laces straight, crossing them over, pulling them tight, making the first bow, and so on). After the therapist has done this several times, the child is manually helped to do only the last step (pulling the two bows tight). After she has been reinforced several times for successfully pulling the bows tight with help, the manual help is gradually dropped and the child is asked to pull the bows alone. After several reinforced successes at this, she is helped to perform the last *two* steps in the sequence (crossing over the bows and then pulling them tight). When she is proficient at these two steps, she begins doing three steps, and so on, until she has progressed backward through the chain of steps and is tying her shoes entirely on her own.

Similar precise training strategies have been developed to teach mentally retarded people to feed themselves, use functional language, use the toilet independently, brush their own teeth, use public transportation, perform some kinds of occupational jobs, and so on. Through these training efforts, the mentally retarded are able to live considerably more independent and meaningful lives. Children who are not mentally retarded, but have more specific and limited developmental delays, have also been helped using this type of training procedure. Examples are children with problems in language development, problems in the fine-motor coordination used in handwriting, and delays in learning to read.

aversive conditioning
(ah-ver'siv)
A method of behavior therapy that involves the use of unpleasant negative stimuli to eliminate abnormal habits such as alcoholism and deviant sexual practices.

Aversive Conditioning

Aversive conditioning is a highly controversial behavior therapy technique. It involves the use of unpleasant, negative (aversive) stimuli to eliminate abnormal habits such as alcoholism and deviant sexual practices. For example, alcoholics who wish to stop drinking sometimes undergo treatment in which alcoholic beverages are mixed with substances that cause nausea and vomiting. Thus, through classical conditioning, the taste of alcohol is associated with the aversive nauseous state. Similar aversive methods have been used with abnormal sexual practices. Men who engage in behaviors such as breaking into women's apartments, stealing underwear, and then masturbating with it are given painful electric shocks while they imagine engaging in these behaviors (Marks & Gelder, 1967).

Although behavior therapists are generally careful to use aversive conditioning only with clients who volunteer after a full discussion of what's involved, these painful methods understandably evoke skeptical, even negative reactions from the public. Aversive conditioning methods appear to give frightening power to behavior therapists to control behavior through pain. The movie *A Clockwork Orange,* for example, was an expression of concern about the use of aversive techniques to control behavior. It's ironic that so much concern has been focused on aversive methods in behavior therapy since, except with a few problems such as sexual molestation of children (Adams & Chiodo, 1984), other methods not using aversive stimuli are often more effective (Kendall & Norton-Ford, 1982). As a result, aversive methods are used less widely today than in the past.

Cognitive Therapy

Cognitive therapy is an important new approach to therapy that rests on the assumption that faulty cognitions—maladaptive beliefs, expectations, and ways of thinking—are the cause of abnormal behavior. Cognitive therapy originated in the cognitive emphasis of contemporary social learning theorists (Bandura, 1977) and contemporary psychoanalysts (Kelly, 1955). It has exerted its greatest influence on the behavior therapy movement and might even be legitimately considered to have been subsumed by that movement. As such, cognitive therapy has greatly broadened the behavior therapy approach.

cognitive therapy
An approach to therapy that teaches individuals new cognitions—adaptive beliefs, expectations, and ways of thinking—to eliminate abnormal emotions and behavior.

Relationship between Cognition and Behavior

Early in the development of behavior therapy, it was assumed that cognitions were relatively unimportant in the origins and treatment of abnormal behavior. For example, if a client came to a behavior therapist because she was unassertive, the conversations with the therapist might reveal that she *believed* (a cognition) incorrectly that her friends would stop liking her if she expressed her true feelings to them. The behavior therapist would feel that it would be unnecessary to change directly this faulty belief, however. The behavior therapist would assume that if the client was taught assertive ways of expressing feelings, then she would see for herself that her friends still liked her and, therefore, change her faulty cognition herself. The cognitive therapy movement, on the other hand, suggests that behavior therapists can be more effective if they directly teach both more adaptive behavior and cognition.

Moreover, cognitive therapists believe that problems do not always stem from inappropriate overt actions. For example, some socially anxious people behave in appropriate, even charming ways in social situations, but they still experience anxiety because they inaccurately *think* of themselves as dull, awkward, and unlikable. Trying to modify their already appropriate overt actions would be fruitless in such cases. Instead, it's necessary to modify their maladaptive cognitions.

OF SPECIAL INTEREST

An Excerpt from Cognitive Psychotherapy

(The therapist is Albert Ellis, clinical psychologist and pioneer in the cognitive approach to psychotherapy.)

Ellis: What's the main thing that's bothering you?

Client: I have a fear of turning homosexual—a real fear of it!

E: A fear of becoming a homosexual?

C: Yeah.

E: Because "if I became a homosexual," what?

C: I don't know. It really gets me down. It gets me to a point where I'm doubting every day. I do doubt everything, anyway.

E: Yes. But let's get back to—answer the question: "If I were a homosexual, what would that make me?"

C: (Pause) I don't know.

E: Yes, you do! Now, I can give you the answer to the question. But let's see if you can get it.

C: (Pause) Less than a person?

E: Yes. Quite obviously, you're saying: "I'm bad enough. But if I were homosexual, that would make me a total shit!"

C: That's right.

E: Now, why did you just say you don't know?

C: Just taking a guess at it, that's all. It's—it's just that the fear really gets me down! I don't know why.

E: (Laughing) Well, you just gave the reason why! Suppose you were saying the same thing about—we'll just say—stealing. You hadn't stolen anything, but you thought of stealing something. And you said, "If I stole, I would be a thorough shit!" Just suppose that. Then, how much would you then start thinking about stealing?

C: (Silence)

E: If you believed that: "If I stole that, I would be a thorough shit!"—would you think of it often? Occasionally?

C: I'd think of it often.

[And later in the same session. . . .]

E: But the reason you're obsessed is the same reason you'd be obsessed with anything. I see people who are obsessed with 5,000 different things. But in every single case, just about, I can track it down; and they're saying, "If I were so-and-so. . . ." For example, "if I got up and made a public speech and fell on my face, I'd be a shit!"—"If I went to school and failed, I'd be a shit!"—"If I tried for a better job and failed, I'd be a shit!" Now, you're doing the same thing about homosexuality: "If I ever did fail heterosexually and became a homosexual, I'd be an utter worm!" Now that will obsess you with homosexuality.

OF SPECIAL INTEREST

C: And that obsession brings me to doubt myself.

E: Well—no. It's part of your general obsession. Your real obsession is: "If (1) I failed at something big, like heterosexuality, and (2) other people didn't like me—they really didn't like me—then I'd be no damned good!" Now, as a subheading under that, you've got the homosexuality. Your general fear is of being worthless—isn't it?

C: Yeah.

E: And you don't only have it in the homosexual area—that's only dramatic and outstanding. What are you working at, at present?

C: I'm a commercial artist.

E: Now, how do you feel about that, when you work at it?

C: Well, I made supervising artist. But I really didn't feel it was good enough. And I just keep going on and on–.

E: Oh. You see: "I made supervising artist, but if I'm not outstanding, I'm a shit!" Is that what you're really saying?

C: (Silence)

E: Think about it, now. Don't agree because I said so. Isn't it something like that?

C: (Pause) I'll go along with it. Because I doubt just everything!

E: Right! But why does anybody doubt everything? Suppose I introduce you to another guy and—I can show you guys who have Ph.D.'s, who have M.D.'s, who are outstanding painters or sculptors, and they feel the same way as you. And some of them have got reputations in their field; they're doing well. They still think they're shits. Now, why do you think they do?

C: (Pause)

E: There's one main reason for shithood. Now what do you think it is?

C: (Pause) Their goals are set too high?

E: Exactly! They're not saying, "I'd like to succeed." They're saying "I've got to! I need an absolute guarantee that I always will succeed. And since there's always a good chance I won't, I'm no damned good!"

C: They're foolish for that.

E: Right. But you're believing that, aren't you?

C: (Pause) Yes, I am.

E: Now the problem is: How are you going to give up that crap?

Maladaptive Cognitions

Psychologist Albert Ellis (1962) and psychiatrist Aaron T. Beck (1976) have described a number of common patterns of maladaptive cognitions that they believe contribute to abnormal behavior and emotions. We look at a few of these to see better how cognitive therapy works.

Ellis suggests that the irrational things we *believe* make us miserable. These irrational beliefs hurt us by leading us to interpret even minor upsets as major catastrophes. Some of the most common irrational beliefs identified by Ellis follow:

1. It is necessary for me to be loved and approved of by everyone in order to feel worthwhile.

2. My personal worth depends upon my being competent, adequate, achieving, and in general good at what I do.

3. It's the end of the world when things don't go exactly the way I want them to.

4. Human happiness is externally caused and people have little or no ability to control or rid themselves of negative feelings.

5. I should have someone around me who is stronger than I believe I am, so that I can depend upon him or her.

6. The past is all important. Once something has strongly affected my life it will continue to affect my life. (Ellis, 1962)

Notice how each of these could lead a person to make mountains out of life's many molehills. For example, take irrational belief No. 1, the belief that I must be loved and approved of by *everyone* in order to be a worthwhile person. Suppose that I should have prepared my class lecture last night, but instead I went to a party and stayed out late. This morning, I did not feel like working, so I procrastinated and didn't prepare. Two hours before class when I finally started to prepare, a friend came in feeling very depressed and I spent all of my time talking to him. By class time I was unprepared and feeling a little down myself, so I grumpily dismissed class without an explanation. Later, one of my colleagues walked into my office, saying she'd heard what I had done with my class, and angrily let me know that she thought I am lazy, unprofessional, and irresponsible.

Such things are going to happen. You cannot go through life without making mistakes and getting criticized for it. These criticisms sting, but generally we get over them quickly. Suppose, though, that I believe I must behave in ways that everyone always approves of: If I *ever* disappoint others, then I am utterly worthless. This belief, which is held by many depressed and anxious individuals, would change the criticism from an upsetting event into a *devastating* one. And if every criticism were devastating, life would become a constantly anxious struggle to please everyone.

To Ellis, the goal of psychotherapy is to persuade clients to abandon such beliefs by pointing out their irrationality. For example, a client who believes in irrational belief No. 1 might be asked to name a person that he is *sure* is worthwhile. When he names one, the therapist might ask if that person always behaves in ways that are approved of by everyone. When the client can see that all people—even the most admired ones—are disapproved of by some people some of the time, it may seem illogical to believe that universal approval is necessary to make a person worthwhile. Similar therapy approaches are taken to dispel other maladaptive beliefs.

Beck has developed a slightly different approach to cognitive therapy that focuses on the illogical patterns of reasoning that characterize depressed and anxious individuals rather than their irrational beliefs. These ways of reasoning lead to unwarranted conclusions that are upsetting to the individual. For example, depressed people often engage in an illogical pattern that Beck calls *arbitrary inference*. This means seeing cause-and-effect relationships—ones that involve the person in a negative way—where there are none. For example, if a business acquaintance fails to show up for an appointment, the individual may take this negligence personally. That is, she may feel that the acquaintance thinks she is a lousy person and therefore skipped the appointment. That might be the reason, but there could be other explanations as well. The person who engages in arbitrary inference, however, is *sure* that every bad thing happens because of his or her faults. In cognitive therapy, the therapist shows the client that such patterns of thinking are both illogical and the source of problems.

R E V I E W

The approach to psychotherapy that is associated with the social learning theory of personality is known as behavior therapy. Abnormal behavior is viewed as learned behavior. It's simply behavior that results from inappropriate learning experiences. The role of the behavior therapist is to serve as a teacher who helps the client unlearn abnormal behavior and learn adaptive ways of behaving to take its place. In systematic desensitization, for example, the behavior therapist teaches clients no longer to fear phobic stimuli by first teaching them to relax deeply, and then gradually exposing them to graduated versions of the phobic stimulus in imagination until the full stimulus does not disturb the state of relaxation. In this way, relaxation becomes the response to the formerly phobic stimulus instead of fear. Flooding provides an alternative to systematic desensitization in which the individual is "flooded" with a prolonged dose of the phobic stimulus until the fear response is extinguished. Other behavior therapy methods use principles of operant conditioning to teach specific skills and aversive conditioning methods to break abnormal habits in individuals who volunteer for treatment.

Cognitive therapy is a therapeutic approach that has grown out of both contemporary psychoanalytic theories of personality and social learning theory; but it has become subsumed by, and has contributed to the expansion of, behavior therapy. While behavior therapists originally believed that the irrational beliefs and ways of thinking (cognitions) that generally accompany abnormal behavior and emotions would simply change when the behavior and emotions changed, cognitive therapists have emphasized the necessity of sometimes changing cognitions first. They believe that behavior and emotional problems will improve when maladaptive cognitions are changed. Consequently, cognitive therapists conduct psychotherapy in an attempt to change cognitions by demonstrating their irrationality to clients. (See *Research Report:* "The Effectiveness of Psychotherapy.")

RESEARCH REPORT

The Effectiveness of Psychotherapy

How effective is psychotherapy? Which is the most effective form of psychotherapy? These seem like simple questions that psychologists should be able to answer, but they are actually quite complicated. Hundreds of experiments have been conducted, but there is still no conclusive answer available. Psychologists Mary Smith and Gene Glass (1977) have attempted to provide tentative answers by using an interesting statistical technique that makes use of data from many different studies. They identified 375 studies in which improvement in patients receiving some form of psychotherapy was compared to a group of patients with similar problems who were not given treatment until after the study was completed. The results of these studies ordinarily could not be directly compared because researchers used patients with different kinds of problems and they evaluated improvement using different criteria. Some studies used therapist's ratings of improvement, some used scores on personality tests, some used direct observations of specific aspects of the patient's abnormal behavior, and so on. Regardless of what criterion was used, however, Smith and Glass calculated a measure of the *magnitude of treatment effect* by comparing the amount of improvement in the treated patients to that of the untreated ones.

While the specific statistics involved are complicated, an effect size of .00 would indicate that treated patients improved no more than untreated patients, while an effect size of 1.00 would indicate that treated patients improved much more than untreated ones.

Table 13.1 shows the average magnitude of effect for the types of psychotherapy described in this chapter, and for *eclectic* psychotherapy in which the therapist blends methods from two or more kinds of therapy.

Note that all of the forms of psychotherapy were effective on the average: All produced average effect sizes that were greater than .00. But note also that there were differences among the kinds of

Other Models of Therapy

Therapy is not always conducted on an individual basis. Some methods of therapy are carried out with groups or entire families, and some programs are designed to prevent rather than treat problems. Moreover, some treatments for psychological problems use medical rather than psychological methods. In this section, we will survey these alternative approaches to the solution of human problems and look at trends oriented away from providing treatment in residential mental institutions and toward treatment in the individual's home community.

R E S E A R C H   R E P O R T

Table 13.1 Average magnitude of treatment effects for different methods of psychotherapy

Methods of Psychotherapy	Average Effect Size*
Psychoanalytic	
Orthodox psychoanalysis	.50
Psychoanalytic (Adlerian)	.71
Behavior therapy	
Systematic desensitization	.91
Operant skills training	.76
Cognitive	.77
Humanistic	
Client-centered	.63
Gestalt	.26
Eclectic psychotherapy	.48

From Smith, M. L. and G. V. Glass, "Meta-analysis of psychotherapy outcome studies" in American Psychologist, 32, 752–760. Copyright 1977 American Psychological Association. Reprinted by permission of the authors.
*See research report text for explanation.

therapy. The behavioral/cognitive methods, client-centered therapy, and the revised psychoanalytic methods based on the approach of Alfred Adler were more effective than orthodox psychoanalysis, Gestalt therapy, and eclectic psychotherapy. Strictly speaking, this cannot be taken to mean that one form of psychotherapy is superior to another since the different psychotherapies did not use the same specific criteria for improvement or the same kinds of patients. It may turn out, for example, that one form of psychotherapy works best for one kind of problem and another is best for other problems. Still, it's encouraging to note that all of the psychotherapies were at least slightly more effective than no treatment and that the ones that had the largest effects also are the ones that used the most rigorous criteria for improvement.

Group Therapy

Psychotherapy is usually conducted on a one-to-one basis, but sometimes it's carried out with groups of clients. One or two therapists work typically with four to eight clients at a time. **Group therapy** is believed to offer therapeutic experiences that cannot be obtained in individual therapy (Yalom, 1975). Some of these advantages are (1) encouragement from other group members; (2) learning that a person is not alone in his or her problems; (3) learning from the advice offered by others; and (4) learning new ways to interact with others. In addition, providing therapy in a group format can sometimes make more efficient use of the therapist's time.

group therapy
Psychotherapy conducted in groups, typically of four to eight clients at a time.

An advantage of group therapy is the opportunity for clients to learn from interacting with other members of the group.

The format of group therapy differs widely depending on the approach taken by the therapist (psychoanalytic, humanistic, or behavioral), but all provide an opportunity for the client to interact with other clients and to learn from these interactions with the help of the therapist. After discussing traditional approaches to group therapy, we describe popular derivatives of group therapy that are used for the personal growth of normal individuals.

Traditional Group Therapy

Each approach to psychotherapy has adapted its own methods for use in groups. Psychoanalysts serve the role of interpreter in group therapy just as they do in individual therapy. They avoid becoming part of the interactions of the group members except to offer interpretations of what these interactions reveal. Humanists use group interactions to help clients develop more accurate self-perceptions through the actions and reactions of other group members toward them. Behavior therapists use groups to facilitate the teaching of adaptive behavior. For example, groups of individuals with problems in social interactions are given instructions in how to relate more effectively, allowed to practice interacting with one another, and then are given feedback and reinforcement from the therapist and other group members.

Psychotherapists from all of these orientations generally believe that the interaction with other group members offers special therapeutic advantages to some clients. Individuals with complex problems that require the full attention of the therapist, or who do not wish to discuss their personal problems in front of others, however, will benefit more from individual psychotherapy.

Group Therapy for Personal Growth

In recent years, group therapy has been offered increasingly as a form of personal growth therapy. Many of these groups focus on a specific topic. For example, normal individuals who feel that they need to improve their ability to express their feelings assertively might become part of an assertiveness training group. Recently divorced individuals might join a group composed of other similar individuals to ease this frequently difficult adjustment. Couples similarly can join groups designed to enhance their sexual and marital relationships.

Encounter groups are an intense form of group psychotherapy.

One of the most popular forms of personal group therapy is designed to improve general self-awareness from the perspective of humanistic therapy. These are known as **encounter groups,** as they seek to provide therapeutic interactions or encounters between the members of the group. The unique flavor of encounter groups stems from their origins in Gestalt therapy. In encounter groups the participants are encouraged to be as honest as possible with one another, dropping the "fake" ways of relating that polite society expects of us. (Remember that Gestalt and other humanistic psychologists believe that society makes it difficult for us to accurately know ourselves.) If you think that Bill is being selfish, pompous, and conceited, you ordinarily would not tell him. But you would tell him in an encounter group. And everyone else would tell Bill what they think of him, too.

Advocates of encounter groups think that this barrage of honesty has two highly important benefits. First, it helps to break down false views of self. If Bill thought he was kind and considerate because he felt that he *should* be that way, but everyone in the group told him that he was actually somewhat selfish, he might gain some needed insight into his true self.

Second, just as important as honesty in encounter groups is the *acceptance* that comes with the honesty. Group members are not only encouraged to be honestly critical, but to express honestly their acceptance and caring for one another. If Bill can see that he is selfish, and everyone knows it, but that the other group members still accept him as a human being—flawed, but worthy of being loved— then Bill may be able to develop a fully accurate view of himself. Sometimes steps are taken in encounter groups to foster this kind of warm acceptance by encouraging touching and hugging to develop a sense of closeness and to break down the barriers that society places on intimacy between strangers. To intensify these interactions, encounter groups are sometimes conducted on a 16- to 48- hour nonstop *marathon group* basis.

Encounter groups are a controversial approach to personal growth. Although they have generally been reported to be helpful when conducted by qualified professionals (Kilmann & Sotile, 1976), they can sometimes precipitate personal problems. Encounter group experiences are intense ones that can be quite upsetting for some individuals (Hartley, Roback, & Abromowitz, 1976).

encounter group
A humanistic group therapy technique designed to improve general self-awareness.

Family Therapy

family therapy
An approach to psycho-
therapy that emphasizes an
understanding of the roles
of each of the members of
the family system, usually
conducted with all members
of the family present.

Another important variation of psychotherapy in which the therapist works with groups of individuals is **family therapy.** In this case, the group is the family composed of parents, children, and any other family members living in the home. Although family therapy is conducted by therapists who take psychoanalytic, humanistic, and behavioral approaches, the approach that we most often associate with family therapy is the *systems* approach of Jay Haley (1976) and Salvador Minuchin (1974).

The family systems view takes the position that it's not possible to understand adequately the psychological problems of an *individual* without knowing the role of that individual in the *family system*. This is thought to be true for two reasons. First, the problem of the individual is often *caused* by problems within the family. For example, a depressed mother or aggressive child may be reacting to the unhappy, conflict-laden relationship of the mother and father. Although the mother or child may be brought to the clinic identified as "the problem," and no mention is initially made of the marital problems, neither the depression nor the aggression can be helped until the marriage problems are resolved.

The second reason that Haley and Minuchin give for needing to understand the operation of the entire family system in order to understand the problems of an individual family member is that the individual's problems may serve a *function* in the family system. For example, the teenage girl who refuses to eat until she has reached a dangerously low weight may be doing so (consciously or unconsciously) to focus concern on her and keep her parents from divorcing. Similarly, parents who blame all of the family's problems on the supposedly wild behavior of their son may be using him as a *scapegoat* to shift attention away from the fact that they are both unemployed alcoholics. Without working with all of the members of the family system, these factors in the origins of the problems of the individual would have been difficult, if not impossible, to uncover.

The family therapist attempts to solve the problems of all of the family members by improving the functioning of the family system as a whole. The therapist attempts to reach this goal in four primary ways. The family therapist works (1) to give the family members insights into the workings of family systems in general and to correct any dysfunctions in their specific family; (2) to increase the amount of warmth and intimacy among family members; (3) to improve communication among family members; and (4) to help family members establish a reasonable set of rules for the regulation of the family. In this way, it's hoped that the family will become a system that provides each member with an accurate view of self, a positive opinion of self, and a sense of belonging.

Medical Therapies

medical therapies
Those therapies—including
drug therapy, electro-
convulsive therapy, and
psychosurgery—generally
designed to correct a
physical condition that is
believed to be the cause of
a psychological disorder.

In addition to psychotherapy, medical therapies are commonly used in the treatment of abnormal behavior. **Medical therapies** are generally designed to correct a physical condition that is believed to be the cause of the psychological disorder. Sometimes, however, it's not clear why a particular medical treatment works; it continues to be used simply because it's effective. There are three general types of medical therapy: *drug therapy* in which medication is used; *electroconvulsive therapy* in which seizures are electrically induced in the brain, and *psychosurgery* in which brain tissue is surgically destroyed.

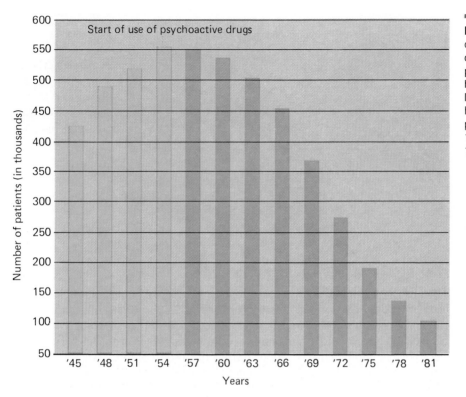

Figure 13.1 The development of effective drugs for treating serious psychological disorders helped make possible the large reduction in hospitalized mental patients that began in the 1950s (Witters & Witters, 1983).

Drug Therapy

By far the most widely used medical treatment is **drug therapy.** The idea that chemicals can be used to treat abnormal behavior dates back at least to the special diets used by Pythagoras around 490 B.C. But the widespread use of effective psychiatric drugs has come about only in the last 30 years. The era of modern drug therapy began in 1954 with the introduction of the *phenothiazine* drugs, such as *Thorazine* for the treatment of schizophrenia. Thorazine gave physicians a tool that for the first time in history substantially improved the lives of schizophrenic persons. So effective is this drug that it's given partial credit for reversing the growth in the number of patients in mental institutions in the 1960s (see fig. 13.1). During the 1960s other drugs were introduced to help in the treatment of depression (antidepressants) and anxiety (tranquilizers).

Today the use of these drugs is widespread. One survey has found that 37 percent of American women and 22 percent of men had used psychiatric medications (especially tranquilizers and sleeping pills) at least once during the preceding year (Parry, Balter, Mellinger, Cisin, & Manheimer, 1973). These figures suggest that Americans may overuse psychiatric medications, sometimes to the point of drug abuse.

In spite of the effectiveness and general acceptance of drugs, they are not without shortcomings. Prolonged use of Thorazine can result in impairment of walking and other serious side effects. Other drugs can be highly addictive.

drug therapy
A medical therapy that uses chemicals to treat abnormal behavior.

Although electroconvulsive therapy, which was introduced in the 1930s, continues to be used with some suicidally depressed individuals, it's not endorsed universally by the mental health profession.

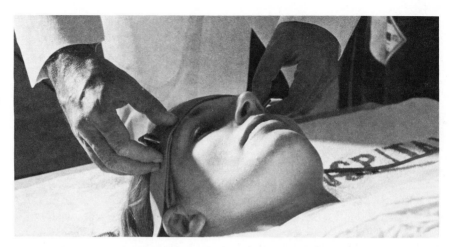

Electroconvulsive Therapy

The idea that people can be "shocked" out of their psychological problems has been around in one form or another for nearly 2,400 years. Hippocrates recommended use of the herb hellebore to induce seizures that supposedly restored balance to the body's four humors. Several different kinds of "shock" treatment were popular in mental institutions during the 1800s; patients were thrown in tubs full of eels, spun in giant centrifuges, and nearly drowned by dropping them into lakes through trapdoors in bridges known as "surprise baths" (Altschule, 1965).

Other forms of shock therapy have also been used, particularly ones in which seizures are intentionally induced. In the 1930s it was noticed that people with epilepsy rarely developed schizophrenia. Several psychiatrists experimented with chemicals that caused seizures to see if they would cure schizophrenia, but camphor, insulin, and other chemicals were found to be of little use with schizophrenics. Italian physicians first used the method of passing an electric current through two metal plates held to the sides of the head to induce convulsive brain seizures. This method, known as **electroconvulsive therapy** or **ECT,** continues in widespread use today. While ineffective with most types of disorders, it's believed by some psychiatrists to be useful with suicidally depressed individuals. But still to this day no one knows for sure how ECT works.

Although ECT has been used successfully for 50 years, the procedure is surrounded by considerable controversy. In large part, this controversy is a holdover from the primitive methods that were used when the procedure was first introduced. The shocks were given without anesthesia and the seizures were so violent that broken bones were not uncommon. Today, the use of anesthesia and muscle relaxants makes ECT a far less unpleasant experience, but temporary or permanent memory loss and confusion are still relatively common side effects (Campbell, 1961). The use of ECT is also controversial, because even after extended use, little adequate research has been conducted to evaluate its effectiveness. The few well-designed studies that have been carried out, however, suggest that it's at least somewhat effective in treating depression (Barton, 1977).

electroconvulsive therapy (ECT)
(e-lek"tro-con-vul'siv)
A medical therapy that uses electrical current to induce controlled convulsive seizures that alleviate some types of mental disorders.

Psychosurgery

Undoubtedly the most controversial medical treatment for abnormal behavior is **psychosurgery.** As with the other medical therapies, there is a historical precedent for the idea that people with psychological disorders can be helped by operating on their brains. In fact, the precedent for psychosurgery is perhaps the oldest of all. Archaeologists have found Stone Age skulls in which holes called *trephines* had been "surgically" cut with crude stone knives. Apparently, these trephining operations—signs of healing indicate that some of these poor souls actually survived the procedure—were performed in an attempt to treat abnormal behavior.

Surgical operations on the brain to treat psychological disorders came into vogue in the 1940s and 1950s. In the most common version, the *prefrontal lobotomy,* a double-edged butterknife-shaped instrument is inserted through holes drilled in the temple region of the skull. Neural fibers are cut that connect the frontal region of the cerebral cortex with the hypothalamus. The theory is that the operation will prevent disturbing thoughts and perceptions from reaching the hypothalamus and related brain structures where they would be translated into emotional outbursts. Lobotomies are not successful in most cases, however, and loss of intellectual functioning and seizures are common side effects (Barahal, 1958). Because of their ineffectiveness and because of the success of drug therapies with schizophrenics, the use of lobotomies and other forms of psychosurgery has declined considerably. However, as late as 1973 some 500 prefrontal lobotomies were being performed in the United States each year (Holden, 1973).

More recently, the development of precise methods of operating on the brain with needle-thin electrical instruments has revived interest in psychosurgery. These instruments are used to operate directly on the hypothalamus and other parts of the brain associated with emotional control. Such operations are performed infrequently, however, and generally used only as a last resort with uncontrollably violent people. Even in such cases, psychosurgery is still a hotly debated procedure. See *Of Special Interest:* "Thomas R." for more on this topic.

psychosurgery
(si''ko-ser'jer-e)
A medical therapy that involves operating on the brain in an attempt to alleviate some types of mental disorders.

The Community Mental Health Movement

In 1963 Congress passed the Community Mental Health Center Act that established facilities in every major city and region in the country to provide services for individuals with psychological problems. The funding of these centers marked a major change in policy for mental health care in the United States. No longer was placement in a residential mental hospital the primary method of treatment of abnormal behavior. Care was given to people in their own communities so they could remain in their own homes, and an emphasis was placed on the *prevention* of serious psychological disturbances.

From Residential Institutions to Mental Health Centers

A primary goal of the community mental health center is to provide treatment to people in their own communities rather than in institutions. Placement in a state or private mental hospital provides care and treatment for people with psychological problems, but it *causes* some serious problems as well. The patients

OF SPECIAL INTEREST

Thomas R.: The Case against Psychosurgery

Advocates of psychosurgery believe it's a necessary form of treatment when all else has failed. Opponents claim that it generally does not work and often causes irreversible damage to the patient. The lines in this argument can be clearly seen in the controversy over Thomas R. Thomas R. was an engineer who was prone to violent, raging attacks against anyone (strangers, friends, or family) who irritated him even slightly. It was decided that the only cure was an operation on a region of the brain called the amygdala (Mark & Ervin, 1970). Although Vernon Mark (1974) described the operation in a psychiatric journal as a success, Peter Breggin (1973), who interviewed Thomas R. and others who knew him well, claimed that this was not the case. Breggin noted that Thomas R.'s violent outbursts continued after the psychosurgery and that he developed epileptic seizures. Moreover, while he had never required hospitalization prior to the psychosurgery, he needed almost constant hospitalization after the operation, lived in constant fear of future operations, and required frequent sedation. While the goal of the psychosurgery was to help Thomas R., Breggin suggests that it did more harm than good.

lose most regular contact with friends and family, robbing them of needed social support. If the institutionalization is for more than a brief period of time, patients often lose their jobs and memberships in clubs and other organizations. And placement in a mental hospital carries a highly negative stigma that may cause others to be frightened or otherwise prejudiced toward former mental patients.

Perhaps the most detrimental effect of institutionalization, however, may be living in the institution itself. Although many newer facilities are greatly improved, the mental hospitals of the 1950s—some of which remain relatively unchanged today—were dreary, regimented, lifeless places. Residential treatment in these facilities frequently made the patients worse rather than better.

Thus, there were many reasons to believe that community mental health centers would result in better care, and in many ways these expectations have been met (Windle, Bass, & Taube, 1974). A motive for their establishment that should not be overlooked, however, was money. Providing treatment in a community-based center is much less expensive to taxpayers than residential treatment. Ironically, severe cutbacks in federal funding of community mental health centers during the 1980s have greatly limited their ability to continue to meet these goals.

Other Community-Based Programs

Other efforts have been made since the 1960s to focus psychological treatment efforts on the communities in which people live. One significant, but still growing, effort is the establishment of *aftercare* programs for former residents of mental hospitals. These provide temporary or permanent places for former patients to

Community mental health centers allow patients to retain regular contact with friends and family and to stay employed while receiving mental health care.

live after leaving the hospital to help them with the sudden transition to independent living. A highly successful example is the Community Lodge Program (Fairweather, Sanders, Cressler, & Maynard, 1969). In this program, former mental patients without homes to live in are set up in a family-style group home. They are trained to handle the responsibilities of independent living (e.g., cooking, shopping, cleaning), to make democratic group decisions, and to manage a budget; they are also helped to set up a business (such as a janitorial service).

The Community Lodge Program has been evaluated by comparing the success of its residents to individuals who receive no aftercare assistance. Forty months after their discharge from the mental hospital, 40 percent of the Community Lodge residents were employed full time compared to 1 percent of former patients without aftercare. Eighty percent of the Community Lodge residents had not required new hospitalization after 40 months, while only 20 percent of the patients without aftercare were living outside of an institution at the time (Fairweather et al., 1969). Unfortunately, far more such programs are needed in the United States than there are funds to provide them.

Community Psychology and Prevention

A movement within psychology that has achieved considerable prominence in the 1970s and 1980s is the *community psychology* movement. Community psychologists resemble clinical psychologists and psychiatrists in that their goal is to reduce human suffering through the application of principles of psychology. But community psychologists work with large groups of people rather than individual clients, and they seek to prevent psychological problems rather than solve existing ones. Community psychology seeks to identify the aspects of a community contributing to psychological disorders and eradicate them before they harm people.

For example, many community psychologists believe racial prejudice creates severe stress that contributes to psychological problems in members of minority groups. They attempt, therefore, to create programs that will reduce racial prejudice. Notable, and somewhat successful, projects to reduce racial prejudice have been conducted in the U.S. Armed Forces and in some school systems. Similar programs are being conducted in industries to reduce sexual prejudice that

OF SPECIAL INTEREST

Selecting a Therapist:
What to Do if You Think You Need Help

All of us face difficult and painful times in our lives. Sometimes we choose to struggle through these stressful periods on our own; sometimes we ask for the support and advice of friends; and at times, we may seek professional help. If you, or someone close to you, are among the many millions of Americans who will use professional mental health services this year, consider these thoughts.

First, you must face the issue of *stigma*—the implication that if you seek professional help that you are not a normal or even fully competent person. If you believe in that myth, then it will be very difficult indeed for you to lift the telephone and make the first appointment. You should know, however, that mental health professionals do *not* believe there is something fundamentally wrong with people who ask for help. They know that a large portion of their clients are completely normal people who are simply asking for assistance in the tricky business of avoiding—or crawling out of—life's pitfalls. So, do not be afraid to ask for help if you think you need it.

Once you have decided to seek help, where do you look for it? As we first mentioned in chapter 1, there are many different mental health professions that operate through a number of different kinds of mental health facilities. The trick is in deciding which kind of professional or facility would be best for you. For college students, this decision is often an easy one: Most colleges and universities have a student counseling or mental health center that provides high-quality services at little or no cost. The professionals who work in these centers are experienced in meeting the mental health needs of students.

In addition, most psychology departments in larger universities operate their own psychology clinics that provide services both to students and to people in the general community. And most cities also have a community mental health center that provides a wide range of services. Both university psychology clinics and community mental health centers generally charge fees that are based on your ability to pay. Often these centers operate 24 hours a day, providing suicide prevention telephone lines that are listed under such titles as "help line," or that can be reached through the telephone operator.

Services are also provided by professionals in private practice. These individuals provide services for a fee like a physician or attorney. Psychiatrists, psychologists, and other professionals in private practice are listed in the telephone book under titles such as "Physicians—Psychiatrists" and "Psychologists." You might want to turn back to chapter 1, page 18 to familiarize yourself with the differences between these and other mental health professions. In most states, only licensed individuals can list their names in the

OF SPECIAL INTEREST

telephone directory as a psychiatrist, psychologist, psychotherapist, counselor, or marriage counselor. But, in some states some of these titles (except for psychologist and psychiatrist) are not regulated by law. This means that anyone—qualified or not—can set up a private practice under one of these titles in many states. You should be careful, therefore, to ask for a referral to one of these professionals from a qualified physician or psychologist if you choose their services.

Referrals are also the best guide to choosing the services of a licensed psychologist or psychiatrist. Like other professions, some are better than others—or are better in dealing with certain kinds of cases—and the advice of someone who knows both you and the professionals in the community could be very helpful. If you do not have access to someone to refer you, it would be wise to ask the psychologist or psychiatrist about "board certification." It's legal in most states for a physician to practice psychiatry without ever having had specific training in that field, but a board-certified psychiatrist has met the criteria of a national board for competence in psychiatry. In psychology, board certification means something different. Only a small proportion of experienced psychologists take and pass a special examination of their skills. They are awarded a diploma by the American Board of Professional Psychology, which is designated in their listing in the telephone directory as "Diplomate in Clinical (or Counseling) Psychology, ABPP." Board-certified psychiatrists and psychologists are not necessarily more competent than those who are not, but it's another way of reducing the uncertainty in choosing a therapist.

For additional information on selecting a therapist, and for information concerning organizations such as Alcoholics Anonymous that provide help for individuals with specific kinds of problems, you may wish to contact one of the following organizations.

Mental Health Association
1800 North Kent Street
Arlington, VA 22209

American Psychological Association
1200 Seventeenth Street, N.W.
Washington, DC 20036

American Psychiatric Association
1700 Eighteenth Street, N.W.
Washington, DC 20009

Suicide Prevention Center
1041 South Menlo Avenue
Los Angeles, CA 90006

makes work adjustment stressful for women in jobs that were traditionally held by men. Other programs identify children with early signs of psychological problems and provide preventive treatment in the schools. Courses for parents are offered in many areas designed to reduce the incidence of inappropriate child-rearing that contributes to juvenile delinquency. And the nationwide Head Start programs provide help to disadvantaged preschool children to prevent later school adjustment problems. As with other community-based programs, these preventive efforts are sadly underfunded in most areas, however.

R E V I E W

One-to-one psychotherapy is not the only approach taken to the solution of psychological problems. For one thing, each method of psychotherapy is sometimes practiced with groups of clients rather than individual clients. Group therapy is practiced primarily because the presence of other people with problems offers advantages to some clients. Other clients provide encouragement, give advice, show the client that he or she is not alone in having problems, and provide opportunities for learning new ways of interacting with others. Group therapy often also makes efficient use of the therapist's time. Individuals with complex problems, or who have sensitive problems that they do not want to discuss in front of others, may be better served by individual psychotherapy, however. In recent years, group therapy has become popular among normal individuals as a form of personal growth therapy. Sometimes this therapy is aimed at a specific topic, such as enhanced sexuality, but the popular encounter group format is designed to use Gestalt therapy methods to improve general self-awareness. Entire families are also often worked with as a group by therapists who believe that the faulty operation of some family systems can cause psychological problems. Family therapy seeks to reestablish proper functioning in these families.

In addition to psychological treatments for psychological problems, physicians often use biological methods. The most widely used medical treatments are drugs. Drugs introduced since the 1950s have been partially responsible for the progress in treating psychological problems, which has resulted in a decrease in the number of institutionalized mental patients in the United States. Electroconvulsive therapy—in which an electric current produces controlled brain seizures—is widely used in the treatment of severe depression. The controversial method of psychosurgery in which parts of the brain are destroyed to prevent excessive emotional reactions is no longer widely used in the United States; but the use of newer, more precise methods may be on the upswing.

Since the early 1960s, the dominant trend for the treatment of people with psychological problems has been away from residential placement in mental hospitals and toward treatment in the individual's home community. Such treatment is less expensive, does not require the loss of employment or termination of friendships, does not involve the negative stigma of hospitalization, and keeps the individual out of the boring, depressing environment of a mental hospital. Other relatively new programs in the community include innovative methods of aiding former mental patients in their readjustment to independent living and community psychology programs designed to prevent the occurrence of psychological problems in large numbers of people.

S U M M A R Y

Chapter 13 outlines the major forms of *therapy* through which individuals are helped with psychological problems.

   I. *Psychotherapy* is the use of methods such as talking, demonstrating, and reinforcing that are based on a theory of psychological disorders to solve human problems.

   A. Freud is the founder of the form of psychotherapy known as *psychoanalysis*, which helps the patient bring unconscious conflict into consciousness.
   1. *Free association* is used to relax the censorship of the ego.
   2. *Dream interpretation* allows the therapist to obtain another "window" on the unconscious.
   3. *Resistance* is any form of opposition of the patient to the process of psychoanalysis.
   4. *Transference* occurs when there is a relatively intense relationship between patient and therapist during therapy; this can be interpreted to give insights to the patient.
   5. *Catharsis* is the release of some of the emotion that is pent up with unconscious conflicts.

   II. Humanistic psychotherapies strive to help the person achieve full self-awareness in order to allow the person's inner-directed tendency to growth to be realized. *Client-centered psychotherapy* and *Gestalt therapy* are two major types of humanistic psychotherapy.

   A. Client-centered psychotherapy helps the client explore unsymbolized feelings and information by providing a safe emotional climate.
   B. Gestalt therapy helps the individual achieve greater self-awareness by using directive techniques such as pointing out inconsistencies in behavior.

   III. *Behavior therapists* use a form of psychotherapy in which they help the client unlearn abnormal behavior and learn adaptive ways of thinking, feeling, and acting.

   A. *Systematic desensitization* and *flooding* are widely used methods of fear reduction.
   B. *Social skills training* and *developmental skills training* are examples of teaching new, adaptive skills using methods derived from operant conditioning.
   C. *Aversive conditioning* uses unpleasant negative stimuli to eliminate abnormal habits.
   D. *Cognitive therapy* rests on the assumption that faulty cognitions cause abnormal emotions and actions.

   IV. Some methods of therapy are carried out with groups or entire families, and some are designed to prevent rather than treat problems.

   A. *Group therapy* makes efficient use of therapists' time, and the presence of other people with problems offers advantages to some clients.
   B. *Family therapy* seeks to reestablish proper functioning within families.
   C. *Medical therapies* are designed to correct a physical condition believed to be the cause of a psychological disorder.
   D. *Community mental health center* facilities provide services for individuals with psychological problems in their own communities and emphasize prevention.

Suggested Readings

1. A description of the major methods of psychotherapy is presented in:

   Kendall, P. C., & Norton-Ford, J. D. (1982). *Clinical psychology: Scientific and professional dimensions.* New York: Wiley.

2. Group psychotherapy is discussed in depth in:

   Yalom, I. D. (1975). *The theory and practice of group psychotherapy* (2nd ed.). New York: Basic Books.

3. A cautionary note concerning encounter groups is provided by:

   Hartley, D., Roback, H. R., & Abromowitz, S. F. (1976). Deterioration effects in encounter groups. *American Psychologist, 31,* 247–255.

4. A major comparison of the effectiveness of different forms of psychotherapy is presented in:

   Smith, M. L., & Glass, G. V. (1977). Meta-analysis of psychotherapy outcome studies. *American Psychologist, 32,* 752–760.

The Social Context

Social Psychology

OUTLINE

KEY TERMS

P R O L O G U E

I vividly remember reading about the death of Kitty Genovese some years ago. I was more than a little disappointed in the human race when I read that she had been beaten and stabbed to death in a residential area of New York City over the course of 30 minutes while 38 of her neighbors came to their windows and watched. Incredibly, no one came out to help her; no one even called the police.

How could such a thing have happened? Did Kitty just happen to live in a neighborhood of uncaring cowards? Social psychologists think that is not the answer. For example, Bibb Latané, John Darley, and Judith Rodin carried out a series of experiments in an attempt to understand the lack of action by bystanders like these. In one experiment (Latané & Rodin, 1969), a female experimenter asked college students to fill out a questionnaire, and while they worked, she went behind a curtain where she staged a fake accident. The students heard her climbing and then falling from a chair. She moaned as if in great pain and begged for someone to help her get her foot out from under a heavy object. When student subjects were alone in the other part of the room, 70 percent came to help her. But when they were in pairs, only 40 percent responded to her anguished pleas. When they were paired with one other student who did not respond to the woman's pleas, only 7 percent tried to help!

In a similar experiment (Darley & Latané, 1968), college students "overheard" a staged epileptic seizure through an intercom. Eighty-five percent of the students tried to find help for the seizure victim when they thought they alone had heard it, but when they thought that others were also listening only 30 percent sought help. As we will see later in this chapter, Darley, Latané, and Rodin do not think that bystanders who fail to help in an emergency are lacking in some personal quality; rather they are influenced in some way by being in a group. It's the nature of people to be with others. We seek out social relationships and are changed by having them. Our social nature is so much a part of our human nature that it's not possible to understand people fully without studying them as they interact with others.

P R E V I E W

Humans are social animals: We enjoy people, need people, and are profoundly influenced by people. Social psychology is the branch of psychology that studies individuals as they interact with others. Taking this social view of human behavior is essential because the process of interacting with others changes us. We have a strong tendency to behave like other members in a group even when we are not asked to conform. Moreover, people can influence us more overtly through the process of persuasion. Interestingly, even frighteningly, the facts and logic of the persuasive argument can be less important than the psychological aspects of persuasion. Perhaps the most disturbing aspect of the power of one person to influence another, however, is our tendency to obey even inappropriate requests from authority figures.

Attitudes are believed to play a key role in social interactions. Other people influence our attitudes, and our attitudes are thought to influence our behavior toward others to some extent. Many of our attitudes are learned from others in the first place and are often changed through the process of persuasion. But social influence is not the only cause of attitude change. When circumstances cause our behavior to change so that it's inconsistent with our attitudes, our attitudes will change under some conditions to make them consistent again with our behavior. Prejudice is a class of attitudes that exerts particularly strong and usually negative influence on social behavior.

To most of us, the most important interactions that we have with others are with the people that we like and love. The perceptions that we form of others are complex combinations of the positive and negative qualities that we see in them. This process is made complex by the facts that our first impressions of a person are often more influential than later impressions, that negative information is more important than positive information, that different people evaluate the same information in different ways, and that we tend to underestimate the role played by situations in influencing the behavior of others. But, other things equal, we are attracted to people who are similar to us (or whose opposite characteristics fit well with our own), who are reasonably competent (but not perfect), who are physically attractive, who we meet when we are in good moods, and who like us, too. Once mutual attraction leads to a relationship, our likelihood of staying in that relationship is determined (1) by how well our expectations of what the person is like continue to be met, and (2) by how fairly balanced the relationship is in terms of how much each person perceives that he or she puts into it and receives from the relationship.

Definition of Social Psychology

social psychology
The branch of psychology that studies individuals as they interact with others.

Social psychology is a branch of psychology that studies individuals as they interact with others. Up to this point, we have studied people as individuals removed from the social context in which they live. But it has been clear all along that people live with other people: Their most important learning comes from others, their most important motives are social motives, and so on.

People are almost always with others. It's part of human nature to be social. Social psychologist Elliot Aronson (1980) reminds us that this insight is among the oldest in psychology. In 328 B.C., Aristotle wrote, "Man is by nature a social

Social psychology is the branch of psychology that studies individuals as they interact with others.

animal. . . . Anyone who either cannot lead the common life or is so self-sufficient as not to need to, and therefore does not partake of society, is either a beast or a god." People need, like, and are profoundly influenced by people. Social psychologists study these attractions, needs, and influences.

Social Influence: People Being Changed by Others

The "bystander" experiment described in the Prologue of this chapter illustrates one way in which people are influenced by groups, but many other examples are possible. Have you ever been to Mardi Gras and watched, or participated in, the raucous behavior of the crowd? Probably very few people in that crowd would behave in the same way if they were in the street alone, even if they had consumed the same amount of alcohol. Have you ever noticed how much easier it is to speak your strongest opinions among a group of friends who hold similar opinions than in a group that hold strongly differing views? Clearly, our behavior is influenced by its social context.

Effects of Being in a Group

Near the turn of the century, William Carr, a black man, was caught killing the cow of a white man in southern Louisiana. A mob of solid citizens took him from the sheriff, who did not resist them, and hanged him without a trial. During the era in which this hanging took place, an average of two black people were lynched each week in the United States. While these lynchings say much about racial prejudice—a topic that we turn to later in the chapter—it also says a great deal about the effects of groups on the behavior of individuals. The members of lynch mobs were almost never men who had murdered before when alone or who would murder alone afterward. Something about being in a group transformed men who were incapable of murder into a mob that was very capable of murder indeed.

Drawing by Stevenson; © 1978
The New Yorker Magazine, Inc.

"The social fabric is extremely fragile around here."

The bystander experiments performed by Latané and others shed a great deal of light on the effects of groups on individual behavior, and are particularly helpful in understanding the behavior of the witnesses to the murder of Kitty Genovese (see Prologue). Many studies have shown that there is a direct relationship between the size of the group and efforts to help by bystanders; the larger the group, the less likely any particular person is to offer to help a person in distress (Latané & Nida, 1981). Why is this so?

Two social factors seem to be primarily responsible for the ability of groups to alter the behavior of individuals (Shotland, 1985).

diffusion of responsibility
The effect of being in a group that apparently reduces the sense of personal responsibility of each group member to act appropriately.

First, groups create a **diffusion of responsibility.** If everyone in the group is responsible for a lynching, then no one person is individually responsible; "I didn't do it, we all just got worked up and did it." In emergencies, a person who is alone is clearly responsible for helping the person in need; but in a group of bystanders, the reasoning is that I do not need to help, because someone else will.

Second, the behavior of individuals in groups is influenced by *modeling* (first discussed in chapter 5, p. 209). It's relatively easy to go along with a lynching (or fail to help a person in distress when in a crowd) when everyone else is doing the same thing. Group members imitate one another. When no bystander is making an effort to help, then it's less likely that any one individual will help. Remember that in the Latané and Rodin experiment 40 percent of the subjects in pairs went to find help for the person who had fallen, but that number was reduced to 7 percent when they were paired with another subject (actually a confederate of the experimenter) who made no effort at all to offer help. In other bystander experiments in which the confederate tried to find a way to help, the subjects were more likely to help, too. Modeling is a potent factor in groups.

In terms of outward behavior, we have a tendency to conform to group norms.

Conformity

Our tendency to behave like others in a group has been further demonstrated in a number of experiments on **conformity.** Conformity is yielding to group pressure even when no direct request to comply has been made. A most informative and now classic study of conformity was conducted by Solomon Asch (1956). He asked college students to serve as subjects in an experiment that he said concerned visual perception. Each subject participated in a group with other "subjects," all of whom were actually confederates of the experimenter. The group was shown four straight lines depicted in figure 14.1. The task was to tell which of the three lines on the right side of the figure was the same length as line A.

The task was intentionally made easy, with line Y being the correct choice. But the real subject was the last one in line as each subject was asked to state his or her choice out loud. One by one, the confederates who were playing the part of real subjects chose line X. The distress of the real subject was immediately apparent. He seemed to be asking, "Am I crazy or are they?" But in an amazing 74 percent of the cases, the subjects conformed to the pressure of the group and gave the wrong answer at least part of the time.

How "deep" was this conformity? Did the subjects know that they were just going along with the group's opinion, or did the group actually change their judgment? Probably a little bit of each goes on when we conform to groups, but we conform mostly in terms of outward behavior. When the same line-judging experiment was conducted in a way that allowed the subjects to make their judgments in private, almost no conformity to the erroneous judgments of other subjects occurred. Apparently, we are able to make up our minds privately in the face of pressure from others, but often go along with the crowd in terms of outward behavior.

conformity
Yielding to group pressure even when no direct request to comply has been made.

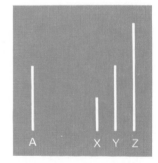

Figure 14.1 Stimuli like the one's used in Asch's study of conformity.

Persuasion

The earliest known work on social psychology was Aristotle's *Rhetoric*. It was an essay on factors that make for persuasive arguments when orators debate. You probably do not listen to many orators debate, but you are often on the receiving end of other kinds of persuasive communications nearly every day. Commercials on the radio, on television, and in newspapers are designed to persuade you to buy the sponsor's products. Political speeches and billboards are trying to persuade you how to vote. Your friend who wants to borrow your car tries to persuade you. And when you ask your professor to let you take an exam early, you try to persuade him or her. **Persuasion** is a natural and necessary part of our interactions with the fellow members of society. But because of the potentially important consequences of persuasive communications (your friend might actually talk you into lending him your car!), it's important to know something about their nature. The persuasiveness of a communication is not only determined by the logical quality of the argument. In fact, logic may be one of the *least important* factors. That is a scary thought because we would like to believe that we live in a world where logic and truth win out. But if you know what makes an argument persuasive, you can at least be on your guard. Notice that the qualities of persuasive communication fall into three general categories: characteristics of the *speaker,* of the *communication* itself, and of the *people who hear it.*

persuasion
The process of changing another person's attitudes through arguments and other related means.

Characteristics of the Speaker

Several characteristics of the speaker are important in determining how persuasive a communication will be.

Credibility. If you listened to a speech on the value of arithmetic, do you think you would be more persuaded if the speech were given by a noted engineer or a dishwasher? Elliot Aronson and Burton Golden (1962) conducted exactly this experiment and found that the engineer swayed opinions considerably more than the dishwasher, even though they gave exactly the same speech. In fact, the same person gave the speech each time, just the introduction identifying his job differed. Many other studies have reached the same conclusion (Aronson, 1980). Our perception of the credibility of the speaker has a great deal to do with the persuasiveness of the communication.

But credibility should not be confused in the above example with being highly educated, intelligent, high in status, or even nice. The key is whether the speaker is a credible source of information *about the specific argument being presented.* Elaine Walster and colleagues performed a clever experiment that forcefully makes this point (Walster, Aronson, & Abrahams, 1966). Subjects were given newspaper clippings of interviews with either a mobster or a politician. Half of the subjects read clippings that argued for more lenient treatment of criminals by the courts, and half read arguments for stricter treatment. When the mobster argued for more lenient treatment, he was completely ineffective and, in fact, slightly swayed attitudes in the opposite direction. When the mobster argued for *stricter* treatment, however, he was as persuasive as the politician. Apparently, the reasoning was that if a criminal (who knows about crime and would not personally benefit from stricter enforcement) thinks we need stricter enforcement of the laws, it must be so.

Thus, the more credible the speaker, the more persuasive the message. But Carl Hovland has qualified this conclusion with the identification of what he called **sleeper effects** (Hovland & Weiss, 1951). Although the attempts at persuasion by speakers who are low in credibility are ineffective at first, they often influence our opinions later. All speakers have the potential, then, to influence our opinions sooner or later.

sleeper effects
According to Hovland, the potential for low-credibility speakers to influence opinion after a period of time.

Attractive, popular, or famous speakers tend to be more persuasive than unattractive speakers. But their persuasiveness seems to be limited to relatively unimportant issues.

Attractiveness. Other things being equal, a speaker who is attractive, popular, famous, and likable will be more effective in changing our opinions than an unattractive speaker. That is why Cheryl Tiegs, Joe Namath, and Catherine Deneuve are paid enormous sums to endorse products in commercials and I am not. Fortunately, the persuasiveness of attractive speakers seems to be limited to relatively unimportant issues—but that includes almost everything that advertisers want us to buy (Aronson, 1980; Chaiken & Eagly, 1983).

Intent. Speakers are generally less persuasive if they obviously intend to change your opinion, particularly if the speaker has something to gain by changing your opinion (Aronson, 1980). If a real estate agent tells you that a lot he wants you to buy is going to rise dramatically in value, you might not believe him. On the other hand, if you overhear two realtors talking at a cocktail party say the same thing, the message would probably be more persuasive since no one is trying to convince you or make a commission from the sale. That is the rationale behind the "hidden camera" testimonials that are included in so many television commercials. Since the people supposedly do not know they are on camera, they do not seem to be trying to sell us anything.

Characteristics of the Message

In addition to the qualities of the speaker, the characteristics of the message are also important determinants of persuasiveness.

Emotional Appeals. Are emotional messages more persuasive than unemotional ones? Adolf Hitler appealed strongly to the emotions of the German people in the speeches he gave to rally support behind his Nazi party. Were the emotions he aroused part of the reason behind his success? The American Cancer Society uses scare tactics in some of the ads they run trying to convince people to stop smoking. Are they going about it in the right way?

Considerable evidence suggests that communications that arouse fear—such as graphic pictures of rotten teeth and gums in messages urging proper dental care—are more effective than the same messages without the fear-provoking images (Baron & Byrne, 1982). Fear can enhance the persuasiveness of a communication, but only under certain circumstances (Mewborn & Rogers, 1979; Rogers, 1975). Listeners will respond favorably to a fear-inducing persuasive communication only if (1) the emotional appeal is a strong one, (2) the listeners think that the fearful outcome (such as rotten teeth or lung cancer) is likely to happen to them, and (3) the message offers an effective way of avoiding the fearful outcome (such as an easy way to stop smoking). If all of these elements are present, emotional appeals can be highly persuasive.

Two-Sided Arguments. There are two sides to most arguments. If, for example, we use more coal in generating electric power, we will reduce our dependence on foreign oil and may be able to keep utility costs from rising as rapidly as in the past. That is good. But if we burn more coal, we will also pollute the atmosphere more, damage a great deal of land and water in the process of strip mining, and lose lives during the mining process. That is obviously bad. If you were trying to convince Congress to support the use of greater amounts of coal, would it be more effective to just tell them the good side of the argument, or to tell them both sides?

There is no simple answer to this question. It depends on how favorable the audience is to your position before you start talking. If the audience is leaning in your direction, your message will be more persuasive if you just tell them about the benefits of burning coal. Telling them about the negative side to the argument may just lose you some supporters. But if your audience is initially unfavorable to your position, it's generally better to give them both sides of the argument. That will make you seem more credible and less biased (Baron & Byrne, 1982). So, the next time somebody does an admirable job of presenting both sides of an issue, you may be dealing with a strong believer in honesty and the democratic process, but you may just be listening to a shrewd operator who is trying to change your mind.

Characteristics of the Listeners

In addition to qualities of the speaker and the message, certain characteristics of the listeners help determine how persuasive an argument will be.

1. *Intelligence.* Generally, less intelligent people are easier to persuade. The exception is when the message is complex and difficult to understand; under this condition, more intelligent listeners are easier to persuade (Baron & Byrne, 1982).

2. *Need for social approval.* Some people have a greater need for social approval (a need to be approved of or liked by others) than other people do. People with a high need for social approval are generally easier to persuade than people who are low in this need (Baron & Byrne, 1982).

3. *Self-esteem.* Under some circumstances, individuals who are somewhat low in self-esteem (have unfavorable opinions of themselves) are easier to convince than people with high self-esteem (Zellner, 1970).

4. *Audience size.* People are generally easier to persuade when they are listening to the message in a group rather than alone. And bigger crowds lead to greater persuasibility than smaller ones (Newton & Mann, 1980).

Obedience: Direct Influence by Authority Figures

One of the most fascinating, and often frightening, lines of inquiry in social psychology has been research on **obedience,** doing what we are told to do by people in authority. This research was prompted in part by the behavior of soldiers in World War II, and later in Vietnam, who committed unthinkable atrocities when ordered to do so. What kind of person would help abuse and murder 6 million Jews during the holocaust? What kind of person would not refuse to obey such an order? The disturbing answer from research is that most of us are that kind of person.

obedience
Doing what one is told to do by people in authority.

Stanley Milgram (1963, 1965) has conducted a series of studies that cast a glaring light on the subject of obedience. Try to imagine that you are a subject in one of his experiments to get the full impact of his findings. You have volunteered for a study of memory. When you arrive at the appointed time, you and another subject, a middle-aged man, meet a somewhat stern, authoritarian experimenter wearing a white lab coat. The experimenter chooses you to be the "teacher" in the experiment and the other subject to be the "learner." The learner will have to memorize a list of word pairs but you have to test him and operate the equipment. The "equipment" is a console labeled "SHOCK GENERATOR" with a bank of switches that are marked from 15 to 450 volts.

Stanley Milgram
(1933–1984)

You help strap the learner into something that looks like an electric chair and you attach electrodes to him that are connected to the shock generator in the other room. The learner asks if the experiment could be dangerous to his heart condition, but the experimenter assures him that while the shocks could be extremely painful, they should cause no physical harm. You return to the next room, take your seat at the console, and are told how you should use the shocks to "help" the learner memorize the list.

You are to listen to him attempt to recite the list over the intercom and shock him by throwing one of the switches after each error. You are to begin with the weakest shock and increase the intensity each time he makes a mistake. You are even given a 45-volt shock to let you see what it feels like (it's unpleasant) and the experiment begins. The learner recalls the list fairly accurately, but makes a few mistakes and you shock him as you have been instructed to do.

What you do not know is that the learner is not really getting shocked. He is a confederate of the experimenter who is acting a role. He is not even talking over the intercom; you are hearing a tape recording instead. But, the important thing is that you *believe* that a man with a heart condition is strapped into an electric chair in the next room and that you are giving him shocks every time he makes a mistake.

The learner grunts and groans some after an intensity of 75 volts has been reached and asks to be let out of the experiment after you give him a 150-volt shock, a request that the experimenter denies. At 180 volts, the learner screams out that he cannot stand the pain, and just as you are about to reach the level marked "Danger: Extreme Shock," he begs you to stop the experiment while pounding on the wall. When you look toward the experimenter expecting him to stop the proceedings, he firmly tells you to administer the next shock.

What would you do? Would you give the extremely dangerous shock even though the learner was begging you to stop? Or would you refuse to continue? Milgram asked a panel of psychiatrists how many subjects they thought would continue giving shocks at this point and they predicted that less than 5 percent would continue. What percentage would you predict? Milgram found that an incredible 65 percent not only gave the next shock but also continued participating until they had given the highest shock.

Further studies conducted by Milgram showed that when the prestige of the experimenter was reduced, the percentage of obedient subjects fell to about 50 percent. When the experimenter gave instructions by telephone rather than in person, the percentage fell to about 25 percent. Furthermore, when the subject was in the presence of two other subjects who refused to give the high-intensity shocks, only 10 percent obeyed the experimenter's instructions to the end. These latter findings are encouraging, but they do not lessen the impact of Milgram's experiments. They are a painful warning against the danger of letting misguided authorities use ordinary people like you and me to obediently carry out their wishes.

R E V I E W

Because people are social animals, we are almost always in the company of others. This is a fundamentally important observation because people can only be fully understood if our social nature is understood; other people influence our behavior and we must understand that process of influence. The very fact of being with others can influence behavior; people behave differently when they are in groups from the way they do when they are alone. Mobs commit crimes that the individuals alone would not commit, and groups of bystanders fail to help people in distress even though the members of that group would have done so alone. Groups change behavior through diffusing responsibility and modeling.

Groups influence individual behavior through our strong tendency to conform with the group even when not asked to do so. We are most likely to conform in terms of outward behavior rather than inward judgments and attitudes, however. Other people can also influence our behavior in more direct ways. Nearly every day someone tries to persuade us to change our attitudes or behavior. The effectiveness of these attempts to influence depends on qualities of the speaker, the message, and the listener. Speakers are more influential when they appear credible, are attractive, and do not appear to be trying to influence us for their own personal gain. We are more likely to be influenced by emotional messages if the emotional appeal is strong, if the listener thinks the fearful outcome is likely, and if reasonable ways of avoiding the fearful outcome are presented. Messages that present some information favoring both sides of the argument are more persuasive, especially with listeners who originally oppose the message. And listeners tend to be more easily persuaded when they are less intelligent, have a high need for social approval, are somewhat low in self-esteem, and are in large groups. Frighteningly, we are all likely to be persuaded to obey even inappropriate requests from a high-prestige authority figure, especially when we face the authority figure alone. (See *Research Report:* "Zimbardo's Prison.")

Attitudes involve beliefs, emotions, and dispositions to behave. The most destructive attitudes are ones involving prejudice towards others.

Attitudes and Social Behavior

Attitudes are a pivotal concept in social psychology. They are of special interest because other people influence our attitudes, and our attitudes are often reflected in our behavior toward others. If I give a speech to parents that changes their attitudes toward discipline (such as, it's better to praise children for their good behavior than to punish them for their bad behavior), they will have a tendency to change the way they actually rear their children, too. As we see shortly, attitudes and social behavior are not perfectly correlated by any means. But there is enough relationship between the two to make attitudes a favorite topic of study of social psychologists, especially attitudes related to important aspects of social behavior such as racial and sexual prejudice.

RESEARCH REPORT

Zimbardo's Prison:
The Power of Social Situations

One of the topics in which social psychologists are most interested is the high degree of influence that social situations can have on our behavior. To a great extent, we behave in the ways that other people want or expect us to behave. Society gives us roles to play and we follow these roles like we are reading parts in a play. You think I am exaggerating? Let me tell you about Philip Zimbardo's prison and then you decide for yourself.

Philip Zimbardo is a social psychologist who teaches at Stanford University. Among other things, he is interested in knowing more about the internal workings of prisons. Why is it that our society, which places so much emphasis on the dignity of the individual, has created a dehumanizing prison system that leaves so many of its inmates more antisocial than before their imprisonment? Why have we failed in spite of good intentions to create a prison system that is truly rehabilitative? Zimbardo feels the answer is that the peculiar social situation of prisons leads to a mistreatment of convicts that worsens their behavior. Consider his description of an experiment that was conducted in 1972 to examine this issue.

In an attempt to understand just what it means psychologically to be a prisoner or a prison guard, Craig Haney, Curt Banks, Dave Jaffe, and I created our own prison. We carefully screened over 70 volunteers who answered an ad in a Palo Alto city newspaper and ended up with about two dozen young men who were selected to be part of this study.

Half were arbitrarily designated as prisoners by a flip of a coin, the others as guards. These were the roles they were to play in our simulated prison. The guards were made aware of the potential seriousness and danger of the situation and their own vulnerability. They made up their own formal rules for maintaining law, order, and respect, and were generally free to improvise new ones during their eight-hour, three-man shifts. The prisoners were unexpectedly picked up at their homes by a city policeman in a squad car, searched, handcuffed, fingerprinted, booked at the Palo Alto station house, and taken blindfolded to our jail. There they were stripped, deloused, put into a uniform, given a number, and put into a cell with two other prisoners where they expected to live for the next two

RESEARCH REPORT

weeks. The pay was good ($15.00 a day) and their motivation was to make money. . . . At the end of only six days we had to close down our mock prison because what we saw was frightening. It was no longer apparent to most of the subjects (or to us) where reality ended and their roles began. The majority had indeed become prisoners or guards, no longer able to clearly differentiate between role playing and self. There were dramatic changes in virtually every aspect of their behavior, thinking, and feeling. In less than a week the experience of imprisonment undid (temporarily) a lifetime of learning; human values were suspended, self-concepts were challenged, and the ugliest, most base, pathological side of human nature surfaced. We were horrified because we saw some boys (guards) treat others as if they were despicable animals, taking pleasure in cruelty, while other boys (prisoners) became servile, dehumanized robots who thought only of escape, of their own individual survival, and of their mounting hatred for the guards.

We had to release three prisoners in the first four days because they had such acute situational traumatic reactions as hysterical crying, confusion in thinking, and severe depression. Others begged to be paroled, and all but three were willing to forfeit all the money they had earned if they could be paroled.*

Zimbardo's prison study clearly points to the power of social situations to influence our behavior. It's an important point to understand. The person you are is determined at least in part by your social situation. But do not forget the individual's own personal qualities. Recall from the chapter on personality theory that behavior is determined by an interaction of both situational and personal qualities. I was exaggerating earlier when I said that we act out social roles "like reading parts in a play" because every person reacts to social situations somewhat differently. But it's important not to underestimate the power of social situations in influencing our behavior.

*From P. G. Zimbardo. Pathology of imprisonment. Published by permission of Transaction, Inc., from Society, Vol. 9, no. 6. Copyright © 1972 by Transaction, Inc.

attitudes
Beliefs that predispose one to act and feel in certain ways.

Social psychologists define **attitudes** as beliefs that predispose us to act and feel in certain ways. Note that this definition has three component aspects: (1) *beliefs,* such as the belief that door-to-door salespeople are generally dishonest; (2) *feelings,* such as a strong dislike for door-to-door salespeople; and (3) *dispositions to behave,* such as a readiness to be rude to them when they come to the door. Where do our attitudes come from, and what causes them to change?

Origins of Attitudes

The origins of attitudes are fairly obvious: We learn them directly from our experiences, and we learn them from others. Some of our attitudes are learned from firsthand experience. Children who are bitten by dogs often carry negative attitudes toward dogs for the rest of their lives, especially toward the kind of dog that bit them. In contrast, the sweet crunch of chocolate chip cookies generally leads to a favorable attitude toward them. In other words, some attitudes appear to be *classically conditioned.* If a stimulus (dogs or cookies) is paired with a positive or negative experience, the attitude will be similarly positive or negative.

Attitudes are also commonly learned from others. Parents who model positive attitudes toward their Chicano neighbors are likely to have children who have positive attitudes toward Chicanos. Children whose best friends think baseball is awful may pick up this attitude through modeling. Similarly, children who are reinforced by their parents and friends for prejudicial attitudes are likely to have these attitudes strengthened. In sum, other people instill attitudes in us through their modeling and reinforcement.

Freud suggested that the role that others play in the formation of our attitudes goes deeper than simple learning, however. He believed that the ego seeks people who appear to be strong, successful, and perhaps even fearful to us. To reduce our anxieties about surviving in the world, we *identify* (see chapter 11, p. 430) with these strong individuals and adopt their attitudes as our own.

Attitudes, Behavior, and Attitude Change

Attitudes are not chiseled in granite; they can change after they have been formed. As we have seen, persuasion is an important source of attitude change, but the discrepancy that often exists between our attitudes and behavior is another key cause of changed attitudes. Even though attitudes are defined in part in terms of a disposition to behave, there is sometimes a great difference between our attitudes and our behavior. For example, during the Vietnam War, many men who held attitudes that were strongly opposed to the war obeyed their draft orders and became a part of the war. Similarly, opinion pollsters know that not everyone who has a favorable attitude toward a product will actually buy it.

The interesting point is when behavior and attitudes are inconsistent, the attitudes often change to match the behavior. Suppose you are a married person who does not particularly like to play bridge. One day, your husband tells you that the two of you have been asked to join the regular bridge group formed by several of his friends at work. You know that bridge is not a big deal to him either, but mostly out of boredom you agree to join. So, you start playing bridge every week even though you do not like it. Do not be surprised if you start liking bridge. When behavior and attitudes are inconsistent, changes in attitudes often "follow" changes in behavior.

However, attitudes only change to become more consistent with behavior under certain circumstances. If the man in the example above had told his wife that his boss had insisted that they join the bridge group, her attitude toward bridge probably would not change. Attitudes only follow behavior when no good explanation exists for engaging in behavior that is inconsistent with the attitude. If her husband's boss had insisted on their joining, she could have easily justified playing bridge as a way of protecting her husband's job. As it was, however, there was no good reason for playing bridge, so her attitudes would be more likely to shift in the direction of her behavior. Two major theories have been proposed to explain our tendency to change attitudes to bring them into harmony with our behavior when there is no obvious explanation for our behavior: cognitive dissonance theory and attribution theory.

Cognitive Dissonance Theory of Attitude Change

Leon Festinger (1957) proposed the theory of **cognitive dissonance** to explain the tendency of attitudes to sometimes shift to be consistent with behavior. This theory states that inconsistencies between attitudes and behavior are *uncomfortable,* so that people will change their attitudes to reduce this discomfort. The woman who started playing bridge even though she did not like it was in an uncomfortable state of dissonance that could be reduced either by not playing bridge or by changing her attitude toward bridge. Often dissonance is reduced by a shift in attitude. The woman would not have been in a state of dissonance if her husband's boss had insisted on their joining the bridge group. She could have justified her behavior: "I don't like bridge, but I'm protecting my husband's job by playing." Because there is no dissonance in this situation, there would not be any attitude change.

cognitive dissonance (dis'so-nans) The discomfort that results from inconsistencies between attitudes and behavior.

Festinger tested the theory of cognitive dissonance in a number of experiments. One of the best known (Festinger & Carlsmith, 1959) involved asking subjects to perform a boring spool-stacking task for an hour. Afterward, the subjects were each asked to tell the next subject that the task was an interesting one. Half of the subjects were offered $20 to say that the task was interesting, and half were offered $1. A third group of subjects stacked spools, but were not asked to say anything to the next subject. Later, all of the subjects were asked how interesting they really thought the task was.

Which group do you think reported the most favorable attitude toward the task? Perhaps surprisingly—but, just as predicted by cognitive dissonance theory—the most positive attitudes were expressed by the group offered only $1. The group offered $20 was not placed in a state of dissonance: "The task was really boring, but I'll lie to the next person to get the $20." The group offered $1 was placed in a state of dissonance, however; there was no good explanation for their stating an opinion about the task that was inconsistent with their attitude, so their attitudes improved to be more consistent with their behavior.

A more recent study shows that cognitive dissonance is relevant to more than our attitudes about stacking spools (Cooper & Mackie, 1983). University students who supported Ronald Reagan in the 1980 presidential election were the subjects in this experiment. They were asked to write an essay favoring an issue that Ronald Reagan opposed (federally sponsored health care) or an essay supporting the candidacy of Jimmy Carter. Half of the subjects were given very little choice about writing the essays. This group of subjects could be expected to experience little cognitive dissonance ("I wrote an essay that was contrary to what I believe, but I had to do it"). The other group of subjects were given much

OF SPECIAL INTEREST

Consistency and Change in Attitudes: What Are the Campus Radicals of the 1960s Like Today?

During the 1960s the divided opinions of the American public about the Vietnam War became highly inflamed emotional issues on many college and university campuses. A considerable number of the students who strongly opposed the war became active in radical organizations that protested the war and the role university research sometimes played in supporting the war effort. Numerous demonstrations and protests were staged that sometimes resulted in the occupation of campus offices, the destruction of property, and in some cases the loss of lives. Where are the campus radicals today, and how liberal are their attitudes?

Collins Vallee was an outspoken opponent of the Vietnam War when he was a student at Tulane University in the late 1960s. As a leader of the Tulane University Front, an organization that organized campus opposition to the war, Vallee was a vocal participant in demonstrations on campus. One such demonstration resulted in an emotional confrontation between protesters and R.O.T.C. students, and a one-semester suspension for Vallee.

Today, Collins Vallee is an attorney practicing general law in downtown New Orleans. His beard and long hair are gone and so are some of his more liberal attitudes. He says that in 1979 he "greatly shocked" his old friends when he supported a Republican candidate for the Governor of Louisiana. Politically, he no longer describes himself as a liberal, but as a "pragmatist." Collins Vallee is now a member of the establishment and is apparently comfortable with it.

Obviously, Collins Vallee's attitudes have changed in the last 15 years. He has had many new experiences since then and it would be surprising if he had not been changed somewhat by them. Still, some of his old attitudes remain unchanged as well. He still would oppose the Vietnam War and still has favorable attitudes about campus protest. Looking back, he said in 1982, "From the standpoint of change, we helped modify some of the codes and rules governing student behavior. They were changes for the better. The draft ended. The war has ended. And the board at Tulane is more responsive to the needs and desires of the student body." Like most of us, 15 years have seen Collins Vallee change in some ways and not in others.

Quotes from the Tulanian, *Spring, 1982, pp. 34–35 (Tulane University Alumni Magazine)*

OF SPECIAL INTEREST

Collins Vallee during a campus demonstration in the 1960s and his New Orleans law office during the 1980s.

more choice as to whether or not they would write the essay. These subjects were likely to experience considerable cognitive dissonance, since they wrote an essay favoring something that they opposed even though they did not have to do so. As Festinger would have predicted, attitudes toward Jimmy Carter and federally sponsored health care changed very little in the low-cognitive dissonance group (the subjects given little choice about writing the essays), but changed significantly more in the high-cognitive dissonance group (the ones given more choice). When the behavior of writing the essays created cognitive dissonance, attitudes changed to be more consistent with the behavior.

It's a little scary isn't it? You probably thought your attitudes were always thoughtfully arrived at and based on reality. If Festinger is right, they may sometimes reflect nothing more than an escape from cognitive dissonance.

Attribution Theory of Attitude Change

attribution theory
(ah-tri-bu'shun)
The theory that states that people tend to look for explanations for their own behavior and that of others.

A rival hypothesis, called **attribution theory,** has been offered to explain why discrepancies between attitudes and behavior often lead to shifts in attitudes. Attribution theory is based on the tendency that we humans have to try to *explain* why things happen, that is, *attribute* them to some cause. If the vase on the table falls off, we want to know why. Was there an earth tremor? Did the cat knock it off? Is the house haunted? Usually, we are not comfortable until we decide on an explanation ("I guess the cat must have done it. . ."). People like to attribute everything to some cause, with no loose ends.

One of the things we are most fond of explaining is behavior. My friend has just invited herself over for dinner for the third time this month—why? Is she broke? Is she a moocher? Does she just like my company? We also feel a need to explain our own behavior. I have been feeling down all day; I must need to get more sleep. Or I must still be upset about what Harold did. Or I guess I am just out of sorts because school has started again. According to attribution theory, we have a tendency to attribute all behavior to some cause.

What does that have to do with changes in attitudes induced by discrepancies with behavior? The answer is that we are particularly likely to look for an explanation for unusual behavior, and behavior that is inconsistent with our attitudes is unusual enough to attract our attention. When subjects in Festinger and Carlsmith's spool-stacking experiment found themselves telling the next subject that the boring task was fun, they needed an explanation for their behavior. The subjects who had been offered $20 could easily say that they were fibbing to get the money, but the subjects who had been offered $1 were not getting enough money to justify lying. If they could not attribute their behavior to the money, they had to attribute it to the task. They had to believe that they were saying the task was interesting because it *was* interesting to make sense of their behavior. In this theory, attitudes do not change to reduce uncomfortable cognitive dissonance, but to fit our explanations of our own behavior.

Proponents of cognitive dissonance theory and attribution theory have offered a number of reasons why they believe that their explanation of attitude change is the better one. The fact is that both of these theories do a pretty good job of explaining this phenomenon. As we see later in the chapter, however, attribution theory is a more general theory that is used to explain a much broader range of phenomena. For this reason, it has become one of the most important theories in social psychology today.

Stereotyping people, such as the "typical" pitchman, detracts from our ability to treat members of a group as individuals, and leads to faulty attributions.

Prejudice

Of all the attitudes that we hold about other people, the kind that is most worthy of improved understanding is **prejudice.** Prejudice is a negative attitude based on inaccurate generalizations about a group of people. The group may be distinguished because they are of a different skin color, religion, sex, age, or any other noticeable difference. In some way, however, the difference is believed by the prejudiced person to imply something negative about the entire group ("They're all lazy, or hysterical, or pushy").

The inaccurate generalization upon which the prejudice is based is called a **stereotype.** We all hold stereotypes of other groups of people. What does a "rock star" look and act like? If you were producing a movie, would you cast Lawrence Welk or Ella Fitzgerald in the role of a rock star? You would not because neither of them fit the stereotyped image of rock stars. What are Russians like? Do you have a stereotyped view of them? Think about it for a second. Would you cast Goldie Hawn in the role of a Russian army officer in a serious dramatic film? Do you hold stereotypes of women, men, Cambodians, blacks, old people, Chicanos?

Stereotypes can either be negative or positive (you could believe that all psychology textbook authors are charming, witty, and attractive), but all stereotypes, positive or negative, are inherently harmful for two reasons.

1. *Stereotypes take away our ability to treat each member of a group as an individual.* When we hold a stereotyped view of a group, we tend to treat each member of that group as if the person has the exact characteristics of the stereotype, whether he or she does in reality or not. Even when the stereotype is partially based on fact, there will be many members of the group that differ from the stereotype in significant ways. Take the view that many of us have of the Chinese: One aspect of the stereotype is that they are highly

prejudice
A negative attitude based on inaccurate generalizations about a group of people.

stereotype
An inaccurate generalization upon which a prejudice is based.

intelligent. While it's true that Chinese do score higher than whites on some specific measures of intelligence *on the average,* not all Chinese are highly intelligent. If a teacher's expectations for a Chinese child of below-average intelligence were based on this stereotype, he might be criticized for not living up to his supposed high intelligence when he was, in fact, performing up to his ability. Stereotyped beliefs that a group is low in intelligence can have even more serious consequences in limiting the educational and occupational opportunities of members of that group.

2. *Stereotypes lead to faulty attributions.* Our stereotypes influence the attributions that we make about other people's behavior. As Elliot Aronson (1980) points out, if a prejudiced white man sees an overturned trash can and garbage strewn around the yard of a white family, he is apt to attribute the mess to a stray dog looking for food. But if he sees the same thing in the yard of a black family, he would more likely attribute it to their supposed lazy, slovenly ways.

    These faulty attributions have the effect of deepening and strengthening our prejudices as we keep "seeing" evidence that "supports" our stereotypes and rejecting evidence that is contrary to them.

R E V I E W

Attitudes are a focus of research for social psychologists because they appear to play a pivotal role in the interactions among people: People influence our attitudes, and those attitudes, in turn, are reflected to some extent in the way that we interact with others. They are defined in terms of three components: beliefs, feelings, and dispositions to behave. Attitudes appear to be learned, sometimes through direct experience with the object of our attitude and sometimes from others. According to Freud, the acquisition of attitudes from others takes place as part of a broader process of identification with powerful figures.

Attitudes are subject to change even after they have been formed. It's not uncommon for us to be persuaded by others to change our attitudes, but discrepancies between our behavior and attitudes provides another potent source of attitude change. There is often a big difference between the attitudes we express and the way we behave: We may feel strongly that money is unimportant, for example, but choose between several job offers on the basis of the highest salary offered. Under some circumstances changes in behavior that create a discrepancy between behavior and attitudes will be followed by a change in attitudes that makes the attitudes consistent with behavior again. This is most likely to occur when there is no obvious external cause of the change in behavior. Two major theories have been offered to explain such changes in attitudes. Dissonance theory states that the discrepancy between behavior and attitudes creates an uncomfortable state that is reduced when the attitudes change. Attribution theory suggests that we seek consistent explanations for our behavior. If we cannot attribute the change in behavior to an external cause, our attitudes change to be consistent with our behavior. Both theories are successful in explaining attitude changes, but attribution theory is a more general theory that has applications to other important phenomena as well.

From the standpoint of social psychology, prejudice is a key attitude that is intricately involved in our social interactions. Prejudice is a negative attitude based on inaccurate generalizations about a group of people. These inaccurate generalizations called stereotypes are inherently harmful because they make it difficult to evaluate members of that group on an individual basis and lead to faulty generalizations about their behavior.

Interpersonal Attraction: Friendship and Love

Who are your friends? Why do you suppose you became friends with them rather than with other people you know? Are you in love with someone, or have you ever been in love? What attracted you to him or her and made you experience such intense feelings? Friendship and love are powerful social phenomena that touch all of our lives in one way or another. As such, they have been of special interest to social psychologists. In this section we look at variables that influence our perception of others, the role played by attribution processes in person perception, the qualities of others that make them attractive to us, and factors that are involved in the maintenance of personal relationships.

Person Perception

The first step to understanding why we are attracted to one person rather than another is to understand something about the process of **person perception.** What factors are important in the way we perceive others? We seem to go through a complex process of "cognitive algebra" to reach an average of all the many factors that enter into our perceptions of others—with some factors contributing more to the average than others (Anderson, 1968; Baron & Byrne, 1982; Kaplan, 1975). We sum up a person as if we assign a weight to each person's positive and negative characteristic in accordance with how important that characteristic is to us and then add them all together to arrive at a total perception of the person. But as the following sections show, the process of person perception is complicated further by the ways we gather and use information about others.

person perception
The process of forming impressions of others.

Individual Differences in the Evaluation of Others

Perhaps the most striking thing about the cognitive algebra of person perception is that different people often seem to be using different equations! Whether a characteristic is considered to be positive or negative and how important a weight it will carry in person perception differs markedly from individual to individual. Jennifer may feel that an interest in sports, nutrition, and philosophy, and an outgoing personality are all highly positive characteristics. Angela may feel that these same characteristics are not very important one way or another. And Lydia might find them all to be highly negative characteristics. If Jennifer, Angela, and Lydia were to meet a man with these characteristics at a party tonight, they would each form a very different perception of him. It's like that for everyone. Because different people evaluate the same characteristics in different ways, some people are going to love you, some are going to dislike you, and the rest will find you so-so. The only difference is in how many people fall into each category. Some people have characteristics that are valued by somewhat more people in our culture than others.

Negative Information: The Bad Outweighs the Good

Other things being equal, we tend to assign higher weights to negative than to positive information (Hamilton & Zanna, 1972). Put yourself in this situation: You are a person who values warmth, physical attractiveness, and honesty in others. You meet a person in class that you find extremely warm and attractive; you have an enjoyable conversation with him after class, but during the course of the conversation he asks you to help him think of a lie to tell his girlfriend explaining where he has been. If you are like most people, your opinion of him will suddenly become quite negative. The fact that he is being dishonest with his girlfriend will overshadow his positive characteristics. Most of us will pass up a delicious looking cake if we know it contains even a small amount of rat poison.

Primacy Effects: The Importance of First Impressions

Our first impressions are usually very important in the person perception process. When you pause for a moment and think about this fact, it's quite disturbing. A factor that is *irrelevant* to the nature of the person we are perceiving—the order in which we learn information about that person—can greatly influence our perception of that person. All of us have our good days and bad days, and it's a shame that the perception that others form of us is influenced so much by whether they form their first impression of us on a good or a bad day.

The first information that we are exposed to about a person tends to be given greater weight than later information (Asch, 1946; Hovland, 1957). This is called the **primacy effect.** If you were introduced to Barbara right after you heard her deliver a polished and interesting talk to your sales group on the importance of ethics in business, your impression would probably be quite positive. Later, if you ran into her in a bar sitting alone, looking forlorn, disheveled, and half-drunk, you would be seeing a very different side of Barbara. But since your initial impression of her was favorable, there would be a strong tendency for you to ignore or "explain away" this new information ("Something awful must have happened to Barbara to make her act this way").

primacy effect
The tendency to weigh first impressions heavily in forming opinions about other people.

First impressions, known as the primary effect, are usually given greater weight than later information in the person perception process.

Suppose, however, that seeing Barbara in the bar was your *first* exposure to her. In that case, your first impression of her would be negative and would tend to dominate your perception of her even after you were exposed to more positive information about her later. If your second meeting with her was hearing her lecture on business ethics, you would tend to discount the positive impression she was giving in that encounter ("She's holding herself together pretty well today—I bet most people here don't know she's really a drunken slob").

First impressions (primacy effects) are not always of overriding importance, however. Their impact is greatly reduced under three conditions.

1. *Prolonged exposure.* Prolonged exposure to a person tends to reduce the importance of your first impression of that person. While it's important to try to make a favorable first impression on the first day of your new job, do not worry about it if you do not. Eventually, your fellow employees will get to know the real you. Information about you gathered over a long period of time will erase any first impressions.

2. *Passage of time.* Like anything else, first impressions tend to be forgotten over time. If a substantial period of time passes between first and subsequent impressions, the more recent impression will be of greater importance. So if you flubbed your first attempt to favorably impress that gorgeous person, wait awhile and try again later.

3. *Knowledge of primacy effects.* When people are warned to avoid being influenced by first impressions, the primacy effect can be reduced (Hovland, 1957). Personnel managers and others to whom accurate person perception is important are educated to the dangers of primacy effects and are often able to eliminate them from their perceptions.

Emotions

Another important factor in person perception that can be irrelevant to the nature of the person about whom we are forming an impression is our emotions. The emotional state that we are in when we meet a person has a great deal to do with our liking that person. Positive emotional states lead to greater attraction to others than negative emotions do. William Griffith and Russell Veitch (1971) had a radio news broadcast turned on as subjects waited for an experiment in interpersonal attraction to begin. Actually the broadcast was taped beforehand so that half of the subjects heard a depressing broadcast and half heard happy news. Afterward, the subjects hearing the sad news did not like strangers that they met in the experiment as well as the subjects who had heard the good news. So, do not introduce yourself to that person that you've been wanting to meet just after your football team has lost a game; wait until it wins one. Chances are he or she will be in a better mood and will like you more (Aronson, 1980). You may want to return to p. 412 and reread "*Research Report:* On Falling in Love on a Swaying Suspension Bridge" for a different look at the effects of emotions on person perception.

OF SPECIAL INTEREST

Question: Do you prefer to be alone or with others?   Answer: It depends.

When Aristotle called us social animals, he was responding in part to the fact that people like to be with other people. There are very few people who actually choose to live the life of a hermit; people usually enjoy the company of other people. But we do not always enjoy being with others, sometimes we just like to be alone. Why is that? Under what circumstances do we prefer our own company to that of others?

Social psychologist Patricia Middlebrook (1980) asked 100 students at Central Connecticut State College whether they preferred to be alone, with others, or had no preference in each of 13 different situations. As you can see in table 14.1, a clear pattern emerged. We most want to affiliate with others at either good times or frightening times; we prefer to be alone or have no preference during less happy times. Contrary to the popular saying, misery does not always want company.

Table 14.1 Student preferences for being alone or with others in 13 different situations

Situations in Which	Percentage of Students Who		
	Wished to Be with Others	Wished to Be Alone	Had No Preference
Most want to be with others			
When very happy	88	2	10
When in a good mood	89	0	11
On Saturday night	85	1	14
When you are in a strange situation or doing something you've never done before	77	13	10
Most want to be alone			
When physically tired	6	85	9
When embarrassed	16	76	8
When you want to cry	8	88	4
When busy	12	70	18
After an extensive period of social contact (after being with others for a long time)	12	75	13
There is no consensus			
When depressed	42	48	10
When worried about a serious personal problem	52	44	4
When mildly ill (e.g., with a cold)	32	49	19
When feeling very guilty about something you have done	45	43	12

From Middlebrook, Patricia Niles, Social Psychology and Modern Life, *2d ed., p. 258. © 1980 Alfred A. Knopf, Inc. Reprinted by permission.*

General Determinants of Interpersonal Attraction

Through the complicated process of person perception, a unique impression of each person is formed. But although person perception is a highly personal process, there are some *general* factors that influence whether or not one person will be attracted to another. These include similar and complementary characteristics, competence, physical attractiveness, and mutual liking.

Similar and Complementary Characteristics

In terms of interpersonal attraction, do "birds of a feather flock together" or do "opposites attract"? Are you more likely to be attracted to someone as a friend or lover who is similar to you in many ways or quite different from you? The answer is *both,* in different ways.

Jennifer probably values people who have an interest in exercise, nutrition, and philosophy because she is also interested in those things. It's enjoyable to have a friend to jog with, who pats you on the back for the healthy way you eat, and shares long, delicious philosophical discussions with you. In general, similarity is highly important in attractiveness. We tend to be most attracted to those people who have similar values, interests, and attitudes (Byrne, 1971).

Opposites can also attract, however, when the opposite characteristic *complements* or advantageously "fits" with one of our own characteristics. Jennifer might also be attracted to the fellow at the party tonight in part because he has an outgoing personality while she is more reserved. She may feel that she is a good listener who gets along better with talkative people than ones who are quiet like herself. And she may feel that when she is with an outgoing person at social gatherings he makes it easier for her to interact with other couples than a quiet man does. Similarly, a dominant person might prefer a submissive person, and a person who likes to nurture and "take care of" others might prefer someone who likes to be taken care of (Winch, 1958).

There is another condition under which opposites attract: when people who are different from you *like* you (Aronson, 1980). It's more flattering and attractive to be liked by someone who holds opposite values and opinions than someone who holds similar ones (Jones, Bell, & Aronson, 1971). But take note that opposites usually do not attract; instead opposites usually repel in personal relationships. A person who intensely advocates liberal causes probably would not like a person who vocally supports conservative causes. And a highly religious person probably would not find a disdain for religion attractive in another person.

Competence

We tend to be more attracted to competent than to incompetent people. Intelligence, strength, social skill, education, and athletic prowess are generally thought of as attractive qualities. But people who are seen as *too* competent may suffer a loss in attractiveness, perhaps because it makes us uncomfortable to compare ourselves unfavorably with them. Elliot Aronson and associates conducted a clever experiment that demonstrates that it's best to be a *little* less than perfect (Aronson, Willerman, & Floyd, 1966). Subjects listened to one of four audiotapes of people who were supposedly trying out to be members of their university's College Bowl quiz team. Two of the people scored over 90 percent correct on difficult questions and were portrayed as being honor students, athletes, and active in student activities. The other two answered 30 percent of the questions and were portrayed as average, unathletic students. Near the end of the tape one of the superior students and one of the average students blundered—each spilled a cup of coffee

R E S E A R C H R E P O R T

Social Bubbles: The Psychology of Personal Space

We may be social animals, but we want most of our social interactions to be at a distance. Having people too close can be very uncomfortable. It's as if we live in bubbles surrounding our bodies that we do not want others to pop (Baron & Byrne, 1982; Hayduk, 1983). However, the amount of personal space we prefer varies considerably depending on the person with whom we are interacting. We like for our lovers to join us in our bubbles, but we are uncomfortable talking to a casual friend at much less than arm's length and are bothered by salesclerks who stand closer than an arm's length and a half.

An unusual experiment examined the impact of invasion of personal space in a way that only males will be able to fully appreciate. In a public men's bathroom with three side-by-side urinals, the experimenter waited for someone to use the left-most urinal and then alternately used the urinal next to the subject or one urinal away. When the experimenter was standing right next to the subject it took significantly longer for the person to begin and complete urination (Middlemist, Knowles, & Matter, 1976). It's disturbing to have someone enter your personal space, especially when your fly is unzipped!

on himself. Who from this group do you think the subjects rated as most attractive? The two superior students were rated higher than the two average students, but the superior student who committed the blunder was rated as most attractive of all. Apparently, the slightly clumsy pratfall made him more endearing to others. However, the blunder did not have the same positive effect for the average student: the one who blundered was rated least attractive of all.

Physical Attractiveness

Other things equal, people tend to be more attracted to physically beautiful people. In the absence of other information, we tend to like beautiful people more, and think of them as nicer, better adjusted, and more intelligent (Dion, 1980). Not only is physical attractiveness important, it seems to be the *most* important factor, at least in the early stages of attraction between dates.

Elaine Walster and colleagues randomly paired male and female college students for blind dates. They rated each student's physical attractiveness and gave them tests to measure attitudes, intelligence, and personality characteristics. After the blind dates, the students were asked how much they liked each other and whether they intended to go out on other dates with one another. The overwhelmingly important variable in determining attraction was physical attractiveness—more so than intelligence, personality, and attitudes. The couples who were most likely to like each other well enough to continue dating were the ones in which both the male and female were attractive (Walster, Aronson, Abrahams, & Rottman, 1966).

Physical attractiveness seems to be the most important factor in the early stages of attraction between people.

One of the key ways that physical attractiveness influences interpersonal attraction was demonstrated in an ingenious experiment (Snyder, Tauke, & Berscheid, 1977). Male and female college students played somewhat different roles in the study. Males were asked to participate in a study of how people get acquainted. They were asked to speak to a woman over a telephone (to rule out nonverbal communication), but each male was given written information describing the woman he was speaking to and a photograph of her.

The female subjects in the study were paired randomly with the males on the other end of the telephone, but the information sheets and pictures had nothing to do with them. All of the information sheets seen by the male subjects were the same, but half of the males saw a picture of a very attractive woman and half saw a picture of a much less attractive woman. After they had talked with her on the telephone, the men who thought they were talking to a beautiful woman rated her as being more sociable, poised, and humorous than did the men who thought they were talking to an unattractive woman. As in previous studies, greater physical attractiveness led to greater likability. But that's not the most interesting finding of this study.

When observers rated tape recordings of the males' conversations, they found that males who *thought* they were talking to a beautiful woman spoke to her in a more sociable way (e.g., warm, outgoing, interesting) and were rated as enjoying themselves more in the conversation. Thus, perceiving the woman as beautiful led the men to be more charming to her.

Perhaps even more interestingly, recorded conversations of the female subjects were also rated. They knew nothing about the pictures the men were seeing, but when the man thought that the woman was beautiful, the women spoke in a more charming, confident manner and were rated as seeming to like the man more. Apparently, thinking the woman was beautiful led the man to not only like the woman better from the start, but to treat her in a way that *induced her to act in her more likable way.* If Alan thinks he will like Eilleen because she is pretty, he will probably speak to her in ways that will bring out her most likable side. It's a lovely self-fulfilling prophecy, *if* you happen to be physically attractive.

But, don't despair; there may be some hope for the rest of us yet! While we might all prefer to be dating Robert Redford or Jacqueline Bisset, people tend actually to choose dates and mates who closely match themselves in degree of physical attractiveness (Berscheid, Dion, Walster, & Walster, 1971). What is more, physical beauty is a highly subjective quality. So, even if you do not think your next-door neighbor is much to look at, chances are that someone else will be coming along soon who thinks he or she is just beautiful.

Perhaps the nicest thing about physical attractiveness and liking, though, is that the relationship goes both ways. Not only is it true that we tend to like people better when we think they are beautiful, but as we get to like people better, we begin to think they are more beautiful (Langlois & Stephan, 1981). So to a certain extent, love *is* blind and beauty *is* in the eye of the beholder. And nothing could be nicer.

Mutual Liking

Let's end this discussion of factors involved in interpersonal attractiveness on an upbeat note. Liking often leads to liking in return. If Vicki likes Neal, she has made herself more attractive to Neal simply by liking him. Neal, if he is like most everyone else, will be more attracted to people who like him than to people who do not like him. Liking someone will not turn you into an irresistible beauty, but it will help.

One reason why this seems to be so is that liking someone will actually make you more *physically* attractive, especially if a little lust is thrown in. You have heard people say that a person is more beautiful when in love, and it's true. Your eyes are more attractive. The pupils are more dilated (opened) when you look at someone you find sexually attractive, and others find large pupils more attractive sexually (Hess, 1975). And your posture and movements are more attractive and seductive. In subtle ways, you are more physically alluring when you are attracted to another.

Another reason that liking tends to lead to liking is that you are nicer to the people that you like, and being nicer makes you more attractive to them. A number of studies show, for example, that we tend to like people more when they praise us or when they have done favors for us. Favors and praise feel nice and we like the giver better for having given them to us. So, send him flowers or give her a record—it might just tip the balance of love in your favor. As you might expect, there are limits on the impact of praise and favors. If they are excessive, and especially if the other person thinks you are insincere and have selfish motives for giving them, praise and gifts will not lead to increased liking and may even lessen the liking (Aronson, 1980).

Attribution Processes in Person Perception

The attribution process that we first encountered in the discussion of attitude change in this chapter is also very much involved in the perception of other people. We try to understand the behavior of others by attributing it to various causes. But the kinds of attributions that we make for the behavior of others have a great deal to do with the perceptions we form of them.

The attribution process is a step toward our ultimate goal in person perception. We want to know what other people are *really* like. We know how they behave but what is the person behind the behavior like? We want to know about the motives, values, and traits that make each person unique. The process of attribution allows us to make these judgments. For example, Sharon calls Bob

OF SPECIAL INTEREST

Is Romance More Important to Men or Women?

It's a commonly held stereotype that women are more concerned with romantic love than men. Men are seen as being interested in sex and domestic help, but not very concerned with romance. Women, in contrast, are viewed as approaching relationships in a more emotional, romantic way. The results of several surveys, however, suggest that not only is the popular stereotype incorrect, but that it may be just reversed. Men rate the desire to fall in love as being a more important reason for beginning a relationship than do women. Women see other qualities of the relationship such as respect and support as being more important. In one survey, two-thirds of male unmarried college students said they would not marry unless they felt romantic love for their prospective wife, while less than one-fourth of college women felt that romantic love was a prerequisite for marriage (Hill, Rubin, & Peplau, 1976; Kephart, 1967; Middlebrook, 1980). Apparently men value the presence of romantic love in their lives more than women.

---

on the telephone and hints strongly that she would go out to dinner with him if he asked. Why did Sharon do that? Is she trying to make her boyfriend jealous? Or is she attracted to Bob? The attribution that Bob makes will have important implications for whether he perceives Sharon as a manipulative or a sincere person.

Dispositional vs. Situational Attributions

Is Fred doing his homework because he loves math or because his parents are making him do it? Perhaps the most important aspect of the attribution process in person perception is deciding whether a person is behaving in a particular way because of some external cause (**situational attribution**) or because of an internal motive or trait (**dispositional attribution**). We tend to attribute behavior to situational causes when it *consistently* occurs in only that situation and when other people behave in the same way in the same situation. Otherwise, we tend to attribute other people's behavior to dispositional causes (Kelley, 1973). But because we often lack information on the extent to which a person's behavior is consistently influenced by situations, attribution can be a tricky business.

The attribution process is made more difficult by two strong *biases in attribution.* First, we have a tendency to attribute the behavior (both desirable and undesirable) of other people to dispositional causes. This leads to a certain amount of inaccuracy in person perception since we tend to underestimate the role of situational factors in determining the behavior of others. Second, males have a self-protective tendency to attribute their own behavior to dispositional causes when the behavior is desirable, but to attribute undesirable behavior to situational factors. This self-protective bias can lead to a serious lack of understanding since it leads to an overestimation of the extent to which desirable behavior is the result of personal characteristics and the extent to which undesirable behavior is the result of external factors.

situational attribution
An explanation for behavior that is based on an external cause.

dispositional attribution
(dis″po-zish′un-al)
An explanation for behavior that is based on a personal characteristic of the individual.

Many females, on the other hand, often do just the *opposite!* Women tend to attribute their successes to situational factors and their failures to dispositional causes (Deaux & Emswiller, 1974). This self-imposed sexist bias in women also leads to inaccurate self-perceptions, but ones that are much more painful than the self-protective distortions common among men.

Maintaining Relationships

We have talked about some of the factors that determine whether you will be attracted to another person. But how about the factors that are involved in maintaining relationships? Assuming that one of the people that you are attracted to becomes your friend, lover, or spouse, what things determine whether you and your partner will stay in the relationship? So many relationships that begin in joy end in a long cry. Why? Two of the major factors are the difference between what you expect to find in a relationship and what you actually find, and the degree to which the relationship is fairly balanced or equitable.

Expectations vs. Reality in Relationships

When you begin a relationship with someone you do not know very well, part of what you fall in love with is what you *expect* the person to be like. Some of these expectations may be based on good evidence. One of his friends has told you that he is an especially nice and fair person, so it's reasonable to expect him to be fair and nice to you. You know that he is in the same profession as you, so you can expect to be able to share your workday experiences easily with him. Other expectations are based on less evidence. He has behaved in a strong, self-assured way so far, so you assume that he will always be this way even though the biggest challenge you have seen him handle is the waiter's mistake of bringing vegetable soup instead of minestrone. You just *know* that he is a wonderful lover even though he has only just kissed you goodnight once. He dresses like an outdoorsman, so you expect him to love backpacking as much as you do. And he is well-educated so you feel sure he will share your love of serious literature.

The point is that, even when your expectations are fairly well-grounded, some of them will turn out to be incorrect. He will not be exactly like you expect him to be before the relationship begins. This is one primary reason why relationships end. If the other person turns out to be significantly different from the person you expected, you may be unwilling to stay in the relationship. This disappointment may not lead directly to an end of the relationship; it may affect the relationship indirectly. Disappointment can lead you to be an unenthusiastic or irritable partner, which can lead to discord and an unhappy ending (Graziano & Musser, 1982).

Relationships that last tend to be based on realistic expectations and on the perception of equity in the relationship.

Even when you know a person fairly well before beginning a serious relationship, differences between expectations and reality can be a problem. People change when the nature of their relationships change, as when children arrive, promotions are received, and so on. The problem of inaccurate expectations, however, is much less likely when the partners know each other well beforehand. (See *Research Report:* "The Unprecedented Divorce Rate.")

Equity in Relationships

Just as we are attracted to people who like us, praise us, and do nice things for us, we tend to stay in relationships in which the good things that we give to our partner are about equal to what our partner gives us. These good "things" that partners give to one another are many and varied. They include compliments, hot meals, back rubs, help with homework, a day off without the kids, flowers, jokes, making love, a willingness to listen about a bad day, kisses, pats on the bottom, and interesting conversations. They even include things like physical attractiveness (a nice looking person is enjoyable to look at), honesty, faithfulness, and integrity.

The commonsense idea that enduring relationships are ones in which the partners give and receive in equal proportion has been formalized and improved by social psychologists (Adams, 1965; Walster & Walster, 1978) under the name of **equity theory.** Equity theory states that partners will be comfortable in their relationship only when the ratio between their perceived contributions and benefits are equal. Equity theory is often summarized by the following equation:

equity theory
The theory that partners will be comfortable in their relationship only when the ratio between their perceived contributions and benefits is equal.

$$\frac{\text{Perceived benefits of person X}}{\text{Perceived contributions of person X}} = \frac{\text{Perceived benefits of person Y}}{\text{Perceived contributions of person Y}}$$

These benefits and contributions cannot be easily translated into numerical terms, but suppose for a moment that person X perceives that she "gives" 10 things to the relationship, while person Y perceives that he only gives 5 things. Would this be an equitable relationship? It would be if person X perceived 10 benefits from the relationship while person Y perceived 5 benefits because the equation would be in balance.

$$\frac{10}{10} = \frac{5}{5}$$

RESEARCH REPORT

The Unprecedented Divorce Rate: Are We Giving Up on Marriage?

Are we growing less interested in having long-term intimate relationships with a spouse? Until recently, the divorce rate in the United States has risen every year that records have been kept, particularly in the 1960s and 1970s. The rate is so high today that approximately 4 out of every 10 marriages end in divorce (National Center for Health Statistics, 1984). At the same time the rate of people living together without ever being married has also risen dramatically. Surveys have found that over 20 percent of all college and university students have lived with a person of the opposite sex without being married (Macklin, 1974). Do these statistics mean that Americans have given up on marriage? Not at all.

Couples who live together without being married rarely see living together as an alternative to marriage, but rather as a stage preceding marriage. Ninety-six percent of all students who live together expect to be happily married some day (Whitehurst, 1977) and more than 50 percent have definite plans to marry the person they are living with at a later date (Danziger & Greenwald, 1973).

Many psychologists also feel that the high divorce rate is not an indication that we are giving up on marriage. Overall, 90 percent of all Americans will be married at some point in their lives (Coleman, 1980). What is even more impressive is that over 80 percent of all divorced people remarry (Coleman, 1980). University of Oregon psychologist Robert Weiss (1975) has suggested that our steep rate of divorce reflects in part a growing determination on the part of Americans to have *good* marriages. Far from avoiding marriage, people with bad marriages are going through the pain of divorce in part to have a chance to try again later with another partner.

There is even some evidence that we may be getting better at making marriages last. For the first time on record, the rate of divorce declined slightly for the past two years for which statistics are available (1982 and 1983) (National Center for Health Statistics, 1984).

There are two important points to notice in the equity theory equation:

First, the benefits that the two people receive from one another do not have to be equal, but the *ratio* between their benefits and contributions must be equal. A person who both gives and receives a lot can be in an equitable relationship with a person who gives and receives much less.

Second, notice that the equation is written in terms of *perceived* benefits and contributions. The only person who can judge how much he is giving and receiving is the person himself. An outside observer might see a relationship as being highly inequitable when the partners themselves are very happy with it. Tender lovemaking might be highly important to one person, but much less important than good cooking to someone else. Unfortunately, people have a tendency to believe that the amount of "good things" that we ourselves should fairly receive is higher than the amount that we think that others should fairly receive (Messick & Sentis, 1979). If we are not careful to compensate for this natural perceptual distortion, it can lead us to perceive an inequity in our relationships when there is none at all.

If either member of a relationship perceives the relationship to be inequitable, that partner will either take steps to restore equity or will leave the relationship. Interestingly, we become uncomfortable in relationships either when we feel that we receive *too little* compared to what we give, *or* when we receive *too much* compared to what we give. In either case, we will be motivated to restore equity by giving more or less, or by asking (or in some other way inducing) the other person to give more or less.

R E V I E W

What determines which people we will like or love? Our perceptions of others can be thought of as being based on a complex cognitive algebra in which we reach a weighted average of all of the positive and negative characteristics we see in others. Person perception is complicated by several factors, however: different people evaluate the same characteristics in a person in different ways, and our emotional state influences person perception; negative information about a person carries more weight than positive information; first impressions usually are more important than later impressions.

Attribution plays an important role in our perceptions of others. We want to know what a person's enduring traits and motives are. We attribute the behavior of others to external causes (situational attributions) when it consistently occurs in only one kind of situation and they consistently react in the same way. Otherwise we tend to attribute the behavior of others to their supposed traits and motives (dispositional attributions). We also tend to attribute our own behavior to dispositional causes, but mostly our desirable behavior. We tend to attribute our undesirable behavior to situational causes, although females are less likely to do this than males.

Although the process of person perception is a highly complex and personal process, there are some general factors that determine whether one person will be attracted to another. Other things being equal, you are more likely to be attracted to a person who has characteristics similar to yours or who has opposite characteristics that complement your own. Other factors in attractiveness include the other person's being competent (but not excessively competent), physically attractive, and the other person's liking and being nice to you.

Once two people are attracted to each other, a number of other factors are involved in whether the relationship will endure. We enter into relationships partly because of our expectations as to what the other person will be like. Since those expectations are generally based on partial information, they are often not met and the relationship fails. Relationships generally fail, too, when they are not equitable. In happy relationships, each person perceives that there is a balance between what they put into the relationship and what they get out of it.

S U M M A R Y

Chapter 14 defines social psychology and explores the influence people have on other people, the nature of attitudes, and interpersonal attraction.

I. *Social psychology* is the branch of psychology that studies individuals as they interact with others.

II. Behavior is influenced by its social context.
   A. Two factors responsible for the ability of groups to alter the behavior of individuals are *diffusion of responsibility* and *modeling.*
   B. *Conformity* is yielding to group pressure even when no direct request to comply has been made.
   C. Persuasion is determined by the characteristics of the *speaker,* the *communication* itself, and the *people who hear it.*
      1. Three characteristics of the speaker are important: *credibility, attractiveness,* and *intent.*
      2. Two characteristics of the message are important determinants of persuasiveness: *emotional appeals* and *two-sided arguments.*
      3. Four characteristics of listeners help determine how persuasive an argument will be: the *intelligence* of the listeners, their *need for social approval,* their *self-esteem,* and the *audience size.*
   D. Research by Stanley Milgram indicates that authority figures can command substantial *obedience* from individuals. Obedience is greatest when we are instructed to do something by a person who is high in status, who is physically present, and when we are alone or in the presence of other obedient individuals.

III. Attitudes are beliefs that predispose us to act and feel in certain ways.
   A. Attitudes are learned from direct experience and from others.
   B. Attitudes can change. One theory that explains attitude change is Leon Festinger's *cognitive dissonance theory.* A rival hypothesis is called *attribution theory.*
   C. *Prejudice* is a negative attitude based on inaccurate generalizations about a group of people. The inaccurate generalization upon which the prejudice is based is called a *stereotype.*
   D. Stereotypes are harmful because they take away our ability to treat each member of a group as an individual and because they lead to faulty attributions.

IV. Friendship and love are powerful social phenomena based on the process of person perception.
   A. The process of *person perception* is complicated by the ways we gather and use information about others.
      1. Different people will perceive the same individual differently because of differences in weighting the importance of the same characteristics and even in viewing them as positive or negative.
      2. Negative information is generally weighted more than positive information in person perception.

3. First impressions (the primacy effect) generally influence person perception more than information learned later.
   a. The primacy effect is generally reduced under three conditions: *prolonged exposure, passage of time,* and *knowledge of primacy effects.*
4. Person perception is influenced by the emotional state of the perceiver.

B. Although many factors ensure that each individual's perception of an individual will be unique, there are some general factors that partly determine to whom we will be attracted: *similar* and *complementary characteristics, competence, physical attractiveness,* and *mutual liking.*

C. The attribution process is involved in the perception of others. One aspect of the attribution process is deciding if a person's behavior is caused by the situation (a *situational attribution*) or by a trait of the person (a *dispositional attribution*).

D. Two major factors in determining if a relationship will last are the difference between what you *expect* to find in a relationship and what you actually find, and the degree to which the relationship is fairly balanced or *equitable.*

Suggested Readings

1. A wonderfully readable, yet scholarly overview of social psychology:
   Aronson, E. (1980). *The social animal* (3rd ed.). San Francisco: W. H. Freeman.

2. The role of cognitive factors in social interactions is described in:
   Wyer, R. S., & Carlston, D. W. (1980). *Social cognition, inference and attribution.* Hillsdale, NJ: Lawrence Erlbaum.

3. Attitude change is discussed in scholarly, but understandable, terms in:
   Zimbardo, D., Ebbesen, E., & Maslach, C. (1977). *Influencing attitudes and changing behavior* (2nd ed.). Menlo Park, CA: Addison-Wesley.

4. An excellent summary of the major concepts of social psychology is found in:
   Baron, R., & Byrne, D. (1982). *Exploring social psychology* (2nd ed.). Boston: Allyn & Bacon.

FIFTEEN

Psychology Applied to Business and Other Professions

OUTLINE

KEY TERMS

A few years ago, Luis Costa was referred by his physician to psychologist Irving Beiman for treatment. On the surface, there is nothing notable about this fact, since thousands of patients are referred to psychologists every day in the United States. But the interesting aspect of this case is that Luis was not referred because of psychological problems; he was referred by his heart specialist for treatment of high blood pressure. Luis was 35 years old at the time of referral and had a three-year history of high blood pressure. His physician had tried to treat his condition with four different medications, but as sometimes happens, the medications had not been successful in reducing his blood pressure.

Luis became part of a new treatment program in *behavioral medicine*, a specialty of clinical psychology that seeks to develop psychological treatments for medical conditions. In Luis's case, his treatment was based on the assumption that his high blood pressure was caused by chronic, or prolonged, stress. As was discussed in chapters 2 and 12, stress produces arousal of the sympathetic division of the autonomic nervous system. In some cases, this is accompanied by increases in blood pressure since the autonomic nervous system not only plays a role in emotions, but also in the regulation of the heart, blood vessels, and other internal bodily organs. If stress is chronic in a person's life—as might happen when an individual holds a stressful job or is involved in a conflict-laden marriage— the high blood pressure can sometimes become chronic. This is not to say that stress always leads to high blood pressure, but it apparently does in some people.

To combat his stress-induced high blood pressure, a program was initiated to teach Luis to relax in the face of stressful situations. Thus he began a behavior therapy called *progressive relaxation training*, a technique originally developed to alleviate anxiety, which will be described in more detail later in the chapter. This involved learning to monitor the amount of tension in different muscle groups and deeply relaxing each muscle group on demand. This was done because relaxation inhibits sympathetic arousal and could be expected to influence Luis's blood pressure. Like learning any new skill, progressive relaxation training requires considerable practice. In Luis's case, seven sessions in the clinic were required during a period of 42 days before he fully mastered deep muscle relaxation. After each practice session, the psychologist also helped Luis identify frequently occurring stressful situations and recommended that he practice relaxing each time those situations occurred.

Happily, Luis's blood pressure steadily fell as he mastered the skill of deep muscle relaxation. Figure 15.1, on the next page, shows his blood pressure as measured both during the contraction of the heart *(systolic blood pressure)* and while the heart rests between beats *(diastolic blood pressure)*. Before treatment began, Luis's systolic blood pressure was about 140 and his diastolic pressure was around 100. As treatment progressed, both blood pressures fell approximately 20 points and remained at that level during several follow-up evaluations conducted during the six months after treatment. These changes dropped his blood pressure into the normal range and kept it there (Beiman, Graham, & Ciminero, 1978). The successful treatment of Luis Costa is just one example of the many ways that psychology has been applied in medicine in recent years. Moreover, many similar applications have been made to business, law, education, and other professions.

P R E V I E W

Psychology is both a scientific and an applied field. The job of many psychologists is to apply the principles and methods of psychology to the solution of human problems. Most applied psychologists work in clinical psychology, and partly as a result we are better able to treat psychological problems today than ever before in history. But clinical psychology is only one of the ways in which psychology has been successfully applied to human concerns.

Psychologists working in business seek to increase the satisfaction we derive from our jobs and to improve our productivity in those jobs. They do so by using their knowledge of psychological assessment to find the right person for the right job, by using knowledge of social relationships to improve methods of managing workers, and by designing the physical characteristics of the job to fit the psychological characteristics of people. Psychologists working in the field of medicine motivate and persuade people to live healthier lives through dieting, exercising, not smoking, and the like. In addition, psychological methods have been used in the direct treatment of some types of medical problems. Psychologists have long been involved in the courtroom practice of law as expert witnesses on questions of insanity, but in recent years have studied the behavior of the people involved in the trial process—jurors, witnesses, attorneys, and others. These studies have shown, among other things, that the psychological characteristics of jurors are related to the likelihood of their voting for conviction and harsh punishments, and that a number of psychological factors are involved even in the presentation of the evidence. Psychologists working in the field of education have used their knowledge of learning and cognition to develop improved ways of educating children, especially those who are slow learners and who might not have previously been able to fully benefit from their time in school. Whenever a profession involves the welfare of *people*, psychology has the potential to help that profession better meet its goals.

Figure 15.1 Changes in systolic and diastolic blood pressure before, during, and after treatment using progressive relaxation training. Dots represent daily blood pressure recorded at home (averaged over two-day periods) and stars represent blood pressure recordings made in the psychologist's office (Beiman, Graham & Ciminero, 1978).

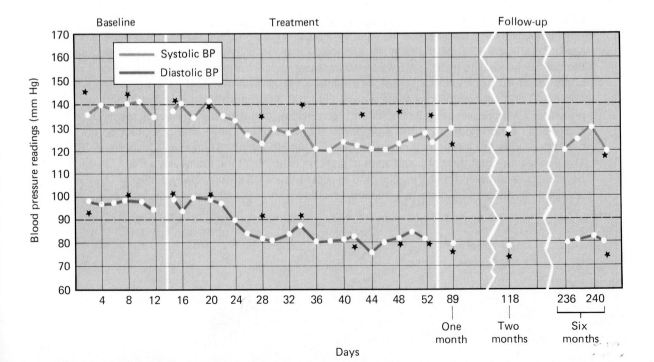

Psychology in Business: Employees Are People, Too

When you think of the word "business," do the words "happiness" and "quality of life" come to mind? No? They should, because business is linked to the quality of our lives in important ways. The standard of living that we enjoy in terms of material goods and services is the end product of business. Your car, clothes, haircut, record album, and newspaper would not exist without the multifaceted business sector. The quality of our lives is also linked to the satisfaction that comes from our work. Most men and women spend a major part of their lives working for pay. The impact that our jobs have on our sense of well-being depends on whether those jobs are boring and demeaning or meaningful and rewarding.

Psychologists who work for business are known as **industrial-organizational psychologists.** They attempt to improve the human benefits of business in a number of ways. For example, they seek ways to help businesses produce more goods and services, to increase job satisfaction by changing methods of management and training, and to fit "the right person to the right job" by modifying methods of employee selection. To be sure, psychological principles are sometimes used to improve profits rather than human lives—such as by developing advertisements that are more persuasive than informative—but such abuses are the exception rather than the rule for professional psychologists in business today.

Personnel departments are where industrial-organizational psychologists can most frequently be found, since employee selection and training is the primary responsibility of these departments. Some large companies employ one or more psychologists to work in personnel, and the undergraduate or graduate education of the personnel manager is often in psychology. Other companies hire the services of industrial-organizational psychologists who work for independent consulting firms. They teach both personnel and general managers to put the principles of psychology to work in helping people contribute more effectively and happily to the goals of the business.

Some industrial-organizational psychologists work for consumers rather than business. They are employed by government or public-interest groups performing such jobs as helping consumers make more informed choices in their purchases.

industrial-organizational psychologist
A psychologist who studies organizations and seeks ways to improve the functioning and human benefits of business.

Industrial-organizational psychologists seek ways to help businesses produce more goods and services, to increase job satisfaction among employees, and to improve employee selection.

Psychologists have learned that applicants with average qualifications rate higher if they are interviewed after two poorly qualified candidates than if they are interviewed after two highly qualified candidates.

Employee Selection and Evaluation

Recall from chapters 1 and 7 that France's Alfred Binet gave us the first practical way of measuring intelligence around the turn of the century. Since Binet's time, numerous useful ways of measuring behavior have been used in educational, clinical, and business settings. In business, the most significant use of psychological measurements has been in the selection and hiring of new employees and the evaluation of current employees so as to make decisions on raises and promotions. The measures most commonly used in employee decisions include interviews, evaluations of biographical data (biodata), paper-and-pencil tests, performance tests, job performance ratings, and the evaluation of simulated job performance in assessment centers.

Interviews

interview
A subjective method of personality assessment that involves questioning techniques designed to reveal the personality of the client.

The traditional heart of the process of evaluating job applicants, **interviews** play a significant role in the assessment of current employees for possible promotion to jobs of higher responsibility. Interviews are more or less structured conversations in which the employee or job applicant is questioned about his or her training, experience, future goals, and so on. The suitability of the individual for the job is evaluated partly in terms of factual answers to questions, but also in terms of the individual's personality, spoken language, potential for leadership, and other personal factors.

The role of the industrial-organizational psychologist has been to educate personnel specialists and other managers as to the nature and limitations of interviews. We discussed some of the problems inherent in interviews, such as the importance of primacy effects or "first impressions," when we discussed the general process of person perception in chapter 14. Industrial-organizational psychologists have discovered a great many other factors that interfere with our

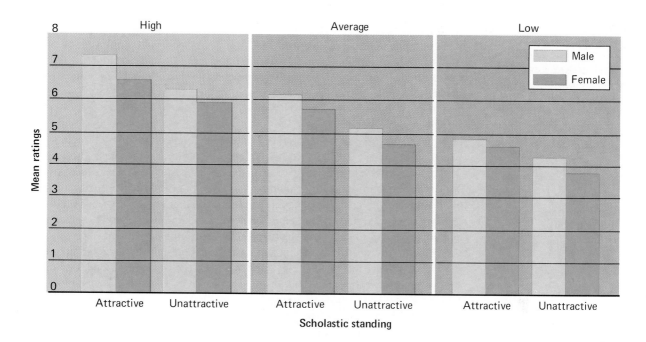

Figure 15.2 Ratings by personnel recruiters from businesses of 12 hypothetical job applicants (six male and six female) who were portrayed as high, medium, or low in academic achievement, and attractive or unattractive (Dipboye, Fromkin & Wilback, 1975).

ability to form objective impressions of people in interviews. For example, the *order* in which job applicants are interviewed sometimes influences our opinion of the applicants. If an applicant of average qualifications is interviewed after two poorly qualified applicants, his or her ratings will be much higher than if interviewed after two highly qualified applicants. The contrast with previously interviewed applicants makes applicants with average qualifications look better or worse than they really are. Fortunately, ratings of highly qualified and poorly qualified applicants are not influenced by previously interviewed applicants. Their ratings are essentially the same regardless of the quality of the applicants who were interviewed just before them (Wexley, Yukl, Kovacs, & Sanders, 1977).

In a study that may hit close to home for you, 30 employment interviewers who recruit on college campuses were shown 12 hypothetical résumés of college students and asked to rate them for a beginning managerial position in a department store. Four of the résumés described individuals with high-scholastic achievement, four described average-scholastic achievement, and four described low-scholastic achievement. In each of these three groups (high-, average-, or low-scholastic achievement), the pictures attached to the résumés were of an attractive male, an attractive female, an unattractive male, or an unattractive female. After reading chapter 14, you will not be surprised by the results of the study. As figure 15.2 shows, scholastic achievement was the most important factor in determining the ratings of the hypothetical applicants. But within each level of achievement, attractive applicants were consistently rated higher than unattractive applicants, and males were rated higher than females (Dipboye, Fromkin, & Wilback, 1975). Although this study used résumés and photos rather than live interviews, physical attractiveness and sex can be expected to play a role in interview evaluations as well. Fortunately, employment interviewers can be trained by industrial-organizational psychologists to reduce somewhat the effects of such irrelevant factors in job interviews (Wexley, Sanders, & Yukl, 1973).

biodata
The biographical
information used by
potential employers to
evaluate a job candidate.

Biodata

The biographical data, or **biodata,** that we give our potential employers on employment application blanks often plays an important role in determining whether we are hired. Examples of biodata are previous job history, hobbies, education, and special skills. Often such biodata is used in the employment selection process in sophisticated ways that are based on careful research. To use a purely hypothetical example, suppose a life insurance company did a study of the biodata of their most and least successful sales agents and found that most of their successful agents are active in sports, attended community colleges, and know how to type, but very few of their unsuccessful agents have these same characteristics. That information might lead the company to give preference in hiring new agents to individuals who have those specific biodata. You can readily see why I had to use a hypothetical example: Companies generally will not reveal the actual biodata they use so that applicants cannot fake their biographical histories.

Biodata is generally used in employee selection only by large companies who employ their own psychologist and who must hire large numbers of employees to perform the same kind of job. This is the case because large amounts of biographical data must be amassed on the characteristics of successful and unsuccessful employees in a specific job before biodata can be used meaningfully. In some instances, the interpretation of biodata is made by a consulting psychologist who has gathered data from the performance of employees in a particular job slot from many different companies.

Paper-and-Pencil Tests

Paper-and-pencil tests are another important part of the evaluation of employees and job applicants. Employers need a wide variety of tests in order to evaluate different characteristics in employees for different jobs. Some highly general tests are used, such as general intellectual ability and personality tests, but tests developed by psychologists to measure specific skills and abilities are also frequently used. For example, spelling and reading tests are often given to applicants for secretarial and clerical jobs, because applicants who are more skilled in these areas can generally be expected to perform better on jobs like typing and proofreading.

Applicants for mechanical and engineering jobs are often given tests like those pictured in figures 15.3 and 15.4 that tap abilities to mentally visualize spatial relationships and to understand mechanical concepts. And applicants for sales positions are frequently given tests of sales aptitude. These tests describe problematic situations that often arise in sales work and require the applicant to choose the best course of action from a number of options. These are only a few of the variety of pencil-and-paper tests that are used today.

Performance Tests

Tests that measure actual manual performance are often used in the selection of assembly-line workers, equipment repair specialists, and the like. **Performance tests** are based on the assumption that the only valid way to find out if applicants can work with their hands is to evaluate them while they are actually working. The Purdue Pegboard is an example of this kind of performance test (see fig. 15.5). In this test, pins, collars, and washers are fitted together in holes in a number

performance test
Employee selection test that
resembles the actual
manual performance
required in a job.

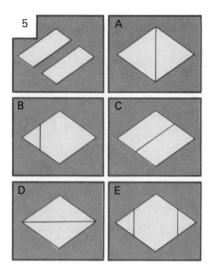

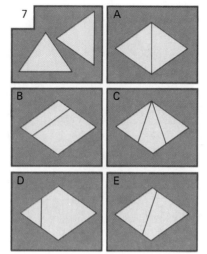

Figure 15.3 Sample items from a test designed to measure an individual's ability to visualize spatial relationships (The Psychological Corporation, 1969).

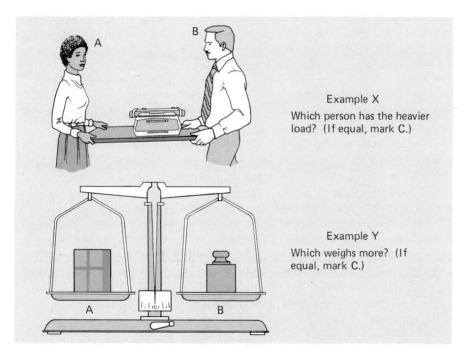

Example X

Which person has the heavier load? (If equal, mark C.)

Example Y

Which weighs more? (If equal, mark C.)

Figure 15.4 Sample items from a paper-and-pencil test designed to measure an individual's mechanical comprehension (The Psychological Corporation, 1982).

Figure 15.5 An example of a performance test that might be used to select employees for a job assembling small machine parts.

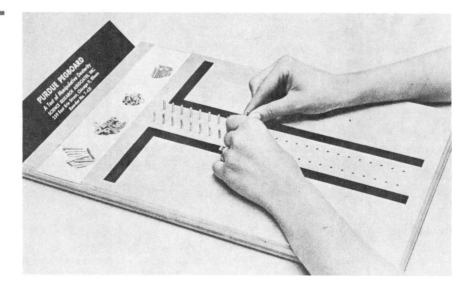

of different ways specified by the tester to evaluate the applicant's manual speed and accuracy. Other types of performance tests may resemble the job to be performed even more. Applicants for typist jobs are asked to type in timed tests; forklift operators are asked to drive forklifts in a prescribed path; and potential recruits for professional baseball teams are given a chance to bat against professional pitchers. Each performance test provides a sample of behavior that can be used to predict actual performance on the job.

Ratings of Job Performance

Not all evaluation methods are used to select the best job applicants; some are designed to evaluate current employees. Such evaluations determine raises, promotions, and even whether the individual will continue to be employed. The most widely used method of assessing current employees is **job performance ratings.** There are a number of different types of performance ratings, but each is designed by industrial-organizational psychologists to transform a supervisor's rating of the employee's actual job performance into a numerical evaluation.

job performance ratings
Ratings of the actual performance of employees in their jobs by supervisors.

In job performance ratings, the employee is rated on a number of different dimensions of job performance. The supervisor checks the statement that best describes the employee from most to least desirable. Three job dimensions from a hypothetical multiple-step rating scale are shown in figure 15.6. The statements are each assigned a value (5, 4, 3, 2, 1) so the ratings can be easily scored numerically and summed across all of the dimensions to obtain an overall evaluation of the employee.

Checklists provide numerical evaluations of job performance in a somewhat different way. Supervisors are asked to read a series of statements such as the following:

_____ Doesn't repeat same mistakes
_____ Orderly in work habits
_____ Effective leader
_____ Has good judgment
_____ Has creative ideas

Dependability				
Unsatisfactory	Below average	Average	Above average	Outstanding
Requires constant supervision to ensure that directions are followed □	Requires considerable supervision. Does not always follow directions □	Requires average or normal supervision □	Can usually be depended upon to complete assignments □	Needs virtually no supervision; completely reliable □
Quantity of work				
Unsatisfactory	Below average	Average	Above average	Outstanding
Consistently below job requirements □	Frequently below job requirements □	Meets job requirements □	Frequently exceeds job requirements □	Consistently exceeds job requirements □
Job knowledge				
Unsatisfactory	Below average	Average	Above average	Outstanding
Unsatisfactory □	Below average □	Average □	Knows job well □	Thorough knowledge □

Figure 15.6 Examples of items from a multiple-step rating scale like those used to evaluate employee performance. The rater marks one category for each item (McCormick & Ilgen, 1980).

The supervisor checks those items that are characteristic of the employee. Each characteristic is assigned a numerical value according to how important it is for the job, with the sum of these values giving the overall evaluation of the employee. Many varieties of job performance ratings are used for the assessment of different types of employees when numerical evaluations are needed.

Assessment Centers

Decisions on the hiring or promotion of managers in large companies are often based in part on evaluations made in **assessment centers.** Assessment centers are conducted usually by a team of upper managers and outside psychological consultants. Several candidates for the same position are brought together in the assessment center so they can be intensively evaluated outside of the usual work environment. Although this technique was developed during World War II to evaluate officer candidates, it has only recently become a popular method of management selection (Bray, Campbell, & Grant, 1974).

assessment center
Center or program for the evaluation of employees that uses simulated management tasks as its primary method of evaluation.

simulated management task
A contrived task requiring managerial skills that is given to candidates for management positions to evaluate their potential as managers.

in-basket exercise
A type of management simulation task in which the individual attempts to solve a problem that is typical of the ones that appear in a manager's "in basket."

Assessment centers use traditional methods of evaluating the candidates for promotion such as interviews and tests, but the distinctive feature of the approach is the evaluation of candidates while they are carrying out **simulated management tasks.** A frequently used simulation is the **In-Basket Exercise.** The candidate is given a problem that might show up in the "in basket" of the new management position. For example, the candidate might be given a memo from a female employee stating that her male supervisor has upset her with his subtle hints that she could rise more quickly in the company if she would have a sexual relationship with him. The candidate would then be asked to discuss the problem with two people playing the roles of the employee and her supervisor. Ratings would be made of the performance of the candidate in this and other simulation exercises and would become a part of the basis for the hiring or promotion decision.

Validity of Job Selection Measures

One major purpose of the measures described above (biodata, performance tests, etc.) is to increase the productivity of industry and government by selecting employees who will better perform their jobs. How good are these methods in improving employee selection? To use a term introduced in our discussion of intelligence tests in chapter 7, how *valid* are these measures?

An excellent summary of the extensive research on this topic has been provided by Michigan State University psychologists John and Rhonda Hunter (1984). Their summary indicates marked differences in the validity of the several measures, with paper-and-pencil tests of intellectual ability generally being the best predictors of later job performance and success in job-training programs. The intellectual ability tests used are sometimes full intelligence (IQ) tests, but are more often less comprehensive tests of more specific intellectual abilities.

Current research suggests that the use of intellectual ability tests considerably improves the selection of employees. For example, Hunter (1979) calculated that if the city of Philadelphia, Pennsylvania, stopped using an intellectual ability test for the selection of police officers, it would lose $170 million over a 10-year period. These dollar losses would result from the increased cost of training officer candidates who could not pass the course or had to be fired later, needing more officers to complete the same amount of work, and the like.

Hunter and Hunter (1984) also found that performance tests, assessment centers, and biodata were valid measures, but were less useful than intellectual ability tests in selecting employees for most jobs. For example, Hunter (1981) indicated that the federal government's use of intellectual ability tests in its hiring of approximately 460,000 new employees each year saves the government $15.6 billion compared to hiring at random. In contrast, the use of biodata—the second most valid method—would save the federal government only $10.5 billion, a loss of $5.1 billion. In addition, interviews generally have been found to be the least valid method of the methods we have discussed for selecting more productive employees. But projective personality tests and handwriting analyses have been found not to be valid at all for employee selection (Reilly & Chao, 1982).

Intellectual ability tests are the most valid selection measures for a wide range of jobs, but not for all jobs. Intellectual ability tests are superior in selecting employees for more complex jobs (sales, managerial, etc.), but performance tests are better when the job is less complex (vehicle operator, semiskilled factory worker, etc.). Supervisor ratings of current job performance cannot, of course, be used to select new employees. However, they can be used when all applicants are given the opportunity to try out for the job. The method of *job tryouts,* however, is both much more expensive and less valid than intellectual ability tests.

Fair Selection of Minority Employees

The use of intellectual ability tests for the selection of employees raises a number of important questions about the hiring of minority applicants. For example, because blacks score lower, on the average, on intellectual ability tests than whites, the use of such tests in employee selection means that a smaller proportion of black applicants would be selected by the test than whites. For example, if an intellectual ability test is used that selects 50 percent of the white applicants, it would select an average of only 16 percent of black applicants (Hunter & Hunter, 1984). Not only does this raise social and ethical questions of fairness, but it also raises legal issues. In some circumstances, this result of the use of intellectual ability tests would be considered illegal.

What is the cause and the proper cure for this dilemma? Hunter and Hunter (1984) offer an informed opinion, but it is not one with which everyone will agree; indeed, it and all conceivable alternatives are sure to generate considerable controversy. To make sense of Hunter and Hunter's proposal, we need to think back to chapter 7 again. Some psychologists have argued that minority groups score lower than whites on intellectual ability tests because the tests reflect information and skills that are emphasized in the white culture and are, hence, biased against people from minority groups (e.g., Williams, 1972). Hunter and Hunter argue, however, that intellectual ability tests are just as valid in predicting job performance for minorities as they are for whites. Although the average scores of black and white groups of applicants are different, a given score on the test predicts exactly the same level of performance for blacks as for whites. Therefore, Hunter and Hunter suggest that differences in intellectual ability scores reflect the disadvantages and prejudice faced by minorities in our society rather than "cultural bias" in the tests.

But, if intellectual ability tests are indeed valid for minorities, what do we do about the inequities in hiring produced by the use of such tests? Hunter and Hunter (1984) argue that if we as a society take the position that hiring equal proportions of minority groups will help eliminate some of the economic disadvantages faced by minorities, then the question is not whether to use intellectual ability tests, but *how* to use them. Their position is based partly on the fact that not using these tests would hurt *all* job applicants—including minority applicants—since they would have to be replaced by less valid selection methods.

How, then, can intellectual ability tests be used in a manner that will promote fair hiring of minority groups? There are two primary alternatives. One is to lower the required score on the test and select qualifying minority and white applicants at random. This approach, according to Hunter and Hunter, would not only result in the employment of many poorly qualified people from all groups, but also would not even ensure that a fair number of minorities would be hired. The alternative is to set quotas for each minority group and then hire the most qualified applicants in each group. Hunter and Hunter suggest that this method would achieve the goal of racial balance at the expense of hiring fewer unqualified individuals. They estimate that if the federal government used the first method, it would cost $13.1 billion to achieve racial balance, whereas the latter method would cost $780 million (one-seventeenth as much). This approach, like all others, however, is sure to generate ethical and legal controversy for some time to come.

Job Satisfaction and Productivity

Psychologists working in business have two inherently important goals: to improve the satisfaction of employees and to improve their productivity. The goals of improved job satisfaction and productivity can be met in two principal ways. As we have just discussed, one is to use methods of employee selection to match the right person with the right job. The other way is to improve working conditions, particularly the ways in which employees are managed and supervised. We first look at the relationship between job satisfaction and productivity, then examine the ways in which supervisory style, and managerial, organizational, and physical conditions are related to these goals.

Are happy workers productive workers? That has been the assumption of industrial-organizational psychologists for many years, but recent research suggests that it often is not the case (Iaffaldano & Muchinsky, 1985). Job satisfaction is not related to how well employees perform in most instances, probably because productivity is influenced by so many different factors (McCormick & Ilgen, 1980). For example, one worker may be highly productive because she is *unsatisfied* with her job as a clerk and hopes her high level of productivity will get her selected for the management trainee program. Another worker may love his job, but may be unproductive because he likes his coworkers and does not want to anger them by producing more than they do.

But although job satisfaction is not directly related to productivity, it's good for the business as well as the employee. High job satisfaction improves the profits of businesses in the following ways:

1. Reducing employee turnover, the rate at which employees quit and seek new jobs;

2. Reducing absenteeism, the frequency with which employees fail to show up for work;

3. Improving relations between labor and management;

4. Improving the ability of businesses to recruit good employees; and

5. Improving the reputation that employees give to a business by what they say about it in the community (Anastasi, 1979).

Management Strategies to Improve Job Satisfaction and Productivity

Thus, although productivity and job satisfaction are not directly linked, keeping employees satisfied with their jobs is indirectly good for business in the ways listed above. This is a happy state of affairs since it gives employers a strong economic reason for improving the job satisfaction of their workers. Fortunately,

Job satisfaction is not directly related to productivity. But it's good for both the business and the employee because it reduces employee turnover and absenteeism.

there is another strong economic incentive for businesses to adopt management policies that enhance job satisfaction: Many of the management practices that lead to higher job satisfaction also improve productivity.

Three major strategies are used to improve both job satisfaction and productivity:

1. *Improving supervisory style.* The most effective managers and supervisors are *considerate* (warm, friendly, and concerned in dealing with employees) and *communicative* (can clearly tell employees what is expected of them and how they will be evaluated on their performance). In addition, the most effective supervisors are also often high in **structuring** (spending a great deal of time organizing and directing the work of their employees). However, being high in structuring is only an advantage when the supervisor is also highly considerate. It may even be a disadvantage when less considerate supervisors closely structure their employees' activities (Anastasi, 1979).

    structuring
    Activities of managers that organize and direct the work of employees.

2. *Improving managerial organization.* In recent years, a great deal of attention has been paid to how the efforts of management are organized. Do messages always come down from top management or are employees involved in decision making to some extent? Are employees told specifically how to work, or are they given specific production goals but allowed freedom in the ways they meet those goals? Does it make any difference? Two strategies of managerial organization that appear to make a significant difference in promoting job satisfaction and productivity are *participative management* and *management by objectives*.

participative management
The practice of involving employees at all levels in management decisions.

In the **participative management** method, employees at every level of the business are actively involved in decision making. For instance, when a dressmaking plant must change over to making a new line of clothes, the sewing machine operators would work out the most efficient ways to do this in discussions with their supervisors. The supervisors would link this decision-making process to higher management by participating in decision-making conferences with their supervisors, who would then participate in decisions with the next level of management, and so on up to the top. In a classic example of the benefits of participative management, employees of the Weldon Pajama Factory showed an almost 50 percent increase in productivity and earning when such a system was introduced (Likert, 1967).

Another effective strategy of managerial organization is **management by objectives.** In this approach, employees are given a specific goal to accomplish—anything from producing 1,000 dishes per month, to reducing air pollution from the factory by 80 percent, to reducing corporate taxes by 20 percent—but they are given considerable freedom in *how* they meet those objectives. This method benefits the company since it ensures that management focuses on what is really important to the company (its objectives). But management by objectives also gives employees a greater sense of independence and an easier way to tell if they are doing a good job of meeting their goals. Often management by objectives is used along with a participative management strategy, allowing employees at all levels to participate in the setting and reviewing of goals. Increasingly, too, the meeting and exceeding of goals is often tied to bonuses, thus giving the employee positive reinforcement for greater productivity in the form of greater monetary income (McCormick & Ilgen, 1980).

management by objectives
The strategy of giving employees specific goals but giving them considerable freedom in deciding how to reach those goals.

3. *Improving physical conditions.* Considerable research has been done by industrial-organizational psychologists on the influence of physical conditions (such as lighting, noise, and temperature) on productivity and job satisfaction. For example, psychologists have found that working in 95-degree temperatures produces significant increases in perceptual and decision-making errors after four to five hours on the job (Fine & Kobrick, 1978). Considerable attention has also been paid to the design of machines that fit well with the psychological characteristics of the human beings who will be operating them. (See *Research Report:* "Environmental psychology" and *Of Special Interest:* "Human factors engineering.")

Industrial-organizational psychologists have done considerable research on the influence of physical conditions at work, such as lighting, noise, and temperature, and on productivity and job satisfaction.

Other Applications of Psychology to Business

We have sampled a few of the ways in which psychology has been applied to business, but there are many others. Psychological principles and methods have been used in developing methods of training new employees and in developing the potential of current employees through continued education. When IBM hires a new person to repair computers, he or she must first be trained to do it. When Prudential promotes a salesperson to a sales management position, he or she must be taught how to manage sales. When McDonald's hires a new management trainee, he or she must be trained in purchasing, hiring, the safe storage of foods, and so on. When the number of employees that need training is multiplied by the number of jobs they must learn, it's easy to see why the efficiency of business depends in part on the efficiency of their training programs.

Psychologists have also contributed to the advertising and marketing end of business. Advertising is almost as old as civilization itself. Excavation of the ruins of the ancient city of Pompeii, for example, found announcements of the availability of products and services painted on the walls of buildings (Anastasi, 1979). And psychologists have been trying to find ways to improve the effectiveness of advertising almost as long as there has been a field of psychology. The first book of the psychology of advertising was published by Walter Scott in 1908.

Psychologists have found that a number of perceptual factors such as size, color, repetition, and spatial position influence the effectiveness of advertisements. For example, half-page magazine ads are noticed by readers only half as often as full-page ads, and full-color ads are read by 50 percent more readers than black-and-white ads (Anastasi, 1979).

R E S E A R C H   R E P O R T

Environmental Psychology:
Psychological Aspects of Architecture and Interior Design

Architects and interior designers strive to create environments where people can live and work more happily, healthily, and productively. In recent years, psychologists have become actively involved in these fields, particularly in the study of psychological reactions to different aspects of the physical environment. Most findings to date have been interesting, but perhaps not surprising. For example, people perceive others in less positive ways and are less interested in socializing in drab, ugly rooms than they are in attractive rooms (Maslow & Mintz, 1956; Russell & Mehrabian, 1978). Adding touches like potted plants and an aquarium to professors' offices makes students feel more welcome (Campbell, 1978). And people are less positive toward others in hot rooms than in comfortable rooms (Griffith & Veitch, 1971).

Other findings have been less expected and have contributed more to architecture and interior design. For example, a popular trend today is to design office space in the so-called *office landscape* format. In this format, offices are laid out in large open spaces and separated from one another only by low movable partitions, desks, and file cabinets. This creates a space that can be flexibly rearranged, is inexpensive to construct, and is attractive in appearance. Contrary to expectation, however, studies of the psychological effects of office landscapes have not painted a positive picture. One study was conducted after a number of workers moved from a building with traditional separate offices into a new building that was equally divided into traditional offices and an office landscape area. After six months, workers who moved into the office landscape area were considerably less satisfied with their surroundings. They reported that they interacted more with each other, but they cooperated less. In addition, they found the new office area less private and noisier, and reportedly accomplished less work (Hundert & Greenfield, 1969).

Another study of the effects of alternative architectural designs has produced interesting results that favor the innovative design. Traditional plans for college dormitories call for a single long corridor onto which a number of small rooms open. Typically, the residents of these rooms share a single common lounge and bathroom that are also located off the corridor. In contrast to this traditional single corridor design, the new look in college dormitories is the suite design. In this concept, three or four rooms are clustered around a small lounge and bathroom shared only by the residents of that one suite. Proponents of the suite design concept suggest that although the same number of people can be housed per square foot in this design (see figure 15.7), it's a far more "human" approach to dense housing. In this case, psychological studies have rather strongly supported the suite design concept. Residents of single corridor dorms spend less time in the dorms, express greater desire to avoid interaction with other residents, and feel that they have less control over what happens in their dormitory than residents of suite design dorms (Baum & Valins, 1977).

Even more impressive is the finding that the effects of living in a single corridor dorm extend outside of the dorm setting. Freshmen living in both types of dorms were brought to a laboratory where they were asked to wait with other students in a waiting room. Residents of single corridor dorms initiated fewer conversations, sat at greater physical distance from the other students, and spent less time looking at the faces of other students. Apparently, their unsatisfactory living environment led them to be somewhat less sociable even outside of the dormitory (Baum, Harpin, & Valins, 1975). If you live in a single corridor dorm, you should not be concerned about lasting damage to your social life, but it may have some minor effect on your current behavior.

R E S E A R C H   R E P O R T

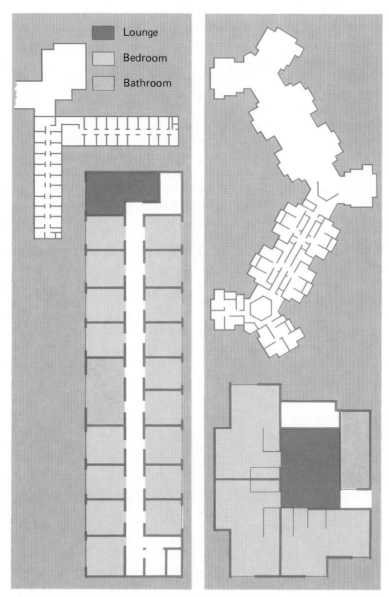

Figure 15.7 Examples of the single corridor and suite design floor plans for college dormitories (Baum & Valins, 1977).

OF SPECIAL INTEREST

Human Factors Engineering

We live in a technological society where more and more of our work is done by machines. But machines must be operated by people, so increasingly the work of people has become the operation of machines. For this reason, one branch of industrial-organizational psychology, known as **human factors engineering**, has as its goal the design of machines that can be more easily and efficiently operated by human beings.

To take a complex example, airplane pilots must operate a number of different manual controls while their eyes are occupied looking at radar, reading gauges, and watching where the plane is going. The job of the human factors engineer is to design manual controls in a way that will make them easier and safer to use. In this case, the controls would probably be designed in a way that makes use of the pilot's sense of touch, because controls do not have to be seen to be perceived. Controls of different shapes can be easily distinguished by touch and are particularly easy to use if their shape is related to their function as shown in figure 15.8. Human factors research has also found controls are more easily operated when they are located next to the dial that they influence rather than in separate clusters (see figure 15.9), and when the direction of turning a control matches the direction of the corresponding dial (see figure 15.10).

Taking a different approach to improving the interface between people and machines, human factors engineers have found that short rest periods greatly improve efficiency in many tasks. For example, workers who need to detect infrequent visual signals, such as an air traffic controller would have to do, have been found to maintain nearly perfect accuracy over an hour and a half when they take a 10-minute break every 30 minutes. When the workers do not take breaks, however, their accuracy in detecting the signals falls below 75 percent after being on the job for more than 30 minutes (Bergum & Lehr, 1962). These examples show only a few of the many ways that human factors engineers help make the marriage between people and machines happier, safer, and more efficient.

human factors engineering
The branch of industrial-organizational psychology interested in the design of machines to be operated by human beings.

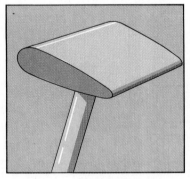

Landing flap

Landing gear

Figure 15.8 An example of controls that are designed to be easily distinguished by touch and related in form to their function (McCormick & Ilgen, 1980).

OF SPECIAL INTEREST

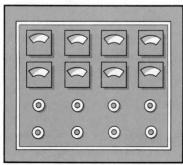
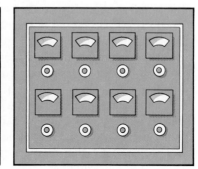

Acceptable arrangement   Preferred arrangement

Figure 15.9 Examples of controls and dials arranged to fit the cognitive characteristics of human operators (McCormick & Ilgen, 1980).

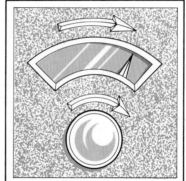
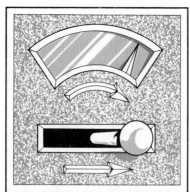
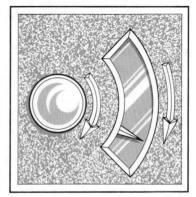

Figure 15.10 Examples of controls designed to operate in a way that is compatible with the direction of operation of the corresponding dial (McCormick & Ilgen, 1980).

Attempts to improve advertising effectiveness often involve emotional appeals. Recall from chapter 14 that fear appeals are sometimes effective in making communications more persuasive. Advertisers of mouthwash, toothpaste, hair dye, and the like would have us believe that if we do not use their products we will be coldly rejected by the people we care about. Manufacturers of boots, bathing suits, perfumes, and sports cars similarly suggest in their ads that if we buy their goods we will be adored by members of the opposite sex.

Psychologists in industry also work to find ways to improve the health and safety of employees by determining the rest periods needed between strenuous work periods, the safest ways to design machines, and so on. Other psychologists conduct surveys to determine the preferences of consumers. Others conduct research to determine the best ways to convey information about the contents of foods and drugs to consumers. Still others concentrate on reducing prejudice and other barriers to equal opportunities for minority groups in business. The roles for psychologists in business are as varied as the business sector of society is itself.

R E V I E W

The quality of our lives is linked to business in terms of both our enjoyment of the goods and services business produces and the satisfaction that we derive from our jobs. Industrial-organizational psychologists help business improve its productivity and help workers obtain more meaning and enjoyment from their jobs. Psychologists most frequently work through personnel departments since they have responsibility for selecting and training employees. They work to improve employee selection (matching the right person to the right job) by consulting with personnel managers on psychological factors that limit the usefulness of interviews, by interpreting biographical data, and by constructing methods of numerically evaluating applicants (and current employees) using tests, job simulations, and performance ratings.

Although job satisfaction and productivity are not perfectly correlated, industrial-organizational psychologists attempt to improve both through essentially the same methods. These methods principally involve helping managers improve managerial style (how they relate to their employees), improving the organizational structure of management (such as through participant management or management by objectives), and by improving the physical conditions of work. Through these and many other methods, psychologists are able to contribute to both worker satisfaction and productivity.

Behavioral Medicine: Psychology Applied to Health

behavioral medicine
A specialty of clinical psychology that provides psychological treatments for medical conditions.

Psychology and medicine have long been related disciplines in the sense that psychiatry is a specialty of medicine devoted to the treatment of psychological problems. It's only in the last decade, however, that psychologists have become actively involved in the treatment and prevention of medical problems. Psychologists have recently found that psychological principles can be used to develop methods that aid physicians in dealing with heart disease, headaches, epilepsy, chronic back pain, and other health problems. Out of this collaboration has come a new specialty within clinical psychology known as **behavioral medicine**.

Psychology and Preventive Medicine

One of the goals of modern medicine is to prevent the development of serious health problems, such as heart attacks, before they have had a chance to damage or kill. There is much evidence that the risk of heart attacks can be substantially reduced by convincing vulnerable individuals to stop smoking, lose excess body weight, and exercise regularly (Farquhar, 1979). The problem faced by physicians, however, is that many people will not actually make such changes in their lives. Psychologists can play an important role in preventive medicine by helping people change their health-related behavior.

For example, a simple but effective method has been developed by psychologists to help people stop smoking (Foxx & Brown, 1979). Because most heavy smokers are physically addicted to the nicotine in the cigarettes, the secret of this method's success is in gradually reducing the individual's dependence on nicotine before asking him or her to stop smoking altogether. In an experimental evaluation of the method, smokers were given a list of cigarettes that stated the nicotine content of each brand. During the first week, the smokers were allowed to smoke their accustomed number per day of their own high-nicotine brand. During the second week, they were asked to smoke the same number of a brand of cigarettes that contained 30 percent less nicotine. During the third week they were instructed to smoke the same number of a brand containing 60 percent less nicotine, and the fourth week brought a change to a brand containing 90 percent less nicotine. At that time 40 percent of the smokers were able to stop smoking permanently and another 30 percent were able to smoke at reduced rates of intake of nicotine and tar. Other methods have been developed to help people stick to their diets, follow regular exercise programs, and so on (Davidson & Davidson, 1980).

Psychologists can play an important role in preventive medicine by helping people change health-related behavior, such as smoking.

Psychological Treatments for Medical Problems

Psychological methods have also been developed recently for the treatment of physical problems that had previously been treated only with drugs and surgery. These problems include high blood pressure, headaches, epilepsy, diabetes, and other forms of pain. The psychological treatments vary, but teaching patients to relax deeply, known as *progressive relaxation training*, and *biofeedback* (first described in *Research Report:* "Biofeedback," p. 56) have proven particularly useful.

Progressive Relaxation Training

Progressive relaxation training, the method used with Luis Costa in the Prologue of this chapter, was designed to teach individuals to relax deeply their large body muscles. Although the method was first developed by a physician in the 1930s (Jacobsen, 1938), the use of a simplified version has been popularized in recent years primarily by psychologists (Rimm & Masters, 1979).

In the progressive relaxation training method, the individual is first taught to sense the difference between tense and relaxed muscles. Stop reading for a second and tense the muscles in your right hand and arm as tightly as you can. Focus your attention on the tension and carefully notice how it feels, then let it go as limply relaxed as you can and notice again how it feels. Now try doing the

progressive relaxation training
A method of learning to deeply relax the muscles of the body.

OF SPECIAL INTEREST

Neuropsychology

Neuropsychology is a new specialty in psychology that is closely related to behavioral medicine. The neuropsychologist is specially trained to administer tests that are used to detect brain damage as might be caused by a head injury, near fatal poisoning, or the growth of a brain tumor. Unlike the neurologist, who is a physician who administers medical tests for the same reason, the neuropsychologist gives psychological tests. The logic behind using psychological tests for this purpose is that damage to the brain will be revealed in a pattern of low scores on some tests from a battery of many psychological tests. In some cases the pattern of deficits can even indicate the location of the damage (Lezak, 1976).

For example, the test item in figure 15.11 is similar to one used in many neuropsychological batteries. The patient is asked to use a pencil to connect the dots and numbers in ascending order (1,., 2,.., 3,..., etc.) as quickly as possible. Patients who have some types of brain damage are much slower and more inaccurate on such tasks than people without brain damage.

Information gathered by neuropsychologists provides a way of assessing the extent of brain damage and its likely impact on the person's life, and even of "looking" into the brain before surgeons decide to operate.

---

same thing with the muscles in *only* your neck while leaving the muscles in your shoulders relaxed. Can you do it? Most people cannot at first, but progressive relaxation training would teach you how.

The therapist slowly takes the individual through all of the muscle groups so that he or she becomes aware how tension and relaxation feel. Over many sessions of practice, the individual becomes more able to achieve a very deep state of relaxation. As a result, progressive relaxation training has been found to be effective in the treatment of insomnia (sleep problems), tension headaches, and general anxiety (Rimm & Masters, 1979).

Biofeedback

biofeedback
(bi″o-fēd′bak)
A technique for providing an individual with precise information about the functioning of an internal organ to help him or her learn to voluntarily control it.

Biofeedback is a method of teaching people to control parts of their bodies that they usually cannot control. If I asked you to raise the index finger on your left hand, you would have no trouble doing it unless you had some kind of physical disability. But try increasing the amount of blood that flows through your temporal artery—the one that runs through your temple. Can you do it? A more appropriate question is how would you know for sure if you *had* increased the amount of blood traveling through the artery? Can you feel changes in arterial blood flow? The answer to that question reveals the secret of biofeedback.

OF SPECIAL INTEREST

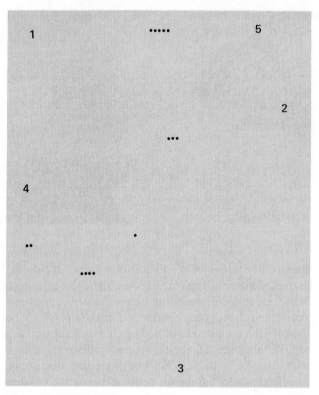

Figure 15.11 An item like those found in neuropsychological test batteries. Use a pencil to connect the dots as quickly as possible in ascending order. Begin with numeral 1, draw a line to the single dot, then to the numeral 2, then to the double dots, and so on.

The term *biofeedback* comes from the fact that the individual is given feedback about a biological process that is ordinarily difficult or impossible to detect. For example, in the treatment of migraine headaches, which result from excessive blood flow to the brain, the individual is given feedback about the amount of blood flow through the temporal artery. A small device that painlessly detects changes in blood flow is placed on the temple. Signals from this detector are used to tell the individual (through changes in a tone or light) whether blood flow has increased or decreased. When a person is given precise feedback on blood flow in the temporal artery, it's possible to learn to control it.

Using biofeedback, we can develop voluntary control over functions of the body that are controlled by the autonomic nervous system. The practical significance of this method is that many individuals are able to reduce the frequency and intensity of migraine headaches in this way (Sturgis, Tollison, & Adams, 1978). Biofeedback has also been used successfully to teach people with epilepsy to control certain brain wave patterns and reduce the frequency of seizures (Lubar & Shouse, 1977).

Recently, the promising application of biofeedback and a variety of other psychological methods to the control of diabetes has been described by psychologists working at Washington University and Duke University Medical Center

Biofeedback helps people develop voluntary control over functions of the body that are normally controlled by the autonomic nervous system.

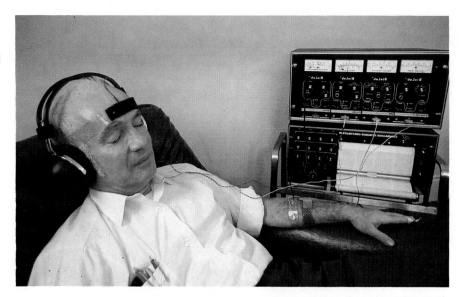

(Fisher, Delamater, Bertelson, & Kirkley, 1982; Surwit, Feinglos, & Scovern, 1983). In the most dangerous type of diabetes, the islets of Langerhans fail to produce sufficient amounts of the hormone insulin or cease to produce insulin completely. As we first mentioned in chapter 2, insulin plays a vital role in metabolism by making the membranes of body cells able to absorb sugar (glucose) from the blood. Without insulin, the cells cannot obtain the necessary glucose. Individuals with this type of diabetes must be given daily doses of insulin; hence, it is termed *insulin-dependent diabetes*. Because it is difficult to manage the delicate balance between blood glucose levels and doses of insulin, it is medically desirable to reduce the patient's need for insulin by controlling blood glucose level through diet, exercise, and the like. Biofeedback provides another method for reducing the size of needed insulin injections.

Because sympathetic autonomic arousal causes, among many other things, the liver to release stored sugar into the blood (see chapter 2, p. 53, for a review), any method that reduces autonomic arousal may reduce blood levels of glucose and decrease the patient's need for insulin. Richard Surwit and Mark Feinglos (1983) used a combination of biofeedback and progressive relaxation training to treat insulin-dependent diabetics who were hospitalized because their blood glucose levels had become excessively high. The biofeedback method was used to help the patients attain deep muscle relaxation by giving them information on the amount of activity in their large body muscles, a method known as electromyograph-biofeedback-assisted relaxation training. As patients learned to relax, they were given continuous feedback on the actual level of activity in their muscles. The results of medical tests after nine days of training indicated that, compared to similar diabetics who did not receive training, biofeedback-assisted relaxation training produced reductions in the amount of glucose released by the liver. Although it is too early to evaluate the value of this new therapy, it offers considerable hope for individuals with insulin-dependent diabetes.

R E V I E W

Psychological methods have been successfully used in the prevention and treatment of medical problems. Methods have been developed to help people exercise regularly, stop smoking, lose excess weight, and make other behavioral changes that reduce the risk of heart attack and other serious diseases. Progressive relaxation training and biofeedback have also been successful in treating problems such as high blood pressure, headaches, epilepsy, and diabetes.

Psychology and Law:
The Behavior of Juries and Witnesses

Psychology and the legal profession have been working together for many years. Psychologists frequently testify as to the competency of an individual to stand trial or as to the sanity of an individual. Moreover, attorneys are necessarily involved in hearings on the involuntary commitment of patients to mental hospitals and in the protection of the rights of psychiatric patients. In recent years, however, psychologists have begun to apply their methods and principles to the *practice* of law in the courtroom. When you think about it, this application of psychology to the practice of law is not surprising. The administration of justice is a process that involves *people*—attorneys, defendants, witnesses, and judges. Any understanding of the profession of law that ignores the human element— the psychology of the people involved—would be an incomplete understanding.

To date, the most extensive psychological study of the legal process has focused on the criminal trial. The findings suggest that, unless they are better understood and controlled, psychological factors in the trial process pose a serious threat to our constitutional guarantee of a fair trial. In addition to the quality of the evidence, the likelihood of conviction depends in part on personal characteristics of the defendant and on characteristics of the jury members. Psychological factors can even influence the quality and convincingness of the evidence itself. The participation of psychologists in the practice of law has been limited thus far largely to the study of the legal process, but psychologists are increasingly serving the role of consultant on jury selection, presentation of evidence, and so on.

Characteristics of Defendants

Other things being equal, you have a greater chance of being acquitted in a criminal trial if you are physically attractive, high in social status, and white. Poor people are more likely to be convicted than affluent ones when charged with similar assault and larceny charges (Haney, 1980). Physically attractive defendants are less likely to be convicted than unattractive ones, unless the attractiveness seemed to play a part in the crime (as in a swindle) (Nemeth, 1981). And racially prejudiced jury members are more likely to convict blacks than whites (Haney, 1980).

The same characteristics of the defendants also play a role in the harshness of the sentence. In first-degree murder cases, blue-collar workers are more likely to be sentenced to death than white-collar workers. And from 1930 to 1979, 2,066 blacks were executed compared to 1,751 whites even though there are four times as many whites in the United States as blacks (Haney, 1980). These findings suggest that justice is not equal for different kinds of defendants, probably because of the prejudices held by jury members about different groups of people. Since characteristics such as income, attractiveness, and race have nothing to do with one's guilt or innocence, these person perception variables make it difficult for all people to receive equal protection under the law.

Characteristics of Jury Members

Certain types of jury members are more likely to vote for conviction and recommend harsher sentences than other types. Jurors who are more conviction-prone and punitive in sentencing are those that are white, older, better educated, higher in social status, more conservative, and believe more strongly that authority and law should be respected (Nemeth, 1981). There is mixed evidence as to whether men are more likely to vote for conviction than women, but there is clear-cut evidence of sex differences in the case of rape. Women are more likely to convict and to be harsher in sentencing than male jurors, while males are more likely to believe that the female victim encouraged the rapist (Nemeth, 1981). There is also evidence that jurors who believe in the death penalty are more likely to convict than those who do not. (See *Research Report:* "Death-qualified Juries" for a discussion of the implications of this fact.)

The evidence on the characteristics of defendants and jurors can be linked in the statement that juries are "kinder to their own kind." Affluent, educated, white jurors tend to be harsher mostly in their treatment of less affluent, less educated, minority defendants.

Psychological Factors in Evidence

It's somewhat reassuring to learn that several studies have suggested that although the characteristics of the defendants and jurors are important in determining conviction or acquittal, the evidence is several times more important (Nemeth, 1981). Unfortunately, facts are not the only important aspect of courtroom evidence; psychological factors are involved here as well.

Eyewitness Testimony

The most convincing evidence to jurors is eyewitness testimony (Buckhout, 1974). Hearing a witness say that he or she saw the defendant commit the crime is almost as convincing as viewing a videotape of the crime in the courtroom. But eyewitnesses are *people*, not video cameras, and a number of psychological factors can lead to inaccurate testimony.

The three men pictured in figure 15.12 were involved in an actual case of double mistaken identity. Lawrence Benson (left) was mistakenly arrested for rape, and George Morales (right) was erroneously arrested for robbery. Both men were arrested because they had been identified in police lineups by eyewitnesses to the crimes. Benson was cleared of the charges, however, when Richard Carbone (center) was arrested and more convincingly implicated in the rapes. After his conviction for rape, he cleared Morales by confessing to the robbery as well (Buckhout, 1974). Although it's easy to see how eyewitnesses could have

 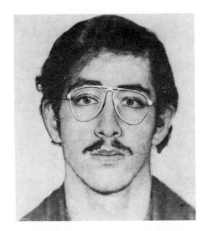 

confused these three similar looking individuals, it's frightening to think that two such nightmarish cases of mistaken identity could happen in the same case. But the scary story about eyewitness testimony is just beginning. Consider the implications of the next experiment.

Gordon Allport of Harvard University conducted a classic experiment some years ago that demonstrated the extent to which our perceptions and memories can be distorted by our prejudices (cited in Buckhout, 1974). Allport had his subjects look briefly at the picture shown in figure 15.13. Look carefully to see who is holding the straight razor. Now be prepared for a shock when you learn that an amazing 50 percent of Allport's subjects later recalled that the black man was holding the razor! Prejudice can obviously play a significant role in determining what eyewitnesses "see." Recall also from chapter 6 on memory that our recollections tend to become distorted and "filled in" with details over time to make the recollection more consistent. If eyewitness testimony is not given immediately—and it rarely is—time will have a chance to work its distortions on the "facts."

Are you losing your confidence in eyewitness testimony? Consider one more experimental finding. A simulated crime was staged in the early 1970s at California State University at Hayward in which a student "attacked" a faculty member (Buckhout, 1974). The staged crime was videotaped to have a record of what happened and then compared to the eyewitness accounts of 141 students who saw the attack. Overall, the witnesses were only accurate on an average of about 25 percent of the facts that they recalled. By now you know that eyewitness testimony is frequently inaccurate. But the more interesting part of this experiment is that the eyewitnesses were later asked to pick out the "attacker" from a set of six photos of similar looking college men. Half of the eyewitnesses were shown the photos under unbiased conditions: All of the photos were head shots facing front and the witnesses were asked *if* the attacker was pictured. The other half of the eyewitnesses were shown the photos in a biased fashion: The photo of the actual attacker was different in head angle and was tilted slightly in the presentation. In addition, the eyewitnesses were told that one of the photos *was* the attacker and were asked to pick him out. Under these biased conditions, 50 percent more of the eyewitnesses chose the attacker. In this case, the presentation was biased against the actual attacker, but the same kind of subtle bias could be unintentionally introduced when an investigator was questioning a witness about

Figure 15.12 Mistakes in eyewitness testimony led to the arrest of the man on the left and the man on the right for separate crimes. Both were cleared following the conviction of the man in the middle for both crimes.

RESEARCH REPORT

"Death-qualified Juries": Are They Fair to Defendants?

Prior to 1968, individuals who had strong objections to the death penalty were routinely barred from serving on juries in cases involving a possible death penalty. In a landmark ruling in 1968, however, an appeals judge commuted a death penalty to life imprisonment in the case of *Witherspoon* v. *Illinois* on the grounds that the jury was composed of only persons who favored the death penalty and was not, therefore, a fair and "representative" jury. In making this ruling, the judge cited a Gallup poll conducted at that time that found that only about 55 percent of the people surveyed favored the death penalty. The judge ruled that prospective jurors could be excluded only when they were so opposed to the death penalty that they would vote against it regardless of the evidence. Was this a good decision? Was the judge correct in assuming that a jury composed only of individuals who favor the death penalty— a "death-qualified" jury—might not give the defendant a fair trial?

Actually, a number of studies support the decision of the judge (Nemeth, 1981). For example, a study was conducted of the relationship between attitudes toward the death penalty and tendency to convict in a sample of 207 industrial workers. They were initially asked to fill out a number of questionnaires including the following:

Capital Punishment Attitude Questionnaire

Directions. Assume you are on a jury to determine the sentence for a defendant who has already been convicted of a very serious crime. If the law gives you a *choice* of death or life imprisonment, or some other penalty: (check *one* only)

☐ 1. I could not vote for the death penalty regardless of the facts and circumstances of the case.
☐ 2. There are some kinds of cases in which I know I could not vote for the death penalty even if the law allowed me to, but others in which I would be willing to consider voting for it.
☐ 3. I would consider all of the penalties provided by the law and the facts and circumstances of the particular case.
☐ 4. I would usually vote for the death penalty in a case where the law allows me to.
☐ 5. I would always vote for the death penalty in a case where the law allows me to.*

R E S E A R C H R E P O R T

Table 15.1 Number of jurors in a simulated trial who voted to convict or acquit, divided according to their willingness to impose the death penalty

Willingness to Impose Death Penalty if Serving as a Juror	Number Voting To	
	Convict	Acquit
Low (1 and 2)	19	40
Medium (3)	59	73
High (4 and 5)	14	2

Source: From Jurow, 1971.

As these subjects did, try to imagine that you have been selected to serve on the jury in a murder trial in a state that imposes the death penalty. Which alternative would you choose?

All of the subjects were then shown two videotapes of mock murder trials that contained all of the standard elements of procedure and evidence. The first concerned a robbery of a liquor store in which the proprietor of the store was killed in the process. The second case was of a man charged with robbing, raping, and killing a college student in her apartment. After each videotaped trial the "jurors" voted to convict or acquit the defendant.

The jurors in this experiment were divided into three groups on the basis of their responses to the questionnaire concerning capital punishment. Jurors scoring low in willingness to impose the death penalty (who checked items 1 or 2) were far more likely to vote for acquittal than conviction in the first trial (see table 15.1). Conversely, jurors who were high in willingness to impose the death penalty (who checked items 4 or 5) were much more likely to vote for conviction. The same pattern was shown in the voting after the second trial, although not as strongly.

Thus, this and other studies finding similar differences do suggest that juries composed only of jurors who are in favor of the death penalty (who are also more likely to be conservative, high status, authoritarian males) are biased in favor of conviction of defendants (Nemeth, 1981). This means that the current practice of excluding only those jurors who are most strongly opposed to the death penalty or of using separate juries for the trial and the sentencing makes good psychological sense.

Figure 15.13 Psychologist Gordon Allport showed subjects this picture for a very brief period of time to test the accuracy of their "eyewitness" testimony in a situation in which racial prejudice might influence their perception.
From Eyewitness Testimony, *by Robert Buckhout.*

a suspect that the investigator falsely believed was guilty. Unfortunately, a number of subtle factors in the questioning of eyewitnesses have been shown to influence their testimony (Haney, 1980). See also *Of Special Interest:* "The Psychology of Interrogating Criminal Suspects."

Order of Presentation of Evidence

Criminal trials are "adversary proceedings." The attorneys for the prosecution and defense each attempt to convince the jury of the guilt or innocence of the defendant as if they were competing in a debate. Since both attorneys cannot talk at the same time, they obviously must make their presentations one at a time. Unfortunately, the *order* in which evidence is presented appears to make a difference in the outcome of the trial. One study investigated the effect of order of presentation in a simulated trial in which law students played the roles of attorneys for the defense and prosecution and undergraduate students served as jurors. The simulated case concerned a man who was charged with murder but claimed he had acted in self-defense. Half of the time, the prosecutor went first, and half of the time the defense attorney went first. The results showed that the attorney who went second held a decided advantage (Thibaut & Walker, 1975). This is not good news if you are falsely accused of a crime, since tradition has it that the prosecutor is allowed to make the last statement to the jury.

Recall from chapter 14 that information you encounter first when getting to know a stranger ("first impressions") is stronger in determining your overall impression of that person *unless* a relatively long time interval elapses between the first and subsequent information. That last qualification may help to explain

OF SPECIAL INTEREST

The Psychology of Interrogating Criminal Suspects

Social psychologist Craig Haney (1980) has analyzed the standard American method of police interrogation to examine its psychological aspects. Police use a number of psychological techniques to increase the probability of a confession. Imagine that you have been taken to a barren interrogating room. You are alone with the interrogators—the room does not even have a telephone—giving you a feeling of being completely cut off from the outside world. The interrogator often stands very close to you, violating your personal space, and giving you a feeling of powerlessness.

The interrogator begins the questioning by pointing out your apparent guilt. But the crime is discussed in such a way as to make it seem so understandable—almost morally justifiable—that you feel that the interrogator would not shame you if you confessed. If the crime is not a big deal, why not just admit to doing it? But the interrogator soon grows impatient with you for not admitting to the crime and storms out of the room. A second officer in the room steps over, though, and asks you to excuse the behavior of the first interrogator—it's been a long and frustrating day. This second officer is very sympathetic to your situation and emphasizes how much easier the court would be on you if you confessed. This officer really seems to feel genuine concern for you. Just then, the first interrogator enters the room again and asks you for a confession. You see anger beginning to build, and you blurt out a confession just to avoid the angry outburst.

This kind of scene is repeated many times a day in police stations across the country, although not always with favorable results. Many suspects are as accustomed to the routine of interrogation as are the police. Haney (1980) asserts, however, that the psychological pressures exerted in such interrogations are powerful enough to elicit false confessions from some individuals. The probability that such interrogation will lead to false statements from witnesses may even be higher.

the findings about the order of presentation of courtroom evidence. It may be that because courtroom arguments are lengthy and complex, recently presented information is more easily remembered and potent. This interpretation is strengthened by the finding that the advantage of presenting in the second position is increased further if an attorney states the most convincing points at the very end of the second presentation rather than at the beginning (Thibaut & Walker, 1975).

Drawing by Lorenz; © 1977
The New Yorker Magazine, Inc.

"The jury will disregard the witness's last remarks."

R E V I E W

Criminal trials are conducted by people so it's not surprising to learn that psychological factors play a role. What may be more surprising—and disturbing—is to see how strong a role they can play. Having different types of people involved in the trial process is likely to produce different outcomes. Poor, uneducated, minority defendants are more likely to be convicted and receive harsher sentences. Jurors who are white, older, higher in social status, more conservative, and more authoritarian than average as well as those who believe in capital punishment are more likely to vote for conviction and impose harsh punishments. The quality of the evidence presented in criminal trials is more important in determining the jury's decision than the psychological characteristics of the defendant and jurors, but psychological factors are also involved in courtroom evidence. Eyewitness testimony can be influenced by the witness's prejudices, by distortions in memory, and by the method of interrogation. Even the order in which evidence is presented can influence the outcome of a trial. Obviously, these factors must be understood and controlled as much as possible if the judicial system is to be fair for all concerned.

Psychology Applied to Education: Better Teaching and Testing

educational psychology
The field in which principles of learning, cognition, and other aspects of psychology are applied to improve education.

Like industrial-organizational psychology, **educational psychology** is almost as old as the discipline of psychology itself. Binet's development of a useful intelligence test for schoolchildren laid the foundation for educational testing, and others, like Edward Lee Thorndike of Columbia University, conducted research on factors that influence school learning and memory during the early 1900s. But while educational psychology is an old field, its current excitement stems from relatively new developments. These innovations promise to particularly improve the education of our slowest-learning children. Psychologists serve education as professors who help train teachers in the psychology of education, as consultants on the development of testing programs, and as specialists employed by school systems (**school psychologists**) to consult with teachers and to test children who may need special educational programs.

Public education was established to implement Thomas Jefferson's philosophy that every American citizen should have equal educational as well as political opportunities. Because citizens need an education in order to govern themselves through democratic institutions, it was decided that education should be available to every American child rather than a privilege of the rich. The most important recent innovations in educational psychology have been ones that help more children benefit fully from their time in school: the mastery learning approach, effective methods of educating economically disadvantaged children, the development of more meaningful tests of achievement, and the integration of children with psychological and physical handicaps into the normal classroom environment, known as mainstreaming.

school psychologist
A psychologist who aids schools by testing children to determine eligibility for placement in special education programs and who consults with teachers and parents.

Mastery Learning

If you were a teacher, would you try to teach a child to add and subtract before he had learned to count? Would you teach trigonometry to a child before she had mastered the basics of plane geometry? It does not make much sense to try to teach a child a new skill before he or she had learned the basic skills that are the foundation for further learning. Yet it happens every day in American education—children are pushed from one subject to another before they are ready to progress. Why? The reason is that in many schools, education is conducted according to group schedules. A certain amount of time is allotted for the group to learn to count, and then the group moves on to addition. Students take plane geometry in the fall semester and then trigonometry in the spring. If an individual child is not ready to progress, he or she must usually move on with the group anyway.

Educational psychologist Benjamin Bloom has been an outspoken critic of this approach and has proposed the **mastery learning** concept to take its place (Bloom, 1974). Quite simply, Bloom insists that children should never progress from one learning task to another until they have fully mastered the first one. If this rule is followed, Bloom suggests that learning will be far more effective in the long run. For example, a group of high school students who were enrolled in a course on automobile mechanics took part in an evaluation of the mastery learning approach. The course was divided into eight units that built upon one another in succession. Half of the students progressed through the units as a group according to a prearranged schedule. The other students—the mastery learning group—moved at their own pace and did not begin the next unit until they had passed a test on the previous unit. At the end of the course, the mastery learning group had learned far more in the same amount of time (Wentling, 1973).

mastery learning
The concept that children should never progress from one learning task to another until they have mastered the more basic one.

Bloom suggests that the mastery learning approach is particularly effective for slow-learning children, but it does not penalize brighter children. In the traditional approach of group scheduling, the top fifth of American students learns three times as much as the bottom fifth by the time of graduation from high school. When students use a mastery learning approach, however, the learning of the bottom fifth improves so much as to cut this difference in half (Bloom, 1974).

R E S E A R C H   R E P O R T

Advance Organizers and the Psychology of Learning from Textbooks

Educational psychologists have devoted most of their research efforts to the study of methods of classroom teaching. A topic that has received increasing attention over the years, however, is the psychology of learning the way you are learning right now—by reading a textbook. What characteristics of a textbook make it easier or more difficult to learn from it? That is a particularly important topic to me as a writer of textbooks, and one to which I devoted a considerable amount of attention before beginning to write this book. Many techniques have been proposed for increasing the ease of learning from written text, such as having review questions at the end of each section and stating objectives for learning at the beginning of each chapter. But unfortunately the research on most of these techniques has not consistently supported the use of such techniques.

One method of increasing the ease of learning from textbooks that has been consistently supported by research is the use of **advance organizers.** Advance organizers are summaries of the general content of the chapter to be read. The previews at the beginning of each chapter in this book are advance organizers. The use of advance organizers is based on a cognitive approach to learning that states that we cannot effectively learn facts until we have learned a general cognitive "structure" on which we can "hang" the facts. Advance organizers summarize the most general concepts in the chapter to give the student an overall cognitive structure for the chapter. There are no detailed facts in the advance organizer; these are all left until later when they can be more meaningfully learned.

advance organizers
Introductory summaries of the content of each chapter that provide the general cognitive structure of the chapter to the learner.

Project Follow Through: Educating Economically Disadvantaged Children

One of the harsher realities of American life is that millions of people live in extreme poverty in spite of the overall affluence of the nation. Who are the poor? Where do they come from? Sadly, most of the people living in poverty today are the children of the last generation of poor people and will be the parents of the next generation of the poor. Poverty tends to run in families.

A key element in the development of a life-style of poverty is educational failure. People who do not learn enough in school to be employable have little chance of rising above poverty. The cycle of educational failure in economically disadvantaged children is an all too familiar story. Each year in school, children from disadvantaged families learn about two-thirds of what the average child learns. This means that they fall farther behind their classmates each successive year in a dangerous downward spiral that often ends in dropping out of school (Becker & Carnine, 1980).

RESEARCH REPORT

This theory was tested by its founder David Ausubel (1960) in a classic educational psychology experiment conducted at the University of Illinois. One hundred and twenty students were divided into two groups. The two groups were initially tested to determine if they differed in their ability to learn from written text. They read a passage on puberty and then answered questions about the passage. There were essentially no differences between the groups in the number of questions that they correctly answered.

In the main part of the experiment, the two groups read a second passage with and without an advance organizer preceding it. The passage covered the properties of carbon steel and contained many facts that were new to the students. To treat the two groups in the same way as much as possible, the group that did not read the advance organizer read a brief passage about the history of metal making while the advance organizer was being read. After both groups had read the passage on carbon steel, they took a brief multiple-choice test covering the facts presented in the passage. As predicted, the group that read the advance organizer scored significantly higher on the test, answering approximately 20 percent more factual questions. Apparently, the advance look at the overall cognitive structure of the passage helped make the memorization of the facts a more meaningful task. That is why previews—advance organizers—were written to precede each of the chapters in this text.

In the mid-1960s a massive experiment was conceived by the U.S. Office of Education to test new ways of educating economically disadvantaged children. Nine groups of researchers were given funds to design and implement what they thought would be ideal educational programs, and independent research organizations were contracted to evaluate their effectiveness. This massive educational experiment—involving tens of thousands of children across the country—was named **Project Follow Through**. This program followed children through the crucial years of kindergarten through third grade, while earlier attempts to help disadvantaged children had stopped at the kindergarten level.

The nine Follow Through projects differed considerably in educational philosophy, and most were clearly unsuccessful in improving educational progress. The most successful of the projects was consistently able, however, to bring disadvantaged children to the national average or above. This project, designed by Wesley Becker and Siegfried Engelmann of the University of Oregon and known as the Direct Instruction project, made simple but powerful use of what is now

Project Follow Through
A federally sponsored program designed to help educate economically disadvantaged children.

Each year in school, children from disadvantaged families learn about two-thirds of what the average child learns. Project Follow Through was designed to test new ways of educating these children.

known about the psychology of education. Becker and Engelmann designed a curriculum based on a knowledge of the cognitive skills needed in reading and other subjects. They also designed a teaching method based on the principles of learning—particularly positive reinforcement—and used practice methods designed to enhance memory for what had been learned. The success of this program is an impressive testimony to the value of the accumulated knowledge of educational psychology.

Criterion-Referenced Testing

The renewed interest in finding better ways to prepare students to lead successful adult lives has also led to the development of a new approach in evaluating how much they have learned in school. In traditional approaches to educational testing, children are compared to one another. For example, a traditional test of computational skills in arithmetic would require children to work a large number of problems. A child who correctly solved the same number of problems as the average for children in his or her grade would be considered to be "on grade level."

criterion-referenced testing (kri-te're-on) Testing designed to determine if a child can meet the minimum standards of a specific educational objective.

The goal of **criterion-referenced testing,** however, is not to compare children but to determine if a given child can meet the minimum criteria for a specific educational objective. Usually these objectives are practical in nature. For example, one criterion-referenced test asks children to fill in a personal information blank like the ones required by most employment applications. The issue in this kind of testing is not how well a child can fill in the blank compared to other children, but simply whether the child can *do* it appropriately. This is a skill well worth teaching to students, since adults who cannot fill out employment forms stand little chance of being hired. Sadly, one study showed that only 61 percent of American 17-year-olds could fill out an employment application form without errors (Mellon, 1975).

Criterion-referenced testing provides the kind of information that teachers need to improve education. If the items accurately reflect the goals of education, then criterion-referenced test scores can provide feedback to teachers on how well they are teaching. If Mary cannot fill out a personal information blank, then the teacher knows that Mary needs more instruction on that skill. If most of the students in a school cannot fill them out, then the school administration knows that a better teaching method must be implemented. Thus, criterion-referenced tests play an important role in evaluating and improving teaching methods. And the fact that only 61 percent of 17-year-olds can fill out employment application forms shows that there is considerable room for improvement.

Mainstreaming: Integrated Education for the Handicapped

During the 1970s, enormous strides were made in the legal standing of children with handicaps such as mental retardation, emotional problems, and physical handicaps. New federal legislation—now famous as *Public Law 94–142*—established that *every* child has a *right* to a public education, regardless of his or her handicap. This means that many more severely handicapped children are being served by public schools than ever before.

Mainstreaming provides handicapped children with a public education in the least restrictive environment. Public Law 94–142 helped get many handicapped children into regular classrooms.

Furthermore, Public Law 94–142 states that the child is entitled to receive that education in the *least restrictive environment*. This legal phrase means that children must receive educational and psychological assistance in circumstances that are as similar as possible to the normal day-to-day environment of nonhandicapped children. Thus, it's no longer legal to isolate handicapped children in separate schools *if* it's possible to educate them in regular schools and allow them to interact with normal children. Whenever possible, in fact, handicapped children must be kept in the regular classroom for as large a part of the school day as possible and removed for special assistance only when necessary. This practice is known as **mainstreaming**, because it keeps handicapped children within the mainstream of normal social and educational development.

In addition to protecting the legal rights of handicapped people, Public Law 94–142 offers some important benefits to all concerned. First, it gives handicapped students an opportunity to learn how to fit into the world of nonhandicapped youngsters. Equally important, it gives children without handicaps a chance to learn firsthand that handicapped children are fully human and well worth having as friends.

mainstreaming
The practice of integrating handicapped children into regular classrooms.

R E V I E W

Educational psychologists have long sought to improve ways of teaching and testing schoolchildren, but the recent excitement in educational psychology stems from new concepts and methods of teaching and testing that promise to help more children benefit fully from the opportunities offered by the educational system. The mastery learning approach provides a way to both enhance learning and decrease the gap between the most and least successful learners; the Project Follow Through experiment has identified effective methods for educating disadvantaged children; and the shift toward criterion-referenced testing provides us with a more meaningful way to evaluate how successful we have been in teaching necessary skills and knowledge to children. In a different way, the mainstreaming approach assures handicapped children of their rightful place in the educational system.

S U M M A R Y

Chapter 15 describes the influence of psychology on four areas: business, medicine, law, and education. The objective is to show that psychology is an applied, as well as a scientific, field.

I. Psychologists who work for businesses are known as *industrial-organizational psychologists*. They are found most frequently in personnel departments.

   A. *Interviews* help managers assess current employees for possible promotion. The role of the psychologist is to educate managers about the nature and limitations of interviews.

   B. Biographical data, *biodata*, is used to help employers in large companies select large numbers of employees who will perform the same kind of job.

   C. *Paper-and-pencil tests* include intellectual ability and personality tests. Tests used to measure specific skills and abilities are also frequently used.

   D. *Performance tests* measure actual manual performance that can be used to predict behavior on the job.

   E. Several methods exist for assessing performance of currently employed workers.

      1. Worker performance is evaluated by supervisors using job performance ratings, such as *multiple-step rating scales* and *checklists*. This method can only be used to evaluate job applicants when job tryouts are used.

      2. *Assessment centers* are frequently used to evaluate applicants or currently employed candidates for management positions in companies.

   F. The most valid method of evaluating job applicants for complex jobs is paper-and-pencil intellectual ability tests, whereas performance tasks appear to be more valid when the job is less complex.

   G. The goals of psychologists working in business are to improve the satisfaction of employees and to improve their productivity. They can accomplish the goals by:

      1. Improving supervisory style.
      2. Improving managerial organization.
      3. Improving physical conditions.

II. In the last decade psychologists have become actively involved in the treatment and prevention of medical problems. This specialty is known as *behavioral medicine*.

   A. Psychologists work for the prevention of medical disorders by helping vulnerable individuals stop smoking, lose excess body weight, and exercise regularly.

   B. *Progressive relaxation training* and *biofeedback* are psychological methods that help in the treatment of physical problems such as high blood pressure, headaches, epilepsy, and diabetes.

III. In recent years, psychologists have begun to apply their methods to the practice of the law in the courtroom.
   A. They have found that the characteristics of defendants affect the like-lihood of conviction and the harshness of the sentence.
   B. They have also found that certain types of jury members are more likely to vote for conviction and to recommend harsher sentences than other types.
   C. Psychological factors are involved in the effectiveness of courtroom evidence. Eyewitness testimony is the most convincing evidence, but eyewitnesses can and do make mistakes.
   D. The order in which evidence is presented appears to make a differ-ence in the outcome of the trial.
IV. Psychologists serve the field of education as professors who help train teachers, as consultants on testing programs, and as school psycholo-gists employed by school systems.
   A. One recent development is *mastery learning*, based on Benjamin Bloom's belief that children should never progress from one learning task to another until they have fully mastered the previous one.
   B. Another development is *Project Follow Through*, a federally funded experiment to test new ways of educating economically disadvan-taged children.
   C. Another new approach is *criterion-referenced testing*, a form of testing designed to determine if a given child can meet the minimum criteria for a specific educational objective.
   D. Public Law 94–142, the *mainstreaming law*, established that every child has a right to public education, regardless of his or her hand-icap. The law states that the education must be in the *least restrictive environment*.

Suggested Readings

1. An excellent overview of industrial-organizational psychology:
   McCormick, E. J., & Ilgen, D. R. (1980). *Industrial psychology* (7th ed.). Englewood Cliffs, NJ: Prentice-Hall.

2. A sophisticated overview of behavioral medicine:
   Doleys, D. M., Meredith, R. L., & Ciminero, A. M. (1982). *Behavioral medicine: Assessment and treatment strategies*. New York: Plenum.

3. For more on the psychology of juries:
   Saks, M. J. (1977). *Jury verdicts*. Lexington, MA: Lexington Books.

A P P E N D I X

Measurement, Research Design, and Statistics

Richard E. Mayer *University of California, Santa Barbara*

The purpose of this appendix is to help you understand some of the basic statistical concepts and research methods used in psychology. Even if you never conduct a psychological study, you need to learn about statistics and research methods in psychology. First, the ability to read and evaluate research that is presented in this textbook or discussed in class helps you to avoid being intimidated by the research data of "experts"; it helps you to tell whether or not an experiment is sound; and it helps you to interpret the results. Second, a basic understanding of psychological statistics and research methods is rapidly becoming a "survival skill" for every educated member of our society. You need to avoid being fooled by "scientific" surveys, government reports, advertiser's evidence, and the like. You need to be able to recognize the difference between a useful study and one that is seriously flawed. Thus, this appendix is designed to help you as a student and as an educated citizen.

For example, suppose you came across the following article in your local newspaper:

TV Viewing Linked to School Failure
Garden City—Researchers at State University have found that students who watch in excess of three hours of television per day get lower grades than other students. The study was based on a survey of students at Garden Valley School. The average student watched approximately two hours of TV per day. Efforts to discourage TV watching have been announced by the school's principal, Mr. George Elliot. "We must get our kids to stop watching TV," Mr. Elliot stated.

As you read this summary of a research study, you should ask yourself such questions as Is this a sound study? and How should I interpret the results? After reading this appendix you will be better able to answer questions like these concerning research studies that you read about.

Descriptive Statistics

One of the basic uses for statistics in psychological studies is to *describe behavior* in a conveniently understood way. This is called *descriptive statistics*. Two common examples of descriptive statistics are as follows:

Describing behavior concerning one variable. For example, a study may report that the "average" student watches two hours of TV per day.

Describing the relation between two variables. For example, a study may report that students who watch more television tend to score lower on tests of school achievement than those who watch less.

Figure A.1 Some uses of statistics.

Use	Situation	Example	Typical statistics
Describing one variable.	There is one score for each subject.	Each of twenty students in Mrs. Perkins's class tells how many hours he or she watched TV yesterday.	Frequency distribution Mean, median, or mode Standard deviation, variance, or range
Describing the relation between two variables	There are two scores for each subject — one score on variable X and one score on variable Y.	Each of twenty students in Mrs. Perkins's class tells how many hours he or she watched TV yesterday, and each student gets a score on the school achievement test.	Correlation

As you can see, descriptive statistics summarize the data for a group of subjects.

Figure A.1 lists the two uses of statistics that will be discussed in the remainder of this part of the appendix.

In the Garden Valley study, the researchers obtained data on only a small number of schoolchildren from just one school; however, the researchers want to generalize their data to all schoolchildren in the United States. Thus, it is important for you to understand the distinction between a *parameter* and a *statistic* as they are used here.

> *Parameter.* Parameters are numbers that describe the behavior of an entire population. A population consists of all possible subjects or objects or cases, such as all schoolchildren in the United States. For example, if we asked every schoolchild in the United States how many hours he or she watched TV per day, then we could develop parameters such as the average number of hours of TV viewing.

> *Statistic.* Statistics are numbers that describe the behavior of only a *sample* drawn out of a larger population. A sample is a portion of an entire population, such as some of the schoolchildren at one school.

Sample statistics—such as the average number of hours of TV watching of some students at Garden Valley School—are rarely identical to population parameters, such as the average number of hours of TV viewing of all U.S. schoolchildren.

Another distinction that you need to understand is the difference between a *variable* and a *score*.

> *Variable.* A variable is a measurable characteristic or behavior, such as age, sex, weight, height, or shoe size. In the Garden Valley study, one variable is the number of hours of TV viewing per day.

> *Score.* A score is the value a given person has for a given variable, such as Joe's age being 27 years or his shoe size being 8½. In the Garden Valley study, Mary watched three hours of TV per day, so her score is 3 on the variable "hours of TV viewing per day."

The data for a study consist of all the scores obtained for each variable that is used.

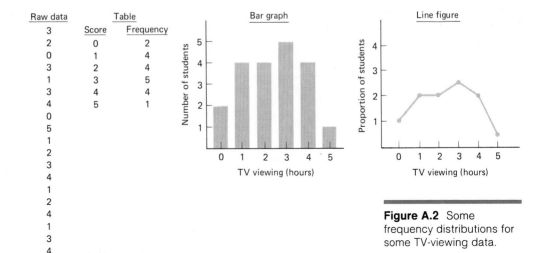

Figure A.2 Some frequency distributions for some TV-viewing data.

Describing Behavior Concerning One Variable

Problem

One of the major uses of statistics in psychology is to describe the behavior of a group on one variable. For example, the Garden Valley study attempted to describe the TV-viewing behavior of schoolchildren. Let's suppose that we go to Garden Valley School and ask twenty students from Mrs. Perkins's class to tell us how many hours they watched TV yesterday. Suppose that we get one answer from each student, as listed in the left panel of figure A.2.

Frequency Distribution

What are the TV-viewing habits of school students? One way to provide data for this question is simply to list the number of hours that each of twenty students reported watching TV. However, since it's hard to make much sense out of a long list of numbers, researchers often organize their data into a *frequency distribution*. A frequency distribution is a table or graph that shows the relationship between score (such as number of hours of TV watching) and frequency (such as the number or percentage of students who gave each score).

Figure A.2 shows some frequency distributions for the TV-viewing data, using the formats of table, bar graph, and line figure. In the table, the first column gives the possible scores (0, 1, 2, 3, 4, or 5) for hours of TV viewing per day, and the second column gives the frequency of each score (that is, how many of the 20 students fell into that category). In the bar graph and line figure, the X-axis gives the possible scores and the Y-axis gives the frequency.

Although the frequency distribution helps you organize data, you may want to summarize the description even further. You could summarize the frequency distribution by giving two numbers—a measure of *central tendency* and a measure of *dispersion*. A measure of central tendency tells where the middle of the distribution is, such as, how many hours do school students watch TV on the average? A measure of dispersion tells you how spread out the scores are, such as, how different are the school students in the number of hours they view TV? These are discussed in the next two subsections.

Figure A.3 Measures of central tendency for some TV-viewing data.

	Mean
	$\Sigma X = 3 + 2 + 0 + 3 + 1 + 3 + 4 +$
	$0 + 5 + 1 + 2 + 3 + 4 + 1 +$
	$2 + 4 + 1 + 3 + 4 + 2 = 48$
	$n = 20$
	$\overline{x} = \dfrac{\Sigma X}{n} = \dfrac{48}{20} = 2.4$

Median

Ranking		Scores in order
1st		0
2nd		0
3rd		1
4th		1
5th		1
6th		1
7th		2
8th		2
9th	Middle of	2
10th	rankings	2
11th		3
12th		3
13th		3
14th		3
15th		3
16th		4
17th		4
18th		4
19th		4
20th		5

Median = point midway between 2 and 3; i.e., 2.5.

Mode

Score		Frequency
0		2
1		4
2		4
3	← Most frequent →	5
4		4
5		1

Mode = 3

Central Tendency

How many hours per day does the "average student" watch TV? There are three major measures of central tendency: mean, median, and mode.

The *mean* is the arithmetic average of all the scores. To compute the mean, you simply add all the scores and divide the sum by the number of scores. The formula for mean is $\overline{X} = \Sigma X/n$, where $\overline{X}$ is the mean, ΣX is the sum or total of the scores, and n is the number of scores. The left portion of figure A.3 shows that the sum of the scores is 48, the number of scores is 20, and the mean is 2.4 hours. One problem with using mean as a measure of central tendency is that it's sensitive to extreme scores. For example, if only the student who reported watching 5 hours per day changed his answer to 24 hours, the mean would increase from 2.4 to 3.35.

The *median* is the score that divides the distribution in the middle, so that half of the frequency is greater than the median and half is less than the median. In order to determine the median, list the scores in ascending (or descending) order, and count down until you reach the score in the middle. An example is given in the middle panel of figure A.3. As you can see, the median is not as sensitive to extreme scores. If the student who watched 5 hours was replaced by a student who watched 24 hours, the median would remain the same!

The *mode* is the score that occurs most often. For example, the mode in figure A.3 is 3 because 5 people watch TV for 3 hours while fewer than 5 watch TV for each other score. There can be ties among modes; for example, the scores 3, 1, 2, 1, 3, 0, 4, 1, 3, 5 have two modes—1 and 3. This is called a *bimodal distribution* because there are two modes. If there is a tie among several scores, such as 1, 1, 2, 2, 3, 3, 4, 4, 0, 0, then there can be several modes—such as 5 modes in the preceding example. This is called a *multimodal distribution*. Although the mode is not often used in research studies, in some cases it may be preferred. For example, the designer of apartments will find it is *more useful* to

	Standard deviation		Range
Raw data	Deviation $(X - \overline{X})$	Square of deviation $(X - \overline{X})^2$	
3	.6	.36	0 ◄——— Lowest
2	− .4	.16	0
0	−2.4	5.76	1
3	.6	.36	1
1	−1.4	1.96	1
3	.6	.36	1
4	1.6	2.56	2
0	−2.4	5.76	2
5	2.6	6.76	2
1	−1.4	1.96	2
2	− .4	.16	3
3	.6	.36	3
4	1.6	2.56	3
1	−1.4	1.96	3
2	− .4	.16	3
4	1.6	2.56	4
1	−1.4	1.96	4
3	.6	.36	4
4	1.6	2.56	4
2	− .4	.16	5 ◄——— Highest
		$\Sigma(X - \overline{X})^2 = 38.80$	

$$S = \sqrt{\frac{\Sigma(X - \overline{X})^2}{n}} = \sqrt{\frac{38.8}{20}} = 1.39$$

Range = (highest − lowest) + 1
Range = 5 − 0 + 1 = 6

Figure A.4 Measures of dispersion for some TV-viewing data.

know that the "modal" family unit is either 1 or 4, than to know that the mean family is 2.5. The builder who includes studio apartments for single adults is likely to rent the available space faster than the builder who believes that only two-bedroom apartments are needed for all those families with 2.5 people.

Dispersion

How different are the scores from one another? There are two major measures of dispersion: standard deviation and range.

The *standard deviation* is a sort of average difference between each score and the mean. It's a statistic that indicates how widely or narrowly scores are spread around the mean on the average. To compute the standard deviation, subtract the mean score from each score, square each of these differences, divide by the number of scores, and then take the square root. The formula for standard deviation is

$$s = \sqrt{\frac{\Sigma(X - \overline{X})^2}{n}}$$

where s is the standard deviation, $\Sigma(X - \overline{X})^2$ is the sum of the square of the differences, and n is the number of scores. The left panel of figure A.4 shows how to compute the standard deviation for TV-viewing scores.

The *range* is the distance between the highest score and the lowest score. To compute range, simply subtract the lowest score from the highest and add 1. The right panel of figure A.4 shows that if the lowest score is 0 and the highest score is 5, then the range is 6; that is, the distance between 0 and 5 is 6 units. The range is rarely used as a measure of dispersion because it's so sensitive to extreme scores. For example, if the student who watched 5 hours of TV was replaced by a student who watched 24 hours, the range would jump to 25.

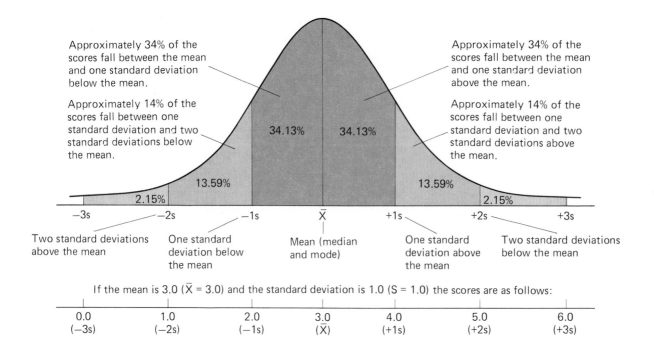

Approximately 34% of the scores fall between the mean and one standard deviation below the mean.

Approximately 14% of the scores fall between one standard deviation and two standard deviations below the mean.

Approximately 34% of the scores fall between the mean and one standard deviation above the mean.

Approximately 14% of the scores fall between one standard deviation and two standard deviations above the mean.

34.13%   34.13%

13.59%   13.59%

2.15%   2.15%

−3s   −2s   −1s   X̄   +1s   +2s   +3s

Two standard deviations above the mean

One standard deviation below the mean

Mean (median and mode)

One standard deviation above the mean

Two standard deviations below the mean

If the mean is 3.0 (X̄ = 3.0) and the standard deviation is 1.0 (S = 1.0) the scores are as follows:

| 0.0 | 1.0 | 2.0 | 3.0 | 4.0 | 5.0 | 6.0 |
| (−3s) | (−2s) | (−1s) | (X̄) | (+1s) | (+2s) | (+3s) |

Figure A.5 The normal curve.

Normal Curve

The scores for any frequency distribution can be plotted on a graph, as in the right-hand panel of figure A.2, and they can take a multitude of shapes. A sort of ideal frequency distribution is the normal curve. It has fascinated scientists and statisticians because many different characteristics in nature tend to be normally distributed—such as adult height, weight, intelligence, and so on. This does not mean they all have the same mean and standard deviation; rather, they all have the same general *shape* of frequency distribution. An example of a normal curve is given in figure A.5.

The normal curve is a frequency distribution that has the following characteristics:

Symmetrical. The right side is a mirror image of the left side.

Bell shaped. The most common scores are near the mean, with scores becoming less common as you move away from the mean in either direction.

68–95–99 density. The area on the normal curve that is within one standard deviation above the mean and one standard deviation below the mean contains 68.26 percent of the cases; within two standard deviations there are 95.42 percent of the cases; and within three standard deviations there are 99.74 percent of the cases.

To make sure that you understand the shape of the normal curve, let's try some examples. Look at the percentages of cases in each area of the normal curve in figure A.5. Suppose that Susan scores one standard deviation above the mean on a test. If the scores are normally distributed, she performed better than ____ percent of the class. Try another one: Tom scored one standard deviation below the mean, so he did better than ____ percent of the class. Finally, try this one: Mary scored better than 98 percent of the other students, so she scored ____ standard deviations *(above/below)* the mean. Look at figure A.6 for the answers.

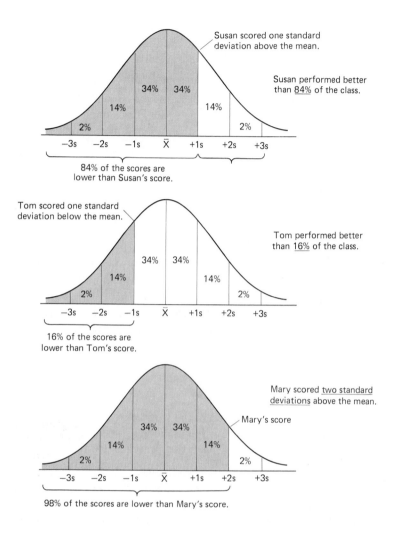

Figure A.6 Some normal curves.

Susan scored one standard deviation above the mean.

Susan performed better than <u>84%</u> of the class.

84% of the scores are lower than Susan's score.

Tom scored one standard deviation below the mean.

Tom performed better than <u>16%</u> of the class.

16% of the scores are lower than Tom's score.

Mary scored <u>two standard deviations</u> above the mean.

Mary's score

98% of the scores are lower than Mary's score.

Flaws in Research Design

When presented with a problem such as the one described at the beginning of this section, you should ask yourself, "What is wrong with the way that the researcher collected data?" A researcher can present you with perfectly calculated statistics and still not be of much help. Your first step in dealing with descriptive data should be to understand any flaws in the research design—that is, in how the data were collected. Some of the more common flaws are described below:

Unrepresentative sample. The people or behavior in the study may not be representative or typical of the larger population. For example, in the TV-viewing study, perhaps the two or three most heavy TV viewers are not included because they are at home watching TV, or perhaps two or three students who watch a lot of TV refused to participate in the study. Mrs. Perkins's class might consist of all "college prep" students who have little time for TV. There might have been some excellent special shows on the night the data were collected, so the students watched more TV than usual.

Experimenter bias. The expectations of the experimenter may influence the data. For example, the experimenter who expects that students watch a lot of TV may inadvertently make errors in posting the data, such as reading one hour as seven hours.

Response bias. The subjects' responses might be influenced by the subjects' general question-answering style. For example, most people prefer to answer yes rather than no, and most people prefer to give socially desirable answers. Thus, students may underestimate their actual TV-viewing time if they think that watching TV is "bad."

Situational bias. Extraneous factors in the research situation may influence the subject's response. For example, the subject might try to give data that are consistent with what the subject thinks the experimenter wants. If the experimenter begins by saying, "Wow, I am happy to see that kids in your class watch a lot of TV," and then asks "how many hours did you watch TV yesterday?" subjects may be more likely to give higher estimates. This type of situational bias is sometimes called *demand characteristics;* in other words, subjects are sensitive to what is demanded by the situation. Other examples of situational bias include the possibility that students will give different answers depending on who the experimenter is, how the question is phrased, whether peers or others are present when the survey is given, and so on.

Invalid scores. The scores used in the study may not accurately measure the subjects' behavior. For example, students may not be able to remember how many hours they watched TV the previous day, or a test may not adequately measure school achievement.

Non-standard conditions. The scores may be obtained under different conditions for different subjects. For example, some students may be asked "face-to-face" by the teacher to tell how many hours they watched TV, while others may be asked to fill out an anonymous questionnaire. If all students are not tested under standard conditions, then there may be differences in their scores that are due to extraneous factors.

Once you are satisfied that you have explored any potential flaws in the research methodology, you are ready to go on and investigate the statistics.

Describing the Relation between Two Variables

Problem

So far you have learned how to describe scores on some variable, using statistics such as mean and standard deviation. Sometimes, however, your goal might be to describe the relation between two variables. For example, in the Garden Valley study, you might want to know whether there is any relation between the number of hours of TV viewing and the score on a school achievement test. Let's suppose we go to Garden Valley School and ask ten students from Mrs. Perkins's class to tell us how many hours they watched TV yesterday and that we get test scores for each student's performance on a school achievement test. Thus, we will have two scores for each of ten students, as listed in the left panel of figure A.7.

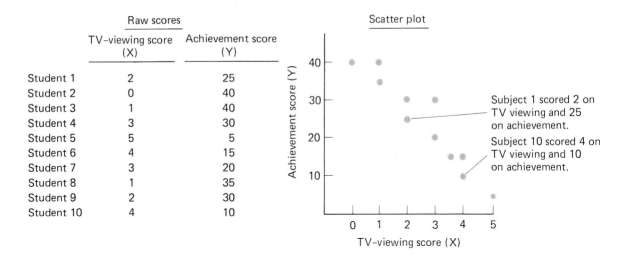

Raw scores

	TV-viewing score (X)	Achievement score (Y)
Student 1	2	25
Student 2	0	40
Student 3	1	40
Student 4	3	30
Student 5	5	5
Student 6	4	15
Student 7	3	20
Student 8	1	35
Student 9	2	30
Student 10	4	10

Subject 1 scored 2 on TV viewing and 25 on achievement.

Subject 10 scored 4 on TV viewing and 10 on achievement.

Figure A.7 Correlation between TV-viewing and achievement scores for ten students.

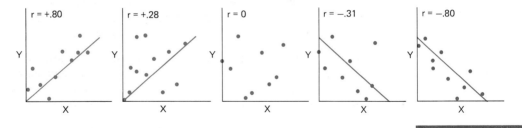

Figure A.8 Five scatter plots.

Scatter Plot

What is the relation between TV viewing and school achievement? One way to provide data on this question is to draw a scatter plot of the scores. A scatter plot is a graph consisting of two axes—such as hours of TV viewing on the X-axis and achievement score on the Y-axis—with one dot corresponding to each score on the two variables. An example for the Garden Valley study is shown in the right panel of figure A.7. As you can see, there seems to be a pattern in which a score on one axis is negatively, or inversely, related to a score on the other; in other words, the higher your TV-watching score, the lower your achievement score.

Figure A.8 shows five scatter plots, ranging from a strong positive relation between the variables to no relation to a strong negative relation. Although scatter plots provide a general description of the relation between two variables, you may want to summarize the data even further. You could mathematically summarize your scatter plot by giving a measure of correlation.

Correlation

The *correlation coefficient* is a number between −1 and +1 that indicates the degree of relation between two variables. A strong positive correlation (such as r = +.8) indicates that TV viewing is strongly related to school achievement, with more TV viewing corresponding to higher achievement. A strong negative correlation (such as r = −.8) indicates that TV viewing is strongly related to school achievement, with more TV viewing corresponding to lower achievement. A neutral correlation (coefficients close to r = .0) indicates that no relation exists between the two variables.

Figure A.8 shows the correlation coefficients for five scatter plots. You can think of correlation in the following way. First, draw a scatter plot. Then, draw a straight line through the scatter plot so that the distance between each dot and the line is minimized. The closer the dots are to the line, the stronger the relationship between the two variables—in either a positive correlation or a negative correlation. If the dots are spread across the whole graph, as in the middle panel of figure A.8, no correlation exists between the variables.

The formula for computing the correlation coefficient is

$$r = \frac{\Sigma xy}{\sqrt{\Sigma x^2 \cdot \Sigma y^2}}$$

where x is the difference between each X variable minus the mean; y is the difference between each Y variable and the mean; Σxy is the sum of the cross products (each x score multiplied by its corresponding y score); Σx^2 is the sum of the squares of the x scores; and Σy^2 is the sum of the squares of the y scores. Figure A.9 shows how to compute the value of r (that is, the correlation coefficient) for the Garden Valley data.

Misinterpretations

Correlation coefficients are useful ways of summarizing the relation between variables, but they can lead to errors in interpretation. Whenever you are presented with a correlation coefficient, you should ask yourself, "How should I interpret this correlation?" Some of the most common errors in interpretation follow:

Failure to recognize curvilinear trends. If you obtain a low correlation, this may be because no relation exists between the two variables or it may be due to other factors. A correlation coefficient looks only for a straight-line relation between two variables; more of one variable is related to more (or less) of another variable. But some relationships between variables change as scores change, producing a curvilinear line that will not be reflected in the coefficient of correlation. Hence, a strong curvilinear relation may exist without producing a strong correlation. An example is shown in figure A.10. In this case, TV viewing up to three hours seems to be related positively with school achievement; thereafter, increased viewing is negatively related with school achievement.

Use of restricted range. A low correlation may also be due to using only a small range of scores along one of the variables. This is because there must be both high and low scores on each variable to see what is related to these scores. For example, if you do a separate correlation for heavy viewers (that is, 3 or more hours) and a separate correlation for light viewers (that is, 0 to 2 hours), the correlation coefficients may be lowered because you included

Subject	TV-viewing score (X)	Deviation (X − X̄)	Squared deviation (X − X̄)²	Achievement score (Y)	Deviation (Y − Ȳ)	Squared deviation (Y − Ȳ)²	Cross product (X − X̄)·(Y − Ȳ)
1	2	− .5	.25	25	0	0	0
2	0	−2.5	6.25	40	15	225	−37.5
3	1	−1.5	2.25	40	15	225	−22.5
4	3	.5	.25	30	5	25	2.5
5	5	2.5	6.25	5	−20	400	−50
6	4	1.5	2.25	15	−10	100	−15
7	3	.5	.25	20	− 5	25	− 2.5
8	1	−1.5	2.25	35	10	100	− 1.5
9	2	− .5	.25	30	5	25	− 2.5
10	4	1.5	2.25	10	−15	225	22.50
	X̄ = 2.5		Σ(X − X̄)² = 22.50	X̄ = 25		Σ(Y − Ȳ)² = 1350	Σ(X − X̄)·(Y − Ȳ) = −16.5

$$r = \frac{\Sigma xy}{\sqrt{\Sigma x^2 \cdot \Sigma y^2}} = \frac{\Sigma[(X - \bar{X}) \cdot (Y - \bar{Y})]}{\sqrt{\Sigma(X - \bar{X})^2 \cdot \Sigma(Y - \bar{Y})^2}} = \frac{-165}{\sqrt{(22.50)(13.50)}} = +.95$$

Figure A.9 How to compute a correlation coefficient.

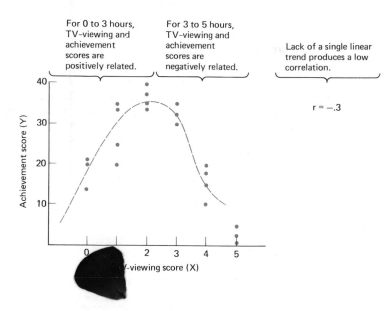

For 0 to 3 hours, TV-viewing and achievement scores are positively related.

For 3 to 5 hours, TV-viewing and achievement scores are negatively related.

Lack of a single linear trend produces a low correlation.

r = −.3

Figure A.10 A curvilinear relation between two variables.

only high scores the first time and only low scores the second time. Since accurate correlations depend on use of scores distributed across the entire range of both variables, restricting the range of one of the variables will artificially lower the correlation coefficient. Similarly, when conducting experiments using college students to see what is correlated with IQ, the experimenter may find low correlation coefficients since college students have mostly high IQ's.

Inferring causation. If you obtain a high correlation (either negative or positive), you may want to make an inference concerning which variable *caused* the values of the other. For example, if TV viewing and school achievement are strongly negatively correlated, you might want to conclude that TV viewing causes poor school achievement. However, such a conclusion is not justified based on correlation coefficients. *Correlation does not mean causation.* It does not indicate that one variable caused the other. Although it's possible that TV viewing causes poor school achievement, it's just as logical to argue that lower school achievement causes increased TV viewing. (Students who do poorly in school are "turned off" to school, so they turn on the TV.) A third possibility is that both TV viewing and low school achievement are caused by a third variable not included in the study, such as family stability or student health.

Inferential Statistics

Thus far you have learned how behavior can be described using statistics. In many cases, however, description of behavior is just the first step.

The second basic use of statistics is to draw conclusions regarding hypotheses based on data. This is called inferential statistics because it involves making inferences about causes of behavior that can apply to the entire population from which the sample was taken.

Problem

In the Garden Valley study, you might want to know whether TV viewing causes poor school performance. In order to test this idea, we could ask twenty students from Mrs. Perkins's class to volunteer for a study of TV viewing and school achievement. We can divide our twenty students into two groups: those who are asked to watch two hours or less ("light group") and those who are asked to watch three hours or more ("heavy group"). This will provide us with two sets of achievement scores that can be analyzed with statistical tests. Figure A.11 shows the score on a school achievement test two weeks later for each of the students in the light group and each of the students in the heavy group.

Research Design

In the preceding example, we have conducted a formal experiment. In order to understand the nature of formal experiments, let's review the following ideas that were introduced in chapter 1.

Independent variable. The independent variable is what the experimenter tries to manipulate, that is, the manipulated variable between the groups (or conditions or treatments). In the Garden Valley study, the independent variable is the degree of TV viewing, and the two groups (or conditions or treatments) are heavy versus light.

Dependent variable. The dependent variable is the measurement that is taken as a result of the manipulations, that is, the score that each subject gives as an outcome. In the Garden Valley study, the dependent variable is the score on the achievement test.

Hypothesis. The hypothesis is a prediction concerning the specific results of the study, in terms of the independent and dependent variables. For example, in the Garden Valley study, the hypothesis might be that heavy and light groups will not differ on school achievement scores.

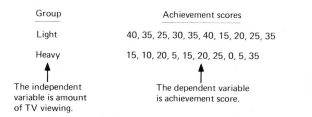

Figure A.11 Achievement scores for ten heavy and ten light TV viewers.

For any formal experiment that is limited to two variables, you should be able to identify the independent variable, the dependent variable, and the hypothesis.

Flaws in Research Design

As you think about the experiment suggested earlier, you should be asking yourself, "Is there anything wrong in the way that the researcher is testing the hypothesis?" One of the most common flaws is *lack of control.* Control refers to the idea that the two groups should be identical in every way *except* for the one thing that is being manipulated in the independent variable. Lack of control refers to the existence of differences between the characteristics or treatments of the two groups other than the independent variable. For example, we may find that the heavy group consists of all boys while the light group consists of all girls, or that the average age of the heavy group is lower than the average age of the light group. Then, we do not know whether differences in school achievement between the groups is due to TV viewing or to other factors, such as age or sex. Similarly, the experimenter may create more favorable testing conditions for the light group as compared to the heavy group. You must be careful to make sure that the experimenter does not overlook the *real* independent variable in an experiment; that is, the variable that causes the differences between the groups might not be the experimenter's independent variable. When another variable is the cause of the difference—such as age or sex or testing conditions—this variable is called a *confounding variable.*

In addition, each of the types of bias discussed for descriptive statistics can play a role in formal experiments.

Tests for Significance

Researchers will calculate the mean achievement score for each of the two groups and compare the results. In the Garden Valley study, the mean achievement score for the heavy TV viewers is 15 while the mean achievement score for the light TV viewers is 30. This does not necessarily mean that heavy TV viewers have lower scores than light viewers. Although it looks like the heavy group scores lower than the light group, in this experiment the difference could be due to chance. For example, if you rolled a die six times with your left hand, you might get 1, 2, 4, 3, 4, 1 for a mean of 2.5; then, if you rolled the same die six times with your right hand, you might get 4, 6, 2, 5, 4, 3 for a mean of 4.0. This does not mean that your right hand is a better die roller than your left. The difference between 2.5 versus 4.0 is due to chance; in this case, if you had rolled the die one thousand times with your left hand and then another one thousand times with your right, you probably would have gotten both means to average very near 3.5. Thus, in formal experiments it's possible to obtain a difference between the groups that is just due to chance. A statistical test can be performed to determine whether a difference between two means is *statistically significant*—in other words, a difference that is probably not due to chance.

A test of significance is used when each subject has one score, and the researcher wants to determine whether the mean for one group is different from the mean for another group. The test will reveal whether the difference between the means is probably due to chance or due to an actual difference between the groups. The researcher will report the results and include a *p-value*, which represents the level of significance. A p-value of .01 means that the difference in mean scores would be expected to occur by chance only one time out of every one hundred trials, and a p-value of .05 means that the difference would be expected on the basis of chance five times out of one hundred. Usually, if a p-value is less than .05, then the differences obtained are tentatively accepted as genuine ones—that is, not due to chance. Such is the case with the Garden Valley data, which show the differences to exceed the .05 level of significance.

Misinterpretations

As with any statistical test, there are many ways to misinterpret the results. Below are some common mistakes.

Multiple tests. If the researcher obtains a significant result, this does not automatically guarantee that the difference is not due to chance. For example, let's suppose that we gave twenty different ability and achievement tests to our heavy and light groups, and then looked for differences between the groups on each test. If we use a p-value of .05, this means that 5 percent of the time (or 1 out of 20) we would expect to find a significant difference that is due to chance. With twenty such tests, we could expect one of them to show a significant result just by chance. Thus, when an experimenter performs many statistical tests, you should be leery of the one or two tests that come out to be significant. To be on the safe side, you might like to see a replication—that is, a repeat of the same experiment with different subjects.

Low sample size. If the researcher fails to obtain significant results, this does not guarantee that there is really no difference between the groups. When very low sample sizes are used (such as, below 15 per group), one or two extreme scores can throw off the results. In general, small sample sizes require a larger difference between the means for the difference to be statistically significant. Thus, before you decide for sure that the difference is not significant, you should allow for a fair test—with several replications and adequate sample size.

Note. If you are interested in reading an actual research report concerning the effects of TV viewing on school achievement, you can read *Student Achievement in California Schools, 1979–80 Annual Report,* available from the California State Department of Education, P.O. Box 271, Sacramento, Calif. 95802. The part of the report dealing with TV viewing shows that the median number of hours of TV viewing per day is two for students in California schools. Furthermore, students who watch over four hours per day perform 10 to 20 percentage points less on tests of mathematics, reading, and written expression as compared to students who watch zero to one hour per day.

GLOSSARY

Pronunciations are from the twenty-fourth and twenty-fifth editions of *Dorland's Medical Dictionary* published by W. B. Saunders Company, in which the following key applies. Unmarked vowels not followed by a consonant are long and those followed by a consonant are short. Long vowels followed by a consonant are indicated by a macron (¯) and short vowels ending a syllable by a breve (·). The syllable *ah* indicates a broader *a*. Primary (') and secondary (") accent marks are used in polysyllabic words, and unstressed syllables are followed by a hyphen.

abnormal behavior
Actions, thoughts, and feelings that are harmful to the person or to others.

absolute threshold
The smallest magnitude of a stimulus that can be detected half the time.

accommodation
(ah-kom″o-da′shun)
The process of adding new information that forces a child to modify existing schemas.

achievement motivation (n Ach)
The psychological need in humans for success in competitive situations.

acupuncture (ak″u-pungk′chūr)
The ancient Chinese practice of inserting needles into specific parts of the body to control pain or cure illness.

adolescence
The period from the onset of puberty until the beginning of adulthood.

adolescent egocentrism
The quality of thinking that leads some adolescents to believe that they are the focus of attention in social situations, to believe that their problems are unique, to be unusually hypocritical, and to be ''pseudostupid.''

adolescent growth spurt
The rapid increase in weight and height that occurs around the onset of puberty.

adrenal glands (ah-dre′nal)
Two glands near the kidneys that secrete epinephrine and norepinephrine and that are involved in emotional arousal.

advance organizers
Introductory summaries of the content of each chapter that provide the general cognitive structure of the chapter to the learner.

affective disorders (ah-fek′tiv)
Psychological disorders involving disturbances of mood.

afferent neurons (af′er-ent)
Neurons that transmit messages from sense organs to the central nervous system.

agoraphobia (ag″o-rah-fo′be-ah)
An intense fear of leaving one's home or other familiar places.

alcoholism
Addiction to alcohol.

algorithm (al′go-rith′m)
A systematic pattern of reasoning that guarantees finding a correct solution to a problem.

amniotic fluid (am″ne-ot′ik)
The fluid within the amniotic sac in which the embryo is immersed.

amniotic sac (am″ne-ot′ik)
The protective covering for the developing embryo.

amphetamine psychosis
(si-ko′sis)
A prolonged reaction to the excessive use of stimulants, characterized by disordered thinking, confused and rapidly changing emotions, and intense suspiciousness.

amphetamines (am-fet′ah-minz)
Powerful stimulants that produce a conscious sense of increased energy and a euphoric high.

anal expulsive personality
A personality type based on anal fixation in which the person is cruel, messy, and disorderly.

anal retentive personality
A personality type based on anal fixation in which the person is stingy, obstinate, and compulsive.

anal stage
According to Freud, the second psychosexual stage (from one to three years), in which gratification is focused on the anus.

angiotensin (an″je-o-ten′sin)
A substance in the blood that signals the hypothalamus that the body needs water.

animism (an′i-mizm)
The egocentric belief of preoperational children that inanimate objects are alive, as the children are.

anterograde amnesia
(an′ter-o-grād)
Disorder of memory characterized by an inability to store and/or retrieve new information in long-term memory.

antidiuretic hormone (ADH)
(an″ti-di″u-ret′ik)
A hormone produced by the pituitary that causes the kidneys to conserve water in the body by reabsorbing it from the urine.

antisocial personality disorder
A personality disorder characterized by smooth social skills and a lack of guilt about violating social rules and laws and taking advantage of others.

anvil
An anvil-shaped bone of the middle ear that helps pass sound waves to the inner ear.

anxiety disorders (ang-zi′ĕ-te)
Psychological disorders that involve excessive levels of negative emotions such as nervousness, tension, worry, fright, and anxiety.

aphasia (ah-fa′ze-ah)
An impairment of the ability to understand or use language.

applied psychologist
A psychologist who uses knowledge of psychology to solve and prevent human problems.

approach-approach conflict
Conflict in which the individual must choose between two positive goals of approximately equal value.

approach-avoidance conflict
Conflict in which achieving a positive goal will produce a negative outcome as well.

Arnold–Ellis cognitive theory of emotion
The theory that emotional reactions are dependent on cognitive interpretations of stimulus situations.

assessment center
Center or program for the evaluation of employees that uses simulated management tasks as its primary method of evaluation.

assertiveness training
A method of behavior therapy that teaches individuals assertive rather than passive or aggressive ways of dealing with problematic situations.

assimilation (ah-sim″i-la′shun)
The process of adding new information to existing schemas.

association neurons
Neurons in the brain and spinal cord that process neural messages.

astral projection (as′tral)
Depersonalization that includes the illusion that the mind has left the body.

attachment
The psychological bond between infants and caregivers.

attitudes
Beliefs that predispose one to act and feel in certain ways.

attribution theory (ah-tri-bu′shun)
The theory that states that people tend to look for explanations for their own behavior and that of others.

atypical sexual behavior
Sexual practice that differs considerably from the norm.

audition (aw-dish′un)
The sense of hearing.

autonomic nervous system (aw″to-nom′ik)
The division of the nervous system that controls the involuntary actions of internal body organs, such as heartbeat and breathing, and is important in motivation and the experience of emotion.

aversive conditioning (ah-ver′siv)
A method of behavior therapy that involves the use of unpleasant negative stimuli to eliminate abnormal habits such as alcoholism and deviant sexual practices.

avoidance-avoidance conflict
Conflict in which the individual must choose between two negative outcomes of approximately equal value.

avoidance conditioning
Operant conditioning in which the behavior is reinforced because it prevents something negative from happening (a form of negative reinforcement).

axons (ak′sonz)
Neuron endings that transmit messages to other neurons.

basal metabolism rate (ba′sal mĕ-tab′o-lizm)
The rate at which the body converts calories into energy.

basilar membrane (bas′i-lar)
One of the membranes that separates the two tubes of the cochlea and upon which the organ of Corti rests.

basket cells
Sensory receptor cells at the bases of hairs that apparently detect pressure, temperature, and pain.

behavior
Directly observable and measurable human actions.

behavioral medicine
A specialty of clinical psychology that provides psychological treatments for medical conditions.

behaviorism (be-hāv′yor-izm)
The school of psychology that emphasizes the process of learning and the measurement of overt behavior.

behavior therapy
Psychotherapy based on social learning theory in which the therapist helps the client unlearn abnormal ways of behaving and learn more adaptive ways to take their place.

binocular cues (bin-ok′u-lar)
Visual cues that require both eyes to allow us to perceive distance.

biodata
The biographical information used by potential employers to evaluate a job candidate.

biofeedback (bi″o-fēd′bak)
A technique for providing an individual with precise information about the functioning of an internal organ to help him or her learn to control it voluntarily.

bipolar affective disorder (bi-po′lar)
A condition in which the individual experiences periods of mania that alternate irregularly with periods of severe depression.

blastocyst (blas′to-sist)
The cluster within the hollow ball of cells that develops early in pregnancy and later becomes the fetus.

blind spot
The spot where the optic nerve is attached to the retina, containing no rods or cones.

bone conduction hearing
Sounds transmitted through the bones of the head directly to the cochlear fluid.

brain
The complex mass of neural cells and related cells encased in the skull.

Cannon–Bard theory of emotion
The theory that conscious emotional experiences and physiological reactions and behavior are relatively independent events.

castration anxiety (kas-tra′shun)
According to Freud, the fear of a young boy that his father will punish his sexual desire for his mother by removing his genitals.

catatonic schizophrenia (kat′ah-ton′ik skiz″o-fre′ne-ah)
A subtype of schizophrenia in which the individual spends long periods in an inactive, statuelike state.

catharsis (kah-thar′sis)
The release of emotional energy related to unconscious conflicts.

causal relationships
Relationships in which one factor causes another to change.

cell body
The central part of the neuron that includes the nucleus.

cell membrane
The covering of a neuron or other cell.

central nervous system
The brain and the nerve fibers that make up the spinal cord.

cerebellum (ser″e-bel′um)
Two rounded lumps behind the medulla responsible for maintaining muscle tone and muscular coordination.

cerebral cortex (ser′e-bral)
The largest structure in the forebrain, controlling conscious experience and intelligence, and involved with the somatic nervous system.

cerebral hemispheres
The two main parts of the cerebral cortex.

chromosome (kro′mo-sōm)
The strip in the cell nucleus that contains genes.

chunks
Units of memory.

ciliary muscle (sil′e-er″e)
The muscle in the eye that controls the shape of the lens.

classical conditioning
A form of learning in which a previously neutral stimulus (CS) is paired with an unconditioned stimulus (UCS) to elicit a conditioned response (CR) that is identical to or very similar to the unconditioned response (UCR).

client-centered psychotherapy
Carl Rogers' approach to humanistic psychotherapy in which the therapist creates an atmosphere that encourages clients to discover feelings of which they are unaware.

climacteric (kli-mak′ter-ik)
The period between about ages 45 and 60 in which there is a loss of capacity to sexually reproduce in women and a decline in the reproductive capacity of men.

clinical method
The method of observing people while they are receiving psychological help from a psychologist.

cochlea (cok′le-ah)
The curved structure of the inner ear that is filled with fluid.

coefficient of correlation
The numerical expression of the strength of a relationship between two variables.

cognition (kog-nish′un)
The intellectual processes through which information is obtained, transformed, stored, retrieved, and otherwise used.

cognitive dissonance
(kog′ni-tiv dis′so-nans)
The discomfort that results from inconsistencies between attitudes and behavior.

cognitive map (kog′ni-tiv)
An inferred mental awareness of the structure of a physical space or related elements.

cognitive therapy
An approach to therapy that teaches individuals new cognitions—adaptive beliefs, expectations, and ways of thinking—to eliminate abnormal emotions and behavior.

collective unconscious
According to Jung, the content of the unconscious mind with which all humans are born.

concepts
Categories of things, events, or qualities that are linked together by some common feature or features in spite of their differences.

concrete operational stage
In Piaget's theory, the period of cognitive development from ages seven to eleven.

conditioned response (CR)
A response that is similar or identical to the unconditioned response that comes to be elicited by a conditioned stimulus.

conditioned stimulus (CS)
A stimulus that comes to elicit responses as a result of being paired with an unconditioned stimulus.

conditioning (kon-dish′un-ing)
A simple form of learning.

conditions of worth
The standards used by others or ourselves in judging our worth.

cones
The 6 million receptor cells located mostly in the center of the retina that transduce light waves into neural impulses, thereby coding information about light, dark, and color.

conflict
The state in which two or more motives cannot be satisfied because they interfere with one another.

conformity
Yielding to group pressure even when no direct request to comply has been made.

conjunctive concepts
(kon″junk-tiv′)
Concepts defined by the simultaneous presence of two or more common characteristics.

conscience (kon′shens)
According to Freud, the moral inhibitions of the superego.

conscious mind
That portion of the mind of which one is presently aware.

consciousness (kon′shus-nes)
A state of awareness.

conservation (kon-ser′vā-shun)
The concept understood by concrete operational children that quantity (number, mass, and so on) does not change just because its shape or other superficial features have changed.

consolidation
The process through which a long-term memory becomes stable.

continuity hypothesis
(kon″ti-nu′i-te)
The view that abnormal behavior is just a more severe form of normal psychological problems.

control group
The group in simple experiments that receives none of the independent variable and is used for comparisons with the treatment group.

convergent thinking
Thinking that is logical, conventional, and that focuses on a problem.

conversion disorders
(kon-ver′zhun)
Somatoform disorders in which individuals experience serious somatic symptoms such as functional blindness, deafness, and paralysis.

cooperative play
Play that involves cooperation between two or more children.

coping
Attempts by individuals to deal with the source of stress and/or control their reactions to it.

cornea (kor′ne-ah)
The protective coating on the surface of the eye through which light passes.

corpus callosum
(kor′pus kah-lo′-sum)
The link between the cerebral hemispheres.

correlational method
(kor″ē-la′shun-al)
A research method that measures the strength of the relation between variables.

creativity
The ability to make human products and ideas (such as symphonies or solutions to social problems) that are both novel and valued by others.

cretinism (kre′tin-izm)
A type of mental retardation in children caused by a deficiency of thyroxin.

criterion-referenced testing
(kri-te′re-on)
Testing designed to determine if a child can meet the minimum standards of a specific educational objective.

critical period
A biologically determined period in the life of some animals during which certain forms of learning can take place most easily.

criticism trap
An increase in the frequency of a negative behavior that often follows the use of criticism that reinforces the behavior it is intended to punish.

cross-sectional design
A research design that compares individuals who are of different ages at one point in time.

cupula (ku′pu-lah)
A gelatinlike structuring containing a tuft of hairlike sensory receptor cells in the semicircular canals.

dark adaptation
Increased sensitivity of the eye in semidarkness following an abrupt reduction in overall illumination.

daydreams
Relatively focused thinking about fantasies.

decay theory
The theory that states that forgetting occurs as the memory trace fades over time.

decenter (de-sen′ter)
To think about more than one characteristic of a thing at a time; a capacity of concrete operational children.

decibel (db) (des′i-bel)
Measurement of the loudness of perceived sound.

deep structure
The underlying structure of a statement that holds its meaning.

defense mechanisms
According to Freud, the unrealistic strategies used by the ego to discharge tension.

delay of reinforcement
The passage of time between the response and the positive reinforcement that leads to reduced efficiency of learning.

delusion
A false belief that distorts reality.

dendrites (den′drīts)
Small extensions on the cell body that receive messages from other neurons.

deoxyribonucleic acid (DNA)
(de-ok″se-ri″bo-nu-kla′ik)
The complex molecule that contains the genetic code.

dependent variable
The variable whose quantitative value depends on the effects of the independent variable.

depersonalization
(de-per″sun-al-i-za′shun)
The perceptual experience of one's body or surroundings becoming distorted or unreal in some way.

depressants
Drugs that reduce the activity of the central nervous system, leading to a sense of relaxation, drowsiness, and lowered inhibitions.

development
The more-or-less predictable changes in behavior associated with increasing age.

dichromacy (di-kro′mah-se)
Color blindness in which the individual is unable to distinguish either red and green or yellow and blue.

difference threshold
The smallest difference between two stimuli that can be detected half the time.

diffusion of responsibility
The effect of being in a group that apparently reduces the sense of personal responsibility of each group member to act appropriately.

directed consciousness
Focused and orderly awareness.

discontinuity hypothesis
(dis-kon″ti-nu′i-te)
The view that abnormal behavior is fundamentally different from normal psychological problems.

disjunctive concepts
(dis″-junk-tiv′)
Concepts defined by the presence of one of two common characteristics or both.

disorganized schizophrenia
(skiz″o-fre′ne-ah)
A subtype of schizophrenia characterized by shallow silliness, extreme social withdrawal, and fragmented delusions and hallucinations.

displacement (dis-plās′ment)
A defense mechanism in which the individual directs aggressive or sexual feelings away from the primary object to someone or something safe.

dispositional attribution
(dis″po-zish′un-al)
An explanation for behavior that is based on a characteristic of the individual.

dissociative amnesia
A dissociative disorder that involves a loss of memory and that has a psychological rather than a physical cause.

dissociative disorders
(dis-so″she-a-tiv)
A category of conditions involving sudden cognitive changes, such as a change in memory, perception, or identity.

divergent thinking
Thinking that is loosely organized, only partially directed, and unconventional.

dizygotic twins (di″zi-got′ik)
Twins formed from the fertilization of two ova by two sperm.

dominant gene
The gene that produces a trait in the individual when paired with a recessive gene.

double approach-avoidance conflict
Conflict that requires the individual to choose between two alternatives that each contain both positive and negative consequences.

Down's syndrome
A human abnormality resulting from a chromosomal malformation of chromosome pair number 21.

dream interpretation
A method developed by Freud in which the symbols of the manifest content of dreams that are recalled by the patient are interpreted to reveal their latent content.

dream sleep
A stage of sleep that typically occurs four to six times each night during which the individual experiences dreams.

drive reduction
The view that motives are based on the body's need to restore homeostasis when its biological needs are unmet.

drug therapy
A medical therapy that uses chemicals to treat abnormal behavior.

dyspareunia (dis″pah-roo′ne-ah)
A female sexual dysfunction in which the individual experiences pain during intercourse.

eardrum
Thin membrane that sound waves cause to vibrate; the first structure of the middle ear.

educational psychology
The field in which principles of learning, cognition, and other aspects of psychology are applied to improve education.

efferent neurons (ef′er-ent)
Neurons that transmit messages from the central nervous system to organs and muscles.

ego (e′go)
According to Freud, that part of the mind that uses the reality principle to satisfy the id.

egocentrism (e″go-sen′trizm)
The self-oriented quality in the thinking of preoperational children.

ego-dystonic homosexuality
(e'go-dis-ton'ik)
Homosexuality that creates discomfort because the homosexual personally considers his or her sexual preferences abnormal.

ego ideal
According to Freud, the standard of perfect conduct of the superego.

eidetic imagery (i-det'ik)
The ability in some individuals to maintain a "visual photograph" of an image after it has been removed from view for more than a fraction of a second.

ejaculatory disorder
(e-jak'u-lah-to''re)
Male sexual dysfunction in which the individual either reaches orgasm and ejaculates sperm too early or not at all.

elaboration (e-lab''o-ra'shun)
The process of creating associations between a new memory and existing memories.

Electra complex (e-lek'-trah)
According to Freud, the transfer of a young girl's sexual desires from her mother to her father after she discovers she has no penis.

electroconvulsive therapy (ECT)
(e-lek''tro-con-vul'siv)
A medical therapy that uses electrical current to induce controlled convulsive seizures that alleviate some types of mental disorders.

electroencephalogram (EEG)
(e-lek''tro-en-sef'ah-lo-gram)
Measures of electrical brain activity recorded on an electroencephalograph.

electromagnetic radiation
(e-lek''tro-mag-net'ik)
A form of energy including electricity, radio waves, and X rays, of which visible light is a part.

embryo (em'bre-o)
The early stage of prenatal life lasting from the second to the seventh week of pregnancy.

emotion
Positive or negative feelings, generally in reaction to stimuli accompanied by physiological arousal and related behavior.

encode (en'cōd)
To represent information in some form in the memory system.

encounter group
A humanistic group therapy technique designed to improve general self-awareness.

endocrine system (en'do-krin)
The system of glands that secretes hormones.

engram (en'gram)
The as yet unidentified memory trace in the brain that is the biological basis of memory.

epinephrine (ep''i-nef'rin)
A hormone produced by the adrenal glands.

episodic memory (ep'ī-sod-ik)
Memory for specific experiences that can be defined in terms of time and space.

equilibrium (e''kwi-lib're-um)
A state of balance when the knowledge of a child fits existing schemas.

equity theory
The theory that partners will be comfortable in their relationship only when the ratio between their perceived contributions and benefits is equal.

escape conditioning
Operant conditioning in which the behavior is reinforced because it causes a negative event to cease (a form of negative reinforcement).

estrogen (es'tro-jen)
A female sex hormone.

exhibitionism
(ek''sī-bish'ū-nizm'')
The practice of obtaining sexual pleasure by exposing one's genitals to others.

experimental group
The group in an experiment that receives some value of the independent variable.

experimental psychologist
A psychologist who conducts basic research.

external auditory canal
The tube that connects the pinna to the middle ear.

external disinhibition
(dis''in-hi-bish'un)
A temporary increase in the strength of an extinguished response caused by an unrelated stimulus event.

extinction (eks-ting'shun)
The process of unlearning a learned response because of the removal of the original source of learning.

extrasensory perception (ESP)
Perception not accounted for by the five senses.

extrinsic motivation
(eks-trin'sik)
Human motives stimulated by external rewards.

extroversion (eks''trah-ver'zhun)
According to Jung, the tendency of some individuals to be friendly and open to the world.

family therapy
An approach to psychotherapy that emphasizes an understanding of the roles of each of the members of the family system, usually conducted with all members of the family present.

fertilization (fer'ti-li-za'shun)
The uniting of sperm and ovum that produces a zygote.

fetishism (fet'ish-izm)
The practice of obtaining sexual arousal primarily or exclusively from specific objects.

fetus (fe'tus)
The stage of prenatal life lasting from the seventh week of pregnancy until birth.

fixed interval schedule
A reinforcement schedule in which the reinforcer is given following the first response occurring after a predetermined period of time.

fixed ratio schedule
A reinforcement schedule in which the reinforcer is given only after a specified number of responses.

flooding
A method of behavior therapy in which the client is confronted with high levels of the phobic stimulus until the fear response is extinguished.

flowing consciousness
Drifting, unfocused awareness.

forebrain
The parts of the brain, including the thalamus, hypothalamus, and cerebral cortex, that cover the hindbrain and midbrain and fill much of the skull.

formal experiments
Research methods that allow the researcher to manipulate the independent variable in order to study the effect on the dependent variable.

formal operational stage
In Piaget's theory, the period of intellectual development usually reached about age 11, and characterized by the ability to use abstract concepts.

fovea (fo've-ah)
The central spot of the retina containing the greatest concentration of cones.

free association
A tool used by Freud in which the patient is encouraged to talk about whatever comes to mind, allowing the contents of the unconscious mind to slip past the censorship of the ego.

free nerve endings
Sensory receptor cells in the skin that apparently detect pressure, temperature, and pain.

frequency of cycles
Rate of vibration of sound waves; determines pitch.

Freud's instinct theory
The theory that aggression is caused by an inborn aggressive instinct.

frustration
The results of being unable to satisfy a motive.

frustration-aggression theory
The theory that aggression is a natural reaction to frustration.

fugue (fūg)
A period of "wandering" that involves a loss of memory and a change in identity.

functional fixedness
A set that interferes with problem solving by focusing thinking on the habitual uses of the elements in a problem.

functionalism (funk′shun-al-izm)
The nineteenth-century school of psychology that emphasized the useful functions of consciousness.

g
A broad general factor of intelligence, a concept endorsed by some investigators of intelligence.

gamete (gam′ēt)
A sex cell that contains 23 chromosomes instead of the normal 46.

ganglia (gang′gle-ah)
Clusters of cell bodies of neurons outside of the central nervous system.

gene (jēn)
The hereditary unit made up of deoxyribonucleic acid.

general adaptation syndrome (GAS)
According to Selye, the mobilization of the body to ward off threats, characterized by a three-stage pattern of the alarm reaction, the resistance stage, and the exhaustion stage.

generalized anxiety disorder
An uneasy sense of general tension and apprehension that makes the individual highly uncomfortable because of its prolonged presence.

generative property of language (jen′ē-ra″tiv)
The ability to create an infinite set of utterances using a finite set of elements and rules.

genital stage (jen′i-tal)
According to Freud, the psychosexual stage (from 11 years through adulthood) in which sexual and romantic interest is directed toward one's peers.

gestalt (ges-tawlt′)
An organized or unified whole.

Gestalt therapy
A humanistic therapy in which the therapist takes an active role (questioning and challenging the client) to help the client become more aware of his or her feelings.

glands
Structures in the body that secrete substances.

glucagon (gloo′kah-gon)
A hormone produced by the islets of Langerhans that causes the liver to release sugar into the bloodstream.

gonads (gō′nadz)
The glands that produce sex cells and hormones important in sexual arousal and that contribute to the development of secondary sex characteristics.

group therapy
Psychotherapy conducted in groups, typically of four to eight clients at a time.

gustation (gus-ta′shun)
The sense of taste.

hallucination (hah-lu″si-na′shun)
A false perceptual experience that distorts reality.

hallucinogens (hah-lu′si″no-jenz)
Drugs that alter perceptual experiences.

hammer
A hammer-shaped bone of the middle ear that helps pass sound waves to the inner ear.

hertz (Hz)
Measurement of the frequency of sound waves in cycles per second.

heuristics (hu-ris′tiks)
A pattern of reasoning that increases the probability of finding a correct solution to a problem.

hindbrain
The lowest part of the brain, located at the base of the skull.

homeostatic mechanism (ho″me-o-stat′ik)
Internal bodily mechanism that senses biological imbalances and stimulates actions to restore the proper balance.

homosexual
An individual who prefers to form intimate and sexual relationships with members of his or her own sex.

hormones (hor′mōnz)
Chemical substances, produced by endocrine glands, that influence internal organs.

human factors engineering
The branch of industrial-organizational psychology interested in the design of machines to be operated by human beings.

humanistic theory of psychology
The psychological view that human beings possess an innate tendency to improve and determine their lives by the decisions they make.

hyperphagia (hi′per-fa′je-ah)
Excessive overeating that results from the destruction of the satiety center of the hypothalamus.

hypnogogic state (hip″nah-goj′ik)
A relaxed state of dreamlike awareness between wakefulness and sleep.

hypnotism (hip′no-tizm)
An altered state of consciousness in which the individual is highly relaxed and susceptible to suggestions.

hypochondriasis (hi″po-kon-dri′ah-sis)
A mild form of somatization disorder characterized by excessive concern about one's health.

hypothalamus (hi″po-thal′ah-mus)
The part of the forebrain involved with motives, emotions, and the functions of the autonomic nervous system.

hypothesis (hi-poth′ē-sis)
A proposed explanation for a phenomenon that can be tested.

id
According to Freud, the inborn part of the unconscious mind that uses the primary process to satisfy its needs and that acts according to the pleasure principle.

ideal self
According to humanists, the person one wishes he or she were.

identification
The tendency to base one's identity on and model one's actions after individuals who are successful in gaining satisfaction from life.

identity crisis
The difficulty encountered by some adolescents in achieving an adult identity.

impotence (im'po-tens)
The inability of some males to achieve or maintain an erection of the penis long enough to have satisfactory sexual intercourse.

imprinting (im'print-ing)
A form of early learning that occurs in some animals during a critical period.

in-basket exercise
A type of management simulation task in which the individual attempts to solve a problem that is typical of the ones that appear in a manager's ''in-basket.''

incentive
An external cue that activates motivation.

incest (in'sest)
Sexual relations between relatives.

independent variable
The variable whose quantitative value can be independently controlled by the researcher.

industrial-organizational psychologist
A psychologist who studies organizations and seeks ways to improve the functioning and human benefits of business.

inference
Logical conclusion based on available evidence.

inhalants (in-ha'lants)
Toxic substances that produce a sense of intoxication when inhaled.

inner-directedness
A force that humanists believe all people possess that internally leads them to grow and improve.

insight (in'sit)
A form of cognitive change that involves recognition of previously unseen relationships.

insomnia (in-som'ne-ah)
Chronic inability to fall asleep in a reasonable amount of time or to stay asleep.

insulin (in'su-lin)
A hormone produced by the islets of Langerhans that reduces the amount of sugar in the bloodstream.

intelligence (in-tel'i-jens)
The cognitive ability of an individual to learn from experience, to reason well, and to cope with the demands of daily living.

intelligence quotient (IQ)
A numerical value of intelligence derived from the results of an intelligence test.

intensity
Density of vibrating air molecules; determines the loudness of sound.

interactionism (in''ter-ak'shun-izm)
The view that behavior is influenced by a combination of the characteristics of both the person and the situation.

interference theory
The theory that states that forgetting occurs because similar memories interfere with the storage or retrieval of information.

interview
A subjective method of personality assessment that involves questioning techniques designed to reveal the personality of the client.

intracranial stimulation (in''trah-kra'ne-al)
Electrical stimulation of the internal structures of the brain.

intrinsic motivation (in-trin'sik)
Human motives stimulated by the inherent nature of the activity or its natural consequences.

introspection (in''tro-spek'shun)
The process of looking inward at one's own consciousness.

introversion (intro-ver'zhun)
According to Jung, the tendency of some individuals to be shy and to focus their attention on themselves.

ions (i'ons)
Electrically charged particles.

iris (i'ris)
The colored part of the eye behind the cornea that regulates the amount of light that enters.

islets of Langerhans (i'lets *of* lahng'er-hanz)
Endocrine cells in the pancreas that regulate the level of sugar in the blood.

James–Lange theory of emotion
The theory that conscious emotional experiences are caused by feedback to the cerebral cortex from physiological reactions and behavior.

job performance ratings
Ratings of the actual performance of employees in their jobs by supervisors.

kinesthetic receptors (kin''es-thet'ik)
Receptors in the muscles, joints, and skin that provide information about movement, posture, and orientation.

Korsakoff's syndrome (Kor-sak'ofs)
A disorder involving both anterograde and retrograde amnesia caused by excessive use of alcohol.

language
A symbolic code used in communication.

latency stage
According to Freud, the fourth psychosexual stage (from about 7 to 11 years), during which sexual energy is sublimated and converted into socially valued activities.

latent content
According to Freud, the true meaning of dreams that is found in the symbols of their manifest content.

law
A strongly supported and widely accepted theory.

learned helplessness
A pattern of learned behavior characterized by a lack of effort to avoid negative events; caused by previous exposure to unavoidable negative events.

learned taste aversion (ah-ver'shun)
Negative reaction to a particular taste that has been associated with nausea or other illness.

learning
Any relatively permanent change in behavior brought about through experience.

learning set
Improvement in the rate of learning to solve new problems through practice solving similar problems.

lens
Transparent portion of the eye that focuses light on the retina.

levels of processing model
An alternative to the stage theory of memory that states that the distinction between short-term and long-term memory is a matter of degree rather than different kinds of memory and is based on how incoming information is processed.

light adaptation
Regaining sensitivity of the eye to bright light following an abrupt increase in overall illumination.

linguistic relativity hypothesis
The idea that the structure of a language may influence the way individuals think.

longitudinal design
A research design in which changes in the same individuals are studied as they reach different ages.

long-term memory (LTM)
The third stage of memory, involving the storage of information that is kept for long periods of time.

mainstreaming
The practice of integrating handicapped children into regular classrooms.

major depression
An affective disorder characterized by episodes of deep unhappiness, loss of interest in life, and other symptoms.

management by objectives
The strategy of giving employees specific goals but giving them considerable freedom in deciding how to reach those goals.

mania (ma'ne-ah)
A disturbance of mood in which the individual experiences a euphoria characterized by unrealistic optimism and sensory pleasures.

manifest content
According to Freud, the obvious, but superficial, meaning of dreams.

mantra (man'trah)
A word or sound containing religious meaning used during meditation.

Maslow's hierarchy of motives
The concept that more basic needs must be met before higher level motives become active.

mastery learning
The concept that children should never progress from one learning task to another until they have mastered the more basic one.

maturation (mach"u-ra'shun)
Systematic physical growth of the body, including the nervous system.

medical therapies
Those therapies—including drug therapy, electroconvulsive therapy, and psychosurgery—generally designed to correct a physical condition that is believed to be the cause of a psychological disorder.

meditation (med"i-ta'shun)
Several methods of focusing concentration away from thoughts and feelings, and generating a sense of relaxation.

medulla (mĕ-dul'ah)
The swelling at the top of the spinal cord responsible for controlling breathing and a variety of reflexes.

menarche (mĕ-nar'ke)
The first menstrual period.

menopause (men'o-pawz)
The cessation of menstruation and the capacity to reproduce in women.

mental processes
Private psychological activities that include thinking, perceiving, and feeling.

metabolism (mĕ-tab'o-lizm)
The process through which the body burns energy.

midbrain
The small area at the top of the hindbrain that primarily serves as a reflex center for orienting the eyes and ears.

mitosis (mi-to'sis)
Cell division resulting in two identical cells.

modeling
Learning based on observation of the behavior of another.

monochromacy
(mon"o-kro'mah-se)
Color blindness in which the individual sees no color at all.

monocular cues (mon-ok'u-lar)
Seven visual cues that can be seen with one eye that allow us to perceive distance.

monozygotic twins
(mon"o-zi-got'ik)
Twins formed from a single ovum; they are identical in appearance because they have the same genetic structure.

morpheme (mor'fēm)
The smallest unit of meaning in a language.

motivated forgetting
Forgetting that is believed to be based on the upsetting or threatening nature of the information that is forgotten.

motivation
Internal state or condition that activates behavior and gives it direction.

motive for affiliation
The need to be with other people and to have personal relationships.

motives
Internal states or conditions that activate behavior and give it direction.

multiple personality
A dissociative disorder in which the individual shifts abruptly and repeatedly from one "personality" to another.

myelin sheath (mi'e-lin)
The protective fatty covering wrapped around part of the neuron.

myoclonia (mi"o-klo'ne-ah)
An abrupt movement that sometimes occurs during the hypnogogic state in which the sleeper often experiences a sense of falling.

natural childbirth
Birth in which the mother is alert, takes an active role, and is not highly anesthetized.

naturalistic observation
A research method based on recording behavior as it occurs in natural life settings.

negative reinforcement
Reinforcement that comes about from the removal or avoidance of a negative event as the consequence of behavior.

neonatal period (ne"o-na'tal)
The first two weeks of life following birth.

nerve
A bundle of long neurons outside the brain and spinal cord.

neuron (nu'ron)
An individual nerve cell.

neurosis (nu-ro'sis)
Psychological disorders that are relatively mild and involve no "loss of contact with reality."

neurotransmitters
(nu"ro-tranz'-mit-erz)
Chemical substances produced by axons that transmit messages across the synapse.

nightmare
A dream that occurs during REM sleep whose content is exceptionally frightening, sad, angry, or in some other way uncomfortable.

night terror
An upsetting nocturnal experience that occurs most often in preschool-age children during deep non-REM sleep.

nocturnal enuresis
(nok"tern-el en"u-re'sis)
Involuntary urination during sleep among children above age four.

nodes of Ranvier (rahn'-vē-ā)
Gaps in the myelin sheath covering
the nerves.

norepinephrine (nor''ep-i-nef'rin)
A hormone produced by the adrenal
glands.

normal distribution
The symmetrical pattern of scores on
a scale in which a majority of the
scores are clustered near the center
and a minority are at either extreme.

norms
Standards (created by the scores of
a large group of individuals) used as
the basis of comparison for scores on
a test.

novel stimulation
New or changed experiences.

obedience
Doing what one is told to do by
people in authority.

objectivity
Lack of subjectivity in a test question
so that the same score is produced
regardless of who does the scoring.

object permanence
The understanding that objects
continue to exist after they have been
removed from view.

observational method
A method of personality assessment
that involves watching a person's
actual behavior in a natural or
simulated situation.

obsessive-compulsive disorders
Disorders that involve obsessions
(anxiety-provoking thoughts that will
not go away) and/or compulsions
(irresistible urges to engage in
specific irrational behaviors).

Oedipus complex (ed'i-pus)
According to Freud, the unconscious
wish of all male children to kill their
fathers and sexually possess their
mothers.

olfaction (ol-fak'shun)
The sense of smell.

olfactory epithelium
(ol-fak'to-re ep''i-the'le-um)
The sheet of receptor cells at the top
of the nasal cavity.

operant conditioning (op'ē-rant)
Learning in which the consequences
of behavior lead to changes in the
probability of its occurrence.

opiates (o'pe-ats)
Narcotic drugs derived from the
opium poppy.

**opponent process theory of color
vision**
The theory of color vision that
contends that the eye has two kinds
of cones that respond to light in
either the red-green or yellow-blue
ranges of wavelength.

**opponent-process theory of
motivation**
Solomon's theory of the learning of
new motives based on changes over
time in contrasting feelings.

optic nerve
The nerve that carries neural
messages about vision to the brain.

optimal level of arousal
The apparent human need for a
comfortable level of stimulation,
achieved by acting in ways that
increase or decrease it.

oral aggressive personality
A personality type in which the
person seeks pleasure by being
verbally hostile to others.

oral receptive personality
A personality type in which the
person seeks pleasure through
overeating, smoking, and other oral
means.

oral stage
According to Freud, the first
psychosexual stage (from birth to one
year), in which id gratification is
focused on the mouth.

organ of Corti (kor'te)
Sensory receptor in the cochlea that
transduces sound waves into coded
neural impulses.

orgasmic dysfunction
(or-gaz''mik dis-funk'shun)
A female sexual dysfunction in which
the individual is unable to experience
orgasm.

oval window
The membrane of the inner ear that
vibrates, creating sound waves in the
fluid of the cochlea.

ovaries (o'vah-rez)
Female endocrine glands that secrete
sex-related hormones and produce
ova, or eggs.

pancreas (pan'kre-as)
The organ near the stomach that
contains the islets of Langerhans.

panic anxiety disorder
A pattern of anxiety in which long
periods of calm are broken by an
intensely uncomfortable attack of
anxiety.

papillae (pah-pil'e)
Clusters of taste buds on the tongue.

paradigm (pār'a-dim)
A pattern or format for conducting
research.

parallel play
Playing near but not with another
child.

paranoia (par''ah-noi'ah)
A nonschizophrenic disorder
characterized by delusions of
grandeur and persecution that are
more logical than those of paranoid
schizophrenics in the absence of
hallucinations.

paranoid schizophrenia
(par'ah-noid skiz''o-fre'ne-ah)
A subtype of schizophrenia in which
the individual holds false beliefs or
delusions—often delusions of
persecution and grandeur—that
seriously distort reality.

parapsychology
(par''ah-si-kol'o-je)
The study of psychic phenomena
such as ESP.

parasympathetic division
(par''ah-sim''pah-thet'ik)
The division of the autonomic
nervous system that generally
"calms" internal organs.

parathormone (par''ah-thor'mōn)
A hormone that regulates ion levels in
neurons and controls excitability of
the nervous system.

parathyroid (par''ah-thi'roid)
Four glands embedded in the thyroid
that produce parathormone.

participative management
The practice of involving employees
at all levels in management decisions.

peak experience
An intensely moving experience in
which the individual feels a sense of
unity with the world.

pedophilia (pe''do-fil'e-ah)
The practice of obtaining pleasure
from sexual contact with children.

penis envy
The desire of a young girl to possess
a penis.

perception (per-sep'shun)
The process of organizing and
interpreting information received from
the outside world.

perceptual constancy
The tendency for perceptions of
objects to remain relatively
unchanged in spite of changes in raw
sensations.

performance test
Employee selection test that resembles the actual manual performance required in a job.

peripheralism (pĕ-rif′er-al-izm)
The theory that thinking is a matter of talking silently to oneself.

peripheral nervous system (pĕ-rif′er-al)
The network of nerves that branch off the brain and spinal cord to all parts of the body.

personal growth therapy
Psychotherapy for normal individuals who want to enhance their personal adjustment, improve interpersonal relationships, learn to react to stress, and so on.

personality
The sum total of the typical ways of acting, thinking, and feeling that makes each person unique.

personality disorders
Psychological disorders that are believed to result from personalities that developed improperly during childhood.

personal unconscious
According to Jung, the motives, conflicts, and information that are repressed by a person because they are threatening to that individual.

person perception
The process of forming impressions of others.

persuasion
The process of changing another person's attitudes through arguments and other related means.

phallic stage (fal′ik)
According to Freud, the third psychosexual stage (from three to six years), in which gratification is focused on the genitals.

phi phenomenon (fī fē-nom′ē-non)
The perception of apparent movement between two stationary stimuli.

phobia (fo′be-ah)
An intense, irrational fear.

phoneme (fo′nēm)
The smallest unit of sound in a language.

physiologist (fiz″e-ol′o-jist)
A scientist who studies the functions of living organs.

pinna (pin′nah)
The external part of the ear.

pitch
The experience of sound vibrations sensed as high or low.

pituitary (pĭ-tu′ĭ-tār″e)
The body's master gland, located near the bottom of the brain, whose hormones help regulate the activity of the other glands in the endocrine system.

placenta (plah-sen′tah)
The structure that holds the fetus against the uterine wall and nourishes it.

pleasure principle
According to Freud, the attempt of the id to seek immediate pleasure and avoid pain regardless of how harmful it might be to others.

polarized state (po′lar iz′d)
The resting state of a neuron when mostly negative ions are inside and mostly positive ions are outside the cell membrane.

pons (ponz)
Part of the hindbrain that is involved in balance, hearing, and some parasympathetic functions.

positive reinforcement (re″in-fors′ment)
Any consequence of behavior that leads to an increase in the probability of its occurrence.

postpartum depression
Major depression that begins immediately following childbirth.

preconscious mind
That portion of the mind that contains information that is not presently conscious but can be easily brought into consciousness.

prejudice
A negative attitude based on inaccurate generalizations about a group of people.

premature ejaculation
A male sexual dysfunction in which the individual reaches orgasm and ejaculates sperm too early.

preoperational stage
In Piaget's theory, the period of cognitive development from ages two to seven.

pressure
Stress that arises from the threat of negative events.

primacy effect
The tendency to weigh first impressions heavily in forming opinions about other people.

primary motives
Human motives for things that are necessary for survival, such as food, water, and warmth.

primary process thinking
According to Freud, the attempt by the id to satisfy its needs by forming a wish-fulfilling mental image of the desired object.

primary reinforcement
Reinforcement from innate positive reinforcers that do not have to be acquired through learning.

primary sex characteristics
Ovulation and menstruation in females and production of sperm in males.

proactive interference (pro-ak′tiv in″ter-fēr′ens)
Interference created by memories from prior learning.

problem solving
The cognitive process through which information is used to reach a goal that is blocked by some obstacle.

progeria (pro-je′re-ah)
A rare disease in which children go through the entire biological process of aging by about 13 years of age.

programmed instruction
Educational materials that incorporate the concepts of operant conditioning, especially positive reinforcement.

progressive relaxation training
A method of learning to deeply relax the muscles of the body.

Project Follow Through
A federally sponsored program designed to help educate economically disadvantaged children.

projection (pro-jek′shun)
According to Freud, a defense mechanism in which unacceptable id desires are viewed as the desires of others and not as one's own.

projective test
A test that uses ambiguous stimuli designed to reveal the contents of the client's unconscious mind.

psychoanalysis (si″ko-ah-nal′ĭ-sis)
A method of psychotherapy developed by Freud based on his belief that the root of all psychological problems is unconscious conflicts between the id, the ego, and the superego.

psychoanalytic theory
Freud's theory that the origin of personality lies in the balance between the id, the ego, and the superego.

psychogenic pain disorders
(si''ko-jen'ik)
Somatoform disorders in which the individual experiences a relatively specific and chronic pain that has a psychological rather than physical cause.

psychological motives
Motives that are related to the individual's happiness and well-being, but not to survival.

psychology
The science of behavior and mental processes.

psychophysics (si''ko-fiz'iks)
A specialty area of psychology that studies sensory limits, sensory adaptation, and related topics.

psychosexual stages
Developmental periods in the personality theory of Sigmund Freud during which the sexual energy of the id finds different sources of satisfaction.

psychosis (si-ko'sis)
Psychological disorders that are relatively disabling and involve "loss of contact with reality."

psychosomatic illness
(si''ko-so-mat'ik)
Bodily illness that is psychological rather than biological in origin (*psycho* = psychological, *soma* = body).

psychosurgery (si''ko-ser'jer-e)
A medical therapy that involves operating on the brain in an attempt to alleviate some types of mental disorders.

psychotherapy (si-ko-ther'ah-pe)
A form of therapy in which a trained professional uses methods based on psychological theories to help a person with psychological problems.

psychotropic drugs
(si''ko-trop'pik)
The class of drugs that alters conscious experience.

puberty (pu'ber-te)
The point in development at which the individual is physically capable of sexual reproduction.

punishment
A negative consequence of a behavior that leads to a decrease in the frequency of the behavior.

pupil (pu'pil)
The opening of the iris.

quantitative (kwon'ti-ta-tiv)
Capable of being measured in numerical terms.

rape
The act of forcing sexual activity on an unwilling person.

rationalization
(rash''un-al-i-za'shun)
According to Freud, a defense mechanism in which stress is reduced by "explaining" events in ways that reduce their stressful qualities.

reaction formation
According to Freud, a defense mechanism in which unacceptable id desires are avoided by transforming them into the opposite desires.

reality principle
According to Freud, the attempt by the ego to find safe, realistic ways of meeting the needs of the id.

recall
The ability to retrieve information from long-term memory with few cues.

recessive gene
The gene that produces a trait in the individual only when the same recessive gene has been inherited from both parents.

reciprocal determination
(re-sip''ro-kal)
Bandura's observation that the individual's behavior and the social learning environment continually influence one another.

recognition
A measure of memory based on the ability to select correct information from among the options provided.

reconstruction theory
The theory that states that forgetting is due to changes in the structure of a memory that make it inaccurate when retrieved.

reflection (re-flek'shun)
A technique in humanistic psychotherapy in which the therapist reflects the emotions of the client in order to help clients clarify their feelings.

regression
According to Freud, a defense mechanism in which tension is reduced by returning to an infantile pattern of behavior.

rehearsal
Mental repetition of information in order to retain it in short-term memory.

relearning
A measure of memory based on the length of time it takes to relearn forgotten material.

reliability
A test's ability to produce similar scores if the test is administered on different occasions or by different examiners.

REM sleep
Rapid-eye-movement sleep, characterized by movement of the eyes under the lids; often accompanies dreams.

repression
Sigmund Freud's theory that forgetting occurs because the conscious mind often deals with unpleasant information by pushing it into unconsciousness.

resistance
Any form of patient opposition to the process of psychoanalysis.

retarded ejaculation
A male sexual dysfunction in which the individual is unable to experience orgasm and ejaculation.

reticular formation
(re-tik'u-lar)
The system of neural structures spanning parts of the hindbrain, midbrain, and forebrain that plays a role in cortical arousal and attention.

retina (ret'i-nah)
The area at the back of the eye on which images are formed and that contains the rods and cones.

retroactive interference
(ret''ro-ak'tiv)
Interference created by memories from later learning.

retrograde amnesia
(ret'ro-grād)
Disorder of memory characterized by an inability to retrieve old long-term memories, generally for a specific period of time extending back from the beginning of the disorder.

reversibility (re-ver'si-bil-i-te)
The concept understood by concrete operational children that logical propositions can be reversed (if $2 + 3 = 5$, then $5 - 3 = 2$).

rods
The 120 million cells located outside the center of the retina that transduce light waves into neural impulses, thereby coding information about light and dark.

role playing
A therapeutic technique in which the therapist and client act as if they are people in problematic situations.

rooting reflex
An automatic response in which an infant turns its head toward stimulation on the cheek.

round window
The membrane that relieves pressure from the vibrating waves in the cochlear fluid.

saccule (sak'ul)
A fluid-filled sac of the vestibular organ that informs the brain about the body's orientation.

Schachter–Singer cognitive theory of emotion
The theory that emotional reactions are dependent on cognitive interpretations of both stimulus situations and physiological reactions and behavior.

schema (ske'mah)
A term used by Piaget to refer to concepts in children's thinking.

schizoid personality disorder (skiz'oid)
A personality disorder characterized by blunted emotions, lack of interest in social relationships, and withdrawal into a solitary existence.

schizophrenia (skiz"o-fren'e-ah)
A psychological disorder involving cognitive disturbance, emotional disturbance, and social withdrawal.

school psychologist
A psychologist who aids schools by testing children to determine eligibility for placement in special education programs and who consults with teachers and parents.

science
Approach to knowledge based on systematic observation.

scientific methods
Methods of gathering information based on systematic observation.

secondary reinforcement
Reinforcement from learned positive reinforcers.

secondary sex characteristics
Development of the breasts and hips in females; growth of the testes, broadening of the shoulders, lowered voice, growth of the penis, and facial hair in males; and growth of pubic and other body hair in both sexes.

selective attention
The mental process of selecting only certain stimuli to be responded to.

self
According to humanists, the person one thinks he or she is.

self-actualization
According to Maslow, the seldomly reached full result of the inner-directed drive of humans to grow, improve, and use their potential to the fullest.

self-concept
Our subjective perceptions of who we are and what we are like.

self-efficacy
According to Bandura, the perception of being capable of achieving one's goals.

self-regulation
According to Bandura, the process of cognitively reinforcing and punishing our own behavior, depending on whether or not it meets our personal standards.

semantic content (se-man'tik)
The meaning in symbols, such as language.

semantic memory (se-man'tik)
Memory for meaning without reference to the time and place of learning.

semicircular canals (sem"e-ser'ku-lar)
Three nearly circular tubes in the vestibular organ that inform the brain about tilts of the head and body.

semipermeable (sem"e-per'me-ah-b'l)
A surface that allows some, but not all, particles to pass through.

senility (sě-nil'ĭ-te)
The physiological deterioration of brain functioning that occurs in some older adults.

sensation (sen-sa'shun)
The process of receiving, translating, and transmitting messages from the outside world to the brain.

sense organs
Organs that receive stimuli.

sensorimotor stage
In Piaget's theory, the period of cognitive development from birth to two years.

sensory adaptation
Weakened magnitude of a sensation resulting from prolonged presentation of the stimulus.

sensory receptor cells
Cells in sense organs that translate messages into neural impulses that are sent to the brain.

sensory register
The first stage of memory that briefly holds an exact image of each sensory experience until it can be processed.

separation anxiety
The distress experienced by infants when they are separated from their caregivers.

serial position effect
The finding that immediate recall of items in a list of fixed order is often better for items at the beginning and end of the list than for those in the middle.

set
An habitual way of approaching or perceiving a problem.

sex chromosomes
Chromosome pair number 23, which determines the sex of the individual.

sexual dysfunction
An inability to engage successfully or comfortably in normal sexual activities.

sexual masochism (mas'o-kizm)
A condition in which receiving pain is sexually exciting.

sexual sadism (sad'izm)
The practice of obtaining sexual pleasure by inflicting pain on others.

shaping
A strategy of positively reinforcing behaviors that are successively more similar to desired behaviors.

short-term memory (STM)
The second stage of memory in which five to nine bits of information can be stored for brief periods of time.

simple phobia
A phobic fear of one relatively specific thing.

simulated management task
A contrived task requiring managerial skills that is given to candidates for management positions to evaluate their potential as managers.

situational attribution
An explanation for behavior that is based on an external cause.

situationism (sit"u-a'shun-izm)
The view that behavior is consistent only as long as situations remain consistent.

Skinner box
A cage for animals equipped with a response lever and a food tray dispenser used in research on operant conditioning.

sleeper effects
According to Hovland, the potential for low-credibility speakers to influence opinion after a period of time.

sleeptalking
Talking during any phase of the sleep cycle.

sleepwalking
Walking and carrying on complicated activities during the deepest part of non-REM sleep.

social clock
The roughly predictable sequence of important events in the adult life span.

social learning theory
The theory that our personalities are formed primarily through learning from other members of society.

social phobia
An intense fear of social interactions, particularly those with strangers and those in which the person might be viewed negatively.

social psychology
The branch of psychology that studies individuals as they interact with others.

solitary play
Playing alone.

somatic nervous system (so-mat'ik)
Division of the nervous system that carries messages from the sense organs, muscles, joints, and skin to the central nervous system, and from the central nervous system to the skeletal muscles.

somatization disorders (so''mah-ti-za'shun)
Intensely and chronically uncomfortable psychological condition that involves numerous symptoms of somatic (bodily) illnesses without physical cause.

somatoform disorders (so''mah-to-form)
Disorders in which the individual experiences the symptoms of physical health problems that have psychological rather than physical causes.

sound waves
Vibratory changes in the air that carry sound.

specialized end bulbs
Sensory receptor cells in the skin whose function is not clearly established.

spinal cord
The neurons in the spinal column.

spontaneous recovery
A temporary increase in the strength of a conditioned response that is likely to occur during extinction after the passage of time.

stage
One of several time periods in development that is qualitatively distinct from the periods that come before and after.

stage theory of memory
A model of memory based on the idea that we store information in three separate, but linked, memories.

standardization
Administering a test in the same way to all individuals.

stereochemical theory (ste''re-o-kem'e-kal)
The theory that different odor receptors can only be stimulated by molecules of a specific size and shape that fit them like a ''key'' in a lock.

stereotype
An inaccurate generalization upon which a prejudice is based.

stimulants
Drugs that increase the activity of the central nervous system, providing a sense of energy and well-being.

stimulus (stim'u-lus)
Any aspect of the outside world that directly influences our behavior or conscious experience.

stimulus discrimination
The tendency for responses to occur more often in the presence of one stimulus than others.

stimulus generalization
The tendency for similar stimuli to elicit the same response.

stirrup
A stirrup-shaped bone of the middle ear that helps pass sound waves to the inner ear.

stress
Any event or circumstance that strains or exceeds an individual's ability to cope.

structuralism (struk'tūr-al-izm)
The nineteenth-century school of psychology that sought to determine the structure of the mind through controlled introspection.

structuring
Activities of managers that organize and direct the work of employees.

sublimation (sub''li-ma'shun)
According to Freud, a form of displacement in which a socially desirable goal is substituted for a socially harmful goal; the best form of displacement for society as a whole.

superego (soo''per-e'go)
According to Freud, that part of the mind that opposes the desires of the id by enforcing moral restrictions and by striving to attain a goal of perfection.

superstitious reinforcement
Reinforcing stimuli that follow a response accidentally.

suppression (sŭ-presh'un)
According to Freud, a defense mechanism in which the ego consciously prevents unacceptable information or feelings from entering the conscious mind.

surface structure
The superficial spoken or written structure of a statement.

survey method
A research method that utilizes interviews and questionnaires with individuals in the community.

symbolization
In Rogers' theory, the process of representing experience, thoughts, or feelings in mental symbols of which we possess awareness.

sympathetic division (sim''pah-thet'ik)
The division of the autonomic nervous system that generally activates internal organs during emotional arousal, or when physical demands are placed on the body.

synapse (sin aps')
The space between the axon of one neuron and the dendrite of another.

syntax (sin'-taks)
The grammatical rules of a language.

systematic desensitization
A behavior therapy method in which the client is taught not to fear phobic stimuli by learning to relax in the presence of successively more threatening stimuli.

tactile discs (tak'til)
Sensory receptor cells in the skin whose function is not clearly established.

taste cells
The sensory receptor cells for gustation located in the taste buds.

telegraphic speech
The abbreviated speech of two-year-olds.

testes (tes'tēz)
Male endocrine glands that secrete sex-related hormones and produce sperm cells.

testosterone (tes-tos'ter-ōn)
A male sex hormone.

thalamus (thal'ah-mus)
That part of the forebrain that primarily routes messages to appropriate parts of the brain.

theory
Tentative explanation of facts and relationships in sciences.

thyroid (thi'roid)
The gland below the voice box that regulates metabolism.

thyroxin (thi-rok'sin)
A hormone produced by the thyroid that is necessary for proper mental development in children and helps determine weight and level of activity in adults.

timbre (tim'ber, tam'br)
The characteristic quality of a sound as determined by the complexity of the sound wave.

traits
Relatively enduring and consistent ways of thinking, acting, and feeling that are believed by some theorists to be the basic units of personality.

transcendental state
An altered state of consciousness sometimes achieved during meditation that transcends normal human experience.

transduction (trans-duk'shun)
The translation of energy from one form to another.

transductive reasoning
(trans-duk'tiv)
Errors in understanding cause-and-effect relationships that are commonly made by preoperational children.

transference (trans-fer'ens)
The phenomenon in psychoanalysis in which the patient comes to feel and act toward the therapist in ways that resemble how he or she feels and acts toward other significant adults.

transsexualism
(trans-seks'u-ah-lizm)
A condition in which an individual feels trapped in the body of the wrong sex.

transvestism (trans-ves'tizm)
The practice of obtaining sexual pleasure by dressing in the clothes of the opposite sex.

trichromatic theory
(tri''kro-mat'ik)
The theory of color vision that contends that the eye has three different kinds of cones, each of which responds to light of one range of wavelength.

trimesters
The three 3-month stages of pregnancy.

Type A personality
A personality type characterized by high n Ach, a sense of time urgency, and hostility.

umbilical cord (um-bil'i-kal)
The structure that connects the fetus to the placenta and through which nutrients pass to the fetus.

unconditioned response (UCR)
An unlearned, inborn reaction to an unconditioned stimulus.

unconditioned stimulus (UCS)
A stimulus that can elicit a response without any learning.

unconscious mind
The part of the mind, of which we can never be directly aware, that is, the storehouse of primitive instinctual motives, and of memories and emotions that have been repressed.

utricle (u'tre-k'l)
A fluid-filled sac of the vestibular organ that informs the brain about the body's orientation.

vaginismus (vaj''i-niz'mus)
A female sexual dysfunction in which the individual experiences involuntary contractions of the vaginal walls, making the vagina too narrow to allow the penis to enter comfortably.

validity
The extent to which a test measures what it's supposed to measure.

variable
A factor whose numerical value can change.

variable interval schedule
A reinforcement schedule in which the reinforcer is given following the first response occurring after a variable amount of time.

variable ratio schedule
A reinforcement schedule in which the reinforcer is given after a varying number of responses have been made.

vestibular organ (ves-tib'u-lar)
The sensory structures in the inner ear that provide the brain with information about movement.

vicarious punishment
(vi-kar'e-us)
Observed punishment of the behavior of a model that also decreases the probability of the same behavior in the observer.

vicarious reinforcement
(vi-kar'e-us)
Observed reinforcement of the behavior of a model that also increases the probability of the same behavior in the observer.

visual acuity
(vizh'-u-al ah-ku'i-te)
Clearness and sharpness of vision.

voyeurism (voi'yer-izm)
The practice of obtaining sexual pleasure by watching members of the opposite sex undressing or engaging in sexual activities.

wavelength
Frequency of light waves; determines the color we see.

Weber's law
A law stating that the amount of change in a stimulus needed to detect a difference is always in direct proportion to the intensity of the original stimulus.

Yerkes–Dodson law
A law stating that effective performance is more likely if the level of arousal is suitable for the activity.

zygote (zi'gōt)
The stable cell resulting from fertilization; it has 46 chromosomes—23 from the sperm and 23 from the ovum.

REFERENCES

Abbott, B. B., Schoen, L. S., & Badia, P. (1984). Predictable and unpredictable shock: Behavioral measures of aversion and physiological measures of stress. *Psychological Bulletin, 96*, 45–71.

Adams, H. E., & Chiodo, J. (1984). Sexual deviations. In H. E. Adams & P. B. Sutker (Eds.), *Comprehensive handbook of psychopathology*. New York: Plenum.

Adams, J. (1965). Inequity in social exchange. In L. Berkowitz (Ed.), *Advances in experimental social psychology* (Vol. 2). New York: Academic Press.

Adams, P. R., & Adams, G. R. (1984). Mount Saint Helens' ashfall: Evidence for a disaster stress reaction. *American Psychologist, 39*, 252–260.

Adelson, J. (1979, February). Adolescence and the generalization gap. *Psychology Today*, pp. 33–38.

Allen, K. E., Hart, R. M., Buell, J. S., Harris, F. R., & Wolf, M. M. (1964). Effects of social reinforcement on isolate behavior of a nursery school child. *Child Development, 35*, 511–518.

Allport, G. W. (1937). *Personality: A psychological interpretation*. New York: Holt, Rinehart & Winston.

Allport, G. W. (1961). *Pattern and growth in personality*. New York: Holt, Rinehart & Winston.

Allport, G. W., & Odbert, H. S. (1936). Trait-names: A psycho-lexical study. *Psychological Monographs, 47* (No. 211), 1–171.

Altschule, M. D. (1965). *Roots of modern psychiatry* (2nd ed.). New York: Grune & Stratton.

American Psychological Association. (1973). *Ethical principles in the conduct of research with human participants*. Washington, DC: American Psychological Association.

Amoore, J. E., Johnston, J. W., & Rubin, M. (1964, February). The stereo-chemical theory of odor. *Scientific American*.

Anastasi, A. (1979). *Fields of applied psychology* (2nd ed.). New York: McGraw-Hill.

Andersen, K. (1983). Crashing on cocaine. *Time*, April 13.

Anderson, N. H. (1968). Application of a linear-serial model to personality-impression task using serial presentation. *Journal of Personality and Social Psychology, 10*, 354–362.

Ardrey, R. (1966). *The territorial imperative*. New York: Atheneum.

Arnold, M. B. (1960). *Emotion and personality* (2 vols.). New York: Columbia University Press.

Aronson, E. (1980). *The social animal* (3rd ed.). San Francisco: W. H. Freeman.

Aronson, E., & Golden, B. (1962). The effect of relevant and irrelevant aspects of communicator credibility on opinion change. *Journal of Personality, 30*, 135–146.

Aronson, E., Willerman, B., & Floyd, J. (1966). The effect of a pratfall on increasing interpersonal attractiveness. *Psychonomic Science, 4*, 227–228.

Arvidson, K., & Friberg, U. (1980). Human taste: Response and taste bud number in fungiform papillae. *Science, 209*, 807–808.

Asch, S. (1946). Forming impressions of personality. *Journal of Abnormal and Social Psychology, 41*, 258–290.

Asch, S. (1956). Studies of independence and conformity: A minority of one against a unanimous majority. *Psychological Monographs, 70* (9, Whole No. 416).

Association for Advancement of Behavior Therapy. (1978). *Ethical issues for human services* (pamphlet). New York: AABT.

Atkeson, B. M., Calhoun, K. S., Resick, P. A., & Ellis, E. M. (1982). Victims of rape: Repeated assessment of depressive symptoms. *Journal of Consulting and Clinical Psychology, 50*, 96–102.

Atkinson, J. W. (1964). *An introduction to motivation*. New York: Van Nostrand Reinhold.

Atkinson, R. C., & Shiffrin, R. M. (1968). Human memory: A proposed system and its control processes. In K. W. Spence & J. T. Spence (Eds.), *The psychology of learning and motivation* (Vol. 2). New York: Academic Press.

Ausubel, D. P. (1960). The use of advance organizers in the learning and retention of meaningful verbal material. *Journal of Educational Psychology, 51*, 267–272.

Ayllon, T., & Haughton, E. (1964). Modification of the symptomatic verbal behaviour of mental patients. *Behaviour Research and Therapy, 2*, 87–97.

Baker, H. (1969). Transsexualism—problems in treatment. *American Journal of Psychiatry, 125*, 118–124.

Bandura, A. (1969). *Principles of behavior modification*. New York: Holt, Rinehart & Winston.

Bandura, A. (1973). *Aggression: A social learning analysis*. Englewood Cliffs, NJ: Prentice-Hall.

Bandura, A. (1977). *Social learning theory*. Englewood Cliffs, NJ: Prentice-Hall.

Bandura, A. (1982). Self-efficacy mechanism in human agency. *American Psychologist, 37*, 122–147.

Bandura, A., Blanchard, E. B., & Ritter, B. (1969). The relative efficacy of desensitization and modeling approaches for inducing behavioral, affective, and attitudinal changes. *Journal of Personality and Social Psychology, 13*, 173–199.

Bandura, A., Ross, D., & Ross, S. A. (1963). Imitation of film-mediated aggressive models. *Journal of Abnormal and Social Psychology, 66*, 3–11.

Banks, M., & Salapatek, P. (1981). Infant pattern vision: A new approach based on the contrast sensitivity function. *Journal of Experimental Child Psychology, 31*, 1–45.

Barahal, H. S. (1958). 1000 prefrontal lobotomies: Five to ten-year follow-up study. *Psychiatric Quarterly, 32*, 653–678.

Barber, T. X. (1969). *Hypnosis: A scientific approach*. New York: Van Nostrand.

Bard, P. (1934). Emotion. I: The neurohumoral basis of emotional reactions. In C. Murchison (Ed.), *Handbook of general experimental psychology.* Worcester, MA: Clark University Press.

Barnes, K. E. (1971). Preschool play norms: A replication. *Developmental Psychology, 5,* 99–103.

Baron, R., & Byrne, D. (1982). *Exploring social psychology* (2nd ed.). Boston: Allyn & Bacon.

Baron, R. A., & Ramsberger, V. M. (1978). Ambient temperature and the occurrence of collective violence: The "long hot summer" revisited. *Journal of Personality and Social Psychology, 36,* 351–360.

Bartlett, F. C. (1932). *Remembering: A study in experimental and social psychology.* New York: Cambridge University Press.

Barton, J. L. (1977). ECT in depression: The evidence of controlled studies. *Biological Psychiatry, 12,* 687–695.

Batshaw, M. L., & Perret, Y. M. (1981). *Children with handicaps: A medical primer.* Baltimore: Paul H. Brooks.

Baum, A., Harpin, R. E., & Valins, S. (1975). The role of group phenomena in the experience of crowding. *Environment and Behavior, 7,* 185–198.

Baum, A., & Valins, S. (1977). *Architecture and social behavior: Psychological studies of social density.* Hillsdale, NJ: Erlbaum.

Bayley, N. (1965). Research in child development: A longitudinal perspective. *Merrill-Palmer Quarterly, 11,* 8–35.

Beck, A. T. (1976). *Cognitive therapy and the emotional disorders.* New York: International Universities Press.

Becker, W. C., & Carnine, D. (1980). Direct instruction: An effective approach to educational intervention with the disadvantaged and low performers. In B. B. Lahey & A. E. Kazdin (Eds.), *Advances in clinical child psychology* (Vol. 3). New York: Plenum.

Becker, W. C., Engelmann, S., & Thomas, D. R. (1975). *Teaching: A course in applied psychology.* Chicago: Science Research Associates.

Behrman, J., & Levy, R. (1970). Neurophysiological studies on patients with hysterical disturbances of vision. *Journal of Psychosomatic Research, 14,* 187–194.

Beiman, I., Graham, L., & Ciminero, A. R. (1978). Self-control progressive relaxation training as an alternative nonpharmacological treatment for essential hypertension: Therapeutic effects in the natural environment. *Behaviour Research and Therapy, 16,* 371–375.

Beiman, I., Majestic, H., Johnson, S. A., Puente, A., & Graham, L. (1976). *Transcendental meditation versus behavior therapy: A controlled investigation.* Paper presented to the Association for the Advancement of Behavior Therapy.

Bell, A. P., & Weinberg, M. S. (1978). *Homosexualities.* New York: Simon & Schuster.

Bem, D. J., & Allen, A. (1974). On predicting some of the people some of the time: The search for cross-situational consistencies in behavior. *Psychological Review, 81,* 506–520.

Benedict, R. F. (1934). *Patterns of culture.* Boston: Houghton Mifflin.

Bennett, W., & Gurin, J. (1982, March). Do diets really work? *Science, 82.*

Benson, H. (1975). *The relaxation response.* New York: Morrow.

Berger, K. S. (1980). *The developing person.* New York: Worth.

Bergum, B. O., & Lehr, D. J. (1962). Vigilance performance as a function of interpolated rest. *Journal of Applied Psychology, 46,* 425–427.

Berkowitz, L. (1983). Aversively stimulated aggression. *American Psychologist, 38,* 1135–1160.

Berkowitz, L. (1984). Some thoughts on anti- and prosocial influence of media events: A cognitive-neoassociation analysis. *Psychological Bulletin, 95,* 410–427.

Berlin, B., & Kay, P. (1969). *Basic color terms: Their universality and evolution.* Berkeley: University of California Press.

Bernstein, B. (1970). A sociolinguistic approach to socialization: With some reference to educability. In F. Williams (Ed.), *Language and poverty.* Chicago: Markham.

Bernstein, I. L. (1978). Learned taste aversions in children receiving chemotherapy. *Science, 200,* 1302–1309.

Berscheid, E., Dion, K. K., Walster, E., & Walster, G. W. (1971). Physical attractiveness and dating choice: A test of the matching hypothesis. *Journal of Experimental Social Psychology, 7,* 173–189.

Bigelow, H. J. (1850). Dr. Harlow's case of recovery from the passage of an iron bar through the head. *American Journal of Medical Science, 20,* 13–22.

Birch, H. C. (1945). The relation of previous experience to insightful problem solving. *Journal of Comparative Psychology, 38,* 367–383.

Birren, J. E., Butler, R. N., Greenhouse, S. W., Sokoloff, L., & Yarrow, M. R. (Eds.). (1963). *Human aging: A biological and behavioral study.* Washington, DC: U.S. Government Printing Office.

Blanchard, E. B., & Epstein, L. H. (1978). *A biofeedback primer.* Reading, MA: Addison-Wesley.

Bloom, B. S. (1974). Time and learning. *American Psychologist, 29,* 681–688.

Blumenthal, J. A., Sanders, W., Williams, R., Needels, T. L., & Wallace, A. G. (1982). Psychological changes accompany aerobic exercise in healthy middle-aged adults. *Psychosomatic Medicine, 44,* 529–536.

Boneau, C. A., & Cuca, J. M. (1974). An overview of psychology's human resources. *American Psychologist, 29,* 821–840.

Bootzin, R. (1973, August). *Stimulus control of insomnia.* Paper presented to the American Psychological Association, Montreal.

Borke, H. (1975). Piaget's mountains revisited: Changes in the egocentric landscape. *Developmental Psychology, 11,* 240–243.

Bosse, J. J., Croghan, L. M., Greenstein, M. B., Katz, N. W., Oliver, J. M., Powell, D. A., & Smith, W. R. (1975). Frequency of depression in the freshman year as measured in a random sample by a retrospective version of the Beck Depression Inventory. *Journal of Consulting and Clinical Psychology, 43,* 746–747.

Bourne, L. E. (1966). *Human conceptual behavior.* Boston: Allyn & Bacon.

Bourne, L. E., Ekstrand, B. R., & Dominowski. (1971). *The psychology of thinking.* Englewood Cliffs, NJ: Prentice Hall.

Bourque, L. B., & Back, K. W. (1977). Life graphs and life events. *Journal of Gerontology, 32,* 669–674.

Bousfield, W. A. (1953). The occurrence of clustering in recall of randomly arranged associates. *Journal of General Psychology, 49,* 229–240.

Bousfield, W. A., & Sedgewick, C. H. (1944). An analysis of sequences of restricted associative responses. *Journal of General Psychology, 30,* 149–165.

Bower, G. H. (1973). Educational applications of mnemonic devices. In K. O. Doyle (Ed.), *Interaction: Readings in human psychology.* Boston: D. C. Heath.

Bower, G. H. (1981). Mood and memory. *American Psychologist, 36,* 129–148.

Bower, G. H., & Mayer, J. D. (1985). Failure to replicate mood-dependent retrieval. *Bulletin of the Psychonomic Society, 23,* 39–42.

Bower, T. G. R. (1971). The object in the world of the infant. *Scientific American, 220,* 30–38.

Bower, T. G. R. (1974). *Development in infancy.* San Francisco: W. H. Freeman.

Bowers, K. S. (1973). Situationism in psychology: An analysis and a critique. *Psychological Review, 80,* 307–336.

Bowers, K. S. (1976). *Hypnosis for the seriously curious.* Monterey, CA: Brooks/Cole.

Bransford, J. D., & Franks, J. J. (1971). The abstraction of linguistic ideas. *Cognitive Psychology, 2,* 331–350.

Bray, D. W., Campbell, R. J., & Grant, D. L. (1974). *Formative years in business: A long term AT&T study of managerial lives.* New York: Wiley.

Breggin, P. R. (1973). Psychosurgery. *Journal of the American Medical Association, 226,* 1121.

Breland, K., & Breland, M. (1961). The misbehavior of organisms. *American Psychologist, 16,* 681–684.

Breuer, J., & Freud, S. (1895). *Studies in hysteria.* New York: Basic Books.

Briere, J., Downes, A., & Spensley, J. (1983). Summer in the city: Urban weather conditions and psychiatric emergency-room visits. *Journal of Abnormal Psychology, 92,* 77–80.

Brown, E. L., & Deffenbacher, K. (1979). *Perception and the senses.* New York: Oxford University Press.

Brown, R. W., & McNeil, D. (1966). The "tip of the tongue" phenomenon. *Journal of Verbal Learning and Verbal Behavior, 5,* 325–337.

Bruner, J. S. (Ed.). (1974). *The growth of competence.* New York: Academic Press.

Bruner, J. S., & Goodman, C. C. (1947). Value and need as organizing factors in perception. *Journal of Abnormal and Social Psychology, 42,* 33–44.

Bruner, J. S., Goodnow, J. J., & Austin, G. A. (1956). *A study of thinking.* New York: Wiley.

Buchsbaum, M. (1983). The mind readers. *Psychology Today, 17(7),* 58–62 (p. 60).

Buckhout, R. (1974). Eyewitness testimony. *Scientific American, 231,* 23–33.

Butcher, H. J. (1968). *Human intelligence: Its nature and assessment.* New York: Harper Torchbooks.

Butler, R. A. (1953). Discrimination learning by rhesus monkey by visual-exploration motivation. *Journal of Comparative and Physiological Psychology, 46,* 95–98.

Byrne, D. (1971). *The attraction paradigm.* New York: Academic Press.

Cahalan, D. (1970). *Problem drinkers.* San Francisco: Jossey-Bass.

Cahalan, D., & Room, R. (1974). *Problem drinking among American men.* New Brunswick, NJ: Rutgers Center of Alcohol Studies.

Calhoun, K. S., Atkeson, B. M., & Resick, P. A. (1982). *A longitudinal examination of fear reactions in victims of rape.* Unpublished manuscript, University of Georgia.

Campbell, D. E. (1961). The psychological effects of cerebral electroshock. In H. J. Eysenck (Ed.), *Handbook of abnormal psychology.* New York: Basic Books.

Campbell. D. E. (1978). *Interior office design and visitor response.* Paper presented to the American Psychological Association, Toronto.

Cannon, W. B. (1927). The James–Lange theory of emotions: A critical examination and an alternative theory. *American Journal of Psychology, 39,* 106–124.

Cannon, W. B., & Washburn, A. L. (1912). An explanation of hunger. *American Journal of Physiology, 29,* 441–454.

Carmichael, L., Hogan, H. P., & Walter, A. A. (1932). An experimental study of the effect of language on the reproduction of visually perceived form. *Journal of Experimental Psychology, 15,* 73–86.

Cates, J. (1970). Psychology's manpower: Report on the 1968 National Register of Scientific and Technical Personnel. *American Psychologist, 25,* 254–264.

Cattell, R. B. (1950). *Personality: A systematic, theoretical, and factual style.* New York: McGraw-Hill.

Cattell, R. B. (1966). *The scientific analysis of personality.* Chicago: Aldine.

Cattell, R. B. (1982). *The inheritance of personality and ability.* New York: Academic Press.

Cattell, R. B., Saunders, D. R., & Stice, G. F. (1950). *The 16 personality factor questionnaire.* Champaign, IL: Institute for Personality and Ability Testing.

Chaiken, S., & Eagly, A. H. (1983). Communication modality as a determinant of persuasion: The role of communicator salience. *Journal of Personality and Social Psychology, 45,* 241–256.

Chapman, L. J., & Chapman, J. P. (1973). *Disordered thought in schizophrenia.* New York: Appleton-Century-Crofts.

Chase, W. G., & Simon, H. A. (1973). The mind's eye in chess. In W. G. Chase (Ed.), *Visual information processing.* New York: Academic Press.

Chomsky, N. (1957). *Syntactic structures.* The Hague: Mouton.

Christensen, A., & Arkowitz, H. (1974). Preliminary report on practice dating and feedback on treatment for college dating problems. *Journal of Counseling Psychology, 21,* 92–95.

Church, R. M. (1969). Response suppression. In B. A. Campbell & R. M. Church (Eds.), *Punishment and aversive behavior.* New York: Appleton-Century-Crofts.

Clarke, A. M., & Clarke, A. B. D. (Eds.). (1976). *Early experience: Myth and science.* New York: The Free Press.

Clemens, S. (1959). *The autobiography of Mark Twain* (C. Neider, Ed.). New York: Harper & Row.

Cofer, C. N. (1972). *Motivation and emotion.* Glenview, IL: Scott, Foresman.

Cohen, L. B. (1979). Our developing knowledge of infant perception and cognition. *American Psychologist, 34,* 894–899.

Colby, C. Z., Lanzetta, J. T., & Kleck, R. E. (1977). Effects of the expression of pain on autonomic and pain tolerance responses to subject controlled pain. *Psychophysiology, 14,* 537–540.

Coleman, J. (1979). *Contemporary psychology and effective behavior.* Glenview, IL: Scott, Foresman.

Coleman, J., Butcher, J., & Carson, R. (1984). *Abnormal psychology and modern life.* Seventh Edition. Glenview, IL: Scott, Foresman.

Collins, A. M., & Loftus, E. F. (1975). A spreading activation theory of semantic processing. *Psychological Review, 82,* 407–428.

Condry, J. C., Simon, M. L., & Bronfenbrenner, U. (1968). *Characteristics of peer- and adult-oriented children.* Unpublished manuscript, Cornell University.

Cooper, J., & Mackie, D. (1983). Cognitive dissonance in an intergroup context. *Journal of Personality and Social Psychology, 44,* 536–544.

Cooper, R. M., & Zubek, J. P. (1958). Effects of enriched and restricted early environments on the learning ability of bright and dull rats. *Canadian Journal of Psychology, 12,* 159–164.

Costa, P. T., & McCrae, R. R. (1976). Age differences in personality structure: A cluster analytic approach. *Journal of Gerontology, 31,* 564–570.

Costanzo, P. R., & Shaw, M. E. (1966). Conformity as a function of age level. *Child Development, 36,* 967–975.

Craik, F. I. M., & Lockhart, R. S. (1972). Levels of processing: A framework for memory research. *Journal of Verbal Learning and Verbal Behavior, 11,* 671–684.

Danziger, C., & Greenwald, M. (1973). *Alternatives: A look at unmarried couples and communes.* New York: Research Services, Institute of Life Insurance.

Darley, J., & Latané, B. (1968). Bystander intervention in emergencies: Diffusion of responsibility. *Journal of Personality and Social Psychology, 8,* 377–383.

Davidson, P. O., & Davidson, S. M. (Eds.). (1980). *Behavioral medicine: Changing health life-styles.* New York: Brunner/Mazel.

Davis, H. P., & Squire, L. R. (1984). Protein synthesis and memory: A review. *Psychological Bulletin, 96,* 518–559.

Deaux, K., & Emswiller, T. (1974). Explanation of successful performance on sex-linked tasks: What is skill for the male is luck for the female. *Journal of Personality and Social Psychology, 29,* 80–85.

Deikman, A. J. (1980). De-Automization and the mystic experience. In J. R. Tisdale (Ed.), *Growing edges in the psychology of religion* (pp. 201–217). Chicago: Nelson-Hall.

Dekker, E., Pelser, H. E., & Groen, J. (1957). Conditioning as a cause of asthma attacks: A laboratory study. *Journal of Psychosomatic Research, 2,* 97–108.

Delgado, J. M. R. (1969). *Physical control of the mind: Toward a psycho-civilized society.* New York: Harper & Row.

Dember, W. N. (1964). Birth order and the need for affiliation. *Journal of Abnormal and Social Psychology, 68,* 555–557.

Dember, W. N. (1965). The new look in motivation. *American Scientist, 53,* 409–427.

Dennis, W. (1973). *Children of the creche.* New York: Appleton-Century-Crofts.

Dennis, W., & Dennis, M. (1941). The effect of cradling practices on the onset of walking in Hopi children. *Journal of Genetic Psychology, 23,* 143–189.

Diamond, E. L. (1982). The role of anger and hostility in essential hypertension and coronary heart disease. *Psychological Bulletin, 92,* 410–433.

Dion, K. K. (1980). Physical attractiveness, sex roles, and heterosexual attraction. In M. Cook (Ed.), *The bases of human sexual attraction.* New York: Academic Press.

Dipboye, R. L., Fromkin, H. L., & Wilback, K. (1975). The importance of applicant sex, attractiveness, and scholastic standing in evaluation of job applicant resumes. *Journal of Applied Psychology, 60,* 39–43.

Dobson, V., Teller, D. Y., Lee, C. P., & Wade, B. (1978). A behavioral method for efficient screening of visual acuity in young infants. *Investigative Ophthalmology and Visual Science, 17,* 1142–1150.

Dodd, D. H., & White, R. M. (1980). *Cognition, mental structures and processes.* Boston: Allyn & Bacon.

Doleys, D. M. (1977). Behavioral treatments for nocturnal enuresis in children: A review of the recent literature. *Psychological Bulletin, 84,* 30–54.

Dollard, J., Doob, L. W., Miller, N. E., Mowrer, O. H., & Sears, R. R. (1939). *Frustration and aggression.* New Haven: Yale University Press.

Duncker, K. (1945). On problem solving. *Psychological Monographs, 58* (No. 5).

Dutton, D. G., & Aron, A. P. (1974). Some evidence for heightened sexual attraction under conditions of high anxiety. *Journal of Personality and Social Psychology, 30,* 510–517.

Ebbinghaus, H. (1885). *Uber das Gedachnis.* Leipzig: Duncker & Humboldt.

Ebert, P. D., & Hyde, J. S. (1976). Selection for agonistic behavior in wild female *Mus musculus. Behavior Genetics, 6,* 291–304.

Egendorf, A., Kaduschin, C., Laufer, R. S., Rothbart, G., & Sloan, L. (1981). *Legacies of Vietnam: Comparative adjustment of veterans and their peers* (Publication No. V101 134P–630). Washington, DC: U.S. Government Printing Office.

Eibl-Eibesfeldt, I. (1973). The expressive behavior of the deaf and blind-born. In M. von Cranach & I. Vine (Eds.), *Social communication and movement.* New York: Academic Press.

Ekman, P., Levenson, R. W., & Friesen, W. V. (1983). Autonomic nervous system activity distinguishes among emotions. *Science, 221,* 1208–1210.

Ekman, P., & Oster, H. (1979). Facial expressions of emotions. In M. R. Rosenzweig & L. W. Porter (Eds.), *Annual Review of Psychology* (Vol. 30). Palo Alto, CA: Annual Reviews.

Elkind, D. (1967). *Children and adolescents: Interpretive essays on Jean Piaget.* New York: Oxford University Press.

Elkind, D. (1981). Understanding the young adolescent. In L. D. Steinberg (Ed.), *The life cycle: Readings in human development.* New York: Columbia University Press.

Elkind, D., & Bowen, R. (1979). Imaginary audience behavior in children and adolescents. *Developmental Psychology, 15,* 38–44.

Ellis, A. (1962). *Reason and emotion in psychotherapy.* New York: Lyle Stuart.

Ellis, H. C., & Hunt, R. R. (1983). *Fundamentals of human memory and cognition* (3rd ed.). Dubuque, IA: Wm. C. Brown Publishers.

Epstein, S. (1982). Conflict and stress. In L. Goldberger & S. Breznitz (Eds.), *Handbook of stress.* New York: Free Press.

Epstein, S., & Fenz, W. D. (1965). Steepness of approach and avoidance gradients in humans as a function of experience: Theory and experience. *Journal of Experimental Psychology, 70,* 1–12.

Epstein, S., & Roupenian, A. (1970). Heart rate and skin conductance during experimentally induced anxiety. *Journal of Personality and Social Psychology, 16,* 20–28.

Erikson, E. (1963). *Childhood and society.* New York: Norton.

Erlenmeyer-Kimling, L., & Jarvik, L. F. (1963). Genetics and intelligence: A review. *Science, 142,* 1477–1479.

Eron, L. D., & Huesmann, L. R. (1984). Television violence and aggressive behavior. In B. B. Lahey & A. E. Kazdin (Eds.), *Advances in clinical child psychology* (Vol. 7). New York: Plenum.

Fagot, B. I. (1974). Sex differences in toddlers' behavior and parental reaction. *Developmental Psychology, 10,* 554–558.

Fairweather, G. W., Sanders, D. H., Cressler, D. L., & Maynard, M. (1969). *Community life for the mentally ill.* Chicago: Aldine.

Fantz, R. L. (1961). The origin of form perception. *Scientific American, 204,* 66–72.

Farber, S. (1982). Genetic diversity and differing reactions to stress. In L. Goldberger & S. Breznitz (Eds.), *Handbook of stress.* New York: The Free Press.

Farquhar, J. W. (1979). *The American way of life need not be hazardous to your health.* New York: Norton.

Fast, J. (1970). *Body language.* New York: M. Evans.

Faust, M. S. (1960). Developmental maturity as a determinant of prestige in adolescent girls. *Child Development, 31,* 173–184.

Faust, M. S. (1977). Somatic development of adolescent girls. *Monographs of the Society for Research in Child Development, 42* (No. 169), 1.

Fenz, W. D., & Epstein, S. (1962). Theory and experiment on the measurement of approach-avoidance conflict. *Journal of Abnormal and Social Psychology, 64,* 97–112.

Fenz, W. D., & Epstein, S. (1967). Gradients of psychological arousal of experienced and novice parachutists as a function of an approaching jump. *Psychosomatic Medicine, 29,* 33–51.

Ferster, C. B., & Skinner, B. F. (1957). *Schedules of reinforcement.* New York: Appleton-Century-Crofts.

Festinger, L. A. (1957). *A theory of cognitive dissonance.* Evanston, IL: Harper & Row, Peterson.

Festinger, L. A., & Carlsmith, L. M. (1959). Cognitive consequences of forced compliance. *Journal of Abnormal and Social Psychology, 58,* 203–210.

Fine, B. J., & Kobrick, J. L. (1978). Effects of altitude and heat on complex cognitive tasks. *Human Factors, 20,* 115–122.

Fisher, E. B., Delamater, A. M., Bertelson, A. D., & Kirkley, B. G. (1982). Psychological factors in diabetes and its treatment. *Journal of Consulting and Clinical Psychology, 50,* 993–1003.

Ford, J. M., & Roth, W. T. (1977). Do cognitive abilities decline with age? *Geriatrics, 32,* 59–62.

Fordyce, W. E. (1978). Learning processes in pain. In R. A. Sternbach (Ed.), *The psychology of pain.* New York: Raven Press.

Foulkes, D., & Schmidt, M. (1983). Temporal sequence and unit composition in dream reports from different stages of sleep. *Sleep, 6,* 265–280.

Fox, S. I. (1984). *Laboratory guide to human physiology: Concepts and clinical applications,* 3rd ed. Dubuque, IA: Wm. C. Brown Publishers.

Foxx, R. M., & Brown, R. A. (1979). Nicotine fading and self-monitoring for cigarette abstinence or controlled smoking. *Journal of Applied Behavior Analysis, 12,* 111–125.

Foy, D. W., Sipprelle, R. C., Rueger, D. B., & Carroll, E. M. (1984). Etiology of posttraumatic stress disorder in Vietnam veterans: Analysis of premilitary, military, and combat exposure experience. *Journal of Consulting and Clinical Psychology, 52,* 79–87.

Freedman, J. L. (1984). Effect of television violence on aggressiveness. *Psychological Bulletin, 96,* 227–246.

Freeman, L. (1972). *The story of Anna O.* New York: Walker Publishing.

French, E. G. (1956). Motivation as a variable in work-partner selection. *Journal of Abnormal and Social Psychology, 53,* 96–99.

Friedman, M., & Rosenman, R. H. (1974). *Type A behavior and your heart*. New York: Knopf.

Furth, H. G. (1966). *Thinking without language: Psychological implications of deafness*. New York: The Free Press.

Galanter, E. (1962). *New directions in psychology*. New York: Holt, Rinehart & Winston.

Gallup, G., & Proctor, W. (1982). *Adventures in immortality*. New York: McGraw-Hill.

Garcia, J., Hankins, W. G., & Rusiniak, K. W. (1974). Behavioral regulation of the *milieu interne* in man and rat. *Science, 185,* 824–831.

Gardner, B. T., & Gardner, R. A. (1971). Two-way communication with an infant chimpanzee. In A. M. Schrier & F. Stollnitz (Eds.), *Behavior of nonhuman primates* (Vol. 4). New York: Academic Press.

Gardner, E. (1947). *Fundamentals of neurology*. Philadelphia: W. B. Saunders.

Gazzaniga, M. S. (1967). The split brain in man. *Scientific American, 217,* 24–29.

Gazzaniga, M. S. (1983). Right hemisphere language following brain bisection: A 20-year perspective. *American Psychologist, 38,* 525–537.

Geen, R. G., & Quanty, M. B. (1977). The catharsis of aggression: An evaluation of a hypothesis. In L. Berkowitz (Ed.), *Advances in experimental social psychology* (Vol. 10). New York: Academic Press.

Gelles, R. J. (1977). *Violence towards children in the United States*. Paper presented to the Annual Meeting of the American Association for the Advancement of Science.

Gelles, R. J., & Strauss, M. A. (1977). Determinants of violence in the family: Toward a theoretical integration. In W. R. Barr, R. Hill, F. I. Nye, & I. L. Reiss (Eds.), *Contemporary theories about the family*. New York: The Free Press.

Gibson, E., & Walk, R. (1960). The "visual cliff." *Scientific American, 202,* 64–71.

Glanzer, M., & Cunitz, A. R. (1966). Two storage mechanisms in free recall. *Journal of Verbal Learning and Verbal Behavior, 5,* 351–360.

Goldfried, M., & Davison, G. (1976). *Clinical behavior therapy*. New York: Holt, Rinehart & Winston.

Goldstein, M. J., & Palmer, J. O. (1963). *The experience of anxiety*. New York: Oxford University Press.

Goleman, D. (1976, March). Why the brain blocks daytime dreams. *Psychology Today*, pp. 69–70.

Goleman, D. (1980, February). 1,528 little geniuses and how they grew. *Psychology Today*, pp. 28–143.

Goodwin, D. W., Schulsinger, J., Hermansen, L., Guze, S. B., & Winokur, G. (1973). Alcohol problems in adoptees raised apart from alcoholic biological parents. *Archives of General Psychiatry, 28,* 238–243.

Goodwin, D. W., Schulsinger, J., Moller, N., Hermansen, L., Winokur, G., & Guze, S. B. (1974). Drinking problems in adopted and non-adopted sons of alcoholics. *Archives of General Psychiatry, 31,* 164–169.

Gottfredson, G. D., & Dyer, S. E. (1978). Health service providers in psychology. *American Psychologist, 33,* 314–338.

Gould, R. L. (1978). *Transformations: Growth and change in adult life*. New York: Simon & Schuster.

Graziano, W. G., & Musser, L. M. (1982). The going and parting of the ways. In S. Duck (Ed.), *Personal relationships 4: Dissolving personal relationships*. London: Academic Press.

Greden, J. F. (1974). Anxiety or caffeinism: A diagnostic dilemma. *American Journal of Psychiatry, 131,* 1089–1092.

Griffith, W., & Veitch, R. (1971). Influences of population density on interpersonal affective behavior. *Journal of Personality and Social Psychology, 17,* 92–98.

Grossman, S. P. (1960). Eating and drinking elicited by direct adrenergic and cholinergic stimulation of hypothalamus. *Science, 132,* 301–302.

Groves, P., & Schlesinger, K. (1979). *Biological psychology*. Dubuque, IA: Wm. C. Brown Publishers.

Guilford, J. P. (1950). Creativity. *American Psychologist, 5,* 444–454.

Guilford, J. P. (1967). *The nature of human intelligence*. New York: McGraw-Hill.

Gustavson, C. R., Garcia, J., Hankins, W. G., & Rusiniak, K. W. (1974). Coyote predation control by aversive conditioning. *Science, 184,* 581–584.

Gutmann, D. (1977). The cross-cultural perspective. In J. E. Birren & K. W. Shaie (Eds.), *Handbook of the psychology of aging*. New York: Van Nostrand.

Haan, N. (1976). ". . . Change and sameness . . ." reconsidered. *International Journal of Aging and Human Development, 7,* 59–65.

Haber, R. N., & Haber, R. B. (1964). Eidetic imagery: I. Frequency. *Perceptual and Motor Skills, 19,* 131–138.

Habif, V. L., & Lahey, B. B. (1980). Assessment of the life stress-depression relationship: The use of social support as a moderator variable. *Journal of Behavioral Assessment, 2,* 167–173.

Haley, J. (1976). *Problem-solving therapy*. San Francisco: Jossey-Bass.

Halikas, J. A., & Rimmer, J. D. (1974). Predictors of multiple drug abuse. *Archives of General Psychiatry, 31,* 414–418.

Hall, C. S. (1951). What people dream about. *Scientific American, 184,* 60–63.

Hall, C. S., & Lindzey, G. (1978). *Theories of personality* (3rd ed.). New York: Wiley.

Hall, G. S. (1904). *Adolescence*. New York: Appleton.

Hamilton, D. L., & Zanna, M. P. (1972). Differential weighting of favorable and unfavorable attributes in impressions of personality. *Journal of Experimental Research in Personality, 6,* 204–212.

Hanawalt, H. F., & Demarest, I. H. (1939). The effect of verbal suggestion in the recall period upon the reproduction of visually perceived forms. *Journal of Experimental Psychology, 25,* 159–174.

Haney, C. (1980). Social psychology and the criminal law. In P. W. Middlebrook (Ed.), *Social psychology and modern life* (2nd ed.). New York: Knopf.

Hanson, D. R., Gottesman, I. I., & Heston, L. L. (1976). Some possible childhood indicators of adult schizophrenia. *British Journal of Psychiatry, 129,* 142–154.

Harlow, H. F. (1949). The formation of learning sets. *Psychological Review, 56,* 51–56.

Harlow, H. F., & Harlow, M. K. (1965). The affectional systems. In A. M. Schrier, H. F. Harlow, & F. Stollnitz (Eds.), *Behavior of nonhuman primates* (Vol. 2). London: Academic Press.

Harlow, H. F., Harlow, M. K., & Meyer, D. R. (1950). Learning motivated by a manipulation drive. *Journal of Experimental Psychology, 40,* 228–234.

Harlow, H. F., & Novak, M. A. (1973). Psychopathological perspectives. *Perspectives in Biology and Medicine, 16,* 461–478.

Harris, T. G. (1973, July). As far as heroin is concerned, the worst is over. *Psychology Today,* pp. 68–79.

Hartley, D., Roback, H. R., & Abromowitz, S. F. (1976). Deterioration effects in encounter groups. *American Psychologist, 31,* 247–255.

Hawton, K., & Osborn, M. (1984). Suicide and attempted suicide in children and adolescents. In B. B. Lahey & A. E. Kazdin (Eds.), *Advances in clinical child psychology* (Vol. 7, pp. 57–108). New York: Plenum.

Hayduck, L. A. (1983). Personal space: Where we now stand. *Psychological Bulletin, 94,* 293–335.

Hayes, K. J., & Hayes, C. (1951). Intellectual development of a home-raised chimpanzee. *Proceedings of the American Philosophical Society, 95,* 105–109.

Hayflick, L. (1965). The limited *in vitro* lifetime of human diploid cell strains. *Experimental Cell Research, 37,* 614–636.

Haynes, S. G., Feinleib, M., & Kannel, W. B. (1980). The relationship of psychosocial factors to coronary heart disease in the Framingham Study. Part III: Eight-year incidence of CHD. *American Journal of Epidemiology, 3,* 37–58.

Hebb, D. O. (1949). *Organization of behavior.* New York: Wiley.

Heider, E. R., & Oliver, D. C. (1972). The structure of color space in naming and memory for two languages. *Cognitive Psychology, 3,* 337–354.

Held, R., & Hein, A. (1963). Movement-produced stimulation in the development of visually guided behavior. *Journal of Comparative and Physiological Psychology, 56,* 23–44.

Hennekens, C. H., Rosner, B., & Cole, D. S. (1978). Daily alcohol consumption and fatal coronary heart disease. *American Journal of Epidemiology, 107,* 196–200.

Heron, W. (1957). The pathology of boredom. *Scientific American, 196,* 52–69.

Herrnstein, R. (1971). IQ. *The Atlantic Monthly, 228,* 43–64.

Hervey, G. P. (1959). The effects of lesions in the hypothalamus in parabiotic rats. *Journal of Physiology, 145,* 336–352.

Hess, E. H. (1975, November). The role of pupil size in communication. *Scientific American,* 110–119.

Heston, L. L. (1966). Psychiatric disorder in foster home-reared children of schizophrenic mothers. *British Journal of Psychiatry, 112,* 819–825.

Hilgard, E. R. (1975). Hypnosis. *Annual Review of Psychology, 26,* 19–44.

Hilgard, E. R. (1978). Hypnosis and pain. In R. A. Sternbach (Ed.), *The psychology of pain.* New York: Raven Press.

Hilgard, E. R. (1980). Consciousness in contemporary psychology. In M. R. Rosenzweig & L. W. Porter (Eds.), *Annual review of psychology* (Vol. 31). Palo Alto, CA: Annual Reviews.

Hilgard, E. R., & Hilgard, J. R. (1975). *Hypnosis in the relief of pain.* Los Altos, CA: William Kaufmann.

Hill, C., Rubin, Z., & Peplau, L. (1976). Breakups before marriage: The end of 103 affairs. *Journal of Social Issues, 32,* 147–168.

Hirst, W. (1982). The amnesic syndrome: Descriptions and explanations. *Psychological Bulletin, 91,* 435–460.

Hogan, R., Mankin, D., Conway, J., & Fox, S. (1970). Personality correlates of undergraduate marijuana use. *Journal of Consulting and Clinical Psychology, 35,* 58–63.

Hokanson, J. E., DeGood, D. E., Forrest, M. S., & Brittain, T. M. (1963). Availability of avoidance behaviors for modulating vascular-stress responses. *Journal of Personality and Social Psychology, 67,* 60–68.

Holden, C. (1973). Psychosurgery: Legitimate therapy or laundered lobotomy? *Science, 179,* 1109–1112.

Hole, J. W., Jr., (1984). *Human anatomy and physiology.* (3rd ed.). Dubuque, IA: Wm. C. Brown Publishers.

Holmes, D. S. (1984). Meditation and somatic arousal: A review of experimental evidence. *American Psychologist, 39,* 1–10.

Holmes, T. H., & Rahe, R. H. (1967). The social readjustment rating scale. *Journal of Psychosomatic Research, 11,* 213–218.

Holyrod, K. A., & Lazarus, R. S. (1982). Stress, coping, and somatic adaptation. In L. Goldberger & S. Breznitz (Eds.), *Handbook of Stress.* New York: The Free Press.

Hopkins, J., Marcus, M., & Campbell, S. B. (1984). Postpartum depression: A critical review. *Psychological Bulletin, 95,* 498–515.

Horner, M. S. (1969, March). Fail: Bright women. *Psychology Today,* pp. 36–38.

Hosken, F. P. (1979). *The Hosken report: Genital and sexual mutilation of females* (2nd ed.). Lexington, MA: Women's International Network News.

House, W. C. (1974). Actual and perceived differences in male and female expectancies and minimal goal levels as a function of competition. *Journal of Personality, 42,* 493–509.

Hovland, C. I. (Ed.). (1957). *The order of presentation in persuasion.* New Haven: Yale University Press.

Hovland, C. I., & Weiss, W. (1951). The influence of source credibility on communication effectiveness. *The Public Opinion Quarterly, 15,* 635–650.

Hubel, D. H. (1979). The brain. *Scientific American, 241,* 44–53.

Hultsch, D. F., & Deutsch, F. (1981). *Adult development and aging: A life-span perspective.* New York: McGraw-Hill.

Hundert, A. J., & Greenfield, N. (1969). *Physical space and organizational behavior: A study of an office landscape.* Paper presented to the American Psychological Association, Los Angeles.

Hunt, M. (1975). *Sexual behavior in the 1970s.* New York: Dell.

Hunter, J. E. (1979). *An analysis of the validity, test fairness, and utility for the Philadelphia Police Officers Selection Examination prepared by Educational Testing Service.* Report to the Philadelphia Federal District Court, Alvarez v. City of Philadelphia.

Hunter, J. E. (1981). *The economic benefits of personnel selection using ability tests: A state-of-the-art review including a detailed analysis of the dollar benefit of U.S. Employment Office placements and a critique of the low-cutoff method of test use.* Washington, DC: U.S. Employment Service, U.S. Department of Labor.

Hunter, J. E., & Hunter, R. F. (1984). Validity and utility of alternative predictors of job performance. *Psychological Bulletin, 96,* 72–98.

Iaffaldano, M. T., & Muchinsky, P. M. (1985). Job satisfaction and job performance: A meta-analysis. *Psychological Bulletin, 97,* 251–273.

Inhelder, B., & Piaget, J. (1958). *The growth of logical thinking from childhood to adolescence.* New York: Basic Books.

Isen, A. M., & Levin, P. F. (1972). The effect of feeling good on helping: Cookies and kindness. *Journal of Personality and Social Psychology, 21,* 384–388.

Iverson, L. L. (1979). The chemistry of the brain. *Scientific American, 241,* 134–149.

Izard, C. E. (1972). *Patterns of emotions: A new analysis of anxiety and depression.* New York: Academic Press.

Izard, C. E. (1977). *Human emotions.* New York: Plenum.

Izard, C. E. (1978). Emotions as motivations: An evolutionary-developmental perspective. In H. E. Howe & R. A. Dienstbeier (Eds.), *Nebraska Symposium on Motivation* (Vol. 26). Lincoln: University of Nebraska Press.

Jacobs, B. L. (1976, March). Serotonin: The crucial substance that turns dreams on and off. *Psychology Today,* pp. 70–71.

Jacobsen, E. (1938). *Progressive relaxation.* Chicago: University of Chicago Press.

James, W. (1890). *The principles of psychology.* New York: Holt.

Janis, I. L. (1983). The role of social support in adherence to stressful decisions. *American Psychologist, 38,* 143–160.

Janis, I. L., & Hoffman, D. (1982). Effective partnerships in a clinic for smokers. In I. L. Janis (Ed.), *Counseling on personal decisions: Theory and research on short-term helping relationships.* New Haven: Yale University Press.

Jensen, A. R. (1973). *Educability and group differences.* New York: Harper & Row.

Jensen, A. R. (1980). *Bias in mental testing.* New York: The Free Press.

Jessor, S. L., & Jessor, R. (1975). Transition from virginity to nonvirginity among youth: A social-psychological study over time. *Developmental Psychology, 11,* 473–484.

Johnson, M. K., Bransford, J. P., & Solomon, S. (1973). Memory for tacit implications of sentences. *Journal of Experimental Psychology, 98,* 203–205.

Jones, E., Bell, L., & Aronson, E. (1971). The reciprocation of attraction from similar and dissimilar others: A study in person perception and evaluation. In C. McClintock (Ed.), *Experimental Social Psychology.* New York: Holt, Rinehart & Winston.

Jones, G. V. (1983). Identifying basic categories. *Psychological Bulletin, 94,* 423–428.

Jones, M. C. (1965). Psychological correlates of somatic development. *Child Development, 36,* 899–911.

Jones, M. C., & Bayley, N. (1950). Physical maturing among boys as related to behavior. *Journal of Educational Psychology, 41,* 129–148.

Jones, M. C., & Mussen, P. H. (1958). Self-conceptions, motivations, and interpersonal attitudes of early- and late-maturing girls. *Child Development, 29,* 491–501.

Jones, R. (1977). *The other generation: The new power of older people.* Englewood Cliffs, NJ: Prentice-Hall.

Julian, J. (1973). *Social problems.* Englewood Cliffs, NJ: Prentice-Hall.

Jung, J. (1978). *Understanding human motivation: A cognitive approach.* New York: Macmillan.

Jurow, G. L. (1971). New data on the effects of a "death-qualified" jury on the guilt determination process. *Harvard Law Review, 84,* 567–611.

Kagan, J. (1978). *The growth of the child.* New York: Norton.

Kagan, J. (1984). *The nature of the child.* New York: Basic Books.

Kagan, J., & Moss, H. A. (1962). *Birth to maturity: A study in psychological development.* New York: Wiley.

Kahneman, D., & Tversky, A. (1982). The psychology of preferences. *Scientific American, 246,* 160–173.

Kalish, R. A., & Reynolds, D. K. (1976). *Death and ethnicity: A psychocultural study.* Los Angeles: University of Southern California Press.

Kallman, W. D., & Gilmore, J. D. (1981). Vascular disorders. In S. M. Turner, K. S. Calhoun, & H. E. Adams (Eds.), *Handbook of clinical behavior therapy.* New York: Wiley.

Kamin, L. J. (1974). *The science and politics of IQ.* Potomac, MD: Lawrence Erlbaum.

Kanfer, F. H., & Phillips, J. S. (1970). *Learning foundations of behavior therapy.* New York: Wiley.

Kaplan, M. F. (1975). Information integration in social judgment: Interaction of judge and informational components. In M. F. Kaplan & S. Schwartz (Eds.), *Human judgment and decision processes.* New York: Academic Press.

Kaye, H. (1967). Infant sucking behavior and its modification. In L. P. Lipsitt & C. C. Spiker (Eds.), *Advances in child development and behavior* (Vol. 3). New York: Academic Press.

Keane, T. M., & Kaloupek, D. G. (1982). Imaginal flooding in the treatment of posttraumatic stress disorder. *Journal of Consulting and Clinical Psychology, 50,* 138–140.

Kelley, H. H. (1973). The processes of causal attribution. *American Psychologist, 28,* 107–128.

Kellogg, W. N., & Kellogg, L. A. (1933). *The ape and the child.* New York: McGraw-Hill.

Kelly, G. A. (1955). *The psychology of personal constructs.* New York: Norton.

Kendall, P. C., & Norton-Ford, J. D. (1982). *Clinical psychology: Scientific and professional dimensions.* New York: Wiley.

Kephart, W. (1967). Some correlates of romantic love. *Journal of Marriage and the Family, 29,* 470–474.

Kilmann, P., & Sotile, W. (1976). The marathon encounter group: A review of the outcome literature. *Psychological Bulletin, 83,* 827–850.

Kilpatrick, D., Resick, P., & Veronen, S. (1981). Long-term effects of rape on the victim. *Journal of Social Issues, 37,* 105–122.

Kinsbourne, M. (1981, May). Sad hemisphere, happy hemisphere. *Psychology Today,* p. 92.

Kinsey, A. C., Pomeroy, W. B., & Martin, C. E. (1948). *Sexual behavior in the human male.* Philadelphia: W. B. Saunders.

Kinsey, A. C., Pomeroy, W. B., Martin, C. E., & Gebhard, P. H. (1953). *Sexual behavior in the human female.* Philadelphia: W. B. Saunders.

Klatzky, R. L. (1980). *Human memory: Structures and processes.* San Francisco: W. H. Freeman.

Kohlberg, L. (1964). The development of moral character. In M. L. Hoffman & L. W. Hoffman (Eds.), *Review of child development research.* Vol. I. New York: Russell Sage Foundation, p. 400.

Kohlberg, L. (1969). Stage and sequence: The cognitive-developmental approach to socialization. In D. A. Goslin (Ed.), *Handbook of socialization theory and research.* Chicago: Rand McNally.

Köhler, W. (1969). *The task of gestalt psychology.* Princeton, NJ: Princeton University Press.

Kolb, L. C. (1977). *Modern clinical psychiatry* (9th ed.). Philadelphia: W. B. Saunders.

Korman, A. K. (1974). *The psychology of motivation.* Englewood Cliffs, NJ: Prentice-Hall.

Kreps, J., & Spengler, J. (1973). Future options for more free time. In F. Best (Ed.), *The future of work.* Englewood Cliffs, NJ: Prentice-Hall.

Krueger, R. W. C. F. (1929). The effect of overlearning on retention. *Journal of Experimental Psychology, 12,* 71–78.

Kübler-Ross, E. (1969). *On death and dying.* New York: Macmillan.

Kübler-Ross, E. (1974). *Questions and answers on death and dying.* Englewood Cliffs, NJ: Prentice-Hall.

Labov, W. (1970). The logic of nonstandard English. In F. Williams (Ed.), *Language and poverty: Perspectives on a theme.* Chicago: Markham.

Lader, M. H., & Matthews, A. (1970). Physiological changes during spontaneous panic attacks. *Journal of Psychosomatic Research, 14,* 377–382.

Lahey, B. B. (1973). Minority group languages. In B. B. Lahey (Ed.), *The modification of language behavior.* Springfield: Charles C Thomas.

Lahey, B. B., & Ciminero, A. R. (1980). *Maladaptive behavior.* Glenview, IL: Scott, Foresman.

Lange, C. G. (1922). *The emotions.* Baltimore, MD: Williams & Williams.

Langlois, J. H., & Stephan, C. W. (1981). Beauty and the beast: The role of physical attractiveness in the development of peer relations and social behavior. In S. S. Brehm, S. M. Kassin, & F. X. Gibbons (Eds.), *Developmental social psychology.* New York: Oxford University Press.

Latané, B., & Nida, S. (1981). Ten years of research on group size and helping. *Psychological Bulletin, 89,* 308–324.

Latané, B., & Rodin, J. (1969). A lady in distress: Inhibiting effects of friends and strangers on bystander intervention. *Journal of Experimental Social Psychology, 5,* 189–202.

Lazarus, R. S. (1982). Thoughts on the relations between emotion and cognition. *American Psychologist, 37,* 1019–1024.

Lazarus, R. S. (1984). On the primacy of cognition. *American Psychologist, 39,* 117–123.

Lazarus, R. S., & Launier, R. (1978). Stress-related transactions between person and environment. In L. A. Pervin & M. Lewis (Eds.), *Perspectives in interactional psychology.* New York: Plenum.

Leboyer, F. (1975). *Birth without violence.* New York: Knopf.

Lenneberg, E. H. (1967). *Biological foundations of language.* New York: Wiley.

Leon, G. R. (1977). *Case histories of deviant behavior: An interactional perspective* (2nd ed.). Boston: Holbrook Press.

Leonard, W. E. (1928). *The locomotive god.* London: Chapman & Hall.

Lepper, M. R., Greene, D., & Nisbett, R. E. (1973). Undermining children's intrinsic interest with extrinsic reward: A test of the "overjustification" hypothesis. *Journal of Personality and Social Psychology, 28,* 129–137.

Levinson, D. J. (1978). *The seasons of a man's life.* New York: Knopf.

Levy, J. (1985). Right brain, left brain: Fact and fiction. *Psychology Today,* May, 38–44.

Levy, J., & Reid, M. (1976). Variations in writing posture and cerebral organization. *Science, 194,* 337–339.

Lewin, K. (1931). Environmental forces in child behavior and development. In C. Murchison (Ed.), *A handbook of child psychology.* Worcester, MA: Clark University Press.

Lewinsohn, P. M., Mischel, W., Chaplin, W., & Barton, R. (1980). Social competence and depression: The role of illusory self-perceptions. *Journal of Abnormal Psychology, 89,* 203–212.

Lewis, M., & Rosenblum, L. A. (Eds.). (1978). *The development of affect.* New York: Plenum.

Lewontin, R. (1982). *Human diversity.* New York: Scientific American Library.

Lezak, M. D. (1976). *Neuropsychological assessment.* New York: Oxford University Press.

Liebert, R. M., Neale, J. M., & Davidson, E. S. (1983). *The early window: The effects of television on children and youth.* New York: Pergamon Press.

Likert, R. (1967). *The human organization: Its management and value.* New York: McGraw-Hill.

Linton, M. (1979, July). I remember it well. *Psychology Today,* pp. 89–98.

Lloyd, C., Alexander, A. A., Rice, D. G., & Greenfield, N. S. (1980). Life change and academic performance. *Journal of Human Stress, 6,* 15–25.

Loftus, E. F., & Loftus, G. R. (1980). On the performance of stored information in the human brain. *American Psychologist, 35,* 409–420.

Long, I. (1976). Human sexuality and aging. *Social Casework, 57,* 237–244.

Lorenz, K. (1937). The companion in the bird's world. *Auk, 54,* 245–273.

Lorenz, K. (1967). *On aggression.* New York: Bantam.

Lou, A. C., Henriksen, L., & Bruhn, P. (1984, August). Focal cerebral hypoperfusion in children with dysphasia and/or attention deficit disorder. *Archives of Neurology, 41,* 825–829.

Lowenthal, M. F., Thurnher, M., & Chiriboga, D. (1975). *Four stages of life: A comparative study of women and men facing transitions.* San Francisco: Jossey-Bass.

Lubar, J. F., & Shouse, M. N. (1977). Use of biofeedback in the treatment of seizure disorders and hyperactivity. In B. B. Lahey & A. E. Kazdin (Eds.), *Advances in clinical child psychology* (Vol. 1). New York: Plenum.

Luchins, K. S. (1942). Mechanization in problem solving: The effects of "Einstellung." *Psychometric Monographs, 54* (No. 6).

Lykken, D. T. (1979). The detection of deception. *Psychological Bulletin, 86,* 47–53.

Maas, H. S., & Kuypers, J. A. (1974). *From thirty to seventy.* San Francisco: Jossey-Bass.

Maccoby, E. E., & Jacklin, C. N. (1974). *The psychology of sex differences.* Stanford: Stanford University Press.

Macklin, E. J. (1974). Cohabitation in college: Going very steady. *Psychology Today, 8,* 53–59.

Maddox, G. L. (1964). Disengagement theory: A critical evaluation. *The Gerontologist, 4,* 80–83.

Mader, S. S. (1985). *Inquiry into life,* 4th ed. Dubuque, IA: Wm. C. Brown Publishers.

Maier, N. R. F. (1931). Reasoning in humans: II. The solution of a problem and its appearance in consciousness. *Journal of Comparative and Physiological Psychology, 12,* 181–194.

Mark, V. H. (1974). The continuing polemic of psychosurgery. *Journal of the American Medical Association, 227,* 943.

Mark, V. H., & Ervin, E. P. (1970). *Violence and the brain.* New York: Harper & Row.

Marks, I. M. (1969). *Fears and phobias.* New York: Academic Press.

Marks, I. M., & Gelder, M. (1967). Transvestism and fetishism: Clinical and psychological changes during faradic aversion. *British Journal of Psychiatry, 119,* 711–730.

Marlatt, G. A., & Rose, F. (1980). Addictive disorders. In A. E. Kazdin, A. S. Bellack, & M. Hersen (Eds.), *New perspectives in abnormal psychology* (pp. 298–324). New York: Oxford University Press.

Marquis, D. P. (1941). Learning in the neonate. *Journal of Experimental Psychology, 29,* 22–40.

Maslow, A. (1967). A theory of metamotivation: The biological rooting of the value-life. *Journal of Humanistic Psychology, 7,* 93–127.

Maslow, A. (1970). *Motivation and personality* (2nd ed.). New York: Harper & Row.

Maslow, A. H., & Mintz, N. L. (1956). Effects of esthetic surroundings: I. Initial effects of three esthetic conditions upon perceiving "energy" and "well-being" in faces. *Journal of Psychology, 41,* 247–254.

Masters, W. H., & Johnson, V. E. (1966). *Human sexual response.* Boston: Little, Brown.

Masters, W. H., Johnson, V. E., & Kolodny, R. C. (1982). *Human sexuality.* Boston: Little, Brown.

Matefy, R. E., & Kroll, R. G. (1974). An initial investigation of psychedelic drug flashback phenomena. *Journal of Consulting and Clinical Psychology, 42,* 854–860.

Mathews, K. E., & Canon, L. K. (1975). Environmental noise level as a determinant of helping behavior. *Journal of Personality and Social Psychology, 32,* 571–577.

Matlin, M. (1983). *Cognition.* New York: Holt, Rinehart & Winston.

Matthews, E. L. (1982). Psychological perspectives on the Type A behavior pattern. *Psychological Bulletin, 91,* 293–323.

Maugh, T. H. (1973). LSD and the drug culture: New evidence of hazard. *Science, 179,* 1221–1222.

McCall, R. B. (1979). *Infants.* Cambridge, MA: Harvard University Press.

McClelland, D. C., & Atkinson, J. W. (1948). The projective expression of needs: I. The effect of different intensities of the hunger drive on perception. *Journal of Psychology, 25,* 205–222.

McClelland, D. C., Atkinson, J. W., Clark, R. W., & Lowell, E. L. (1953). *The achievement motive.* New York: Appleton-Century-Crofts.

McClelland, D. C., & Winter, D. G. (1969). *Motivating economic achievement.* New York: The Free Press.

McConaghy, M. J. (1979). Gender permanence and the genital basis of gender: Stages in the development of constancy of gender identity. *Child Development, 50,* 1223–1226.

McConnell, J. V., & Malin, D. H. (1973). Recent experiments in memory transfer. In H. P. Zippel (Ed.), *Memory and transfer of information.* New York: Plenum.

McCormick, E. J., & Ilgen, D. (1980). *Industrial psychology* (7th ed.). Englewood Cliffs, NJ: Prentice-Hall.

McGaugh, J. L. (1983). Preserving the presence of the past: Hormonal influences on memory storage. *American Psychologist, 38,* 161–174.

McGraw, M. B. (1940). Neural maturation as exemplified in achievement of bladder control. *Journal of Pediatrics, 16,* 580–590.

McKinlay, S. M., & Jeffreys, M. (1974). The menopausal syndrome. *British Journal of Preventive and Social Medicine, 28,* 108.

McWilliams, S. A., & Tuttle, R. J. (1973). Long-term psychological effects of LSD. *Psychological Bulletin, 79,* 341–351.

Meichenbaum, D. H. (1966). Sequential strategies in two cases of hysteria. *Behaviour Research and Therapy, 4,* 89–94.

Mellon, J. C. (1975). *National assessment and the teaching of English.* Urbana, IL: National Council of Teachers of English.

Melzack, R., & Dennis, S. G. (1978). Neurophysiological foundations of pain. In R. A. Sternbach (Ed.), *The psychology of pain.* New York: Raven Press.

Messick, D. M., & Sentis, K. P. (1979). Fairness and preference. *Journal of Experimental Social Psychology, 15,* 418–434.

Mewborn, C. R., & Rogers, R. W. (1979). Effects of threatening and reassuring components of fear appeals on physiological and verbal measures of emotion and attitudes. *Journal of Experimental Social Psychology, 15,* 242–253.

Meyer, M. E. (1979). *Foundations of contemporary psychology.* New York: Oxford University Press.

Middlebrook, P. N. (1980). *Social psychology and modern life* (2nd ed.). New York: Knopf.

Middlemist, R., Knowles, E., & Matter, C. (1976). Personal space invasions in the lavatory. *Journal of Personality and Social Psychology, 33,* 541–546.

Milgram, S. (1963). Behavioral study of obedience. *Journal of Abnormal and Social Psychology, 67,* 371–378.

Milgram, S. (1965). Some conditions of obedience and disobedience to authority. *Human Relations, 18,* 57–76.

Miller, G. A. (1956). The magic number seven, plus or minus two: Some limits on our ability to process information. *Psychological Review, 63,* 81–97.

Miller, N. E. (1944). Experimental studies of conflict. In J. McV. Hunt (Ed.), *Personality and the behavior disorders* (Vol. 1). New York: Ronald Press.

Miller, N. E. (1978). Biofeedback and visceral learning. *Annual Review of Psychology, 29,* 373–392.

Miller, N. E. (1980). Effects of learning on physical symptoms produced by psychological stress. In H. Selye (Ed.), *Selye's guide to stress research.* New York: Van Nostrand Reinhold.

Milner, B., Corkin, S., & Teuber, H. L. (1968). Further analysis of the hippocampal amnesic syndrome: 14-year follow-up study of H. M. *Neuropsychologia, 6,* 215–234.

Mineka, S., Davidson, M., Cook, M., & Keir, R. (1984). Observational conditioning of snake fears in rhesus monkeys. *Journal of Abnormal Psychology, 93,* 355–372.

Minuchin, S. (1974). *Families and family therapy.* Cambridge, MA: Harvard University Press.

Mischel, W. (1968). *Personality and assessment.* New York: Wiley.

Mischel, W. (1981). *Introduction to personality* (3rd ed.). New York: Holt, Rinehart & Winston.

Mischel, W. (1984). Convergences and challenges in the search for consistency. *American Psychologist, 39,* 351–364.

Mohr, J. W., Turner, R. E., & Jerry, M. B. (1964). *Pedophilia and exhibitionism.* Toronto: University of Toronto Press.

Monroe, L. J., Rechtschaffen, A., Foulkes, D., & Jensen, J. (1965). Discriminability of REM and NREM reports. *Journal of Personality and Social Psychology, 2,* 456–460.

Moody, R. (1976). *Life after life.* Covington, GA: Mockingbird Books.

Morell, P., & Norton, W. T. (1980, May). Myelin. *Scientific American,* pp. 88–118.

Morgan, S. W., & Mausner, B. (1973). Behavioral and fantasized indicators of avoidance of success in men and women. *Journal of Personality, 41,* 457–470.

Mosher, F. A., & Hornsby, J. R. (1966). On asking questions. In J. Bruner (Ed.), *Studies in cognitive growth.* New York: Wiley.

Moss, H. A., & Susman, E. J. (1980). Longitudinal study of personality development. In O. G. Brim & J. Kagan (Eds.), *Constancy and change in human development.* Cambridge, MA: Harvard University Press.

Mowrer, O. H., & Mowrer, W. M. (1938). Enuresis: A method for its study and treatment. *American Journal of Orthopsychiatry, 8,* 436–459.

Munjack, D. J., & Staples, F. R. (1977). Psychological characteristics of women with sexual inhibition (frigidity) in sex clinics. *Journal of Nervous and Mental Diseases, 163,* 117–129.

Murchison, C. (Ed.). (1929). *Foundations of experimental psychology.* Worcester, MA: Clark University Press.

Myers, D. H., & Grant, G. A. (1972). A study of depersonalization in students. *British Journal of Psychiatry, 121,* 59–65.

Nachman, M. (1962). Taste preference for sodium salts in adrenalectomized rats. *Journal of Comparative and Physiological Psychology, 55,* 1124–1129.

Nachman, M. (1963). Learned aversion to the taste of lithium chloride and generalization to other salts. *Journal of Comparative and Physiological Psychology, 56,* 343–349.

National Center for Health Statistics. Births, marriages, divorces, and deaths, United States (1983). *Monthly Vital Statistics Report* (Vol. 32, No. 12), DHHS Pub. No. PHS-84-1120.

Neale, J. M., & Oltmanns, T. F. (1980). *Schizophrenia.* New York: Wiley.

Nelson, L. P., & Nelson, V. (1973). *Religion and death anxiety.* Paper presented at the Society for the Scientific Study of Religion, San Francisco.

Nemeth, C. J. (1981). Jury trials: Psychology and law. In L. Berkowitz (Ed.), *Advances in experimental social psychology* (Vol. 14). New York: Academic Press.

Neugarten, B. L. (1964). *Personality in middle and late life.* New York: Atherton Press.

Neugarten, B. L. (1968). The awareness of middle age. In B. L. Neugarten (Ed.), *Middle age and aging.* Chicago: University of Chicago Press.

Neugarten, B. L., & Hagestad, G. O. (1976). Age and the life course. In R. H. Binstock & E. Shanas (Eds.), *Handbook of aging and the social sciences.* New York: D. Van Nostrand Reinhold.

Newton, J. W., & Mann. L. (1980). Crowd size as a factor in the persuasion process: A study of religious crusade meetings. *Journal of Personality and Social Psychology, 39,* 874–883.

Norton, A. J. (1974). The family life cycle updated: Components and uses. In R. F. Winch & G. B. Spanier (Eds.), *Selected studies in marriage and the family.* New York: Holt, Rinehart & Winston.

Nuckolls, K., Cassel, J., & Kaplan, B. H. (1972). Psychological assets, life crisis, and the prognosis of pregnancy. *American Journal of Epidemiology, 95,* 431–444.

Nydegger, C. N. (1973, November). *Late and early fathers.* Paper presented to Annual Meeting of American Gerontological Society, Miami Beach.

Offer, D. (1969). *The psychological world of the teenager: A study of normal adolescent boys.* New York: Basic Books.

Offer, D., & Offer, J. (1975). *From teenage to young manhood.* New York: Basic Books.

Offer, D., Ostrov, E., & Howard, K. I. (1981). *The adolescent: A psychological self-portrait.* New York: Basic Books.

O'Hara, M. W. (1980). *A prospective study of postpartum depression: A test of cognitive and behavioral theories.* Unpublished doctoral dissertation, University of Pittsburgh.

Ohman, A., Erixon, G., & Lofberg, I. (1975). Phobias and preparedness: Phobic versus neutral pictures as conditioned stimuli for human autonomic responses. *Journal of Abnormal Psychology, 84,* 41–45.

Olds, J., & Milner, P. (1954). Positive reinforcement produced by electrical stimulation of septal area and other regions of rat brain. *Journal of Comparative and Physiological Psychology, 47,* 419–427.

Olsen, K. M. (1969). *Social class and age-group differences in the timing of family status changes: A study of age norms in American society.* Unpublished doctoral dissertation, University of Chicago.

Osherson, D. N., & Markman, E. (1974). Language and the ability to evaluate contradictions and tautologies. *Cognition, 3,* 213–226.

Pahnke, W. N. (1980). Drugs and mysticism. In J. R. Tisdale (Ed.), *Growing edges in the psychology of religion* (pp. 183–200). Chicago: Nelson-Hall.

Parkes, C. M. (1972). *Bereavement: Studies of grief in adult life.* New York: International Universities Press.

Parry, H. J., Balter, M. B., Mellinger, G. D., Cisin, I. H., & Manheimer, D. I. (1973). National patterns of psychotherapeutic drug use. *Archives of General Psychiatry, 28,* 769–783.

Patterson, F. (1977). The gestures of a gorilla: Language acquisition in another primate species. In J. Hamburg, J. Goodall, & L. McCown (Eds.), *Perspectives in human evolution* (Vol. 4). Menlo Park, CA: W. A. Benjamin.

Pauly, I. (1968). The current status of the change of sex operation. *Journal of Nervous and Mental Disorders, 147,* 460–471.

Paykel, E. S., Emms, E. M., Fletcher, J., & Rassaby, E. S. (1980). Life events and social support in puerperal depression. *British Journal of Psychiatry, 136,* 339–346.

Perls, F. S., Hefferline, R. F., & Goodman, P. (1951). *Gestalt therapy.* New York: Julian Press.

Petersen, A. C. (1979, January). Can puberty come any faster? *Psychology Today,* pp. 45–56.

Petersen, R. C., & Stillman, R. C. (1978). *Phencyclidine (PCP) abuse: An appraisal* (National Institute on Drug Abuse Monograph No. 21). Washington, DC: U.S. Government Printing Office.

Peterson, L. R., & Peterson, M. J. (1959). Short-term retention of individual items. *Journal of Experimental Psychology, 58,* 193–198.

Phillips, D. P., & Feldman, K. A. (1973). A dip in deaths before ceremonial occasions: Some new relationships between social integration and mortality. *American Sociological Review, 38,* 678–696.

Phillips, J. D. (1933). *Salem in the seventeenth century.* Cambridge, MA: Riverside Press.

Piaget, J. (1972). Intellectual development from adolescence to adulthood. *Human Development, 15,* 1–12.

Piaget, J., & Inhelder, B. (1963). *The child's conception of space.* London: Routledge and Paul.

Pines, M. (1980, December). The sinister hand. *Science, 80,* 26–27.

Pines, M. (1981, September/ October). Genie. *Dallas Morning News.*

Pines, M. (1983, September). The human difference. *Psychology Today,* p. 52.

Plutchik, R. (1980). *Emotion: A psychoevolutionary synthesis.* New York: Harper & Row.

Pope, K. S. (1978). The flow of consciousness. In K. S. Pope & J. L. Singer (Eds.), *The stream of consciousness: Scientific investigations into the flow of human experience.* New York: Plenum.

Pope, K. S., & Singer, J. L. (Eds.). (1978). *The stream of consciousness.* New York: Plenum.

Pope, K. S., & Singer, J. L. (1980). The waking stream of consciousness. In J. M. Davidson & R. J. Davidson (Eds.), *The psychobiology of consciousness* (pp. 169–191). New York: Plenum.

Posner, M. I. (1973). *Cognition: An introduction.* Glenview, IL: Scott, Foresman.

Prentice, W. C. H. (1954). Visual recognition of verbally labeled figures. *American Journal of Psychology, 67,* 315–320.

Quay, H. C. (1959). The effect of verbal reinforcement on the recall of early memories. *Journal of Abnormal and Social Psychology, 59,* 254–257.

Rabkin, J. G., & Streuning, E. L. (1976). Life events, stress, and illness. *Science, 194,* 1013–1019.

Ranken, H. B. (1963). Language and thinking: Positive and negative effects of naming. *Science, 141,* 48–50.

Raugh, M. R., & Atkinson, R. C. (1975). A mnemonic method for learning a second-language vocabulary. *Journal of Educational Psychology, 67,* 1–16.

Ray, O. S. (1974). *Drugs, society, and human behavior* (2nd ed.). St. Louis: C. V. Mosby.

Reeves, A., & Plumb, F. (1969). Hyperphagia, rage, and dementia accompanying a ventromedial hypothalamic neoplasm. *Archives of Neurology, 20,* 616–624.

Reilly, R. R., & Chao, G. T. (1982). Validity and fairness of some alternative employee selection procedures. *Personnel Psychology, 35,* 1–62.

Reisenzein, R. (1983). The Schachter–Singer theory of emotion: Two decades later. *Psychological Bulletin, 94,* 239–264.

Reiss, I. L. (1980). *Family systems in America* (3rd ed.). New York: Holt, Rinehart & Winston.

Resick, P. A., Calhoun, K. S., Atkeson, B. M., & Ellis, E. M. (1981). Social adjustment in victims of sexual assault. *Journal of Consulting and Clinical Psychology, 49,* 705–712.

Reynolds, A. G., & Flagg, P. W. (1983). *Cognitive Psychology* (2nd ed.) Boston: Little, Brown.

Riegel, K. F., & Riegel, R. M. (1972). Development, drop, and death. *Developmental Psychology, 6,* 306–319.

Rimm, D. C., & Masters, J. (1979). *Behavior therapy* (2nd ed.). New York: Academic Press.

Rock, I., & Kaufman, L. (1972). The moon illusion. In R. Held & W. Richards (Eds.), *Perception: Mechanisms and models.* San Francisco: W. H. Freeman.

Roffwarg, H. P., Muzio, J. N., & Dement, W. C. (1966). Ontogenetic development of the human sleep-dream cycle. *Science, 152,* 604–619.

Rogers, C. R. (1951). *Client-centered therapy: Its current practice, implications, and theory.* Boston: Houghton Mifflin.

Rogers, D. (Ed.). (1980). *Issues in life-span human development.* Monterey, CA: Brooks/Cole.

Rogers, R. W. (1975). A protection motivation theory of fear appeals and attitude change. *Journal of Psychology, 91,* 93–114.

Rollins, B. C., & Feldman, H. (1970). Marital satisfaction over the family life cycle. *Journal of Marriage and the Family, 32,* 20–28.

Rolls, E. T., Burton, M. J., & Mora, F. (1976). Hypothalamic neuronal responses associated with the sight of food. *Brain Research, 111,* 53–66.

Rosch, E. (1973). Natural categories. *Cognitive Psychology, 4,* 328–350.

Rosch, E. H., Mervis, C. B., Gray, W. B., Johnson, D. M., & Boyes-Braem, P. (1976). Basic objects in natural categories. *Cognitive Psychology, 8,* 382–439.

Rosenman, R. H., & Chesney, M. A. (1982). Stress, Type A behavior, and coronary disease. In L. Goldberger & S. Breznitz (Eds.), *Handbook of stress.* New York: The Free Press.

Rosenweig, M. R. (1984). *Cognition.* New York: Holt, Rinehart & Winston.

Rossi, A. S. (1980). Aging and parenthood in the middle years. In P. B. Balter & O. G. Brim (Eds.), *Life-span development and behavior* (Vol. 3). New York: Academic Press.

Rowland, K. F. (1977). Environmental events predicting death for the elderly. *Psychological Bulletin, 84,* 349–372.

Rubenstein, E. A. (1983). Television and behavior: Research conclusions of the 1982 NIMH report and their policy implications. *American Psychologist, 38,* 820–825.

Ruble, D. N., & Ruble, T. L. (1980). Sex stereotypes. In A. G. Miller (Ed.), *In the eye of the beholder: Contemporary issues in stereotyping.* New York: Holt, Rinehart & Winston.

Rumbaugh, D. M., & Gill, T. V. (1976). The mastery of language-type skills by the chimpanzee *(Pan).* In S. Harnad, H. Steklis, & J. Lancaster (Eds.), *Origins and evolution of language and speech.* New York: New York Academy of Sciences.

Russell, J. A., & Mehrabian, A. (1978). Approach-avoidance and affiliation as functions of the emotion-eliciting quality of an environment. *Environment and Behavior, 10,* 355–387.

Russell, M. A. H. (1971). Cigarette smoking: Natural history of a dependence disorder. *British Journal of Medical Psychology, 44,* 1–16.

Sachs, J. D. S. (1967). Recognition memory for syntactic and semantic aspects of connected discourse. *Perception and Psychophysics, 2,* 437–442.

Salapatek, P. (1977). Stimulus determinants of attention in infants. In B. Wolman (Ed.), *International encyclopedia of psychiatry, psychology, psychoanalysis, and neurology* (Vol. 10). New York: Aesculapis Publishers.

Santrock, J. W. (1981). *Adolescence: An introduction.* Dubuque, IA: Wm. C. Brown Publishers.

Santrock, J. W., & Yussen, S. R. (1984). *Children and adolescents: A developmental perspective.* Dubuque, IA: Wm. C. Brown Publishers.

Sarason, I. G., Johnson, J. H., & Siegel, J. M. (1978). Assessing the impact of life change: Development of the life experiences survey. *Journal of Consulting and Clinical Psychology, 46,* 932–946.

Saxe, L., Doughterty, D., and Cross, T. (1985). The validity of polygraph testing: Scientific analysis and public controversy. *American Psychologist 40,* 355–366.

Scarr, S., & Salapatek, P. (1970). Patterns of fear development during infancy. *Merrill-Palmer Quarterly, 16,* 53–90.

Scarr, S., Webber, P. L., Weinberg, R. A., & Wittig, M. A. (1981). Personality resemblance among adolescents and their parents in biologically related and adoptive families. *Journal of Personality and Social Psychology, 40,* 885–898.

Schachter, S. (1959). *The psychology of affiliation: Experimental studies of sources of gregariousness.* Stanford, CA: Stanford University Press.

Schachter, S. (1971). Some extraordinary facts about obese rats and humans. *American Psychologist, 26,* 129–144.

Schachter, S., & Singer, J. E. (1962). Cognitive, social and physiological determinants of emotional state. *Psychological Review, 69,* 379–399.

Schaffer, H. R. (1971). *The growth of sociability.* London: Penguin.

Schaie, K. W., & Labouvie-Vief, G. (1973). Generational and cohort-specific differences in adult cognitive behavior: A fourteen-year cross-sequential study. *Developmental Psychology, 9,* 151–166.

Schaie, K. W., & Parham, I. A. (1977). Cohort-sequential analyses of adult intellectual development. *Developmental Psychology, 13,* 649–653.

Schiffman, H. R. (1976). *Sensation and perception: An integrated approach.* New York: Wiley.

Schreiber, F. R. (1973). *Sybil.* New York: Henry Regnery.

Schwartz, N., & Clare, G. L. (1983). Mood misattribution, and judgments of well-being. Informative and directive functions of affective states. *Journal of Personality and Social Psychology, 45,* 513–523.

Scott, W. D. (1908). *Psychology of advertising.* Boston: Small, Maynard.

Scoville, W. B., & Milner, B. (1957). Loss of recent memory after bilateral hippocampal lesions. *Journal of Neurology, Neurosurgery, and Psychiatry, 20,* 11–21.

Sechehaye, M. (1951). *Reality lost and regained: Autobiography of a schizophrenic girl* (G. Rubin-Rabson, Trans.). New York: Grune & Stratton.

Segall, M. H., Campbell, D. T., & Herskovits, M. J. (1963). Cultural differences in the perception of geometric illusions. *Science, 139,* 769–771.

Seligman, M. E. P. (1975). *Helplessness: On depression, development, and death.* San Francisco: W. H. Freeman.

Selye, H. (1976). *The stress of life.* New York: Knopf.

Serbin, L. A. (1980). Sex role socialization: A field in transition. In B. B. Lahey & A. E. Kazdin (Eds.), *Advances in clinical child psychology,* (Vol. 3). New York: Plenum.

Sheffield, F. D., Wulff, J. J., & Backer, R. (1951). Reward value of copulation without sex drive reduction. *Journal of Comparative and Physiological Psychology, 44,* 3–8.

Sheppard, W. C., & Willoughby, R. H. (1975). *Child behavior.* Chicago: Rand McNally.

Shotland, R. L. (1985). When bystanders just stand by. *Psychology Today,* June, 50–55.

Simmons, R. G., Rosenberg, F., & Rosenberg, M. (1973). Disturbance in the self-image at adolescence. *American Sociological Review, 38,* 553–568.

Skeels, A. M. (1966). Adult status of children with contrasting early life experiences. *Monographs for the Society for Research in Child Development, 31,* 1–65.

Skinner, B. F. (1953). *Science and human behavior.* New York: Macmillan.

Skolnick, A. (1966). Stability and interrelations of thematic test imagery over 20 years. *Child Development, 37,* 389–396.

Slobin, D. I. (1979). *Psycholinguistics.* Glenview, IL: Scott, Foresman.

Smart, R. G., & Fejer, D. (1972). Drug use among adolescents and their parents: Closing the generation gap in mood modification. *Journal of Abnormal Psychology, 79,* 153–160.

Smith, D. E., King, M. B., & Hoebel, B. C. (1970). Lateral hypothalamic control of killing: Evidence for a cholinoceptive mechanism. *Science, 167,* 900–901.

Smith, E. M., Brown, H. O., Toman, J. E. P., & Goodman, L. S. (1947). The lack of cerebral effects of *d*-tubocurarine. *Anesthesiology, 8,* 1–14.

Smith, M. L., & Glass, G. V. (1977). Meta-analysis of psychotherapy outcome studies. *American Psychologist, 32,* 752–760.

Snyder, M., Tauke, E. D., & Berscheid, E. (1977). Social perception and interpersonal behavior: On the self-fulfilling nature of social stereotypes. *Journal of Personality and Social Psychology, 35,* 656–666.

Snyder, S. H. (1974). *Madness and the brain.* New York: McGraw-Hill.

Sokolov, E. N. (1977). Brain functions: Neuronal mechanisms of learning and memory. *Annual Review of Psychology, 28,* 85–112.

Solomon, R. L. (1980). The opponent-process theory of acquired motivation. *American Psychologist, 35,* 691–712.

Sorenson, R. C. (1973). *Adolescent sexuality in contemporary America.* New York: World.

Spearman, C. E., & Wynn-Jones, L. (1950). *Human ability.* London: Macmillan.

Speisman, J. C., Lazarus, R. S., Mordokoff, A. M., & Davison, L. (1964). Experimental reduction of stress based on ego-defense theory. *Journal of Abnormal and Social Psychology, 68,* 367–380.

Sperling, G. (1960). The information available in brief visual presentations. *Psychological Monographs, 74,* 1–29.

Sroufe, L. A. (1978). The ontogenesis of emotion. In J. Osofoslay (Ed.), *Handbook of infancy.* New York: Wiley.

Stagner, R. (1958). The gullibility of personnel managers. *Personnel Psychology, 11,* 347–352.

Stark, E. (1984). To sleep, perchance to dream. *Psychology Today,* October 16.

Steinmetz, S. K., & Strauss, M. A. (Eds.). (1974). *Violence in the family.* New York: Harper & Row.

Stephan, W., Berscheid, E., & Walster, E. (1971). Sexual arousal and heterosexual perception. *Journal of Personality and Social Psychology, 20,* 93–101.

Sternbach, R. A. (Ed.). (1978). *The psychology of pain.* New York: Raven Press.

Sternberg, R. J. (1979). The nature of mental abilities. *American Psychologist, 34,* 214–230.

Sternberg, R. J. (1981). Testing and cognitive psychology. *American Psychologist, 36,* 1181–1189.

Sternberg, R. J., & Gardner, M. K. (1982). A componential interpretation of the general factor in human intelligence. In J. J. Eysenck (Ed.), *A model for intelligence.* Berlin: Springer.

Sternberg, S. (1969). Memory scanning: Mental processes revealed by reaction time experiments. *Acta Psychologica, 30,* 276–315.

Stevens, C. F. (1979). The neuron. *Scientific American, 241,* 54–65.

Strongman, K. T. (1973). *The psychology of emotion.* New York: Wiley, 1978.

Sturgis, E. T., Tollison, C. D., & Adams, H. E. (1978). Modification of combined migraine-muscle contraction headaches using BVP and EMG feedback. *Journal of Applied Behavior Analysis, 11,* 215–223.

Surwit, R. S., & Feinglos, M. N. (1983). The effects of relaxation on glucose tolerance in noninsulin-dependent diabetes care. *Diabetes Care, 6,* 176–179.

Surwit, R. S., Feinglos, M. N., & Scovern, A. W. (1983). Diabetes and behavior: A paradigm for health psychology. *American Psychologist, 38,* 255–262.

Tanner, J. M. (1970). Physical growth. In P. H. Mussen (Ed.), *Carmichael's manual of child psychology* (Vol. 1). New York: Wiley.

Tanner, J. M., Whitehouse, R. H., & Takaishi, M. (1966). Standard from birth to maturity for height, weight, height velocity, and weight velocity. *Archives of Diseases in Childhood, 41.*

Tarpy, R. M., & Mayer, R. E. (1978). *Foundations of learning and memory.* Glenview, IL: Scott, Foresman.

Tart, C. T. (1975). *States of consciousness.* New York: Dutton.

Terman, L. M. (1925). Mental and physical traits of a thousand gifted children. In L. M. Terman (Ed.), *Genetic studies of genius.* Stanford: Stanford University Press.

Terrace, H. S. (1980). *Nim.* New York: Knopf.

Thibaut, J., & Walker, L. (1975). *Procedural justice: A psychological analysis.* Hillsdale, NJ: Erlbaum.

Thomas, M. H., & Drabman, R. S. (1975). Toleration of real-life aggression as a function of exposure to televised violence and age of subject. *Merrill-Palmer Quarterly, 21,* 227–232.

Thurstone, L. L. (1938). Primary mental abilities. *Psychometric Monographs,* No. 1.

Tollison, C. D., & Adams, H. E. (1979). *Sexual disorders: Treatments, theory, research.* New York: Gardner Press.

Tolman, E. C., & Honzik, C. H. (1930). Introduction and removal of reward, and maze performance in rats. *University of California Publications in Psychology, 4,* 257–275.

Tolman, E. C., Ritchie, B. F., & Kalish, D. (1946). Studies in spatial learning. I: Orientation and the shortcut. *Journal of Experimental Psychology, 36,* 13–25.

Tulving, E. (1972). Episodic and semantic memory. In E. Tulving & W. Donaldson (Eds.), *Organization and memory.* New York: Academic Press.

Turkat, I. D., & Calhoun, J. F. (1980). The problem-solving flow chart. *The Behavior Therapist, 3,* 21.

Turnbull, C. (1962). *The forest people.* New York: Simon & Schuster.

Turner, J. H. (1970). Entrepreneurial environments and the emergence of achievement motivation in adolescent males. *Sociometry, 33,* 147–165.

Tversky, A., & Kahneman, D. (1973). Judgment under uncertainty: Heuristics and biases. *Science, 185,* 1124–1131.

Uhr, S., Stahl, S. M., & Berger, P. A. (1984). Unmasking schizophrenia. *VA Practitioner, 1,* 42–53.

Van De Graaff, K. (1984). *Human anatomy.* Dubuque, IA: Wm. C. Brown Publishers.

Varca, P. E., Shaffer, G. S., & Saunders, V. (1984). *A longitudinal investigation of sports participation and life satisfaction.* Unpublished manuscript, University of Georgia.

Velten, E. (1968). A laboratory task for induction of mood states. *Behaviour Research and Therapy, 6,* 473–482.

von Frisch, K. (1953). *The dancing bees: An account of the life and senses of the honeybee.* New York: Harcourt, Brace, & World.

Wald, G. (1950, August). Eye and camera. *Scientific American,* pp. 1–11.

Wallace, B., & Fisher, L. E. (1983). *Consciousness and behavior.* Boston: Allyn & Bacon.

Wallace, R. K., & Benson, H. (1972). The physiology of meditation. *Scientific American, 226,* 85–90.

Walster, E., Aronson, V., & Abrahams, D. (1966). On increasing the persuasiveness of a low prestige communicator. *Journal of Experimental Social Psychology, 2,* 325–343.

Walster, E., Aronson, V., Abrahams, D., & Rottman, L. (1966). Importance of physical attractiveness in dating behavior. *Journal of Personality and Social Psychology, 5,* 508–516.

Walster, E. W., Walster, G. W. (1978). *Equity: Theory and research.* Boston: Allyn & Bacon.

Warrington, E. K., & Weiskrantz, L. (1968). A study of learning and retention in amnesic patients. *Neuropsychologia, 6,* 283–292.

Warrington, E. K., & Weiskrantz, L. (1978). Further analysis of the prior learning effect in amnesic patients. *Neuropsychologia, 16,* 169–177.

Watson, J. B. (1925). *Behaviorism.* Chicago: University of Chicago Press.

Watson, J. B., & Rayner, R. (1920). Conditioned emotional reactions. *Journal of Experimental Psychology, 3,* 1–4.

Watson, R. I. (1971). *The great psychologists* (4th ed.). Philadelphia: J. B. Lippincott.

Webb, S. B., & Collette, J. (1975). Urban ecological and household correlates of stress-alleviative drug use. *American Behavioral Scientist, 18,* 750–769.

Webb, W. B. (1968). *Sleep: An experimental approach.* New York: Macmillan.

Webb, W. B. (1982). Sleep and biological rhythms. In W. B. Webb (Ed.), *Biological rhythms, sleep, and performance* (pp. 87–110). New York: Wiley.

Webb, W. B., & Bonnet, M. H. (1979). Sleep and dreams. In M. E. Meyer (Ed.), *Foundations of contemporary psychology.* New York: Oxford University Press.

Wechsler, D. (1955). *Manual for the Wechsler Adult Intelligence Scale.* New York: Psychological Corporation.

Weiss, R. L. (1975). *Marital separation.* New York: Basic Books.

Wentling, T. (1973). Mastery versus nonmastery instruction with varying test item feedback treatments. *Journal of Educational Psychology, 65,* 50–58.

Wexley, K. N., Sanders, R. E., & Yukl, G. A. (1973). Training interviewers to eliminate contrast effects in employment interviews. *Journal of Applied Psychology, 57,* 233–236.

Wexley, K. N., Yukl, G. A., Kovacs, S. Z., & Sanders, R. E. (1977). Importance of contrast effects in employment interviews. *Journal of Applied Psychology, 56,* 43–48.

Whitehurst, R. N. (1977). Youth views marriage: Awareness of present and future potentials. In R. W. Libby & R. N. Whitehurst (Eds.), *Marriage and alternatives: Exploring intimate relationships.* Glenview, IL: Scott, Foresman.

Whorf, B. L. (1956). Science and linguistics. In J. B. Carroll (Ed.), *Language, thought, and reality: Selected writings of Benjamin Lee Whorf.* Cambridge, MA: MIT Press.

Wickens, D. D., Born, D. G., & Allen, C. K. (1963). Proactive inhibition item similarity in short-term memory. *Journal of Verbal Learning and Verbal Behavior, 2,* 440–445.

Williams, R. L. (1972). Abuses and misuses in testing black children. *Journal of Black Psychology, 4,* 77–92.

Wilner, A., Reich, T., Robins, I., Fishman, R., & van Doren, T. (1976). Obsessive–compulsive neurosis. *Comprehensive Psychiatry, 17,* 527–529.

Wilson, J. R., Kuehn, R. E., & Beach, F. A. (1963). Modification in the sexual behavior of male rats produced by changing the stimulus female. *Journal of Comparative and Physiological Psychology, 56,* 636–644.

Winch, R. F. (1958). *Mate-selection.* New York: Harper & Row.

Windle, C., Bass, R. D., & Taube, C. A. (1974). PR aside: Initial results from NIMH's service program evaluation studies. *American Journal of Community Psychology, 2,* 311–327.

Witters, P. J., & Witters, W. L. (1983). *Drugs and society: A biological perspective.* Monterey, CA: Wadsworth.

Wolman, B. B. (Ed.). (1977). *Handbook of parapsychology.* New York: Van Nostrand Reinhold.

Wolpe, J. (1958). *Psychotherapy by reciprocal inhibition.* Stanford, CA: Stanford University Press.

Yalom, I. D. (1975). *The theory and practice of group psychotherapy* (2nd ed.). New York: Basic Books.

Yankelovich, D. (1974). *The new morality: A profile of American youth in the seventies.* New York: McGraw-Hill.

Zajonc, R. B. (1980). Feeling and thinking: Preferences need no inferences. *American Psychologist, 35,* 151–175.

Zajonc, R. B. (1984). On the primacy of affect. *American Psychologist, 39,* 117–123.

Zellner, M. (1970). Self-esteem, reception, and influenceability. *Journal of Personality and Social Psychology, 15,* 87–93.

Zubek, J. P. (1973). Review of effects of prolonged deprivation. In J. E. Rasmussen (Ed.), *Man in isolation and confinement.* Chicago: Aldine.

C R E D I T S

Photographs

Part Openers

Parts One, Five, Six, and Seven: © Tom Bean; **Part Two:** © W. H. Hodge/Peter Arnold, Inc.; **Part Three:** © Robert Madden/Folio, Inc.; **Part Four:** © Margaret Fava.

Chapter 1

page 8: top left, © Martin Bruce/Tom Stack Associates, **top right,** © Bill Gallery/Stock, Boston, **middle left,** © Ron Cooper/EKM-Nepenthe, **middle right,** © Paul Damien/Click, Chicago, **bottom left,** © Mike Button/EKM-Nepenthe, **bottom right,** © James R. Holland/Stock, Boston; **page 13:** Courtesy, National Library of Medicine; **page 14: top,** Courtesy, National Library of Medicine, **bottom,** Bettmann Archives; **page 16:** Culver Pictures; **page 17:** Bettmann Archives; **page 19: top,** © Christopher S. Johnson/Stock, Boston, **middle,** Bettmann Archives, **bottom,** Courtesy, National Library of Medicine; **page 27: left,** © Don and Pat Valenti/Tom Stack and Associates, **right,** © Martin and Ginney Garst/Tom Stack and Associates, **page 37:** © Gabor Demjen/Stock, Boston; **page 39:** © Michael Sullivan/Texa-Stock.

Chapter 2

page 46: top, © Manfred Kage/Peter Arnold, **bottom,** UPI/Bettmann Newsphotos; **page 58:** © Manfred Kage/Peter Arnold; **Figure 2.12a:** Igaku Shoin, Ltd.; **Figure 2.12b:** © Manfred Kage/Peter Arnold; **Figure 2.18a and 2.18b:** Courtesy of Dr. Monte Buchsbaum; **Figure 2.19a and 2.19b:** Courtesy of Drs. Lou, Henricksen, and Bruhn; **Figure 2.20:** Courtesy, National Library of Medicine; **page 75: top,** © Leonard Lee Rue III/Click, Chicago, **bottom,** UPI/Bettmann Newsphotos; **Figure 2.22:** Courtesy, the Upjohn Company; **page 77: both,** © Manfred Kage/Peter Arnold; **Figure 2.23:** Courtesy, the Upjohn Company; **page 81: left,** © Betsy Cole/Picture Cube, **right,** © Philip Jon Bailey/Stock, Boston.

Chapter 3

page 93: top, © G. Palmer/Image Bank, **bottom,** © Elizabeth Wenscott; **page 94:** © Michael Sullivan/TexaStock; **page 97:** AP/Wide World Photos; **page 99:** © Pete Pearson/Click, Chicago; **page 103:** AP/Wide World Photos; **page 107:** © Jeff Albertson/Picture Cube; **page 115:** © Elizabeth Wenscott; **page 123:** © Elizabeth Wenscott; **page 126: all,** © Elizabeth Wenscott; **page 128: both,** Bettmann Archives; **Figure 3.23:** © William Vandivert.

Chapter 4

page 141: © Owen Franken/Stock, Boston; **page 143:** Sleep Lab/University of Florida; **page 147:** Courtesy, Ernest Hartmann, M.D. Tufts University School of Medicine and Lemuel Shattuck Hospital, Boston; **page 149:** © Howard Sochurek/Life Magazine © Time, Inc.; **page 160: left,** © Bill Gallery/Stock, Boston, **right,** © Barbara Alper/Stock, Boston; **page 163:** © Barbara Van Cleve/Click, Chicago.

Chapter 5

page 173: © Roy Roper/EKM-Nepenthe; **page 174:** Bettmann Archives; **page 179:** © Elizabeth Wenscott; **page 183:** © David Kennedy/TexaStock; **page 187:** © Jim Brandenberg; **page 198:** © Gregg Mancusco/Stock, Boston; **Figure 5.10:** Courtesy, B. F. Skinner; **page 191:** © Annie Griffiths; **Figure 5.12:** © Bob Daemmrich/TexaStock; **page 202:** © George Mars Cassidy/Click, Chicago; **page 204:** © Owen Franken/Stock, Boston; **page 209:** © Peter Marler; **page 212:** © John Running/Stock, Boston; **page 213: all,** Courtesy, Albert Bandura; **page 214:** courtesy of John Hallett.

Chapter 6

page 221: © Bill Gillette/Stock, Boston; **page 223:** © Bill Gallery/Stock, Boston; **page 226:** © William Means/Click, Chicago; **page 227:** © Bill Ray/Life Magazine © Time, Inc.; **page 232:** © Charles Gupton/Stock, Boston; **page 237: left,** © Elizabeth Wenscott; **right,** © Michael Bertan/Click, Chicago; **page 243:** © Jeff March/Tom Stack and Associates; **page 246:** © Roy Armstrong/Click, Chicago.

Chapter 7

page 257: © Gabor Demjen/Stock, Boston; **page 259:** © Bob Coyle; **page 261:** © Greg Nikas/Picture Cube; **page 266:** © Ellis Herwig/Stock, Boston; **page 269:** © Jean-Claude Lejeune/EKM-Nepenthe; **page 271:** © C. T. Seymour/Picture Cube; **page 274: left,** © Bob Daemmrich/TexaStock, **right,** © Bob Eckert/Stock, Boston.

Chapter 8

page 279: left, © Chris Brown/Stock, Boston, **right,** © Lynn McClaren/Picture Cube; **page 280:** Bettmann Archives; **page 284:** Bettmann Archives; **page 290:** © Gabor Demjen/Stock, Boston; **page 299:** © Ellis Herwig/Stock, Boston; **page 300:** © Terry Eiler/Stock, Boston; **page 301:** © Bob Eckert/EKM-Nepenthe; **page 303: top,** © Sybille Kalas, **bottom,** Courtesy, University of Wisconsin Primate Lab; **page 304:** © Martin Rogers/Stock, Boston; **page 305:** © Bob Coyle; **page 308:** Bettmann Archives; **page 309:** © George Zimbel, Monkmeyer Press; **page 311:** Courtesy, Harvard University News Office; **page 312:** UPI/Bettmann Newsphoto; **page 315:** © Cary Wolinsky/Stock, Boston; **page 319:** © Donald Yaeger/Camera M. D. Studios; **page 321:** © Julie O'Neill/Picture Cube; **Figure 8.4:** © David Linton; **page 324:** © Peter Menzel/Stock, Boston; **page 325:** © David Woo/Stock, Boston; **Figure 8.5:** © William Vandivert; **page 329:** © Eric Roth/Picture Cube; **page 332:** © Mimi Forsyth/Monkmeyer Press.

Chapter 9

page 339: © Janice Fullman/Picture Cube; **page 344:** © Billy E. Barnes/Click, Chicago; **page 346:** © Paul Conklin; **page 349:** © Adams/Click, Chicago; **page 351:** © George Riley/Stock, Boston; **page 353:** © Herta Newton/Click, Chicago; **page 356:** © Peter Fronk/Click, Chicago; **page 357:** © Steven Stone/Picture Cube; **page 361:** © Paul Conklin; **page 363:** © Tom Borden/Click, Chicago; **page 365: both,** © L. L. T. Rhodes/Click, Chicago; **page 367:** Bettmann Archives.

Chapter 10

page 379: © L. L. T. Rhodes/Click, Chicago; **Figure 10.2:** Courtesy of Teitelbaum and Campbell; **page 381:** © Jeff Albertson/Picture Cube; **page 384:** © Rhoda Galyn/Photo Researchers; **page 387:** © Jeff Albertson/Picture Cube; **page 391: both,** University of Wisconsin, Primate Lab; **page 393:** © Peter Vandermarks/Stock, Boston; **page 395:** © Edward Miller/Stock, Boston; **page 402: top left,** © Oliver Rebbot/Stock, Boston, **top right,** © John Lei/Stock, Boston, **bottom left,** © Peter Southwick/Stock, Boston, **bottom right,** © Andrew Brilliant/Picture Cube; **page 405:** © Brian Seed/Click, Chicago; **page 411: all,** UPI/Bettmann Newsphotos; **pages 412, 413:** © Tom Kitchen/Valan Photos; **page 415:** © Cary Wolinsky/Stock, Boston.

Chapter 11

page 423: UPI/Bettmann Newsphotos; **page 428:** © Chuck Feil/Stock, Boston; **page 430:** © Paul Conklin; **page 432:** © Bob Coyle; **page 434: left,** © Paul Damien/Click, Chicago, **right,** © Oliver Rebbot/Stock, Boston; **page 439:** Courtesy, Albert Bandura; **page 441:** © Peter Southwick/Stock, Boston; **page 443: left and middle,** UPI/Bettmann Newsphotos, **right,** Three Lions; **page 446:** © Steven Stone/Picture Cube.

Chapter 12

page 465: © R. P. Kingston/Stock, Boston; **page 466:** © Mary Messenger; **page 469:** © Bob Coyle; **page 475:** © Bob Coyle; **page 480:** © Paul Conklin; **page 481:** Bettmann Archives; **page 491:** © John H. Anderson/Click, Chicago; **page 493:** © Mary Messenger; **page 500:** © Dave Schaeffer/Picture Cube; **page 504:** © Mottke Weissman/Photo Researchers; **page 509:** © Beckwith Studios/Taurus Photos; **page 515:** AP/Wide World Photos.

Chapter 13

page 528: © Bob Coyle; **page 529:** Historical Pictures Service; **page 532:** © Bob Coyle; **page 539:** © Deke Simon/Real People Press; **page 540:** © Lucasfilms, Ltd.; **page 550:** © Stacy Pick/Stock, Boston; **page 551:** © Bob Coyle; **page 554:** Courtesy, NIMH; **page 557:** © James Ballard.

Chapter 14

page 569: © Donald Dietz/Stock, Boston; **page 571:** © R. P. Kingston/Picture Cube; **page 573:** © Bob Coyle; **page 575:** © Eric Kroll; **page 577:** © M. Timothy O'Keefe/Tom Stack & Associates; **page 583: both,** Courtesy, Tulane University; **page 585:** © Bob Coyle; **page 588:** © Donald Smetzer/Click, Chicago; **page 593:** © Stacy Pick/Stock, Boston; **page 597:** © P. O. Malibu/The Image Bank.

Chapter 15

page 605: © Cary Wolinski/Stock, Boston; **page 606:** © Jim Pickerell/Click, Chicago; **page 610:** Courtesy, Science Research Association; **page 615:** © Nancy Simmerman/Click, Chicago; **page 617:** © Dan McConnell/Click, Chicago; **page 623:** © Paul Conklin; **page 626:** © Owen Frankin/Stock, Boston; **Figure 15.12:** New York Times News Service; **page 638:** © Barbara Van Cleve/Click, Chicago; **page 639:** © David Strickler/Picture Cube.

Line Art, Tables, Quotations

Chapter 1

Figure 1.4: From Matthews, K. E. and L. K. Cannon, "Environmental noise level as a determinant of helping behavior" in *Journal of Personality and Social Psychology, 32,* 571–577. Copyright 1975 American Psychological Association. Adapted by permission of the author.

Chapter 2

Figures 2.4, 2.8: From Hole, John W., Jr., *Human Anatomy and Physiology 3d ed.* © 1978, 1981, 1984 Wm. C. Brown Publishers, Dubuque, Iowa. All Rights Reserved. Reprinted by permission.

Figure 2.9: From Sturgis, E. T., C. D. Tollison and H. E. Adams, "Modification of combined muscle contraction headaches using BVP and EMG feedback" in *Journal of Applied Behavior Analysis,* 1978, *11,* p. 220. Adapted by permission.

Figure 2.15: From Levy, Jerre and M. Reid, "Variations in writing posture and cerebral organization" in *Science,* Vol. 194, p. 337, Fig. 1, October 15, 1976. Copyright 1976 by the American Association for the Advancement of Science, Washington, D.C. Reprinted by permission.

Figure 2.17 a & b: From Peele, T. L., *Neuroanatomical Basis for Clinical Neurology 2d ed.* © 1961 McGraw-Hill Book Company, New York. Reprinted by permission.

Figure 2.24: From Batshaw, M. L. and Y. M. Perret, *Children with Handicaps: A Medical Primer.* Baltimore: Paul H. Brooks, 1981. Adapted with permission.

Chapter 3

Figures 3.5, 3.6, 3.7, 3.12: From Hole, John W., Jr., *Human Anatomy and Physiology 3d ed.* © 1978, 1981, 1984 Wm. C. Brown Publishers, Dubuque, Iowa. All Rights Reserved. Reprinted by permission.

Figure 3.9: From Hole, John W., Jr., *Essentials of Human Anatomy and Physiology.* © 1982 Wm. C. Brown Publishers, Dubuque, Iowa. All Rights Reserved. Reprinted by permission.

Table 3.2: From Schiffman, H. R., *Sensation and perception: An integrated approach.* © 1976 John Wiley & Sons. Reprinted by permission of John Wiley & Sons, Inc. and Brown, E. L. and K. Diffenbacher, *Perception and the senses.* Copyright © 1979. Reprinted by permission of Oxford University Press.

Chapter 4

Figure 4.1: From *Foundations of Contemporary Psychology,* edited by Merle E. Meyer. Copyright © 1979 by Oxford University Press, Inc. Reprinted by permission.

Chapter 5

Figure 5.4: From Allen, K. E., et al., "Effects of social reinforcement on isolate behavior of nursery school child" in *Child Development,* 1964, *35,* 511–518. © Society for Research and Development, Inc.

Figure 5.5: Reprinted with permission from Allyon, T. and E. Haughton, "Modification of the symptomatic verbal behavior of mental patients" in *Behavioral Research and Therapy,* *2,* 87–97. © 1964 Pergamon Press, Ltd.

Figure 5.11: Reprinted from *Programmed Reading* by Sullivan Associates. Copyright 1973, with permission of Webster/McGraw-Hill.

Figures 5.15, 5.16: Adapted from Tolman, E. C., B. F. Ritchie and D. Kalish, "Studies in spatial learning I: Orientation and the short-cut" in *Journal of Experimental Psychology,* 1946, *36,* 13–25.

Figures 5.17, 5.18: From Tolman, E. C. and C. H. Honzik, "Introduction and removal of the reward and maze performance in rats" in *University of California Publications in Psychology,* 1930, *4,* 257–275. Adapted by permission of the University of California Press.

Figures 5.19, 5.20: From Harlow, Harry F., "The formation of learning sets" in *Psychological Review,* 1949, *56,* 51–56.

Chapter 6

Figure 6.3: Based on Peterson, L. R. and M. J. Peterson, "Short-term retention of individual items" in *Journal of Experimental Psychology, 58,* 193–198. Copyright 1959 American Psychological Association. Adapted by permission of the author.

Figure 6.4: From *Foundations of Learning and Memory* by R. M. Tarpy and R. E. Mayer. Copyright © 1978 by Scott, Foresman and Company. Reprinted by permission.

Figure 6.5: Based on Glanzer, M. and A. R. Cunitz, "Two storage mechanisms in free recall" in *Journal of Verbal Learning and Verbal Behavior,* 1966, *5,* 351–360. By permission of Academic Press, Orlando, Florida.

Figure 6.6: Adapted from Wickens, D. W., D. G. Born and C. K. Allen, "Proactive inhibition item similarity in short-term memory" in *Journal of Verbal Learning and Verbal Behavior,* 1963, *2,* 440–445. By permission of Academic Press, Orlando, Florida.

Figure 6.7: From Carmichael, L., H. P. Hogan and A. A. Walter, "An experimental study of the effect of language on the reproduction of visually perceived form" in *Journal of Experimental Psychology,* 1932, *15,* 73–86.

Chapter 7

Figures 7.2, 7.3: Based on fig. 25, p. 146 of Wolfgang Köhler, *The Task of Gestalt Psychology.* Copyright 1969 by Princeton University Press. Redrawn by permission of Princeton University Press.

Figures 7.4, 7.5: From Bourne/Ekstrand/Dominowski, *The Psychology of Thinking.* © 1971, p. 52. Reprinted by permission of Prentice-Hall, Inc., Englewood Cliffs, NJ.

Figure 7.8: © THE NOBEL FOUNDATION 1974.

Chapter 8

Figure 8.1: From McGraw, M. B., "Neural maturation as exemplified in achievement of bladder control" in *Journal of Pediatrics,* 1940, *16,* 580–590. Reprinted by permission of C. V. Mosby Company, St. Louis, Missouri.

Figure 8.2: Based on text from *Review of Child Development Vol. I,* Eds., Hoffman & Hoffman. Copyright © 1964 by Russell Sage Foundation. Adapted by permission of the publisher.

Figure 8.6: Adapted from Mosher, F. A. and J. R. Hornsby, in J. S. Bruner (ed.), *Studies in Cognitive Growth.* New York: John Wiley & Sons. By permission of J. S. Bruner.

Chapter 9

Figure 9.1: From Tanner, J. M., R. H. Whitehouse and M. Takaishi, "Standard from birth to maturity for height, weight, height velocity, and weight velocity" in *Archives of Diseases in Childhood,* 1966, *41.* By permission of the British Medical Society, London, England.

Figure 9.2: From Olsen, K. M., "Social class and age-group differences in the timing of family status changes: A study of age norms in American society." Unpublished dissertation, 1969. Courtesy of Dr. Kenneth M. Olsen.

Figure 9.3: From Rollins, B. C. and H. M. Feldman, "Marital satisfaction over the family life cycle" in *Journal of Marriage and the Family,* Vol. 32, pp. 20–28. Copyright 1970 by the National Council on Family Relations, St. Paul, Minnesota. Reprinted by permission.

Figure 9.4: From Phillips, David P. and K. A. Feldman, "A dip in death before ceremonial occasions: Some new relationships between social integration and mortality" in *American Sociological Review,* 1973, *38,* 683. Reprinted by permission of the American Sociological Association.

Chapter 10

Figure 10.1: From Murchison, C., (Ed.), *Foundations of Experimental Psychology,* 1929, p. 437, fig. 1. Clark University Press.

Figure 10.3: From Hervey, G. P., "The effects of lesions in the hypothalamus in parabiotic rats" in *Journal of Physiology,* 1959, *145,* 336–352. Reprinted by permission.

Figures 10.7, 10.8: From Solomon, R. L. "The opponent-process theory of acquired motivation" in *American Psychologist, 35,* 691–712, 1980. Copyright 1980 by the American Psychological Association. Reprinted by permission of the publisher and the author.

Figure 10.9: Data (for diagram) based on Hierarchy of Needs in "A Theory of Human Motivation" in *Motivation and Personality 2d ed* by Abraham H. Maslow. Copyright © 1970 by Abraham H. Maslow.

N A M E   I N D E X

SUBJECT INDEX